DOS<—>UNIX Networking and Internetworking

New Yo

Associate Publisher: Katherine Schowalter
Editor: Diane Cerra
Associate Managing Editor: Jackie Martin

This text is printed on acid-free paper.

Printed in the United States of America

10 9 8 7 6 5 4 3 2

Dedicated
to
Our Wives
Bonnie and Gini
and to Our Children
Jessica, Justin, Nicholas, and Natalie
Rachel and Emily

Contents

10   Emulating DOS   235

11   Connecting Printers   251

Contents

Preface

Why We Wrote This Book

We believe there is a real need among small businesses, consultants, and large corporations alike to unite DOS and UNIX machines. PCs running DOS make up the single largest operating system base in the world, and UNIX represents the fastest growing segment of the computing marketplace. The voice of the business community rings loud and clear; they want these two operating systems working together. In *DOS—UNIX Networking and Internetworking* we attempt to meet this need head on.

We wanted to write a book that gets right down to the nuts and bolts of using DOS and UNIX together. After some investigation, we discovered most networking books either cover only DOS networking or only discuss UNIX networking. What the marketplace lacks is information on how to make UNIX and DOS work together on a practical level. That's what this book is all about.

With that in mind, we take a slightly unusual approach. We spend little time on the theoretical issues behind networks and operating systems, and do our best to avoid technological babble. Rather, we concentrate on specific solutions for specific problems. Though we provide some primer information in the first three chapters, you won't find discussions about the technical superiority of Ethernet over Token-Ring, or even an in-depth tutorial on how they work. We leave these discussions to those many good books already on the shelves.

This book is solution oriented. Business people do not solve problems with theories, concepts, or debates. They solve them by getting into the trenches—usually, with a product. The last half of the book is an in-depth evaluation of many products on the market. However, even in the how-to chapters, we are frequently product specific. Whenever appropriate, we provide detailed tables on products and their capabilities.

We provide cost and time-to-install information wherever we can. We, like you, are concerned about cost in the decision-making process. We respect its impact. We know businesses must often use the hardware and software on hand and cannot always afford an entirely new system or an expensive consultant.

While this is neither a UNIX networking book nor a PC LAN networking book, you will find information to help you with UNIX network setup, printer sharing, NetWare administration and other issues related to LANs. We also help you if you happen to have stand-alone machines on either side of the fence.

Finally, we consider this book a part and parcel of the client/server craze, although we choose to adopt the broad industry definition of client/server technology. In our context, a client is any machine/program requesting services or information from another machine. In many respects, this describes much of what happens in DOS—UNIX networking and internetworking. We don't worry about whether it meets everyone's strict definition of client/server computing—our goal is to show you "how to do it."

This unique approach has minor drawbacks. First, because we are working with more than 100 different products, we recognize the impossibility of being in sync with the latest release of every product. We worked hard to get the most recent version of each product before the book went into production.

In addition, some specifics may be outdated within one or two years. New products or methodologies inevitably replace older ones. For example, the shift from TSR-based TCP/IP programs to the Windows Socket API (WinSock) was just gaining momentum while we were writing the book.

The benefits of our approach outweigh any drawbacks. For many of you, working with what you have already installed is a necessity. Small businesses cannot afford to upgrade to the newest version. In many cases, earlier versions still perform the job adequately. Good business management means upgrading as needed—not necessarily all in one shot.

How to Use This Book

This book can be used in a variety of ways. A newcomer to the dual environment of DOS and UNIX can choose it as an overall primer on the subject. Software purchasers will find the product evaluations useful in their own selection process. Implementors can profit from the network setup hints woven throughout the book.

The first three chapters are primers. If you need some background in either DOS or UNIX as an operating system, read Chapter 1. Those with only a vague understanding of networks will benefit from the simple approach to networking theory in Chapter 2. Chapter 3 outlines an entire decision process—the many choices you face when incorporating DOS or UNIX into your network. This chapter should be read by everyone.

Chapters 4-12 cover the mechanics of DOS—UNIX networking and internetworking. We talk about hardware and software—but avoid discussions of vaporware. These chapters deal with the practical aspects of installation, setup, usage, and maintenance of DOS and UNIX working together. We think it is easier to learn how to do something by really doing it, so many of our examples revolve around real installations, real hardware, and real software products.

Chapters 13-18 contain the evaluations of key product groups. This is where you turn to find out about the latest products on the market and how easily you can use them. In almost every case, we loaded the software, or installed the hardware, and tested it for its intended use. We attempted to be fair, noting both when we liked and did not like a product, and why. Not every product on the market is good and we want to help you sort the wheat from the chaff. Tables at the end of these chapters compare the features of the products, simplifying your selection process. We made every attempt to contact vendors right up until production time. However, because products change continuously, always double check with the vendor if you need a specific feature we did not mention.

Appendix A contains a small gold mine of UNIX and DOS operating system information. Turn there if you need to get a quick background in commands and procedures, or use it for occasional reference. Finally, we provide several pages of vendor addresses in Appendix B to assist you in your quest for more information.

We try to give the book a readable flavor. Throughout the book, we provide simple diagrams describing complicated concepts. We explain the concepts from a bottom-line point of view. When we talk about hardware, we provide a picture of a sample product whenever possible. When we discuss software, we give you a screen shot. In the product chapters particularly, we use screen shots to help you get a feel for the various user interfaces. Throughout the book, we supply a variety of hot tip boxes and warning boxes to alert you to items of special interest.

We try to avoid being grim-faced about networking. Business people need a little humor, since they have to pay real money for computer networks. Implementors need to know that we have been where they are. We wish to act as guides, not instructors. For these reasons, we have tried to write as comfortably as possible, using "you" and "we," ... and we confess that we are not above poking fun occasionally. Nevertheless, we take our research seriously. We know it means time, money, and productivity to our readers.

Formatting issues are minor, but you should be aware of those we use. We differentiate from DOS and UNIX commands by making all DOS commands capitalized since DOS is not CAPS sensitive. We bold all commands. When we list a short script or set of commands separately, we place them in a smaller program font to set them off from the text. Italics are occasionally used for emphasis.

Our Network Layout

Within the confines of our laboratory, we matched real business situations as closely as possible. We always maintained a Novell NetWare 3.11 network with 1 to 4 NetWare clients, a SunSelect PC-NFS TCP/IP network with 2 to 4 PC clients, a Sun SPARCstation IPC, and an IBM RS/6000 on the network as shown in the accompanying figure.

In addition, at various times we used a Microsoft LAN Manager network, a Microsoft Windows for Workgroups network, a Windows NT network, and a LANtastic network, running over our same set of cables. Different UNIX hosts included SCO OPEN DESKTOP 2.0 and 3.0; UnixWare Application Server and Personal Edition; and a DECstation 3100. We also installed an IBM OS/2 PC, X terminals from NCD and Tektronix, and character-based terminals from Wyse Technology. At any given time, we had 10 to 13 different hardware platforms running 3 to 5 different

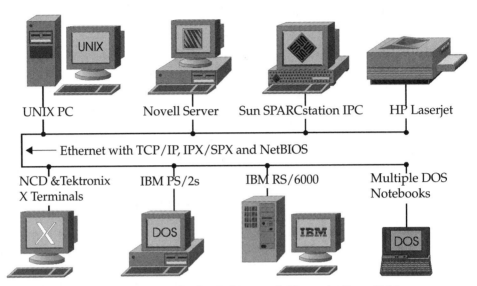

FIGURE P.1 Our Test Lab—Multiple Machines and OSs on the Same Cable

operating systems during our testing. We spent hours on the phone getting technical support. Many products did not always work as they should. Reliable delivery, we discovered, didn't necessarily mean that *we* knew where our information ended up; it went somewhere, we're certain, but where, only our software seemed to know. Networks right out of the box may be just around the corner, but don't throw away those working gloves just yet.

Acknowledgments

We have many people to thank for the content and production of this book, *DOS— UNIX Networking and Internetworking*. Certainly when we set out to examine over 100 products, we needed to have support from the vendors, and we got it without exception. We are especially grateful to Rose Kearsley at Novell, Beth Beyers at Sun-Select, Barbara LoFranco at SCO, and Melanie King at Univel/Novell for their support on the software side.

We also need to thank a number of hardware vendors who loaned us equipment at various times to enable us to complete our testing. We want to thank IBM Corp. for loaning a number of PS/2s and an RS/6000 Model 320; NCD Corp. for an NCD 17c X terminal; Tektronix Inc. for an XP337 X terminal; Sun Microsystems Inc. for a Sun SPARCstation IPC; Digital Equipment Corp. for a DECstation 3100; Best Power Systems for three Fortress UPS systems; Zenith Data Systems for a Z-note 386 notebook; Keydata for a Keynote notebook; Xircom for portable LAN adapters and print servers; U.S. Robotics for modems; Standard Microsystems Corp. for numerous Ethernet adapters; Eagle Technology for more Ethernet adapters; Pacific Data for a multiprotocol print accelerator; and Hewlett-Packard Company for LaserJet boards and a font cartridge.

We are also grateful to Frame Technology Corp. and Corel Systems Corp. for supplying software for the production of our manuscript. We used CorelDraw 3.0 for Windows; CorelDraw 2.1 for UNIX; Framemaker for OpenLook; and Framemaker for Microsoft Windows. Fiona Rochester at Corel Systems and Yolana Leinson at Frame Technology were especially helpful and courteous.

The production of the book is due to many helping hands. Nearly all the drawings and diagrams were done by Bruce Pierson, our technical assistant and artist-in-residence. He did a fantastic job, and without him our pages would have been bland, to say the least. We are also grateful to Gini Phillips for her work in formatting, editing, and organizing the production of the book. We would not have a book without the contributions of these two.

Those at John Wiley who helped us in the process include our patient and thoughtful editor, Diane Cerra; her assistant, Tammy Boyd, who helped keep us on track, and Jackie Martin, the managing editor who made sure our camera-ready disks were just right. Thanks as well to Rik Farrow, UNIXWorld's Technical Editor for his review of some critical UNIX system administration issues.

Finally, our family and friends in Bozeman, MT deserve our applause and gratitude. We thank our wives, Bonnie and Gini, for their support and patience during those long, extra hours of product testing. Jessica, Justin, Nicholas, Natalie, Rachel, and Emily were great for helping us to remember the important and satisfying things in life. In many ways this book has been a family endeavor.

Michael J. Burgard
Kenneth D. Phillips
Comments can be directed to the authors via e-mail:
        mjburgard@mcimail.com (Mike)
        602-2316@mcimail.com (Ken)
or, by mail to:
        3017 Secor Avenue
        Bozeman, MT 59715

1

DOS and UNIX Primer

Introduction

Whenever you cross into the realm of internetworking, you encounter a whole new set of issues—not the least of which is the learning curve. The very concept of internetworking implies more than one operating system and more than one type of hardware box. You may have a large number of IBM PS/2s connected to a single Sun Microsystems server, or you may have a network of DECstations and need to add some low-cost PC clones for a particular task.

Unfortunately, most of us have a rather well-defined job, and it usually revolves around a specific set of hardware and software. When we venture outside this arena, we find ourselves unable to speak the language and groping for the information needed to solve a specific problem. In Chapters 1 and 2, our intention is to provide information which you may need before you delve into the world of internetworking.

Chapter 1 outlines basic information on UNIX and DOS, as well as some other related hardware and software issues. If you are a UNIX guru but short on DOS knowledge, you might skip the sections on UNIX and just read the MS-DOS and Windows sections. Similarly, if you run a large DOS network but have no idea what UNIX does, you can concentrate on the UNIX portion. The DOS and UNIX sections cross reference similarities where they exist in order to help the new user understand foreign-sounding terms. There is also a DOS to UNIX command cross-reference and other information in Appendix A.

In any case, we make no attempt to replicate the volumes of information about these operating systems. There are excellent books available on UNIX, MS-DOS, Windows, and each of the network operating systems from a variety of sources. These include *Modern UNIX* by Alan Southerton (John Wiley & Sons, Inc. books), *Running MS-DOS* by Van Wolverton (Microsoft Press), and *Running Windows* by Craig Stinson (Microsoft Press). These books and others are listed in Appendix B.

Instead, we cover the operating systems basics and discuss some of their similarities and differences. If your project is small, the knowledge you gain from these chapters and the hands-on information provided in later chapters should allow you to get up and running. Bigger projects may require you to invest in some general background references. Our goal in this chapter is to to get you started.

The UNIX Operating System

The widespread popularity of the UNIX operating system is relatively recent. This popularity stems from many different factors, but includes UNIX acceptance by the education community, its ability to run on a variety of platforms, its openness, the stability of the operating system kernel, and a dozen other items. Following is a brief overview of what UNIX is and what it has to offer. See Appendix B for a list of books to give you an in-depth treatment of UNIX.

Origin and History

UNIX is an operating system developed by researchers at AT&T's Bell Labs in 1969. For many years, UNIX was a trademark of AT&T, though later it came under the auspices of UNIX Software Laboratories, or USL, which was purchased by Novell, Inc. in 1993. While originally created for a PDP-7 (a mini-computer manufactured by Digital Equipment Corporation) in PDP assembler language, UNIX quickly spread beyond this proprietary hardware, once it was ported to the C language.

There were a number of reasons for UNIX to grow beyond its dependance upon a single hardware system. UNIX quickly evolved into a portable and scalable operating system. That is, you could "port" it to any kind of processor, whether from Motorola or Intel or SPARC or MIPS, and it would run on a machine constructed with that processor. One of its inventors, Dennis Ritchie, once said that "it was easier to port UNIX to a new hardware machine than an application to a new operating system." It is also scalable, which means it runs on small machines like laptops as well as big machines like supercomputers. In these days of linking big networks together, administrators prefer worrying about as few operating systems as possible.

For the first 10 years of UNIX's existence, its position in the commercial marketplace was insignificant. No one attempted to resell UNIX until Interactive Systems did so in 1977, eight years after its genesis—a lifetime in operating systems longevity. Even the formation of The Santa Cruz Operation, Inc. in 1981 and Sun Microsystems in 1982, did not quickly change the landscape. Instead UNIX grew slowly during the go-go days of the PC in the mid-1980s, taking a position of importance in scientific and engineering situations, but not making a large impact on the general business computing environment. As Table 1.1 shows, the UNIX market has grown steadily yet substantially since those early days.

UNIX experienced a splitting of the ranks so to speak when in the early 1980s, the University of California, Berkeley, created a version of UNIX based on AT&T source code. This new version of UNIX became known as Berkeley UNIX and, because universities could get the source code for a low price, it became a popular variant. Sun Microsystems adopted Berkeley UNIX for its line of workstations and lengthened its life considerably. When it is important, we point out differences between Berkeley UNIX and AT&T System V UNIX (known just as System V).

Table 1.1: **History of UNIX**

YEAR	UNIX MILESTONES
1969	UNIX created in AT&T Bell Labs
1977	Interactive Systems first company to resell UNIX to end-users
1981	SCO collaborates with Microsoft on XENIX for PCs
1982	Sun Microsystems founded, uses Berkeley UNIX
1983	Total UNIX systems: 70,000 computers
1985	International Data Corp. estimates UNIX market at $3.6 billion
1985	Tandy ships 14,000 XENIX-based systems (at one time, Tandy had the biggest installed base of UNIX machines)
1986	System V Release 3
1987	UNIXWorld estimates UNIX market at $5.5 billion
1987	Total UNIX systems: 750,000
1988	System V Release 4 (SVR4) released
1990	IDC estimates the UNIX market at $117 billion
1991	AT&T spins off UNIX to UNIX Systems Laboratories (USL)
1993	USL is purchased by Novell Inc.
1994	IDC estimates the UNIX market at $160 billion

Basic Components of UNIX

UNIX consists of a number of components making up the complete operating system. A working knowledge of the UNIX operating system helps when attempting to physically internetwork UNIX with DOS machines. However, you do not need to be a UNIX expert to understand this book, since our discussions in later chapters are not highly technical in nature, nor do they require programming knowledge. There are some products we found which challenge even the knowledgeable UNIX administrator.

The Kernel

The central component of any UNIX operating system is the *kernel*. The kernel loads into memory at the time the computer is booted or started up. In MS-DOS the kernel roughly equates to the hidden files. In UNIX, the kernel can have a different name for each operating system and multiple kernels can be present on the system at the same time. However, only one kernel can load and run at any given time.

The kernel serves an important function handling nearly all control activities, such as managing demand paging, swapping memory to disk, running processes, running or operating the filesystem, and managing device drivers.The kernel keeps track of the system and the other programs and processes in order to facilitate processor time and memory allocation. Each program or continual operation in UNIX is called a process. Because UNIX is multiuser and multitasking, there can be many processes running at the same time. UNIX is a true preemptive, multitasking environment where each process runs separately—a unique and important aspect of UNIX. The kernel relies on other files during the time your machine is coming up.

Daemons

Daemons (pronounced "demons") are special processes that run continually while the UNIX system operates. They may handle any number of tasks including controlling a print spooler, managing the sharing of files with a Network File System (NFS), or handling communication options. Daemons are background processes, similar to DOS Terminate and Stay-Resident (TSR) programs. The major difference is that UNIX OS directly supports daemons; and, therefore, daemons seldom cause problems with other processes. In DOS, TSRs are occasionally the cause of system crashes and lock-ups, because DOS is not equipped to handle multiple processes. Most daemons are automatically loaded at start-up time through the start-up scripts.

The Shell

UNIX uses a *shell* to isolate the kernel from the user. The shell is simply a program that runs on top of the kernel and handles all the input from the user. The MS-DOS counterpart is COMMAND.COM. Different users logged into the same system can be using different shells. UNIX supports many different shells, of which three different types are popular. They are called the C shell, the Bourne shell, and the Korn shell. More similarities than differences exist between these three shells. Each accepts commands from the user directly at the command prompt or from a shell script. Shell scripts are similar to DOS batch files. Associated with shells is a complete programming language that includes IF statements, variables, and other control statements. Many of the commands are the same in all three shells. For further reference, examine the many good books on programming shell scripts, including *UNIX Shell Programming* by Lowell Arthur (John Wiley & Sons, Inc.) or *UNIX Power Tools* by Jerry Peek, Mike Loukides, and Tim O'Reilly (O'Reilly & Associates).

The Bourne shell (written "sh") was named for its inventor, Stephen Bourne, and represents the easiest of the shells to learn. Normally, when logged into a UNIX system under the Bourne shell, your prompt is a dollar sign ($). The Bourne shell provides the lowest common denominator among all three shells. A shell script written in Bourne shell works with the Korn shell, though not with the C shell without alteration.

The C shell (written "csh") more closely resembles the C language and provides much more power than does the Bourne shell. It was written in the early 1980s by

Bill Joy, one of the cofounders of Sun Microsystems Inc. The percent (%) sign is the usual prompt for the C shell. The C shell is the most powerful of the three shells. It includes command history editing and a powerful scripting language.

Following the invention of the C shell came the Korn shell (written "ksh"). Its inventor, David Korn, attempted to combine the compatibility of the Bourne shell with the power of the C shell. As a result, his Korn shell is growing to be the standard shell shipped with many UNIX systems. The prompt sign is a dollar sign ($), the same as for the Bourne scripts. The few scripts discussed in later chapters are all Bourne scripts. We leave the script writing to books on UNIX.

Startup Files

Depending on the shell you are using, UNIX uses different startup files to get your overall environment up and running. Each user on the UNIX system can have his own environment set up through their own start-up scripts. If you are using the Bourne shell, the **.profile** will be in your home directory. This is the only file used. For C shell users, **.cshrc** is invoked first followed by the **.login**. These files always work in conjunction with each other. Both of these files resemble the **CONFIG.SYS** and **AUTOEXEC.BAT** files in MS-DOS. They set user paths, parameters, and run certain background programs. The Korn shell uses the **.profile** and a second file called **.kshrc**. The main reason for two files has to do with starting a sub shell after you are logged in. The C shell and Korn shell only invoke their secondary file when you start a new shell. This is for the sake of convenience. Start up files associated with the X Windows System are discussed later.

Security and the Superuser

For login, UNIX uses user names and passwords—providing many security benefits over the relatively vulnerable MS-DOS. In a well-managed system, these security features keep unauthorized people from getting on the computer and using (or abusing) the data. UNIX assigns each user the ability to create, use, change, and save only certain files and directories. This ability is referred to as permissions and provides an additional level of security beyond login protection. However, in order for all this to work, there needs to be one user who can change anything. In UNIX, this user is called *root* or the *superuser* (su). Root and superuser are interchangeable terms, so most documentation makes no distinction between the two. When you are logged in as root, your system prompt is the pound sign (#) rather than the prompt of the specific shell.

The superuser must have a private password and is, out of obvious necessity, the most tightly controlled user. If anyone of a deviant nature logs into your system as the superuser . . . well, we leave the damage to your imagination. Because nonnetworked DOS machines do not have passwords, permissions, or other controls, users moving from DOS to UNIX over an internetwork need additional training on how a UNIX system works. Partly for this reason, UNIX users are seldom enamored with connecting up with their less secure DOS brethren.

Multiuser

Another major difference between UNIX and MS-DOS is that UNIX is a *multiuser* operating system. With UNIX, many users can all log onto the same CPU. Users can access different applications simultaneously or even the same application simultaneously. The UNIX kernel manages the different users by scheduling the use of the processing time as well as swapping programs and data in and out of memory through paged memory and virtual memory to disk. The most important fact to remember is that the number of concurrent users depends on the amount of memory installed in the computer. In UNIX, each user must have a certain amount of memory set aside for his work unless everyone is willing to tolerate slow response. The amount varies depending on the tasks a user needs to accomplish.

Networking

Networking exists as an inherent part of the UNIX operating system. For MS-DOS systems you need to add hardware in the form of a network interface card and software in the form of communications protocols in order to network. Under UNIX, the interface is built into workstations (but not PCs running UNIX) and communications software is usually part of the operating system. Standard hardware provides the network interface. The Transport Control Protocol/Internet Protocol (TCP/IP) is the standard networking protocol available in UNIX. A significant portion of this book discusses how the protocol works in conjunction with PCs. Chapter 2 discusses the protocol's place in networking, with further discussion in Chapter 5.

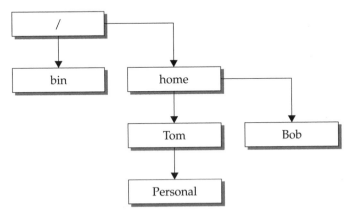

FIGURE 1.1 UNIX directory structure

Filesystems

UNIX stores and maintains its files in a *filesystem*. There can be more than one filesystem mounted on or available to each system. In concept, a filesystem resembles the designated drive names in DOS. For example, a typical UNIX system might have a root filesystem (/), a user filesystem (/**usr**), and a home file system (/**home**). These might all be on the same hard disk, or they can be on multiple disks. Although filesystems can be created either on floppy disks or tapes for backup and other specialty tasks, for all practical purposes, UNIX filesystems exist only on hard disks.

UNIX uses the same hierarchial directory structure found in DOS. As shown in Figure 1.1, the topmost directory is / with the directories cascading down from that point. If you want to store files in Bob's directory, they would be in **/home/Bob**. Moving between directories is done just as in DOS.

X Windows System

The *X Windows System* was developed by MIT in the 1980s. The X Windows System provides an underlying windowing protocol display of graphical or character-based information across a network. We can't begin to describe the X Windows System in a few paragraphs but we can give you an understanding of how it works.

X has a number of features that sets it apart from earlier attempts to create a windowing environment. X is does not care about the network itself. It is network-transparent. While X is often associated with TCP/IP, it can be used with DECnet, IBM's SNA, and any other networking protocol. X uses a communication protocol that works within the confines of other network communication protocols. Second, X is device independent. X is not restricted to any particular type of hardware. X servers and X clients can run on RISC machines, VAXes and PCs. While X is associated with UNIX, it is also operating-system-independent. It can run on MS-DOS, VMS, Macintosh, OS/2, and other operating systems.

What this does for the average networking environment is open the world to standard applications and lower costs. You don't have to have a different application for every different type of hardware platform. For example, the Informix Wingz spreadsheet on the Sun workstation (with the proper license) works on all the other network platforms through an X server. The learning curve is reduced by using common applications. All applications use a similar interface so training is simplified. Standardization helps reduce maintenance and training costs across the board. The X Windows System has many benefits in a networked computing environment.

While the latest release of The X Windows System is X11 Release 5, many workstation vendors still use X11R4. The release number of X is comparable to any OS new release. If a vendor chooses to write an application that works only with the latest version, you need that version. The same is true of X. However, it is our experience that nearly all common X clients work with X11R4 since most workstation vendors still ship this version of X and there is a large installed base of applications.

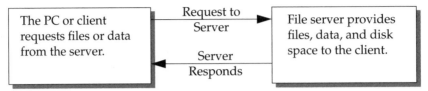

Typical Client/Server Scenario has your local machine requesting files and programs from the remote host or server.

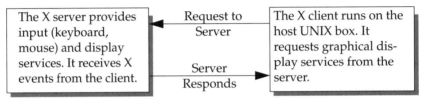

In X Windows Client/Server terms, the local machine is the server and it responds to requests by the remote host for display and input services.

FIGURE 1.2 Standard client/server model compared to X Windows System

The X Server

One major difference when working with X is the terminology and the way X looks at applications. Normally, you think of yourself as the client and the host machine as the server. This is particularly true in a PC-LAN when you store programs on the Novell file server and your machine is the client. In the world of X, this concept is turned around as Figure 1.2 shows. X applications are the *clients* requesting services of the network. The *X server* provides these services in the form of graphics to the X client. The X server handles the input and output including keyboard, mouse, and display. An X server can reside on the same physical machine as the X client. Or an X server can be on a different machine—another workstation, an X-terminal, a PC running X server software. The X server provides the application with services such as display and keyboard input. The X server can serve more than one X client from whatever machine it is running on. The actual processing of the application takes place on the client side, but any screen actions, input, and output all work through the X server.

The X Client

The *X client* is also an application. The X client can reside anywhere on the network. The host machine does not even need the ability to display graphics or have a display at all. The X client uses its host machine for its disk, RAM, and processing. It does not use the host machine's display facilities—the single exception is when the host machine is also the X server. The X client requests services from multiple X servers when more than one user is using the X client. In general, we consider the X client to be the application like FrameMaker or Lotus 1-2-3 that a user is using. The client communicates with the server via the X communication protocols.

However, X does not provide the window manager, the desktop, nor any of the desktop tools. These are provided by other parties in the chain. If you are familiar with MS-DOS and MS-Windows, consider the diagram in Figure 1.3. This shows the place of UNIX graphical components in comparison with DOS components. You can see that the UNIX side is much more component-oriented than is the DOS side. A good description of the X Windows System from a user's view can be found in *The Joy of X* by Niall Mansfield (Addison-Wesley Publishers Ltd.) while those more interested in the heavy-duty aspects will find O'Reilly's *X Windows Series* (O'Reilly & Associates) to be the definitive word on the X Windows System. Other books are listed in Appendix B.

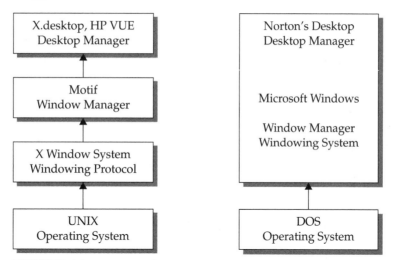

FIGURE 1.3 Diagram of X Window System on UNIX compared to MS-DOS

The Window Manager (Motif)

Unlike Microsoft Windows and the Macintosh, X offers the options of plugging in other components of the windowing system. The X library toolkit is used by developers to create these components, hidden from the user. The user interface or *window manager*, also known as the *GUI*, is responsible for how the user alters windows on the screen. X provides a window manager, but almost every one uses a commercially supported window manager. Once there were two competitors for the user interface in UNIX (see following discussion on COSE), but for all practical purposes the only window manager now available in UNIX is Motif (although the OPEN LOOK GUI will be available for a few years yet). The window manager is responsible for how the borders and title bars look on each window, how you move and size windows, and what keyboard and mouse actions do with respect to the windows. The window manager does not affect the application nor interact with specific files or icons. The latter job is left for the desktop manager.

The Desktop Manager

The next component of the typical UNIX graphical environment is the *desktop manager*. The desktop manager has the task of actually handling how the screen is presented to the user, how icons look, how icons operate, and what services are available graphically to the user. In UNIX, desktop managers usually handle a range of functions. These include the creation of desktops where you can place icons; selecting icons and start-up applications; moving, copying and linking files via icons; dragging certain icons and dropping them onto other icons for specific actions (like printing a file by dropping the file on a printer icon); and creating icons with specific object behavior. Common desktop managers in UNIX include IXI Limited's X.desktop, Hewlett-Packard's VUE, and Visix' Looking Glass.

The Startup Files

X requires some of its own start-up files. Normally, a file called **xinit** actually starts the X server on your machine. This file is usually found in **/usr/bin/X11**. However, often the command **xinit** is found within another script that also sets some environment variables for your X session. For example, on a Sun SPARCstation running OpenWindows, the file is called **openwin**. Once the X server starts, it looks for **.xinitrc**. This is a script file where all the major customizing occurs for your X environment. The window manager, desktop manager, and other start-up clients are usually listed here. This file is called **.startxrc** on SCO and **.olinitrc** on UnixWare. One other method to start up an X server is to use **xdm**. This is explained in Chapter 8 where PC-based X servers are discussed.

The UNIX OS Shuffle

We conclude our short discussion of UNIX by identifying growth and diversity in the UNIX market. While UNIX is portable, it is not always the same from platform to platform. Many vendors have taken the basic UNIX system from AT&T and made significant changes (enhancements in the vendors' eyes). As a result, not every UNIX system is compatible with another system. This contrasts with the ability of a DOS machine to be able to run any piece of DOS software without recompiling or porting the software because the standard is the same across all machines. In addition, UNIX runs on a wide variety of architectures and processors which make it difficult for developers to create a single version of a software package to run on all these different workstations and computers.

UNIX operating systems come in many different flavors. There are the semi-proprietary versions designed to work only with the specific hardware of the vendor. These include IBM's AIX, DEC's Ultrix, Data General's DG/UX, Apple's A/UX, and Hewlett-Packard's HP/UX. Each operates only on the hardware manufactured by its respective company. These tend to be larger hardware companies that have minicomputers and workstations sold with UNIX installed. Also, these versions tend to be the ones most altered from the standard vanilla UNIX. We use some of these in our book because they are popular. In particular, we tested networking products using IBM AIX and Sun Solaris 1.1 (SunOS 4.x). Where we discovered differences important to interoperability and internetworking, we try to point them out.

On the other side of UNIX, there is System V UNIX from USL designed to run on Intel platforms. The most popular Intel-based UNIX operating system is SCO UNIX System V Release 3.2 and its Motif-based product, Open Desktop. SCO possesses a commanding share of the Intel UNIX market from its long history of supporting only PCs. Other vendors include Interactive UNIX System V (now owned by Sun Microsystems) and UnixWare from Novell (formerly Univel). There are at least one hardware vendor and numerous software vendors reselling SVR4 for Intel platforms.

There are a couple of other UNIX options worth mentioning. OSF/1 from The Open Software Foundation is a truly non-platform specific version of UNIX. However, other than DEC, we are not aware of any vendor using it. Sun Microsystems has moved from BSD UNIX in SunOS to SVR4 for its new OS, Solaris 2.x. Solaris 2.x has combined the operating system, X Windows System, and GUI-based desktop all rolled into a single product. Solaris runs on both Intel-based PCs and on all Sun platforms. Sun also plans to port Solaris to the new PowerPC chip being produced by Motorola, Apple, and IBM.

COSE and X/Open

In the spring of 1993, the major UNIX vendors decided to further close the gap on UNIX differences. Up until that point, two GUIs—Motif from OSF and OPEN LOOK from Sun Microsystems Inc.—had competed head to head. This resulted in further fragmentation and application incompatibility. The spring 1993 agreement adopted the Common Operating System Environment (COSE) in the hopes of providing UNIX users with a single desktop and GUI. This is in direct response to the introduction of Microsoft Windows NT. The major result from COSE is the likely abandonment of OPEN LOOK by Sun Microsystems and its subsequent adoption of Motif. From a user's perspective, however, changes to the UNIX desktop may be a long time in coming. Our book discusses both Motif and OPEN LOOK applications. Other than some minor command variations in screen shots, the COSE initiative does not affect internetworking information, at least based on its preliminary objectives.

The second recent event is the decision by Novell to release the UNIX trademark to X/Open, a standards organization. This occured in October of 1993. Again, this is seen as a step towards providing further compatibility across different types of UNIX. Only vendors that meet X/Open's branding process will be allowed to call their product UNIX. Vendors also agreed during this time frame to common application binary interface (API) calls that will make it easier for vendors to offer their application on various versions of UNIX. While it does not guarantee shrink-wrapped applications that will work on any version of UNIX, it does insure the vendor can easily move an application from one version to another.

The MS-DOS Operating System

MS-DOS is the operating system of choice for most of the Intel-based PCs of the world. If you have ever touched a computer, you have likely heard something about MS-DOS. MS-DOS has become a household word, much to the disdain of many UNIX lovers who see the operating system as less than adequate. Intimately tied to the history of the IBM PC, we provide UNIX users not familiar with DOS a brief overview of its history and its components.

Origin and History

For a number of reasons, MS-DOS represents a much less complicated operating system than UNIX. DOS originated in 1981 from the then-puny Microsoft Corporation. At that time IBM asked Microsoft to write an operating system for the as-yet-unannounced IBM PC. Many stories have circulated over the years about the beginnings of this relationship. While much of the tale is nothing more than hearsay, here are two basic facts. While IBM did consider using Digital Research Corp. (inventor of DR DOS) to do the new operating system, for some reason this did not happen. Microsoft, in the meantime, purchased a portion of their operating system code from another small developer in Seattle for about $20,000.

From these inauspicious beginnings, Microsoft grew into the largest software company in the world. This is in sharp contrast to the liaise-faire approach of AT&T with its UNIX code. DOS resembles in some ways, both UNIX and CP/M, an earlier microprocessor operating system that was popular in the late 1970s and early 1980s. In particular, Microsoft had created Xenix, a variation of UNIX, and then went on to incorporate some of the features such as the similar subdirectory structure and configuration files. Most of these changes were incorporated in DOS 2.0 back in 1983. The longest running version of DOS was the 3.x series, particularly 3.3. Version 3.0 was introduced with the AT line of computers in 1984 to handle larger disks and faster processors, and when updated to 3.3, remained the primary version of DOS well into 1991. DOS 4.x added a shell program, but had many reported bugs and was not adopted by most vendors. DOS 5.0 released in 1991, included new memory features, an improved shell, and new device drivers. DOS 6.0, released in 1993, has disk-doubling options, virus protection, an auto-configuration option, and better memory management.

Basic Components of MS-DOS

DOS does not break out into neat compartments as easily as does UNIX. This is partially due to its simplicity—no multiuser or multitasking ability. It is also partly due to its heritage. Even so, we draw some parallels to UNIX when looking at DOS.

Hidden system files (the kernel)

DOS uses two hidden files at boot time. These are **io.sys** and **msdos.sys**. For all practical purposes, these files, in conjunction with the firmware BIOS built-into every PC, make up the DOS kernel. They load at the time of start-up and allow the command processor to run. Unlike UNIX, these files are not rebuildable or alterable. You can install device drivers in DOS, but you cannot change the kernel.

COMMAND.COM (the shell)

The equivalent of the UNIX shell in MS-DOS is **COMMAND.COM. COMMAND.-COM** is more commonly referred to as the command processor. It processes the commands you enter at the **C:>** prompt. When you run programs from DOS and then return to DOS, the system must be able to find **COMMAND.COM** and reload it back into memory. The DOS shell also supports a command language similar to the essence of the UNIX shell. Known as the DOS Batch language, files with a **.BAT** extension are considered executable by the command processor. The Batch language is not as powerful as UNIX scripting, but does support conditional statements and variables. In the early years of PCs, the batch language was used for many tasks. Now, low cost utilities often provide many times the functions in addition to direct support. However, batch files are still very common and very useful.

DOS services (daemons and UNIX system calls)

Because DOS is not multitasking, it cannot have multiple processes (daemons) working in the background like UNIX. However, DOS does use services that allow programs to interact with the computer. These services include basic input/output services (BIOS), print services and file services. DOS services use what is known as an interrupt to the microprocessor. This interrupt concept allows terminate-and-stay-resident (TSR) programs. TSRs can set quietly in the background and appear when the user requests them. Though not nearly as clean or flexible as UNIX daemons, TSRs provide DOS with the ability to run more than one task at a time.

Startup files

DOS uses two configurable startup files. They are **CONFIG.SYS** and **AUTOEXEC.-BAT**. They support functions similar to startup files in UNIX like the **.profile** and the

.cshrc file. The **CONFIG.SYS** has the task of loading installable device drivers and other system parameters which must run at boot time. The device drivers might be for a CD-ROM drive or a sound board. The **AUTOEXEC.BAT.** starts applications automatically for the user, handles logins for network software, and places information in the PC's environment. In some cases, no clear cut delineation exists between which commands go into the **CONFIG.SYS** and which go into the **AUTOEXEC.-BAT**. In general, the **CONFIG.SYS** holds only device drivers, special commands provided with DOS, and memory managers.

Limitations

MS-DOS is a *single-user* operating system. It is designed to operate on machines using the Intel Corp. line of 8086 line of microprocessors including the 8088, 8086, 80286, 80386, 80486, and the new Pentium (80586). Unlike UNIX, DOS cannot directly support a large network of users. But because DOS and PCs became so popular, many network operating systems were designed in the mid-1980s to network DOS machines together, working around the operating system limitations through software.

DOS is limited in its memory usage. From the beginning, DOS was designed to allow only the first 640 kilobytes of memory to be used for application programs, even though only 1 megabyte of memory was addressable. This seems absurdly low to the average UNIX workstation user who is accustomed to a relatively unlimited amount of system memory. To current DOS users, 640 kb has proven to be inadequate as well. The latest version, DOS 6.0, has special memory management tools and techniques built in to allow programs additional memory. Additionally, an entire counter-culture of memory management tools have been developed which allow programs to use more memory under previous versions of DOS. These include Quarterdeck's QEMM386 and Qualitas Inc. 386Max.

Closely tied to the limitation on memory is DOS's inability to run more than one program at a time. The nature of DOS requires one program to end before another one begins. Again, the ingenuity of programmers has worked numerous tricks to get around this limitation. For one, TSRs can load into memory and stay throughout a session. These are similar to UNIX daemons in that they are background programs available for use by other programs. However, many programmers have parented poorly-behaved TSRs, which are unstable, or can cause multiple problems with other programs. Lack of standards has given TSRs a bad reputation. Sometimes a TSR itself is reliable, but does not work well with other TSRs. A second solution to the single application shortcoming has been task switching programs like Software Carousel and the original Microsoft Windows. These allow you to quickly move between different applications that are frozen in RAM or on a hard disk swap space. Though certainly not multitasking, they are much better than nothing. Nevertheless, the only solution that attempts multitasking is Microsoft Windows which we discuss shortly. You should understand that no matter what Microsoft says, Microsoft Windows is not an operating system. DOS remains the operating system and Windows is simply a user interface with lots of flexibility.

Security Shortcomings

DOS also evinces a lack of concern for security or networking. There are no passwords, login files, encryption, networking hooks, mail programs, communication programs, or any of the other tidbits UNIX users have come to take for granted. This security shortage presents a particularly difficult problem in a networked environment. Most network operating systems have put security measures on top of DOS. These typically involve logins and access permissions to the programs on the server. DOS now comes with a program called SHARE that controls access to the same file by multiple users over a network. Still, each individual DOS machine is inherently susceptible to viruses, rogues, and security leaks.

Ease of Use

How did DOS become so popular (well over 100 million copies by now)? The answer is a combination of marketplace luck, good PR, low cost, and ease of use. Precisely because DOS had no encumbrances and because IBM put DOS on its PCs, anyone could easily buy a machine and put DOS on their desk. The DOS batch language which resembles shell scripts in UNIX allowed nonprogrammers to write simple programs and interfaces. DOS itself is not that easy to use, but the programs created to run under MS-DOS were themselves understandable to the computer illiterate individuals of the world. Additionally, the low cost of entry gave everyone an advantage over the more technically correct, but harder to use, UNIX variants.

DOS Variants

Microsoft does not make the only versions of DOS. IBM has a license to create DOS which runs on IBM PS/2 computers and is called PC-DOS. Up until DOS 4.0, there were only minor differences between MS-DOS and PC-DOS. Since that time, there has been more divergence by the two companies. In the late 1980s, a number of DOS multiuser versions appeared on the market including VM-386 and CMOS. The only major competitor to MS-DOS in the single machine market is DR-DOS from Digital Research. Yes, that is the same company, now owned by Novell Inc., that was involved in the original discussions with IBM that crashed and burned. Essentially, DR-DOS has jumped a release ahead of MS-DOS when it comes to new capabilities and technologies. DRI guarantees the compatibility of DR-DOS with programs designed for MS-DOS. There have been a number of multiuser variants of DOS out for years, including DR Multiuser DOS, PC-MOS, and VM-DOS. It is an unanswered question whether we will see the variety of DOS versions that we have seen in the UNIX market.

Microsoft Windows and Windows NT

Microsoft Windows, Windows for Workgroups, and its recently released, powerful cousin Windows NT, are all an integral part of DOS-UNIX internetworking. The vast majority of applications we tested were Windows-based. While the number of Windows PCs remains small compared to the total PC installed base, it is growing at a tremendous rate. According to Dataquest Corp., there have been over 25 million copies of Microsoft Windows shipped worldwide compared to an installed base of an estimated 140 million or more PCs of all types.

Origin and History

In a manner similar to DOS, the genesis of Windows tells a fascinating tale of non-existent products and marketing maneuvers. Microsoft first announced Windows in 1985, long before any product really existed. It was originally designed as an interface to handle peripherals and other devices but quickly became an operating environment. The first release of Windows occurred in 1987 and was virtually ignored by the entire industry. There were only a few applications available, including Page-Maker from Aldus Corp. Subsequent versions did not fare much better. It wasn't until 3.0 was released in early 1990 and then 3.1 in mid-1991 that the product became a hit. These two versions, in combination with falling memory prices, allowed PC users to run multiple Windows programs on a single PC without compromising speed. At one point in its history, Windows was designated as the low-end desktop solution with OS/2 touted as the upgrade for power users. The divergence of Microsoft and IBM have placed Windows and OS/2 as direct competitors.

Basic Components of Windows

Microsoft Windows is more than just the X Windows System look-alike for DOS. Like X, it is not an operating system, but rather an operating environment. You have to use MS-DOS for all Windows products except Windows NT. Windows goes beyond X by also supplying the window manager and the desktop manager in a single package. Microsoft has a monopoly of sorts on the PC operating system business. Windows handles the graphical aspects of all applications including graphical system calls, window movement, and application interaction. This makes it much more complete then any single component on the UNIX side.

We avoid describing all the components and nuances of Windows 3.1, the latest release of Windows for the desktop. Again, there are excellent books for the Windows user including *Using Windows 3.1* by Ron Person & Karen Rose (QUE) and *Windows 3.1 Secrets* by Brian Livingston (IDG Books). Livingston's book is particularly useful for making Windows work well, though at nearly 1000 pages it is quite a volume to pore through.

The main components of Windows 3.1 that affect internetworking are the Program Manager, File Manager, Control Panel, and the Print Manager. The Program Manager represents the equivalent of the desktop manager in UNIX; you load new applications and invoke current applications there. The File Manager is akin to the Sun OpenWindows File Manager—allowing you to copy, move, and generally work with individual files. Neither the Program Manager nor the File Manager is a great program. Each accomplishes the task, but does so somewhat cumbersomely. This shortcoming has given rise to a large aftermarket of products that provide an improved desktop and file management user interface. In this regard, the Windows 3.1 market is similar to the X market in that there are many desktops and utilities available that operate similarly but are not standard.

Windows 3.1 operates in three different modes. The Real Mode is seldom used by any applications and is of little value in today's market. The standard Mode allows Windows to do multitasking, but still operate in the nonprotected mode of the 386 Intel chip. You cannot run DOS programs in the background or use all of Windows memory management options when running Standard Mode. Most DOS emulators that run Windows on a UNIX machine only allow Windows to run in Standard Mode. The Enhanced Mode runs in the 386 protected mode of the Intel processor. This allows Windows to invoke virtual machines when running DOS applications in Windows. The Enhanced Mode aspect of Windows 3.1 improves the stability of the overall Windows session.

You use the Control Panel to make changes to Windows including fonts, printers, and networking. It offers a simple set of icons with specific functions. We refer to the Control Panel at various times and each time we have given you detailed information on how to use it. The Print Manager handles the printing of Windows Applications and does its own spooling. Some print services are managed from the Print Manager while others are handled from the Printer Icon within the Control Panel. See Chapter 7 for more detailed information about Windows and Chapter 11 for Printer specific information.

Windows Networking

One of our purposes in writing this book was to deal with the inherent networking deficiencies in Windows. For the most part, the original design of Windows fails to take networked PCs into the equation. As a result, only limited networking support is built into Windows 3.1. Microsoft has responded in at least three areas. One is the creation of Windows for Workgroups (WFW). WFW is the basic Windows 3.1 product with some networking. It supports peer-to-peer networking with other WFW clients. This means you can share your hard drive with another WFW user and they can share yours. Besides peer-to-peer, WFW supports scheduling and mail functions across the network and the TCP/IP support in Windows NT.

A second option at Microsoft is the Windows Socket Application Programming Interface (WinSock API). This specification allows networking vendors to let their network software interact directly with Windows without having to rely on TSRs and other tricks of the trade. Wherever appropriate, in Chapters 5 and 8, we show how vendors handle connecting to Windows and whether a particular methodology causes a problem. Chapter 7 also provides a more detailed discussion of how products interact with Windows when making a UNIX connection.

Windows NT

The third networking solution supported by Microsoft is Windows NT. Windows NT is much more than just a networking solution. It is a complete preemptive multitasking operating system and does not use MS-DOS at all. It was built from the foundation up. While Windows NT uses Win32 as its interface, to the user it looks exactly like Windows 3.1. NT supports most Windows applications, runs DOS programs and supports some degree of networking. Windows NT is not a multiuser operating system unless you purchase the Windows NT Server product which bundles in LAN Manager. However, NT does include some networking options to allow NT machines to communicate with other machines.

Windows NT supports the complete peer-to-peer capabilities found in Windows for Workgroups. NT also provides limited TCP/IP support in the form of outgoing TELNET options. There are no NFS facilities in NT nor is there any ability to login to an NT platform from UNIX machines. The server version has access to UNIX machines running LAN Manager products like SCO through the LAN Manager portion of NT. We discuss Windows NT as a connectivity solution in Chapter 14.

Lots of hype has been said and written about Windows NT. From the DOS—UNIX internetworking perspective, we see a few points of interest to all users. First, Windows NT is not designed to replace Windows 3.1. All sorts of numbers have been bandied about, but we expect Windows NT to replace maybe 10 percent of the Windows 3.1 desktops in the next year. So there is no danger of Windows 3.1 applications suddenly becoming obsolete. Second, most Windows 3.1 applications work fine with NT, so comments made in our book about these applications still apply if you choose to purchase NT. Third, UNIX multiuser networks can not switch to Windows NT because it does not support multiple users unless you purchase the Server option (which is nothing more than LAN Manager, not a very serious challenger to UNIX). This means UNIX systems will still find a home. Fourth, it will take the marketplace some time to generate the extent of NT-specific (Win32) applications necessary to challenge the speciality applications available on UNIX.

The OS/2 Operating System

Windows, DOS, and UNIX do not represent the only operating systems involved on the desktop. As we have already seen, there are a number of UNIX variants which run on Intel PCs. Worth noting is OS/2 from IBM Corp. Originally a joint venture between Microsoft and IBM, OS/2 was intended as the replacement for DOS. Along the way, Windows popularity and OS/2 1.1's dismal acceptance convinced Microsoft to bail out. Meanwhile, IBM stuck to its guns and moved forward with OS/2—developing it not only as a DOS replacement, but also as substitute for Windows.

OS/2, now available as 2.1, has a number of positive aspects. It is a new operating system that does not rely on DOS. Preemptive in nature, unlike UNIX, applications are protected from crashing the system. OS/2 runs Windows 3.1 applications, DOS applications and OS/2 32-bit applications. It does not run Windows NT 32-bit applications. OS/2 uses an interface called the Workplace Shell in conjunction with the Presentation Manager GUI. They operate in a fashion similar to MS-Windows.

We limit our treatment of OS/2 for three reasons. First of all, by the spring of 1992, IBM had sold only about 2 million copies of OS/2 2.0 according to International Data Corp., as compared with the approximately 25 million copies of Windows sold by Microsoft. Secondly, OS/2 was designed as a server platform and in many cases finds its place in large corporations that design and build in-house applications. These do not represent the primary readers of our book. Thirdly, because the focus of the book is on DOS—UNIX internetworking, we had to make some tough decisions and a limit on OS/2 coverage was one of them.

Hardware Platforms

While this primer has concentrated on the software side of computing, there are a few hardware tidbits you should be knowledgeable about before beginning the trek into DOS—UNIX internetworking. In general there are two types of hardware architectures involved in desktop and client/server computing. The patriarch is Complex Instruction Set Computing (CISC). While many semiconductor firms manufacture CISC chips for many types of computers, the primary desktop chip comes from Intel Corp. and its line of x86 chips. The newcomer is Reduced Instruction Set Computing (RISC). Again, though supported and manufactured by many firms, RISC is most closely allied with Sun Microsystems Inc. and the SPARC chip. Here we give you a sweeping overview of history and the significant issues. We don't believe either of these two architectures is technically or morally superior. It is our opinion you need to know some of the basics and go about your business of choosing the best platform without regard to the technical arguments.

Intel Architecture

Intel Corp. was founded in 1968 by a group of engineers from Fairchild Semiconductor. Intel's first products were DRAM and SRAM (Random Access Memory) chips. The first microprocessors appeared in 1971. The first chip that was a direct descendant of the current 486 and Pentium chips was the 8086 created in 1978 (or the 8080 in 1974). Intel, and to a certain degree other semiconductor vendors, owes its success to the introduction of the IBM PC in 1991. Using the Intel 8088 chip, the PC was widely successful. The reason the PC was popular, and still is today, is due to its relative low cost and ease of use. Certainly for most of the 1980s, DOS applications were cheaper and easier to use than UNIX. The ability to control your own computing power was also a big driving force. Shortly after the IBM PC appeared, a number of clone computers appeared, the most successful of which is Compaq. Today, many computer companies support the Intel chip on the Industry Standard Architecture (ISA) or Extended ISA (EISA). With the exception of Apple Macintosh, all PCs use an Intel or Intel-compatible chip.

The original purpose behind the IBM PC was as another method of getting to the IBM mainframes. The original PC had no hard disk, 128 kilobytes of RAM, and an 80-character monochrome monitor. If any single event changed the role of the first PCs, it was the introduction of Lotus 1-2-3, a spreadsheet that let users do all manner of computing tasks at their desk without using the expensive mainframe. Soon thousands of applications became available to the PC user.

The 80x86 line of chips from Intel (and clone manufacturers like Advanced Micro Devices and Cyrix) all use CISC design. CISC chips use relatively complex instructions given to it by the software and run the instructions. In the case of CISC, these instructions require more work from the microprocessor to complete a set of actions. Some of the differences between RISC and CISC are highlighted below.

RISC Workstation Architecture

The success of UNIX workstations and companies like Sun Microsystems Inc. is in no small part due to the success of Reduced Instruction Set Computing (RISC). RISC is based on the concept that microprocessors can be faster and more efficient when provided with simpler instructions to execute. The first RISC chips were created in the early 1980s and the first commercial RISC chip was shipped by MIPS in 1985, but did not meet marketplace success until Sun introduced the SPARC (Scalable Processor Architecture) chip design in 1989. Now nearly every major hardware manufacturer supports a RISC chip (IBM—PowerChip; Hewlett-Packard—PA-RISC; DEC—Alpha; Silicon Graphics Inc.—MIPS). Many of these companies have attempted to form independent standards around their chip design. Sun has been the most successful with the formation of SPARC International in 1989. Other companies have followed suit.

What separates a RISC workstation from a regular CISC machine provides the stuff for esoteric debates among engineers and theorists. Certainly, CISC people will say CISC chips can incorporate many of the components of RISC design. No argument there. However, there are a few points on which you can hang your hat in order to be better informed. RISC chips are generally simpler to design because they handle only simple commands. Studies found that most software used only a small portion of the commands available on the hardware processor. RISC chips are optimized to take advantage of that knowledge. The nature of the design allows RISC chips to be faster than comparatively priced and sized CISC chips. Other differences include shorter RISC design cycles and the ability to use multiple chip designers. Of course, until just recently, RISC chips and RISC machines were more expensive.

Without a doubt, both RISC chips and CISC chips will be around for a number of years, so any debate on merit is without purpose. In a typical environment, mixed workstations (from Sun, IBM, HP, DEC and SGI) internetwork with Intel PCs and Apple Macintoshes on a continuous basis. Depending on price, processor speed, and other variables, a RISC machine may or may not be faster than a CISC machine. In general, workstations tend to be fitted with higher performance peripherals—SCSI drives, network interfaces, high performance graphics—all of which add to their price. Armed with this basic background, you can relax from the processor debate and worry about other more pressing issues.

2

Network Primer

Introduction

It seems the author of every networking book on the market feels the need to discuss the basics of networking and present the Open Systems Interconnection (OSI) seven layer model. We too feel the burden of this obligation, but we hope to broaden the approach and make internetworking more understandable. We refer you to other books on each issue of importance for a more in-depth treatment of any particular subject. This enables us to focus on hands-on solutions, not technical specifications or the superiority of one protocol over another.

You should read this chapter if you do not know much about networking. Perhaps you are a DOS user without any networking knowledge. Or maybe you have been thrust into a networking position after the previous expert left. Maybe you work with a network but just don't know anything about the basics. When you are finished, you should know the following: 1) the essence of physical topology, 2) the most common types of cabling options, 3) the difference between various logical topologies, 4) the definition of a network driver, 5) the definition of a network protocol, and 6) definition of a network operating system.

LAN Basics

Every book and every vendor has a definition for a LAN (Local Area Network). And as if LAN isn't enough, we now are faced with WANs (Wide Area Networks), MANs (Metropolitan Area Networks), Enterprise LANs, and so on. It is enough to make anyone who is not already a computer expert turn to using an abacus.

What Is a LAN?

Here are some simple thoughts for defining a LAN. A LAN is the connection of two or more computers or workstations in a manner which allows users to share files, programs, or data with a minimum of effort. A LAN is usually local; that is, the machines are located in one physical location—like a building or one floor of the building. A LAN also tends to use a single set of networking options. For example, a

LAN generally uses one network operating system, one type of cable, and one logical topology. A LAN usually works within either a small business or a specific group of a larger company, like accounting or marketing. A LAN is not limited to any particular operating system. DOS, Macintosh, and UNIX can all be run across a LAN.

What Is Not a LAN?

We intentionally have left the definition of a LAN broad enough to encompass a wide variety of software and hardware solutions. However, we also need to define what is not a LAN. First, connecting a number of computers through a print buffer to share a common printer is not a LAN. This is a cost-effective method of sharing an expensive peripheral, but it does not constitute a LAN. Second, connecting a lone PC to another completely different system—be it a UNIX system, a mainframe, or a mini—is not a LAN. This is often an important part of sharing systems, but don't confuse it with a LAN. Third, dragging together hundreds of machines from a wide variety of locations running a variety of operating systems is not a LAN.

Client/Server Computing

Client/server computing is critical in the world of internetworking. It is also the latest buzzword among vendors and users. Everyone wants their application to be client/server. We have neither the interest nor space to engage heavily in the client/server debate, particularly in the parts that attempt to define what is client/server technology and what is simply old-fashioned host-based processing.

The classical definition of client/server computing says that one machine initiates a request (usually from a desktop) to another machine located somewhere else. The client's request is typically in the form a database query to the server's master database. The query is formed, modified and sent by the client, the server computes the answer, and the answer is passed back to the client for display or output.

As we saw in Chapter 1, the X Windows System fits the client/server definition even if it does confuse the terms. But in the most basic sense, a Novell NetWare network is client/server as well. NetWare clients are requesting file services from the Novell server. In the same way, we see PCs requesting file, print and application services from a UNIX host as falling into the client/server role. If you have a set of PCs connected to a Sun Sparcstation via TCP/IP and NFS, this is client/server computing. Same with using serial-based terminal emulation or using a UNIX host as a Novell server. Most, but not all, of the technologies presented here are client/server.

The OSI Model

We feel compelled to present the Open Systems Interconnection (OSI) model, if for no other reason than to have a point of reference. OSI and all its related standards and specifications are the creation of a committee—in this case, the International Standards Organization (ISO). As such, it has some tremendous theoretical advantages, but practically speaking it is less useful than intended by its creators. Many people do not realize that OSI represents not only a model of networking but also an implementation. Just as there are TCP/IP products on the market, there are OSI products. Because it provides a standard, OSI is part of the U.S. Government's standard networking requirements, known as GOSIP.

However, the reality remains far from the theory. OSI is experiencing only limited success in Europe, in the U.S. consumer market, and even among U. S. government purchasers. According to a survey conducted by *Government Computer News,* (March 15, 1993) only 2% of the U.S. Government installations are using the OSI protocol.

We present the OSI model, shown in Figure 2.1, because you see and hear about it in many different places. Its greatest benefit lies in a layered approach to networking. These layers help differentiate parts of the network. However, the real world does not follow the OSI layering model. Vendors build their products in layers, but most components do not match the OSI model. Instead, other factors play an important role.

The Seven Layers of OSI

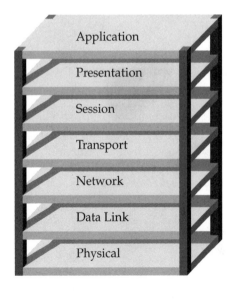

OSI Reference Model

You can think of the OSI model as layers built on top of each other. If a vendor produces an OSI product, strict adherence to the model requires that every communication pass through each layer, not skipping any as is common in MS-DOS programming. In reality, even some OSI products or protocols skip certain layers.

The most critical layers are the physical layer, the data link layer and the transport layer. Every network has these components. In real world networks, combinations of the other layers can be skipped or missing depending on the network and its design.

FIGURE 2.1 Open Systems Interconnection Model

Physical Layer

The lowest layer of the OSI model carries the weight of the other layers figuratively and literally. The *physical layer* is responsible for the electrical and mechanical aspects of the data transfer. This primarily means how the bits are transmitted and how the related voltages, timing and other electrical nuances are handled. By definition, the OSI model physical layer says nothing about the actual cable used to transfer the data or how the cable is physically laid out in the network. We raise these issues later in Chapter 2 because they are crucial to success in networking.

Data Link Layer

The most critical yet most confusing of all the layers, the *data link layer* is responsible for host-to-host communications, taking the data or packets and placing them into frames for transmission across the network. The data-link protocol is responsibility for ensuring the packets or frames of data arrive safely. There are many different data-link protocols including serial protocols like Xmodem or Ymodem (discussed in Chapter 9), IBM mainframe protocols like Synchronous Data Link Control (SDLC) or X.25 (discussed later in Chapter 2). These are referred to as flow control protocols.

The data link layer of the OSI model is frequently divided into two sub-layers—logical link layer and media access control (MAC). The MAC sub-layer is concerned with how the data uses the physical media, and is also known as the logical topology. We spend a significant amount of time discussing the various logical topologies which includes Ethernet and Token-Ring. It lays closest to the physical layer. The logical link layer brings the information delivered by the MAC driver to the correct communications protocol.

Network Layer

The *network layer* is responsible for finding the best route to the destination node. In a single LAN, the network layer services, while present, seldom do much work, since there is no routing by definition. In a network with subnets or in a wide-area network, the network layer works with assorted software, routers, bridges and gateways to find the most expedient method of moving the packets.

Transport Layer

The *transport layer* is an important layer and is always involved in a network scenario. It makes sure the data gets to where it is going in the shape it was sent. Think of it as the Federal Express tracking system. It makes sure it gets there by 10:30 or else! If there is a problem with the network, the transport layer looks for alternate means of delivery. In network terms, the transport layer makes sure the packets are received, there are no duplicates, and they are placed in the correct order after they are received. We spend more time on the services provided by the transport level when we talk about specific communication protocols later in the chapter.

Session Layer

The next three layers provide services to the applications in different ways and are less involved in the transmission of the data. When two machines are connected, there is a logical session. Managing this session is the job of the *session layer*. The session layer controls the flow of data and handles the termination of the session. Session services include logging on and providing security.

Presentation Layer

The *presentation layer* acts as the interpreter between interfaces, translating the information received from the session layer into something the receiving machine can understand. This can involve character translation (ASCII to EBCDIC), encryption, compression, and formatting. Programs familiar to the user such as the GUI may be responsible for presentation layer actions.

Application Layer

Layer 7, the *application layer*, is seldom the user's application, as is often thought. Rather, the user's application communicates to some network services provided at the application layer. These services can be file transfer, terminal emulation, network management and electronic messaging. Many utilities provided with TCP/IP packages work at the application layer.

The MBKP Practical Decision Model

The best place for the OSI model is in a pure OSI environment where OSI equipment and software are being used. As for the rest of the world, we need a different model. Now, we are not so presumptuous as to suggest we can propose something better than a committee of experts could create over a number of years. But we can give you something innovative to sink your teeth into and perhaps make understanding networks a little easier.

For the sake of discussion, let's call our model the MBKP Practical Decision Model (see Figure 2.2). Its premise is one of realism and simplicity. It has seven components rather than seven layers. The components are organized by what you really need to know when building/working with networks; particularly when working in the DOS—UNIX internetworking environment. The remainder of this chapter uses the model as its guide and explains these topics as they relate to networking and internetworking. We do not refer to the model outside of this chapter.

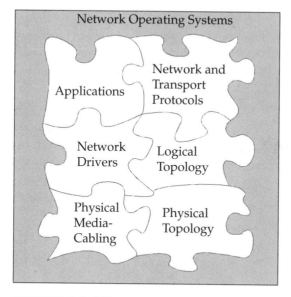

MBKP Practical Decision Model.

This model looks like a puzzle because putting together a network is somewhat like building a puzzle. You need to consider different components of a network decision process. These same decisions are required when connecting DOS to UNIX. We present each component in a semi-orderly fashion to familiarize you with the terminology of the network wizard. However, the decision-making process can begin at different places in the puzzle.

FIGURE 2.2 MBKP Practical Decision Model

What Is a Physical Topology?

The confusion between physical topologies and logical topologies haunts nearly every network neophyte. Often, people speak about topologies in general without having a specific meaning in mind. The phrase "physical topology" refers to how you lay out the different machines or nodes on the network. When you read books on the theoretical aspects of networking, you find many different layouts suggested. However, in practical terms, we believe there are only three physical layouts worth discussing—bus, or daisy chain; ring; and star. We discuss each briefly.

Bus or daisy chain

Perhaps the most prevalent physical topology is the linear bus or *daisy chain*. Its popularity relates directly to its simplicity. As Figure 2.3 shows, each node connects to the next node on the chain. With the *bus topology*, there are always two ends to the chain. Each end terminates the chain. This method is common among Ethernet installations, particularly those using thinnet cable, also known as 10Base2. In an Ethernet thinnet network, each node connects with a BNC T connector—a T-shaped device to connect the network adaptor to the cable.

The bus topology has become popular with small networks because it is easy to install. Just run a single cable from one machine to the next, forming a chain. The signals do not travel in one direction, but go out in both directions from each node. However, the biggest problem with a daisy chain is the "one down, all down syndrome." If you experience a cable break on the network, all the machines go down. If you disconnect a workstation, the network remains running as long as you have only disconnected the cable from the machine and not broken the cable.

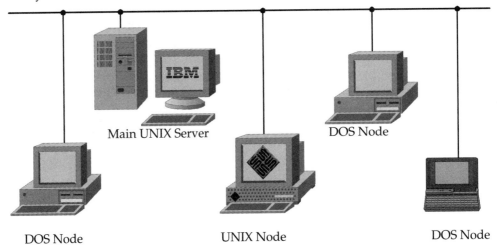

Main UNIX Server   DOS Node

DOS Node   UNIX Node   DOS Node

FIGURE 2.3 Bus topology with PCs and a central file server

Ring

The second physical method of layout is a *ring topology*. As the term indicates, the ring represents a closed circle of nodes. Normally, network traffic moves in only one direction. This reduces the possibilities of data getting lost in *collisions*— a problem when two data packets run into each other. As Figure 2.4 shows, the ring method also provides a simple layout. It too suffers from the same problem associated with the bus topology—one bad connection brings down the network.

The ring topology allows for high speed data movement because the collision detection aspects can be simpler. In most cases, a ring uses some type of token passing scheme (see Token Ring under Logical Topologies); however, a token passing scheme does not necessarily use a ring topology. In many cases, the ring is never physically created but instead is done through some type of concentrator and shows itself as a star topology.

Star

Quickly becoming the leading network physical topology for PCs is the star method. A central host, concentrator, or controller is the centerpiece of a *star topology*. Each node communicates directly with the central node (see Figure 2.5). The traffic goes from the node to the central hub and back. It is easy to see that a star configuration is going to use more cable because every node has a string of cable returning to the

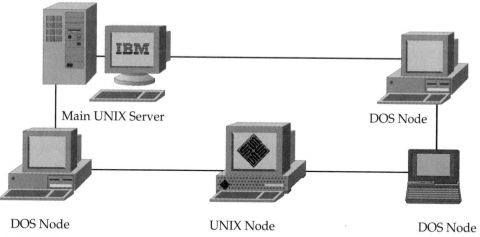

Main UNIX Server   DOS Node

DOS Node   UNIX Node   DOS Node

FIGURE 2.4 Ring topology

central host. However, if the cable for one station is bad, the remainder of the network stays up. You can also use a lower grade network cable since the connection needs to handle only the traffic of one node. For this reason UTP is commonly used in a star topology.

In a simple UNIX scenario using a star topology, the UNIX host can act as the hub or central host with all the nodes going off of it. In other more common PC or mixed network scenarios, the central controller for a star topology is a device called a hub or concentrator. In the world of Token Ring, the Multistation Access Unit (MAU) is the controller that connects all the nodes.

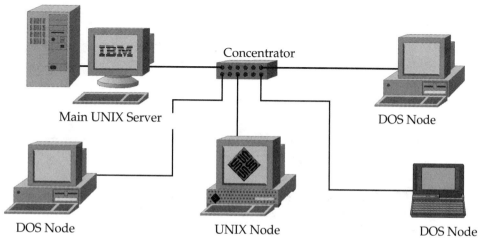

Concentrator

Main UNIX Server   DOS Node

DOS Node   UNIX Node   DOS Node

FIGURE 2.5 Star topology with a concentrator at the center

What Is Physical Media?

Unrelated to the layers of the OSI model, but important in the selection of the network options to be used by your company, is the physical media, or *cable*. There are many cable options (see Figure 2.6), and while some cables function in any type of networking environment, others require specific networking solutions. In Chapter 4, we cover specifics on how to use and install cabling, particularly UTP and coaxial. Here, we give you an overview of the cable types. If you already have cable in place from your current network, your choice becomes easier. If not, your cable decision will be made early in the overall network decision-making process.

Twisted Pair—Shielded and Unshielded

Perhaps the most misunderstood and misapplied cable type is *twisted pair*. Often touted as the cheapest and easiest to work with, twisted pair cable is not always so. Often people confuse twisted pair with other similar cables like multiconductor cable or Quad telephone cable. Multiconductor cable, suitable for serial connections, is discussed in Chapter 9. Quad is the type of cable used in residential phone wiring. Neither of these cable types is suitable for LAN communications.

Twisted pair, as the term connotes, comprises a pair of wires twisted around each other to reduce electrical interference. There can be two, four, or more pairs in a single wrapper. Commonly found in newer buildings as the primary communication option, twisted pair is often associated with PBXs and telephone connections. Twisted pair comes in two varieties, shielded (STP) and unshielded (UTP) with UTP generally considered the easier to use. Signals on twisted pair travel at 10 mbps to meet Ethernet standards. In addition, since twisted pair can handle only one channel of data, it is baseband or single channel in nature. The connections on twisted pair

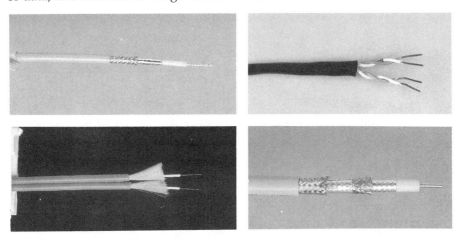

FIGURE 2.6   Clockwise from upper left: thinnet, UTP, thicknet, and fiber optic cable

usually require RJ-11 or RJ-45 modular connectors, the same connectors used for telephone purposes. Chapter 4 discusses how to make these connections.

STP is commonly used in IBM's Token Ring Network (see later in this chapter) and, because of the shielding, costs substantially more than UTP. STP provides a lower interference problem than UTP and often operates at higher speeds, up to 100 mbps under proposed Fast Ethernet standards. However, it is also bulkier and more difficult to work with. UTP, also known as 10Base-T when used with Ethernet, is commonly used in a star or hub topology. The small bandwidth and slow speed represent relatively minor problems when running from the hub to a single workstation. Be advised that the UTP cable already existing in your office can sometimes be used if there are extra twisted pairs of wires not in use and the cable is data grade. However, this convenience is frequently overrated and can result in picking the wrong cable for the job.

Coaxial Cable

Coaxial cable (*coax*) is probably the most popular type of cabling for LANs and internetwork. The basic design of coax remains the same regardless of its use. An insulator, usually plastic, surrounds an inner conductor, usually stranded, but it can be solid. Around the insulator is a wire mesh acting as the second conductor. This is all wrapped in a jacket (made of PVC or other material) as shown in Figure 2.7. Coaxial cable handles transmissions faster than twisted pair because coaxial has less impedance or electrical resistance. Also, due to its wider bandwidth, coax can be used for broadband or multiple channel communications. There are many kinds of coaxial including TV cable, thick, ARCnet, and thin coaxial. We describe thick and thin coax since these are the varieties you encounter in a DOS—UNIX internetwork.

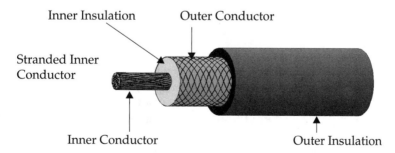

FIGURE 2.7 Drawing of Coaxial Cable

Thick coaxial

Thick coax is a heavy, frequently yellow-colored cable used as the network backbone in Ethernet installations. Known formally as standard Ethernet PVC coax (or 10Base5), thick coax can be difficult to work with because of its weight and lack of flexibility. While seldom used as the direct connection to the workstation, thick coax is often used as a *backbone* cable. The backbone runs through a building and is tapped by other cables. Tapping a thick coax cable is difficult but can be done with the right tools. Because of its size, thick coax costs plenty, but it can handle faster speeds (like all coax) than twisted pair cables because of its lower electrical resistance. It can also handle many channels of data and, as such, can be used in a broadband network situation. A thick coax cable may be as long as 500 meters and increased to 2500 meters with *repeaters*—providing the possibility of many nodes.

Thin coaxial

The more common coaxial cable is the thinner cable, known as RG-58. It also goes by the names 10Base2, cheapernet, and *thinnet*. The 802.3 Ethernet specification itself calls for RG-58 A/U stranded-core coaxial. Depending on the vendor, you can find it called solid-core RG-58U, stranded-core RG-58 A/U and thinnet. Some cable vendors charge more depending on the specification. While the Ethernet specification is stranded-core, many people use solid core RG-58. You will be safe if you say you want stranded-core RG-58 for an 802.3 thin Ethernet installation.

On the other hand, thinnet does differ from RG-62, the cable specification used with ARCnet networks. thinnet can be used in a bus and ring topology since it is relatively easy to work with and uses T-connectors to make the connection to each workstation. It has an impedance of 50 ohms and is relatively immune to noise. We discuss how to make and install thinnet cable in Chapter 4 and recommend it in many DOS—UNIX connectivity scenarios. Thin coax is designed to handle speeds up to 10 megabits per second in an Ethernet environment. Even faster speeds are now possible with the more expensive LAN adapter hardware.

Fiber-Optic

The most expensive, albeit the most promising, cabling technology is *fiber-optic* cable. Also used by telephone companies and cable TV companies, fiber-optic cable provides the major advantage of being able to push multiple signals (high bandwidth)—perhaps 100 or more—through a single fiber. In the last few years, it has become possible not only to use fiber-optic cable as the corporate backbone, but also to run it to the workstation. Fiber cable can have many times more nodes on a single network than can a coaxial or UTP-based Ethernet. Fiber-optic comes in many varieties and combinations. Generally, the fibers are either glass or plastic and surrounded by a plastic or glass cladding. Fiber also represents the fastest option available, because it offers no resistance to the signals. Unlike copper wiring, fiber optic experiences no electrical loss during transmission.

In addition, fiber provides a high level of security since the cable cannot be tapped like a copper cable. If you tap into a fiber cable, the continuous pulse of light is disrupted and the signal ends. On the down side, this same security advantage makes it difficult to use fiber in place of coaxial cable in many situations. If you add more nodes, you cannot simply tap into the fiber (although there are some recent advances in that area). Fiber-optic cable is lightweight and unbothered by such environmental dangers as water and heat, which threaten copper cable. Because of its small size and tremendous bandwidth, fiber promises to be one of the primary cables of the future.

In the past, creating a fiber-optic finished cable required a professional, but not so now. The existence of the AMP LightCrimp tool kit makes it possible for anyone to learn how to put connectors on fiber optic cable. However, the kit runs you around $1000, and the other needed peripherals like adapters are still expensive. In most DOS—UNIX internetworking scenarios you will find fiber-optic cabling too costly and difficult to work with except when used as a high-speed link between wiring closets across buildings and installations.

Wireless

The final cabling scheme we mention actually represents a non-cabling scheme. We are referring to *wireless* LANs. Wireless LANs are becoming increasingly popular because of their improvements in technology and ease of installation. A wireless LAN is, in reality, only partially wireless. Each workstation communicates to a hub or concentrator using either radio frequencies or infrared light. Infrared connections must be line of sight while radio frequencies are subject to interference and both can be slow for application interoperability. The hub is still connected to the network with standard cabling. Wireless arrangements are more expensive than standard cabling options. However, their success and position in the marketplace is likely guaranteed because certain large corporations are backing the concept. For example Motorola with their Altair system, NCR with their WaveLAN, and Xircom with their Netwave are all advocates of wireless connections for portions of the LAN equation.

What Is a Logical Topology?

The next link of the networking chain is the *logical topology*. Logical network topology refers to the method of data transport around the network. It is also known as *access method*, *access scheme*, or *logical network*. The logical topology roughly equates with the data link layer in the OSI model. The OSI data link layer is concerned with the method used to convey the data—in effect what we have termed a logical topology. You can often use a different physical topology with different logical topologies with some restrictions. In addition, you might choose your logical topology before choosing any other aspects of our network. Logical topologies include Ethernet, Token Ring, ARCnet, and FDDI (Fiber Distributed Data Interface). Although other topologies exist (such as X.25), we only briefly mention them because they are not commonly used in DOS—UNIX internetworking.

Ethernet

The most common topology is *Ethernet*. Designed in the 70s by Xerox Corp., Ethernet was popularized in the 80s by its acceptance as IEEE 802.3. Here again, however, we see where terminology is confusing and not consistent. The IEEE 802.3 standard is not exactly the same as what many people refer to as Ethernet. We try to clear up some of the differences in the next few paragraphs. Ethernet is used by all UNIX hosts and workstations and is the primary topology when considering DOS—UNIX internetworking. Ethernet represents a broadcast network; in other words, every node receives every transmission. It uses the CSMA/CD (carrier sense multiple access/collision detection) baseband method of moving packets on the network.

Here's roughly how it works. Every node on the network listens to see if the network is transmitting before sending a *packet*. If the network is busy, the node waits until there are no signals present. When the network is quiet, the node transmits its packet. However, since nodes are at different locations, two different nodes can end up transmitting during the same silent time. The result is a packet collision. If a collision is detected, both nodes send out a jam signal over the network, and all the nodes stop transmitting and go into a wait mode. Then on a random basis, they go back to listening/transmitting. The packets caught in the collision are re-sent when there is an opportunity. The random restart helps to make sure there are not more collisions immediately when all the nodes start to retransmit.

Ethernet transmits information in frames or packets called *datagrams*. Ethernet packets have a particular structure underlying how the data and routing information are packaged inside. This is where Ethernet and the 802.3 standard have become somewhat muddled. Figure 2.8 shows a typical true Ethernet frame, as originally created. However, the IEEE 802.3 standard has altered the packet as compared with true Ethernet. The main difference is that the frame type field in Ethernet has been replaced with a byte count field. True Ethernet frames are used by nearly all TCP/IP products and can also be called *DIX Ethernet*, or *Ethernet II*. Novell, on the other hand, uses *802.3* frames. Both frames can travel over the same cable, but you need a different communication protocol for each type of frame. NetWare is fundamentally incompatible with TCP/IP setups unless you change NetWare to use the TCP/IP frame type or run dual protocol stacks. Dual stacks involve running two different protocols at the same time and are explained later in the chapter. All this causes the confusion we hear when people refer to their network as using 802.3 Ethernet. Are they using 802.3? Or Ethernet? Although we recommend careful attention to the frame type, go ahead and call it all Ethernet.

Ethernet is highly susceptible to slow-downs on the networks when the number of nodes increases. More nodes mean more collisions, and collisions slow down the overall effectiveness of the network. This is one reason your actual throughput is often much less than the 10 megabits per second rating of Ethernet. There is more than one type of Ethernet network—referring to the overall network implementation. The common Ethernet types are 10Base-T (10 mbps, baseband, UTP cable), 10Base2 (10 mbps, baseband, thin coax cable), and 10Base5 (10 mbps, baseband,

Destination Address: 6 Bytes	Source Address: 6 Bytes	Type: 2 Bytes	Frame Data: 46 - 1500 Bytes	CRC: 4 Bytes

Ethernet II

Destination Address: 6 Bytes	Source Address: 6 Bytes	Packet Length: 2 Bytes	Frame Data: 46 - 1500 Bytes	CRC: 4 Bytes

IEEE 802.3 Ethernet

FIGURE 2.8   Ethernet II vs. 802.3 Ethernet packets

thick cable). Faster Ethernet specifications for up to 100 mbps per second are under consideration by various standards committees, and some products are available now. Broadband or multiple channel Ethernet standards also exist.

Token Ring

Token Ring is based on the IEEE 802.5 standard which comes from the developmental work of IBM in the early 80s. IBM Token-Ring Network provides the most popular and only significant commercial implementation of the token ring logical topology. Instead of using collision detection, token ring networks use a token passing scheme to avoid collisions. A free token is passed around the network to each node in turn. When a node wants to transmit, it grabs the token and attaches its packet or frame to it. Now the token is unavailable to the other stations until the data arrives at its destination, and the originating station removes the data. The token goes around the network in a specific order and every station is polled in that order.

Token Ring can be a confusing topology to understand. Its physical topology is almost always a star layout with a Multistation Access Unit (MAU) acting as the hub. "Wait a minute!" you say. "How can it use token passing in a star configuration?" The answer lies in the logical ring occurring inside the hub. This gives the ring-within-the-star topology. Most often token ring uses STP cabling, but it can use UTP. The two speed standards are 4 mbps and 16 mbps, but don't expect to make direct comparisons with Ethernet on speed. Basically, there is little consensus among the industry when it comes to comparisons. Factors such as cabling, distances, number of nodes, amount of traffic, etc., all influence true loads and throughput. IBM's Token Ring network is the industry leader. There also exists an IEEE standard for a Token Bus network, IEEE 802.4.

ARCnet

ARCnet was developed by Datapoint in the 70s and was made popular by Standard Microsystems Inc. It uses a token passing scheme combined with broadcast. The token is passed to all stations with each station having a specific broadcast number. ARCnet normally runs at 2.5 mbps. While this does not represent very high throughput, there is a new 20 mbps ARCnet standard now available. ARCnet uses RG-62 coaxial cable (although a twisted pair option is available) and lower cost adapters than Ethernet. ARCnet uses a star physical topology—limited to 2000 feet between stations and uses active and passive hubs with each node no further than 100 feet from a passive hub. Its biggest problem is lack of acceptance by the IEEE and the growth of Ethernet in the 80s. ARCnet cannot run across the same cabling as Ethernet and thus is seldom used in a DOS—UNIX internetworking environment.

Fiber Distributed Data Interface (FDDI)

FDDI is a scheme dependent on the use of fiber optic cable (although a copper-based FDDI proposal is in the works, called CDDI). It relies on two concentric rings each operating at 100 mbps and using token passing in a variation of 802.5. The one ring can be a backup, or the rings can divide up the tasks of send and receive—sending the data in different directions. With the FDDI scheme, you can have up to 1000 stations on the network. FDDI is not directly compatible with Ethernet, but Ethernet packets can be encapsulated within an FDDI packet. FDDI is not an IEEE standard and therefore competes with 802.6, IEEE's Metropolitan Area Network (MAN) specification. FDDI is popular as a backbone topology.

WAN Topologies

There are many more topologies used when creating wide-area networks (WANs). These include ISDN, ATM, X.25, Frame Relay, and Fast Ethernet. Each of these has its place and we mention them briefly here. However, DOS—UNIX internetworking across high cost, high speed WAN topologies is beyond our range of discussion. *ISDN* is Integrated System Digital Network and is a topology designed to use high speed phone lines to transmit digital voice data. ISDN can be used for data, voice, and video, but it appears as if other technologies are going to pass it by. *ATM*, Asynchronous Transfer Mode, is a high band-width technology that has potential to move data at 600 Mbps or higher. ATM derives from a specification for broadband ISDN. ATM uses small fixed-length packets and is not a contention-based topology like Ethernet or Token Ring. ATM does have actual interface cards available and can be used at the LAN level, but is extremely expensive.

   X.25 is packet-switching standard that is popular in Europe. X.25 is not used in LAN environments. It is most commonly used in large public networks. X.25 defines the connection between the data terminal equipment and the public network. *Frame Relay* is a variation on X.25 with faster message acknowledgment and therefore faster transmission. It, too, is used in packet-switching networks and not found in LAN technology. *Fast Ethernet* is nothing more than a set of concepts being proposed to the IEEE 802.3 committee. There are two main contenders that claim speeds of 100 Mbps. One proposed method runs over 4-pair UTP but does not use the CSMA/CD associated with classic Ethernet. The other proposed standard uses Type 5 cable specified by FDDI but proposes technologies that are as yet untested. Neither of these Fast Ethernet technologies are readily available in any size, shape or form, although vendors promise products by early 1994.

What Are LAN Adapter Drivers?

No topic has been more ignored or mistreated than LAN adapter drivers (also known as network drivers). The LAN adapter driver is the piece of software that allows the network interface card (NIC) to communicate with the network communications protocol (discussed in the next section). The NIC is the actual physical board inserted in your PC or workstation that connects to the network cable. Normally, network drivers coincide with the upper half of data-link layer of the OSI model called the Media Access Control (MAC) layer. Drivers don't present much of an issue on a UNIX workstation, because workstations come equipped with a manufacturer-provided adapter. However, drivers are a key issue with PCs. One confusing issue becomes the variety of network driver types and the different sources for drivers. Network adapter vendors always supply a set of drivers with their product; other sources include the PC network operating system and TCP/IP products meant to connect DOS and UNIX. You need to know the main types of adapters and how they differ. Depending on your circumstances certain drivers make your life easier. The following information gives you some firm footing to traverse the slippery slopes of the network driver landscape.

Driver Fundamentals

In the interest of making the marketplace a fun place for purchasers and installers of network equipment, vendors decided to introduce network drivers. (This means the vendor wants to lock you into their software.) There are four main driver types that you might encounter in your own selection process—NDIS (Network Driver Interface Specification), ODI (Open Datalink Interface), ASI (Adapter Support Interface), and Packet drivers. Each has unique features as pointed out in the following sections. However, they are more alike than different.

Each driver is a piece of software designed to act as the intermediary between the network interface card (NIC) and the communications protocol (like TCP/IP or IPX/SPX). The network driver handles interrupts, I/O, and other issues at the MAC sub-layer of the data link layer of the OSI model. Thus, they are occasionally called MAC level drivers. Different drivers have different layers or components. However, regardless of the number of components found within the driver, its main job remains constant. It picks up the packets or frames from the NIC and gives them to the communications protocol. Some drivers allow you to have more than one protocol running (called dual stacks or multiple protocols). The driver determines which protocol needs a particular frame and passes it on to the correct one. This dual proto-

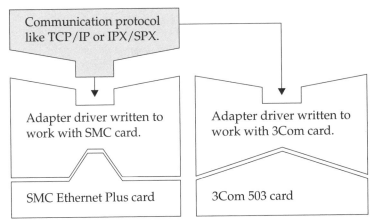

FIGURE 2.9 LAN adapter drivers fit between the adapter card and the communication protocol.

col ability is particularly useful in DOS—UNIX internetworking where two different protocols are not uncommon.

It is critical to realize that a driver is designed to work with a particular NIC. As shown in Figure 2.9, the driver is written to a specific NIC or series of NICs. The driver talks to the NIC on one end and talks to the communication protocol on the other end. This allows the communications protocol to use the wide variety of NICs on the market without having to make special exceptions for each one. With the correct driver, any NIC can work with your communication protocol.

One good source of information on network drivers for laymen comes from FTP Software Inc. in their handy *Interoperability Guide*. See Appendix B for more information. Most books on networking and manuals from vendors give only cursory treatment of network drivers.

NDIS

In 1988, Microsoft and 3COM created the NDIS driver specification. Its primary purpose was to support LAN Manager and 3COM networks. Even though 3COM no longer sells a network operating system, and LAN Manager does not have a large market share, NDIS was adopted by many vendors and remains a popular solution in DOS—UNIX internetworking.

NDIS uses an extra program called the protocol manager (**PROTMAN.SYS**) to connect the MAC or network drivers to the communications protocol. Like a traffic cop, **PROTMAN.SYS** directs the packets to the correct communications protocol. This is one of the reasons NDIS is so useful in multiple protocol environments. The protocol manager is available in the public domain but is usually provided by the TCP/IP or communications protocol vendor. The biggest problem with NDIS is the particular sensitivity of **PROTMAN.SYS** as loaded in the **CONFIG.SYS** file.

ODI

ODI drivers were a direct response by Novell to Microsoft's NDIS drivers. As you might expect, ODI works primarily on a NetWare network. ODI also allows multiple communications protocols to operate on the same machine. There are two layers to ODI, the MLID (Multiple Link Interface Driver), which is the actual MAC driver supplied by the card manufacturer, and LSL (Link Support Layer), which is provided by Novell. **LSL.COM** rides on top of the driver and passes the packets to another program called **IPXODI.COM.**, whose job is to get the packets to the correct communications protocol. ODI drivers are nearly always used in a pure Novell network, but can be used in a TCP/IP network that is connecting UNIX machines to a Novell NetWare setup. Most TCP/IP products support ODI drivers.

Packet

Packet drivers were a common driver available for multiple protocols and many TCP/IP networks in the mid-80s. They are often referred to as the Clarkson drivers, because Clarkson University has collected and maintained a large number of them—available in the public domain. The packet driver is a simple concept. It comes as a single piece of software that loads either as a TSR or a DOS device driver (depending on how it is written), allowing multiple protocol stacks by reading each packet and passing it along to the proper communications protocol. Packet drivers can figure out specifics about the network card; for example, the hardware interrupt or address space. This makes installation easier than some of the other driver options. While these drivers do not come from a specific vendor, the drivers are specific to each vendor's card. There are many different packet drivers available. However, packet drivers are not always supported by the TCP/IP vendors and notes to that affect are found in many TCP/IP packages. We found packet drivers provided only one advantage not found in NDIS or ODI for internetworking; they take the least amount of memory on your DOS machine, an important consideration for some.

ASI

The Adapter Support Interface was created by IBM for its Token-Ring networks in the mid-80s. It differs from the other types in that it only works with Token-Ring networks and not Ethernet. There are two parts to ASI, the adapter support device driver and the interrupt arbitrator. The interrupt arbitrator sits on top of the NIC and passes the packets to the device driver. The driver then loads from the **CONFIG.SYS** file. Other vendors such as 3Com, Proteon, and Standard Microsystems supply ASI drivers. If you are using OS/2 on a Token-Ring network, you might be using IBM's Communication Manager drivers. It would be unlikely for those to be used in a DOS—UNIX environment.

What Are Communications Protocols?

The next part of the puzzle is important and often confused by those new to the networking world. Communications protocols are responsible for packaging the data and formatting it for transmission to the destination as well as insuring it gets to the right place in the fastest manner. Communication protocols allow data to get from one node or machine to another machine in a standard format. Communication protocol products tend to correspond to the network and transport layers of the OSI model. For example, with respect to TCP/IP, the IP portion fits within the network layer, and the TCP portion fits into the transport layer. However, not all protocols fit nicely in a specific layer of the OSI model. Depending on a variety of interpretations, communication protocols can also overlap session and presentation layers.

The communications protocol is often referred to as the *protocol stack*. When someone says he or she is using a *dual stack*, that person is referring to the situation in which the machine uses two incompatible communications protocols simultaneously. In that case, a LAN adapter driver is directing the packets to the correct protocol for further processing. We avoid a detailed technical discussion of all the different protocols available today. There are only two or three protocols which have much impact in the DOS—UNIX internetworking field.

TCP/IP

TCP/IP (Transmission Control Protocol/Internet Protocol) is the core set of protocols used in DOS—UNIX internetworking. Because of its importance, we provide a bit of history, a discussion of the key components of TCP/IP and information about the Internet. If you would like to know the most intimate details of TCP/IP, in particular, see *Internetworking with TCP/IP* by Douglas Comer (Prentice Hall) or *Troubleshooting TCP/IP* by Mark E. Miller (M & T Books).

History

TCP/IP originated in the 70s as research funded by the U.S. Department of Defense's Advanced Research Project Agency (DARPA) which itself was born in 1969. At the time, the Defense Department needed a non-proprietary means of moving data across various types of media including serial lines. For most of the 70s, DARPA's work was limited to researchers. TCP/IP got its biggest boost in the early 80s due to two events. First, the Department of Defense mandated the use of TCP/IP for its interconnections. Second, because universities were using BSD UNIX, TCP/IP was ported to run UNIX and most vendors shipped the TCP/IP protocol free of charge with BSD UNIX. This provided strong impetus in the marketplace for TCP/IP's acceptance since it was free and could be used on nearly any size machine. In the mid 80s, PC versions of TCP/IP began to appear from companies like FTP Software Inc. TCP/IP is the main protocol of choice when internetworking between DOS and UNIX. The majority of solutions discussed in later chapters rely on TCP/IP.

One major result of DARPA is the *Internet*. The Internet (with a capital I or referred to as the connected Internet by some) is a collection of networks using TCP/IP to route information, files and e-mail around the U.S and around the world. In order to participate on the Internet, you have to have an address and a method to tie into an Internet network node. Nearly all universities and military sites are Internet nodes as well as many commercial businesses. The Internet relies on TCP/IP and is a packet-switched network of networks. You can find out more about the Internet in Chapter 12 and Chapter 18 as well as from the books in Appendix B.

Description

TCP/IP is really made up of two protocols. The TCP portion operates at the transport level of the OSI model. TCP adds a destination port and other information to the outgoing data, and puts the resultant group of information in what is called a TCP segment. IP operates at the network level. It picks up the segment from the transport level along with destination information. It adds specific routing information (whether to deliver the packet directly or through a router), and the data is now a called an IP datagram. Finally, the IP *datagram* is passed to the network driver at the data-link layer, and further heading information is attached. The datagram becomes a packet or a frame ready for transmission across the network.

Some attributes of TCP/IP are, first, it is a reliable protocol. It guarantees the packet is received by the destination. If the packet is not received, it notifies the sending node. After the notification, TCP/IP resends the packet. It is also an open protocol. In other words, it is available to any and all comers—not tied to any particular vendor. This openness has allowed TCP/IP to become the standard in UNIX networking even though OSI is the officially recognized international standard. The IP portion of TCP/IP may not be used if the destination node of the packet is on the same physical network as the sending node.

The Internet Protocol Suite

TCP/IP is a part of a larger picture called The TCP/IP Internet Protocol Suite. Besides the communication protocol aspects of TCP/IP, there are higher level services which can be important for different functions. These include Standard Mail Transport Protocol (SMTP), used for e-mail; File Transfer Protocol (**ftp**), used in the transfer of large files; **telnet**, the telecommunications emulation protocol, used in logon situations; and a set of other utilities. NFS (Network File System) from Sun Microsystems is not a formal part of TCP/IP, but it is built on it. Any standard TCP/IP implementation contains all these elements. Detailed discussions of these utilities can be found in Chapter 5.

A variation of the TCP/IP protocols are a set of serial line protocols. The original specification, SLIP (Serial Line Internet Protocol) has been replaced by PPP (Point-to-Point Protocol). Both of the protocols allow a user to make a connection to a TCP/IP network via a direct serial connection or over a modem. But if you give vendors an inch, they take a mile. Because of performance problems with PPP, two additional proprietary protocols have appeared. Tektronix Inc. has developed Xpress and NCD Inc. has developed Xremote. Both of these protocols allow X terminals and PC-based X servers to use serial lines to communicate with a TCP/IP network.

IPX/SPX

IPX/SPX (Internetwork Packet Exchange/Sequenced Packet Exchange) is the communication protocol developed by Novell for its NetWare networks. It is a subset of the Xerox Network Services (XNS). IPX/SPX is similar to TCP/IP in terms of function and compatibility with the layers on the OSI model. IPX is the network protocol for a Novell network while SPX is the transport layer protocol. You can use IPX/SPX to interconnect Novell to UNIX by a number of different options. The most common is to give the UNIX host IPX/SPX capability.

SPX provides guaranteed delivery, similar to TCP, by tracking the transmissions and resending them if no acknowledgment was received. SPX works closely with IPX, the real workhorse portion of Novell's communication suite. The NetWare shell prepares packets of information before handing them to IPX. IPX addresses and routes packets to their destination. IPX then uses the LAN driver to send the packet over the network. IPX works with many different boards and drivers, though it is partial to ODI drivers. Incoming packets are read by IPX and directed to the proper layer in the NetWare server or client.

NetBIOS and NetBEUI

Information about *NetBIOS* (Network Basic Input Output System) and *NetBEUI* (NetBIOS Extended User Interface) is difficult both to find and to understand. IBM developed NetBIOS in 1984 as part of its original PC Network and the subsequent PC LAN. Later, with the introduction of its Token-Ring Network, IBM expanded NetBIOS to NetBEUI. Many vendors, particularly in the PC market have adopted NetBIOS, including OS/2 LAN Server, Microsoft LAN Manager, Artisoft LANtastic and other DOS-based peer-to-peer networks.

NetBIOS is not a true communications protocol. It operates at the session and presentation layer and is charged with establishing sessions and providing the ability to send and receive information on a peer-to-peer network. NetBEUI extends the capability of NetBIOS to act more like a communication protocol in the transport layer. There is an Internet RFC (Request For Comment) that proposes a NetBIOS to TCP/IP connection. We found no products using this standard.

SNA

System Network Architecture (SNA) is the overall networking model created and supported by IBM. Because of IBM's massive presence in the marketplace, it has been able to make SNA a de facto standard in the marketplace. SNA uses numerous specific protocols within its realm—such as synchronous data link control (SDLC). The main success of SNA lies in connecting IBM mainframes to other IBM systems—such as the System/3x with the AS/400. SNA is now part of IBM's grandiose scheme called Systems Application Architecture (SAA) to interconnect various IBM and non-IBM computers. Overall, SAA has not met with the success of SNA due to widespread acceptance of open standards. Outside of the mainframe world, there exists little support for SAA, even where IBM equipment is involved.

DECNet

DECNet, formally known as Digital Network Architecture, is a protocol designed by Digital Equipment Corp. to connect different types of computers, including IBM mainframes and DEC VAX. They also are used to bring together wide-area networks and various LANs. DECnet uses Ethernet as its primary topology but also supports X.25. While DECNet existed before the OSI model, DEC has made efforts to form its protocol around OSI standards. The bottom five layers of DECNet generally look exactly like the OSI model. In a strong DEC environment, DECNet makes a lot of sense, but for most DOS—UNIX internetworking, you would not likely purchase a DECNet solution.

What Is a Network Operating System?

Our final topic in this network primer is the concept of Network Operating Systems. Perhaps somewhat foreign to UNIX users, the Network Operating System (or NOS) is a necessity in the PC world for a very simple reason. MS-DOS is a single user operating system—no file sharing, no remote logins, no e-mail, no file transfer. This shortcoming did not go unnoticed, and the 80s produced a plethora of NOS choices. We mention the more common operating systems here. A NOS encompasses many of the parts we have discussed earlier in the chapter.

An NOS is usually independent of the physical media, the logical topology and the physical topology. However, some NOSs are limited by design to certain types of set-ups. In any case, an NOS has to encompass each of the technologies discussed in this chapter. The NOS provides the basic software to make it all happen.

We have no intention of supplying detailed information on these complex products. Instead we limit ourselves to a brief discussion of the most popular NOSs and the ones we discuss in later chapters.

Novell NetWare is the most popular NOS among PC users. NetWare is available in at least 4 different forms. Three of the products, NetWare 2.x, 3.11 and 4.0 are all client/server technologies. This means there is one or more NetWare servers where all the NetWare clients access services. The file server stores all the data files and services the requests of the client for programs or data. The fourth product, NetWare Lite, is a peer-to-peer network allowing every machine to share files and peripherals. By virtue of Novell's commanding share of the marketplace, many of the concepts and products we review use a Novell server in one fashion or another.

Banyan VINES is a PC NOS based on the UNIX operating system. It is similar in features to NetWare. Banyan is best known for its network services. These services, known as ENS (Enterprise Network Services) allow VINES to manage all the resources on multiple networks as a single network. This makes VINES and ENS a good fit for larger corporations.

Microsoft LAN Manager and IBM OS/2 LAN Server are very similar. They both run on OS/2 and have the same genesis. Both products provide the whole suite of NOS functions including security, file sharing, resource sharing, and directory services. Neither product enjoys significant market success; however, they are used in many circumstances. LAN Manager is also available to run on a UNIX server, making it a worthy choice to consider in a DOS—UNIX internetwork. In particular, LAN Manager has numerous UNIX offerings which we discuss in Chapter 14.

Artisoft LANtastic is a popular peer-to-peer network for DOS PCs. A peer-to-peer network lets each machine act as either the client or the server depending on the direction of the request. Software is loaded in memory on the PC and when booted, it searches the network for other machines. Once found, these machines exchange information about the available resources. Great for small networks, peer-to-peer in the DOS world has significant limitations in size and performance in larger networks. There are a wide variety of peer-to-peer networking operating systems for DOS PCs including NetWare Lite, LANtastic, and SilverNet.

3

A Decision Primer

Introduction

The goal of Chapter 3 is, quite simply, to help you in the network decision-making process. All of our testing, hands-on tips, product reviews, and internetworking information is little more than not-so-flowery prose if you remain unable to solve your DOS—UNIX internetworking problems. In order to meet this goal, we have tried to present a useful paradigm to help you find the best solution for your particular internetworking needs. In this chapter, there is no product hype, no vendor cheerleading, no touting of the best technological solution. We simply lay out internetworking solutions based on your current situation and your potential needs.

The question of whether or not you need a LAN is not a part of this chapter. There are many tomes on this subject including *LAN Local Area Networks Developing Your System for Business* by Donne Florence (John Wiley & Sons, Inc.). Our guess is that you either already have a LAN or at least have done this part of your networking homework. We also do not make any attempt to convince you about the merits of internetworking DOS and UNIX. You likely know the needs of your particular situation. In addition, unlike many vendors and authors, we have no ax to grind with regard to UNIX being better than DOS, Windows NT being better than UNIX, or any such comparisons. Each operating system has its pros and cons.

We realize that in most small and large businesses resources are limited. This is especially true in the "do more with less 90s." With this in mind, we approach DOS to UNIX internetworking solutions from a combination of perspectives. First we ask the question, "What do you want to do?" This functional approach sets the groundwork for all your decisions. Next, we look at the questions that often impact on function. These are, "What is it going to cost?" "What can you do with what you have?" and "How much work can you reasonably stand?" While these questions present some overlap, breaking down your problem in this way lets you easily see your business's needs and make an honest evaluation of potential solutions.

We can hear the purists argue that all computer decisions should be made from a functional point of view—nothing else makes sense. Needs analysis, functional requirements, top-down. . . ad nauseam. Well, yes, in a perfect world, all purchases are based on fulfilling functional requirements. But in the real world, most businesses work with the concurrents of time, money, experience, and knowledge. We chose to attack the problem of internetworking DOS and UNIX with these considerations in mind.

The performance of your network must fit into the overall decision-making process. We chose to weave performance throughout our questions and our model. Performance is often, though not always, related to cost. Performance can also be a bottleneck depending on the frequency of a function's use. For example, if you are transferring hundreds of files per day, you may need a high performance solution even though your task is a simple one. Additionally, functions that are on a higher level of complexity (like application sharing) require faster performance.

The options we suggest are only broadly outlined. Supplementing each section is a table with the advantages and disadvantages of various options. We also refer you to various parts of the book which discuss these options in detail. Our goal in Chapter 3 is to point you in the direction that best fits within your constraints while satisfying your requirements. We hope you find it useful.

What Do You Want to Do?

The most important question is that of function. What do you want to accomplish with respect to DOS—UNIX internetworking? We divide functional needs into five relatively common categories—file exchange, printer sharing, corporate communication (or e-mail), application sharing, and application interoperability. No function is automatically more important than another. Each has a place in a mixed-platform environment. Do not let a salesman convince you to purchase a complex solution when you need to solve a simple problem. Some of these solutions are not networks at all. They merely allow you to solve a particular problem in the most efficient manner. If you anticipate future complexity, relax; almost every option we suggest leaves you room to grow.

A word of explanation is necessary. With some exceptions, we present each function in a relatively progressive relationship. That is, the communications function is more complicated than the printer sharing function, and so on. Additionally, in most cases, the solutions we suggest at any given point often include the ability to handle the earlier functionalities. For example, application sharing options can also do e-mail, printer sharing, and file exchange in many cases.

File Exchange

The simplest function between UNIX and DOS is the ability to copy or move a file from one machine to another. In many situations, data files occasionally need to be used by someone else. Maybe you keep a spreadsheet of vacation days on your PC. Once per quarter your boss wants to examine the spreadsheet on his UNIX workstation. Or, you might have a UNIX multiuser host that collects manufacturing information. The monthly reports need to be given to the accounting department so they can analyze the results on their PC LAN.

Option 1: Floppy Disk

In many cases, a simple floppy disk carried back and forth between machines does the trick. Nearly all UNIX computers come equipped with the ability to read and write DOS floppies, though DOS computers are not set up to read UNIX disks. If your access needs are infrequent, this should be satisfactory, and you avoid those extra wires and cables. But there are significant drawbacks which we list in Table 3.1. Also, see Chapter 12 and Appendix A for some specific guidance on floppy disk transfer or sneakernet.

Option 2: Serial Connection

Another option is make a simple serial connection between the PC and the UNIX host. Using a serial emulation program (also known as terminal emulation) on the PC, you make a connection to the UNIX host and use the emulation program to download a file, usually in ASCII format. This can be done with a direct connection or with a modem. See Chapter 16 for a discussion of serial products that also include UNIX components to make file transfer simple.

Table 3.1: File Transfer

	Serial Connections	Floppy Disk Transfers
PROS	Easy to setup	No Setup
	Inexpensive Cabling	No cost in most situations
	No need to alter the UNIX host in many cases	No alterations needed for any computer
CONS	Slow for large files	Slow for all files
	Possible transfer errors if no UNIX component for error correction.	Files cannot be larger than disk size
	Not always easy to use	Can have incompatible diskette formats

Printer Sharing

The next link in the networking chain is the ability to share peripherals—particularly printers. While the average laser printer is coming down in price, it still represents a sizable investment and remains one of the most under-utilized pieces of equipment in the office. If your goal is to share expensive resources such as laser printers, you have three options (see Table 3.2). We present detailed information in Chapter 11.

Option 1: Print Buffers

If you have a multiuser UNIX host running character applications and you want to share printers with PCs, consider using a print buffer. A print buffer simply receives input from many different machines and re-routes it to the appropriate printers. This provides you with a low-cost, low-hassle approach to sharing printers. A typical print buffer costs between $300 and $800 and services upwards of 20 or more stand-alone machines. Set-up is easy and cost is low.

Table 3.2: Printer Sharing Options

	Print Buffer	Switching Printer	Print Servers & Adapters
PROS	Inexpensive	Handles different protocols	Inexpensive
	Uses cheaper serial cabling	Switches to Post-Script or HCL	A variety available on the market
	Has large RAM buffer	Single-vendor solution	Keep current printer
	Controls multiple printers	Easy configuration	
CONS	No PostScript/PCL switching	Expensive	Limited functional-ity
	Not always as simple as they look		Most require extra printer RAM
	No UNIX specific settings		Must have both DOS and UNIX on same network

Option 2: Auto-Switching Printers

When you have a PC LAN and UNIX workstations, one of your options is to purchase an automatic, protocol-switching printer. These printers, from Compaq, Hewlett-Packard, and QMS to name a few vendors, can be hooked up on a network running both TCP/IP and Novell NetWare protocols. The printer automatically senses where the job is coming from and switches to the correct protocol for receiving that job. Additionally, many of these printers automatically switch between PostScript and HP's PCL, the two most common printer languages. Another variation of the auto-switching printer can receive input over both an Ethernet port and the standard serial or parallel port. This allows you to use the network connection and still attach a stand-alone workstation to the same printer.

Option 3: Print Servers and Adapters

A third option is to use one of the many third-party adapters and print servers available. These adapters either fit into an internal slot in the printer or attach externally to the parallel port. They often have the network protocol-switching built into the firmware. These allow a Novell NetWare and TCP/IP network to share the same printer if they are sharing the same network cable.

Corporate Communications

Human beings, being social creatures, require communication with each other, person to person. So of course they require such a function of their DOS—UNIX internetworks. Electronic mail, usually called e-mail, allows two or more people to exchange messages, notes, and information back and forth without having to leave their desks. With regard to an e-mail solution, the computer is merely a conduit. In a pure DOS LAN environment, many e-mail product options exist.However, once you want to use e-mail between DOS and UNIX boxes, your options become more limited. Table 3.3 shows the pros and cons of each option.

Option 1: Local Serial Connection

If you have just a few PCs needing an e-mail connection to a local UNIX network, you can use a serial connection from the PC with terminal emulation. PC users receive a UNIX login and mailbox on the UNIX host. They use the UNIX mail system to communicate with other users on the UNIX network. Chapter 16 outlines serial emulation products. In particular, serial desktop products best fit this description.

Option 2: Public Mail System

When you need to communicate with UNIX or DOS users in distant locations on a non-real time response mode (only 1 to 2 times a day), a public e-mail service provides an excellent option. Rarely will you have extra cabling and network expenses other than the cost of a modem and communication software. Chapter 18 provides a synopsis of public e-mail options. The most prevalent e-mail systems for UNIX are the Internet and UUNET. On the DOS side, MCI Mail and CompuServe represent two common services. All four services can make connections to each other.

Option 3: Multi-Platform E-Mail

When you have a large number of PC and UNIX users, an e-mail system that crosses both platforms is your best option. The connectivity between these platforms must use TCP/IP over Ethernet or Token Ring—due to both speed requirements and the fact that TCP/IP represents the only protocol available for both platforms. Unfortunately, as Chapter 18 points out, there are only a few products on the market which meet these requirements. But the ones we test are well worth considering.

Option 4: E-Mail Gateway

If you already have a mix of e-mail products, an e-mail gateway might be an appropriate solution. A gateway is designed to join two different systems, say Microsoft Mail on a PC and UUCP on a UNIX host. Most e-mail gateways tend to concentrate on connecting enterprise-wide networks, but there are some products available in the smaller scale DOS—UNIX internetworking arena. See Chapter 12 for additional information on gateways.

Table 3.3: E-Mail Solutions

	Serial Connection	Public Mail System	Multi-Platform E-Mail Connection	E-Mail Gateway
PROS	Low-cost or no cost	Low cost -small monthly fee	Everyone is on same system	Uses current e-mail system
	Uses present UNIX e-mail software	Many user-interface options available	Real-time messaging	No new training
	No special routing requirements		No e-mail protocol issues to be concerned about	
CONS	PC users have to learn UNIX mail program	Not fast enough for frequent contact	High initial cost	Difficult to setup
	No PC-to-PC e-mail	Expensive to transfer large messages	Few products on the market	Expensive in some cases
	Requires new cabling	Ties up a phone line	UNIX users may need to learn a new product	May require a leased line for connecting various sites

Application Sharing

Perhaps the most commonly-sought networking capability is program and file sharing. That's probably why you have a LAN in the first place. If you use Novell Netware, Lantastic, LAN Manager or some other PC network, you already share files and programs. For example, you may have only one copy of a word processor, but if it is licensed for ten users, all ten can access the program from its central repository—the file server. In many cases, application sharing is nothing but a form of client/server computing. We prefer to think of application sharing as a small subset of the client/server world. We discuss it more specifically in the preface and Chapter 2.

When looking at application sharing between DOS and UNIX platforms, we categorize the options depending on how you want to share applications. There are four possible scenarios. Options are listed under each of the four scenarios. Table 3.4 summarizes all options.

PC Users Share PC Applications Through a UNIX Server

Option 1: NFS on a TCP/IP Network

NFS (Network File System), the creation of Sun Microsystems Inc., lets you connect PCs to PCs with UNIX (or some other machine) in the middle acting as the file server. NFS is supported by most of the TCP/IP products we discuss in Chapter 13. A UNIX-based NFS server gives a number of PCs common access to programs with large amounts of disk storage. It requires a complete network environment, including Ethernet cable and network cards. See Chapter 6 for more information on NFS.

Option 2: Non-NFS PC-LAN Solutions

There are a limited number of non-NFS solutions that allow UNIX hosts to store DOS programs. In essence, from your PC-based LAN you can access DOS programs residing on a UNIX server. These include products based on Microsoft LAN Manager like SCO LAN Manager and DEC PATHWORKS. These products all meet a special need in the marketplace and we discuss them further in Chapter 14.

UNIX Users Share UNIX Applications Through a Non-UNIX Server

Option 1: PC LAN Networking Products

This solution involves storing UNIX programs on a PC LAN server and allowing various UNIX users to access the programs. Though different options exist for this solution, all involve a PC LAN. Products like UnixWare and NetWare NFS allow the Novell server to store UNIX programs which can then be used by UNIX users. Generally, these products are costly and require extensive administration. They are discussed in Chapter 14.

UNIX Users Execute DOS Programs Residing on PC Servers

Option 1: Single Machine DOS Emulation

Don't buy a 747 for puddle jumping to the next town. If you need to provide DOS access to a single UNIX user, consider a DOS emulation package. The UNIX user gets to run popular DOS packages without having to bother about network issues and without giving up workstation horsepower. These products are relatively cheap if you only need to supply a couple of users. Most PC UNIX packages such as SCO UNIX and Novell UnixWare supply DOS emulation as part of their distribution product. However, there are performance drawbacks to nearly all these products. See Chapters 10 and 17 for further discussion.

Option 2: DOS Servers

DOS emulators are great for limited access, but if you have a large number of users, providing a different type of connection with DOS capability makes sense. The idea of a DOS server is relatively new. The concept involves setting aside part or all of a DOS machine for access by UNIX users. Desqview/X is probably the best example of this technology and is discussed in Chapters 14 and 17. Be forewarned, however, it is a relatively new market and many products have yet to reach reliable maturity.

PC Users Execute UNIX Programs Residing on a UNIX Server

Option 1: Serial Terminal Emulation

Do you have character-based UNIX applications that your PC users need to use? A simple serial connection may make the most sense. Use it in conjunction with one of the terminal emulation programs discussed in Chapter 16. Serial connections are easy to install and low in cost.

Option 2: TCP/IP and Terminal Emulation

It could be that you already have network connection, perhaps through Novell or LAN Manager. In this case, you may need more speed or throughput than a serial product offers. Your second choice might be a TCP/IP product to makes the connection over Ethernet. This option gives you increased speed, though you pay more in cost and complexity. You can use a TCP/IP product on a single PC like those considered in Chapter 13, or you might consider a LAN-wide solution as discussed in Chapter 14. The terminal emulator serves as your view into the UNIX applications. Sometimes the options provided with the TCP/IP product suffice to meet your needs.

Option 3: X Servers

Perhaps the most flexible option for running UNIX applications from a PC is a Microsoft Windows-based X server. The X server allows you to run graphical X Window applications on the PC. In Chapter 15, we look more closely at a half dozen X servers which operate under MS Windows. While X servers exist that operate under DOS, we find them to be less than satisfactory. The X server gives you access to every text and graphical-based application on the UNIX network, though a TCP/IP connection is required (There are now some viable options for a X server serial connection using special protocols).

Interoperable Applications

Our last functional category, interoperable applications represents the final frontier. For the sake of our discussion, we refer to interoperability as the capacity to bring information from one application on one machine and join it to another application on another machine (or possibly the same machine)—in other words, the ability to interconnect applications. To a limited degree X servers provide this function. Interoperability can involve client/server computing, but a client/server scenario may not involve interoperability.

The best example of interoperability within the DOS world is Microsoft's OLE (Object Linking and Embedding). OLE allows you to open a spreadsheet program from within your word processor, make some changes to a table, and return to your word processor without ever knowing where the other application came from. Another example is Microsoft's DDE (Dynamic Data Exchange) which requires far more programming than OLE and provides only limited support. Another group of products, the Remote Procedure Call (RPC) products, builds the framework for cross-platform interoperability. Sun produces a product called ToolTalk that provides interoperability tools. The Object Management Group (OMG) also is working on a level of interoperability which is object-oriented. Terminology includes groupware, workflow, and client/server technology. No matter what top-level technology you use, you still need a connection between different platforms. If interoperable solutions are your goal, not only do you need the best TCP/IP network available, but you need to remember that interoperable applications still require a fair amount of programming. Until the technology becomes more standard, you need a team of programmers in addition to your foundational TCP/IP network. Look for interoperability support in products evaluated in Chapters 13 and 14.

Table 3.4: Sharing Applications

		NFS Products	DOS Emulators & Servers	Serial Emulation	TCP/IP & Emulation	PC LAN Network Products	X Servers
PROS		Complete resource & application sharing	Only a single monitor on each desktop	Inexpensive	Full-speed Network Connection	Many options available	Runs all graphical applications
		Proven technology	Cheaper than a new computer	Easy to setup	Good base for future upgrades	Can save money on hardware	Uses TCP/IP
		Saves hardware dollars		Supports many machines	Cheaper for multi-nodes than serial	Uses TCP/IP in many cases	Integrates with MS-Windows
		Uses TCP/IP				Interfaces many users at one time	
CONS		Expensive for small numbers	Slow w/o accelerator (hardware)	Slow transmit speed	No graphical support	Expensive	Expensive
		Difficult to administer	Do not run all DOS programs	Can only run character applications	Expensive for small numbers	Difficult to set up	Difficult to set up
			Memory Hog		Difficult to set up	Tied to single PC NOS	Performance and compatibility problems in some cases

What Is It Going to Cost You?

Sometimes the cost factor, both in terms of time and money, comes to the forefront of your decision-making process. Nothing unusual about that. Everyone wants the best network money can buy, but only some can pay for it. However, within the context of internetworking DOS and UNIX, there are plenty of options at all cost levels. We deal with the cost issue arbitrarily—in terms of low, medium, and high cost. Although we try to talk in absolute terms, attaching real numbers, it is not hard to imagine scenarios where a low-cost option might exceed a medium-cost option. For example, a DOS emulator represents a low-cost solution for the single user, but multiply that by 20 or 30, and the cost is out of line for the additional functionality. Also, your time is worth something, and if you have to hassle with complicated installations, slow speed, and incomplete implementations, that "lower cost" solution may cost you more in the long run.

When we speak of tangible costs, we refer not only to the software, but also to the networking hardware aspects of a particular implementation—including the cables, the network cards, and the time to set up. In general, we exclude the cost of the platform itself—its RAM, hard disk space, and processor speed. The platform does come into play, and we address that subject a little later on in this chapter. But we assume that you already have many of the basic components since you now have a need to internetwork them.

One final word about cost. Cost relates closely to network performance. If you need a fast network, you have to spend more money. With only minor exceptions, the more costly an internetworking option, the greater the throughput and performance available to you.

Low Cost Solutions

When you find yourself constrained by price limitations, consider being innovative. Don't concern yourself with providing every last ounce of functionality, but rather use the Parado Rule (the last 20% of any project requires 80% of the work) and target something less. Table 3.5 illustrates this balancing act. For example, when looking to share printers with a serial-based UNIX host, look to the $300-$800 print buffers. You can simply hook your PCs to the print buffer with low-cost multi-conductor cable, and be off and running. Or don't purchase a new printer if the old one works fine on your Ethernet. Instead, buy a protocol switching print server. At only $499, these allow both DOS and UNIX networks to share the same printer.

Serial connection often provides the cheapest way to accomplish internetworking. You can use multi-conductor cable (as cheap as 15 cents a linear foot). All PCs come with a serial port. Thus, if your UNIX host has an extra serial port or already uses a multiport board, your only large expenditure is a terminal emulation program. Don't automatically purchase the $495 variety of terminal emulation. Evaluate your needs; a less expensive one may be sufficient. Chapter 16 gives you some guidance on terminal emulation. There are still zillions of character-based programs running on UNIX machines and PCs. If you are off-site, you will need a modem. A typical 9600 bps modem costs $200 to $400. See Chapter 9 for more information.

Table 3.5: Low Cost Considerations

PROS	You still get the basic features of a complete network.
	Sharing a printer or using a serial connection is easy to administer.
	There's not a lot of wiring to worry about.
	Total costs and costs per user may both be low depending on the implementation.
CONS	You can only use a single serial connection.
	You cannot run graphics applications across the serial cable w/o special protocols.
	The serial options are slower and have fewer upgrade routes than a TCP/IP network.

Medium Cost Solutions

Medium-cost solutions make up the bread and butter of networking. If you have several machines to hook up, or you need fairly complete functionality, figure on spending some money (see Table 3.6). Consider yourself lucky if you already have your PCs set up with NICs (Network Interface Cards). At $150-$400 a pop, these can represent some of your largest expenditures. Cabling is also costly. While the party line says that UTP is the cheapest form of cabling, we find thinnet coaxial to be thrifty in certain situations. If you can't use UTP in your building because the cable is not data-grade, already has all its lines in use, or is not accessible, you must resign yourself to a costly cable purchase. Chapter 4 provides some breakdowns, definitions and information on cabling. Figure on paying 20-35 cents per foot for coax cable and 15-60 cents for UTP cable (depending on the grade) and lots more money for installation charges. In a small business, you may be able to save dollars by installing the cable yourself, but in many cases hiring a professional is inevitable, and may prove cheaper in the long haul.

There are other cost issues to consider when trying to bring multiple PCs into a UNIX environment. You may have to use transceivers, repeaters, bridges, or routers to connect the networks. These hardware boxes are not cheap. While a simple transceiver used to connect a UNIX workstation to a thinnet line can be found for under $100, bridges and routers typically cost $2,500 to $25,000. Chapter 4 gives some information about these pieces of equipment used to cross-connect networks.

The need for TCP/IP software can also drive up costs. Say that you have a 100-node Novell NetWare LAN. Even with a special purchase, 100 TCP/IP packages might cost nearly $10,000. Consider buying only for the necessary nodes; or better yet, look at the LAN-based solutions discussed in Chapters 7 and 14. Whenever you internetwork two LANS or protocols (like IPX/SPX and TCP/IP), you introduce potential problems. You had better plan for more system administration time.

Table 3.6: Medium Cost Considerations

PROS	Data travels faster across Ethernet or Token Ring than serial lines.
	You can connect multi-protocol networks together, increasing productivity.
	You get a larger variety of features such as terminal emulation, file transfer, and multiple remote logins.
	A TCP/IP network handles many more users than a low cost solution.
	Graphical applications and interoperable applications are easily used.
CONS	The cabling is more elaborate and will require more time to install.
	The overall software and hardware costs are significantly higher.
	The network will require more system administration time and perhaps more training.

High Cost Solutions

So why would any one want to spend more money? Speed, speed, speed. Throw in some flexibility. Included in this list of potential high fliers are fiber optic networks, ATM, and Fast Ethernet (all defined in Chapter 2). While they are attractive, such technologies are more practical for large corporations. As Table 3.7 shows, some technologies are not yet available at reasonable cost. Fiber optic cable and adapters are the most readily available while other systems have limited vendor support.

Table 3.7: High Cost Considerations

PROS	These technologies produce the fastest network by far.
	You can use them as enterprise-wide management tools.
	Fiber can handle a huge number of users.
	You can use multiple protocols on the network.
CONS	Currently, it is expensive hardware and software.
	You are at the frontier of technology, which increases the risk.
	Installation and administration is often difficult.

As marketplace standards gel, these technologies will become cheaper and more available. Cost and availability prohibited us from testing or evaluating these technologies. Fiber optic cabling is still reasonably high priced, $1.25-$1.50 per foot, and difficult to install. The nature of its connections will probably dismay most do-it-yourselfers. Fiber optic NICs cost about $700 or more, and therefore are used much less than other NICs. Fiber tends to be used as the backbone in a campus-wide installation. Using FDDI as the logical topology, fiber optic networking has met with success as the corporate backbone in a large Ethernet environment.

ATM and Fast Ethernet are two technologies hoping to push the speed of networking into the 100 mbps realm. ATM cards are available but cost over $2000 per unit as of the Spring of 1993. Fast Ethernet remains in the standards stage, although companies like Wellfleet Communications and Optical Data Systems intend to support 100Base-VG (a version of fast Ethernet) whether it becomes a standard or not. These prices will drop quickly as the marketplace begins to implement these technologies, but don't expect them to be as cost effective as Ethernet and Token Ring for a number of years.

What Can You Do with What You Have?

Network books often assume you already have all the right machines. Our experience in business suggests otherwise. Although it would be ideal to replace less desirable machines for the sake of your new networking plan, often you have to live with what you have. So, here are some suggestions about what you can do with your existing hardware. Of course, you can change equipment, but why spend money if you don't need to?

Standalone Configurations

By "standalone" we mean those situations where you do not already have a complete TCP/IP or Novell NetWare network already in place. You might have a number of independent PCs or a multiuser UNIX system with character-based terminals.

Situation: Pre-386 PC

Older machines cannot run MS-Windows in Enhanced Mode or with adequate performance, and many of your networking options from DOS-UNIX require Windows. That's not to say you can't connect older, slower PCs. Serial products work well with older machines when you need UNIX access. Print sharing can easily be done. However, we hesitate to recommend connecting slower machines via a full TCP/IP network solution. They will work, but you may be disappointed in your return on investment. If you have graphical applications to run, you might be better off selling your older machines and investing in low-end 486 machines.

Situation: Fast PC

With newer and faster PCs you can do just about anything when it comes to internetworking. The one major advantage is the ability to use MS-Windows X servers. These graphical products require Microsoft Windows, lots of memory, and fast processors. But they yield tremendous flexibility. See Chapters 8 and 15 for discussions about X servers and product evaluations. Of course, NFS and full TCP/IP implementations make perfect sense for connecting 386 or faster PCs to a UNIX network.

Situation: Character-Based UNIX Host

Many small businesses find themselves with a UNIX-based accounting system, manufacturing system, or tracking system running on an Intel platform using SCO UNIX, SCO Xenix, or another PC version of UNIX. These same businesses also have DOS-based PCs, but the two sets of machines cannot communicate with each other. If you are in such a position, and you want to make use of your resources by, at the very least, doing some file transfer and peripheral sharing, here are some of your options. Use serial terminal emulation products and a multiport board to allow your PCs use of the UNIX system. Try using a printer buffer to connect the UNIX machine and your PCs to the same printers. If you have only a few connections to make and no plans to move to a graphical environment, avoid TCP/IP. 9600 baud serial lines are not speedy, but few character applications push the limits of these connections.

Multi-Node Configurations

A multiple node configuration exists anytime you already have your PCs linked together in some type of network. We distinguish between some of the brand names because the type of network makes a big difference on the available options.

Situation: Novell NetWare Server

If you find yourself with a Novell NetWare network, you are in luck. By virtue of being the market leader of PC network services, NetWare generates a sizable list of potential DOS—UNIX connectivity options. The Novell-related products we reviewed work with NetWare 3.11 (and with 4.0 in most cases) unless otherwise noted. If you have only a few NetWare users needing access to UNIX, dual stack TCP/IP communication protocol products are the cheapest solution. They provide TCP/IP capability to individual workstations while able to run in conjunction with the IPX/SPX protocol. We give you information about these in Chapters 5, 6, and 13. If you need to provide access to nearly everyone on the network, LAN-based network products become your best option. These are discussed in Chapters 7 and 14.

Situation: LAN Manager/IBM LAN Server/Banyan Vines

If you are running a PC-based network operating system other than Novell NetWare, you have fewer options. This is merely a factor of the marketplace—supply and demand. However, don't despair. Options are available. Many of the TCP/IP products discussed in Chapter 13 run with a LAN Manager client. You can also find LAN-wide options, such as DEC PATHWORKS or SCO LAN Manager. However, don't expect to use the PC server as a file server for UNIX programs.

Situation: Peer-to-Peer Networks

Peer-to-Peer networks still represent a popular option even in large enterprises. These include Artisoft LANtastic, Novell NetWare Lite, and Microsoft Windows for Workgroups. We discuss some solutions in Chapter 14. With some DOS-based peer-to-peer networks products it is impossible to make TCP/IP connections, with others it is only difficult. However, serial terminal emulation is always an option particularly where you have only a few PCs.

Situation: UNIX Workstations

If you have UNIX RISC-based workstations, such as Sun SPARCstations or IBM RS/6000s, you already have available TCP/IP protocol and probably Ethernet as well. In such cases it makes sense to continue down the path laid before you. Sun SPARCstations running Solaris 1.x have the most options available to them in terms of connectivity to PC-LANs. However, all of the TCP/IP and NFS products discussed in later chapters work with any UNIX workstations. We recommend you take the plunge and equip your PCs with NICs and TCP/IP software.

Enterprise-Wide Configurations

What do you do with IBM Mainframes or DEC Vaxes or IBM minicomputers? Well, you are probably not reading this book to develop a corporate-wide networking plan, but we can go out on a limb and give you a little advice anyway.

Situation: IBM Mainframe, Minis or PCs

When your office or business revolves around IBM hardware, you need to give careful consideration to IBM's chosen topology solution—Token Ring. While it is not difficult to connect IBM PCs to, say, an IBM RS/6000 UNIX workstation using Ethernet, it makes sense to look closely at Token Ring. If you also have AS/400s and other IBM hardware, we believe Token Ring provides major advantages in terms of support and continuity. You can always use UNIX-to-mainframe specific solutions like those offered by Systems Strategies Inc. or Cleo Communications. These boards and/or software solutions plug into your UNIX box and offer direct IBM connectivity using the proprietary IBM protocols like LU6.2 and SNA.

IBM mainframes do support TCP/IP options that can be purchased direct from IBM. There are also NFS products available for IBM mainframes and DEC Vaxes. DEC also supports TCP/IP, even though it prefers to use DECNet. The biggest difficulty with supporting TCP/IP on big iron is whether the MIS shop is willing to move from SNA or another proprietary protocol.

Situation: UNIX, DOS, Macintosh, VAX, and Others

If you have a slew of different machines from a variety of vendors, we believe a TCP/IP network using Ethernet is your only long term solution. Nearly every other option limits you to certain platforms, specific operating systems, or a specific vendor. While some vendors and consultants consider OSI products the only way to go, their availability is still too low and price too high to recommend them in any situation. TCP/IP is going to be the standard of the 90's and beyond for internetworking.

How Much Work Do You Want to Do?

Whether you are a UNIX guru, a PC power user, or the designated computer expert of your company, you want to be as effective as possible. Here are some aspects of networking that can make your life miserable. Don't bite off more than you can chew. If you think you might need help, buy from a source where support is readily available. Remember, functionality is often directly related to cost and complexity. Low-cost, simple-to-install products often function on a lower level. But if they provide what you need, consider yourself a happy camper.

Simple Challenges

If you don't know much about computers, and don't want to learn, call a consultant who gives you good references and offers a reasonable price for services. If you are stuck doing some or most of the work on your own, consider a few pointers. The easiest solutions to get up and running have certain traits in common. If you don't know UNIX, avoid those products which alter the UNIX kernel or load various daemons on your system. We had experiences in which a product forced us to make significant changes to our system before that product would work properly. In many cases, all that work is not worth the result. We also found times when two different networking products running on the UNIX host caused each other problems.

Look for those products that do not involve much wiring or changes in your present system. Anytime you change the basic environment of any computer, you can have problems. You probably remember occasions when a simple 15 minute install turned into a 3 to 4 hour mess. Sometimes, days after an installation, we discovered that an internetworking program was bringing down the network or fouling up the printer. In some cases, it was a product with a nasty bug, but in most cases the product required an ideal working environment that wasn't satisfied by our arrangement (nor likely by yours).

Some hardware solutions can also be handled simply. The easiest of the bunch is direct serial connections and terminal emulation software. Just like Jello—no-hassle (almost). Go with four wire cable and save money. Even if you have a UNIX multiport port board or terminal server to set up, you should find it a fairly simple task for serial installations. Nevertheless, most network situations fall into the class of average difficulty. Remember that you have a choice of cabling media for the higher-throughput Ethernet. Using what you may already have in place generally makes more sense than pulling in new cable.

Average Challenges

Some DOS—UNIX internetworking scenarios require more work and added complexity than our previous simple situations. If you are connecting a single PC LAN to a set of UNIX workstations, you need to expect a few days of work over a period of a few weeks. Installing NICs and TCP/IP networking software in PCs running DOS and Windows can be a trying process if you are not a network specialist. Most users should be able to do these installations, but expect to have some incompatibilities or incorrect switch settings before all the bugs are worked out. Consider going about the process in a piecemeal approach. Get one machine up and running in the internetwork, then connect a second machine and so on. No point in trying to do everything at once and not be able to isolate the problem.

We expect many installations to use products which load daemons on the UNIX host at boot time or perhaps even alter the UNIX kernel. Our experience indicates that while sometimes you can do this with only limited knowledge of UNIX, most of the time you need to understand the UNIX startup files and how they are altered by different products. In particular, products that join UNIX to PC LANs tend to be difficult to install and require patience.

Hardware issues become more time consuming when you need to intermix types of cabling, brands of LAN adapters, and varieties of network drivers. We recommend you consider using the same type of network drivers on all your machines and try to keep the same kind of cabling and adapters. If you use communication servers and LAN-based modems, serial connections rise in difficulty compared with average serial installations.

Using the X Windows System on the UNIX side and Microsoft Windows on the PC side also adds complexity to the scenario. Character-based applications tend to be easier to set up in an internetworking scenario than are graphical applications. We had far more difficulty running X clients on our PCs than we did running simple UNIX character applications.

Complex Challenges

Creating an enterprise-wide internetwork can be complicated. We recommend that anyone developing their corporate MIS policy read more than a single book. Some networking topologies and technologies require a tremendous amount of research and preparation. This often includes such monumental tasks as re-wiring the enterprise with fiber optic cable. Almost without exception, a vendor or manufacturer's representative is involved, as well as an implementation team from the corporate staff.

For our purposes, we include in the complex installation category those situations in which multiple networks in different locations are connected. The use of routers, bridges, brouters, gateways, and the like are rarely used in the average small installation. If you have multiple PC LANs or a large UNIX installation, joining these systems together will require a well-laid implementation plan, lots of time, and a substantial monetary investment.

Recommendations

Certainly we have not answered every question with respect to planning DOS—UNIX internetworking. What we did want to do is steer you toward your likely solutions. Now you need to go to the how-to chapters. Then take a look at the product chapters and see which of the products on the market have the right features for your situation. Keep your sense of humor handy (along with your tech support numbers), and have fun.

4

Assembling Ethernet Hardware

Introduction

Installing any type of computer hardware can be scary to the uninitiated. Networking hardware in particular has a high level of mystique, because networking is usually left in the hands of the gurus. In this chapter, we send the message that you can install networks fairly easily with a few tools, even if you would not consider yourself a 'guru.' We describe the common components you will deal with, how to install them, and how to make sure the network is viable when you are through.

Your choice of network hardware should be made concurrently with your choice of software. The functionality you desire will determine the hardware you need. Conversely, the expense of the hardware may determine the level of functionality you must live with. Refer to Chapter 3 for assistance in preparing a plan of attack.

This chapter gives attention to the primary type of network hardware: Ethernet. Ethernet networks work hand-in-glove with TCP/IP networking software (the defacto standard for UNIX networking) and provide the high throughput needed for file servers and X servers. Chapter 2 briefly introduced you to the theory of Ethernet. Here we name the components again briefly and discuss how to put it all together.

Ethernet Components

By way of review, Ethernet uses thin coax, thick coax, fiber-optic, or UTP cabling. Newer wireless technology also supports Ethernet. Ethernet permits a maximum of 1024 nodes on the network, or signalling problems begin to occur. (To attain this many nodes you must use devices called multiport repeaters—later in the chapter.)

In large installations, *backbones*, also known as *spines* or *trunk cables*, are built from fiber-optic cable (in many new installations) or thick coaxial cable—chiefly to allow long overall distances in the network and many nodes. A thick Ethernet backbone (according to the 10Base5 standard) is laid as a linear bus segment, a maximum of 500 meters in length. Up to 4 additional segments (*ribs*) can be joined to the backbone with repeaters, allowing a total length of 2500 meters and up to 100 direct MAU connections (discussed later) per segment. Thick Ethernet cable is built ruggedly and has double shielding, so it is quite stiff (what backbone isn't?) and difficult to install. However, this shielding protects against noise. Computers are attached to flexible drop cables off of the backbone. Since large installations have cabling specialists and/or vendors to assist them, we do not discuss thick coaxial, fiber-optic, or wireless Ethernet in detail.

In smaller installations, the backbone and drop cables may be ignored in favor of using the same cable throughout—thin Ethernet cable (shielded coaxial *thinnet*) or unshielded twisted pair (UTP). Using only the smaller cable has advantages; it is much cheaper, and it requires less variety in adapters and equipment. However, thin Ethernet (according to the 10Base2 specification) is limited in length to 185 meters per segment (5 segments, 925 meters total) and only 30 directly-attached devices per segment. If you use cable/components that have low decibel loss (10-11dB), these limits can be extended to 300 meters and 100 nodes per segment. Thin Ethernet is very flexible, so it is always run directly to each computer or other device. However, just as for thick coax backbones, it uses the linear bus topology.

The 10Base-T Ethernet specification uses UTP cable installed in a the star topology. A *hub* or *concentrator* is placed at the center of the star. 10Base-T allows the same throughput as thin coaxial Ethernet, and the same number of nodes, but allows more wiring flexibility, as well as an intelligent, collision-reducing hub. UTP's star topology is also much more forgiving than the linear bus, in that one node's malfunction cannot down the entire network. This chapter concentrates on cabling for the smaller installations using thin Ethernet or UTP.

LAN adapters connect computers to the network cable. There are three general types of PC adapters, depending upon the architecture of the PC—EISA, ISA, and MicroChannel Architecture (MCA). Vendors usually supply similar adapter models for each type of PC, so you don't have to fumble through differing manuals and configuration procedures unless you inherited a variety or bought them piecemeal. Adapters can be either internal (a board you insert into an open slot in the PC—see Figure 4.1) or external. External adapters are of two types: parallel port adapters, and transceivers. You would typically use a parallel port adapter for (1) a laptop computer, which does not have space inside for a card, or (2) temporary connections.

A transceiver, sometimes called a Medium Attachment Unit (MAU), attaches to a thick coax or fiber-optic backbone and provides the drop cable to a computer, terminal, repeater, or printer. You might also commonly use a transceiver to attach certain UNIX workstations to thin Ethernet or UTP. Internal LAN adapters generally have an on-board transceiver, making external transceivers unnecessary on thin Ethernet or UTP LANs. However, to connect to a backbone, you can disable the on-board transceiver and use the drop cable/MAU wiring scheme.

In addition to the bus architecture and internal/external differences, adapters can also have different types of connectors to match the network cabling:BNC, UTP, Dual ST, N-series, and AUI. BNC connectors are the silver, bayonet-style barrels that connect to "T" adapters onRG/58 coaxial cable. UTP ports are for use by the telephone-style RJ-45 modular plugs and unshielded twisted pair cable. (Token-Ring cards use this cabling exclusively.) ST connectors (a pair) attach fiber-optic cable. N-series male connectors are for use with thick Ethernet. AUI jacks are 15-pin, female, D-style connectors, and have a sliding latch to firmly affix transceiver drop cable.

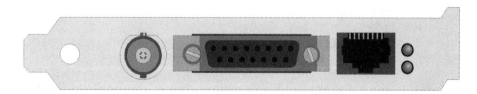

FIGURE 4.1 End view of a 'Combo' adapter, with BNC, AUI and UTP (RJ-45) ports

Installing Ethernet Cable

Many businesses today purchase pre-made cables. Others make their own cables. There are reasons for each. Here are a few reasons to build and lay your own cable:

- The company will require many cables over time, costing a lot of money. Savings of 40% - 85% in materials can be realized by making versus buying.
- The cables must be run through plenums and/or between floors, making it time-consuming to estimate lengths in advance.
- It is usually aggravating, sometimes impossible, to run pre-made cables (having the connectors mounted) through tight places and building conduit. The only alternative under these conditions is to hire an outside contractor.
- Time can be saved by building cables in-house versus ordering them.

On the other hand, cabling the company network yourself has drawbacks:

- Running cables through walls, ceilings, and plenums takes time.
- Some vendors may not support a workplace with self-installed cable.
- Flawed material purchasing decisions, or flawed materials, means waste and re-installation time.
- If there is a problem that cannot be traced easily, no one else will make it right.

If you are unsure of your abilities, or only need a few cables, by all means, buy them. If you desire to make cables in-house, you need two things primarily—(1) quality components and tools, and (2) good fine-motor skills. If you, or the designated builder, are handy with small tools (not everyone is), making one or two cables provides all of the practice needed. The procedure and parts are uncomplicated, and there are ways to test the finished product before actually installing it.

Selecting the Cable

Avoid inferior-quality cable and connectors by buying from a reputable vendor. The cables may be in service for several years, and it would be a shame if the insulation were to fail prematurely. Faulty connectors can also cause intermittent problems, which are difficult to spot. The vendor should sell products that meet the U.S. government specs.

RG-58 coaxial cable handicap cable are the two most popular cable types for Ethernet networks. Transceiver cable is often needed as well to connect some computers to the backbone. Here are some specifics about each.

RG-58 A/U or C/U cable (thinnet) has a stranded center conductor, an insulation layer, a foil shield, an outer braided wire conductor which also acts as shielding, and a PVC or plenum-rated outer jacket. It is flexible and used BNC connectors. The lower grade RG-58U cable has a solid center conductor, no foil shield, less outer conductor, and is usually cheaper and easier to work with, but it does not comply with the thin Ethernet standard. However, many smaller installations use nothing but RG-58U. The Ethernet standard also specifies different connectors for thinnet than for RG-58U. However, the connectors are exactly the same style and, practically speaking, there is negligible difference in size, so vendors sometimes sell one connector for use with either cable.

Plenum-rated thinnet cable has a tougher jacket and greater rigidity. Because plenum cable is harder to flex without putting strain on the connectors, you might find it more difficult to work with, especially if you are running the cable all the way to the computer/terminal or are connecting to Ethernet adapters in tight spaces. You can end up moving boards around in the computer just to provide enough room to connect the Ethernet cable on the outside. However, building codes usually require plenum cable to be used in conduits, in ceilings, and in other airspaces (plenums). Again, make sure the connectors you buy work on your cable.

UTP cable is used for10Base-T Ethernet and Token Ring. It uses the star topology, requiring gobs of cable, but the cable is inexpensive and the star provides flexibility. Companies almost always make their UTP cables. Get the data-grade variety, which is rated for 10M/sec data throughput. UTP uses modular RJ-45 phone plugs.

Transceiver (*drop*) cable is specially shielded, multiconductor cable. Its purpose is to attach devices with AUI (Attachment Unit Interface) ports to external transceivers (MAUs). Self-manufacture is not recommended due to the added complexity of the shielding and additional conductors. Drop cables can be up to 50 meters long.

How to Make Thin Ethernet Cables

Purchase enough thinnet RG-58 bulk cable to stretch between computers, allowing extra length for flexibility. Thinnet lengths can be as short as 18 inches. Purchase two male BNC crimp connectors and one BNC "T" (tee) with female ends on the two top-arms (the straight-through parts are for connection to cables) and a male connector on the single down-leg (for connection to the Ethernet adapter). If this will be the first or only cable in the network, you will need an extra T, two male terminators, and, if your workstation uses an AUI-style connection like those on a Sun SPARCstation, a transceiver and drop cable.

We have seen RG-58 cable costs between 20 and 35 cents per foot in bulk (1000' rolls). You can get BNC male crimp connectors for $1.25-$3.00, Tees for $3-$9, and terminators for $1.50-$15.00. The range of prices often seems ludicrous. Obviously, what you pay depends upon quality, quantity breaks, and the vendor's credibility.

Two basic styles of BNC connectors can be used: screw-on and crimp. The screw-on style requires a wrench; the crimp-on style requires a crimp tool, which can also vary widely in price ($25-$70). You will need a coaxial cable stripper for either type ($15-$32). We prefer crimp connectors because the twist-on connectors tend to loosen up over time. A loose connector can cause the entire network to fail. However, twist-on connectors will do in a pinch.

Assembly

Refer to Figure 4.2. First, prepare the cable end. If you are using crimp-on ends, place the hollow, cylindrical crimp sleeve over the end of the cable now (it would be more difficult later) and push it back out of the way. Open the cable stripper and lay the end of the cable in the groove so that it just reaches the far edge of the stripper. Note that there are two blades at different heights in the stripper. If no diagrams are furnished with the stripper, just remember that the blade which cuts deeper into the cable should be toward the end of the cable. Gently lower the stripper jaw onto the cable—do not squeeze it down. The stripper cuts the cable like a copper pipe cutter. Turn the stripper slowly around the cable 3-4 turns, until resistance lessens. Leaving the stripper closed, pull the cable out. The cable should resemble the diagram in Figure 4.2. If the cuts are too deep, i.e., if the outer braid is partly gone or the inner conductor has been cut, cut off the end with wire cutters and try again. This may take a few tries.

If you use crimp connectors, find the tiny gold-plated pin and place it over the end of the stranded inner conductor (or solid conductor wire, if you have RG-58U). Position it in the appropriately-sized groove on the crimping tool and carefully squeeze the tool until it reaches the end of its travel. The pin should now be firmly attached. Place the connector over the end, pushing its stud down between the white insulation and the shielding/outer conductor. There may be a slight pop when the connector is fully on—this is caused by the gold pin seating itself in the connector. If there is no pop and the pin does not extend fully through the end of the connector, it is likely that the cable insulation was not stripped back far enough. Remove the connector, and use the stripper to cut a little more off the cable, but just a little—1/16" or so (you already mounted the pin).

When the connector fits snugly onto the cable, push the crimp sleeve back down the cable until it covers the copper braid and stud of the connector. Use the appropriately-sized groove on the crimping tool to crimp the sleeve in place. You should not

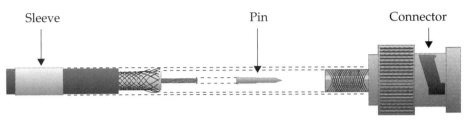

FIGURE 4.2 Assembly diagram of crimp-on thin Ethernet connector

be able to pull the connector off except with unusual force. Cut the cable to length, then mount a connector at the other end.

If you are using twist-on connectors, simply twist the end on (clockwise) until it stops. You will need a wrench to do this. Other styles of twist-on connectors require two wrenches to hold separate halves. Still others require the pins to be soldered on.

Testing

Before you install all of your cables into the ceiling, test them on the floor. You will have to warn any users who remain on the network to cease computing. Also, make sure no automated communications are using the network.

You can perform a basic test of cable connectivity immediately after you build it. Obtain an OHM meter (or continuity tester), set the selector to read resistance (Ohms, the upside-down horseshoe), then touch one test probe to the center post (pin) on one end of the cable and the other test probe to the matching center post on the other end of the cable. The meter should indicate a positive value, perhaps close to zero, but not infinity. An infinity reading (no change on the meter) means that there is an open connection, not a complete circuit. (The cable may have an improperly installed connector, or perhaps a conductor was broken somewhere along the cable.) Make the same continuity test at the connectors themselves: you should get similar readings.

You can also test for a short-circuit in the cable. Test the center post on one end and the connector on the other. This reading SHOULD be infinity.

If the cable has already been laid, you can place a terminator at one end (see Figure 4.3) and test at the other. The terminators and cable are rated at 50 ohms *impedance*, so you should get a reading within about 2 ohms of that if you test the center post against the connector case. You can test several new cables at once by connecting them with BNC T connectors. (The resistance should not significantly change over several cables.) If the cable you are testing is (or was) already in use, a reading taken at a T with both ends terminated should show 25 Ohms. (This reading can fluctuate if the network is not silent.) If your readings are far different, you should look for a cable fault. See Wavetek's book, *Handbook of LAN Cable Testing*, if you need to do serious testing and you have a bent for electronics.

Coaxial Ethernet cable requires the linear bus topology. When you lay new cable, it is to your advantage to locate the server in the middle, if you have a choice.

FIGURE 4.3 BNC tee and terminator for thin Ethernet connections

That way, if you have to do any cable repairs on one side during work hours, at least half of the users can still reach the server. (Warn all users to log off, place a terminator at the repair spot, then let the bulk of users back on.)

Connect each cable end to a horizontal arm of a T. At each end of the total length you must attach a terminator. Attach the bottom of the Ts to the network adapters. You do not have to attach each T to a network adapter—the network will be viable as long as the arms are all connected.

How to Make Unshielded Twisted-Pair Cables

When you purchase UTP, be sure to buy data-grade cable (level 4 or 5). Only the data-grade cable is rated for Ethernet's 10 megabit per second data transfer. The cable should be 24 AWG solid conductor, but 22 or 26 gauge wire can often be used. Usually this wire has a round, gray jacket (or transparent-white for plenum use) and is called telephone station wire. This is not the same as the 'silver satin', sometimes flat, modular telephone wire that you might lay along the floor behind furniture—do not use that. UTP costs only 15-30 cents per foot for 4-pair cable. Plenum-rated UTP is twice that. However, the 10Base-T standard only requires 2 twisted pairs. In some situations, you can use leftover cable from a 3- or 4-pair wall jack, already installed in the building.

You also need RJ-45 modular plugs (8-pin, non-keyed) at 35-50 cents each, and an RJ-45 crimp tool ($20 for a cheap one, $160 for the ritz). The crimp tool should have cutter and stripper blades. You may need new RJ-45 wall jacks if you use the building wiring. If you have a wiring closet and lots of nodes in the network, you should terminate all station cables on punch-down 66-blocks (with a punch-down tool), and add more cable from there to the wiring center. See Concentrating on UTP, below, for further details.

Assembly

UTP cables should be wired straight-through; e.g., pin 1 to pin 1, etc.—no crossing. Color codes for the pairs can vary by manufacturer, but do not matter to the network. Generally, the first pair is white/blue and the second is white/orange. If you are using existing building station wire, you will just have to see what is available at the wall jack.

To crimp on a connector, place the cable between the stripper blades, close the tool, and pull the wire out, stripping off the outer insulation. You do NOT want to damage the insulation on the inner conductors. Fan and flatten the pairs, placing the white/blue pair on the left and the white/orange pair on the right. Cut the ends off squarely, leaving about one-half inch of the colored conductors visible past the gray outer insulation. Grasp the RJ-45 plug with the gold pins away from you and the clip underneath. Insert the conductors carefully into slots 1,2,3, and 6. If you have 4-pair wire, place the white/green pair in slots 4 and 5 and the white/brown pair in slots 7 and 8. Those pairs can be used for telephone lines. Make sure that all conductors are pushed in fully, and that they line up perfectly in the slots. Insert the plug into the crimper and squeeze the handles, pressing the golden knife blades in the plug down onto the conductors. Repeat for the other end of the cable.

Testing

Testing UTP cable with a continuity tester is not easily done, because there are twice the conductors, and probes may be too thick to touch them, anyway. (If you do check impedance, the OHM meter should indicate 100 Ohms, plus or minus 15%.) The easy way to perform a basic test is to connect the cable between the computer's LAN adapter and the concentrator. You can do this while other users are on the LAN. Both the LAN adapter and the concentrator should show link integrity by lighting green LEDs. If they indicate a fault, check the ends visually. If a gold knife is positioned between conductors, there is a good chance that you found the offender. Cut off that end and replace it.

Useful Cable Adapters

You can generally do all of your network cabling with the parts mentioned above. However, you may run into situations in which the cabling must be physically altered. An adapter may exist to help.

For example, is your thinnet coaxial cable too short to reach to the next node? You can extend it with an extra length of cable and a T, or try a cable and a female-female or male-male straight connector instead. (You can also solve gender problems with these connectors.) Do you have an extremely tight space on the back of your computer for connecting the cable to the LAN adapter? Perhaps it won't tolerate a T with two plenum cables attached? Try placing right angle adapters on the end of the plenum cables, or if you can find one, try a Y or F instead of the T. Do you want to use the building conduit instead of dangling cable from the ceiling? Get bulkhead connectors and wallplates.

You can even adapt one cable type to another using *baluns*. For example, a balun can convert thinnet cable (BNC connectors) to unshielded twisted pair cable (RJ-45 connectors), letting you switch media for up to 350 feet. Or, adapt your UTP cable to the coax that runs to the wall plate.

HOT TIP

Keep the Noise Down

Avoid noise and electrical interference problems, especially if you use unshielded cables. If you are running cables through ceilings or equipment closets, route the cables away from fluorescent light fixtures, air conditioners, pumps, broadcast equipment, and other electrical devices. UTP is especially vulnerable to noise at junction points where it becomes temporarily untwisted.

Concentrating on UTP

Cables are not all you need for a star wiring scheme with unshielded twisted pair— you also need a wiring center. The wiring center, also called a *hub, multiport repeater*, or *concentrator*, is the clearing house for Ethernet packets. It is usually placed in a wiring closet, sometimes the telephone equipment closet. Wiring centers can feed other wiring centers, creating large and flexible networks. Wiring centers isolate networks of computers from other networks. They also isolate misbehaving equipment from the network, so if one computer develops a bad connection, the rest can still carry on. Ethernet collision detection occurs in the wiring center. Depending upon the model, hubs, and concentrators can knot computers together in the star through coax or fiber-optic cable, as well as UTP.

UTP cable may be cheap, but you had better factor this major piece of equipment into your budget. Hubs are the least expensive wiring centers, at $300-400 for the simple, 8 port, single media variety. They can be linked together, but usually support no more than 48 total ports.

Concentrators have more capabilities, and a higher price tag ($1000-$3000). Concentrators are sold with plug-in modules. For example, one module may provide 12 twisted-pair ports, and you might add modules to a maximum of 132 ports. You can also mix wiring types with concentrators, something not usually done on hubs. You may have 3 modules for twisted-pair, 2 for fiber-optic, and two more for Token Ring twisted-pair. You can manage most concentrators, and some hubs, from remote stations via the Simple Network Management Protocol (SNMP). This capability requires LAN Management software, discussed in Chapter 12.

Attaching PCs to Ethernet

Each PC to be attached to the network requires a *network interface card* (NIC) or external adapter suitable for use with thin coax, transceiver (AUI), fiber-optic, or unshielded twisted-pair cable. You can obtain a partial list of companies which manufacture NICs or external adapters from Appendix B.

Select a network interface card/adapter for each PC, verifying that each is supported by the TCP/IP software you want to run on the PC (FTP, PC-NFS, SCO UNIX System V/386, SCO Open Desktop, etc.) Check with your software vendor(s). Most provide a list of supported hardware on request. The adapter must also have a connector to match your cable type. Virtually all provide both an AUI port and one for BNC, UTP, or fiber-optic cable. Finally, unless you are networking XTs that have only 8-bit slots, always choose a 16- or 32-bit card as an internal adapter. You will get significantly better performance than if you used an 8-bit card, due to the wider I/O path.

Internal Adapters

The installation steps for network interface cards are similar from product to product. We used 3Com EtherLink II, SMC 16 Elite Combo, and Eagle NE2000 adapters in our desktop PCs like the one in Figure 4.4.

Setting jumpers on the card

Configure the adapter hardware if necessary. On some boards, such as SMC's Elite16 Series, all configuration can be done through software. However, many boards require you to set jumpers or DIP switches to configure some or all of the board's attributes. Here are the five commonly set parameters.

- *I/O base address*—Each Ethernet adapter requires a small contiguous memory space for input/output registers. The base address is the starting location for this space, expressed in hexadecimal notation in increments of 20 (32 bytes). Several PC devices require their own I/O addresses, including LPT and COM ports, expansion units, disk controllers, and video display drivers. You must make sure they all use different address locations. On the 3Com EtherLink II, the I/O base address jumper can be set for 2E0 through 300. On the SMC Elite, you can have 200-3E0. The typical factory default is usually 280, but this can conflict with the Wyse 2108 PC LCD display. The safest addresses to use are typically 280,220,240,2A0,2C0, and 340.

- *Shared memory (RAM) base address*—The RAM base address provides a device with a large area of RAM that serves as a temporary storage area (buffer). These devices include network adapters, video display cards, BIOS, and expanded memory. Network adapters use the shared memory area for data transfer between the adapter and the PC. The RAM area ranges from address A0000 to 100000, and interface cards consume it in increments of 4000 hex (16K

FIGURE 4.4   Standard Microsystems Elite Combo Ethernet Adapter

bytes). Don't be confused if the addresses may be expressed as A000 to 10000, and the RAM requirement as 400—the final zero is frequently dropped in the literature, and it means the same thing. Typically, you can select an address of D000, D400, D800, or DC00, as long as this does not conflict with any other device. Be aware that some VGA cards use the area C000-DFFF, which would conflict. If you use a memory management utility such as EMM386 or QEMM, you MUST direct it to exclude your chosen memory space. You can also disable shared memory for the network adapter, in which case it may use DMA. Use shared memory if you can, because it is faster than DMA.

• *Direct Memory Access Channel*—PCs use a DMA controller to transfer large amounts of data quickly. The DMA controller moves data from an external device (such as a network adapter) into RAM, without help from the CPU. Each device requires its own channel—1, 2, 3, or disabled. Packet drivers (as opposed to NDIS or ODI) support shared memory, but not DMA. See your network software manual for recommendations.

• *IRQ level*—Interrupt levels must be assigned to PC hardware devices, including network adapters. The possible choices are 2-5, 7, 10, 11, and 15. The EGA/ VGA board sometimes claims IRQ 2, COM2 gets 3, COM1 is on 4, LPT2 uses 5, and LPT1 uses 7. This leaves 10, 11, and 15 unused on most PCs, unless you do not have LPT2 (the second parallel port) installed, in which case 5 is fair game. The same goes for COM2 (the second serial port) and EGA/VGA irks.

• *Output port*—In many cases there is a switch to select the output port, whether AUI (for transceiver drop cable), BNC (for 10Base2 thin coax), or UTP (for 10Base-T twisted pair).

You can often leave the adapter set to the factory defaults, but you should make sure they do not conflict with other devices and installed boards. If you find any setting to be identical, change the settings on the new board. You should always keep a record of how the boards are configured for reference.

If you don't have records available, you can check settings on the other boards/ devices in one of several ways. The fastest and best method is to use a system diagnostic software tool such as those described in Chapter 5 under How to Obtain PC Hardware and Memory Information. These tools can provide lists of what the machine has for hardware, and how it is all configured. LAN management tools with automatic inventory capability can do this as well, from a remote location (see Chapter 12). If you do not have such a tool, install the board as is and watch the hardware initialization messages during boot—usually the board settings are displayed. The third, and most time-consuming, method is to go through the manuals for each of the other boards and identify the settings visually on those boards, by removing them if necessary. If you cannot easily determine the settings, go ahead and install the board anyway—you will discover later if there is a problem (no harm done—the boards in conflict just won't work). Be careful to write down the settings for later reference during software installation—otherwise, you may have to pull the card out of the PC just to verify those settings.

Handle Electronics With Care

PC boards can be fried by one spark of static electricity. Use care when handling and installing them. Ground yourself on an unpainted part of the computer chassis first. (The computer should remain plugged in, but not on.) Be sure to store cards in their static- protected packaging when they are not installed.

Installing the card

Install network adapter according to the manufacturer's instructions. Usually, the only tool required for installing an internal card is a Phillips screwdriver. The power to the computer should always be off when altering the hardware. Remove the screws on the back of the PC and slide off the case. Several card slots will be located on the motherboard, some of which will be used. Choose a slot that accommodates the card. Some cards are 8-bit and require one 3-inch slot for seating. 16-bit cards require both a 3-inch and a 2-inch slot. If you are using coax cable, try to choose a slot some distance from previously installed cards because the BNC T connector consumes more than its share of space behind the computer. If you run into a problem attaching the T, you might need to move the cards around to make room. Remove the screw holding the blank plate in place. (Don't drop the screw inside!)

Guide the adapter gently into the slot; then push it straight in firmly. Replace the screw you just removed, fastening down the end of the board. Replace the cover.

Connect the cabling to the adapter from the back. Occasionally you will find too little room at the back of the computer to attach an Ethernet T amid other cables. One solution is to move the boards around; another is to replace the T with a more expensive F or Y connector which can accomplish the same purpose.

HOT TIP   **A Lesson in Magnetism**

Contrary to popular belief, you CAN use a magnetized screwdriver near a computer. This tool makes it easy to fasten down boards, or retrieve errant screws. Just keep it away from the floppy disks, which store data magnetically. If you don't, you can lose entire disks of data!

External Adapters

Due to their small size, most laptop PCs do not have room for an internal network interface card. We easily connected our laptop PCs using Xircom Pocket Ethernet Adapter II's attached to the laptops' parallel ports (as shown in Figure 4.5).

Make sure you buy the proper model for your network cable. Xircom, Intel, and others also manufacture 'credit card' adapters for PCMCIA card slots, which are used on tinier palmtop computers.

External adapters for parallel ports require no tools for installation. On a laptop, simply open the I/O panel (usually on the back of the computer) and press the adapter onto the standard 25-pin D-style port. The Xircom has a rubber belt you turn to secure the adapter. If a parallel printer is already attached, you can obtain a Y (multiplexer) adapter from Xircom to let you keep that connection while still attaching the computer to the network. Then attach the network cable. Because they attach

---

CAUTION
WATCH YOUR STEP

Tapping the Hornets' Nest

Be careful when disconnecting cables from a thin Ethernet network adapter! If you break the line during an exchange of traffic, data may be lost, LAN servers may become confused, and enemies may be gained. The safe place to disconnect the cable is at the base of the tee, where it connects to the adapter, NOT on either arm. If you must add/replace a section of cable during business hours (which we do not advise), broadcast a message to the users to save what they are doing and logoff. (Actually, they should not have to logoff or even get out of their applications, as long as their applications do not attempt to reach the server, or can recover from such an attempt. But, it is safest to have them logoff, or work after hours yourself.)

FIGURE 4.5   For people on the go: Xircom's handy Pocket Ethernet Adapter II

to the parallel port rather than the PC system bus, there are no jumpers to set for I/ O base memory, IRQ, etc.

The main thing to know about parallel port adapters is that their performance depends largely on the port. Standard parallel ports are designed for sending data primarily in one direction (out to a printer). It only receives a little, such as paper out signals. The parallel port network adapter CAN use standard ports. However, newer parallel ports on laptops support a bi-directional mode which can improve the data transfer rate by up to 50%—a noticeable improvement. This bi-directional capability is called Enhanced Parallel Port (EPP) technology. If your laptop supports EPP, an EPP-compatible adapter will supply a driver to capture the extra performance. We placed Xircom's **EPP.COM** on the laptop and executed it from **AUTOEXEC.BAT**.

Configuration and Testing

Turn on the computer. The new adapter will likely display a message during the boot process, indicating the success or failure of initialization. Some products, including 3Com's EtherLink II and SMC's Elite 16 Combo, provide configuration software which you should now run. The EtherLink II software allows you to set the interrupt level (range = 2 to 5), DMA channel (range = 1 to 3), and transceiver type (use the onboard transceiver for thin Ethernet, external transceiver for thick Ethernet). If you are not sure about a setting, accept the factory defaults for now.

If the PC accepts the new hardware, the next step is to install the adapter's software driver(s). Network drivers provide the link between the network operating system and the adapter hardware. Every LAN adapter comes with a diskette containing drivers for different hardware/software scenarios. The typical installation procedure involves copying files onto the hard drive from the disk and placing lines of instructions in the **AUTOEXEC.BAT** and **CONFIG.SYS** files. Other configuration files can be affected as well; and, of course, networking software must also be installed to make use of the hardware by talking to the driver.

At this point we are going to bail out of the subject of software configuration, since this chapter concentrates on hardware. We direct you to Chapter 5 for an in-depth discussion of how to get the software end up and running.

The Oldies Are Not Always Golden

Most networking software products provide drivers for common LAN adapters and will install one for you. However, their drivers may be outdated with respect to your particular adapter, preventing you from establishing connection with your host. If you need a current driver, either find one on the diskette supplied with the adapter, or call your adapter vendor. The vendor may offer a bulletin board service which has all of the current drivers.

Running diagnostics

Often, manufacturers, such as SMC, provide a diagnostic utility with the adapter in case of difficulty. Figure 4.6 shows a screen shot of this utility. Before you perform any diagnostics, these utilities may require you to remark-out any lines in your **AUTOEXEC.BAT** and **CONFIG.SYS** files that load memory-resident programs. This will help to rule out problems with the adapter itself, if you have trouble.

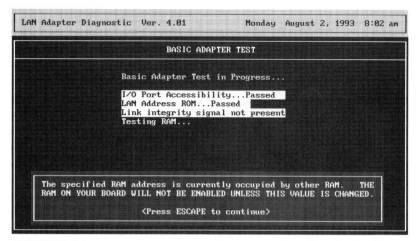

FIGURE 4.6 Diagnosing adapter conflicts with SMC's Diagnose

Attaching UNIX Workstations to Ethernet

Many workstations, such as the RS/6000 models, come with Ethernet network cards that plug into the workstation's bus. The board in our RS/6000 has both AUI and BNC ports. We had to remove the card in order to check the jumper setting—it was configured for the AUI port. Since we had a BNC T-connector waiting (no thick Ethernet backbone) we switched it to BNC. Then we were ready to configure the RS/6000's software (discussed in Chapter 5).

A Sun SPARCstation IPC, on the other hand, has a built-in network adapter with only the AUI port. Attachment Unit Interface ports connect the computer to the network cabling via a transceiver and drop cable.

Transceiver Hardware

A short length of transceiver drop cable (specially-shielded twisted pair) connects the workstation to the transceiver, but it can be up to 50 meters (165 feet) long if need be. Eight-foot transceiver cables cost $25-$50; 50 meter plenum drops can go as high as $300. (You can eliminate this cost by purchasing a transceiver that connects directly to your AUI port.) Transceivers adapt drop cable to thin or thick Ethernet, UPT, or fiber-optic cable; but not all do, so you need to make sure you order the correct model. If you are adapting to thick coax, you will need a special device called a tap (N-type is about $8) to attach the transceiver to the coax.

We bought a private-label transceiver for BNC from a mail order firm that specialized in inexpensive foreign goods. The label was so private, we couldn't find it! While this product worked with no problem, we would have felt more comfortable having at least a phone number to call if we had trouble. We also tried a transceiver from SMC that worked well and came with a company address and model number. Transceivers usually cost $100-$200. Don't expect much in the way of instructions to come from the manufacturers, however. With such simple devices, they sometimes presume that you can figure out how to attach the cables.

Transceiver Installation and Testing

Make sure there is no traffic on the network before you break the line to insert the transceiver. The AUI transceiver cable attaches to the 15-pin D connectors on the transceiver and the AUI port at the computer.

Turn the power back on to the workstation. There is usually a series of LEDs on the transceiver which indicate its status (similar to a modem), but there are few or no switches. Our no-name transceiver has LEDs for power (+12V coming from the computer), transmit (data going to the network), receive (data coming back from the network), collision (detects simultaneous transmit and receive; then notifies the computer to wait and retry—should normally be off), and Signal Quality Error status (on or off). SQE is a "heartbeat" function that is disabled when used with a repeater. Some SMC transceiver models also have a Link LED to indicate the integrity of the UTP or fiber-optic cables to which they are attached. Our SMC transceiver also had a switch to enable SQE; you can set it with a pencil point. When used with UPT, transceivers filter line noise to eliminate false collision detection.

Getting More Distance with Repeaters

Repeaters contribute to internetworking by boosting the signal strength of packets. They essentially repeat messages at louder volume. When packets are transmitted over the network, the electrical signals dissipate as the distance of travel increases. To accommodate this limitation, the maximum recommended thick Ethernet segment length is 500 meters—not enough distance for many companies with large campuses. In order to give a packet enough 'oomph' to traverse another segment, a *repeater* joins each segment with the next. This enables Ethernet LANs to grow beyond their natural length limits, up to 2500 meters. No more than four repeaters can be used on any LAN, because each one (along with its cable) introduces a slight delay in signal re-transmission. Going beyond the 2500 meter length limit with repeaters causes a synchronization problem: a host at one end listens to the line and hears nothing, even though a host at the other end just started transmitting. Then the first host starts transmitting and a collision occurs.

Repeaters can have multiple ports, allowing you to connect more than two segments (like a fork in the road), rather than being strictly linear. This feature allows both extended distance on the backbone (two segments joined) and service to other media such as thin coax (a third segment branching off). Multiport repeaters are often called *hubs* (see Concentrating on UTP, earlier). Repeaters connect to thick coax via an MAU transceiver and transceiver drop cable. Alternately, in smaller operations, thin coax can be used in place of a backbone between two repeaters. Or, as a third scenario, eliminate the backbone and second repeater altogether—the repeater itself can act as the backbone for perhaps up to 20 segments. Note that you must disable the SQE 'heartbeat' test at the transceivers, if you use repeaters. Operating at the lowest level of the OSI model (the Physical Layer), repeaters are unintelligent enough to be grouped with the cabling. Multiport repeaters cost about $1000-$1300, from manufacturers such as 3Com Corporation.

Assembling Your Network

By this time you should have a fair idea of how everything fits together, but just to make things easy, here are some diagrams. Figure 4.7 shows a small thin Ethernet network between a PC, a workstation, and a printer (note the terminators). Figure 4.8 pictures a UTP-based wiring scheme utilizing wall jacks and a wiring closet. Figure 4.9 shows a portion of a thick Ethernet network.

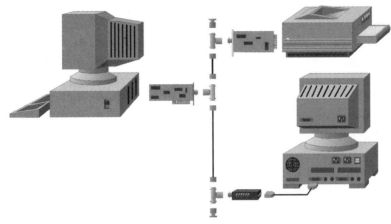

FIGURE 4.7　Connecting a PC, printer, and workstation with thin Ethernet

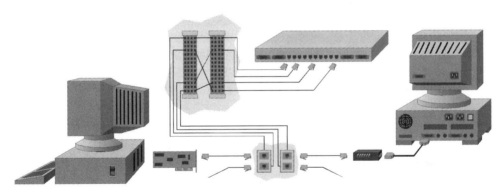

FIGURE 4.8　All machines talk to the hub in a UTP environment

Directing Network Traffic

Once you have your machines physically and mentally connected over Ethernet, you must concern yourself with *traffic*. Traffic on the network is, of course, the stream of data packets flowing between machines. When traffic gets heavy, there are *collisions*, and the entire network slows down. (At least there is no gawkers-block; packets don't stop to stare.) Collisions are not due to installing a bad network driver, they are simply a normal part of life, accounted for in the Ethernet specification. Chapter 2 provides background information on how data is transmitted over Ethernet. In this chapter we start a new discussion of network traffic and tell you how to direct it.

To begin, here is one quick rule of thumb: once your traffic grows to about 60% of capacity, collisions begin to occur with regularity. As traffic increases, so do the collisions, resulting in slower and slower responses over the network. It is to your advantage to reduce traffic jams, because it makes all of your users more productive. Products exist to help you monitor the level of traffic and diagnose problems. You can also obtain devices to route or restrict traffic for maximum efficiency. Here are some key types of products that you should be aware of.

FIGURE 4.9 Transceivers and drop cables connect computers to a thick Ethernet backbone

LAN Analyzers

You can find many tools to help you analyze in detail the traffic on your network. These tools are known by many names: *LAN analyzers, protocol analyzers traffic monitors*, and *network management systems*. You may find it difficult to compare these products with each other because their feature sets can be widely different. Such tools can, among other things, (1) show you what types of packets (corresponding to specific protocols) are being sent over the network, and in what quantity; (2) record histories of traffic patterns; (3) map nodes on the network graphically; (4) help you detect faulty equipment and cables; and (5) alert you to network slowdowns or other misfortunes as they happen. Any system administrator with 100 or more nodes (or network slowdowns) should give some thought to purchasing a network management tool that has traffic monitoring capabilities.

We have chosen to not discuss LAN analyzers and other network management tools in a detailed fashion here. Please turn to Chapter 12 to find out more on that subject, and to learn about automatic network inventory and remote configuration.

Bridges

Bridges are hardware products which organize large networks into sub-networks (or, conversely, organize networks into large internetworks). Bridges are useful when network performance drops due to the number of computers on the network. Larger networks are usually composed of regional (local) servers networked together. Most computers need to talk primarily with their local server, such as a PC exchanging bookkeeping data with the Accounting Department server. However, without some means of setting boundaries for the packet, it would transmit across the entire network. Perhaps it would collide with a data packet from the Engineering server to a CAD station, requiring both to be re-sent. The network becomes congested, resulting in slower response time for everyone. A bridge acts as a boundary, isolating entire networks from other networks. However, packets specifically addressed to a destination on the other side of the bridge are happily sent through, maintaining complete networkability for all nodes. Bridges are similar to repeaters in that they link segments of a large network. However, repeaters pass every packet through in either direction; bridges are selective. Bridges operate at Layer 2 of the OSI model, one step above repeaters.

Bridges are transparent. That is, network nodes do not know bridges exist, so setup is easy. Bridges teach themselves which hosts are on the isolated side. They also do not care which protocol sends and receives the packets, whether TCP/IP, IPX/SPX, DECnet, AppleTalk, or whatever—all are treated the same. They only look at the packet frame header to check the destination (the MAC, or Ethernet address), then forward the packet across the bridge as necessary.

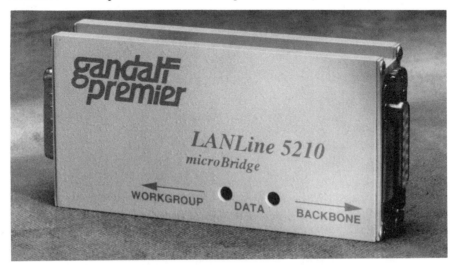

FIGURE 4.10 Gandalf Premier LANLine 5210 Micro Bridge—tiny package, big job

Many companies manufacturer bridges for Ethernet, and they are simple to install. For example, see Figure 4.10 for a picture of the tiny Gandalf LANLine 5210

Micro Bridge from Premier. Each end of the Microbridge has an AUI port, one for the main network ("To UNIX Host"), the other for the sub-network ("To Isolated Computers"). On the host side you would typically connect an AUI cable from the bridge to a hub or multiport repeater; on the isolated side you would usually connect to a transceiver on the subnet backbone. The bridge draws its power from the hub or the backbone, not through a wall outlet. During the first 90 seconds of its life on the LAN, the 5210 learns who is who on the network—which computers it is isolating. The bridge requires no configuration. If you have a network manager, it should convey that network traffic outside of the isolated subnet has decreased and performance has increased. LEDs on the 5210 indicate the traffic and collision rates on either side of the bridge as visual references.

Routers

One step up from a bridge, a *router* performs the same functions, but has more brains for decision-making. Operating at the Network level of the OSI model (Layer 3 or higher) routers can be configured to filter packets far beyond what bridges do with the destination addresses. Routers can restrict traffic based upon packet type (such as SMTP for e-mail), and can direct the packet down the best route (least expensive, least busy, or fastest) to reach its destination. They are aware of the existence of other routers and make use of them. Router capabilities hinge on the programming—they must be configured by software. They have their own network addresses, and are known to the nodes they service. Routers only listen to packets that are addressed to them, ignoring all others (but preventing their passage across to another subnet). Routers are much more expensive, as you might expect. The hardware cost is $10,000-$100,000, and there is some setup cost as well for routing daemons and tables. Cisco Systems, Inc. is well-known for its routers, such as the new Model 4000 in Figure 4.11.

FIGURE 4.11 Cisco Systems' Cicso 4000 Multiprotocol Router

The definition of a router lays heavy on translation between peer protocols, and signal adjustment. In other words, where there is a large gap in the technical specifications, due to frame format or size, addressing, error detection methods, etc., the router manages the conversion. Routers join two incompatible networks, and are designed to support particular protocols, such as NetWare and DECnet.

The ability of routers to restrict packet travel based upon type, or protocol, is a boon to internetworking. If a packet has business on another subnet, such as the e-mail example, or SNMP for network management, it may pass through. If a Novell IPX packet arrives at the router, it won't be allowed to clutter the UNIX TCP/IP network unless the administrator has created a NetWare server there.

The term *gateway*, or *IP gateway* is interchangeable with *router*. Many people have been confused by vendors, who attempt to differentiate their products using terminology.

As you would guess, a *brouter* is a combination bridge/router. If you have an SNA network, you must use a bridge, rather than a router, to internetwork. Brouters accommodate these IBM bridges while providing multiprotocol support as a router. Proteon is one example of a company which manufactures bridging routers.

If you have specific questions about whether to use a bridge or router in your particular situation, contact a vendor for suggestions. As with all computer products, you will be weighing performance against cost, only in this case the entire network and all users' salaries come to bear.

Troubleshooting

Troubleshooting communications hardware is difficult to do without software. There are only a few things you can do to check yourself in the early stages. Usually you don't know if there is a problem until you get your network driver and network operating system installed. Nevertheless, here are some low-level troubleshooting ideas for your adapters and cables. We also discuss the major causes and fixes for network slowdowns.

Checking the Components

If you suspect an adapter problem, here are some general hints to pursue before you have Sarah ring Tech Support. See Chapter 5 for additional troubleshooting with regard to network drivers.

Localize the trouble

•Make sure other network nodes are not experiencing the same problem? Is the network server up? If all nodes get slow responses, check the following section on Network Slowdowns. If all nodes have suddenly collapsed, check for a missing terminator on one of the ends, or a disconnected cable somewhere in between.

Check the obvious (the cable)

• Is the network cable connected? If you are using coaxial Ethernet cable, is the T reliable? If you are using twisted pair cable, do the adapter and wiring center indicate a valid link status? If you are attached to a thick coax backbone, is the transceiver working, and is the LAN adapter set to use the AUI port? Can you swap in another computer, with a different LAN adapter, to test the cable?

• If you suspect the cable, break the segment and test each side with an Ohm meter. Each side should read very close to 50 Ohms. If one side is far off, say 42 Ohms, reconnect the cable and move along in that direction. Break the cable and test both halves again. Repeat until you have isolated the cable length that does not read 50 Ohms. Replace the cable.

Check initialization

• Does the board initialize properly at boot time? Is the board properly seated in its slot? Do any other boards indicate a conflict of I/O address, IRQ channel, or shared memory address? Verify jumper settings, or software configuration. Try changing the configuration. If the adapter is set for shared memory, remember to exclude that memory space from any memory management utility that is installed.

• Has the network driver been installed, and the protocol stack drivers for the network operating system? Are the drivers compatible with the adapter and with each other? Has a ROM chip been installed on the adapter, and is it appropriate for this machine? Does this machine require boot image files to be installed on the server?

Run diagnostics

• Run any diagnostics that the vendor provided with the adapter. Such programs may provide loopback tests for testing the connection between two nodes. If the test passes, the problem may be with the file server. If the test fails, the cabling or local adapter is at fault.

Check transceiver status

• If you have a transceiver on the network, check to see if the collision LED is staying on. If it is, disconnect the new adapter from the network cable and see if the situation clears. If it clears, the adapter is probably defective.

• If all the transceiver lights are off, it is not being powered from the node to which it is attached. Swap in a new AUI cable and/or LAN adapter. If all the lights are on, there may be no viable connection with the network cable—

reconnect the network cable. If you have repeaters on the network, disable the SQE heartbeat.

Network Slowdowns

Slowdowns can be caused by a few factors, including faulty LAN adapters, intermittent cable connections, electrical noise on the cables, overloaded servers, and too many users. Network Management software can sometimes help you pinpoint these causes (see Chapter 12). Look for unusually high rates of errors or lost packets.

Heavy traffic

- When a network reaches approximately 60% of capacity, collisions start occurring regularly. If there is too much traffic on the network, isolate users (create subnetworks) using a bridge. This will speed up the entire network by lowering the overall traffic and the collision rate.

- You can graph the packet rates to indicate the busiest time of day. One alternative to more hardware is to schedule users around the busy time.

Equipment failure

- With the help of traffic monitoring software, you might spot brief periods of time in which the traffic count goes to zero. These periods, if uncharacteristic for the LAN, could signify an intermittent connection in the coax network.

- On the other end of the traffic spectrum is the *broadcast storm*. Broadcast packets have no designated recipient, but go to all hosts on the network. Some broadcast packets require a response by all hosts. If a broadcasting host sends out a stream of broadcast packets, the resulting milieu is called a broadcast storm—there is a downpour of returning packets, clogging the drainpipes of the network for a period of time. *Jabbering* is a similar problem. Occasionally, a network adapter or repeater can get "stuck" transmitting packets and slow the network with the extra traffic. Network monitoring software can help you pinpoint the offending host, or there may be rapidly flashing transmit lights on one of the network adapters/transceivers. You can try shutting off or swapping out suspected equipment to see if the problem ceases. Jabbers can be caused by a buggy network driver, so before you toss a card, try getting an updated driver.

- If a computer will not communicate, or not boot properly, traffic monitors can check for packets transmitted by that computer. If there are none, the adapter hardware may have failed. If packets were transmitted, perhaps an error exists at the server.

- Disk errors on network drives, station lockups, traffic-less slowdowns, time- or location-dependant problems, and similarly unfathomable events are the most difficult problems to deal with. These problems are usually due to cable trouble: induced electrical noise, flawed or damaged cabling, mixed cable types, or merely coincidental combinations of electrical characteristics in the cable. Determining the exact nature of these problems can require electronic expertise and special test equipment. Assuming you don't have expertise and equipment, the easiest way to deal with such a problem is to replace the suspected cable segment—preferably with a longer or shorter one, and re-route the cable away from any type of lighting or equipment. For UTP installations, noise could be entering at a connection box, where the "twist" is temporarily lost.

Application-dependant slowdowns

• If only some users complain of certain applications, use a trace program (or personal interviews) to see what they might be doing differently than the rest. For example, the users may be running overlay files on the server instead of on their own machines, creating more server access.

• Some applications may be poorly written for networks, inefficiently handling requests. The only solution for this problem is to replace the application with another that performs the same task.

• You may find that applications needed by many users frequently take up a lot of CPU time at the file server, causing delays for all. If you have more than one server, re-distribute the busy applications from the current server to one or more file servers that are less busy.

• If you have an application that regularly crashes, network management software can help you trace the reason. Turn on the history function for that application so that you can observe the traffic pattern that leads to its demise.

5

Setting Up a TCP/IP Network

Introduction

TCP/IP (Transmission Control Protocol/Internet Protocol) sounds boring. But is it just one more acronym? If you are planning a network between DOS and UNIX, plan on liking it. Practice saying it: T-C-P-I-P. As introduced in Chapter 2, TCP/IP is the primary software conduit for UNIX networks, through which passes all network information. These two combined protocols supply the low-level rules for communication with the hardware and its drivers, roughly similar to what Novell's IPX/SPX does on the PC (DOS) LAN side. TCP/IP is a widely-adopted networking standard which connects dissimilar computer systems of every hardware type and operating system: workstations, PCs, Macintoshs, mainframes, and minicomputers. The Internet literally exists through TCP/IP, and Client/Server architecture depends heavily upon it. Nearly all of the connectivity products mentioned in this book either supply TCP/IP functionality or depend on its availability.

For all of these reasons and more, creating a TCP/IP network is the starting point for most of the networking solutions available to your operation. In this chapter we show you how to create a TCP/IP network between UNIX workstations and PCs.

What You Gain from TCP/IP Networking

The TCP/IP specifies a basic set of communication utilities, or *Internet services*. These services, along with every other detail about TCP/IP, are defined in documents called RFCs (Request for Comments). The main variances between TCP/IP networking products for PCs are the utility selection and the ease of access to those utilities. For example, one product may provide a Microsoft Windows graphical user interface with icon point-and-shoot access to its utilities. Another product may only provide a DOS command-line interface, but with a couple more utilities. The DOS version requires more extensive knowledge about the parameter syntax for each utility. (However, most products now provide some level of Windows interface.)

In addition to utilities, the protocol by itself can be a valuable product. The protocol *stack* is the underlying kernel, or communication layer, for the utilities. Each utility talks to the stack, which in turn packages the information so that TCP/IP servers across the network can read it. Applications can be written which talk directly to the TCP/IP stack, enabling client/server communications. Many vendors sell both a full-blown TCP/IP package, complete with stack and utilities, and a stack-only version for use by compatible applications. Vendors can also supply software development kits to help you write TCP/IP-aware applications.

Here is a list of the more important TCP/IP utilities and support protocols which compose the TCP/IP protocol suite. We also list related applications which you typically use through TCP/IP. The names of some utilities may change from product to product as vendors seek market differentiation.

Remote Login

telnet—remote login as a terminal. The **telnet** utility provides UNIX terminal emulation without much in the way of features. As you can see from Figure 5.1, **telnet** is not very dressy. You use this simple utility to remotely connect to other machines

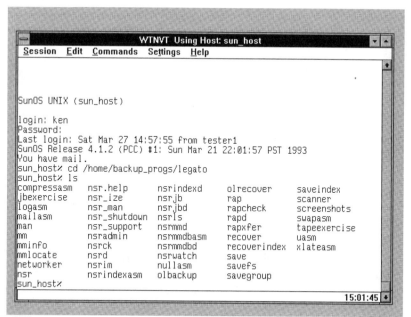

FIGURE 5.1 Telnet from PC to Sun via FTP Software's PC/TCP

(often using different operating systems) on the network—be they Sun SPARCstation, DEC VAX, IBM mainframe, PC, or whatever supports TCP/IP. Vendors supply a variety of terminal emulation modes including VT100-320, ANSI, and tn3270 (a stripped-down 3270 emulation). **telnet** allows you to configure a limited set of session options to effect communications, but the session will not offer one of those fancy desktops you have seen on X-terminals. Many TCP/IP products also let you remap the PC keyboard to match what you are used to, as shown in Figure 5.2.

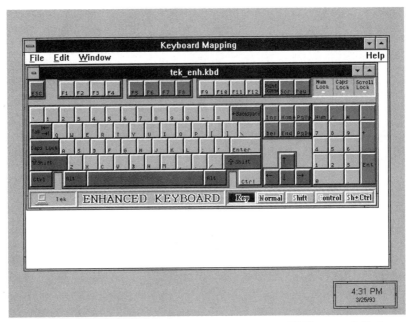

FIGURE 5.2 One of the best keyboard remappers—Wollongong's Pathway Access

Remote Commands—rlogin is a remote login similar to **telnet**, but with more flexibility. This utility circumvents the normal login/password verification by setting up remote user names equivalent to local names, allowing faster connection and automated access by software programs. The local machine's environment can also be communicated to the remote machine, making the session look more like a local session. In **telnet**'s favor, however, is the fact that **rlogin** can only be used between UNIX systems—**telnet** can work between differing operating systems. The remote shell command, called **rsh** by BSD UNIX, **rcmd** by System V, is a variant of **rlogin**, and executes a program on a remote host without stopping for interactive login. When the program completes its execution, the command and link terminates. **rexec** is similar to **rsh**, but asks for a login first. **Rcp** is a special-purpose remote command for remote copy. However, it is not as robust for file transfer as **ftp**.

File and Resource Sharing

ftp (File Transfer Protocol)—basic file and directory services. This utility performs a login; then it allows remote filesystems to be perused and files to be transferred in either direction. Figure 5.3 shows Novell's implementation of **ftp**. The Trivial File

Transfer Protocol (**tftp**) is a utility with a subset of **ftp** capabilities (no authentication password, single file transfer only) and is sometimes placed in ROM to boot diskless workstations on the network. You typically use **tftp** for booting X-terminals, for example. Some TCP/IP products for Windows allow file transfers to occur in the background of their regular work, but this capability is thanks to Windows, not the **ftp** protocol.

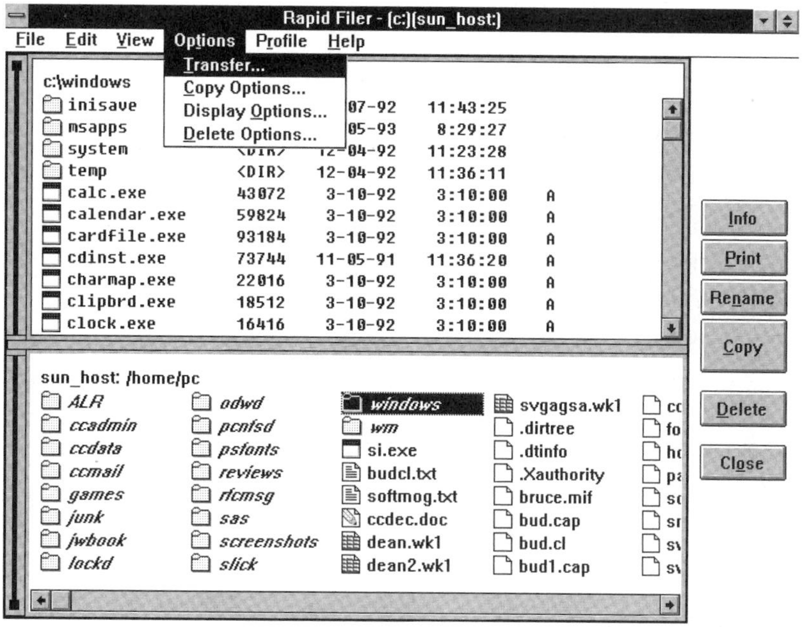

FIGURE 5.3   UNIX ftp never looked this easy—Novell LAN WorkPlace for DOS

NFS (Network File System)—transparent access to remote filesystems. With NFS you may execute programs and share data files on remote machines as if they were local resources. The user does not necessarily know that the computer he or she is sitting at has no "E:" drive (see Figure 5.4). NFS is not a TCP/IP utility, but rather an important specification in its own right that relies on TCP/IP. However, NFS functionality is often packaged with TCP/IP products for PCs, so we introduce it here. Chapter 6 is devoted entirely to NFS.

Network Management

SNMP (Simple Network Management Protocol)—obtains statistics on network traffic and computer configuration. Most network analyzer or management software requires an SNMP agent to be running on each managed computer in the background as a terminate-and-stay-resident program (TSR). If you have a larger network you should have SNMP capability at each node.

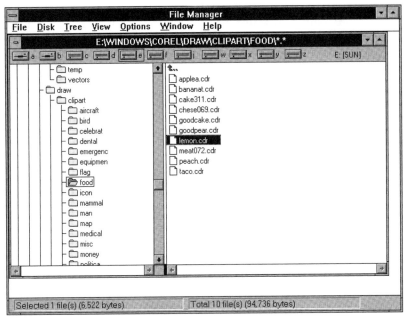

FIGURE 5.4 NFS satisfies the hunger for disk space—Windows finds UNIX drives

PING—network testing utility. This utility sends packets to another computer to see if a viable connection exists. Here is an example of pinging machine **laptop** from the Sun:

```
sun_host% ping laptop
laptop is alive
sun_host%
```

NETSTAT—network statistics utility. Traffic on the network (number of packets sent and type, number of errors) can be viewed in a statistical fashion.

FINGER— shows information about a network user such as login, home directory, project, when mail was last read, etc.

WHOIS—shows who is currently logged in to the network.

Mail and Messaging

SMTP (Simple Mail Transfer Protocol) support—electronic mail between remote machines. This standard protocol is in use by the Internet and is common among UNIX machines. Most UNIX E-mail software requires SMTP compatibility in order to send and receive mail. Figure 5.5 shows one SMTP-based mail package for PCs.

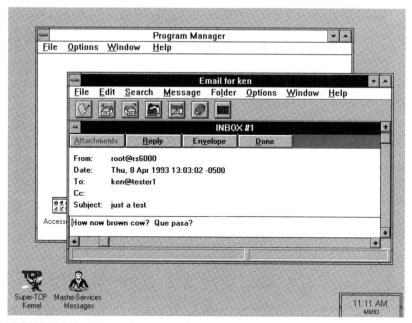

FIGURE 5.5 The mail must go through—Frontier Technologies' Super-TCP

Console messaging—Called by various names such as TALK, SEND or CHAT, this function lets you transmit short messages to other machines on a simpler level than electronic mail. The utility may allow interactive (conversational) communications. It is not a part of the TCP/IP applications, but vendors often included it.

Printing

The following utilities are a part of UNIX, but not part of the TCP/IP specification. TCP/IP products for PCs provide access to UNIX printers through these utilities. (For more on printer connections, see Chapter 11.)

LPR—enables you to print to any UNIX network printer which is managed by an LPD Server. LPR creates print job files from your document and places them in a spool directory.

LPD Server—makes the computer function as a network print server. LPD (for line printer daemon) watches for print jobs spooled by LPR and creates sub-processes to print them. LPD also provides queue management and printer control services. This server daemon is available on BSD-based UNIX operating systems. SVR4 UNIX uses a slightly different system of print service; however, the service can accommodate LPR requests.

Printing via PCNFS—printer output can be redirected from a machine's local port to a printer connected via NFS. The process uses the LPR protocol to print, but PCNFS supplies the niceties of browsing for printers and controlling remote queues.

Selecting a TCP/IP Networking Product

TCP/IP is a well-defined standard, extensively tested, and not any one vendor's idea of utopia. This means that any TCP/IP networking product will do for connecting a DOS PC to a UNIX computer, regardless of the vendors involved. The products are interchangeable if you need only the basic **telnet** and **ftp** capabilities. You can mix and match TCP/IP networking products from several vendors on the same TCP/IP network. This compliance with a standard leaves you free to select a TCP/IP product based upon ease of installation, ease of use, the feature set, and compatibility with non-UNIX networks. Looking at those qualities, important differences between products exist—it pays to shop around. Prices range from $250 to $400. We provide an extensive comparison guide to TCP/IP products for PCs in Chapter 13. Here are some major issues to pursue with the vendors as you shop.

NFS Support

The TCP/IP suite of protocols (utilities or capabilities) is sometimes packaged by vendors into several products. Be sure to nail down what is included in your chosen package, especially in regard to NFS. NFS is often sold as an option to a TCP/IP product; e.g., Frontier Technologies markets Super-TCP and Super-NFS; FTP Software sells PC/TCP and Interdrive. SunSelect's PC-NFS provides all functions in one package. If you already have a TCP/IP network running on a target machine and only wish to add NFS functionality, you need to obtain the NFS option from the TCP/IP vendor, or switch to another TCP/IP product if NFS is not available. A TCP/IP product with NFS costs slightly higher—$350-500.

Network Support

The TCP/IP software you choose should be compatible with other network operating systems that may also be on the network. Novell Netware, Microsoft LAN Manager, Banyan Vines, DCA 10Net, DEC PATHWORKS, and others usually require special configuration procedures. Most of these configurations depend upon the use of particular network drivers, such as NDIS, ODI or packet drivers (discussed later).

If you connect your computer to the network via serial cable or modem, remember that the TCP/IP product must support SLIP or PPP. See Chapter 9, Setting Up Serial Connections, for a discussion of these protocols.

Windows Support

"Windows compatibility" is used carelessly by some vendors in order to make their products look more advanced than they really are. Almost every DOS program is Windows-compatible in the sense that it will run in the MS-DOS Prompt window. However, that approach does not take advantage of Windows' graphical environment and memory management services— you are temporarily hopping out of Windows. Make sure you understand what your vendor means.

The TCP/IP *kernel*, or *protocol stack*, is important to consider from the standpoint of system memory. Some kernels are implemented as DOS *TSR* (Terminate-and-Stay-Resident) programs, which consume part of the limited memory allocated for DOS and its programs. This situation can prevent a machine from loading all of the other programs it needs. (DOS programs run almost exclusively in the first 640K of memory.) On the other hand, kernels implemented as Windows *DLLs*, (Dynamic Link Libraries) utilize Extended Memory along with other Windows applications. This allows many programs to be available to the user at once. Sometimes a TSR can be loaded into upper memory, saving DOS memory for the foreground programs, but you need to check with the vendor. DLLs are considered to be slower than TSRs because DLLs must switch back and forth between *real* and *protected mode*. Whether or not most users will detect this difference in real life is debatable. However, the problem of lack of memory will almost certainly be noticed.

A disadvantage to DLLs is that they only run under Windows. You cannot run TCP/IP utilities implemented as DLLs from DOS, or even from Windows' DOS-compatibility box. On the other hand, TSR-based TCP/IP kernels load from the DOS command line, and are available to both DOS and Windows. This distinction is moot, however—if you have the Windows GUI, why would you not want to use it?

Of course, if you do not have Windows (and the extra memory to run it), you must either get Windows or stick with DOS TSR-based products. However, the popularity of Windows indicates to us that DLL programs are preferable for the long haul. The transition from TSR-based programs to DLL programs is in full-swing, with many vendors offering both DLL and TSR solutions in one package.

Another wrinkle has been added to the TSR-DLL debate—the *VxD*. Windows VxDs (Virtual Device Drivers) solve both the memory problem of TSRs and the performance problem of DLLs. VxDs are 32-bit implementations, unlike the 16-bit TSRs and DLLs. Frontier Technologies is the first vendor to offer VxD technology, for their Super-TCP/NFS for Windows. You need to check with vendors if the TSR issue is important to you (and we think it should be) in order to insure they have made the transition to DLL or VxD.

You should be aware of one other facet of Windows support—the Windows Socket specification (currently at version 1.1.) The WinSock API (Application Program Interface) allows one vendor's Windows application to use the capabilities of another vendor's Windows application. For example, since Frontier Technologies Corp. SuperTCP/NFS has a Windows Sockets interface to their TCP/IP protocol stack, your company can develop an in-house, Sockets-compatible, client/server application that uses Frontier's TCP/IP stack for communications. **WINSOCK.DLL** contains the library of API calls. Eventually, all TCP/IP stacks will be WinSock compliant making connections much easier for developers and users.

Finally, Spry, Inc. has developed a new specification as well—*APP2SOCK*. As the name implies, APP2SOCK is an API interface between applications and WinSock, as well as Novell's WLIBSOCK and SunSelect's TKLIB DLLs. It supports both TSR- and DLL-based TCP/IP transports. APP2SOCK is a public specification which simplifies programming efforts, and developers should take note.

Preparing for Installation

A variety of hardware items may be required for a TCP/IP network, most of which are also common to PC LANs. Ethernet is the desirable medium for a TCP/IP network. If you are familiar with Ethernet network wiring and adapters, you already have a good grasp of the territory. Regardless of your experience level, installation of the TCP/IP network hardware is usually a simple matter. See Chapter 4 if you need assistance in setting up an Ethernet LAN. Or, as an alternative to Ethernet, Chapter 9 can help you make low-performance serial connections.

TCP/IP network software installation involves four main processes: 1) determining the TCP/IP configuration parameters, 2) installing the TCP/IP software and LAN adapter driver on the PCs, 3) readying the UNIX servers, and 4) testing and completing the network paths. On the UNIX side, TCP/IP drivers are built into the operating system on many systems such as Sun SPARCstations. In these cases it is not necessary to load any software drivers. Other systems such as SCO UNIX 3.2.4 and UnixWare require the TCP/IP support package to be installed as a subsequent act—follow loading instructions in your UNIX system network administration manual. Then, configure the UNIX server by referring to the information to follow.

PCs require installation of a software package such as SunSelect's PC-NFS, Frontier Technologies' Super TCP, or NetManage's Chameleon. Again, see Chapter 13 for reviews of these and other TCP/IP products. The installation programs are typically menu-driven and supplied on floppy diskettes. Many of these products are easy-to-use Microsoft Windows applications. Helpful background information on TCP/IP from a PC perspective usually comes with the software, but don't expect to find much to help you with the UNIX side.

TCP/IP Configuration Parameters

In order to install or maintain TCP/IP networks, you have to master a small body of knowledge. At install time you are either prompted for this information by the PC driver installation program, or you have to edit the information into data files to complete the software configuration. Many TCP/IP products provide worksheets for this purpose. Before loading the installation media, take a few minutes to view the following list of common TCP/IP terms and jot down the appropriate responses. Most, but not all, items may be required for your particular setup.

Host Information

Each computer must have access to a data table that defines other computers on the network. This can be provided either through a **hosts** file stored on the local drive of each computer node or through *name servers* located on one or more machines in an existing TCP/IP network. Name servers, also called *domain name servers*, are preferred for larger networks because they are easier to maintain. Entries in the name server's name table show understandable machine names associated with the less obvious Internet numeric addresses. All nodes communicate with other nodes by machine name, trusting the name server to resolve the names to addresses and enable the communication to be routed properly. If you make a change or addition to the network, the name server makes the new information available to all users.

If a name server is available, the UNIX system administrator can provide the appropriate Internet address of that unit for entry into the TCP/IP configuration file. If not, construct a **hosts** file on each networked computer in the **/etc** directory. As with name servers, this file also contains the list of computers that will be connected via TCP/IP, including the particular computer being configured and all addresses. If you do not define a computer in this file (or on the name server), you cannot reach it from this node. The format of the **/etc/hosts** file is as follows:

```
# Sun Host Database
# If the NIS is running, this file is only consulted when booting
#
127.0.0.1       localhost
#
192.9.200.1     central_host    loghost
192.9.200.2     danny           tektronix_xterm
192.9.200.3     elizabeth       ncd_xterm
192.9.200.4     troy            386_1
192.9.200.5     laserjetIII     printer_1
192.9.200.6     teri            386_2
192.9.200.7     laptop          laptop
192.9.201.1     slip_gate
192.9.201.2     on_the_road
```

Here are descriptions of the three fields:

Internet Address (also called *IP Address*): This unique address is composed of four numbers, each separated by a dot (period). The address is divided into two portions. The first one to three numbers compose the Network Number and are assigned by the Network Information Center, an agency which protects the internetworking viability of TCP/IP. You assign the last one to three numbers, called the

Host Number. Each set of digits can range from 1 to 254 (8 bits—0 and 255 are reserved for broadcast addresses). For example, the following Network Number pertains to a Class C (small) network: 192.51.108. One additional set of digits (an "octet", or an 8-bit number) will be tacked on the end as the Host Number; e.g., if this node is the first, you might call it "1". Taken as a whole, this unique address (192.51.108.1) is affixed to all information packets received by and sent from this node. Communication of any sort between nodes depends upon the address being known to both the sender and the receiver. If your network has not yet been assigned a Network Number by the Network Information Center, see Chapter 12 (Obtaining an Internet Network Number) for information on how to apply for a number. Subnets can be defined for any Network Number; these subnets make use of a user-defined subnet mask to modify the host portion of the Internet number, but the overall format of the number will not be changed.

Host Name: Each computer requires a host name to be associated with its unique Internet address. This name can be anything which identifies the computer: function, type, location, operator, etc., as long as it uniquely identifies the machine to the local network. The host name can be used interchangeably with the Internet number when describing and diagnosing the network, providing the advantage of designations which can be remembered more easily than addresses.

Nickname(s): Alias(es) by which this node is known in addition to the host name. Aliases are not usually required.

The **Hosts** file can be edited or created on the PC using DOS editors such as **EDIT** or **EDLIN** (see Appendix A: Editing Files Under DOS and UNIX); however, some TCP/IP software products build this file for you during configuration. On the UNIX side, **vi** can be used for the purpose of modifying the /**etc/hosts** file.

Network and Other Information

Other information may be required for the installation process. Here is a list of items that you are likely to encounter:

Broadcast Address: The broadcast address is composed of the Network Number, followed by filler values (255s) in the host ID portion. In the case of a Class C network, the broadcast address is usually something like 192.9.200.255, the first three octets being the Network Number. (Due to a mistaken default value in an early version of Berkeley UNIX, some UNIX variants, notably Sun, default the host octets to 0 instead of 255. While not standard, it is permitted.) A node can send a packet (message) simultaneously to every other node via this address. Another form of the broadcast address limits the broadcast to the local network, without knowing the network IP address (255.255.255.255). UNIX computers use the Address Resolution Protocol (ARP) to locate other machines on the network via the broadcast address. Servers advertise their services to the network via the broadcast address, and clients find resources in the same manner.

Subnet Mask: You use this mask only if the network is divided into subnets. Subnets allow one network Internet IP Address to service several small physical networks. This is accomplished transparently by dividing the local or host portion of the IP address into subnet bits (which identify the sub-network) and a host identifier. For example, if the network uses a class C address such as 192.9.200.0, 192.9.200 is the network portion and 0 is the host portion. In binary, the final 0 would appear as the 8 bits 00000000. If you implement subnets, you might allocate the four leading bits for subnet identification, allowing 16 possible combinations or sub-networks. (Four binary bits yield 16 possible combinations.) Four bits remain for the host, allowing 16 hosts per sub-network. In this example, a subnet mask would have 1s for all network and subnet bits in the address, e.g. 11111111 11111111 11111111 11110000 in binary or 255.255.255.240 in decimal (Internet) notation.

Number of Subnet Bits: This number is not important unless the network is divided into subnets. An IP Address, and potentially the Subnet Mask, are 32-bit binary numbers. This number ordinarily includes the number of bits in the network number plus the actual subnet-determining bits in the host number. It equals the number of 1s in the subnet mask. A class A address has a maximum of 8 subnet bits; class B, 16 bits; class C, 24 bits.

Host Table Path and Name: Ordinarily, the Hosts file is located in the same directory as the installed driver software. However, with many products you can place this file in another directory, under another name. Some products do not store host information in a separate data file.

Name Server Internet Address: Two types of name servers exist, *domain name servers* and old-style *name servers*. The UNIX Systems Administrator will know if either type has been set up.

Domain of this Host: A domain name, set by the UNIX Systems Administrator, combines with your host name for use by a domain name server.

Time Server Internet Address: If a time server is not available to set the official time, you may wish to respond to other prompts which ask for the timezone and offset in minutes from Greenwich Mean Time.

Print Server Internet Address: A printer may be attached to the TCP/IP network. An Internet address or host name accesses this device, as it does for computer nodes.

Gateway Internet Address: A router may be used to connect this TCP/IP network with another.

Login Name: This name automatically informs other hosts of your login ID as you make connection.

Installing TCP/IP on a DOS/Windows PC

Good PC software products provide a completely menu-driven installation. Poor ones require you to make modifications by executing DOS programs from the command line and editing data files with a text file editor. Since each product is different from the next (meaning that you cannot lay out a step-by-step plan), we have taken a topical approach to the discussion.

General Procedure

You must cover some pretty rough terrain when preparing your stand-alone PC to run TCP/IP. Here is the installation procedure, at a glance. If you have trouble at any point along the way, refer to the associated sections to follow.

Preparations

First, make sure you have a PC with enough muscle to run the software. TCP/IP products do not make big demands on system resources, so you could use a lowly XT in a pinch for non-Windows (DOS) products. However, if you want Windows capability you should have a minimum of a 386 with a VGA color monitor. 2M of memory is a waste of time—get 4M. You should upgrade the operating system software to DOS 5.0 or 6.0 and Windows 3.1.

Before you begin, it is a good idea to create a bootable disk for the computer just in case it has a nervous breakdown. If your computer ever gets into a confused state where it cannot remember how to boot, you will be glad you have it. In addition to the operating system, you might also place **EDLIN** and **FDISK** on it. If you haven't created a bootable diskette, find the original DOS diskette set and use disk one.

Moving files

Copy the TCP/IP product software into a newly made directory on the PC. An installation program usually creates the directory, copies the files, and configures most or all of the environment for you. The install program is typically named **SETUP** or **INSTALL**. For the least confusion, exit from Windows completely; then, at the DOS prompt, type **A:SETUP**, or something similar, to start the install. Some products are designed to be installed from within Windows; in that case, select **File/Run** on the Windows Program Manager action bar and type in **A:SETUP**, or whatever the vendor says. These installation programs may or may not do most of the grunt work for you. We can practically guarantee that you will have some startup file editing to do later on.

TCP/IP software often comes in two packages: Runtime and Applications. The Runtime package includes the kernel (operating system) and adapter/protocol drivers. Applications include programs such as **telnet** and **ftp**. Install the Runtime first. Vendors may also break down the installation process into two stages—installation and configuration. If the vendor follows this two-stage approach, the installation stage mainly unpacks files onto the PCs hard drive.

Network configuration

As you run the install program(s) you will likely be asked questions regarding the PCs IP address, the server IP address and the server name. The host information is often worded in such a manner that you have no idea which machine the vendor is referring to—server host or PC host—so try to pin down the appropriate responses by looking at the manual, or by viewing the on-line help. Most other questions will be intuitive.

LAN adapter configuration

You usually need to perform two steps in regard to your LAN adapter. The first is to supply its hardware configuration parameters to the installation program so that the program can create the configuration data files. We discussed these parameters in Chapter 4—you should have a list of them.

The second step is to select a network driver that works with your adapter. Use the NDIS driver if one is available. If you have NetWare, make that ODI (see Selecting the LAN Adapter Driver, to follow). Most adapters have NDIS- or ODI-compatible drivers. After selecting the driver, the install program should copy it and any accessory files to the appropriate directory on the PC and modify your startup files appropriately. If the install program leaves those tasks to you, copy the driver files to the root directory of the boot drive, then go to work editing files.

How to Obtain PC Hardware and Memory Information

If you install a PC networking product for TCP/IP, you need to know a few of the technical details about your computer hardware and its current configuration. This information can include LAN adapter addresses, device interrupts, and much more. If you don't have software to help you, and you have more than one computer to inventory, this takes awhile, and can be aggravating.

Even more frequently, you need information about your RAM usage. Most DOS products are designed to use low DOS RAM (addressed from 0-640K.) After you are through packing one of these networking products onto your system, you may find that the PC won't even load the systems properly because it is out of DOS RAM.

There are a several ways to obtain hardware configuration information about a PC. Some computers can provide general information through the system setup (CMOS) utility, but this information is usually not extensive. **MEM**, a memory analysis program shown here, comes with newer versions of DOS. **CHKDSK**, another DOS program, tells you how much disk space you have, and can fix some abnormalities in the filesystem. If you run Windows 3.1, try running **MSD** (Microsoft Diagnostics), shown in Figure 5.6. This utility tells you all kinds of interesting things, including when the PC became obsolete (calculated as two months after you bought it.) It can also tell you how memory is being consumed at any point in time. Even though it comes with Windows, **MSD** should be run from the DOS prompt outside of Windows. Memory management products usually include a similar utility. For

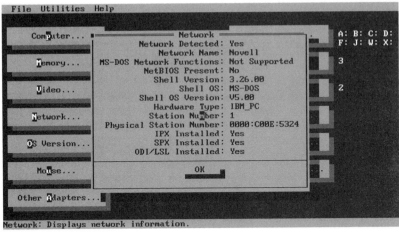

FIGURE 5.6 Viewing a PCs network configuration with Microsoft Diagnostics

example, QEMM from Quarterdeck provides Manifest (Figure 5.7) for system hardware and memory usage. Qualitas' 386MAX 5.0 includes a memory-analysis utility called **386UTIL**. Other alternatives for hardware information include Central Point PC Tools for Windows, or diagnostic software such as QAPlus, from DiagSoft, Inc.

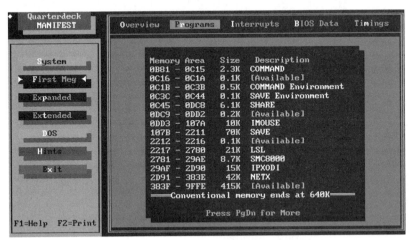

FIGURE 5.7 Quarterdeck's Manifest displays ODI drivers' memory consumption

PC UNIX users have other options. For example, SCO UNIX provides **hwconfig** for hardware information. Use **sysadmsh** (System Report and other options) to view and edit hardware configuration. General UNIX utilities include **df, ifconfig** and others. **Fsck** performs a filesystem check similar to DOS **CHKDSK**, and can perform filesystem repairs.

Selecting the LAN Adapter Driver

The driver is a crucial software program that provides a layer of communication between chips on the adapter (the media) and software applications which transact business through the adapter. A diskette of drivers usually accompanies each adapter, but you can also get an assortment of drivers from the TCP/IP software vendor which work for many brands of adapters. If a vendor has the right driver for your needs, the product will usually install it for you, saving you a little work.

Depending upon the networking environments you have, there are several different types of device drivers to choose from. We discuss the three most common types here: Packet, NDIS, and ODI. (Chapter 2 supplied background information on these.) In addition, dedicated IPX drivers, which are not device drivers in the same sense, are very common for Novell NetWare installations and perform the same function. Each driver type or dedicated IPX driver has its own strengths and weaknesses. The following sections can help you sort out what you need.

Using packet drivers

Packet drivers have been around for years and may be the easiest drivers to obtain and use. Clarkson University maintains the primary repository of packet drivers, and makes the drivers available over the Internet. The Clarkson drivers generally consume the least ram of all driver types—in the neighborhood of 4K—because they are tuned to one hardware adapter. They also do not require the assistance of other supporting software such as Protocol Manager or Link Support Layer (see later).

A packet driver can be used with Novell NetWare if you obtain the **PDETHER** packet driver-to-ODI converter, or shim, from Novell. Another shim, **ODIPKT**, converts ODI drivers to packet driver format for use by some TCP/IP stacks. Or, you also have the possibility of generating a packet driver-aware **IPX.COM** shell. The main problem facing packet drivers is that Microsoft and Novell have come up with their own widely-marketed driver protocols (NDIS and ODI), so packet drivers are slowly being phased out of the products we see.

Packet drivers offer the best value when you can't tolerate much consumption of low DOS memory. They are board-specific, so they cut out most of the overhead you would have with other drivers. They have **.COM** or **.EXE** filename extensions.

Using NDIS drivers

NDIS allows multiple packet types to be handled simultaneously through one network adapter. However, NDIS drivers also consume about 10 times the RAM of packet drivers (40-50K). Microsoft and 3Com jointly created NDIS (Network Driver Interface Specification) for LAN Manager and NetBIOS-compatible networks. The marketplace has been securely hooked by the NDIS specification, so they are the most prevalent drivers on the LAN adapter scene. Several network operating systems including 3Com's 3+Open, DEC PATHWORKS, and Banyan VINES are written to support the NDIS standard. All of them use the same LAN adapters and drivers, and NDIS-compatible TCP/IP networking products integrate with them. Versions of

NDIS drivers are available for OS/2. NDIS drivers are commonly used over DOS Token-Ring networks in place of ASI drivers. Banyan VINES networks often use their own VINES device drivers, but later versions (4.1+) can use NDIS.

If you don't have strict memory restrictions, NDIS drivers make a good choice. The NDIS standard gives you greater flexibility than the packet driver approach. A driver written to the Network Driver Interface Specification allows its corresponding LAN adapter hardware to be easily controlled by NDIS-speaking network software. The network software only needs one API—Application Program Interface—to talk to NDIS-compliant adapters from many manufacturers. (The packet driver approach requires a separate API for each adapter.) All network software that we tested support NDIS drivers, and all newer LAN adapters include them. If you have an older board that is not NDIS-compliant, you should see if the network software supports that adapter. Some TCP/IP networking products or product versions, such as NetManage ChameleonNFS 3.1, ONLY support NDIS drivers, with converters for Novell. NDIS drivers have the **.DOS** or **.OS2** filename extension.

Using ODI drivers

Novell, Inc. and Apple Computer, Inc. developed the ODI (Open Data-Link Interface) driver specification for NetWare. ODI is similar to NDIS in some respects. Currently Novell is the only real promoter of ODI, but that is good enough—hundreds of products can optionally link to NetWare through ODI drivers, with some products, such as NetWare Lite 1.1, requiring ODI. Like NDIS, ODI allows multiple packet types simultaneously on a single adapter, but it also requires more memory than packet drivers. ODI drivers are available for OS/2, and can be used with IBM Token-Ring networks. ODI drivers have **.COM** filename extensions.

If you will be accessing Novell NetWare concurrently with TCP/IP, you must have drivers to serve both IPX packets (for Novell products) and IP packets (for TCP/IP). Every TCP/IP kernel automatically provides the IP packet driver. You have four options for setting up the IPX side:

- Install an ODI adapter driver, **LSL.COM** and **IPXODI.COM**.
- Install an NDIS adapter driver and an NDIS-to-IPX shim.
- Install a packet adapter driver and a packet-to-IPX shim.
- Generate an IPX shell specifically for your adapter and/or packet driver (see the following section).

If an NDIS-compatible LAN comes into the fray, forming a three-protocol LAN, you can handle this connection through the NDIS-to-IPX shim.

If the adapter is not one of the main-line brands, find out if it supports your frame type(s): Ethernet_II for TCP/IP, and (usually) Ethernet_802.3 for NetWare. We have found that not all adapters support both. If you need to know more about setting up drivers and frame types for NetWare, see Chapter 7.

Using dedicated IPX drivers

IPX.COM can be generated by your NetWare administrator specifically for your LAN adapter. This program loads from **AUTOEXEC.BAT**, before the NetWare shell (**NETX**) loads. Some TCP/IP vendors provide **IPX.COM** with their products.

Editing Startup Files

Most of the following discussion applies to the two main files, **AUTOEXEC.BAT** and **CONFIG.SYS**, both found in the root directory of the PCs boot drive (usually in C:\.) You may have to edit additional files, depending upon your scenario. There are primarily two **PROTOCOL.INI** for NDIS, and **NET.CFG** for ODI. Each of these latter files contain similar data, but in different formats. They accomplish a similar purpose as well—providing a single, user-modifiable file in which to fiddle with the adapter configuration. If you need help in locating an editor, look in Appendix A.

How adapter and network protocol drivers load into memory

The drivers are executed in the order of their appearance. First, drivers mentioned in **CONFIG.SYS** are started, then the drivers mentioned in **AUTOEXEC.BAT**. In general, the low-level hardware driver is loaded first (with supporting software), followed by non-TCP/IP network protocols (kernels or shells), then the TCP/IP protocol, then Windows.

The order in which you load drivers sometimes determines which driver or protocol gets first crack at handling a packet being sent or received. The low-level adapter and adapter-support drivers are the first to process an incoming packet. When sending packets, the last network kernel in the list is the first to examine packets. If the TCP/IP kernel is loaded last, TCP/IP must process only its own packets and let NetWare (IPX) packets pass on to **NETX**, the NetWare kernel. If you experience trouble in communicating on a multiprotocol network, try varying the order of the network kernels in **AUTOEXEC.BAT**. Novell's **NETX** is considered by many to be courteous to other networks—a safe bet to place last. If you use NDIS drivers and the Protocol Manager, the priority can be set in a data file.

Drivers also consume memory in different ways. Memory can be corrupted if you disobey vendor instructions, causing system "hangs" (lockup) or failure to boot. Products which let you unload them from memory usually provide instructions on how to go about it. Generally, you should unload the most recent program last.

Setting DOS environment variables

Enough environment space must be available for new paths and variables required by your TCP/IP software. Some drivers and TSR programs claim environment space when they load. The line **SHELL=C:\COMMAND.COM /E:512 /P**, placed in your **CONFIG.SYS** file, sets environment space of 512 bytes (usually more than enough). Type **SET** from a DOS prompt to see what is in your environment at that time.

Increase your environment space if you get an **Out of environment space** error during boot.

Configuring expanded memory managers

You may be required to alter any line in **AUTOEXEC.BAT** or **CONFIG.SYS** which loads an expanded memory driver. If a network adapter is configured to use shared memory, its memory space must be kept out of reach of the memory manager. Memory conflicts can cause inexplicable errors or hanging. Here is an example for the memory manager, EMM386, that comes with DOS and Windows.

```
DEVICE=C:\WINDOWS\EMM386.EXE NOEMS D=64 X=D800-DBFF
```

The example shows that the address range **D800-DBFF** is to be excluded from the supervision of EMM386.

Problems with Windows Share.Exe

SHARE, loaded from **AUTOEXEC.BAT** for the sake of Windows, may conflict with the act of installing certain drivers. You may have to remove it from your startup process temporarily, until you get the new product loaded. To do this, place **REM** in front of that line in **AUTOEXEC.BAT**.

Using a packet driver

Packet drivers can be installed with one line in **AUTOEXEC.BAT**. No accessory files are needed. The following sample loads a Western Digital (SMC) packet driver:

```
wd8003e 0x61 5 0x280 0xd000
```

The first parameter, *0x61*, is an *interrupt vector* that is always set through software. Interrupt vectors are used for communication between the network protocol stack and the device driver. The number is usually in the range of 60-79, typically 61. The product you are installing may use this vector as the starting number for a series of 2 or 3 vectors. Other communications boards can require their own interrupt vector(s) as well, so make sure they don't conflict.

5 (or **0x5**) is the *IRQ interrupt number*, **0x280** is the *I/O base address*, and **0xd000** is the *shared memory base address*. Some adapters do not require some or all of the entries. Additional parameters may be supported by your adapter. The most used is the *-n* switch, to tell the adapter to use the Ethernet_802.3 frame type (Novell) in addition to the standard Ethernet_II frame type.

When Novell NetWare is involved, the packet driver specification can be implemented by vendors in different ways. Distinct Corporation's TCP/IP provides two methods. The following listing from **AUTOEXEC.BAT** shows a packet-driver aware **IPX.COM**. Note that if you use the Ethernet_II frame type on your NetWare LAN, you must remove the *-n* switch from the packet driver parameter list.

```
REM -----Next line is the packet driver for the Western Digital/SMC adapter
\DISTINCT\ETC\WD8003E.COM -n -w 0x62 0x3 0x280 0xD800
\DISTINCT\ETC\IPX.COM
REM -----Next line loads the TCP/IP stack
\DISTINCT\ETC\DISTINCT.EXE
NETX.COM
F:LOGIN NOVELL/KEN
```

In the next example, Distinct provides an ODI-to-Packet converter, **ODIPKT.-COM**, which loads before the Distinct TCP/IP stack. If you already have an ODI driver in place on the PC, but the vendor does not support ODI, the vendor may get around that problem using the converter. However, it is not as efficient as the first method.

```
LSL.COM
REM -----Next line is the ODI driver for the Western Digital/SMC adapter
SMC8000
IPXODI.COM
\DISTINCT\ETC\ODIPKT.COM
REM -----Next line loads the TCP/IP stack
\DISTINCT\ETC\DISTINCT.EXE
NETX.COM
F:LOGIN NOVELL/KEN
```

Using an NDIS driver: PROTMAN, NETBIND, and PROTOCOL.INI

There are two major components to the NDIS specification: the Protocol Manager, and Media Access Control drivers, also called MACs. It is Protocol Manager's job to manage the MACs and communication protocols, binding the low-level hardware with the higher level transport protocol. There are two major releases of the Protocol Manager—version 1.1, which binds protocols statically to the hardware, and version 2.x, which binds dynamically.

Under the older static-binding Protocol Manager (**PROTMAN**), as the boot script (**CONFIG.SYS**) loads each protocol driver, that program registers itself with **PROTMAN**. **PROTMAN** tells the protocol driver where to find **PROTOCOL.INI**, which has the driver's configuration information. This information can be used for many purposes, depending upon the driver; for instance, many LAN adapter drivers find information in **PROTOCOL.INI** for configuring the LAN adapter. **PROTMAN** also sets up a vector table with the driver's address at the top of low DOS memory, just beneath where **COMMAND.COM** resides, to know later where the driver is located in memory. It leaves this information there like secret plans dropped in a dumpster for the foreign agent, hoping that the information will be picked up at a discrete moment (the **NETBIND** stage). However, just as a city garbage crew might empty the dumpster before the foreign agent arrives, any other program may decide to use that memory space as well, covering over the data and causing **NETBIND** to fail when it executes.

NETBIND issues a command to **PROTMAN** to bind all registered protocols to their appropriate MAC drivers. The instructions on how to do this come, again, from **PROTOCOL.INI**. If there is a single protocol to bind to the board, the protocol binds directly with the NDIS (MAC) driver. **PROTMAN** can mostly sit back and relax after that, because the protocol driver and MAC driver talk directly to each other. If there are multiple protocols, **PROTMAN** binds with the MAC driver, then binds with each protocol. After this, the adapter alerts **PROTMAN** to any new packets received. **PROTMAN** passes the packet to each protocol driver in its vector table in turn, until the appropriate protocol accepts it. The Priority field in **PROTOCOL.INI**, if present, controls the order.

This process can bind more than one transport protocol to a single adapter, enabling concurrent connections between, say, a TCP/IP server and a Novell server. If **NETBIND** fails, there is no communication over the adapter. There are two important rules of thumb to make the process work: 1) always load **PROTMAN** ahead of the adapter's device driver in **CONFIG.SYS**, and 2) place **NETBIND** as close to the start of **AUTOEXEC.BAT** as possible.

The problem of intervening programs clobbering the vector table has been corrected by **PROTMAN** V2.0. This version uses **LOAD** and **UNLOAD** commands to dynamically bind the protocols to the hardware. **NETBIND** is not used. It is a safer method than that for version 1.1, but as of this book's writing, very few TCP/IP networking products use the 2.0 **PROTMAN**. Each product usually supplies the 1.1 **PROTMAN** and **NETBIND** versions, often installing them in \LANMAN.

The following example loads an NDIS driver for use with Beame & Whiteside's BW-NFS. We can note several things from the listings:

- **PROTMAN** loads before the protocol drivers. **PROTMAN** learns where to find **PROTOCOL.INI** using the /I parameter. Then the NDIS driver is loaded.

- Each vendor may load additional drivers in **CONFIG.SYS**. In this case, **ETHDEV.SYS** is BW's NDIS protocol interface, and **TCPIP.SYS** is their TCP/IP protocol driver.

- **NETBIND** was called as quickly as possible in **AUTOEXEC.BAT** to avoid conflicts with other programs.

- None of the startup files, including **PROTOCOL.INI**, are case-sensitive, for the most part. However, section names and parameter values in **PROTOCOL.INI** are critical—spell them exactly.

Here are the listings of **CONFIG.SYS**, **AUTOEXEC.BAT**, and **PROTOCOL.INI**:

```
REM -----Lines at the end of CONFIG.SYS
DEVICE = C:\BWTCP\NDIS\PROTMAN.DOS /I:C:\BWTCP
DEVICE = C:\BWTCP\NDIS\SMCMAC.DOS
DEVICE = C:\BWTCP\ETHDEV.SYS
DEVICE = C:\BWTCP\TCPIP.SYS 1460
```

```
REM -----Lines in AUTOEXEC.BAT
REM -----BW install placed this line near the beginning
C:\BWTCP\NDIS\NETBIND

REM -----BW install placed these lines at the end to serve Remote Procedure
REM -----calls and NFS
C:\BWTCP\BWRPC
C:\BWTCP\BWNFS tester1 /D:10 /R:4096 /W:4096

REM -----Lines I added later to authenticate and mount drives under NFS
net register *tester1
net link G: \\sun_host\/home/pc
rem net link H: \\rs6000\/home/pc
net link lpt1: \\sun_host\serial_for_PCs


; -----Protocol.ini
[protocol manager]
 drivername = PROTMAN$

[SMCMAC_NIF]
 drivername = SMCMAC$
 irq =5
 ramaddress = 0xD800
 iobase = 0x280
 receivebufsize = 4096

[ETHDEV]
 driver = ETHDEV27
 bindings = SMCMAC_NIF
```

NDIS drivers can also be used with NDIS-aware dedicated IPX drivers for connectivity with NetWare. In the following example, Netmanage, Inc.'s Chameleon-NFS loads the NDIS driver in **CONFIG.SYS**, then uses **IPX** instead of **IPXODI** in **AUTOEXEC.BAT**. Note the extra binding in **PROTOCOL.INI**, labeled **IPX NDIS**.

```
REM -----Lines at the end of CONFIG.SYS
DEVICE=C:\NETMANAG\PROTMAN.DOS /I:C:\NETMANAG
DEVICE=C:\HARDWARE\SMCMAC.DOS
DEVICE=C:\NETMANAG\NETMANAG.DOS
REM -----(No TSR TCP/IP stack for Chameleon - 100% DLL stack)


REM -----Lines at the end of AUTOEXEC.BAT
C:\NETMANAG\IPX
C:\NETMANAG\NETBIND
```

```
; -----Protocol.INI
[PROTOCOL MANAGER]
DRIVERNAME=PROTMAN$

[SMCMAC_NIF]
DRIVERNAME=SMCMAC$
IRQ=5
IOBASE=0x280
RAMADDRESS=0xD800

[NETMANAGE]
DRIVERNAME=NETMNG$
BINDINGS=SMCMAC_NIF

[IPX NDIS]
DRIVERNAME=IPX$NDIS
BINDINGS=SMCMAC_NIF
```

HOT TIP   **Pause to Reflect on the Installation**

When editing the **AUTOEXEC.BAT** file, **PAUSE** is an extremely useful command to insert after each of your new lines. On boot, the **PAUSE** command causes the script to stop execution until any key is pressed, preventing screen messages from being scrolled off of the screen before you can read them. Being able to verify execution of the software is necessary, especially if you get an error message. You can remove the **PAUSE**'s after the network is operational.

You can place another command, **@ECHO OFF**, at the start of **AUTOEXEC.BAT** to reduce the amount of junk that displays. **SET**'s and other inconsequential commands will not be echoed to the console.

Using an ODI driver: IPXODI and NET.CFG

Novell runs the driver show entirely from **AUTOEXEC.BAT**. There are three levels of programs which execute. The ODI driver is on the lowest (MAC) level. This is also called a Multiple Link Interface Driver, or MLID. On the topmost level are the protocol stacks for IPX and TCP/IP. In between, joining the two, is **LSL**, the *Link Support Layer*. In the **AUTOEXEC.BAT** file, however, the order of execution is always 1) **LSL**, 2) ODI driver, and 3) the stacks, which commonly includes one called **IPXODI**. **IPX-ODI** contains both the IPX and SPX protocols, and works in place of the dedicated IPX driver **IPX.COM**.

LSL reads **NET.CFG** to know how to bind the protocols to the drivers. You only need to edit **NET.CFG** if you have changed the default settings on the LAN adapter, or if a TCP/IP product prepared a **NET.CFG** for you. (They generally don't do it correctly.)

Here is an example of an ODI driver configuration for Wollongong's PathWay. Wollongong provides the ARP protocol in addition to IP, so this must be bound to the adapter as well. This configuration uses two frame types, so not only must each protocol be bound to an adapter, it must also be assigned a frame type. (Note: versions of LSL before 2.0 used the words "envelope type" instead of "frame".)

```
REM -----Lines at the end of AUTOEXEC.BAT
LSL.COM
REM -----Next line is the ODI driver for the Western Digital/SMC adapter
SMC8000
IPXODI.COM
NETX.COM
F:LOGIN NOVELL/KEN

SET PATH=C:\PATHWAY\;$PATH%
PWCONFIG -n:65
ODI -l:5
REM -----Now load Wollongong's TCP/IP stack
PWTCP


# -----NET.CFG
Protocol IPX
          Bind SMC8000

Protocol IP
          Bind SMC8000

Protocol ARP
          Bind SMC8000

Link Driver SMC8000
          Port #1 280 20
          Mem #1 000D8000 2000/10
          Int #1 5
          Frame Ethernet_802.3
          Protocol IPX 000000000000 Ethernet_802.3

          Frame Ethernet_II
          Protocol IP 000000000800 Ethernet_II
          Protocol ARP 000000000806 Ethernet_II
```

If your NetWare server uses *Ethernet_II*, you can probably get away with very little in your **NET.CFG**, such as in the following example. All protocols will assume they use *Ethernet_II*, which is fine with TCP/IP. If you were to leave out the Frame field, or select *Ethernet_802.3*, your TCP/IP stack would not be able to communicate.

```
# -----NET.CFG
Link Driver SMC8000
          Port #1 280 20
          Mem #1 000D8000 2000/10
          Int #1 5
          Frame Ethernet_II
```

An Ounce of Prevention: Hints to Save Time and Frustration

When the installation or configuration program finishes, it may or may not tell you that you need to reboot. You need to. However, before rebooting, there are some things you should do automatically. (We are not troubleshooting yet!) Believe us, going through this checklist will save you time:

1. Edit **AUTOEXEC.BAT**. If you start Windows from this file, you will almost invariably find at least one error. The **WIN** line should come AFTER any new lines inserted by the Install program, so that the TCP/IP software can be loaded before you start Windows. If you are using an NDIS driver, **NETBIND** should appear early in the file—definitely ahead of any network or anti-virus software executables. Place a **PAUSE** statement before and after each new executable to help you during the debugging phase. Look at the **PATH** statement to see if a new directory was added to the list. Also look at the new lines to see if a directory path was placed before any file names. Jot these down. If you have more than one networking product loaded on the same machine, it is usually better to avoid global paths in the **PATH** statement. Instead, specify the path with the filename.

2. Edit **CONFIG.SYS**. Make sure that you do not have two lines (one old, one new) loading the same or similar device driver. Check the paths and filenames on the new line(s). Jot these down. The **DEVICE=...PROTMAN.DOS...** line MUST appear before any NDIS device driver line. These lines should be placed at the end of the file.

3. Edit **PROTOCOL.INI**. You can find its location by looking at the path ending the **DEVICE=...PROTMAN.DOS...** line in **CONFIG.SYS** (after the /I.) If there is no /I, look in **\LANMAN**. Note the new lines and jot them all down. If you know that your LAN adapter has different settings than what you see in the file, change the lines to match the card. Usually the settings are only standard defaults; and, in all likelihood, the IRQ, I/O base address or memory address is wrong. If you are not using an NDIS driver, you probably will not have this file, although at least one product, Walker, Richer & Quinn's TCP Connection, uses it for general purposes.

4. If a **NET.CFG** was created in the root directory for use by an ODI driver, edit that file. Check the Link Driver section to make sure it has the correct adapter infor-

mation. The Link Driver name does not always correspond to the name of adapter vendor's ODI driver file. Check the literature to find out what it should be called. The Frame type is fundamentally important, commonly set to *Ethernet_II* (DIX Ethernet) for TCP/IP products. (The DIX Ethernet specification is defined in RFC-894.) Novell NetWare typically uses *Ethernet_802.3*. If your NetWare server uses Ethernet_II frames (although few do), all you need in **NET.CFG** for the sake of protocols are these lines:

```
Link Driver NE2000
            Frame Ethernet_II
```

Be aware that some adapters only support Ethernet_802.3. Next we show a sample Link Driver section from **NET.CFG** for use with two frame types. Notice that in this case you must specify which protocol uses which frame type. See your Novell manuals for specific details about these and other **NET.CFG** parameters.

```
Link Driver NE2000
            Frame Ethernet_II
            Frame Ethernet_802.3
            Protocol IP 8137 Ethernet_II
            Protocol IPX 0 Ethernet_802.3
```

5. Look at the list of paths and programs you have made. Go to each of the named directories and make sure that the named files are there. This prevents surprises. If you are missing a file, dig through the Install manual to see if there is something else you must load separately. This frequently happens when you use an NDIS driver. You often must hand-copy **PROTMAN** and **NETBIND** from a supplemental disk or another source.

6. Check the listed items to see that the device driver for your LAN adapter is correct. Occasionally a TCP/IP product sets up an incorrect driver or an outdated one. This frequently occurs for SMC adapters, formerly Western Digital. (We all make mistakes!) It is sometimes difficult for the TCP/IP vendors to time their software releases with the availability of new drivers. The correct driver is supplied with the adapter, but the software product can supply an acceptable copy as well.

7. The product may require you to enter the Windows Setup program from a DOS prompt in order to configure Windows for using a vendor-specific network driver. (These files have the extension **.DRV**.) For example, if you wish to run SunSelect PC-NFS 5.0 with Windows 3.1, make sure this configuration will provide, among other things, a Network window on the Control Panel (see Figure 5.8), displaying features of PC-NFS that you can control. The options you gain vary from network to network, and not all products use this interface mechanism. Usually, the File Manager makes any mounted network drives available without this step. **SYSTEM.INI** is the primary affected file.

Setting Up a TCP/IP Network

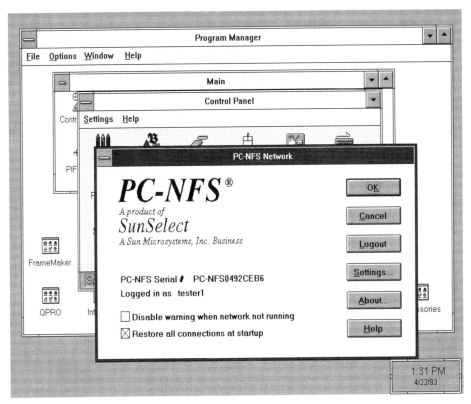

FIGURE 5.8 Configuring SunSelect's PC-NFS on your Windows PC

8. Exit Windows, if you have not done so already, and power down the computer. Turn the computer back on and, as each **PAUSE** is reached, verify that the particular operation performed was successful. If everything goes as hoped and the LAN adapter gives encouraging messages (including its settings), begin to test the product's features. If some aspect fails during boot, you can easily isolate it. Cheer up—it rarely goes right the first time! See the Troubleshooting section at the end of this chapter for additional tips.

Tips on Loading Software into Upper Memory

Once you get your programs working together, you should try to move them from low DOS memory (0-640K, sometimes called conventional memory) to upper memory—the 640K to 1M range. (You may have to do this BEFORE the programs will work!) The upper memory area is designed for use by shadow RAM, video controllers, LAN adapters, and other hardware expansion cards, but some of the space remains unused on the typical PC. If you have a *memory manager*, you can command many device drivers to load themselves in this high memory area instead of conventional memory. Otherwise, you may get into a situation in which you use up your conventional memory loading TSRs, and cannot load your main application. Special utilities that come with the memory managers can help you find free space. See also How to Obtain PC Hardware and Memory Information, earlier in this chapter.

HOT TIP	**Switching to Another Network**
	Windows 3.1 only allows only ONE network driver to be loaded at a time. (Windows for Workgroups and Windows NT do allow multiple networks.) This means that you have to change your network driver in Windows Setup every time you need to switch networks. Some products such as Wollongong's Pathway can give you the NetWare driver in addition to their own. This problem can also be eliminated by using the add-on product from Cogent Data Technologies, WinNET plus. For evaluations of these products, see Chapter 13.

Not every program can be moved into upper memory, for three reasons. First, TSRs require *contiguous* memory, so even though total unused space is large enough, you may not have enough memory grouped together. Second, some programs require more memory for *initialization* than for their final state. Again, the initialization size may be too large to fit the available space. Third, some programs fail when loaded high because of their internal design. If they cannot be loaded into upper memory, one of two things will happen: 1) DOS will load it into low memory anyway, or 2) the programs just won't work and you will have to change them back.

Most network drivers can be loaded high. The list includes NDIS, ODI, and packet drivers, **PROTMAN.DOS**, **LSL.COM**, **IPXODI.COM**, **IPX.COM**, and **NETX.COM**. Note that **NETBIND.EXE** is not a *resident* program (remaining in memory), so do not try to load it high. Many vendor-specific drivers can be moved.

Before you make any attempts to load high, be sure that you have a DOS diskette you can boot off of in an emergency (if you hang during **CONFIG.SYS**). For a specific example of loading vendor-specific TCP/IP & NFS programs into high memory, see the FTP Software evaluation in Chapter 13. Here are the general configuration instructions for the most popular memory managers.

MS-DOS 5.0

DOS 5 includes a memory manager called EMM386. This program should not be confused with the EMM386 that comes with Microsoft Windows. The two programs are not the same, and some software only works with the DOS version. To set up EMM386, enter lines such as the following at the start of your **CONFIG.SYS** file (see the DOS manual for particular parameter changes):

```
DEVICE=C:\DOS\HIMEM.SYS
DOS=HIGH,UMB
DEVICE=C:\DOS\EMM386.SYS RAM
DEVICE=C:\WINDOWS\SMARTDRV.EXE /DOUBLE_BUFFER+
DEVICEHIGH=...
DEVICEHIGH=...
```

You can use **DEVICEHIGH** instead of **DEVICE** to load device drivers into upper memory. **ANSI.SYS** and some TCP/IP drivers qualify. The drivers **HIMEM.-SYS, EMM386.EXE** and **SMARTDRV.EXE** (if used) should be loaded first and NOT loaded high. If you are using NDIS drivers, **PROTMAN.SYS**, the adapter driver, and related drivers also cannot be loaded high. DOS can be loaded high using the format **DOS=HIGH**.

Use EMM386's **LOADHIGH** in **AUTOEXEC.BAT** and other .BAT files to make use of upper memory. Simply place **LOADHIGH** in front of the program names (not **SET** or **PATH** statements.) **SHARE** can be loaded high. Other possible candidates include mouse drivers, miscellaneous TSRs, and TCP/IP or NFS modules. If you run NetWare, the workstation shell **NETX.COM** cannot be loaded high (45-50K), but its alternative versions **EMSNETX.EXE** and **XMSNETX.EXE** will tuck themselves neatly out of the way into Expanded and Extended memory respectively. (Some programs automatically load into upper memory without **LOADHIGH**, based upon their construction or a user-specified command tail). ODI drivers, **LSL.COM**, **IPX-ODI.COM**, and adapter board drivers cannot be loaded high. NDIS driver files (**NETBIND.EXE**)—same story.

MS-DOS 6.0

DOS 6.0 is newly released. While many changes have been made to DOS, one of the additions is a useful tool called MEMMAKER. This utility examines your **CONFIG.-SYS** and **AUTOEXEC.BAT** files and modifies the command lines, moving many programs from conventional memory into upper memory. This is attractive to anyone who prefers not to stomp around in scripts. However, you are still at the mercy of the third-party TCP/IP vendor, because some of the programs MEMMAKER moves may not work in upper memory. It is still a trial-and-error process, utility or not.

QEMM-386 7.0

Quarterdeck's memory manager, QEMM-386 has a strong reputation for flexibility and for getting the most out of your high memory. For most network situations, we recommend it as the optimum solution. Here are some tips.

Use the Manifest program provided by Quarterdeck or the **LOADHI** command to determine what is in your high memory and how much memory is available contiguously. Just as for DOS **EMM386**, you must load the memory manager, called **QEMM386.SYS**, in **CONFIG.SYS**. After that, in **CONFIG.SYS** you can load a device high by setting a line with **DEVICE=C:\LOADHI.SYS (other device name to load high)**. You can load TCP/IP TSRs high from **AUTOEXEC.BAT** as well, using the command **C:\QEMM\LOADHI (TSR name and parameters)**.

The best way to configure QEMM is to use a combination of the Optimize and Stealth programs. Optimize figures out the best use of upper memory and Stealth uses some advanced techniques to get more available memory out of your machine (by stealing reserved memory which is, nevertheless, not being used). However, we found that not every machine will let you use Stealth.

We provide additional hints on QEMM in the review of Desqview/X in Chapter 14. One thing is for sure, use Quarterdeck's tech support if you get stuck. There are enormous permutations and you can easily get caught in a loop.

Qualitas' 386Max 7.0

386MAX users require **385MAX.SYS** to be loaded as a device in **CONFIG.SYS**. This is the memory manager itself. Another device, **386LOAD.SYS**, can then be loaded with the *prog=* parameter set to the name of a TCP/IP device driver that should be loaded high. From AUTOEXEC.BAT, load programs into upper memory using the **386LOAD** command, again, specifying the name of the TSR (this time without *prog=*) and the TSRs normal parameter line. Use **386UTIL** to analyze memory.

Readying the UNIX Server

You probably thought you were done. Wrong-O! Now we start on the UNIX server side.

Install the TCP/IP Module

UNIX operating system software for workstations such as Sun Solaris includes all software necessary for TCP/IP network communications. No other third-party software need be loaded onto the workstation for TCP/IP (although NFS for PCs may require the pcnfs server daemon to be loaded separately—see Chapter 6). However, if the workstation has always been a stand-alone, there is a chance that it is not yet configured (see the next section).

If you run UNIX on a PC, you need to pay closer attention, because TCP/IP may not be installed. You may have to purchase TCP/IP as an additional module. For example, SCO OPEN DESKTOP is supplied with TCP/IP while SCO UNIX 3.2.4 is not. In either case, however, you must install the networking options. Here are the general steps which must be performed to complete the setup.

●Install the TCP/IP modules included with the UNIX operating system. For SCO OPEN DESKTOP, you do this from **custom** or **sysadmsh** by loading the Networking Services. Novell UnixWare supplies a TCP/IP module which you install from the Desktop window.

•Configure the software with the communication parameters. Under SCO OPEN DESKTOP you use the **netconfig** utility to do this. With **netconfig** you prepare a TCP/IP chain first. Select the appropriate driver for your network interface card. Enter the driver parameters according to the settings of the board at installation, such as I/O base address, DMA channel (or shared memory base address), and IRQ interrupt number (or interrupt vector). When you have finished with this first chain, create a second chain to link NFS to TCP/IP. Then tell **netconfig** to rebuild the kernel.

Configure the Network Interface

The easiest course of action (if you are on an existing network) is to follow the premise, "innocent until proven guilty." Assume the network is set up properly, and go about your business. If you find at test time that something does not work, step through the Troubleshooting section of this book and/or your Network Administration manual. Each UNIX operating system differs from the rest in such areas as file names and locations. Furthermore, individual servers may have files missing, daemons remarked-out of startup scripts, etc. The flexibility and low-level compartmentalization of UNIX also creates a maze of data and executable files which can be intimidating.

Having said that, there are steps you can take to scope out the network, especially if the workstation is a stand-alone. IBM provides a helpful utility for setting up system parameters and data files on an RS/6000 workstation: SMIT, or **smitty**. Figure 5.9 shows a sample display. We would recommend using it to set up TCP/IP parameters, users, hosts, and for getting help. Select the category Communication Applications and Services. HP-UX users have the SAM utility. (Who's next? Li'l Abner?) Sun users do not have the luxury of making changes from a single utility unless they have the limited **admintool** of Solaris 2.x.

If you have made changes for networking, reboot the workstation. The boot process runs the program **ifconfig**, and sets up all TCP/IP links. Watch for the console messages generated by **ifconfig** during boot; **ifconfig** shows the status and parameters of the network interface. The same information can be obtained from the prompt at any time on a Sun by typing **ifconfig le0** or **ifconfig -a** (for the standard Ethernet interface or all interfaces). On an IBM RS/6000, type **ifconfig en0** (IBM's standard Ethernet designation) or use SMIT. Here is the Sun version:

```
sun_host% ifconfig le0
le0: flags=63<UP,BROADCAST,NOTRAILERS,RUNNING.
            inet 192.9.200.1 netmask ffffff00 broadcast 192.9.200.0
            ether 8:0:20:9:79:d0
sun_host%
```

The flags should indicate that the interface is up, broadcasting, and running. **Inet** shows the Internet address or host name of this host, or else **ether** will show the hardware address (**ns** on IBM). The **netmask** is the subnet mask described earlier,

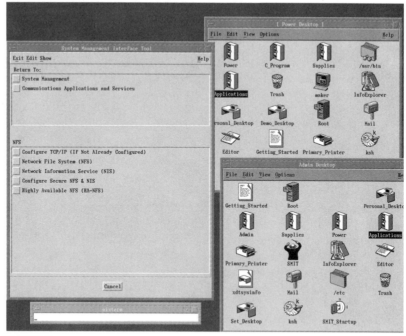

FIGURE 5.9 Setting up TCP/IP with IBM's SMIT—it beats editing files by hand!

and the **broadcast** address is given as well. You can change any option by typing **ifconfig (interface#) (option)**. For example, **ifconfig le0 broadcast 192.9.200.0** sets the broadcast address. **ifconfig le0** up sets the UP flag. Other lesser-used options can be set as well (see the **ifconfig** manual page).

Setting host and user information: NIS or /etc files

We discussed the **/etc/hosts** file earlier as a means to identifying particular machines with their network (Internet) addresses. Usually, however, only the small organizations use such a system. Larger organizations use the Network Information System (NIS) to keep track of hosts names, IP addresses, users, passwords, etc. Formerly called the Yellow Pages by Sun, NIS provides central management for crucial pieces of network information. The administrative databases that compose the NIS can be located among several machines across the network.

NIS is made available through the server daemons, **ypserv** and **ypbind** (**yp** for Yellow Pages), along with several other supporting daemons. The data is stored in text files called **maps**, which are roughly equivalent to the files in **/etc** on non-NIS machines: **hosts**, **ethers**, **passwd**, **group**, **services**, **protocols**, **aliases**, **netmasks**, and more. Your System Administrator will know what changes to make to the map files and can distribute the changes properly. See your Network Administration manual for more information about NIS.

If there is no NIS, update the UNIX server's **/etc/hosts** file with the new PC node Internet Address and Host Name. Set up entries in **/etc/passwd**, and possibly **/etc/ group**, on the non-NIS UNIX server for the new PC user. These files control logins and permissions on the UNIX host. If the user has an existing account, no changes are needed. Be sure that the user is given a suitable group ID that enables rights to their intended filesystem.

After editing the files you should be able to login as the new user and receive the appropriate filesystem rights. If not, go back and check the NIS maps or **/etc** files for errors. Set a password for the new user by using the **passwd** command.

Preparing for remote commands

If you wish to use **rlogin**, **rsh/rcmd**, or other remote commands, you must set up the UNIX host with the necessary information to let you in. Two files on the UNIX host control remote user authentication. You can set up either one, or both.

The first file to be checked when a remote command is to be authenticated is **/ etc/hosts.equiv**. On an IBM RS/6000 you can use SMIT to create the file. On a Sun, enter the host name, followed by an optional user name. You can use + or - to make modifications to either field. Here is a sample file with a variety of simple entries:

```
tester1 james
rs6000 +
-public
+ ken
+ @netgroup_name
```

The first entry lets user *james* in from host *tester1*. The second entry allows any user in with a host name of *rs6000*. The third eliminates any access from the machine called *public*. The fourth lets *ken* in from any host. The last entry allows any user in the specified NIS network group in. If any of the entries conflict, the first will prevail.

In addition, users can set up a **.rhosts** file in their home directory for the purpose of letting remote users into a particular account. This file uses specific host and user names, not the + and - formats. This file should have read/write permission for the owner of the account only (**chmod 600 .rhosts**).

As you might guess, these files create a potentially sizable hole in security. There is no password to enter, and the equivalent hosts can be as broad as the wide world. For the sake of your system, you should consider not allowing remote commands.

Configuring RARP and BOOTP Servers

Attaching diskless computers, print servers, and terminals to the TCP/IP network presents a problem—no place at that machine to store disk-based startup files. In this case, a boot image must be transferred from the server computer to the diskless station. Sometimes devices (particularly PCs and print servers) only need to get their IP address. Similar to the newly-hatched chick who asks "Are you my mother?" a

RARP (Reverse Address Resolution Protocol) or **BOOTP** (BOOT Protocol) client at a PC, print server, or terminal broadcasts a message asking for help from any machine that knows it. If any **RARP** or **BOOTP** server gets the message, it begins a dialogue with the device that needs assistance. Note that if you are using a SLIP direct serial connection to the host, or a SLIP or PPP dialup connection, you cannot use **BOOTP** or **RARP**. SLIP and PPP servers can dynamically assign IP addresses to the computers as they connect.

Configuring a RARP server

Reverse Address Resolution Protocol makes use of the unique physical hardware address attached to each Ethernet adapter. (As a point of interest, the first three bytes—6 digits—correspond to the manufacturer. Sun's code is 08:00:20.) When a **RARP** client boots, it broadcasts its hardware address in a **RARP** Ethernet packet. Any **RARP** server that knows that hardware address will respond, sending back the matching IP address to the hardware address. From that time on, the client station uses the IP address for further communication. **RARP** enables system administrators to manage network IP addresses from a central location, making large network maintenance much simpler.

Most TCP/IP products for PCs support RARP servers. In order to take advantage of **RARP** servers there are some things you must do:

• Verify that **RARP** is running, if you don't know already. This can be done by looking in the list of running processes for **rarpd**. Type **ps -ax** on a Sun, or **ps -Al** on an IBM RS/6000. On the Sun, this daemon is usually started from the /**etc/rc.local** script if a /**tftpboot** directory exists (the use of **tftp** implies *RARP*). If **rarpd** is not running, you can start it with /**usr/etc/rarpd -a**, presuming **rarpd** is in that directory.

• Create an entry for the new machine in /**etc/hosts**. Assign an IP address there. If there is no /**etc/hosts** file, the Network Information Service map files have the entries.

• If you have a BSD-based UNIX machine and are not using NIS, create or edit the UNIX host's /**etc/ethers** file to include 1) the Ethernet address, and 2) the host name of the **RARP** client machine. (NIS also maintains an ethers map.) The /**etc/ethers** file looks like this for one model of X-terminal and a print server:

```
# ethers
08:00:11:01:61:8e        xp337
00:80:72:00:10:FD        pserver
```

Configuring a BOOTP server

PC's can use **bootp** to obtain network information including: IP address, subnet mask, and addresses for network time servers, domain name servers, log servers,

HOT TIP   **Ethernet Addresses**

YOU MUST USE COLONS between the digits of Ethernet addresses, rather than the periods you habitually use for IP addresses. If you use periods, **rarpd** won't complain, but it won't find the address, either. You can usually find the Ethernet address stamped somewhere on the device, or on a card included with the documentation.

gateways, print servers, etc. The PC's use their own DOS hard drives to boot. FTP Software's PC/TCP is one product that can use **bootp** in this way

A couple of ways exist to tell the station how to find a server which will help it boot. With X-terminals, critical addresses and boot paths can be entered into the terminal's non-volatile memory designed specifically to hold that information. This allows the terminal to contact the server directly, accessing the filesystem and boot files using a simple transport mechanism, **tftp**. Perhaps half of all X-terminals use this method to boot—mostly sites with few terminals to maintain.

The second method allows the terminal to be unboxed, placed on the user's desk, and booted without entering any parameters into the terminal. This is accomplished using **BOOTP**. Sites with many terminals prefer this method to save on installation and maintenance time.

BOOTP is a preferred alternative to **RARP**. **BOOTP** provides extra information: a startup program to execute (for terminals) and server addresses. **BOOTP** makes use of UDP (User Datagram Protocol), rather than **RARP** packets. The client machine sends a UDP packet to the limited broadcast IP address (255.255.255.255). The **BOOTP** server sends the needed information back to the same limited broadcast address. **BOOTP** helps the client to find vendor-supplied boot code on the host's filesystems.

X-terminals such as the Tektronix XP337 alternately try **RARP** and **BOOTP** on startup until success is achieved. If unsuccessful after a lengthy period of time, they revert to the boot monitor prompt. From the monitor you can enter parameters that will help the X-terminal make connection if the server daemons are not responding.

Here are the steps for setting up a **BOOTP** server on the UNIX host, regardless of the type of device, PC, or terminal:

• You may not be able to see **bootpd** running in a process list because it can be configured to fire up only in response to a boot request. On a Sun, place the following line in **/etc/inetd.conf:**

```
bootps dgram udp wait root /etc/bootpd bootpd
```

If it is already there, tftp may be missing. Check that the following line is there.

```
tftp dgram udp wait root /usr/etc/in.tftpd in.tftpd -s /tftpboot
```

The *-s /tftpboot* portion is called a secure path by Sun, required for tftp file transfers. This secure path is, intentionally, the path to the boot files. Make sure that **bootpd** can be found in **/etc**, or that you supply a new path to it. If you want **bootpd** to run all the time, place this line into **/etc/rc.local** instead:

```
/etc/bootpd -s; echo -n ' bootpd'
```

•The **bootpd** must be provided with port numbers so that it can listen for boot requests. You do this by placing the following lines in **/etc/services** for the boot server and client port, if not already there:

```
bootps 67/udp
bootpc 68/udp
```

•Create an entry in **/etc/bootptab** for the client terminal or PC. This file is as touchy as **/etc/printcap**, so be careful of willy-nilly modifications. Read the **bootptab** manual page carefully to sort out the options. Here is a sample entry for the Tektronix XP337, which we named *xp337*:

```
xp337:\
                    :ht=Ethernet:\
                    :hd=/tftpboot:\
                    :hn:\
                    :bf=/XP330/os:\
                    :ha=08001101618e:\
                    :ip=192.9.200.6:
```

•If you are booting a terminal, load the terminal vendor's boot software on the UNIX server according to instructions. You will have to do additional configuration to establish the window manager, fonts and tools. See Chapter 12 for further information specific to X terminals.

Establishing Communications Between DOS and UNIX

After the hardware and software have been installed and configured, establishing a communications link over the TCP/IP network is a simple matter. The primary means of testing the links is to **ping** the nodes.

Basic Testing

Ping is a TCP/IP network testing program that is almost invariably included with TCP/IP products for PCs. Begin testing by typing **ping (host name)**, e.g., **ping 486**, where *486* is the name of this machine. The computer should return a message stating that the link is active. Then ping the other nodes on the network (especially the server), substituting the host names of those nodes into the ping command. This will demonstrate viable links FROM this computer TO the others, but not necessarily true in reverse. Go to each other node and do the same procedure again. If all nodes indicate attachment to the nodes they were planned to reach, you have a successful installation.

HOT TIP   **Ping, Ping**

If the first attempt at pinging another node results in failure, try again. Sometimes the first ping fails although there is nothing technically wrong with the link.

The first application to try is **telnet**. The **telnet** utility establishes a session on a remote host. Type **telnet (hostname)**, then enter your user name and password at the login prompt. A successful login will place you in your home directory, with your own brand of shell, as defined in the remote host's **/etc/passwd** file. You can then do anything on the remote host that your user group allows.

Network Monitoring and Diagnostic Programs

You can use programs such as **netstat** (and variations) to find out what is happening on your network. On the Sun and IBM RS/6000 workstations, **netstat -i** is helpful to show network activity. The IN packets (packets received) and OUT packets (packets transmitted) should be increasing continuously with network traffic. **netstat -r** and **netstat -rs** provide other statistics which may be useful. If there are a significant number of errors there may be a conflict between the LAN adapter interrupt and that for another device. For example, most LAN adapter cards default to interrupt 3—the same as that used by the second serial port. Here is netstat output from a Sun:

Name	Mtu	Net/Dest	Address	Ipkts	Ierrs	Opkts	Oerrs	Collis	Queue
le0	1500	sun-ether	sun_host	54544	1	52648	0	0	0
lo0	1536	loopback	localhost	6230	0	6230	0	0	0

PC products often supply their own versions of netstat. Figure 5.10 shows one such product.

The program "**ifconfig** provides general information about network links. At a Sun workstation type **ifconfig (device number)** for information on a specific node (e.g., **ifconfig le0**), or **ifconfig -a** for information on all nodes. Note the broadcast address in particular—it should show your correct network address. The broadcast address is used to find remote resources. If a broadcast address was entered incor-

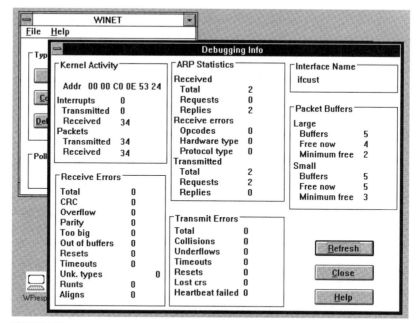

FIGURE 5.10 FTP Software's PC/TCP gathers network traffic counts

rectly, communication on the network will not exist for that node. Be wary when dealing with Suns—your PC software (e.g., FTP Software PC/TCP) may default to the 255 broadcast address (host ID portion) instead of Sun's 0.

LAN management software can be invaluable to monitoring the vitality of your network. Many handle multiple protocols. See Chapter 12 for details.

Troubleshooting

Assuming that all has not gone as hoped, here are some troubleshooting hints. There is a lot of wide-ranging material to cover, because network operating systems touch many areas. This section is organized topically, under (hopefully) relevant-sounding categories.

Cabling problems

• Check to see that the machine's LAN adapter is connected to the network cabling. If you are using twisted-pair cabling, the hub should indicate a viable link to the LAN adapter. See Chapter 4 for Ethernet troubleshooting hints.

• If you are using a serial link, between machines, make sure that you are using a null modem cable (wires 2 & 3 are crossed), not a straight-through cable. Also check that the serial ports on both computers are configured to the same baud rate, parity, data, and stop bits. On a PC, the port should either be managed by the TCP/IP product (you had to enter the serial port parameters), or else a statement such as **MODE COM1:9600,N,8,1** should be in the **AUTOEXEC.BAT** file.

Drivers do not load on boot

•If you get the message "Bad command or file name" at boot time, view the startup files (**AUTOEXEC.BAT** and **CONFIG.SYS**) to identify which file failed to load. Check the spelling, then the path. The **PATH** has three ways to go wrong: 1) the **PATH** statement in **AUTOEXEC.BAT** may be incomplete, 2) a path on the front of a file name in **AUTOEXEC.BAT** or **CONFIG.SYS** may be incorrect, or 3) you are not in the directory that you thought you were in, the one that contains the file. In the latter case, look for a CD (change directory) command as a potential culprit.

•Outside of command line parameters used by packet drivers, there are two files for NDIS and ODI drivers which contain LAN adapter settings. **PROTO-COL.INI** or **NET.CFG** (whichever is used) must agree with the actual adapter settings for shared memory, interrupt and I/O base address. If you edited either of them, do a cold reboot. The adapter may require a hard reset, perhaps remaining off for several seconds, before it will behave properly. These files also use filenames as parameters, so make sure the paths are included either with the filenames or in the **PATH** environment variable in **AUTOEXEC.BAT**.

•If you edit the frame type, or some other parameter, in a **PROTOCOL.INI** or **NET.CFG**, but the item does not change during boot, you probably have a stray path statement. Search for an extra path and files, and remove them.

•If **NETBIND** fails you could have several problems. Check **CONFIG.SYS** to make sure that a **PROTMAN** device is loaded ahead of your LAN adapter device. Place the **NETBIND** command at or near the beginning of **AUTOEX-EC.BAT**, ahead of other programs. Also check to see that the NDIS and **PROT-MAN** versions match. NDIS 2.x drivers cannot be used with **PROTMAN** 1.1, but the reverse is true.

•The startup files governing the driver loading process can easily get messed up if you switch drivers by hand from one type to another, say, from NDIS to ODI. You should do a complete re-install of a product if you need to switch driver types, unless 1) you have a lot of experience, 2) you are a lucky person, or 3) the product provides a utility for that purpose. Reinstallation is usually the quickest and safest way because the install program will copy the needed files and (hopefully) insert lines into startup files. Just keep a copy of your old setup, if it worked, just in case you need to refer to it again.

•If you are attempting to move a driver into upper memory at startup, it may not properly load there. Load it in conventional memory.

•Memory conflicts are frequently to blame when you have inexplicable problems at boot time. Drivers may be attempting to load out of sequence or load unnecessarily, and may corrupt the memory that another driver expects to keep. The drivers may or may not give an explanation for their collapse. Or, programs last in the list (such as Windows) may fail because there is not enough DOS memory available (the lowest 640K of memory). If lack of memory is your problem, try loading as much as possible into high memory.

•Check **CONFIG.SYS** for **EMM386.EXE** or another memory manager. If you are using shared memory on the adapter you need to use the /X parameter to exclude the shared memory from use; for example, **DEVICE=C:\WINDOWS\EMM386.EXE X=D800-DBFF.**

•If a machine has had more than one set of networking software installed, it may execute programs of the same name from the wrong network. For example, **rtm** can be supplied by more than one vendor, but only works with its originating vendor's software. The path to the old network's **rtm** comes ahead of the path to the new **rtm** in the **PATH** statement, so at boot time the old **rtm** is found and executed. The **rtm** says that it is loaded, but it is the wrong **rtm**. You probably will not get an error message under these conditions.

Machine locks up on boot

•There may be a conflict between your memory manager and a new network protocol or adapter driver. Boot from a floppy, then remove one or the other to confirm the conflict. Exclude memory in conflict from the memory manager. You may have to use the trial-and-error method for other parameters.

•If the PC has a grand mal seizure right after you load network software—such as not recognizing that it has a hard drive—chances are that the software modified **CONFIG.SYS** or **AUTOEXEC.BAT** by placing a program out of order with another program. Or, perhaps you inserted a program that you should not have. No permanent damage is done, but it may cost you a couple of Tylenol. We had dreadful experiences on our EISA machine—the machine lost its configuration information for the SCSI hard drive on two separate occasions. On the first, a TCP/IP product placed **PROTMAN** after a LAN adapter driver in **CONFIG.SYS**. **NETBIND** failed, then the system hung on loading the mouse driver. On reboot, the machine could not find the hard drive, and it had to be booted from a floppy and reconfigured. The second experience came when we haphazardly converted from an NDIS driver to an ODI driver, leaving a couple of **CONFIG.SYS** lines unREMmed.

Unable to establish connection: ping fails

•Verify that the remote host is running. Check to see that the network interface is working on that host. To do this, go to that host and type **ping (hostname)** or **ping localhost** to see if it finds itself (localhost is alive).

• If you get the message "Bad command or file name" on a PC, you are simply not finding the **ping** program. Change to the TCP/IP software's directory first, or set that directory into the **PATH** in **AUTOEXEC.BAT**.

• When a PC has been moved from another location, it may have TCP/IP already installed, or partially installed. You may get a message similar to "Transport protocol has not been loaded", even though you verified that all modules loaded correctly on boot. In this case, you probably found another program's **ping** instead of your own. The solution is to clean out the old software, including its lines in **CONFIG.SYS** and AUTOEXEC.BAT, and remove the directory from the **PATH** statement.

• Instead of typing **ping (host name)**, try typing the alternate form **ping (Internet address)**, e.g., **ping 192.51.108.2**. If this works, the pinged host name was either not spelled correctly, or the name was not entered correctly into the **hosts** file.

• Sometimes a **ping** to this machine works but fails to all others. This usually means that the hardware is not configured properly. For example, many LAN adapters offer a choice of AUI (DB15 connector), BNC (bayonet connector), or UTP (RJ-45 connector) interfaces. A jumper on the adapter may be prescribing the wrong cable interface.

• If you are pinging from a Sun workstation, **ping** with the -s parameter, e.g., **ping -s (host name)**. This method pings continuously until you press **CTRL-C**. At that point, diagnostics will be displayed which indicate how frequently the host being pinged dropped the packets. If you are pinging from a PC, see the TCP/IP vendor's reference manual for variations of **ping**.

• Typically, if there is no connection **ping** will show that packets were transmitted but NONE were received. This can be caused by many factors, including a missing cable terminator, a faulty cable connection, a bad tee (very insidious), a faulty LAN adapter or adapter installation, OR by using the wrong or outdated device driver for the adapter. See Chapter 4 for further information about hardware troubleshooting.

Common problems under MS-Windows

• The most commonly observed problem with applications for Windows is that they install lines in the **AUTOEXEC.BAT** file AFTER the line which starts Windows, and therefore, the application, or one of its components, is never executed. This usually results in a message saying that important files are not loaded. Use an editor to move the **win** line to the end of the file and reboot. The same problem occurs if a batch file is executed by name before **win** is encountered—the parent batch file (**AUTOEXEC.BAT**) dies. In that case, place **CALL** ahead of the batch file name, or move the called batch file's contents into **AUTOEXEC.BAT**.

•If the failing product has both an MS-Windows GUI utility and an MS-DOS command-line utility, try the DOS utility. For example, if the product does not work under Windows, completely exit from Windows to the DOS prompt. (Do not use a shell.) Check the product documentation to determine the DOS command syntax. If the product now runs properly, you may have localized the problem to the MS-Windows configuration process. The error may be in the PIF (Product Information File) for that program icon. Run the PIF Editor in the Main group /**File/Open** to select a PIF).

•Certain products may generate "Share violation" errors. If you get a message during Windows boot that there was an "Error loading ____" and the computer goes back to the DOS prompt, this could also be caused by a sharing violation. **REM**ark-out **SHARE** if it is executed in **AUTOEXEC.BAT** or **CONFIG.SYS**, then do a hard reset of the computer.

Connection buffer errors

•TCP/IP requires packet buffers for basic communication. Packet buffers are a maximum of 1514 bytes in length, and provide temporary storage for a packet received from the remote server if it cannot be processed immediately. This should be enough space in most cases. However, if packets come back too quickly and all packet buffers are filled, an "Out of Buffers" error will be generated by the TCP/IP software. Use the configuration utility to increase the buffers. Bear in mind that this will consume more of your low (DOS) memory.

•TCP and UDP connection buffers for **telnet** sessions are typically small—128 bytes. However, the accompanying structure can consume perhaps 2K bytes. You need one telnet session buffer per session. If you need more DOS memory and do not need multiple sessions, you can limit the number of connection buffers.

Login and printer access is denied

•Check the remote hosts **/etc/passwd** file. You must have an account before attempting to login or use the printer.

Permission denied

•When using TCP/IP utilities, you may receive "permission denied" errors. This signifies that either you belong to a group that does not have permission to execute the command, or that the file is set with the wrong permission flags. Use **chgrp** or **chmod** at the UNIX host.

File transfer problems

•If the host is slow to respond, try increasing the number of packet buffers, if you can, for your TCP/IP product. Use shared memory instead of DMA on your LAN adapter.

•Older **ftp** servers on UNIX hosts may not support commands such as **pwd**, **mkdir**, or **rmdir**. This requires an upgrade to the server.

•The DOS **APPEND** program can, if loaded, interfere with file transfer by redirecting transferred files to the wrong location, and can overwrite files of the same name. Remove it from **AUTOEXEC.BAT**.

•BSD 4.3 UNIX can truncate transferred files. If this occurs, get the file transfer fix for 4.3.

•**Tftp** is not supported by all UNIX hosts. BSD 4.2 UNIX **tftp** has bugs.

6

Installing NFS Products

Introduction

The Network File System (NFS) specification allows files on local disks to be shared across a network. It is a *distributed file system*, similar to the Remote File Service (RFS) of System V UNIX and the Server Message Block of Microsoft LAN Manager. Sun Microsystems, maker of the Sun SPARCstation, deserves credit for inventing NFS and placing the specification in the public domain. NFS has been wholeheartedly adopted by the UNIX community, and is a defacto standard for resource-sharing across multivendor platforms as well.

Ethernet

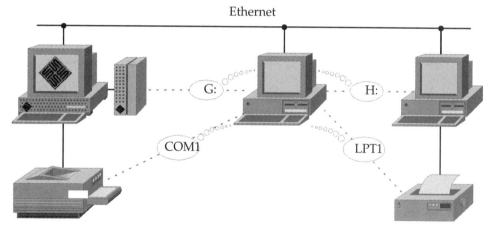

FIGURE 6.1 The transparency of NFS—using drives and printers of NFS server computers

The key thought on NFS (and any distributed file system) is *transparency*—NFS makes files located on one computer to be equally and immediately available to another, all without special effort on the part of the users. UNIX computers are the primary users of the technology to re-distribute the wealth of expensive and large hard drives to other servers on the Internet. However, PC installations have also adopted NFS, primarily to sponge resources off their powerful UNIX cousins. Conversely, some products allow UNIX computers to make use of PC file servers via

NFS. Figure 6.1 illustrates how a PC (in the middle) uses drives and printers actually located on other machines, through NFS.

NFS networking products provide PCs with access to UNIX filesystems, making a UNIX drive appear to the PC as if it were a local drive. Therefore, a network of PCs running NFS can use the UNIX workstation as a file server and data repository. Normal UNIX login and file locking protect files and filesystems. (NFS has no file locking facility of its own.) A special daemon gives PCs access to network printers. NFS does not put UNIX or UNIX applications on the PC! NFS gives PCs access to UNIX hardware, not software.

Due to these important features, NFS provides a level of functionality higher than TCP/IP. Indeed, TCP/IP (and Ethernet) forms the underlying environment over which NFS works. TCP/IP provides the conduit, NFS makes it mostly invisible. As Figure 6.1 shows, a PC user may not know that the drive known as "G" is actually on a machine down the hall, and he or she can select the network printer just as easily as the dot matrix by his or her desk. NFS is such a terrific facility that it is frequently bundled with the TCP/IP protocol and utilities needed by PCs joining the UNIX network. One such example is the popular PC-NFS 5.0 from SunSelect.

Why NFS Makes Sense for DOS PCs

DOS PCs are very different from character-based terminals or X-terminals. PCs are autonomous, each sporting its own CPU, memory, input/output devices, and disk storage—similar (on a lesser scale) to a UNIX workstation. When a PC runs an application, the application is usually read off its own disk into memory, where the CPU finds it and performs its instructions.

A terminal on a UNIX network usually has no need or ability to call an application into its own memory for execution. There are limited exceptions. X-terminals do download a boot image and start a locally-resident window manager. Newer character-based terminals also have a limited set of utilities which run without outside help. However, if we may speak in generalities, a terminal is a client, which purchases execution time from the server's CPU and memory. File transfers to terminals do not happen after boot, because they do not have a great local file storage capacity or, indeed, any REASON to store files. Terminals are only consoles with display and data-entry capabilities. They are windows into the UNIX server, which has all of the brains (or most of them—see Chapter 12 under X-Terminals.) The UNIX server is both multitasking and multiuser—it can run programs for many users at once by slicing a little CPU time for each. Plain vanilla DOS does not have this capability, so one CPU can execute only one application at a time.

On a PC network, the central host computer is a PC, usually dedicated only to file serving. Each PC requests a file transfer of its needed application, which the server sends down. As the PC executes the application, it may, if the user has permission, manipulate and update common data files on the server by locking them briefly for exclusive use. Several PCs can run copies of the same application at one time (such as word processing or general ledger), access common data files by taking turns, print documents at a network printer, or dial out on a modem.

The major difference between X-terminals and PCs, namely local intelligence, is the reason why NFS fits into DOS scenarios so well. Any computer, whether mainframe, mini/midrange, workstation, or PC, can use NFS to gain access to drives and browse for printers across the network. With the proper protocol-adjusting software (TCP/IP) and NFS, a UNIX computer can be used as a file server for PCs, whether the PCs are currently stand-alones or networked in a LAN.

There is a cost to NFS. Sharing PC files from the UNIX drives increases network traffic, since the server must habitually transfer large executable files. If there are a lot of PCs on the network regularly asking for 400K files to be sent down, all network users may experience some annoying delays. But the advantages of sharing files far outweigh any slowdowns (which are fixable in other ways). However, we don't recommend serial connections between host and PC under an NFS relationship—the data transfer rate to that PC is just too slow.

How NFS Works

The NFS protocol makes use of two separately-defined mechanisms called XDR (eXternal Data Representation) and RPC (Remote Procedure Calls). Together, these two specifications form the basis of client/server architecture for distributed computing. They are also indispensable to NFS.

XDR provides a means to translate data from one format to another—such as when the most significant byte of a two-byte data value is stored in the high memory address on one machine and the low memory address on another. This service allows data representations to be machine-independent.

RPCs are procedure calls written into programs to request services from a remote computer. The request-maker is called the client. Each client application has certain routines which call (make requests of) remote procedures or services. Before sending the RPC across the network to the remote computer, the client must obtain a directory of TCP/IP services advertised by that computer. The *portmap server* on the remote host tells the client which TCP/IP protocol port should be the destination for the RPC. The client then affixes the destination port to the packet. Meanwhile, the server portion of the application waits for a client RPC to appear. It has also informed the portmap of the TCP/IP ports it is listening on, as well as what RPC numbers it will accept. An RPC server on a Sun is known by its **rpc** name prefix, as in **rpc.mountd**, the mount daemon. When an RPC does appear, the server determines what information is required and sends it out as another network packet to the client. Therefore, a client/server program executes on two machines at once—hence the term distributed computing.

NFS is a client/server program, using both XDR and RPCs. This combination allows NFS to provide file services across a network between Sun, DEC, IBM, Intel PCs, and other dissimilar computers. XDR insures that data on one machine can be read by another, even though each represents data in a different format. The RPCs, being standardized according to specification between vendors, insure that each UNIX vendor's NFS server will pass files properly to another vendor's client.

Varieties of NFS Products for the PC

UNIX machines can easily support NFS connections with each other, provided the TCP/IP and NFS options are installed. When it comes to networking PCs, however, NFS needs help. Not only does DOS not support NFS, but the UNIX computers have to take special pains to maintain filesystem security.

Many TCP/IP product vendors provide an NFS client, which lets PCs use UNIX drives under NFS. Some of the vendors integrate NFS client capability, while others provide add-on NFS client modules, perhaps even as third-party products. Fewer vendors supply the PC authentication (security) component for the UNIX side.

Some products enable a PC to function both as a client and as an NFS server to other computers. In fact, two PCs running both client and server NFS can cross-mount each other's drives, similar to the peer-to-peer networking concept of resource sharing.

When you look for connectivity between UNIX and PC LANs, rather than UNIX and stand-alone DOS machines, NFS options can take on new guises. At least one product makes a Novell NetWare file server function additionally as an NFS server. This capability enables UNIX computers to use the NetWare server's disk space.

NFS Server Daemons

UNIX daemons are the rough equivalent of DOS TSRs (terminate-and-stay-resident programs). These programs execute and listen in the background for service requests. On a UNIX system, daemons are a way of life—crucial to a multiuser and multitasking environment. An NFS server requires four primary daemons to be running: **inet**, **portmap**, **nfs**, and **mount**. The first two daemons run automatically on a UNIX system and require no intervention from you. The latter two run on a Sun if the **/etc/exports** file exists (a list of filesystems to export to other machines). On a System V machine, you activate remote resource-sharing by setting the run level to 3 in **/etc/inittab**, or by typing **telinit 3** from the command line. You should know a little about what these daemons do. You may also have to install a **pcnfs** daemon for the sake of the PCs, if one is not already running.

You can verify the availability of running daemons by typing **ps -ax** at a Sun, **ps -A** at an IBM, or **ps -a** at an SCO machine to view the active processes. Or append **grep pcnfs** to find just the pcnfs daemon. Use **| more** if you do not have scroll bars to let you review what scrolled off the window/display—the complete list is quite long.

NFS Daemon

Nfsd starts filesystem request daemons to serve NFS clients. On a Sun, for example, **nfsd** is usually started by the **rc.local** script and brings a default of 8 request servers to life, each of which services NFS requests from many clients. If more than 8 NFS servers are needed to handle demand, the number of servers can be increased in **rc.local**. **Nfsd** works hand-in-glove with **biod** (the block I/O daemon), which manages read/write buffering.

Pcnfs Daemon

Rpc.pcnfsd is the typical name for the **pcnfs** daemon. (You need this as well as **nfsd**; it is not an alternative daemon.) Sun developed this daemon for use by their PC-NFS 1.0 product, and released the specifications to the market in general. Beame & White-side supplies their own daemon under the name **bwnfsd**, and Wollongong provides **nfsad**, but they are nearly the same as **rpc.pcnfsd**. This daemon is needed only for the purpose of interfacing the multiuser NFS daemons with DOS, which is not a multiuser operating system. The primary function of this daemon is to authenticate the remote DOS user and, consequently, to provide access to the NFS server daemons. An NFS user is the same as any other user—the **/etc/passwd** file, **/etc/group** file, and file and directory permissions govern which files may be accessed or executed. The PC software encrypts the user's name and password for the authenticator; then the authenticator returns user and group IDs (if validated). The secondary purpose of **rpc.pcnfsd** is to support authentication, queue management, and browsing for network printers. These functions are illustrated in Figure 6.2.

Without NFS, the user at the PC supplies a machine name to the TCP/IP software during installation, and logs in with a password whenever he or she begins a telnet session. If NFS client capability is also installed on the PC, the procedure is a little different. When the system boots, the PC NFS software will ask for the password up front, so that it can immediately, automatically mount drives and printers for the user. Only one computer is designated as the authentication server, so only one **rpc.pcnfsd** need be running on the network. However, running more than one can be an advantage in case the authentication server or a gateway goes down. Software such as SunSelect's PC-NFS can broadcast to find an authentication server.

Two versions of **pcnfs** exist. Version 1 supplied the user authentication and basic print services for PC-NFS 1.0 users. You may find it running on your system, or no **rpc.pcnfsd** at all. Version 2 supplies significant advantages over Version 1, which are designed mostly for the benefit of Windows 3.x users. If the PC runs Windows, Version 2 provides network browsing for printers as well as expanded print queue man-

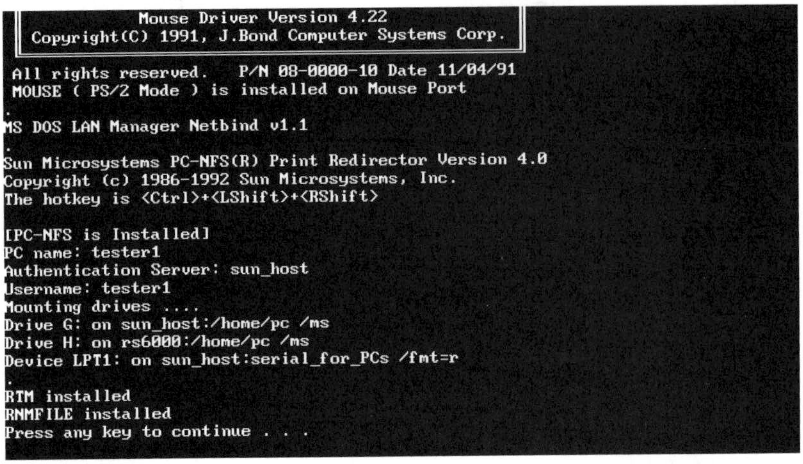

```
        Mouse Driver Version 4.22
   Copyright(C) 1991, J.Bond Computer Systems Corp.

   All rights reserved.   P/N 08-0000-10 Date 11/04/91
   MOUSE ( PS/2 Mode ) is installed on Mouse Port

   MS DOS LAN Manager Netbind v1.1

   Sun Microsystems PC-NFS(R) Print Redirector Version 4.0
   Copyright (c) 1986-1992 Sun Microsystems, Inc.
   The hotkey is <Ctrl>+<LShift>+<RShift>

   [PC-NFS is Installed]
   PC name: tester1
   Authentication Server: sun_host
   Username: tester1
   Mounting drives ....
   Drive G: on sun_host:/home/pc /ms
   Drive H: on rs6000:/home/pc /ms
   Device LPT1: on sun_host:serial_for_PCs /fmt=r
   .
   RTM installed
   RNMFILE installed
   Press any key to continue . . .
```

FIGURE 6.2 Authentication and drive/printer mounting at boot time

agement. The **pcnfs** daemons supplied by Beame & Whiteside and SunSelect are Version 2 compatible.

Rpc.pcnfsd can be found in several directories, depending upon your system: **/ usr/etc, /etc, /usr/lib, /bin, /usr/bin**. On a Sun system it is executed at startup as a part of **/etc/rc.local**. You can recompile the source code to support non-Sun UNIX systems, with help from the UNIX vendor. Beame & Whiteside's **bwnfsd** comes with "make" files for supporting the common varieties of UNIX.

Mount Daemon

All filesystems, both local and remote, must be mounted before they can be used. Mounting is the term applied to the process of attaching a filesystem to an existing directory or *mount point*. The mount daemon is called **mountd** or **rpc.mountd**. When a mount occurs, the filesystem directory structure is inserted under the drive letter/ directory name you select. Note that if the directory is not empty, mounting another filesystem there temporarily makes those files inaccessible until unmounted (using **umount**). Unmounting may be impossible without a reboot if the filesystem is currently being used for another purpose, so always mount on an unused directory.

Under NFS a filesystem mount takes the form **mount hostname:pathname mount_point**. For example, our Sun could mount a filesystem from the NFS-serving IBM RS/6000 by our issuing the command (in its simplest form):

    mount RS6000:/home /home/RS6000

The remote **/home** directory appears on the Sun as **/home/rs6000**. A PC may do a **mount sun:/home/pc G:** to make the server's **/home/pc directory** accessible as the root directory of a virtual drive, G. **Rpc.mountd** is usually started on the NFS-serving UNIX system from the **rc.local** startup file. See the *mount(8)* manual page for information about mount options.

Portmap Daemon

This daemon gives client programs the direction they need to find their servers. **Portmapd**, or portmapper as it is sometimes called, acts as a directory for Remote Procedure Calls. Servers declare themselves to the portmapper, and remote clients seek directions from the portmap for their Remote Procedure Calls. **Portmapd** is started on the UNIX server before the **inetd** daemon, since **inetd** starts many Internet servers (defined in **inetd.conf**). Several products, such as ChameleonNFS from NetManage (see Figure 6.3) provide a portmap server for the PC, as well the ability to view a remote portmap list.

Inet Daemon

Always running, **inetd** is the name for the Internet services daemon. Its function is to listen in on the Internet (LAN users, mostly) and *spawn* (start) new daemons as needed to satisfy requests for services. Available services are advertised in portmap. At startup (from **rc.local**, on a Sun) **inetd** reads configuration information from **/etc/inetd.conf** about the daemons available to be enabled. When a service is requested, **inetd** starts that service (if enabled) or refuses the connection. For example, when a

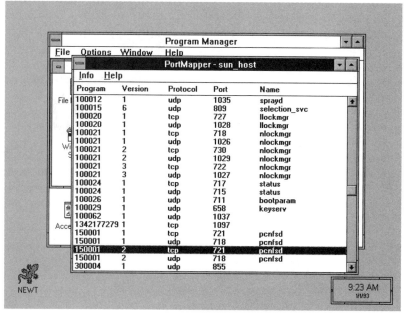

FIGURE 6.3 Looking at the Sun's portmap from a PC via ChameleonNFS

user opens a telnet session on the host, the telnet client (at the user's location) requests telnet service and **inetd** spawns a new **telnetd** for the remote user. Several **telnetds** may be running at any time, one for each open session. Other server daemons commonly started by **inetd** include **ftpd**, **tftpd**, **fingerd**, **rshd**, **rlogind**, and **rexecd**.

You may get the impression that these servers can only run on UNIX machines—not so. As one example, Beame & Whiteside's **INETD** runs in the background on a PC, turning it into a server for **ftp**, **telnet**, **finger**, and other services. You can configure each service for TCP or UDP protocol, port number, and other optional parameters. Of course, if the PC gets many requests, its regular user will be robbed of processing speed.

Other NFS-Related Daemons

NFS is called a *secure* network service if the users, not just their computers, are qualified before they are admitted to the filesystem. If your site uses the Network Information Service, when the login program obtains the user's password, it looks up that user's encryption key in the NIS, decrypts it, stores it in **keyserv** for safekeeping, and passes the encrypted key to the client. The client uses the key to encrypt a time stamp, which it affixes to each NFS request. At the NFS-serving host, the request is compared to the stored key, and if it is valid, the request is honored.

Where an Internet domain name server is used, **in.named** supplies that service. The lock daemon, **rpc.lockd** is desirable when more than one user can use the same data at the same time. **Rpc.statd** represents a network status monitor—used with **rpc.lockd** to inform clients when a system is off-line. SunSelect provides updated lock daemons to support PC-NFS on a Sun.

SunSelect's PC-NFS provides an optional **msgserv** daemon to support a quick-and-dirty inter-machine messaging capability. Such capability is often called chat.

Exporting Filesystems

No PC or UNIX computer user can just knock on the door of a remote host and expect to be given a filesystem. The host must *export* a filesystem first. **Exportfs** (called from the startup script **rc.local**, on a Sun) becomes the export agent, and **/etc/exports** is the shipping manifest. Any exported filesystem must appear in the **exports** file. If the **exports** file does not exist, the **nfsd** daemon will not be started at boot time. To see what is currently being exported type **exportfs** or **cat /etc/exports**. Here is a sample **/etc/exports** file:

```
# exports
/home/pc                              # no options, open to all comers
/var/spool
/usr -access=fin1:fin2:eng1,rw=eng2     # limited access
```

You may restrict access to only certain PC hosts by adding the parameter **access=(PC1):(PC2)**. Read-only permission is given by **-ro;-rw=(PC1):(PC2)** gives read-write permission to two PC hosts while the rest remain read-only. All exports should be restricted for security. See the *exports(5)* manual page for further information about root access privileges and secure access to exported directories.

HOT TIP

Getting into the Export Business

PC applications can gobble up disk space in a hurry. Type **df** to see if the exported directory has enough disk space available to service its users. Also, symbolic links should not be used as exported filesystem names—some PC products cannot access them.

When you use NFS with DOS PCs you might think that the PC will be able to run UNIX programs—not true. Only a serious programming project can port a UNIX program to run on a DOS/Windows platform because the two operating systems are completely different. A DOS PC uses only the executables and data files that are designed for DOS. Such files should be placed in an exported directory away from UNIX executables and data files which a PC user could potentially alter by mistake. The reverse is also true—you don't want UNIX users to accidentally fall into the PC users' directories and alter files.

The main value of NFS is in using the large UNIX hard drives as file server disks for PC-only files. In other words, all PCs on a TCP/IP network can store executable programs in one place and keep common databases. You should export a **/home/pc** or similarly-named directory for the exclusive use of PCs. The PC users create subdirectories and load software within that filesystem. **/home/pc** can be used as the home directory for most or all of the PC users. (The **/etc/passwd** file must be edited for each PC user, in part to set their home directory. See later discussion.)

Steps for Configuring an NFS Server

Most NFS products for DOS machines do not include PC authentication server software. Instead, they assume the server is installed already. Consequently, for PC users with no background in UNIX, installing NFS client products is a little like playing "Pin the Tail on the Donkey"—they don't know if it will work until they try it. Our SunOS 4.1.2 documentation does not discuss the add-on **pcnfs** daemon at all. In fact, most PC NFS products do not even provide instructions related to PC NFS authentication servers, and some flatly refuse to provide telephone support on the topic. If you need the **pcnfs** server daemon, make sure you get one with the NFS product you buy. Here is the scoop on NFS servers.

Serving PCs from a UNIX Workstation

The first step is to make sure the UNIX host is configured for TCP/IP, especially if it has never been networked before. Typing **ifconfig -a** at a Sun or **ifconfig en0** at an RS/6000 will tell you the status of the network. The network is activated on a Sun through the **/etc/rc.boot** file—the **ifconfig** line. See the system manual pages and Chapter 5 for assistance.

For the sake of discussion we are assuming you do not run an NIS (Network Information Service). An NIS becomes a more complicated scenario. If you have NIS, we assume you know how to set it up.

If you are preparing an IBM RS/6000 for use as an NFS server, type **smitty** or **smit** from the command line to configure NFS, export filesystems, and user groups. When using HP-UX, type **sam**. SCO machines provide the **sysadmin** utility for these purposes; UnixWare provides Setup utilities. These vendors recommend you use the utilities rather than directly editing the files. Suns running Solaris 2.x have the **admintool** for setting up users, groups, hosts, and other databases, but this utility does not help with network interface configuration or filesystem exports. (Fortunately, NFS generally needs no configuration.) If you are on a Sun running SunOS 4.1.x you have no utility—you must do everything the "Armstrong" way, editing files by hand. If you have not already logged into the UNIX host as **root** or superuser, then do so. The following discussion applies primarily to Sun users.

Prepare a PC group and directory

Since DOS and UNIX files don't mix well, you should take care to keep them separate. The first step is to create a user group in **/etc/group** for general PC users. In this way you can give them separate rights from UNIX users. Here are sample lines for a group file:

```
pc:*:106:
softnet:*:107:mike,ken,supervisor
```

We created the **pc** group specifically for users who gain access from PCs via NFS. The second field is for the group password (rarely used—enter * or nothing), then comes the group ID, followed by an optional member list. Customarily, you should use group ID numbers between 100 and 60,000. One networking product we tested, Puzzle SoftNet Utilities, created its own entry for users we specified. If you use NIS, a **+:** may be present as the last line, indicating that the NIS group file is to be added there.

Next, create a private directory for the PC group—a "home away from home." Type **cd /home**, if **/home** is the name of your chosen filesystem, then **mkdir pc**. Type **chgrp (PC group name) pc** to let the PC group own this directory. Then set PC user write permission with **chmod g+w /home/pc**. (You can see the results with **ls -l /home**.) Create a similar directory for use by the print spool program. Typically the spool directory is **/var/spool/pcnfs** or **/usr/spool/pcnfs**, but you can place it in a sub-directory of **/home** as well.

Export the private and print spool filesystems for the PC group. To do this you must edit **/etc/exports**, then run **exportfs (exported directory)**. If **/etc/exports** did not previously exist, it is easier to reboot (after you complete the rest of these instructions), since the related daemons must also be started.

Identify the PC users and their machines

Create an entry in **/etc/passwd** for each PC user. The records are structured in this fashion: username, password (encrypted), user ID, group ID, user's real name, home directory and login shell. Place a "*" in the password field—a starting password can be set later. Enter a unique user ID number and the PC group ID. Enter the exported PC directory as the home directory, or give the user a personal directory in that filesystem. Use the same shell as for other UNIX users. Utilities such as **smit** make this process much simpler than editing by hand. Here are some sample lines from an **/etc/passwd** file (not ours, of course):

```
ken:HewHkwcpIXM:304:20:KenP:/home/ken:/bin/csh
mike:YYfgUnCVbkZsiOj:305:20:MikeB:/home/mike:/bin/csh
gini:*:306:106:GiniP:/home/pc:/bin/csh
valuept:Hot2qrclYPYAw:307:106::/home/pc:/bin/csh
```

We assigned the last two users to group *106*, the *pc* group. Their home directory is */home/pc*. Some PC NFS client products allow users to mount drives without entering passwords, such as if *gini* did not even have the "*". However, most require them, for good reason. You should always use passwords to maintain security.

Check the work you have just done for groups and users by logging in. Set a starting password for the users that had "*" by typing, for example, **passwd gini**, and entering the password. Ctrl-D to logout as root, then enter one of your new PC user names. Type **pwd** after login—you should be in the **/home/pc** directory (the user's home directory). If you cannot gain a terminal session, double-check your group ID in **/etc/passwd**. You must be able to log into each NFS server you need to access, so you must modify **/etc/passwd** (and **/etc/group**) on each of those machines unless you use an NIS server.

Edit **/etc/hosts** file to include the hostname and IP addresses of the attaching PCs. If you use *RARP* to boot PCs (diskless workstation situations), you must edit the ethernet adapter addresses into the **/etc/ethers** file on the **RARP** servers.

Start the daemons

Verify the existence of the NFS and **pcnfs** daemons, as outlined in the previous section on NFS Server Daemons. If you had to build the exports file from scratch, the NFS daemons may not presently be running. You should reboot if that is the case, as the daemons may now be triggered by **/etc/exports** or **/etc/inittab**.

If **rpc.pcnfsd** is not in the process list; you need to install it from the PC. (If your NFS client product does not supply this daemon, its time to get on the phone to your workstation vendor.) Installing the daemon involves moving source code to the workstation and executing commands to compile it. SunSelect's PC-NFS shows you how to edit the **rc.local** startup script to automatically run it on boot. Only one host on the network need run this daemon, although several can. Some vendors (SunSelect, Beame & Whiteside) provide the DOS user with an **rcpinfo** command to check the host's **pcnfsd** version.

Mount the UNIX drives at the PC

Install the NFS client on the DOS computer according to the vendor's instructions and test. This includes establishing a TCP/IP connection if the machine is new to the network (see Chapter 5). If the NFS client does not do a mount for you from the installation utility, you must issue a command from the DOS prompt such as **MOUNT SUN:/HOME/PC G:** (syntax can vary by vendor). If successful, you will be able to type **cd (drive letter assigned with mount):**, then **DIR** to see a directory of the UNIX drive. You can manipulate directories and copy files using regular DOS commands. Depending upon your NFS client software you may have to do a cold or warm reboot on the PC if there is a problem recognizing the existence of the remote host. If the mount still fails or hangs, verify the above steps and/or try the connection from another machine. The message, Permission denied means that the user/machine is not a valid name on the host's **/etc/passwd** list.

Complete the link from Microsoft Windows

Under Windows, enter the Main program group, locate the File Manager icon and double click. Then choose **Disk/Network Connections** (see Figure 6.4). The Browse button can help you find a host's exported filesystems. When you have specified a host name, filesystem, virtual drive letter, and password, press **Connect**. If successful, a new drive icon will appear in the main File Manager window. Similarly, printers can be mounted from the Print Manager. However, if you mount drives and printers only from within Windows, not the DOS prompt (or **AUTOEXEC.BAT**), they will not remain mounted if you exit Windows. See Chapter 7 for detailed information about interfacing with Microsoft Windows.

Serving PCs from Another PC

Some products allow you to set up a PC as an NFS server for other PCs or UNIX workstations. (But don't bother mounting a 40 megabyte drive for your RS/6000—it won't help you much!) This configuration creates, in essence, a PC peer-to-peer LAN similar to Artisoft's LANtastic or Microsoft's Windows for Workgroups.

If your NFS product has this capability, the NFS Server installation on the PC usually occurs without your intervention. It happens at the same time that you install TCP/IP and the NFS client, so there is very little, if anything, to do on a DOS

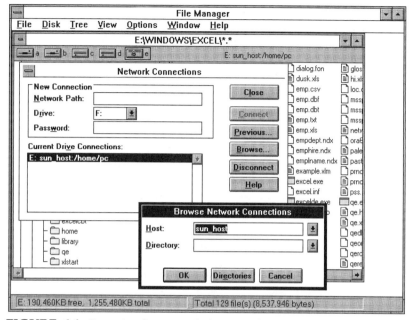

FIGURE 6.4 Browsing for network drives with Microsoft Windows File Manager

machine for setup. Two good NFS-serving products are ChameleonNFS, from Net-Manage Inc., and BW-NFS, from Beame & Whiteside Software Ltd.

Installing DOS Software on a Workstation File Server

Once NFS is running you can easily move DOS software and data files onto the UNIX file server. The UNIX filesystem appears to the DOS side as just another drive, and you use the common DOS commands **COPY**, **DIR**, etc. To install a software package from DOS, simply substitute the letter of the new drive into the install procedure. For example, if the manual says to type **INSTALL C:**, type instead **INSTALL G:** (or whatever letter you mounted the drive as). If you install the program under Windows and it is Windows-compatible, go into the Program Manager, select **File/Run** and enter the drive letter and name of the product's installation program.

When the files are installed on the UNIX drive they show the ownership of whichever PC user installed them, using **ls -l (directory)** from the UNIX station. If the PC users have all been placed in the same group there is no technical barrier preventing any user from accessing the files, other than an application's normal file locking, since the users all have the same rights. (There could be licensing issues—you must usually license the number of copies you need.) However, if the users are assigned to other groups they may not have permission to run the software. Or, the software may not have set the proper permissions for the users. You can rectify permission problems using three commands:

- As super-user or owner of the file, execute the command **chgrp (groupname)** to assign the file to another more all-encompassing group. Use **chgrp -R (groupname)** to assign an entire directory with subdirectories.

- As the super-user or owner of the file, execute the command **chmod (new permissions) (file or directory)** to change the permissions level on a file or directory. Permissions can be set with numeric syntax, but the alphanumeric syntax is easiest to remember. Permissions can be set for user/owner (u), group (g), others (o), or all (a). Three permissions are available: *read* (r), *write* (w), and *execute* (x). Use + to add permission or - to take it away. For example, to give all **pc** group members write permission to all files in the current directory, use the command **chmod g+w ***. However, most files should have read-only permission to avoid file sharing violations between multiple users—you should give write permission only to the files that need that permission (usually shared data files). You shouldn't need execute permission on DOS executables, because they are copied down to the PC before execution, anyway. You can tell the current permission level of a file or directory by using the **ls -l** command: **drwxrwxrwx** indicates full read/write/execute permission on a directory (x gives permission to search the directory). **-rw-rw-r--** indicates read/write for the owner and group, but read-only for all others.

- As the super-user, type **chown (new owner) (file or directory)** to switch owners entirely, although this may not accomplish much in your situation.

Troubleshooting

If you experience problems mounting drives or printers, or running programs installed on your network drive, this section lists some possible solutions. Your NFS client vendor may supply additional tips.

NFS or other programs do not load

- The modules were not loaded in the correct order. A generally usable order is: hardware drivers, non-TCP/IP network software, TCP/IP kernel, NFS, mount command, and finally, Windows. Check your PCs **AUTOEXEC.BAT**.

- Some products modify the path statement in **AUTOEXEC.BAT**. If you install the product on a network drive, make sure that the path to that product is set *after* the drive is mapped. If you don't do this, you can have problems that are difficult to trace. For example, we installed LAN WorkPlace for DOS on a Net-Ware server drive J:. The **PATH** statement thus included **J:\WKPLACE**, but **PATH** was executed before we ever logged in to NetWare. The drive **MAP** command displayed drive J: sometimes, but sometimes not, depending upon how much DOS environment space we were using at the time. It could not be reliably accessed by other programs later in **AUTOEXEC.BAT**, although we could always login to J: when **AUTOEXEC.BAT** was done. To fix this problem, place the statement **SET PATH=J:\WKPLACE;%PATH%** after your login.

"Access Denied" or authentication failure error message

- The authentication daemon is not running on the UNIX server.
- UNIX server's **/etc/hosts** file or NIS name service does not know the PC.
- UNIX server's **/etc/exports** file does not export the directory that you wish to mount (or a parent of your chosen directory).
- The PC host name does not have access to the exported directory.
- The exported directory is a symbolic link, and the PC product does not support symbolic links.
- Another user may have locked a shared file.

"File Creation Error"

- The PC account does not have permission to do the requested file operation.
- The UNIX host is out of disk space in the mounted filesystem.

Mount commands time out

- Not all UNIX NFS server daemons are not running.
- The domain name server daemons are not running on the UNIX host, and you have configured the PC software to use a domain name server.
- You have specified a default gateway (router), but the gateway is not functional, the gateway address is incorrect, or the server return route is incorrect.

Mounted drives appear to be empty

- Load NFS after the other networking software.

"Permission Denied"

- The UNIX host's **/etc/passwd** file does not know your login name or grant the rights you require for the file operation.
- The file permissions may not allow the operation you requested.

7

Linking UNIX with PC LANs

Introduction

If you've been waiting for the internetworking part of the book title, here we are. This chapter discusses internetworking—the networking of networks, focusing particularly on internetworking UNIX TCP/IP networks with PC-based LANs. As you can imagine, when you link two networks using the inner secrets of the network operating system(s), the end result depends a lot on the creativity and good sense of the engineer. The linking products have a dual character, or split personality, capturing the best of two worlds. Some products are network operating systems in their own right. Others simply extend existing networks across protocol boundaries.

We concentrate here on laying the groundwork, not so much theoretically as practically. We provide a background in the common PC LAN attributes which UNIX system administrators must understand in order to internetwork. There is not a lot here for PC LAN administrators, since UNIX networking has already been discussed in detail in Chapters 5 and 6. We introduced router-based internetworking products in Chapter 4, but to limit the scope of this book we do not deal with that subject thoroughly. However, everyone can benefit from this discussion of the critical points of contact between UNIX and DOS networks, as well as the multiprotocol troubleshooting hints.

Why Link Networks?

You already know some of the benefits to linking networks since you are reading this chapter. Here we add some advantages from our point of view.

DOS and Windows applications are easy to use, generally easier to install than UNIX software, and there are LOTS of them. For breadth of software, PCs have a huge lead over UNIX machines. Why not tap in to those applications, while retaining the mission-critical programs and raw processing power of UNIX?

UNIX programs are multitasking as well as multiuser, allowing you to run several programs at once. Windows NT allows multitasking on PCs, but lags behind UNIX when it comes to multitasking applications. UNIX systems also have more options than those provided by PCs: more memory, larger disks, and tape and CD-ROM drives as standard equipment.

Linking networks can give users access to both worlds without investing in more machines and desktop real estate. It takes advantage of the strengths of each. If the interface is good, users may not even know they are using a foreign system.

Purchasing Considerations

The world of LAN to UNIX products is somewhat difficult to sort out, partly because of new jargon you may have to learn and partly because there are so many ways of fitting products together. Modern software is increasingly adopting the "open systems" philosophy. Manufacturers design Application Program Interfaces (APIs) for their products which allow more-or-less universal connections with other products. This approach resembles the invention of replaceable gun parts. Products which plug easily into existing systems are easy on the pocketbook, so users buy them. Of course, if you are a manufacturer following a widely accepted standard, there is always the chance that a competitor's product will supplant yours—let the chips fall where they may.

Yet even with more generic connections between applications, the increasing variety of APIs provides an abundance of alternatives for making those connections. For example, in connecting NetWare with UNIX you can find software that is either Novell- or UNIX-based, as well as other products that convert the host to either a server or client of the other. Here are some points to consider as you shop for network-linking products.

Operating System Requirements

Does the product require OS/2, DOS, or Windows? Perhaps other operating systems such as Banyan Vines? Most products are manufactured for compatibility with DOS and Windows, but Windows compatibility is often a matter of degree. If your users are Windows-oriented, seek a product that integrates well with Windows.

Multiuser vs. Single-User Station

Most products allow all network nodes of the same class to access the contrasting server. However, some products are designed to make the connection between single stations and the server. This may be an architectural matter, not just a licensing one. For example, most TCP/IP products for PCs, such as Distinct Corporation's TCP/IP, are single PC to UNIX networking products. Puzzle SoftNet Utilities, on the other hand, gives NetWare PCs blanket access to the UNIX workstation as a NetWare server—a limited form of internetworking. See Figure 7.1 for pictorial representations of the networking/internetworking scenarios.

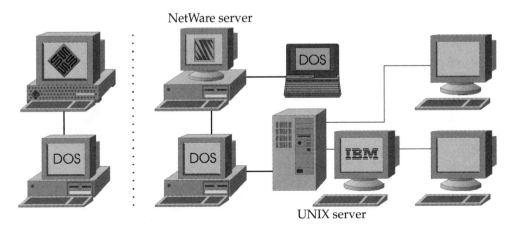

FIGURE 7.1 UNIX networking versus multiprotocol internetworking

Client/Server

It is easy to be confused over this terminology. *Server* and *client* carry slightly different connotations to a UNIX person than to a PC LAN person, so it is imperative that you understand both viewpoints. On a PC LAN, the server and client are often discussed as machines—the server machine is a file repository for the client machines. which use the server are called clients. On a UNIX network, however, the terms *server* and *client* have very specific technical meanings. They are halves of a program, not machines. The server component serves many client components, which may run on a machine across the network, or on the server's own machine, or both. (This enables distributed computing.) In order to grasp the mumbo-jumbo of product literature, you must determine the context of what the vendor is telling you. Some products create servers, others clients. For the most part, our discussion in this chapter is oriented toward the 'machine' connotation of these terms. For example, Spry NetWare Client for UNIX turns the UNIX workstation into a Novell client, capable of communicating with a NetWare file server. On the other hand, Puzzle SoftNet Utilities converts a UNIX workstation into a NetWare file server for access by NetWare client PCs. The latter case is depicted in Figure 7.2.

One of the tougher questions to tackle is this: if you need to bring UNIX and DOS applications together on one hardware platform, to which user group do you cater, UNIX users or PC users? Do you make UNIX machines act like DOS PCs or vice versa? There is no one-size-fits-all answer, but we suggest that you choose a product that encourages the growth of your primary LAN, the LAN you will standardize on for the future. If the users on the primary LAN need additional primary LAN resources, choose a product to create a server out of a machine on the secondary LAN. If the users on the secondary LAN need primary LAN resources, make them clients. In the end, since each environment has a lot to offer the other, you may end up with products of both types.

FIGURE 7.2 UNIX workstation acting as NetWare file server

Utilities

When you create a server on a machine as a "second language," not all of the vocabulary may be transferred. In other words, network utilities you are accustomed to may not be supplied for the new server. This is not necessarily important, however. For example, SunSelect's NetWare SunLink provides many utilities normally found on a NetWare server, but Puzzle's SoftNet Utilities assumes you will move the utilities from your current NetWare server if you need them. If the underlying network software is 100% compatible, you can copy over some utilities. Also, if you attach a new server rather than login to it as the default server, you retain the utilities of your current server.

Printing

Although printing is a prime motivation for networking, it is not likely to be a differentiating factor in your purchase, since there usually is little difference in capability between products. It is true, however, that print functions often take more time to set up than the other server functions. Since most products serve either UNIX or DOS, but not both, they also usually supply the capability to print from only one direction—the PC LAN job to a UNIX printer, or a UNIX job to a PC LAN printer. Nail down the printing capabilities with your vendor before you buy. One other important question to ponder: do you want to print both PostScript and PCL files on the same printer? (See Chapter 11, Connecting Printers.)

Bi-Directional Servers

A few products provide a high-level gateway between LANs, transmitting data across cabling schemes and protocols in either direction—similar to a low-level hardware gateway. UNIX clients see UNIX servers, PC LAN clients see PC LAN servers.

These products can be either hardware- or software-oriented. TCP Gateway 386, from Network and Communication Management, Inc., is one example of a hardware-oriented solution. This product links two physical LANs by connecting them to a single PC, with software to manage multiprotocol communications between

LANs. Figure 7.3 shows a hardware-based gateway. Mini-Byte Software Inc. provides a software-only product.

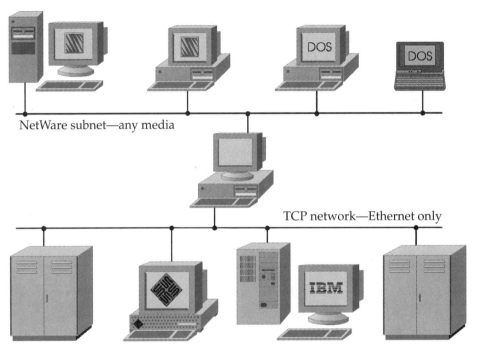

FIGURE 7.3 A hardware gateway can link two physically dissimilar networks

Linking UNIX with the Novell NetWare Environment

The following section outlines the major issues you must understand in order to link UNIX with Novell NetWare. NetWare is an easy-to-manage, as well as full-featured, PC network operating system. These qualities have propelled NetWare to the forefront of PC LAN popularity. For information about other types of PC network operating systems, such as Microsoft LAN Manager, see Chapter 14.

About the NetWare Server

Here is a little background on the Novell NetWare file server, written from the perspective of internetworking. You may never have to set up a NetWare file server, but this section tells you what sort of a kingdom it is and how to get your bearings should you need to. Then again, some products build a NetWare server inside a UNIX filesystem, which is a little like building a broiler inside a microwave, but it works.

IPX/SPX—the Novell counterpart to TCP/IP

IPX stands for Internetwork Packet eXchange, and is responsible for the connections between software and network hardware. Sequenced Packet eXchange supervises IPX transmissions. Since data often transmits in multiple packet-loads, SPX has the job of making sure all packets get through. The IPX protocol compares to UNIX IP, and SPX to TCP. The formats of the low-level IPX and IP data packets are different, but can be accommodated through software to allow internetwork communications.

Network and server identification

NetWare makes use of an internal 8-digit hexadecimal address (1 to FFFFFFFF) to identify the network. This number is arbitrarily set at the time of NetWare installation. You can view the number from a NetWare station using **SLIST** or **SYSCON**. Note that a **BIND** statement in the system **AUTOEXEC.NCF** file may set a second physical network number, which you should use in place of the internal network number.

File servers are identified with names up to 47 characters long, also assigned at installation time. Names are used for attaching servers, logging in, and mapping drives. Again, use **SLIST** or **SYSCON** to see the names of operable servers.

Server startup files and server shutdown

When the file server powers up, DOS controls the boot. Once NetWare is in control, you do not see the DOS prompt again at that machine. (The new system prompt is a colon.) The first script to activate is **AUTOEXEC.BAT** (**CONFIG.SYS** is unnecessary). Its only real job is to change to a **\NOVELL** directory and execute **SERVER.-EXE**. **SERVER** runs **STARTUP.NCF**, which is a script for loading the disk drivers, similar to **CONFIG.SYS**. **STARTUP.NCF** mounts volume *SYS*, then finds and runs **AUTOEXEC.NCF**. This script sets network identification and loads the bulk of the NetWare operating system and options. NetWare file servers run on dedicated PCs or non-dedicated UNIX workstations.

To shutdown the file server, go to the system prompt and type **DOWN**. This will notify the NetWare users and give them time to logoff of that file server. When the server is down, type **EXIT**.

Server console and remote server console

Some network maintenance tasks, such as loading NetWare Loadable Modules (NLMs), copying files to the NetWare directories, or downing the server, can be performed only from a server console at the system prompt (:). This is not the same as **SYSCON**, the System Console which you can run from any machine. The **MONITOR** is a system utility which displays currently connected users, allows you to edit startup files, etc. Most users leave this running at the server console all the time. If the monitor is not running, type **LOAD MONITOR** at the system prompt to start it.

NetWare allows you to access the server console from your local NetWare client node, rather than physically going to the server. To do this, place the following lines in **AUTOEXEC.NCF:**

```
LOAD REMOTE (PASSWORD)
LOAD RSPX
```

Then reboot the server console. After that, as Supervisor, type **RCONSOLE** to gain the same capabilities as at the server (except for the floppy disk drive). You can even reboot the server remotely if you add the **REMOVE DOS** command to **AUTOEX-EC.NCF**. The NetWare NFS product also allows X Window terminals to function as remote consoles.

Filesystem organization

Novell filesystems are broken into *volumes*. The only required volume is **SYS**, and it is created at installation time for holding system, utility and login files. This volume should usually be kept to a small portion of the server's hard drive, but no less than 40 megabytes. Create an additional volume(s) to contain most user applications.

The NetWare installation process creates several *directories* on the **SYS** volume (the only volume which you MUST have). Note that path names under DOS and Novell NetWare use "\" instead of "/", as used by UNIX. Here is a brief sketch of each directory:

●**SYS:\LOGIN** is required for user logins. If a login fails, through bad password or otherwise, the user is left in this directory. **SLIST** is available to show which servers can be connected via **LOGIN** or **ATTACH**.

●**SYS:\MAIL** serves network mail systems. Each user has his or her own mail box. The directory also stores user login scripts.

●**SYS:\PUBLIC** contains utility programs for general access by NetWare clients. Examples include **SYSCON**, **PCONSOLE**, **SALVAGE**, and **USERLIST**. The system login script is also stored here. Small public applications and DOS files can be stored in subdirectories of **PUBLIC**.

●**SYS:\SYSTEM** contains NetWare Loadable Modules and other files of interest to NetWare and the Supervisor user. This directory is the Supervisor's home directory on login. **SYS:\SYSTEM** also contains a sub-directory for each print queue defined in **PCONSOLE**.

SYSCON creates an additional directory in **SYS** for each user defined, e.g., **SYS:\KEN**. This directory becomes the home directory of that user on login. By convention, **SYS:\ETC** (when used) contains files such a **/etc/hosts** and **/etc/networks** that would be used by UNIX TCP/IP applications. NetWare does not support symbolic link capability.

Name Space

DOS names are limited to 8 characters, with a 3-character extension. Extra name space can be reserved for long UNIX names under NetWare. To enable this support, load **NFS.NAM** or **FTAM.NAM** on the Novell server. (See NLMS below.) Make sure you enter the lines into the **STARTUP.NCF** script from **SYSCON**.

NetWare Loadable Modules (NLMs)

NLMs make the NetWare world go round. They are programs that can be added or subtracted from the NetWare operating system on the fly, without downing the file server. NetWare NLMs come in four fundamental varieties, and consequently, four different file extensions: disk drivers (**.DSK**), network drivers (**.LAN**), name space modifiers (**.NAM**), and management utilities (**.NLM**). NetWare stores these modules in the **SYS:\SYSTEM** directory. Third-party products can supply additional NLMs for special purposes, and these may be stored anywhere.

To load an NLM immediately, go to the system console (or use **RCONSOLE**), and at the console prompt ':' type **load (path\NLMname parameters)**. Various amounts of the server's memory is used by each loaded NLM. To unload, type **unload (NLMname)**. Unloading a module releases its allocated server memory. If you unload any NLMs that are not management/server applications (in other words, **.NAM**, **.LAN** or **.DSK** modules), observe precautions for the sake of your users.

NLMs are usually loaded automatically when the server is booted. To do this, edit the **AUTOEXEC.NCF** file (system startup script) from **SYSCON**. An example is shown in Figure 7.4.

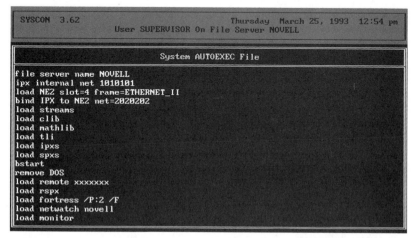

FIGURE 7.4   Editing the NetWare server's startup script, AUTOEXEC.NCF

Configuring a NetWare Client

Chances are good that you will someday have to configure a NetWare client. It may be either a PC or a UNIX workstation, but either way, it has to speak IPX. This discussion starts with setting up the protocol drivers for PCs and works into logins and other matters of consequence to any NetWare client machine.

PC network drivers

If you are preparing a PC, you must load three layers of hardware and protocol drivers. The first of these layers, the ODI driver, forms the link with the hardware LAN adapter. Chapter 5 provides information about loading this driver and its related files **LSL.COM**, **NET.CFG**, and **IPXODI.COM**. The **NET.CFG** file is particularly important. It provides startup data for binding the adapter drivers to your network protocol. However, before you jump into that installation process, read about the IPX layer and modifying NetWare's frame type, both discussed below.

The IPX layer

The second layer of drivers establishes the IPX protocol. The **IPX.COM** driver manages the packaging of data in IPX protocol packets for transmission to the server. It also unwraps packets received from the server. **IPXODI.COM** performs similar functions to **IPX.COM**, but in a slightly different way. You need one or the other on a PC, but not both. If you are preparing a UNIX workstation to be a NetWare client, the IPX protocol driver is usually supplied by the client software vendor as a platform-specific UNIX program under a different name.

The first practical difference between these two PC-based IPX protocol drivers is that you usually generate **IPX.COM** yourself, using Novell-supplied utilities and source code files, for a particular adapter. You usually get **IPXODI.COM** from Novell or a third-party vendor. Secondly, because **IPX.COM** is generated for the exact hardware in the machine, it needs to read no external data file to configure itself at boot time. On the other hand, **IPXODI.COM** requires the Link Support Layer (**LSL.COM**) and an ODI driver to be installed, as well as the **NET.CFG** configuration file to help LSL bind the protocol(s) to the adapter. Thirdly, if you use the **IPX.COM** workstation shell in a multiprotocol environment, your machines must all use the same frame type, or you will be unable to talk to some of them (probably the TCP/IP machines, since they don't use NetWare's default frame type). If you use **IPXODI.-COM** with **LSL.COM** and **NET.CFG**, you can bind more than one frame type to the same LAN adapter and communicate with all machines.

IPX.COM and **IPXODI.COM** go by version numbers. According to one vendor, **IPX.COM** version 2.0 has a bug that can prevent the NETX version number and mapped drives from being communicated to their software. If you need to, you can find out your version number by typing **IPX I** or **IPX ?** for help.

The NetWare shell

The NETx NetWare shell is the highest-level protocol driver for NetWare. This software component, sometimes called a redirector, is the first point of contact between a network-aware application and devices across the network. It makes the file server's disk drive accessible to the client machine.

NETX.COM/.EXE (or **NET3**, **NET4**, **NET5**, depending upon DOS version) intercepts an application's requests for DOS services. If the request can be handled by DOS locally, it passes the request on to the normal DOS routines for servicing and pretends not to be nosy. If the application requests services which are located across the network, such as a request for a shared file, **NETX** redirects the request to the file server, circumventing DOS. To do this, **NETX** first converts the request into NetWare protocol, then passes it to IPX which transmits the request to the server. The requested file comes from the file server back to IPX, then to **NETX**, then to the calling application.

Other versions of **NETX** are provided by Novell to take advantage of **LIM/EMS** expanded memory (**EMSNETX**) and extended memory (**XMSNETX**). You must be aware of different release levels of **NETX** also. Windows 3.1 Setup recognizes four different phases of **NETX** development, pre-3.01, pre-3.21, 3.21 or higher, and 3.26 or higher. To find out which version you are using, type **NETX I**, or **NETX ?** for help.

Modifying NetWare's frame type

NetWare defaults to a frame type called Ethernet_802.3. Nearly all UNIX networks use Ethernet_II (DIX Ethernet) as the frame type. If there is no communication with the Novell server, i.e, **NETX** displays a message that "A file server could not be found", check for a frame type conflict between the workstation's **IPX.COM** or **NET.CFG** and the server. The Novell server's frame type is displayed in the LAN Information section of the Monitor program at the server console. Use Novell's **econfig** command to view the frame type at the workstation (for **IPX.COM**, or variant such as Microsoft's **MSIPX.COM**), e.g., **econfig ipx.com**. If the frame types are different, you can do one of three things:

- Use **econfig** to alter the frame type in **IPX.COM**, e.g. **econfig ipx.com shell:e** to change to Ethernet_II, or use **shell:n** for Ethernet_802.3.

- Reset the frame type on the Novell server to Ethernet_II. This also requires changing the frame type at each NetWare client machine.

- Place two frame types in **NET.CFG**, if ODI drivers are used, and bind each network to its own frame type via the Protocol statement. Here is an example:

```
Link Driver NE2000
Frame Ethernet_II
Frame Ethernet_802.3
Protocol IP 8137 Ethernet_II
Protocol IPX 0 Ethernet_802.3
```

Connecting to NetWare file servers

You can connect a NetWare client to any NetWare file server. To find out what servers are available on your network, run **SLIST** from a NetWare client. If the server you are looking for does not appear on the list, that server may have been configured to use another frame type. See Chapter 5 for more details.

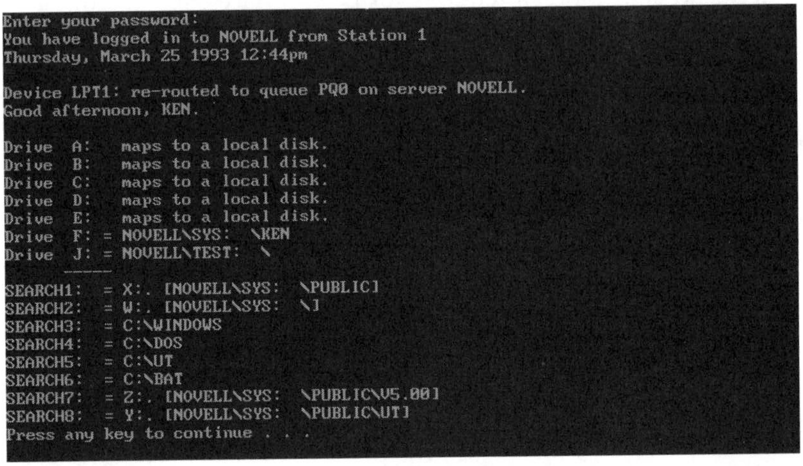

```
Enter your password:
You have logged in to NOVELL from Station 1
Thursday, March 25 1993 12:44pm

Device LPT1: re-routed to queue PQ0 on server NOVELL.
Good afternoon, KEN.

Drive  A:    maps to a local disk.
Drive  B:    maps to a local disk.
Drive  C:    maps to a local disk.
Drive  D:    maps to a local disk.
Drive  E:    maps to a local disk.
Drive  F: = NOVELL\SYS:  \KEN
Drive  J: = NOVELL\TEST:  \

SEARCH1:   = X:. [NOVELL\SYS:  \PUBLIC]
SEARCH2:   = W:. [NOVELL\SYS:  \]
SEARCH3:   = C:\WINDOWS
SEARCH4:   = C:\DOS
SEARCH5:   = C:\UT
SEARCH6:   = C:\BAT
SEARCH7:   = Z:. [NOVELL\SYS:  \PUBLIC\V5.00]
SEARCH8:   = Y:. [NOVELL\SYS:  \PUBLIC\UT]
Press any key to continue . . .
```

FIGURE 7.5 Login messages and drive mappings from a NetWare file server

You can connect to servers in two different ways: through login and attachment. Login requires **LOGIN.EXE** to be located on the server in the **SYS:\PUBLIC** directory. Here are sample driver startup and NetWare login lines from **AUTOEXEC.-BAT**, using an ODI LAN adapter driver (line two):

```
LSL
SMC8000
IPXODI
NETX
F:LOGIN NOVELL/KEN
```

When you login, the system or user login script on that server governs what drive mappings are performed, among other things. See the example in Figure 7.5.

Logging in to a second server automatically logs you off the first server. Again, if you get an "Unknown file server" message, check the frame type.

After you login to a server, other servers can be attached using the **ATTACH** command. Execute **ATTACH** commands from either the command line, or more permanently from the login script. (See System Console below.) Then use **MAP** to map the volume/drive to a particular drive letter, as viewed from your client station. Here is an example for the Puzzle SoftNet Utilities server, as you might enter it in the system login script:

```
ATTACH PUZZLE/%LOGIN_NAME
MAP K:=PUZZLE/SYS:%LOGIN_NAME
```

When you wish to leave the computer, you should **LOGOUT**. This properly terminates the connection with the Server.

Drive mapping

When a NetWare client boots, NetWare always looks for a **LASTDRIVE=** command in its **CONFIG.SYS**. It then maps the first server volume (typically **SYS**) as the next drive after **LASTDRIVE**, the second volume to the following drive letter, and so on. In the absence of a **LASTDRIVE** command, NetWare assigns **F:** to the first volume. Some or all of the volumes can be mapped to specific letters defined by the login scripts. Search drive mappings are also controlled by login scripts, but are assigned backwards from **Z:**. (Refer back to Figure 7.5.)

Such a scheme works well unless you integrate Microsoft LAN Manager, or LAN Manager-compatible, networks. These networks map drives up to and including **LASTDRIVE**. If you have both types of networks available to a PC, the LAN Manager network drives must map to lower drive letters than Novell. This means the LAN Manager product may not be able to access all Novell drives, and vice-versa.

DOS Environment

DOS provides storage space called the environment. This space stores paths and variables from the **PATH** and **SET** statements in **AUTOEXEC.BAT**, as well as variables from executing programs. (See Chapter 5, Setting Up a TCP/IP Network.) NetWare does not use the DOS environment, but the DOS environment can affect NetWare. (See Drive Mapping in the Troubleshooting section.)

Ordinary NetWare Supervision

Outside of setting up a NetWare file server, which you may never do, there is still the matter of everyday system administration, which you certainly will do. This will help you get going.

Using the system console

SYSCON controls most features of the NetWare environment. To modify the environment, login as Supervisor, then type **SYSCON**. Navigate the menu-driven screens using the arrow keys to locate on a listed option, as shown in Figure 7.6, Return (Enter) to select, and Escape to exit. **SYSCON** allows you to easily control accounting, file servers, group and user information, and other options. If you login as other than the Supervisor, you may only view most information. UNIX-based NetWare servers have their own utilities to configure the interface between NetWare and UNIX. For example, SunSelect's NetWare SunLink (which has a tight integration

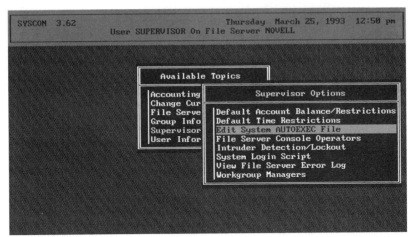

FIGURE 7.6 The supervisor can set network options from any NetWare node

with NetWare) provides both a standard **SYSCON** and **sconsole**. **Sconsole** makes the final connections to UNIX.

User accounts

You must set up a user account for each potential user. Run **SYSCON** as supervisor to set up new user accounts, including passwords and account restrictions. This process creates a user directory on the server in the **SYS** volume. On most NetWare LANs, anyone can login as the user **GUEST** without a password. This account has many restrictions, but allows access to public programs and printers.

NetWare passwords are not case-sensitive, because DOS is not case-sensitive. They are independent of any UNIX account passwords the user may also have. Use **SYSCON** to set up initial passwords for new users. Users run **SETPASS** to change their passwords.

NetWare 3.x encrypts user passwords, but NetWare 2.x does not. Many UNIX applications for NetWare connectivity do not support encrypted NetWare passwords, either. You may need to set a software switch to allow unencrypted as well as encrypted passwords, for the sake of these applications. To do this, place the line **set allow unencrypted passwords = ON** in the NetWare servers **AUTOEXEC.NCF** startup script. As supervisor, you can edit the file from **SYSCON**. Then down and restart the server.

Installing PC software on NetWare file servers

User application software is loaded on the server from a client PC, not from the server console. (The server console does not provide a DOS prompt.) Note the following directions: login to the server; then go to the proper drive by typing the drive letter followed by a colon. Use the **MD**, **RD**, and **CD** commands to make, remove and change to directories. Copy files using the **COPY** command. However, DOS/

Windows software generally provides an installation utility that performs these operations for you. Additional changes may be made to initialization and startup files on the local PC—these do not affect the NetWare fileserver.

Check disk usage before you attempt to load software. The DOS utility **CHKDSK** will not work on a NetWare drive. Instead, use **CHKVOL** and **CHKDIR** to obtain information on disk usage. On a user-by-user basis you can restrict disk space using **USERDEF** or **MAKEUSER**. If your server is located on a UNIX workstation, you can check disk usage for entire filesystems from a UNIX console using the **df** command.

Do not load UNIX software into filesystems allocated for DOS because NetWare clients cannot run it. The converse is also true.

Once the software has been loaded, make sure that all intended users can access the directory and files with the proper privileges. Make these Trustee Directory Assignments from **SYSCON**. See the example in Figure 7.7.

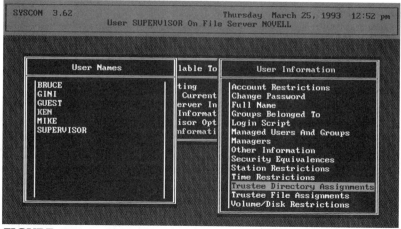

FIGURE 7.7 Assigning directory rights with SYSCON

DOS versions 3.1 and higher support file locking to permit file-sharing. Novell NetWare supports locking on both the file and record level. The applications determine how files are opened and locked.

File characteristics

LAN-to-LAN products must deal with the difference in file characteristics between DOS and UNIX. The three major differences are in naming, attributes, and file structure. Novell (DOS) files are named using the 8.3 convention: 8 character primary name followed by a dot (period) and a 3-character extension. Certain extensions are reserved, such as **EXE**, **COM**, and **BAT** for executable program, command, and batch files. Other extensions indicate a file's function (**DAT**, **INI**, **ERR**), format (**TXT**, **ASC**, **BIN**, **PCX**), or source code (**C**, **BAS**, **ASM**). You are free to make up new extensions or not use them, but their use is preferred. You should avoid punctuation in filenames, although many characters are legal. Filenames are not case-sensitive—everything converts to uppercase automatically. DOS filenames can be viewed under UNIX without modification, but long UNIX filenames must be converted for viewing under DOS. See Name Space below.

DOS supplies only four file attributes: Archive, Read-Only, Hidden, and System. These can be revealed using the **ATTRIB** (filename) command. Novell adds many more attributes for networking purposes: Copy Inhibit, Sharable, Read-Write, etc., including attributes for directories. Use **FILER** to view and set attributes, or **NDIR** to view only.

Textual DOS files are structured differently than UNIX text files. DOS text files add a Carriage Return (**ASCII 13** or **0x0D**) to the end of each line before the linefeed character (**ASCII 10** or **0x0A**). When a file is converted from DOS to UNIX format, the Carriage Return must be stripped off; or added back if converted from UNIX to DOS. There can be other changes as well, such as CTRL-Zs to end a file, and others. Most versions of UNIX supply text file conversion utilities, but they may not make 100% of the changes you need.

Printing

Use **PCONSOLE** to configure your network printers, servers, and print queues. The queues-and-servers structure allows your print jobs to be sent to different printers, depending upon document content, speed of the printer, or printer location.

You can find detailed information about configuring your NetWare network for printing in Chapter 11. In brief, you must first create a print queue, or a print job storage area, for each printer. Then, define a print server to actually deliver those print jobs to the printer as they arrive. One server definition can be tied to several queues. Finally, start the **PSERVER** program on a dedicated workstation, on the file server, or (rarely) on a bridge.

Many installations use the **CAPTURE** command to redirect parallel port output to a print queue. It allows you to print files from the command line and use the Shift-PrntScr key to print screens. You can place **CAPTURE** in the system login script for the sake of all network users. **NPRINT** is similar to **CAPTURE**, but prints files from the command line.

Miscellaneous utilities

NetWare provides a long list of utilities for NetWare clients. These are stored in the **SYS:\PUBLIC** directory, and include such utilities as **SALVAGE**, **CAPTURE**, **SYSCON**, **PCONSOLE**, and printer definition files. Seek more information from the NetWare Utilities Reference manual. Products such as SunSelect's NetWare SunLink provide the same utilities, but others such as Puzzle SoftNet Utilities do not.

Linking UNIX with the Microsoft Windows Environment

This section describes major points about Windows 3.1 connectivity. It does not, however, deal with the newer networking versions of Windows, namely Windows for Workgroups 3.1 and Windows NT. For information about those products and the connectivity transformations they have undergone, see Chapter 14. Most of the world still uses plain Windows 3.1, so we devote attention to it here.

Windows 3.x itself does not do any resource-mounting for you—that is almost always performed from your PC startup script **AUTOEXEC.BAT**, or batch files called from **AUTOEXEC.BAT**. However, you must inform Windows of these resources by 1) connecting remote drives and printers, and 2) installing any network driver supplied by the network vendor. As a network integrator, you need to have basic knowledge of certain Windows utilities and procedures.

Starting the Network on a Windows PC

Always start Windows after you have started the network(s). If you start the network(s) from within Windows you will likely be disappointed when either it, or Windows, doesn't run. After you install any network product, and especially if you start windows automatically on boot, check your **AUTOEXEC.BAT** file. If the install program placed lines for the network after the **WIN** line you will have to move them ahead of it. Most installation programs for TCP/IP products change **AUTOEXEC.-BAT** for you, but very few get this right.

AUTOEXEC.BAT usually invokes all remote drive and printer mounts as well. Mounts, login, and user authentication nearly always occur before Windows is started. Some networks allow you to login/logout from the Networks utility in the Control Panel, but most do not.

Using the File Manager

After you install an NFS product, test it under Windows from the File Manager. Any remote drive that has been mounted and connected shows up as another drive icon, and you may click on it to see the contents. If you have not connected the drive yet, but it has been mounted from a startup file, you can select Disks from the menu bar, then Network/Browse to see what is available (see Figure 7.8). Select the drive and press Connect.

Once you establish a connection, Windows remembers it for next time and connects the drive automatically, until you Disconnect it.

Disconcerting Disconnect

Do not Disconnect a drive while its files may be in use by another application. This is a good way to hang your computer and lose data.

File Manager is sensitive to low memory/swap space conditions, so if you are just squeaking by on memory it may show up there first—File Manager won't load when you click on its icon. If this happens, read about 386 Enhanced Virtual Memory below.

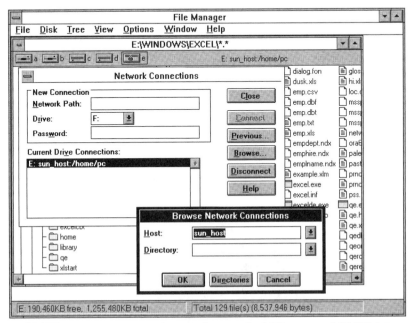

FIGURE 7.8   File Manager lets you browse for NFS-mounted UNIX drives

Under Windows 3.0 the File Manager mistakenly converts host names and file-system names to uppercase characters before attempting connection. As any UNIX administrator knows, this makes 3.0 practically useless in a UNIX environment, where almost every name is lowercase. Beame & Whiteside's BW-NFS compensates for this by re-converting the name to all lowercase, but that does not correct the flaw 100%. Upgrade to Windows 3.1.

Using the Print Manager

The Print Manager allows you to connect network printers and manage network print queues. In order to connect to network printers from Windows applications, you need to have installed the vendor's network driver. The Print Manager printer connection windows are similar to those for the File Manager (see Figure 7.9). Select Options Network Connections to Browse for printers. Or, find the same windows from the Printers icon on the Control Panel. Once you have connected a printer, Windows tries to re-establish that connection each time you start Windows. Browsing for UNIX printers depends upon the capabilities of the network driver you have loaded

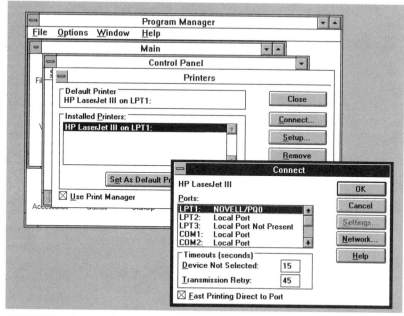

FIGURE 7.9 Windows Printers utility finds a NetWare print queue

and the version of the **pcnfsd** daemon running on the remote UNIX host. **Pcnfsd** must be version 2 to permit printer browsing.

For additional information about installing printers, see Chapter 6, Installing NFS, and Chapter 11, Connecting Printers. Also see the evaluations of specific products for hints.

Configuration for Networks

You only see the Networks icon on the Control Panel if a network driver has been loaded. Network vendors are responsible for supplying a Windows-compatible driver for their network. Along with it, they can supply a custom window for their product, which displays when you click on the Networks icon. (Consequently, your Windows User's Guide has almost nothing to say about this icon.) Some vendor windows are mostly informational, others provide tidbits of useful options. Some go so far as to let you login/logout from the network or send messages to other network users. With most products you rarely need to invoke this window. See the Novell NetWare example in Figure 7.10.

The Networks utility depends upon a network driver being loaded in Windows Setup. Only one network driver can be loaded at a time. However, Beame & Whiteside does something a little tricky. BW-NFS lets you load the NetWare driver first, then load BW's driver over the top of it. BW keeps both, allowing you to see both

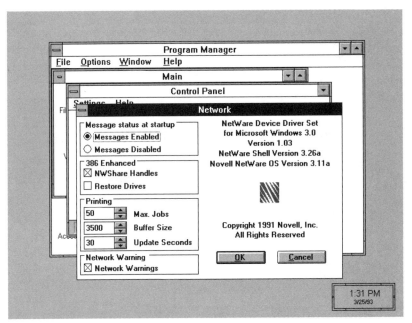

FIGURE 7.10   Enabling Netware messages under Windows is easily done

screens from the Networks utility. For other enhanced multinetwork support, see the
Cogent Data Technologies WinNet Plus product evaluated in Chapter 13.

386 Enhanced Virtual Memory

Microsoft Windows in 386 Enhanced mode makes use of a hard disk swap area.
Installing a lot of RAM (12-20 megabytes) is the best way to prepare for running
Windows, but if you don't have it, Windows uses a swap area to store and retrieve
information to and from memory. This enables Windows to keep many applications
open at once, including non-Windows applications running in the background. 386
Enhanced mode cannot be used by 286 computers. The alternative to 386 Enhanced
mode is Standard mode, which does work on 286s, but which does not use virtual
memory or allow non-Windows applications to run in the background.

The more disk space you allocate for Virtual Memory, the faster Windows will
perform, but the less disk space you have available for applications. If your hard
drive is nearly full, do some housecleaning; delete old stuff you don't need or back it
up onto floppies. Or, you can use another logical or physical drive such as **D:**, if you
have one, for the swap area (as long as it is not a network drive). Permanent swap
space is faster than temporary swap space because it avoids disk fragmentation. Figure 7.11 shows the Virtual Memory setup windows.

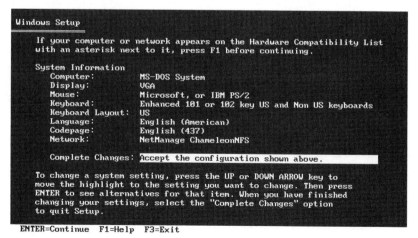

FIGURE 7.11   Setting swap space with the Virtual Memory window

Using the Windows Setup Utility

You load network drivers through Windows Setup. While you can run Setup off of the Windows Accessories window, most products recommend you run it from the DOS prompt after first exiting Windows. Figure 7.12 shows the Setup menu.

```
Windows Setup

     If your computer or network appears on the Hardware Compatibility List
     with an asterisk next to it, press F1 before continuing.

     System Information
          Computer:            MS-DOS System
          Display:             VGA
          Mouse:               Microsoft, or IBM PS/2
          Keyboard:            Enhanced 101 or 102 key US and Non US keyboards
          Keyboard Layout:     US
          Language:            English (American)
          Codepage:            English (437)
          Network:             NetManage ChameleonNFS

          Complete Changes:   Accept the configuration shown above.

     To change a system setting, press the UP or DOWN ARROW key to
     move the highlight to the setting you want to change. Then press
     ENTER to see alternatives for that item. When you have finished
     changing your settings, select the "Complete Changes" option
     to quit Setup.

  ENTER=Continue  F1=Help  F3=Exit
```

FIGURE 7.12   Loading the NetManage network driver via Windows Setup

If the network installation program does not install the driver for you, your network vendor will supply instructions on how to do it by hand. However, we have gotten stuck in loops using Setup. This happens when Setup asks you for a diskette which does not have the drivers you are requesting. If it asks for a Windows diskette, and you are sure you have the right Windows diskette in the drive, try specifying an alternate path such as **C:\WINDOWS\SYSTEM**. Depending upon your situation, the drivers may already be loaded there. You might also try specifying the directory where the network programs are located.

Installing UNIX Software (for the UNIX Novice)

Here is a word for those who might have to load UNIX software—thinking particularly of those creating Novell NetWare file servers on a UNIX workstation. Installing software on UNIX computers can be more complicated and confusing than installing software on PCs. First of all, you should select the proper filesystem. Usually, the root (/) and **/usr** filesystems are reserved for UNIX system software, so don't install software there unless instructed to by the vendor. Usually the workstation has a large filesystem, often on a large external drive, for the purpose of installing the bulk of applications. This filesystem may be called **/home** or some other name. To see how much space is available in each of the UNIX filesystems, type the **df** command from a UNIX prompt.

Startup scripts may require editing. The **/etc/rc.local** file typically contains the lines that load server daemons. The **.cshrc** (for c-shell), **.profile**, or **.login** files usually set the environment variables and paths needed by applications. See Chapter 1 and Appendix A for further details.

Occasionally, a networking software installation program builds a new kernel, or operating system shell for the UNIX host. Rebuilding the kernel (called **/vmunix** on Sun SPARCstations), including new source code, may be required to integrate new networking capabilities with UNIX. For example, SunSelect's NetWare SunLink's new kernel loads drivers for IPX, SPX, and other NetWare protocols. If you must rebuild a kernel, specific instructions will be provided to you by the vendor. Save a copy of your original kernel under another name as a safeguard, but be aware that a kernel is very large in size—store it in a filesystem that has ample room.

Troubleshooting

Since many of the errors and troubleshooting techniques are the same as for troubleshooting TCP/IP networks, you may find answers to your questions in Chapter 5, Setting Up a TCP/IP Network. Look here for solutions to several common Novell internetworking problems. Titles in quotes are Novell error messages. Many of the hints will also apply to other PC LANs. This section identifies the most likely troublemakers.

"Could not find a board that supports IPX"

- The IPX protocol has not been assigned a frame type. A Protocol statement is needed in **NET.CFG**.

"A file server could not be found"

- You may have loaded the wrong ODI LAN adapter driver or IPX shell (they don't always tell you).
- For ODI, the **NET.CFG** entry for the driver may be incorrect or missing.
- The frame type may be set incorrectly.
- The server may be down.

Drive mapping error

- This problem occurs when a drive you have mapped in the login script does not display at login time. This problem may be intermittent, depending upon the contents of your startup scripts. It often leads to another problem—the TCP/IP kernel or other program on that drive will not load from **AUTOEXEC.-BAT**. Look for a statement in **AUTOEXEC.BAT** that uses a drive/path before logging into that file server. This can easily happen if you load a TCP/IP networking product on a network drive; the install program sets the **PATH** in **AUTOEXEC.BAT** without intelligently checking login first.

Login Failure: Access Denied

- The user you specified may not have an account on the target system. Use **SYSCON** to create a User account. Also make sure that the user name and password were entered correctly. Enter the password for a NetWare LAN user via **SYSCON**. This password is not directly linked to any UNIX account password.

Login Failure: Unencrypted Passwords

- The product has tried to login to the Novell server using an unencrypted password. You must set the server to allow unencrypted passwords, because the product trying to login probably has no capability to encrypt.

"Invalid drive specification"

- If the "**F:**" (or similar) login command generates this error, although it was working before you installed a TCP/IP product, you have a **LASTDRIVE** problem in **CONFIG.SYS**. **LASTDRIVE** was probably set to Z for the sake of a Microsoft-based redirector program, which uses all drives up through **LAST-**

DRIVE. Novell claims the first drive after **LASTDRIVE.** Change **LASTDRIVE** to **E** or another letter—it will pose no problem to NFS or TCP/IP. If there is no **LASTDRIVE**, Novell will use drive **F:** for the first network drive. If you do set **LASTDRIVE** to a new letter, make sure your login command in **AUTOEXEC.-BAT** looks to the right drive, which is usually one letter after **LASTDRIVE.**

Unreliable or non-existent communications with the NetWare file server

•Both the TCP/IP vendor's kernel and NetWare's **NETX** redirector wait for packets to transmit from the application to the file server. The last of these to load is the first to intercept packets being transmitted. If the packet is not for that program's network, it must allow the packet to pass by to the other network. Check to see which is loaded last, the TCP/IP kernel or **NETX.** Load **NETX** last if possible, as it has a reputation for being well-behaved.

•Avoid using interrupt vector 64 for communication between the TCP/IP protocol driver and the IPX driver. That vector reportedly passes all information except for the flags, which may be needed. You are rarely given the opportunity to change this number by any product, but if you are, change the interrupt in the TCP/IP setup program to 61 or another number not in use by another PC application.

Failure to attach print queue

•A print queue is needed for each print server. Use **PCONSOLE** to define a print queue.

Print queue does not empty to the printer

•The print server is not functioning, or no print server has been assigned to service this queue. Use **PCONSOLE** to check the Currently Attached Servers. If you are sending print jobs to a print server on the UNIX system, check to see that the print server process is running, using the **ps** command. If it does not appear in the process list, start it. If it is in the process list, kill it, and restart it. If you are using a DOS-based print server, make sure **PSERVER** is running.

"Unknown file server"

•The network number you entered on the UNIX side may be incorrect.

•The name of the file server is incorrect.

•The frame type of the file server may be different than the client.

•The UNIX file server daemon is not running.

A DOS application on the network drive will not run

•Check in **SYSCON** to see that the user has rights to the directory containing the application. As a test, see if the Supervisor (who has all rights) can run the program.

•The application directory may need to be placed in the search path. Check the login script(s) for search drive mappings.

8

Using X Servers on PCs

Introduction

Sometimes you need more than file sharing and printer sharing between your DOS and UNIX systems. You need to share applications as well as the underlying data and peripherals. When you want to go from a DOS PC (stand-alone or networked) to the UNIX host, solutions come at you from all directions. There are the character-based terminal emulation programs, Microsoft Windows serial interfaces like VisionWare's PC-Connect, and Windows-based X servers. Each finds a niche in a particular situation. However, if your goal is to take full advantage of the graphical environments on both sides of the DOS—UNIX computing world, you have only one good choice—a Microsoft Windows-based X server. Here we describe a Microsoft Windows-based X server, go over the installation issues, and examine some of the problems you might face putting these products to work for you.

X Windows System

We discuss X Windows System and client/server computing in Chapter 1. If these concepts tend to confuse you as much as they do the rest of the world, take a peek at that discussion again. As a quick refresher, X is a standard method of communicating across a network between two applications—the X client and the X server. Remember that X is independent of both hardware and operating system. While generally associated with UNIX, there is no reason any operating system or piece of hardware cannot run X. This single factor contributes greatly to its popularity. If you need more information about how X works or how to configure your X environment from the UNIX side of the house, check out the Appendix for the many good books on X and configuring your X environment.

The X Client

The X client represents an application—with all of its respective data, functions, and menus. For example, a word processor such as WordPerfect for Sun or a visualization program such as PV-WAVE running in UNIX can be the X client. The X client can reside anywhere on the network. The host machine does not need the ability to display graphics; it may not even have a display at all. The X client uses the host machine for its disk, RAM, and processing. It does not utilize the host machine's display facilities unless the host machine is also the X server.

The X Server

The X server is a separate software application that handles the input and display activities of the X client. This includes video output, mouse movements, and keyboard input. Communication over the network between the server and the client occurs using the X protocol. An X server can be running from a workstation such as an IBM RS/6000, or it can be running on an X terminal such as those manufactured by NCD Inc. or Tektronix Inc. However, these are examples of hardware boxes dedicated to running X applications. What if you already have the PC and want to keep your PC applications, but you need access to X applications without multiple machines on your desktop? The Windows-based X server becomes your answer. A software product running under Microsoft Windows, the Windows-based X server uses the existing hardware display and graphics adapter of the PC as part of the equation. Figure 8.1 shows you how this might fit on your network.

The X Server Market

According to the X Business Group Inc. (Fremont, Calif.), the PC X server market is expected to grow from only 50,000 units sold in 1991, evenly split between DOS X servers and Windows X servers, to over two million units by 1996, nearly all Microsoft Windows-based X servers. They predict this growth based on the strength of Microsoft Windows and on the continued need of corporations to internetwork DOS and UNIX. We cover Windows-based offerings almost solely, simply because

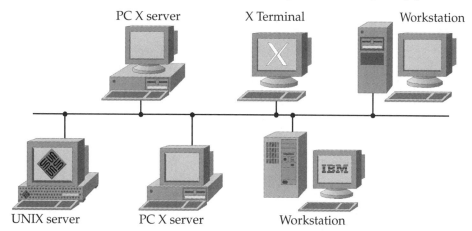

PC X server   X Terminal   Workstation

UNIX server   PC X server   Workstation

FIGURE 8.1 A typical network with PC X servers

Windows-based machines comprise almost the entire market of new machines sold. Users needing access to the graphical world of X applications seldom use DOS as their primary working environment. However, there are DOS-based X servers on the market as well. While we do not review them in Chapter 15, we have tried to mention when a vendor has a DOS companion X server.

In 1991, the last year for which full statistics are available, the X Business Group indicated the following as the leading vendors of PC X servers: Hummingbird Communications (Exceed/W), VisionWare Limited (XVision), NCD (PC-XWare), AGE Logic (Xoftware), and Integrated Inference Machines (X11/AT). These products form the backbone of our testing and are all evaluated in Chapter 15.

While the latest release of the X Windows System server is X11 Release 5, some PC X server products still use X11R4. The release number of X11 is comparable to any OS new release. If a vendor chooses to write an application that only works with the latest version, you need that version. The same is true of X. However, it is our experience that nearly all common X clients work with X11R4 since most workstation vendors still ship this version of X.

The forthcoming Windows NT also adds a degree of difficulty to our evaluation process. At the time of our final copy, Windows NT was still in beta and not shipping (early summer 93). It is highly likely that when you read this book, NT will be shipping. Some vendors have committed to shipping NT X servers, and these are mentioned in Chapter 15 where appropriate. We did evaluate the beta copy of Windows NT in Chapter 14. Since there are over 20 million users of Windows 3.1, many will continue to use Windows 3.1 as their primary desktop interface for some time. In addition, all X servers that run under Windows 3.1 also run under Windows NT. The major advantage of NT and a 32-bit X server relates to performance. If you choose the TCP/IP connections provided by Microsoft, you will need an appropriate driver from the X server vendor.

Why Choose a PC X Server?

Making the decision to support Windows-based X servers in your organization requires careful consideration. As our later discussion shows, X servers are not trivial products, both in terms of resources required and potential problems. But these difficulties should not prevent you from looking at the advantages of using a Windows-based X server.

Advantages

There are situations in which you should choose an X server over the alternatives. The primary consideration in most cases is whether you want to keep your Intel-based PC and DOS/Windows applications without having an extra machine on the desk. An X server also enables you to:

• Access critical graphical UNIX applications that are not available on a DOS PC;

• Avoid investing in new silicon—such as X terminals or workstations;

• Share information between a DOS application and a UNIX application, when creating true interoperable applications takes more time and money than you can afford;

• Optimize the use of under-utilized UNIX CPU power on the network by running some applications on the UNIX CPU;

• Continue using your currently-owned copies of DOS and Microsoft Windows programs.

Limitations

The limits to a Window-based X server are apparent. On a workstation, the X server is an integral part of the GUI. Therefore, to the average user, the client and server seem to function together. However, in the case of connecting a PC to an X-based workstation, the differences become pronounced. Here are some of the limitations:

• If you do not already have the TCP/IP connection between your PC and the UNIX network, a PC X server can be expensive.

• For graphics-intensive and processor-intensive applications, an X server may challenge the snail for slowness. In some cases performance may simply be inadequate. We noticed abrupt differences in performance when running certain applications on a Windows-based X server vs. the same applications on an NCD X-terminal, even when the PC was a 486 50MHz machine.

• PC screen sizes tend to cluster around the 14 or 15-inch area with 800x600 resolution being the highest possible on such a small screen. This often makes an X application, designed to roam about on a 17 or 19-inch screen, difficult to use. Some applications may not work correctly on a smaller screen, because they need at least 1024 x 768 resolution.

Basic PC Requirements

X servers require more resources and computer power than other DOS—UNIX connectivity options. The main reasons are visibly obvious—Microsoft Windows and X. These two graphical environments make significant demands on the processor and system memory. Constantly redrawing the screen and moving information around takes its toll on even the fastest machine.

While many vendors quote the typical Windows system specifications as the machine size necessary to operate an X server, we suggest you do not run an X server on a machine with anything less than our suggested requirements. On a machine with less than 6M of RAM, we find performance unacceptable.

A video accelerator card with Windows drivers should also be considered a mandatory requirement. The X server puts tremendous pressure on the screen redraws in Windows. A variety of video cards fit the definition of a Windows accelerator card. The list includes the ATI Graphics Ultra (ATI Technologies Inc.) and the Paradise Accelerator Card (Western Digital Corp.). Other than the 2 to 4 M of disk space required for the X server products files, there is no specific disk requirement for running X applications. We base our disk recommendations on what a typical Windows PC needs for effective operation.

If you have less powerful machines in your possession, such as 286 machines, or if your needs tend towards character-based connectivity, consider some of the other connectivity options such as serial interfaces discussed in Chapter 16.

Windows-Based X Server Minimum Configuration

386SX processor running at 20 MHz or faster
4M RAM
80M Hard Disk
14-inch Super VGA monitor
Ethernet Card
TCP/IP Software
Mouse
Windows 3.1, DOS 3.3

Windows-Based X Server Preferred Configuration

386DX processor running at 25 MHz or faster
8M RAM
120M Hard Disk
17-inch Super VGA monitor
Windows Video Accelerator Card w/1M RAM
Ethernet Card
3-button mouse
TCP/IP Software
WIndows 3.1, DOS 6.0

The Costs

What can you expect cost-wise to get an X server up and running? It can be relatively cheap. However, if you are beginning with only a stand-alone PC minus the network connection, expenses run up quickly. Here's the break down.

First, you need a PC that meets minimum requirements for speed, memory, and storage. Count on $1000 being your low-end cost, and closer to $2000 if you buy the preferred configuration model. Of course, in most cases, an X server makes sense only if you already have the PC. If you don't really need the PC in all situations and don't have one, purchase an X terminal from a vendor like NCD or Tektronix, or consider a diskless workstation. We discuss X terminals in Chapter 12.

Second, you need a network connection (of the TCP/IP variety) to your UNIX host. Figure on $100-$200 for a simple 8-bit network interface card—about $25 for the cabling and connectors, and $100-$450 for the TCP/IP software. Software cost varies widely depending on the number of machines you intend to utilize, the variety of TCP/IP utilities you desire, and the particular vendor you choose. A thorough discussion of the TCP/IP options is provided in Chapter 5 and Chapter 13.

Third, the X server itself typically costs about $495 retail. Mail order shopping reduces the price, but you usually have to purchase the product from a mail order firm that caters to UNIX. Few PC mail order firms carry X servers.

HOT TIP	Purchasing UNIX Software
	You don't have to buy UNIX software from that high priced, value-added reseller anymore. Within the last two years, UNIX mail order houses have appeared. These firms make buying UNIX software as easy and cheap as buying PC software has been for years. Products are usually well-stocked, and the sales people, knowledgeable. Check the Appendix for vendors.

Finally, you need X-based applications. This represents the forgotten cost of getting an X server up and running. Presumably you have some applications on your UNIX workstations. However, depending on the license agreement, many products like FrameMaker (Frame Technology Corp.) and IslandWrite (Island Graphics Corp.) require more licenses if you have additional users. Licensing comes in a variety of forms. On a UNIX workstation, a license can exist for each individual user; this is termed a "per user" license. A more popular option on UNIX networks is to procure a floating license. In this case, you purchase a set number of licenses based on maximum desired users. Any user on the network can use the product, though once all licenses are in use, no more users are allowed until someone releases a license. The third type of licensing depends on the size of your platform and not the number of users. We recommend you stay away from applications that do not offer a floating license or a per user license.

In either case, you need to figure in the cost of additional licenses. An extra license can run anywhere from 25% to 100% of the original cost of the first license (depending on the number of licenses purchased, the original price of the product, and the platform being used). Historically, the cost of UNIX single user applications have been higher than comparable PC applications. This is changing as more and more PC vendors sell into the UNIX marketplace. WordPerfect is an example of a vendor who sets similar prices for both platforms. Figure about $300 per application and probably two applications for every installation just as a guide.

The grand total is over $4,000 if you are starting from scratch and nearly $2,000 when starting with the PC. The total cost is far more reasonable if the PC network connection is already available or part of a planned purchase. In this scenario, an X server costs about $800 per PC. Still not cheap, but it gives you one of the most flexible workstations on the market. Where else can you get DOS, Windows, and UNIX-based X clients all within a single desktop?

Installing Your Windows X Server

If you do not have a TCP/IP connection up and running, go back to Chapter 5 and find out what you need and how to set it up. The process of installing an X server could try the nerves of the Man of Steel, so we advise you to set aside some time to be sure that your network runs properly. The individual X server vendors provide detailed information about how to install their product. In general, they do a good job. Even so, there are a variety of issues that warrant your special attention. The most difficult installation issues become the use of additional drivers by the Windows X servers and how to best make use of memory and installation order. Here we provide some pointers.

Working with TCP/IP

The most difficult problem in getting an X server to work involves the underlying TCP/IP network and communications. There is a wide disparity among vendors on handling communications to Windows. Many TCP/IP networks do not have explicit Windows support. Here we describe the various options; your choice will depend on the network communications software you are using.

The TCP/IP software can be DOS-based. These products use a TSR-based method of communication. In order for a Windows-based X server to talk to the communication protocol, it must load a TSR before Windows is loaded, since Windows takes up precious low DOS memory. The X server talks to its own DLL, which in turn talks to its own TSR, which in turn talks to the TCP/IP TSR. See Figure 8.2 for a pictorial representation of this chain.

A second option, the communication protocol, is Windows-aware. In this case, the communication vendor can uses a DLL-based stack (with or without an additional TSR-stack). The X server again talks to its DLL which in turn talks to the communication protocol DLL. This saves one step in the process, but depending on the number of layers, some disadvantages in terms of speed are possible. Additionally, the X server vendor must have a DLL for every communication protocol vendor.

A third option is quickly gaining ground with all vendors. Microsoft now has an API toolkit available for vendors to write standard DLLs. It is called the WinSock

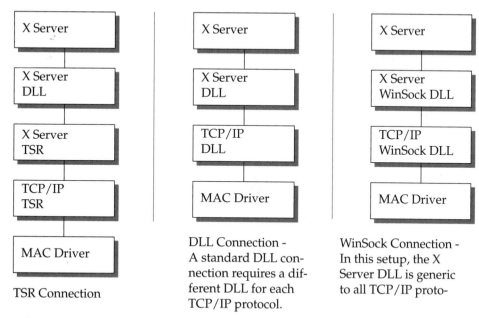

FIGURE 8.2 Three ways to make an X server connection to the network

specification. If the communication protocol vendor has written its DLLs to the Win-Sock specification, the X server's job becomes much easier. Many TCP/IP vendors are now writing their drivers to the WinSock specification. In this case, the X server vendor needs only to provide a single WinSock-specific DLL to connect with any protocol supporting WinSock. This makes your whole installation process smoother. In this case, the X server talks to its own DLL which in turn talks to the WinSock-compliant DLL from the communications vendor. No low DOS memory is used by any of the components.

WinSock API DLLs are still in process for most vendors. The table listed at the end of Chapter 15 provides the latest information about each X server's support for WinSock. By publication date, more vendors will support WinSock DLLs. However,

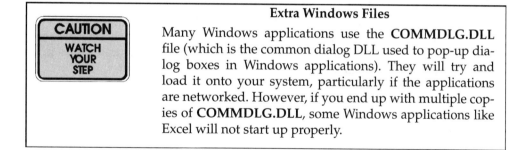

Extra Windows Files

Many Windows applications use the **COMMDLG.DLL** file (which is the common dialog DLL used to pop-up dialog boxes in Windows applications). They will try and load it onto your system, particularly if the applications are networked. However, if you end up with multiple copies of **COMMDLG.DLL**, some Windows applications like Excel will not start up properly.

vendors will still support the older TSRs and DLLs, due to the many TPC/IP software packages still installed out there.

Changes to System Files

PC X server installation programs often make changes to your system files—including your **CONFIG.SYS**, **AUTOEXEC.BAT**, **WIN. INI**, and **SYSTEM.INI** files. Depending on your perspective, this can be good or bad. When the product gives you an opportunity to see modifications and save your old files, the procedure helps hurry along the installation. However, if mistakes are made in the auto install and you have to debug them, you might wish for a little less help. In Chapter 15, we mention some specific changes and problems that occur during installation of particular products. Consider the following when installing X servers:

CONFIG.SYS

Any special communication drivers required for an X server will load in the **AUTOEXEC.BAT** file or the **WINSTART.BAT** file. No changes need to be made in the **CONFIG.SYS** file with the exception of **FILES** and **BUFFERS**. Both of these should be at least 25 and 15 respectively.

AUTOEXEC.BAT

Most X servers installation programs want to modify your **PATH** statement. Not all of them do it correctly. This occurs partly due to the multiple level of subdirectories involved with networking products. Look for bad **PATH** statements if you have errors like Cannot find xyz module or Unable to load xxx.dll. We also found that some X servers attempt to substitute their programs for ones provided by the TCP/IP vendor. This is often the case when using X servers with SunSelect's PC-NFS. In particular, the **RTM.EXE** and **RNMFILE.EXE** files are susceptible to automatic or manual substitution. DO NOT use the files provided by the X server vendor. In almost every case, you are better off using the versions supplied by Sun with PC-NFS; you can lock up your PC using the wrong versions of the **RTM.EXE** and **RNMFILE.EXE**.

If you use a TSR, it is normally inserted in the **AUTOEXEC.BAT** file, and it should be the last entry in the file before Windows is loaded. You can also create a separate batch file if you only want to load your X server occasionally. DOS 6.0 provides a special configuration feature that allows you at boot time to select various configuration options. Rather than having multiple **CONFIG.SYS** and **AUTOEXEC.BAT** files for different network setups, you create one file with specified options. The entire process is extremely simple and requires no programming. For any one using multiple protocols or various network configurations, DOS 6.0 is a life saver.

Corrupted Substitutes

Avoid using the X server's version of any TCP/IP programs. Use the copy provided by the TCP/IP vendor. In almost all cases, this is the better decision. Note this especially with PC-NFS based networks.

WIN.INI

Some X servers, such as X11/AT require you to run a program from within **WIN.-INI**. You insert the command on the **RUN** line which falls right after the first couple of lines in the file. These programs (nettask for X11/AT) can run in any order on the run line. eXceed/W also adds a product-specific list of information under its own program heading in **WIN.INI**. These change set directories and dictate which fonts are the default with eXceed/W. These changes seldom cause any problems.

SYSTEM.INI.

The **SYSTEM.INI** file gets hit by many different X servers. The resulting changes vary greatly from product to product and often relate to the use of TSRs needed for the TCP/IP stack rather than DLLs. To help you in such a situation, we have listed some of the potential changes you might see in the **SYSTEM.INI** FILE. Some products do a good job of explaining the particulars and what each command means while others just make the changes and figure you would rather not know. You usually do not have to worry about making any changes once the product is installed, but it is a good idea to create backups of your **SYSTEM.INI** and **WIN.INI** file once the X server has made its changes.

Sample Changes to the **SYSTEM.INI**:

```
[boot] heading:
network.drv=C:\EXCEEDW\SUN\PCNFS.DRV

[386Enh] heading:
device=C:\EXCEEDW\SUN\PCNFS.386
InDOSPolling=on
UniqueDOSPSP=true
PSPIncrement=5
TimerCriticalSection=1000
```

Here is an explanation of these changes to the Windows **SYSTEM.INI** file. **NET-WORK.DRV** represents the driver used with the network. Some networks do not require a driver to be set in **SYSTEM.INI**. Some X server products provide their own drivers for the appropriate networks. The **InDOSPolling** parameter is set to On or Yes when the network software needs access to *INT21*, a common interrupt used in networking. When **UniqueDOSPSP** is set to True, Windows gives each DOS session (virtual machine) a unique starting address in memory. This is necessary because some networks can get confused if multiple virtual machines start at the same address. The **PSPIncrement** represents actual memory offset, in 16-byte increments, that must to be added to each DOS session. **TimerCriticalSection** says how long windows should wait in order for network functions to continue. This helps smooth out some of the problems when Windows and the network clash for resources. You can survive just fine without knowing the specifics of these changes to your files, but it certainly doesn't hurt to know where an application is messing with your system.

HOT TIP	**DOS 6.0 Auto Configuration Menu**
	A great reason to buy DOS 6.0. When you boot, you can easily load different configuration files. If you only occasionally use an X server, you can avoid multiple startup files and confusing copy commands by using the new DOS 6. 0 configuration menus. They do not require any batch file programming.

Memory Management

X servers and TCP/IP networks provide excellent reasons for buying a third party memory manager. The standard memory utilities provided with DOS versions before 6.0 and with Windows (**HIMEM.SYS** and **EMM386.SYS**) do not provide enough options to handle the variety of requirements available in this environment. We tested Quarterdeck's QEMM. Depending on your network, you can expect either mediocre or excellent results. Discussions on the memory impacts of network setups can be found in Chapter 5. Here we limit our discussion to what happens when you try to load X server TSRs in high memory.

Memory managers are not panaceas; they do not solve all of the problems with the DOS limitation on 640K of memory. First, they can only use the memory between 640 and 1024K. Known as upper or high memory, this 384K of memory is also in demand by video adaptors, system ROM, and network cards. Second, memory managers can only load a program in contiguous areas of memory. If you have a driver that is 32K in size, and the largest free memory area available is 28K, you will not be able to load the driver high. This becomes a problem with X server TSRs for certain networks. For example, many of the TSRs used with SunSelect's PC-NFS 4.0 or earlier are 100K or more in size. In these cases, it is unlikely that your machine has a block of memory large enough. Other network TSRs, however, require less memory.

Using Quarterdeck's **LOADHI** command, you can determine the largest space available. You should first load the TSR to see how much low memory it requires. DOS 6.0 and QEMM both have a method to automatically place those drivers in high memory that fits. Even if you cannot load the driver, it might be worthwhile to purchase a memory manager so other drivers can be loaded high. In general, you can often load high device drivers for your mouse, a CD-ROM, and a sound card. Many of the network device drivers located in the **CONFIG.SYS FILE** cannot be loaded high. In particular, **PROTMAN.SYS**, **PCNFS.SYS**, Microsoft's **SMARTDRV,** and **MIRROR.COM** represent some of the drivers that usually will not load high.

HOT TIP   **WINSTART.BAT**

A little known file is the **WINSTART.BAT** file. It loads after the **WIN** command when starting windows, allowing Windows-specific TSRs to load without using low memory. Some X servers support the use of **WINSTART.-BAT** directly while others work if run from **WINSTART.-BAT** with special parameters set.

Window Managers

X servers provide a visual flexibility not available in other products. Melding an X-based graphical environment with a MS Windows environment gives you some choice when it comes to the window manager. Generally speaking, there are three different options.

Window Manager Options

All the PC X servers on the market provide the choice of using a local window manager or a remote window manager. The local window manager is either Windows itself or a Windows look-alike put into place by the X server. In this scenario, most frequently called *multiple windows mode*, each application (whether an X client coming over the network or a local Windows application) is placed inside its own window. This is the way Microsoft Windows works with Windows applications when an X server is not running. Since each X client can be iconized or placed over other applications, the screen is easier to manage. For this reason, a local window manager is our preferred method of running X applications from a PC.

Using a remote window manager is a second option—known as *single window mode*. Normally, your choices are Motif or OPEN LOOK, but OPEN LOOK applications are destined to disappear. With a remote window manager, every X application runs under the client window manager (usually Motif), but all the X applications run inside one larger MS Windows' window. We find less incentive to take this course of action, since it puts the window manager on the host and increases the network traffic. Also, many users find having all X applications sitting under one Window both awkward and inconvenient. If you want to open one X client, you must bring up the entire desktop first and then bring up your client, which is more work for the user.

This choice could be to your advantage, however, if you are already familiar with the client window manager and prefer using any special features it provides.

A third option, supported by X11/AT, is to allow both a local and a client-based window manager to run simultaneously. For example, MS Excel would be running within a MS Windows windows manager, yet Z-Mail uses Motif as the window manager. Every application gets its own window and every application uses its native window manager. This is a compromise of the other two methods. If you like Motif, this method is a good route to go.

Panning and Scrolling

Along with the design of a window manager, come various other options. For example, you can set up particular scrolling and panning abilities in certain scenarios. Scrolling only applies if you run your X server in single window mode. Scroll bars attach to the side of the X window. Panning works in either window mode. Panning allows you to move parts of an application window off to the side of the screen simply by moving the mouse off the screen. It becomes a quick way to increase screen size as shown in Figure 8.3.

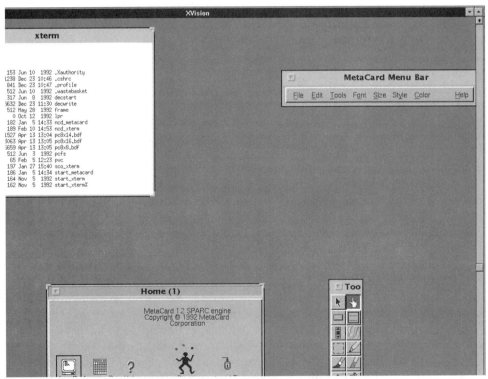

FIGURE 8.3 X server using large virtual root window with panning

A virtual root window is another way of increasing screen size. Root window is the term for the background on an X Windows display. Let's say you are running in 800 x 600 pixel mode on a 17-inch monitor. You could designate a virtual display of 1024 x 768 by making the selection in the appropriate configuration box. This increases the root window and allows larger clients to display. See our example in Figure 8.3. Notice how some of the applications have Windows partially off the screen. Notice also, the title of the X server in the title bar. It appears this way because virtual screens work only in single window mode. You can pan or scroll the virtual root window simply by moving the mouse. One advantage of the virtual screen is the ability to run X applications which require a larger screen space than is typically found on smaller PC screens.

Another aspect of the PC X server is the control it exerts over the root window. When in multiple window mode, the X server takes over the background of your display, and the root window becomes the entire screen. What this means is the screen is now an X root window and not under the control of Microsoft Windows. This often causes the cursor to be a 3-D X when it moves over the background (the same as it would be on a UNIX workstation) rather than the standard MS Windows cursor. It also means the Windows task manager cannot be called up via the mouse. This is because Microsoft Windows no longer has control over the background window. You can, however, call up a task manager with the Ctrl-Esc key sequence.

Xterm

The simplest way to run an X client from your PC is to use an **xterm** window. An **xterm** is nothing more than a graphical terminal emulation window into the UNIX workstation. An **xterm** gives you the opportunity to launch X applications or monitor system events or run character-based applications. The **xterm** has more flexibility than just using a **telnet** window into the UNIX host because an **xterm** is an X client that you run from the UNIX host. It is not a service provided as part of the X server. Every UNIX hardware or operating system vendor provides an **xterm** as part of the standard distribution. However, you cannot always find it in the same place from system to system. In some cases, **xterm** is located in /**usr/bin/X11** with other the X clients. In Sun's case, the standard **xterm** is in /**usr/openwin/lib**. Different vendors also provide substitute **xterm**s in an attempt to provide added enhancement over the standard **xterm** provided with X11R4. Table 8.1 shows information about how some different UNIX systems handle their **xterm**.

The **xterm** does a number of things for the PC user to avoid many of the UNIX problems associated with terminal emulation. (See Chapter 9.) When you use terminal emulation, UNIX applications need to know how your terminal defines and uses its keys. Terminal types are registered either in the **termcap** file or in the **terminfo** database found on the UNIX host. These special files tell the application and terminal how to work together. Terminal emulation packages termcap and terminfo and imitate common UNIX terminals to provide access to applications. **xterm** is a special terminal emulator that every UNIX system and application expects to see on the system. **xterm**, or scoterm or cmdtool or any other **xterm** variant, is found in the **termcap** file like standard terminal types. Consistency is the key. Every application expects to see the same information and can use the **xterm** terminal emulator. This makes it easier for future software developers.

Table 8.1: **UNIX xterm variations**

Platform	xterm location	xterm replacement	Location
Sun Solaris 1.x	/usr/openwin/lib	cmdtool	/usr/bin
IBM AIX	/usr/lpp/X11/bin	aixterm	/usr/lpp/X11/bin
SCO ODT	/usr/bin/X11	scoterm	/usr/bin/X11
UNIXWare	/usr/X/bin	None	

Xterm Configuration

With the standard **xterm**, you get a set of handy-dandy pop-up menus that allow you to make some on-the-fly changes to the window. To access one of these menus, push the Ctrl key and one of the three mouse buttons. Sometimes an **xterm** does not support all three menus. Your menu may look similar to the one shown in Figure 8.4.

FIGURE 8.4 xterm with pop-up menu displayed from IBM RS/6000

One of the more useful menu options puts a set of scrollbars on the **xterm**. These allow you to scroll back and look at other information. Such available options vary depending on the OS, and they are a function of the **xterm**, not of your X server software. Here we provide a brief rundown of the more common commands available. With an **xterm**, a standard layout enables the scrollbar, auto wraparound, jump scroll, and curses emulation. Other features can be added as needed. **xterm** also accepts command line input. While there is a large variety of **xterm** options available, there remains an unfortunate lack of documentation on how to use them. Most workstations do not have a manual page for **xterm** and most UNIX user books ignore X and **xterm** all together. One excellent source for learning more about your options is *Modern UNIX* by Alan Southerton, while O'Reilly's *X Window Programming* series provides another, more technical, presentation.

Common xterm Menu Options

Scrollbar	Puts a scroll bar on the side of the **xterm** window
Reverse Video	Switches the video on the **xterm** window
80/132 Column	Allows 132 columns to display on window
Jumpscroll	Enables speed scrolling
Auto Wraparound	Wraps long text and commands to the next line
Status Line	Display a single status line at the bottom of the **xterm**
MarginBell	Toggles the bell that rings when you exceed the right margin
Curses Emulation	Allows you to run a character-based program using curses

Opening an xterm

The simplest method for getting an **xterm** window up and running is to open a **telnet** window to the host and enter the **xterm** command. However, you cannot just type **xterm** at the command line. First, you should always run **xterm** in the background. In UNIX, that merely means placing an & after the command and its parameters. Second, you must indicate on which physical display or x server the **xterm** is to appear. If you simply say **xterm** &, the **xterm** window opens on the host, and you will not see it on your X server. The following command opens an **xterm** on the X server named **mike**.

xterm -display mike:0 &

The **-display** parameter is necessary anytime you run an X client on a different X server. Immediately following the parameter comes the name of the host. You can also set the display variable at start-up in the .profile. When you login via an X server, a DISPLAY variable in your **.profile** automatically sets the proper display as your X server. This ensures all X clients started during the current session display on the proper X server. If there is no alias or host name, you must use the internet address. The :0 always represents the current display of the named X server. If you login from various machines under the same user name, you need to have a script separate from the **.profile**.

X Clients

The application you run is called the X client or X application. Examples are Frame-Maker, Sun Mailtool, xclock, and Wingz. You need to know that not all X applications run correctly in a Windows-based X server. Our moderate testing indicated you should prepare for a variety of possible problems depending on your UNIX host, X server software and hardware. Some of the difficulties we encountered were independent of the X server while others were definitely related to the X server. In any case, be prepared for a few challenges in getting X servers up and running.

We had problems with cc:Mail for UNIX under nearly all the X server products. cc:Mail is extremely font sensitive. For example, under X11/AT, the title bars flickered rapidly. eXceed/W had problems as well and could not get cc:Mail to run consistently. In addition to cc:mail, MetaCard from MetaCard Inc. proved to be a problem application for X servers. XVision, for example, did not correctly handle MetaCard's multiple fonts, and occasionally other X servers crashed while attempting to run it. NCD's older X server product, PC/XView, could not run MetaCard at all. Another product, DECwrite for Sun SPARCstations, did not cooperate in many cases. DECwrite works fine on our Sun SPARCstation, but intermittently on an X server. Some of our actions crashed it, and the menus did not always work as advertised. In this case, we suspect DECwrite as the problem. Z-Mail from Z-Code Software Corp. usually worked, but at times the entire application seemed to drag and wait for the cursor to catch up.

Some OPEN LOOK applications using the NeWS server on Sun SPARCstations are not going to run on an X server or on an X terminal. The reason is simple. In the late 80s, Sun Microsystems attempted to support their own windowing system, called Network Extensible Windowing System (NeWS). It was not compatible with the X Windows System. Sun experienced only minor success in the marketplace and was forced to offer X on all SPARCstations. Sun did this by producing a combination server that supports both X and NeWS. While most applications use X, some still make use of the NeWS server—such as FrameMaker for OPEN LOOK. These applications do not work on other X server platforms—including both a PC running an X server and an X terminal. If you have such applications, you need to purchase a pure X Windows version of the product or use a Sun Workstation as the server.

The reasons for variability among application success on an X server is as different as the products. In some cases, we are confident the X server does not correctly follow the X11R4 or X11R5 specifications. In other cases, the X client is the problem. Our recommendation is simple. If you have X applications you need to run on an X

server, get a written guarantee that the application works in your configuration. Then test it before committing to the X server software.

HOT TIP	**X Client Won't Run On Sun**
	If you are using a Sun workstation, you might get a message like Library not found: SO4. You have to set the **LD_L-IBRARY_PATH** in your **.profile** equal to the path of the X libraries. On a standard installation, these are located in **/usr/openwin/lib**. This allows the Sun to find the X files it needs to open an xterm and run applications in an X server. Often, a Sun workstation does not have the environment variables set to use the standard X utilities.

Autostarting X Applications

The simplest method of making a connection between your PC and the UNIX host with an X server is to choose the **telnet** option with your X server, login to the host and then open an **xterm** window. Once you have an **xterm** window open, you can run X clients by invoking them from the command line and putting them into background. For example, bringing up Z-mail can be done by typing **zmail -gui &** at the command line. Certainly this is not difficult, but you may find it somewhat troublesome to remember commands and to get at the programs you want to run. Every Windows-based X server provides at least two alternative options for entering information each time you want to use an X application.

Many X servers, like XVision and HCL-eXceed, provide a utility which automatically loads X applications. Called Program Starter or Launch, these simplify the application startup process. The autoloader stores the application name, user login, user password, host id, and application startup script. This allows you to launch or start an X application with the mere click of your mouse. You can often store this information within a specific icon.

There are a couple of ways these autoload programs supply the need for more information. One method requires that you type all the needed commands on the command line of the dialog box. Generally, this method works when only one line is required to open an application. X11/AT follows this approach with its Launch command. Loading an **xterm** might look like the line below.

```
c:/windows/iim/launch 192.9.200.1 mike /usr/lib/X11/xterm -display mike:0 &
```

A problem with this approach is the 60 character limitation of Program Manager when it applies to parameters. This means any line can only contain 60 total characters. Given path names, internet addresses and UNIX variables, you can run into the limit quickly. If you do run into the limit, use a MS-DOS batch file where the character limit does not apply.

X servers such as Xvision and HCL-eXceed/W give you the opportunity to attach a parameter file to their launch programs. You usually provide information such as your login, user name, password, and command information about the specific application. Each parameter file opens a different X client but can be selected directly from an icon. In many products, you can create application-specific icons by placing an icon in the a Program Manager group and invoking it like any other Windows application. If the X server is not running, it is automatically started.

A second approach to starting up X clients involves creating a script in UNIX. With this method the command in the X server program starter is simple. For example, if you need to run FrameMaker from an X server, you could simply issue the command **frame** from the X server autoload program. After the connection opens, the script called **frame** executes. It sets any paths or variables needed and then executes the maker command, opening framemaker on the correct X server. The script might look something like the one listed here. Any changes or custom options can be handled within the script clearly and easily.

```
!#/bin/sh
FMHOME=/home/frame
PATH=:$FMHOME/bin:$PATH
export FMHOME PATH
if [ -z "$OPENWINHOME" ]; then   # FMHOME
   OPENWINHOME=/usr/openwin     # FMHOME
cd /home/mike
nohup /home/frame/bin/maker -display mike:0 &
```

HOT TIP   **Using Nohup**

Depending on your X server and your host, you may need to use the **nohup** command. **nohup** prevents applications started in the background from closing if your original **telnet** session is closed. If your X client does not stay open, try using the **nohup** option.

X Display Manager

Using UNIX scripts and X server-based autostart programs to load X clients is not trouble free. First, you need icons for every X client. Second, often you want to load a specific set of X clients every time you log on. Thirdly, logging on can be a difficult task for the non-computer-literate. If you have many X servers on your network, you probably want to give users some type of simple login procedure. The X Windows System provides a way around this difficulty. All MS Windows X servers provide support for X Display Manager (**xdm**) and its accompanying X Display Manager Control Protocol (XDMCP). Support for XDMCP was included as a part of X11R4.

To understand **xdm**, think of a scenario where character terminals are connected to a single host. A user turns on the terminal and is greeted with a login. When the user name and password are entered, the user is then logged into the system and often into a specific application or into some type of menu where application selections are made. The advent of X-terminals, PC-based X servers, multiple hosts, and a proliferation of networks have made this model impractical in a graphical-based multiple host environment. But there are still instances where you want to provide a direct and controlled method of logging onto the network. This is where **xdm** comes in. It provides a method for automatic logins and automatic client start-up.

You are unlikely to set up **xdm** without help from the UNIX system administrator. Most of the Windows-based X server manuals give only cursory coverage to **xdm** and none of them show you how to set it up on the UNIX host. If you are going to use **xdm**, you have a number of tasks. First, you configure the X server to choose a startup method. Second, you create or alter two X configuration files located on the UNIX host. Finally, you create an X session script to start up X clients and set your environment. Here we walk you through the basics that might just get you up and going without too much of the trouble associated with creating UNIX scripts.

Choosing a Startup Method

The first step is to establish the X server connection. Test it using the **telnet** login to insure there are no underlying TCP/IP or cable problems. Also make sure you can use some type of remote login procedure and run a client application on the host using an **xterm**. Some X servers like eXceed/W and XVision provide options on their start-up programs for choosing a method of XDMCP startup. XDMCP is a communication protocol used only when your X server attempts to make contact with a host or hosts running **xdm**. The main purpose of XDMCP is to make the connection without the hosts having to know all the X servers on the network. Under older versions of X11, the host had to continually send connection requests over the network looking for an X server trying to log on. There are three XDMCP connection methods supported by most X servers.

XDMCP query (direct)

In a single host environment, the best way to make an XDMCP connection is with a direct query. When the X server starts, it sends an XDMCP message over the network to a specific host. If the host is properly configured and willing to accept a connection from your machine, a set of responses are sent back and forth with the XDMCP protocol. Once a session is initiated, XDMCP no longer is used and the connection is turned over to **xdm**. **xdm** provides a login screen where you login by providing user name and password, no matter what type of connection is started.

XDMCP broadcast

If you have multiple acceptable X hosts, Broadcast mode may be the best connection method. Your X server broadcasts to the network and any properly configured host picks up the query and responds to the X server. If multiple hosts respond, the X server uses an arbitrary method to select a host and sends a request packet to **xdm** on the selected host. If accepted, the host provides the login. XVision has a variation on the arbitrariness of selection. It provides you the option of selecting the first host that answers a request or XVision displays a list of available hosts and lets you choose the host. All other X servers choose the first available host. If **xdm** is not running on any host or no host is willing to start a session, you cannot log in using the X Display Manager. You could still come in via **telnet**.

XDMCP indirect

The final method, indirect XDMCP, allows your X server to make a direct request to a single host. This host in turn passes the request on to other hosts on the network. These additional hosts actually make the connection. In a fluid network, this is a convenient method of tying all the X servers to a single host and only having to make changes on that host with respect to available hosts.

Editing X Configuration Files

Setting up **xdm** is normally a function for the UNIX system administrator. But your system administrator may not be familiar with **xdm**. Here are the basic scripts and steps needed to get a session started.

xdm-config

You have to be using X11R4 or higher since support for XDMCP did not exist prior to this release. (Check the UNIX system documentation.) The first host file to configure is **xdm-config**. This master configuration file sets the resources which apply globally to **xdm** as well as some resources that apply to specific X server displays. Its main job is to tell **xdm** where to find everything else. On a SVR4 host, **xdm-config** is located in /**usr/lib/X11/xdm** while in a SunOS SPARCstation it is located in **$OPEN-WINHOME/lib/xdm**. It follows the same format as the standard X resource files. The **xdm-config** file is often supplied with your operating system but does not come with every version of UNIX. Some X terminals also supply this and other configuration files. We list two sample host files.

Sample **xdm-config** from SunOS (BSD UNIX).

```
DisplayManager.errorLogFile: /usr/tmp/xdm-errors
DisplayManager.pidFile: /usr/tmp/xdm-pid
DisplayManager.servers: $OPENWINHOME/lib/xdm/Xservers
DisplayManager*resources: $OPENWINHOME/lib/xdm/Xresources
```

```
DisplayManager*session: $OPENWINHOME/lib/xdm/Xsession
DisplayManager*authorize: true
DisplayManager*reset: $OPENWINHOME/lib/xdm/Xreset
DisplayManager._0.xrdb: $OPENWINHOME/lib/xdm/xrdb.sh
DisplayManager._0.authorize: true
DisplayManager._0.userPath: ":/etc:/bin:/usr/bin:/usr/ucb:$OPENWINHOME/
          bin"
DisplayManager._0.systemPath: "/etc:/bin:/usr/bin:/usr/ucb:$OPENWINHOME/
          bin"
```

Sample **xdm-config** from UNIX SVR4.

```
DisplayManager.errorLogFile:usr/lib/X11/xdm/xdm-errors
DisplayManager.pidFile:/usr/lib/X11/xdm/xdm-pid
DisplayManager.authDir:/tmp/xdm-auth
DisplayManager.servers:/usr/lib/X11/xdm/Xservers
DisplayManager*resources:/usr/lib/X11/xdm/Xresources
DisplayManager*session:/usr/lib/X11/xdm/Xsession
DisplayManager._0.startup:/usr/lib/X11/xdm/Xstartup
DisplayManager._0.reset:/usr/lib/X11/xdm/Xreset
DisplayManager._0.authorize:true
DisplayManager*authorize:false
```

Explaining the xdm-config

The meanings of the various resources are the same on all systems.

authorize: This resource turns off and on the ability to use the security features of xdm. _0 turns on display authorization for the local machine. *authorize turns on the authorization scheme for other displays.

authDir: The location of the directory where security items are placed. This includes the location of the magic cookie.

errorLogFile: The name and location of a file that stores all your login errors. If you are not successfully completing an **xdm** session, this file is the first place to look for answers.

pidFile: The location of the **xdm** process daemon.

reset: This resets the console control once a user logs out of a session. It changes the console ownership back to root.

resources: The name and location of the resource file needed when starting up **xdm**. This will be explained in more detail shortly.

servers: A list of X servers that must be managed directly by **xdm**. These are X servers not using XDMCP.

session: This is the name and location of the system-wide default Xsession. If there is no .xsession file in your home directory, **xdm** uses this file to start a session.

xrdb: Tells **xdm** which X resource database to use. If none listed, it uses the default.

_0 vs. *: The use of the _0 signifies this resource applies only to a particular server while the * is a global resource.

Xresources

The Xresources file is one of two files listed in the **xdm-config** where you may need to make some adjustments. It sets up the login screen which you receive when using **xdm** from a remote X server. Different resources determine the colors used, the width of the border, the greeting, and what happens if we want to bypass the normal session. The sample shown here is off a Sun, but would work on any machine. You would normally find this file in the same directory as **xdm-config**. This file follows the rules of normal X resource files. The colors can be changed and the greeting can be changed. The **login.translations** resource is a trick to allow you to use the F1 key to circumvent your **.xsession** script if there is some problem logging into the system. It guarantees that you won't be stuck without being able to get into the UNIX host.

```
xlogin*login.translations: #override\
    <Key>F1: set-session-argument(failsafe) finish-field()\n\
    <Key>Return: set-session-argument() finish-field()
xlogin*borderWidth: 3
xlogin*greetColor: blue
xlogin*failColor: red
xlogin*Foreground: white
xlogin*Background: grey
xlogin.Login.greeting: Welcome to OpenWindows
```

Creating an X Session Script

The **.xsession** script forms the main element of an **xdm** session. Here, your applications are set up, environment variables invoked, and resources specified for your X session. The **.xsession** script resembles the functions of the **.profile** and **.xinitrc** files on most UNIX machines. It is similar also to the **AUTOEXEC.BAT** file or the **WIN.-INI** file for Microsoft Windows machines. The script sets up the user environment, starts up certain programs, and specifies what runs where on the UNIX host.

Usually, there is an Xsession file located in the **/usr/lib/X11/xdm** directory. **xdm** always look for the Xsession file and runs it first. Normally, the Xsession routine passes off control to the user's **.xsession**. If there is no **.xsession** file in the user's home directory, Xsession has a default startup. The default is often limited to starting a window manager and executing an **xterm**. The listing here typifies an **.xsession**. We left this script intentionally simple and did not use any branching or other shell script techniques likely to be found in similar scripts.

Sample script

```
#Startup file for xdm

# Download resources if there are any
resources=$HOME/.Xresources
if ( -f $resources ); then
xrb -load $resources
fi

# Start up an analog clock with a second hand:
xclock -geometry 150x150-10+10 -update 1 &
sleep 2

# Start up a calculator below digital clock:
xcalc -geometry 170x200-10+220 &
sleep 2

# Create an xterm with log-in shell
xterm -geometry 80x55+10+16 -1s &
sleep 2


mwm
```

Explanation of script

The first portion of the script asks if there is a resources variable set; if so, then load that database. This lets you set your own resource file separately from the system resources. We load three X applications. These are usually available on every system. The **sleep 2** command lets 2 tenths of a second pass between command starting. This just helps from having commands fall over each other when they begin to open on the X server. The parameters are miscellaneous X positioning and sizing commands. Each X client is started in the background. The last line (**mwm**) loads the window manager.

The Last Line

The only way an **xdm** session can quit is when the last client is no longer available to **xdm**. This means the last command (usually an **xterm** or the window manager) in the .xsession script must be run in foreground. You then close down your **xdm** session by closing the final application.

Starting and Stopping an X Session

In order to keep you out of trouble, we now mention a few points about beginning and ending an XDMCP session. If your Windows-based X server is set up in XDMCP broadcast mode, your host always looks for the connection. As soon as the Windows X server starts up, a connection attempt is made to one or more hosts on the network. For this to happen, **xdm** must be running on the host. **xdm** can be set up to run automatically at boot time, or it can be invoked by the superuser. In most cases, no parameters need be established for **xdm** to work. You can instruct **xdm** to use a specific **xdm-config** file at start-up time.

How does **xdm** know when a session ends and your X server is no longer needing any control? You provide the cue when you close the X application that is started in the **.xsession** running in the foreground. It is the foreground application that keeps the session open. When the foreground session closes, **xdm** senses the change and disconnects that server from the network. For this reason, it is important to run either an **xterm** or the window manager in foreground. (Omitting the ampersand as the last parameter places the application in the foreground.) If you use an **xterm** as the defining client, it becomes the last client in the **.xsession** file. In this case, when you close the **xterm** window your **xdm** session also closes—possibly causing you to lose the rest of your clients. Try the safer approach and use the window manager as the foreground client. When you want to exit from **xdm**, simply select **exit** from the window manager's pop-up menu. The window manager then closes, and the XDMCP connection shuts off as well.

Cutting and Pasting

A major advantage of using a GUI like Microsoft Windows or X is the ability to easily cut and paste information across applications. Granted, cut and paste does not exactly represent tight application interoperability. However, until the vendors can create standards in their own environments, cut and paste may be the method of choice. More sophisticated methods of sharing data like DDE (dynamic data embedding) and OLE (Object-Linking and Embedding) are still gaining support. DDE never quite caught on in Windows because of its complexity. OLE should fare better, but its users may still find it difficult as well as limited in availability.

Moving data from X to Windows and vice versa can best be done with cut and paste. Windows has a cut and paste facility which places text or graphics in the Windows clipboard. X stores its cut and paste information in one of a series of buffers called the X selection. Each X client decides on which buffer for storing information. Most use the **Primary X** selection, but there are a number of others available—including the **Secondary X** selection and **Cut_Buffer0** all the way up to **Cut_-Buffer7**.

The job of the X server is to get the information back and forth from Windows to X when you need only pieces of a file. The simplest method is to copy a section of text from the X client to the X selection. You can usually do this by highlighting the text with the left mouse button and releasing the button. The menu button (upper left hand corner of the title bar in the window manager) of the X client invariably has an edit menu option driven by the X server. One option allows you to copy the X selection. This takes the contents of the X selection and places it in the Windows clipboard. Now go to your Windows applications and choose Edit Paste to move the information into your application.

Other options offered by different X servers might better fit certain needs. A copy rectangle option (found in eXceed/W and XVision) lets you take a picture of a section of text or graphics and place it directly in the Windows clipboard. A second option enables you to capture the entire visible screen and transfer its contents to the Windows clipboard. Make sure an X server meets your primary needs with regard to smoothly moving blocks and samples of text across the two operating.

HOT TIP   **X Cut and Paste**

X does not use a single clipboard buffer as Microsoft Windows does, but rather a series of buffers. The X client itself determines which buffer to use. For most, the **Primary X** buffer is selected. You can cut and paste in an **xterm** by highlighting the text with the right mouse button, moving the cursor to the command line and pressing the middle mouse button.

Keyboards

Keyboards are frequently particular to specific hardware. Only recently has there been an attempt to standardize keyboards across different operating systems. Macintoshes, PCs, and UNIX workstations are tending towards the standard 101 keyboard layout made popular by IBM. This change helps eliminate potential conflicts when using a UNIX-based X client on a PC through an X server. However, differences still exist, and you should know how keyboard mapping works in order to smooth out potential problems. UNIX administrators are generally much more familiar with this subject than PC power users. If your PC uses a non-standard keyboard, consider mapping to insure your applications work correctly.

Mapping

Keyboard mapping is the process of matching keystrokes sent by your PC to the X client. All X servers provide some type of keyboard mapping facility through the X client **xmodmap. xmodmap** comes as part of the standard release of X11R4. Each MS Windows-based X server uses a standard keyboard map provided by the X server, normally based on the language of the keyboard (English, German, etc.). This map outlines what each key, shifted key, and two other variations display when pressed. Each key generates a unique keycode which becomes the raw scan code. The keyboard sends the raw scan code when you press a key. The scan code is keyboard dependent but fairly consistent across manufacturers, particularly PC keyboard manufacturers. The keycode often maps to a virtual keycode in the X server product. The extra layer is required because the X server runs on top of Windows and must do its own translation.

If you want to see a list of the keyboard map for your host, type the command listed here at the command prompt and you will see a listing similar to ours.

sun_ipc # xmodmap -pk | more

keycode	keysym	keysym
68	0x0064 (d)	0x0044 (D)
69	0x0065 (e)	0x0045 (E)
70	0x0066 (f)	0x0046 (F)
71	0x0067 (g)	0x0047 (G)
72	0x0068 (h)	0x0048 (H)
73	0x0069 (i)	0x0049 (I)
74	0x006a (j)	0x004a (J)
75	0x006b (k)	0x004b (K)

Each **keysym** is similar to a specific keycode or scancode but works with X. The **keysym** represents X specific keycodes. For example, 0x0064 is the **keysym** for 'd'. When you strike the little 'd' key on the keyboard, it generates the keycode 68. The X server receives this code from Windows and using the keyboard map, translates it to the matching **keysym**. Finally, the X application receives the **keysym** and produces a 'd' and sends it to the server where it is displayed. If you want to have the 'j' key produce a 'g', you can enter at the command line **xmodmap -e "keysym j = g"**. When you strike the 'g' key, it sends the scancode 71 which is then mapped by the **xmodmap** as 0x006a or ' j'. The most pointed places to make these changes is for special keys like function keys or modifier keys.

Shortcut Keys

A potential conflict between X servers and Microsoft Windows occurs when you use a host-based window manager like Motif. Normally, the X server passes all special key sequences on to MS Windows. This is true of the Alt+<key> shortcut keys used by Windows. For example, the Alt-Tab key switches from one application to another. When running in single window mode (all X applications under a single MS Windows window), you might want to pass these keys onto Motif rather than Windows, since Motif uses the keys in a fashion similar to Windows. In many X servers, a configuration dialog option makes this change. You will want to maintain the Windows shortcut keys if you always use the local (Microsoft Windows) window manager. If you use the remote window manager with your X applications, you might want to disable the Alt key compatibility option so the Alt key combinations work correctly within Motif.

Fonts

Fonts can be a problem with an X server for a variety of reasons. First, the creators of X did not anticipate many of today's software requirements so the font support is not strong. X11R5 begins to counter some of those problems with a font server. Secondly, vendors stray from the MIT font standards. Some vendors do this to get around shortcomings in the MIT X fonts, others do it to provide the customer more flexibility. The end result is a proliferation of incompatible applications and fonts.

A third problem occurs with the mixing of fonts from two different systems, Microsoft Windows and X. Windows applications are full of font technologies including TrueType, Bitstream fonts, and Adobe fonts. However, there are some things you can do to alleviate your problems.

Font Helps

Here are some ideas to help you get past various font roadblocks:

a. Have plenty of disk space (maybe 25% more than whatever the vendor recommends as minimum) wherever you load an X server. This allows you to load all the available fonts. Because they require a lot of space, you might be tempted to skimp on which fonts to install. Don't. You never know when you might need the extra flexibility. Most X programs give you no explicit information about which fonts they use and how. Generally, you want to avoid a font problem by having a large number of fonts available on your PC.

b. Your X server automatically creates a font directory. Within the font directory on your PC, there is a file called **fonts.dir**. **always? The purpose of this file is to list all the available fonts stored in the directory. We show the syntax here. The first number in the file represents the number of fonts in the file.

```
45
<filename>    <font logical name>
symb14.fon    -ADOBE-Symbol-Medium-R-Normal..
courb10.fon   -Adobe-Courier-Bold-O-Normal..
```

All X servers but X11/AT refer to their font files with a **.fon** extension. The fonts provided by X server vendors are X11 fonts (normally provided as **.bdf** format) compiled to work under Microsoft Windows. X11/AT from IIM uses **.snf** for server natural fonts. **snf** is the internal format of X11 fonts found in Release 4 and earlier. When you add other fonts to the X server, you must place the font logical name and the specific file name in the **font.dir** file, otherwise the X server does not know they are available. All X11 fonts need to be compiled before they can be used by a Windows X server. Besides **.snf** fonts, fonts can be in **.bdf** (Bitmap Distribution Format) and in **.pcf** (Portable Compiled Format) which is the internal font format for X11 Release 5.

c. Another helpful file is the **fonts.ali**. The idea behind the **fonts.ali** file is simple. In this file you provide alias names for specific fonts. An alias is a method to provide an alternate name for the same font or provide a substitute font for one that is not available. For example, you can substitute Helvetica for Courier if your application wants Courier but your system does not have it. This can be important when you have an X client looking for a specific font not available in your X server. If you place the font substitution in the **fonts.ali** file, the application always finds a font. Xoftware for Windows contains a **fonts.ali** file that makes fonts available in Framemaker and Open Look Window Manager.

   d. You may need to compile fonts in a case where your X client provides a set of X Windows fonts in **.bdf** format, and you need to use them with your X server. You would only compile these fonts, however, if it included a number of different fonts and you did not want to use the substitute fonts in your **fonts.ali** file. Not all X servers provide a font compiler, but for those that do the process is easy:

   1. Copy the **.bdf** fonts from the UNIX host to your PC into the subdirectory where you want them to reside. You can use **ftp** or NFS to copy the files. It is usually a good idea to create a new subdirectory.
   2. Run your compiler program. In all cases, the compiler is a **.exe** file normally available from an icon. The compiler lets you select fonts and compile them either individually or in a group.
   3. If not already created, create a **fonts.dir** file with a list of all your new fonts. The X server probably provides a utility to do this automatically.
   4. Add the new fonts to the default font path in your X server.

   e. X11R5 supports a font server. As shown in the table in Chapter 15, some of the X servers use X11R5 and more soon will. The font server allows you to store all your fonts on the UNIX host. This alleviates many of the problems such as the amount of disk space used by fonts, trying to maintain many different font directories on a variety of machines and insuring applications have fonts available. When possible, we recommend you use the font server.

Using X11 Fonts

With almost all X servers, you can use the X server-provided fonts in standard Microsoft Windows applications. This can be a real benefit. While the price of fonts has tended downward, you still can pay plenty for new fonts. In many cases, Windows-based X servers provide a larger selection of fonts than exist on your PC. Making use of them in standard Microsoft Windows applications requires some work.

Windows font basics

In Windows, there are two basic font types—screen fonts and printer fonts. Screen fonts display correctly on your screen. The compiled fonts provided by X servers are screen fonts. Printer fonts reflect what your printer is capable of producing. The print driver you select in a Windows application knows what printer fonts are available for your particular printer. For example, a Hewlett-Packard IIIP printer comes with a set of scalable printer fonts.

The fonts, whether printer or screen, come in two varieties. Bit-mapped fonts (also known as raster, nonscalable, or fixed) are stored as a fixed map of dots. Bit-mapped fonts can be reproduced without distortion only at their normal size. In Windows, fonts like Courier and Times Roman are bit-mapped fonts. The second variety, scalable fonts (also known as outline or vector), are generated at the time of drawing and stored as a mathematical formula. Each time you draw the character, it is recalculated. Thus, scalable fonts take longer to create but can be made in any size without having the font on the disk. TrueType fonts like Courier New are scalable fonts.

Installing in the control panel

The process of installing your X server fonts in Windows is straightforward.

1. Open the Control Panel.
2. Double-click on the Fonts icon.
3. As shown in Figure 8.5, a list of installed fonts displays in the dialog box.
4. Select the Add button.
5. A new dialog box appears with a directory window in the left hand corner. Choose the directory where your X server fonts are located.
6. From the list, select one or more fonts you want included in Windows. In most situations, unselect the Copy Fonts to Windows Directory box since the fonts are already located on your machine.
7. Select OK, and the fonts are added to your Windows font list. These fonts are now installed in Windows and available for use.

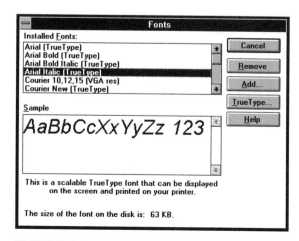

FIGURE 8.5 Microsoft Windows Fonts window

Using X11 fonts in windows applications

With X11 fonts now installed in Windows, not all Windows applications automatically use the fonts. Certain applications list these new fonts in their font boxes. For example, Microsoft Excel lists all the fonts, and they are usable simply by selecting them from the font list., because Excel displays screen and printer fonts. Other applications take a different approach. Word for Windows, FrameMaker for Windows, and many word processors only display printer fonts. Selecting Format Character or choosing the font list off the ribbon bar does not show your new fonts since they are not printer fonts. However, you can still use them simply by typing in the font name and font size. The fonts display properly on the screen. When the document prints, your word processor substitutes the closest available printer font. The major advantage to using X server fonts is on-screen consistency.

Colors in X

Each X application can provide its own colormap or color palette. This tells the window manager what colors to display in the application. Because competing applications and colors can work to the user's disadvantage, the best place to resolve color problems is in the window manager. If the window manager handles the colors, each application appears consistent. For example, Microsoft Windows manages its colors. The X server tries to balance the best of both worlds. All Windows-based X servers give you some flexibility. In most cases, your best bet is to use the defaults.

There are five color mechanisms normally found in an X server. They are PseudoColor, DirectColor, StaticColor, StaticGray and TrueColor. In general, working with color mechanisms directory is something done at the programmer's level and not at the application level. For many scenarios, PseudoColor or the color map default provided by your X server is sufficient. PseudoColor provides a default colormap, and the Windows system colors are used by X clients. This keeps every window consistent. True color and direct color work with monitors that support more than 256 colors.

Troubleshooting

Login problems with telnet or xterm

•Watch out for display-intensive applications. Applications that use a lot of fonts, redraw the screen frequently or place complicated graphics on the screen may not work. Try loading all the X server fonts on your PC. See if your X server can compile X fonts provided by the application.

●If you cannot open an **xterm**, first check the X server side of the equation. Check that you have the correct information in the login boxes. Also check that you have the correct access method selected.

●If you have a solid TCP/IP connection, but still are having problems with making a connection, try using the IP address instead of the host name.

●When the X client is not displaying on your machine, make sure you have a DISPLAY variable properly set. Login via a **telnet** session and do a **env**. Look for DISPLAY=hostname:0. You can set the display variable on the command line or in a script that calls your application. See the examples under **xterms**.

●Check the host UNIX machine to insure it has your machine in its **/etc/hosts** file or you are properly listed in NIS.

Xdm Login does not come up or wrong applications load.

●Check to be sure you have a **.xsession** in your home directory

●Make sure the default Xsession file has an **if** statement directing **xdm** to your own **.xsession** file if it exists.

●Look for the presence of additional Xresources or **xdm-config** files that are being invoked rather the your own. X-terminal software often loads its own files.

●Make sure **xdm** is running as a daemon on the UNIX host.

●Make sure your X server is using the correct method of XDMCP and has the correct host name.

9

Making Serial Connections

Introduction

Have you ever bought a product—perhaps a stereo system—and got it home only to realize you now had more than you needed? You can have the same experience with networking. If you are connecting a PC to a UNIX system, you will likely hear the virtues of using TCP/IP and Ethernet until you think these vendors are running for President rather than selling you a network solution. And yes, Ethernet is a great solution, otherwise we wouldn't spend most of our book discussing it. Yet it is neither required nor appropriate for every business computing problem. In more than one circumstance, a simple asynchronous RS-232 serial connection can meet all your needs. Review Chapter 3 if you are unsure whether or not a serial connection represents the right choice for your situation; then let's plow ahead with the issues. In this chapter we give you information on when to choose a serial connection, discuss the key software installation and configuration issues, and look at setting up your PC and UNIX host for serial communications. For the devoted do-it-yourselfers, we provide information about making your own serial cables and connectors (a relatively simple task, though daunting at first glance).

Choosing Serial Connections

The decision to use a serial connection between DOS and UNIX is often just a matter of looking at your application and considering the costs. If the applications on your UNIX host are standard character-based programs, a serial connection represents a good solution. Many small businesses running turn-key accounting, inventory, job cost manufacturing, and distribution applications fall into this category. Contrary to popular belief, there are still hundreds of thousands of character-based UNIX users around the world. Using any of the applications mentioned in this chapter and Chapter 16, you can access the UNIX host and run UNIX programs from the comfort of your PC, as shown in Figure 9.1.

However, there is no reason why you cannot mix and match serial connections with Ethernet. Terminals, remote users, and some PCs may access the system over serial cables and/or phone lines, while other users are attached via Ethernet.

Figure 9.2 displays a possible scenario which allows each technology to do what it does best. One possible variation involves connecting terminals and PCs to a terminal server which in turn connects to the Ethernet. This scenario, discussed in Chapter 12, is common in larger businesses with multiple networks or large numbers of users.

Our configuration comprised a mix of computers and connections. We used an Insight 486 50MHz PC and a Keydata laptop as our main PCs. We used a U.S. Robotics Sportster FAX modem, a U.S. Robotics Courier modem, and a Logicode Quicktel fax modem for our modem connections. We tested most packages by installing them on a PC, then connecting them directly to an IBM RS/6000 Model 340 with two serial ports. We also tested connections to a Sun Microsystems SPARCstation IPC and to an SCO OPEN DESKTOP machine.

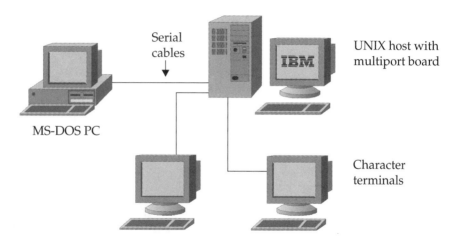

FIGURE 9.1 Plain serial network

Advantages

Cost and simplicity make up the primary advantages of using a serial connection. Even though the popularity of GUI-based applications which require the throughput of Ethernet is spreading rapidly, serial still has a lot to offer. Remember, there are plenty of previously-installed UNIX and DOS character-based applications out there which work just fine for the problems they were designed to solve.

- You may already have terminals running off your UNIX box—connected to a multiport device. If you have extra connections on the board, spending money on any new network cards for either the UNIX host or the PC won't be necessary. Every PC comes with at least one serial port.

•Cabling for serial connections comes cheaper than either thick or thin coaxial cable. Usually, serial cable is even less expensive than using unshielded twisted pair (UTP) in a 10Base-T scenario (although you can still use UTP).

• Depending on your requirements, terminal emulation software may be cheaper than buying a full-fledged TCP/IP product like those in Chapter 14.

•The simplicity of serial connections represents a major advantage. On a PC, the installation and use of a terminal emulation program involves little work. Unlike the TCP/IP products for PCs, there are no interrupts to configure, TSRs to run, or cryptic network error messages to work through.

•With serial connections, you have portability, because you can use a modem to dial-in while away from the office—either from your home or hotel.

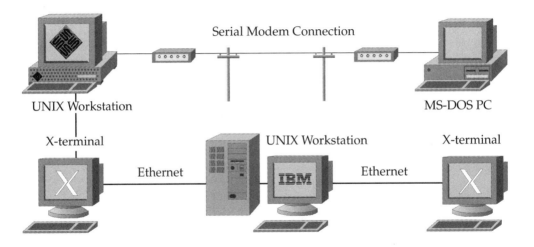

FIGURE 9.2 Serial network using a modem tapped into an Ethernet connection

Disadvantages

Despite all our hoopla, we can offer you no free lunch—even with serial connections. Along with low cost and simplicity come some disadvantages. You simply cannot get full functionality with serial connections in most circumstances.

•Serial connections are slower than Ethernet. While Ethernet is rated 10 million bits per second, the standard serial connection only rates from 9,600 to 38,400 bits per second.

•A regular serial connection cannot run X applications or other graphical environments; the connection is just too slow to move the massive amount of information associated with graphical applications. There are, however, at least four protocols available to overcome this limitation, although none of them run as fast as regular Ethernet. These are discussed later in the chapter.

• A standard serial connection also eliminates the option of using NFS between your PC and UNIX system. Almost all terminal emulation products support the ability to do file transfer between systems; but, because of file size, *sharing* files and applications becomes impossible.

Installing and Configuring Software

Now, back to some good news—installing and configuring serial-based terminal emulation products is a straightforward process. Conflicts with other programs are rare, and you should encounter no more than minor difficulties choosing the correct configurations.

PC Terminal Emulation Products

Putting DOS and Windows programs onto the disk and readying them to run becomes a snap with PC terminal emulation. None of the programs we tested required any difficult configurations. The installation itself almost always runs from a simple script. Most DOS and Windows products automatically make changes in the startup files **AUTOEXEC.BAT** and **WIN.INI**, and the better programs let you see changes before they are made. We installed over a dozen emulators and did not find the process difficult. Still, you may want to review certain pieces of information before beginning the installation process since many products request them during configuration. We cover these in the following sections.

COM port

You need to know which **COM** port your PC uses for communications. In 90% of the cases it is going to be **COM1:** or **COM2:**. Look for a label to that effect on the back of your machine or run a simple diagnostic program like **MSD** that comes with Windows. If for some reason you cannot be certain of this designation, note that every product lets you change the port after the program opens. We provide more information on this topic in the section on setting up PC hardware.

Terminal emulation

If you are connecting to a UNIX host for a specific application, the terminal emulation mode is often important. Many custom UNIX applications support only a limited set of terminal emulation modes. If you don't know your correct one, you may end up frustrated trying to get the screen to work correctly. It's a good idea to be armed with terminal emulation mode information before purchasing a product.

Network connections

You need to know beforehand what type of network connection you are making. For most situations, RS-232 (also known as serial connection) is the standard option. However, if you use a Novell network and a communication server, you might require NASI, NCSI, or other options. Your situation may demand emulation over a TCP/IP connection or your proposed product might ask whether the connection is direct or via modem.

Baud rates/speed

Finally, you need to know at what speed you are going to set the connection. On the software side, your best choice is to set the baud rate for higher than the actual connection. As discussed in the Setting up UNIX section of this chapter, UNIX cycles through a variety of baud rates looking for the right match; many modems do the same. Setting speed in the terminal emulation package only controls the speed of the PC **COM** port.

Using Serial Emulation Over a Network

If you require a serial connection from a Novell network, don't think you need a modem on every PC. Many methods exist for creating a communication server on your network. A communication server consists of a dedicated hardware box, a multiport adaptor for multiple modems, and software. The most common communication server is Network Communication Services Interface (NCSI) from Network Products Corp. NCSI is also repackaged as Novell's NACS communication server. A communication server allows a client on the network to dial out over a serial line without having an individual modem. NCSI supports nine simultaneous connections.

There are a variety of API interfaces supported in a communication server environment. Besides NCSI, there is INT 14 IBM-PC, INT 14 J&L, 3Com BABI, and INT 6B (also known as NETCI from Ungermann-Bass). Each of these interfaces is used by the client PC to communicate with the server. If you have a communication server with a specific type of interface support, you need a terminal emulation package with that support. You also need to insure that your software can provide multiple sessions if you want such a feature.

Once a communication server is installed, setting up the client presents no real problems. During the configuration stage, many terminal emulators ask you for the type of connection. Instead of choosing **COM1** or **COM2**, choose the appropriate communication server interface. If you choose NCSI, or NCSI-like interfaces, you may have to complete additional information. The server name is the name given for a specific communication server. This becomes important if you have more than one server and want to restrict access to a single server. In the case of a server, a general name is given to a group of modems or connections. For example, **a** special long distance set of phone lines may be listed as **W_GRP** in the server while regular phone lines might be called **REG_GRP**.

We found the PC-centric programs, like Smartcom and Dynacomm, provided more Novell environment network options than did the UNIX-centric products, like Blast and TERM. If you have a communications server on the network, purchase a program with the exact network solution you require. Remember, you don't need a product with support for 20 different network communication options—just sufficient support for the one you use.

Terminal Emulation with a UNIX Component

When there is a UNIX component to a terminal emulation product, its usual purpose is to provide better file transfer capability. Normally, the product supports its own file transfer protocol or a proprietary protocol. If you are a DOS user stuck trying to install the UNIX portion of a DOS product, here are a few hints to overcome the pathetic nature of UNIX installation scripts.

- You need to have root or superuser privileges for most programs to install.
- UNIX usually refers to disks by their capability. For example, **fd196ds9** is the 1.44M 3.5 inch floppy. **196** stands for tracks and **9** represents the number of sectors. A 5 1/4 inch high density floppy (1.2M) is **fd096ds15**, and **fd048ds9** is a 360K floppy disk.
- The difference between **rd** (raw device) and **fd** (floppy device) is usually immaterial when using the floppy disk drive.
- The **umask** command is often used to insure proper permissions, but if you are logged in as root, it is usually not a problem.
- Many installation manuals do not refer to a specific device name, but rather tell you to use "the appropriate device name." When in doubt, try one of the names listed above for the floppy.
- Some install programs first off-load a small file called **install** or something similar. Once the script is on your hard disk, you then run it. Don't forget to type **./** in front of the name to tell UNIX to look in the current directory for the file.
- Programs with the ability to self-upload the UNIX host component from the PC tend to work sporadically. Allow yourself lots of time.

Cabling Basics

A serial connection requires cables—just like an Ethernet network. You can build your own or purchase ready-made cables. Reasons to consider making your own cables include:

•You truly can save significant money. For example, serial cables with 7 conductors pre-made by a national catalog firm specializing in cables cost about 50 cents a foot for 50 foot lengths. This is 3-4 times the cost of buying components.

•Running a pre-made serial cable through walls and plenums with the connectors hard-wired is no easy task. For long distances, these cable almost always have to be made on site.

•Serial connections vary depending on what you are connecting. In all likelihood, even if you buy cables, you are going to do much of the legwork anyway.

But let's assume you decide to buy cable. Here are a few simple things to keep in mind. (For those who want to investigate making your own cables, complete instructions are found at the end of the chapter.)

•PC to Modem cables are the easiest to purchase as a complete set. Modem cables can be purchased for $8-$20 depending on the length and source.

•Don't pay for expensive cable if you don't require it. Most serial situations gain no benefit from using shielded cable (also known as extended distance cable). You also don't need LAN grade UTP. Plain multiconductor cable works fine for smaller sites, although for expansion you may want to consider using UTP.

•When connecting a PC to a UNIX host, buy cable with only 4 or 7 conductors. You don't need to connect all the pins on your serial port. Except for modem connections, 7 conductors are the most you should ever need, and 4 do the trick in most cases.

•Make sure you know which of your machines are DTE (Data Terminal Equipment) and which are DCE (Data Communication Equipment)—if you have any non-standard equipment.

•Connecting from a PC to a UNIX host usually requires a null modem cable— one in which pins 2 and 3 are crossed in the connectors.

HOT TIP   **Communications Tutorial**

Data Bits: The number of bits for each character—it can be either 7 or 8. The full ASCII character set requires 8 bits, but most text data uses only the bottom half of the set. This means 7 data bits work fine.

Stop Bits: The number of bits at the end of each character. It can be 1 or 2, but almost always 1.

Parity: Built-in error detection. Parity can be odd or even or none. None is preferred whenever file transfer already has error correcting.

Preparing the PC

Setting up the PC is a relatively easy part of the DOS to UNIX serial formula. Aside from installing the software, your main concerns are: installing a serial port (if one does not exist), making sure DOS or MS Windows recognizes the port, and setting the serial addresses.

COM 1 or 2

Generally, setting up the PC serial port requires relatively little work. All newer PCs come with at least one, and often two, serial ports. MS-DOS refers to the first serial port as **COM1** and the second as **COM2**. Unlike UNIX, with its support for multiple serial ports, DOS supports only two serial ports under normal circumstances. Even though DOS 3.3 and higher has support for **COM3** and **COM4**, we had a problem finding usable new interrupts. Some applications support the use of **COM3** and **COM4,** and you can use them through the first two serial ports. There is also a share-ware program called **COMRESET.EXE** that lets your PC recognize **COM3** and **COM4** if your **BIOS** supports it. We assume you use **COM1** or **COM2**.

If you are using a DOS-based terminal emulation program, as opposed to a Windows program, you need to set the **MODE** command in the **AUTOEXEC.BAT** file. The **MODE** command contains information about which **COM** port you want to use, baud rate, data bits, stop bits, and parity. The following represents a typical command for a 9600 baud connection, with 8 data bits, 1 stop bit, and no parity.

```
Mode COM1: 9600,8,1,n
```

Windows uses its own method of setting up the **COM** ports. You do not use the **MODE** command at all—although, if you are using a combination of DOS and Windows communication programs, you still need the **MODE** command. Within Windows itself, however, everything is handled in the Control Panel. Under the ports options, Windows lists **COM1** through **COM4**. These normal settings mirror the options found in the DOS **MODE** command—except for flow control, discussed later. You can also set the address and interrupt under the advanced settings.

Jumpers and Addresses

Even though you should have no major configuration problems, two items of concern are the address and the interrupts used by your serial card. The address indicates the memory address of the card. Each **COM** port needs to have a particular place in DOS memory. Standardization for the memory address of each **COM** port makes for easy installation of your cards. For example, **COM1** uses **03F8** and **COM2** uses **02F8**. These addresses are in the first 1024 bytes of DOS memory. This is specifically set aside for these and other DOS features. Network cards, sound boards, and other devices do not use these addresses. They use the memory between 640K and 1024K called Upper Memory.

Interrupts represent how the card communicates with the **BIOS** and operating system. An interrupt defines how the serial port breaks into the computer's work-flow and then tells it either to receive or send data. Only limited, standardized inter-rupts are available for serial communications. **COM1** should be assigned interrupt 4; and **COM2**, interrupt 3. If you install a new serial card, you have to set these inter-rupts (usually with hardware pin jumpers on the board itself). On most new machines, however, these have been correctly preset. The biggest problem comes when the interrupt has been set incorrectly, or another card—a network card, for example—is set for interrupt 3 or 4.

What if the connection was successful, but the screen never seems to correctly sync up? When it comes to PC serial ports, be on the lookout for a potential problem which may be difficult to diagnose. Check the UART chip (Universal Asynchronous Receiver/Transmitter) which handles the actual communications. Introduced many years ago, UART chips have changed over the last few years. However, there is a set of older UART chips (usually the 8250) often found in 286 PCs that don't work well with bi-directional computing. Symptoms include: keystrokes which—when dis-played on the video—fall behind, slightly garbled data fields, and mixed-up screens.

HOT TIP   **Slow Communications Chips**

You may need to replace the serial board in your PC if you are using a 286 or older PC, and you are having troubles making the connection work properly. Older serial cards can have problems keeping up with the speed of 9600 baud The newer chips (UARTs) are the 16550 and 16450. The older chip is an 8250. The best way to determine which is installed is to run the **MSD.EXE** program pro-vided with Microsoft Windows or DOS 6.0.

Often, the serial card works fine with a serial printer where the one-way com-munication is the norm, and it functions adequately with 2400 baud and slower modems. However, when faced with a 9600 baud connection with significant two way communication, the UART chip fails to handle all the information. In this case, first double check the cable, the connection, and the communication settings (by attaching to another machine with the same setting). If this fails to fix the problem, purchase a new serial card with a UART 16550 chip. Mail order companies offer them for between $20 and $60.

Preparing the UNIX Host

Readying the UNIX host for serial communications poses a much more difficult task than setting up the PC. This is good news for the UNIX system administrator but bad news for the PC power user trying to get a UNIX box to recognize the PC. Every UNIX machine goes about the process differently. This section is for the part-time UNIX system administrator who has never connected a PC to a UNIX host either via direct connection or through a modem. If you find yourself not knowing enough about the UNIX system because you lack a true system administrator (not an unusual situation), refer to the Bibliography in Appendix B. Included in the appendix are some excellent UNIX administration books. Our goal here is to give you a road map for getting your PC connected to your UNIX host.

The Initialization File

Every version of UNIX sets up the serial ports differently. In System V, changes are made to the **/etc/inittab** file, while in BSD it's the **/etc/ttytab** file. **Inittab** keeps track of devices available to the UNIX system. Devices include terminals or serial ports, and the system console. In the case of a serial port, these are known as *ttys*. In SCO UNIX (System V, release 3.4), the first two serial ports are **tty1a** or **tty2a**. For the IBM RS/6000 running AIX, **tty0** and **tty1**; for SunOS 4.x(BSD), **ttya** and **ttyb**.

	Breaking the Baud Rate
	If you have the right baud rate but still are getting junk on the screen, it is possible that your system is not syncing with the UNIX host—usually a symptom when the UNIX host does not pick up on the right baud rate. If you use Ctrl-Break once or twice, often that will sync the systems. Sometimes, you simply have to hang up and call the system again.

In many versions of UNIX, the vendors have provided specific methods for setting up the serial port. Without all the gory details (found later), if you do a **cat /etc/ inittab**, you see a line similar to the following, depending on your system, usually near the end of the file. There are other lines setting the states of different devices.

```
SCO        t1A:2:off: /etc/getty -t60 tty1A 3
IBM        tty0:2:respawn:/etc/getty /dev/tty0
SUN        ttya "/usr/etc/getty std.9600"   unknown        off local secure
```

If you have to edit the files yourself, as some UNIX hosts require, the key point is not to change the first or second field for the SCO or IBM options. The third field should read *respawn* if you are dialing into the host and the fourth field calls on the

getty program (discussed next). In the case of the Sun, the third field is the terminal type and the fourth field is either off or on. The fifth field is *local* as opposed to *network* to allow serial connections. The *secure* means root login is permitted.

HOT TIP   **Changing inittab**

Even if your UNIX system has a neat way of setting up the serial port, you can look at the **inittab** file through the **cat** command or change it in an editor. Find the line with the correct tty. The third field (in SVR4, SunOS, AIX, and SCO UNIX) will be a one word command. **Off** means the port is not enabled, and you cannot connect a terminal or dial in via a modem. **Respawn** tells UNIX to send a **getty** through the serial port. The getty is constantly looking for a login. Other possible options are **wait, once, boot,** and **power.** These do not apply to serial port devices and are found in other devices in **/etc/initab**.

Getting a Getty

UNIX machines can have many different serial ports. Frequently these ports are tied to terminals. You have to enable the ports in order for each port to receive input. The **enable** command is used in some UNIX versions like SCO. It tells UNIX that a certain port is functioning and to expect input from that port. In SCO UNIX the command is **enable tty1a**. The **enable** command edits the **/etc/inittab** file, tells the init process a change has been made and sends out a **getty**. This allows a remote user to log into this port, the first serial port.

When a port is enabled, a **getty** becomes associated with the port. **Getty,** a UNIX process (program), waits for a signal from the port. If **getty** can open the port , it sends out a login prompt. At the login prompt, getty accepts the user's name and starts the login program which asks for the password. The login program then runs the program listed in the last field of the passwd file which might be **.login, .profile, .cshrc,** or other start-up files.

If you want to dial out of a UNIX port with a modem, in many cases you need to disable the **getty** that is listening to the port. If not, the **getty** is constantly going out through the port causing interference to outgoing communications. For example, it might start-up a login process locally. If you want to use a port for both incoming and outgoing communications, your work is more difficult. One solution is to write a short UNIX script that enables and disables the port depending upon its use. Better yet, purchase a UNIX terminal emulator which handles that task for you. Many programs will do this automatically.

The Gettydefs File

UNIX can answer your modem no matter at what baud rate you dial in. (This assumes the receiving modem can handle the baud rate.) In the **/etc/gettydefs** file, each baud rate is usually associated with a single letter code or a string like 19200. The entries are structured so that if you dial into a port at 2400 baud which normally expects 1200 baud, **getty** reads **gettydefs** and cycles through all the available baud rates. This cycling is done because each field in the **gettydefs** file refers to another field in the file. This allows different speed modems to dial into the same port without making alterations for each user. Under normal circumstances, the **gettydefs** file should not be altered, but you can edit it to make your own autosyncing options. The **gettydefs** also contains a number of commands for setting up your terminal or serial port and the specific login prompt. (If you want to alter the initial login prompt, you can do it in the **gettydefs** file.)

Unfortunately, autosyncing does not always work. First, in order to make getty recognize your presence you need to hit keys like the ENTER or Ctrl-Break. However, that does not always work. We have seen certain UNIX systems insist on picking up at 1200 baud even though the modem is calling at 2400 baud. We have seen other scenarios where autosyncing just plain fails. In those cases where the autosyncing does not appear to work, go to your UNIX documentation and determine how to change your **/etc/inittab** entry to pick up at a specific baud rate. Then the getty picks up at that specific baud rate.

Termcap and Terminfo

When using a serial connection and terminal emulation, you might run into some problems with the type of terminal emulation. We can't begin to cover all the idiosyncracies of terminal emulation and the termcap file and the terminfo databases, but if you are from the DOS side of the world, you need someone to set you straight, otherwise you can flail around for hours. Because vendors make their own rules, every character terminal works differently. The result is you have to tell UNIX what

---

HOT TIP

Lock Files

UNIX places a lock file on the serial port in use. The lock file is usually found in the **/etc/locks** directory. For example, if the port is **tty1a**, then while the port is in use, a file called **LCK..tty1a** exists in the **/etc/locks** directory. This file vanishes when you shut down your emulation program. If no one is using the port, and you find a lock file, simply delete it with a **rm LCK..tty1a**. The lock file can cause problems with UUCP or certain UNIX communication programs. In particular, we have seen programs such as Blast not work properly if a lock file exists on the port.

type of terminal you are using. Common terminal emulation modes include VT100, VT220, Wyse60, TeleVideo 955, and SCO ANSI.

HOT TIP

Getting the Right Emulation

Terminal emulation can be a problem. If you are having trouble, try VT100 emulation. Almost all programs support it, even though it provides limited functionality. On the UNIX side use **TERM=vt100;export TERM** for systems using the **termcap** file under Bourne Shell and **setenv TERM=vt100** in the C shell to reset the UNIX environment. Using the **env** command tells you what terminal environment your login is presently using.

Normally, your emulation mode is set in the **.profile** file. You need to make sure that the PC emulation software matches this emulation. If the TERM variable is set for Wyse60, then your PC software has to be using Wyse60. If not, certain applications may not work correctly. The application also examines the TERM variable and expects certain keystrokes to mean certain actions. This mismatch can cause graphics to be drawn incorrectly, function keys not to work, and selections to produce the wrong action

In some cases, your application might require a particular terminal emulation mode. Some of the newer SCO UNIX applications require SCO ANSI or Wyse60 mode because they make use of certain keys. On the other hand, we have seen turn-key applications that only work with a limited number of terminal emulation modes. In those cases, even if your PC terminal emulation software mode matches the environment variable, the application may still work incorrectly. Test a copy of the emulation program against your programs before making a purchase.

Setting Up the IBM RS/6000

Making a serial port work, as well as getting a connection to a PC on the IBM RS/6000, requires you to use **smit** (System Management Interface Tool), IBM's answer to SCO's System Administrators Shell. Start **smit** at the command line with **smit** or in an xterm with **smit -C**. In **smit**, select **Devices, TTY, Add a TTY. Smit** gives you the option of choosing which port to add, either an **RS232** or an **RS422** Asynchronous Terminal. Choose RS232. Next, select the serial port, normally **serial port 1** or **serial port 2**. The final screen contains a set of configuration option boxes. Your selection should match the parameters of the PC and your modem. You also have to select the port number. Your choices are **s1** or **s2**. Nearly all of the other settings in the menu are self-explanatory. This menu contains only one potential glitch; IBM does not provide a list of acceptable terminal types. The default type is a dumb terminal, but make sure that you type in a name recognized by the RS/6000 **termcap**. **Vt100** is always a safe bet.

When you dial into an RS/6000, you may find it best to set the Enable login option in **smit** to **delay**. This gives the modem time to pick up the call and sync up on the baud rate before the login is sent to modem. We experienced problems with leaving the login option at **enable** while using a modem. The RS/6000 ports lock up easily and requires frequent removals of **/etc/locks/LCK.tty0** and **/etc/objrepos/config_lock**. With different modems, we also experienced the inability of the RS/6000 to properly interpret the DSR and DCD signal in providing a **getty**.

On the cabling side, we experienced serious problems finding the right pinouts. We were unable to make a direct connection from our PCs to the RS/6000 running AIX 3.2.2 with only three conductors. We succeeded when we used five conductors and connected 20 on the PC to 6 and 8 on the RS/6000 and vice versa. The RS/6000 wants to use the DTR and DSR signals to send a login to the modem or the PC. IBM does have a new version of the **tty** subsystem that fixes some of these problems. In any event, you need to be aware that you may need five wire cable to connect serially to an IBM RS/6000.

The RS/6000 does not use a **gettydefs** file. Instead **smit** handles all of these options. If you want to do autosyncing of the baud rate, you type in 9600, 2400, 1200, 300 in the baud rate option box. The **STTY** attributes tell the device driver how to behave. You might find it beneficial to insert **-clocal** in the list of options. This causes the device driver to pay attention to the modem control lines like carrier detect, hardware handshaking. **+clocal** ignores DTD and DCD.

Setting Up SCO UNIX Hosts

The SCO manuals are inadequate when it comes to the process of adding either a terminal or a PC using terminal emulation. Thankfully, the process is not complicated, just more interactive than we would like. First you need to insure that the serial card is configured. Use the **hwconfig** command. The serial card should be a configured hardware option. If so, there is a **name=serial** as one of the options. If not, go into **sysadmsh**, select **System**, **Configure**, **Hardware**. Choose **Serial card**. You need to know the address and interrupt of your serial card.

Once the card is configured, set up the port to respond to an incoming call or serial connection. SCO uses different port designations for serial ports with modem control and for those without modem control. Serial ports set up for modem control are **/dev/tty1A** and **/dev/tty2A**. Non-modem control changes the capital A to a small a, as in **/dev/tty2a**. The first step is to disable the port by typing:

```
disable tty1a
disable tty1A
```

Next you have to edit the **inittab** file. SCO does not provide a menu driven method to make changes. You have to do it with **vi** or another editor. Once in **/etc/inittab**, find the line that begins **t1A**, **t1a**, **t2A**, or **t2a** depending on which serial port you are using. At the end of the line, you need to type in the correct code for the syncing action to be used. A **3** at the end of the command means 2400 baud, a **2** means 1200 baud, and an **m** means start with the entry called **m** in the gettydefs file which is 9600 baud. Use **m** for a direct connection. The line should look like the following if you are using a 9600 baud direct connection on serial port 2.

    t2a:2:off: /etc/getty -t60 tty2A m

Once finished in the **/etc/inittab** file, you need to make the same changes in the **/etc/conf/init.d/sio** file. This is the backup file and the one the operating system uses when it reboots. If you don't make the changes here, the changes do not come up next time the system restarts. After making the changes, type:

    enable tty2A

The port is ready for business. You can also use **init q** to inform the system to reread the **inittab** file. If you have a modem attached and activated, you will see the DTR (or TR) light go on. If the DTR light does not go on, the port is not working properly. If it lights up, you should be ready to dial in or log in from a direct connection. You may need to hit the Return key a couple of times when making a direct connection. The **getty** from the SCO UNIX side has an initial delay time when first logged on or after breaking a connection.

Setting Up SunOS SPARCstations

Like most UNIX machines, setting up SunOS 4.x for a direct serial or modem connection requires manhandling some commands. No utility or menu driven method is available. The generic Sun kernel is already configured to use both serial ports. You only need to reconfigure the kernel if you have changed the default kernel and removed these devices.

Hardware connections

The Sun DIN to DB-25 connector ends in a female connection. This requires you to have a gender changer if you purchase a modem cable since standard modem cables expect a male DB-25 on the computer side. Make sure you have a DIN to DB-25 adaptor from Sun. Sun's use of a DIN connector for the serial port provides another example of hardware manufacturers doing the strangest things. Sun supports RS-422 protocol which we discuss later. It means you can use faster communications if you have the other components in the system.

Run mknod

If you are creating direct serial connection and do not plan on using a modem, you can skip running the **mknod** command. **mknod** creates an alternative device and allows your modem to support incoming and outgoing calls. The syntax for **mknod** follows.

```
mknod cua0 c 12 128
```

The name of the device is **cua0**. You always use **cua0** for the first modem you want to connect to the system and **cua1** for the second modem. This is regardless of the particular serial port the modem connects with. The second parameter, a standalone **c** means this is a *character* or *raw* device. The 12 and 128 are the major and minor device numbers. You find these by running the command **ls -l /dev/ttya** (or **ttyb** for the 2nd serial port) and receiving a response like:

```
ls -l /dev/ttya
crw--w--w- 1 root          12,          0 Jun 3 17:00 /dev/ttya
```

The major device number is 12 in our example. The minor device number is 0. You always add 128 to the minor device number. You need to change the ownership and permissions on this device. Give uucp ownership, and make the file writable.

Edit ttytab

In SunOS 4.x, the **/etc/ttytab** file is similar to the **/etc/inittab** file in SVR4. It contains the devices that are available. You need to open the file and change the **ttya** or **ttyb** line. Without providing detailed explanations, we show the various options you might want to consider.

```
Direct Login:
ttya            "/usr/etc/getty std.9600        direct          on local

Fixed Dialup Baud Rate:
ttya            "usr/etc/getty std.2400         dialup          on remote

Flexible Dialup Baud Rate:
ttya            "usr/etc/getty D2400            dialup          on remote
```

If you have a modem than runs faster than 2400 baud (very likely), you have to create new entry in the **/etc/gettytab** file. This file is similar to the **gettydefs** file on a SystemV. The Sun defaults to 7 data bits, even parity, 9600 baud for direct connections. You can either change these settings on the Sun, or simply change your communication software to work with these settings.When you finish altering the **/etc/ttytab**, you have to inform **init** of the changes. This requires you to type **kill -1 1** (one, not L). This resets the **ttytab** file.

Modems—Buying and Installing

A modem, like the one shown in Figure 9.3, is primarily a device to convert digital signals to analog and then convert them back again. You can easily see why this is necessary, since nearly all phone lines use analog technology to send signals while computers use digital signals. What if you don't have a modem? No trouble. The successful marketing by Hayes Microcomputer Products Inc. along with advances in integrated circuits have reduced purchasing a modem to a simple and inexpensive task. Here we present some pertinent considerations for buying a modem, both for the PC and the UNIX host. We also mention some of the standards that apply. Your main concerns are compatibility, speed, data compression, and fax support. We don't recommend any particular brand of modem. We use four or five different brands and have found they all perform similarly.

Compatibility

The ability of your modem to communicate with your software is critical. In most environments, there is only one answer—Hayes compatibility. Specifically, you want your modem to support the Hayes command set. This is the set of AT commands which allows you to communicate with your software. Note that modem speed remains a separate issue. Nearly all modems have a Hayes-compatible mode.

Speed

"Speed Kills" was an ad campaign of years ago. With modems, a lack of speed kills time and money. Originally expressed as *baud rate*, most modems now use *bps* (bits per second) to identify their speed. Technically, baud and bps are not the same measures and, therefore, are not interchangeable. However, nearly everyone uses them interchangeably. There are two ways to increase your communication speed. One involves the physical line transmission rate. The other utilizes compression.

Transmission rate

Early PC modems started out at 300 bps with the Bell 103 standard and moved to 1200 bps with the Bell 212 standard. These two standards were quickly overwhelmed by the 2400 bps modem, known as *V.22bis*. 2400 bps still represents the most commonly used communication speed for PC-based communications. Nearly all 2400 bps modems are backwardly-compatible to 1200 and 300 bps. You seldom find an electronic service or other machine that cannot handle a call at 2400 bps.

On the next rung up the speed ladder are the 9600 bps modems, known as *V.32*. These modems improve by fourfold the throughput of the earlier 2400 bps modems. Up to this point, none of these speeds or standards involve any compression or encoding.

FIGURE 9.3 U.S. Robotics Courier V.32bis modem

Compression

Confusion results when one tries to differentiate transmission speed, data compression, and error correction. V32.bis is considered a *compression* standard as is the next CCITT standard, *V.42bis*. V.42bis increases the throughput by a factor of four—regardless of the original transmission rate. Therefore, using a V.32 modem at 9,600 with V.42bis compression produces a throughput of 38,400 bps. You can even use V.32bis encoding with V.42bis compression to increase maximum throughput to 57,400 bps. Be aware that there is one common compression scheme used before the V.42bis standard was in place. Developed by Microcom, *MNP 5* remains a popular compression standard used by many modems.

Error correction can be the *V.42* standard or Microcom's *MNP* error correcting protocols. MNP 1-4 is used by many manufacturers. What your modem uses for standards depends on what it connects up with. If you have a modem using MNP 4 error correcting and you link it with another MNP 4 modem, then the modems will use MNP 5 compression. Conversely, if these modems link up with V.42 error correction, they use V.42bis compression.

Further complicating actual throughput are factors such as the type of file transfer protocol used. The discussion on file transfer protocols later in this chapter provides advice on actual connections.

Fax Support

Many modems on the market support fax send and receive in addition to standard data communications. The worldwide fax standard, Group III, transmits the fax at 9600 bps. Modem fax options come from the addition of a single chip to the modem circuit board which seldom causes any problems. However, we have seen fax modems that do a poor job of resetting themselves after sending a fax. Subsequent data communications may then require a manual reset to the modem. You need software that supports both send and receive in order to use fax from your computer.

Internal vs. External

Modems come in two forms—internal and external. Internal modems fit into one of the expansion slots within your PC and are generally cheaper than external modems. In addition, internal modems have more speed potential since they do not have to deal with the serial port and its speed limitations. You can purchase an internal modem for less than $100. However, there are some negatives. You do not have as much flexibility in setting the configuration of a modem when it is internal. In addition, an internal modem can have interrupt conflicts, particularly in SCO UNIX machines. You almost always have to assign it one of the interrupts that belonged to a serial port, causing you to lose a serial port.

What To Do?

We recommend that you purchase a modem with everything—one which supports V.32bis, V.42, and MNP 4 error correction, and V.42bis and MNP5 data compression. This means you are getting 9600 throughput at a minimum with a maximum throughput of 57,600. While slightly more expensive, external modems provide more flexibility, are easier to configure, and cause fewer conflicts. Also, go ahead and get a fax modem. Even if you don't have any use for it today, it won't cost you anything and can become an option for the future. Modems with these combinations can be purchased for between $250 and $500.

	Internal Modems— Not!
CAUTION WATCH YOUR STEP	SCO recommends that you do not use internal modems with SCO UNIX or SCO OPEN DESKTOP. The modem causes problems by flooding the system with spurious interrupts, and it lacks support for certain features.

Modem Switch Settings

Appropriate switch settings depend somewhat on the modem and on what you intend to do with that modem. Listed in Table 9.1 are the common settings. Most manufacturers have eight DIP switches that can be set manually based on Hayes Smartmodem compatibility. U.S. Robotics Sportster and Telebit Trailblazer represent two other commonly-used modems. U.S. Robotics products usually support the same switch settings as Hayes. Some U.S. Robotics modems have 10 switches. In

Modems—Buying and Installing

221

those cases, the ninth switch lets the modem hang up with a +++, and the tenth switch loads the factory defaults as opposed to the NVRAM defaults.

Table 9.1: Hayes Smartmodem Settings for UNIX Computers

Switch Number	1	2	3	4	5	6	7	8
Switch Name	DTR Required	Codes in English	Result Codes	Commands Echoed	Auto answer	Carrier Detect Asserted	Single Line Phone	Dialing Commands
Setting	UP	UP	Down	Up	Up	Up	Up	Down
Definition	A DTR signal is required from the Computer.	Result codes will be displayed in English	Result codes (xxx) will be displayed.	Commands will not be echoed by the modem.	The modem is set to answer the phone.	The carrier is detected and displayed.	The modem is being used on a single line phone.	The AT command set will be enabled

Confusing the Baud Rate and Serial Port Rate

With all the options available in baud rates, compression, and error correction, there are a variety of ways to make a connection. When you use a modem with V.42 and V.42bis, the actual throughput capability of the modem is much higher than the *baud rate* or the signal rate. A modem using a phone line signal rate of 9600 bps can achieve a throughput of 57,600 bps as we discussed earlier. However, if your communications software has the serial port set for 9600 bps, you get your data at that speed and no faster. This can explain why you may not be getting the file transfer rate you expect.

If you are using a high-speed modem, such as a V.42 modem, you need to adjust your communications software to handle the higher throughput. Modem manufacturers and communication program vendors all give different advice. The best course of action is to set the *serial port communications rate* (often just called the baud rate by the software) for either 38,400 or 57,600. If your software has an automatic baud detection option, turn it off. Otherwise, it will lower your port throughput to the same speed rate as the modem signal.

When you set the baud rate higher than the true phone transmission rate you actually fool your software into thinking you are connecting at 38,400 bps. In fact, between the modem and the CPU, you really are communicating at 38,400 bps. Between the two modems, you use 9,600 bps—with error detection and data compression providing the remainder of the throughput.

File Transfer Protocols

Here we provide a brief overview of asynchronous file transfer protocols. If you are using either PPP or SLIP connections, you want to use **ftp** or **tftp** protocols. The most basic file transfer is ASCII where no compression or error correcting is done. Although ASCII remains sufficient for some uses, most DOS to UNIX file transfers require a more accurate protocol. If you want a more technical discussion of these protocols, consider *Business Data Communications* by Fitzgerald, Dvorak's *Giant PC Communications*, or *Enterprise-Wide Computing* by Madron.

XModem Family

Like the oldest kids in the neighborhood, the Xmodem family of protocols were the first to venture around the block. Basic Xmodem was designed as a microcomputer-based file transfer protocol, but it can be used on UNIX systems. It packages the data in a frame or block with a header character, the data, and a checksum for error correction. As the oldest protocol, it often becomes the common denominator in attempts to transfer across different machines. Xmodem CRC adds *cyclical redundant check* (CRC) to the standard Xmodem protocol and, with it, improves accuracy. Xmodem-1k expands the speed of basic Xmodem by increasing the size of the blocks to 1024 bytes from 128 bytes.

Ymodem provides an improvement over Xmodem-1k by adding CRC-16 error checking. Ymodem-G is still another variation—this time designed to work with error correcting modems. Ymodem-G can also send multiple files in the same transfer. Zmodem is a protocol not directly descended from Xmodem. It has all the advantages of Ymodem-G and Xmodem, except that it also uses a sliding window protocol and only retransmits a portion of the file in case of an error. Ymodem-G and Zmodem represent the two best protocols for BBS (Bulletin Board Systems).

uucp

uucp stands for UNIX to UNIX copy. It is a single program found in nearly all UNIX operating systems and has been used for a number of years by UNIX users when sending files and e-mail to different platforms. UUCP in capital letters refers to a entire set of utilities designed to handle **uucp** transfers and activities. There are DOS-based programs that run **uucp** and allow you to connect to UNIX machines. The level of error correcting in **uucp** is rudimentary. However, **uucp** does provide the method of file transfer for usenet—a cooperative network of UNIX machines sending and receiving mail—rather like a giant, unmanaged bulletin board system. Usenet is further discussed in Chapter 18.

Blast

Blast is a proprietary protocol, supported by U.S.Robotics and incorporated as part of its communication software also called Blast. Blast uses a sliding window protocol and an ANSI CRC-16 error correcting routine. It has become well-known for its ability to overcome such obstacles as noisy lines and line delays due to satellite transmissions. Since it works in full duplex, acknowledgments can be sent back while data is sent out. Blast is more reliable than most of the Xmodem family protocols.

DOS To UNIX File Transfer

When sending or receiving text files between UNIX and DOS systems, you need to be aware that UNIX files have only a line feed at the end of every line while DOS files insert a carriage return and a line feed. The long and short of it is if you don't tell your terminal emulation program to make some type of conversion, you get a double-spaced file when going from DOS to UNIX and a long file going the other way. Many programs, such as DynaComm, allow you to determine what to do with CR and LF when doing an ASCII transfer.

Kermit

Kermit was developed by Columbia University as an error-free file asynchronous transfer protocol available across many different systems. It packages data similarly to Xmodem—in packets instead of blocks. Kermit is freely distributed so there are no royalties. Kermit transmits all data in ASCII, and it works nicely on any systems that support RS-232.

Serial TCP/IP Protocols

What if you desperately need to have TCP/IP support over a serial line? This time, you're in luck! There are at least four methods available to you, each with its pros and cons. All the protocols must emulate the routing, deliver, and datagram services of TCP/IP protocol over a non-dedicated serial line. Serial Line Internet Protocol (SLIP) is the original standard for using IP over serial connections. Although it is extremely slow and only works at 9600 bps, SLIP is widely supported. The second protocol, Point-to-Point Protocol (PPP), has become the replacement for SLIP. It also has the stamp of approval from the keepers of the Internet Protocol.

Challenging both SLIP and PPP are two proprietary protocols. Tektronix markets their own protocol called Serial Xpress, and NCD Inc. has put out XRemote.

Both of these protocols not only support their own line of X-terminals, but are available in MS-Windows X server packages. (See Chapter 15 for a discussion of these packages.) Both of these are faster than SLIP or PPP and are generally easier to set up. In addition, both can work over either a modem or a direct serial connection. The main disadvantages of Serial Xpress and XRemote are the proprietary nature of their protocols. When using these protocols, it is best not to use the compression techniques built into the modems, but you do need to have a 9600 bps modem.

The primary use of SLIP or PPP in our minds is to make a direct connection to the Internet from a modem or to login into your company's network while traveling. However, it is unlikely you can work with WordPerfect over the serial connection because of serial line noise and the slowness of SLIP. Attempting to use an NFS connection could result in substantial delays while loading and saving files.

Setting Up a SLIP or PPP Connection

There is a base of common elements when establishing a SLIP or PPP network. First, the machines using SLIP must be on a separate network from your remaining machines. For example, if your primary network is 192.9.200 (named "primenet"), then the SLIP machines must be on a separate network or subnet, maybe 192.9.201 ("slipnet"). The server on the original network serves as the gateway to the SLIP subnet. This has to be done before attempting to make any connections.

Your PC must now be configured to use SLIP or PPP. This is a product-specific task varying from one TCP/IP stack to another. Not all TCP/IP products directly support SLIP or PPP, or if they do, provide clear documentation on setting up the PC. Two vendors—FTP and SunSelect—provide detailed information. Because some of the more common uses of SLIP and PPP are for terminal emulation tasks, you also need to insure your favorite terminal emulator supports these protocols.

In addition, each host you dial into must be configured to receive a SLIP or PPP connection over the serial line. This is in addition to the proper NFS and TCP/IP protocols running on the host. For an SCO Open Server host, the information needed makes minor additions to the TCP/IP setup. With SCO, you can have four SLIP and four PPP lines installed at one time. Specifically, you need host and destination IP addresses, baud rate, and a SLIP netmask. For a Sun Solaris network, there is a detailed setup procedure that prepares the ports for SLIP connections. Sun assumes you are using PC-NFS from SunSelect and the only documentation comes from Sun-Select—not from the operating system documentation.

Rolling Your Own Serial Connection

Buying ready-made cabling is not always an option. If you are connecting a lone PC via modem to a UNIX host, it makes sense to just purchase the cable and plug it in. But many scenarios are more complicated. One challenge common to many small businesses is connecting PCs to a UNIX host running character-based applications. Other complications arise when you must run serial cable to a printer-sharing device. In these and other situations, you often cannot buy ready-made cable. You either make it or hire someone else to come in and make it. Our goal in the following sections remains practical—to help you get a serial connection up and running between your PC and UNIX host. There are many detailed books that dive into the inner workings of serial connections and modem communications. For a more detailed understanding of serial topics, see the books in Appendix B.

Serial Standards

Making a set of serial connections requires some background knowledge. You do not need to be an expert in data communications, but it helps to know some of the terminology. Here we examine some basic terms you need to know if you dive very deeply into serial connections and cable making.

RS-232 and RS-422

The RS-232 (or RS-232c) standard defines how a serial interface is supposed to work. It outlines what each wire in a connection is does. Created by the Electronic Industries Association (EIA), RS-232 represents a common term in the industry. Unfortunately, in practice you will find the standard both loosely interpreted and applied. Nearly any type of serial interface is often considered to be RS-232. Different manufacturers implement different ways of connecting to the PC. The two most common arrangements are 25 pin connectors and 9 pin connectors. RS-422 is a standard that allows faster communications over greater distances than RS-232. You may find it mentioned with products like terminal servers. It works with RS-232 and is compatible.

DCE versus DTE

The exact function of each wire in RS-232 depends on the type of device which sends or receives the data. These devices fall into two categories—Data Terminal Equipment (DTE) and Data Communications Equipment (DCE). The two terms define what the equipment sends or expects from the connection. In general, DTE equipment originates the data, and DCE represents the communication device. The standard pin-out for 25-pin DTE connections is shown in Figure 9.4. Notice that some of the pins remain unmarked. These pins have no function for data communication. Notice the differences between the 9-pin and 25-pin connectors.You need to know which pieces of equipment are DTE and which are DCE before making your connections—though, of course, vendors have decided not to follow any exact method of applying these terms. Still, we have some guidelines that should help you. Modems are always DCE. Terminals are always DTE. Many people will tell you that computers—PCs or UNIX hosts—are always DTE. Not so. We are familiar with older machines (some from Kaypro and certain notebook computers from Toshiba, for

Making Serial Connections

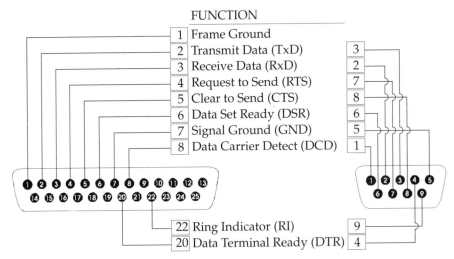

FUNCTION

1	Frame Ground
2	Transmit Data (TxD)
3	Receive Data (RxD)
4	Request to Send (RTS)
5	Clear to Send (CTS)
6	Data Set Ready (DSR)
7	Signal Ground (GND)
8	Data Carrier Detect (DCD)

22	Ring Indicator (RI)
20	Data Terminal Ready (DTR)

FIGURE 9.4 RS-232 Standard connections for 25 pin and 9 pin D connectors

example) that have the serial ports configured as DCE. Most computers are DTE, but if you want to be sure, check the manual and compare the serial pinout with the diagram above. Without a guarantee of what you are using, you can run into a load of troubles. Remember also, if you have a multiport board on your UNIX host, it can be *either* DCE or DTE. So before you begin, get to know your equipment.

Going with the Flow

Invariably, when working with serial communications, you will run into the terms *handshaking, hardware handshaking,* or *XON/XOFF*. Handshaking describes the process of two electronic devices communicating back and forth about the status of their transmission. Remember those college lectures (usually right before the final), when you tried to take notes as fast as your professor spoke? Eventually, some desperate student raised their hand with a, "Whoa, slow down, I can't write that fast." In modems and serial communications, handshaking is that student. The receiving end of the conversation (usually) sends start and stop information to the sending end— regulating the flow of information.

Hardware flow control

Hardware handshaking involves using the RS-232 connection as well as specific wires for control lines. Only two of the lines in a 25 wire RS-232 cable are actually used for data transfer. The rest serve as control lines. Hardware handshaking becomes particularly important for certain types of equipment. A modem, for example, almost always depends on hardware handshaking. The first handshake is often the computer telling the modem, "I am ready to start a session." Typically, the computer sends a signal to data terminal ready (DTR). When the modem then makes a connection with another computer, it signals your computer with a data carrier detect (DCD) signal.

Once data is in the process of being sent, there often arises a need to control the flow or speed of data (hence, the term *flow control*). In the context of hardware hand-shaking, this involves wires RTS and CTS. Vendors disagree about the need for hard-ware handshaking in every circumstance. Our experience indicates that modem connections require hardware handshaking, but direct connections do not require it.

XON/XOFF flow control

If you do not or cannot use hardware handshaking, most terminal emulation pro-grams support a method of controlling the communications called *XON/XOFF*. Implemented only in software, **XON/XOFF** must be supported on both ends of a connection. If one machine begins to overload, it sends a Ctrl-S to the other machine that says, "Wait until I can catch up!" When the first machine is ready to receive more data, it sends a Ctrl-Q. Less reliable than hardware handshaking, software flow control is also difficult to implement if you are uncertain about the setup of the com-puter on the other side.

HOT TIP

Go with the Flow

Often when logging in by modem to a UNIX machine that you do not control from a PC, you may need to experi-ment with flow control options. If you are receiving gar-bage on the screen or are not able to login, check the baud rate first. If that rate is correct, try logging in with a differ-ent type of flow control.

Cabling and Connections

The how, what, and where of making a serial connection always begins with the cable. Even if you choose not to make or even install your own cable, you can benefit by knowing your options. Unlike the more complicated Ethernet, serial connections involve fewer choices, and most are relatively cheap based on a per-foot cost.

Types of Cable

You can use UTP LAN grade cable for serial connections. If you do, our guidelines still apply. But the extra cost does not provide any direct advantages except in terms of expandability. We assume you will use either either modular cable (often called telephone cable or quad) or simple multiconductor RS-232 cable. If you are working with DB-9 or DB 25 connectors on both machines, you can use either cable type. If you have modular connections (usually RJ-11), modular cable makes more sense.

Quad/phone cable, seen in Figure 9.5, comes in 4, 6, or 8 conductor. You should choose whichever fits your setup, but in most cases 4 conductor is used with RJ-11 connections. You can expect to pay in the range of 10 to 20 cents per foot. Multiconductor cable comes in both shielded and unshielded forms, with many combinations of conductors. We have seen 4, 7, 8, 12, 16, 25, and 50 conductor cable. Even though a DB-25 connection has 25 pin settings, you frequently can get by with 4 conductor. If flow control is an issue, 8 conductor represents the most you should need. Four conductor cable costs about 15 cents a foot for the unshielded variety and around 20 to 25 cents for shielded. Eight conductor runs closer to 35 cents a foot, while 25 conductor can be nearer to 80 cents a foot. As you can see, 25 conductor is more than double the cost for wiring you may not need. Depending on your source, you may get Level 4 UTP for a similar price.

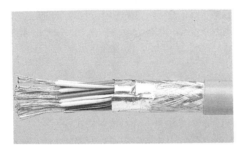 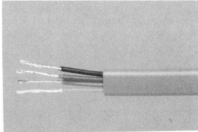

FIGURE 9.5   Photo of multiconductor cable and Quad cable, courtesy of Black Box

Length of Run

There is no firm consensus in the industry regarding how much cable you can run before needing a line booster or repeater. Yes, the RS-232 standard says 50 feet without repeaters or signal boosters. However, only a minority of sources suggest you adhere to these figures. Many opinions permit you to go higher. *The Technical Aspects of Data Communications* (Digital Press, 1982) by McNamara suggests you can go to 1000 feet for shielded cable and 500 feet for unshielded cable at 2400 baud. Our experience indicates that no matter what type of cable you use, 100 to 200 foot long cables should never produce a problem. We suggest that if you use 9600 baud direct connections you can easily go to 250 feet without worry. If you want safety beyond that distance, purchase shielded cable, and distances of 1000 feet with no loss of data or garbled characters between your UNIX host and PC should be possible.

Connector Types

There are numerous options within each of the connector groups. For D-shell (DB-25 or DB-9) connectors, shown in Figure 9.6, you can use solder connectors. We person-

FIGURE 9.6 Dshell connectors, courtesy of Black Box Corporation

ally don't like soldering (too much of a mess), and it doesn't seem worth the hassle. Solder connections are generally cheaper than other options if you do not include the cost of solder, soldering gun, band-aids, and so on.

We prefer, as a second option, crimp-style connections. With these you crimp the pins on the wire and then push the pins into their shells with a pin tool (about $3). If you are going to do a number of connections, you will want a crimp tool which can cost close to $100; but, shop around, and you might find one for closer to $20. The shells cost about 60 cents for plastic ones and close to $1.50 for metal shells.

A third option is the IDP D-shell connectors. Also known as quick connect, they can only be used with ribbon cables. If you need to connect from a DB-25 or DB-9 connector on the PC or UNIX host to a modem, this works well.

Modular connectors come in two common varieties. Crimp connectors allow you to place the wires inside the housing and clamp down with a modular crimping tool. The connectors run only about 50 cents, but the crimping tool runs anywhere from $10 for a simple RJ-11 crimper to a $100 for a multipurpose modular crimper. Buy the cheaper version if you only have RJ-11 connectors. Snap-on modular connectors are also available. These cost close to $4 per connector. Though initially more expensive, if you need only a few connections, snap-ons can save you the price of a crimping tool as well as extra hassle. Chapter 4 provides more information on using RJ-11/RJ-45 connectors.

Finally, you can use modular telephone cable (even when you have DB connectors on your machines) by purchasing DB to RJ modular adaptors. These adaptors cost only a couple of dollars and allow you to run telephone cable (or UTP) while still plugging into DB-25 slots. Though multiple options are available, choose the ones with pins already on the DB end. Then all you have to do is push them into the shell. This saves you the cost of the crimping tool. We think this route has some real advantages even if you still need a crimper for RJ-11 connections.

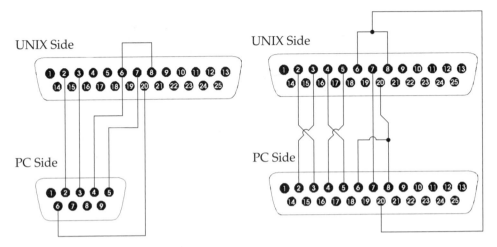

FIGURE 9.7 DB-25 to DB-9 connection and DB-25 to DB-25 connection—all DTE

Standard Pin Outs

We hope to provide some relief from the aggravation of determining correct pin outs. The options we list do not cover every possible PC to UNIX connection—but certainly the majority. Even if you are not going to make the connection, you can provide this information to the technical person building the cable since they often ask, "How do you want the cable built?" We'll help you look good by showing you the answer. While the advice here specifically talks about D-shell connectors, the same information applies if you are using 4 wire and RJ-11 jacks.

Connecting a PC to a UNIX host

Even "easy tasks" are not always easy. When connecting a PC to a UNIX host, you may find different types of connections at each end. In addition, you will have to cross certain wires to convince the host you can communicate. There are many opinions on the number of wires you need in order to insure a solid connection. Some say you need to have nine different wires connected for PC to UNIX serial communications. Others tell you to get by with four, and still others, three. The correct answer is—it depends. In general, you can get by with three wires. In the Figure 9.7 shown here, the three critical connections are (from the PC side) Pin 2 (TD), Pin 3 (RD), and Pin 7 (GND). You have some choice about the remaining connections. First, you can just leave them off. In nearly all non-modem communications, this works just fine. With the second option you can short-out the connections on each side. That is, connect 20 to 6 and 8, and connect 4 to 5 on the same connector with a small piece of wire. Do the same on the other side. This tricks both machines into thinking they are receiving RTS, CTS, DTR, DSR, and DCD signal. Some terminal emulation vendors will tell you this could cause data problems. In theory this is possible, but we have not experienced any such problem. Create a third option by using eight conductor wire and making all the connections. This approach is guaranteed to work—as long as you get all the connections correct and don't multiply mistakes by connecting the wrong items. Our nine pin PC to UNIX connection is shown with only five conductors while the 25 pin connection has all eight. We recommend you try the simplest approach first.

HOT TIP   **Gender Changers**

Always keep a supply of 9 and 25-pin gender changers on hand as well as a couple of DB-9 to DB-25 adaptors. Not every PC and UNIX manufacturer follows the same standards, and many times we have stood at the end of a wiring job looking at two of the same connectors. For example, the IBM RS/6000 has DB-25 male connections to their serial ports, while Sun SPARCstations supply DB-25 female connections. Gender changers are cheap (around $2-$6 in most electronics catalogs), and you will go through them like candy if you have multiple setups.

The main concern in connecting a PC to a UNIX host over a direct serial connection is to insure the transmit pin on the PC side goes into the receive pin of the UNIX side. If both machines are DTE, this requires pins 2 and 3 to be crossed. Our diagram outlines the ideal situation with these pins crossed. Pins 4 and 5 are also crossed to accomplish the same purpose with the CTS and RTS signals. Ditto for 20 to 6 and 8. The easiest place to make the swap is at the PC—since multiple cables often leave from the UNIX host. We feel better knowing that the mess of cables all go out straight through and that the twisted end concludes at a single machine. You can save yourself some trouble by keeping a color-coded list of the wires at each end. This step eliminates those frustrating memory outages which always seem to occur when you need to make wiring changes.

HOT TIP   **Crossed Wires**

What if it does not work? Before trying anything else, switch pins 2 and 3. In the confusion of building the cable and trying to determine which of what was correct, you may have these two wires turned around. You may have a DCE port in the DTE spot. Perhaps you crossed the connection twice, or a pre-existing cable had already crossed 2 and 3 at some other point in the line.

However, when connecting a DB-9 directly to a DB-25 on the UNIX host, you do not have to cross 2 and 3. This is because pin 2 represents Receive Data and pin 3, Transmit Data on a DB-9 connector. Though we do not show it here, a DB-9 to DB-9 does require the crossed pins.

Connecting a PC or UNIX machine to a modem

This is the simplest connection. Buy a modem cable. These cables are pre-fabricated and provide the correct wiring for PC to modem. Your cost should be only $10 to $20. If you have a number of connections that support a 25 DB connector, you can purchase a length of 25-wire ribbon cable and the correct number of quick connects (IDP connectors). The cable runs straight through to both connectors. These connectors clamp down on the ribbon cable with the blow of a hammer. Don't purchase 25 wire multiconductor cable. If your PC has a DB-9 connector, purchase one DB-9 to DB-25 adaptor. The adaptor handles the change between DB-25 and DB-9 so you do not have to worry about pin outs. Also, a modem does not use all 25 wires, so you can get by with nine conductors as shown in Figure 9.8. However, the pinouts shown here will do the job if you insist on building your own cable. This is true of both connections—on the PC side and the UNIX host.

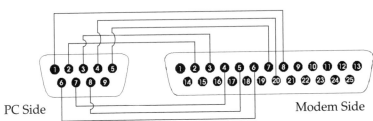

PC Side   Modem Side

FIGURE 9.8   PC DTE port with DB-9 connector to DCE modem with DB-25 connector

Connecting a terminal to UNIX

We mention connecting a terminal to UNIX only because you may need this connection in the same workflow as connecting PCs. With a terminal, you can always get by with just ground, send-data, and receive-data connections. Most terminals use a female DB-25 pin connector. They also represent DTE equipment in all cases we have ever seen. Since you are connecting DTE to DTE, you need to make sure that 2 and 3 are crossed. The third connection is 7 to 7.

Test Boxes

Before you actually delve into a swarm of cables and connectors, you need one more piece of equipment. This is the *breakout box*. Known by many names—including RS-232 Tester, Test Box, Cable Tester, and Status Activity Monitor—these little devices can be lifesavers. Their purpose is simple. They determine whether or not you have the correct connections. You first plug the breakout box into the cable run at one end or the other. A series of LEDs indicate which lines are correctly configured. For example, if lines 2 and 3 are improperly configured, you will get no lights on these lines, meaning that no data can get through. When you connect a serial port to a modem in a straight-through cable, nearly all the lights will light up. If you send keystrokes to the modem from within a terminal emulation program, the outgoing line (normally 2 from a DB-25 connection) blinks, showing transmission. If the receiving device has any response, this shows up on line 3. When using a null modem cable (one with the transmit and receive wires crossed), the main LEDs of interest are 2 and 3. If these are not lit up, the connection was performed incorrectly.

Multiport Problems

If you are using a multiport serial board, you have extra work. There is no standard wire layout when using RJ-11 or RJ-45 connections with a multiport board. The vendor may use the wires in a different order than you are familar with. And even if the multiport board uses DB-9 connectors, there is no guarantee the vendor follows the RS-232 standard in terms of pinouts. Be sure to check with the vendor on the meaning of each pin.

You can pay upwards of $200 for a sophisticated breakout box. Expensive ones provide more options as well as allowing you to configure the connection. However, you probably only need the $20-$30 model without all the bells and whistles. Look for it in electronics catalogs, Radio Shack stores, and small electronics stores. Ninety out of one hundred of your problems will be either a poor cable connection or a crossed connection. A breakout box easily identifies both problems. A typical box has a male and female connector as well as a set of LEDs to show the connections. Buy one; the small expenditure will save you hours of time.

Troubleshooting Serial Communications

- Check your cable for tight connections.

- Make sure that pins 2 and 3 are crossed, if they should be.

- Check the owners manual to see if your port is DCE instead of the expected DTE. If only one machine is DCE, wires 1 and 2 should not be crossed.

- Make sure the MODE command is set if you are using DOS applications.

- Don't strip the sheathing too far back from multi-conductor cable. This is especially true when using crimp-on D-shell connectors. If too much bare wire shows, the wires may touch inside the D-shell. Cut back only about 3/8 of an inch—just long enough to fit into the crimp pin.

•Double-check your cable functionality. Attach the cable to another machine capable of making the connection, and then try it. (This is easy to do if you have a laptop that can be used as a portable tester.)

•If using a modem, make sure it works on a test machine. Plug it into a working COM port.

•Check to see whether the COM port is disabled in the ROM BIOS setup. In many new machines (laptops especially), the COM port might be shut off.

•If using Microsoft Windows, use the simple Terminal Program to check the port. Test both COM ports.

•Check that the COM2 jack is correctly attached to the board inside the PC.

•Check the jumper settings for memory and address on the serial port. Run a diagnostic program like MSD to determine the settings. Insure they are standard as discussed in the Preparing Your PC section. Make sure you do not have a network card using the same interrupt or address.

•Consider replacing the serial card if you have an older machine. Run a diagnostic program to determine the UART chip name. Refer to our earlier discussion on the symptoms of an older chip.

•Confirm that you are using the same data bits, stop bits, baud rate and parity settings as the receiving machine. When you are unable to login, try sending a control-break signal.

•Determine that you are communicating to the correct COM port, not trying to use COM1 when your modem cable is connected to COM2.

10

Emulating DOS

Introduction

This chapter presents a topic of interest to UNIX shops—emulating DOS. UNIX machines can be outfitted to run DOS, just like any PC.

Why would anyone want to turn their SPARCstation or RS/6000 into a low-life PC? Applications!! Even those who spend most of their time in UNIX might be interested in financial planning with a Borland Quattro Pro spreadsheet or writing letters using Microsoft Word for Windows. Figure 10.1 shows Microsoft Excel for Windows running on a Sun SPARCstation. Most customers buy DOS emulation because they must use a particular DOS application frequently, but don't want to buy a PC and have it vying for desktop space.

DOS and Windows applications account for the vast majority of all commercial applications. Whether or not you like PCs, you have to appreciate the overwhelming availability of their applications. The average business or academic person has greater familiarity with PC programs than with UNIX programs. Because of the huge market ($$$), competition has driven DOS/Windows software developers to out-perform one another in terms of capability, reliability, ease of use, connectivity, interoperability, and price. As a general rule, DOS/Windows products are easier to install and use than UNIX products. Some large DOS software vendors, such as Lotus and WordPerfect, are moving their products to UNIX, but the DOS market will be ahead in variety and distribution for a long time.

In this chapter we explain the basics of installing DOS emulators. Read Chapter 17, DOS Emulation Products, for evaluations of particular products. There aren't many of these complicated, niche market products to choose from.

DOS Emulation Described

Emulating DOS means that you actually duplicate a DOS PC within the confines of the UNIX computer. You can run DOS or Windows applications just as if you were seated at a PC, without modifications of any sort to the applications. Screen layout, icons, mouse control, commands, menus—everything is the same.

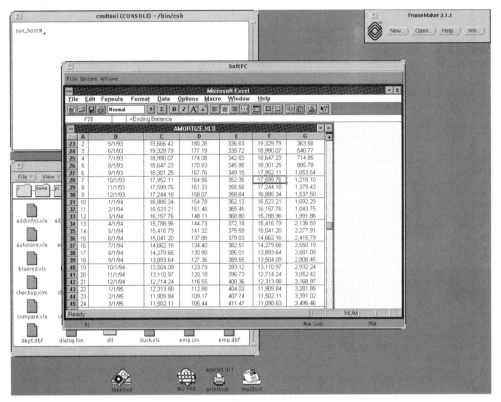

FIGURE 10.1 Running a Microsoft Excel spreadsheet on a SPARCstation—no problem!

However, DOS emulators don't convert your entire workstation to DOS; they just use part of the resources like any other UNIX process. DOS is given its own window that can be sized to encompass the entire display or minimized to an icon. You can ride the mouse back and forth between DOS and UNIX windows, running programs here and there concurrently.

We make an arbitrary distinction between *DOS emulators*, which run at the local machine, and *DOS servers*, which provide DOS services across the network. DOS emulators can indeed also be DOS servers in the sense that they can provide multiple sessions to X-terminals or other workstations. However, there is a real difference to note from the standpoint of hardware. DOS emulators must clone the PC hardware, while DOS servers usually do not—the servers are generally PCs themselves, somewhere on the network. DOS servers display DOS consoles remotely. Most of what we have to say in this chapter is in regard to the former group, DOS emulators. Chapter 17 evaluates some of both for you.

Limitations of DOS Emulation

The only significant difference between real DOS and DOS emulation is how you access the outside world. Using local printers and floppy drives does take some extra fiddling. Some DOS emulators can network as clients nodes of Novell NetWare, and (hopefully soon) Banyan Vines and other PC network operating systems. However, some do not provide network protocol drivers and so cannot network.

We must also clarify that DOS emulation is NOT NECESSARILY a synonym for Windows support. Windows is a GUI that runs over the top of DOS, and not all DOS emulators do Windows. Some products let you run Windows and Windows applications with complete compatibility on the UNIX workstation. The rest only provide a pure DOS compatibility box, similar to Windows' MS-DOS Prompt feature.

PC Hardware

DOS emulation requires compatibility not only with DOS software, but with PC hardware as well. PC hardware is much different than UNIX RISC hardware. The PCs Intel CPU has an entirely different instruction set, so you need software to handle those instructions as Intel would. Also, PC video cards provide varying levels of software-accessible display drivers—from Monochrome Hercules to Super VGA. DOS expanded memory must be duplicated, plus mouse, floppy drive, and communication ports.

There are four ways to supply the needed PC hardware to a DOS emulator:

- Run UNIX on a PC.
- Install an accessory board with an Intel processor in the UNIX workstation.
- Use PC equipment remotely from across the network. (We call this a DOS server.)
- Duplicate the hardware circuit traces in software.

We can find real-life examples of each. SoftPC, from Insignia Solutions, clones the hardware entirely in software. Locus Merge (shipped with SCO Open Desktop and Novell UnixWare) has an easier job, because its UNIX operating system already runs on the PC platform. Others, including Puzzle's Synergy II and SunSelect's SunPC, off-load the hardware problem onto an add-on board with an Intel processor mounted on it (a PC on a board). These particular boards are designed for installation in Sun SBus workstations. Logicraft manufactures the Omni-Ware server, which packs several PCs into one box through multiple expansion boards, and exports DOS sessions across the network, first-come, first-served. Quarterdeck's Desqview/ X serves DOS from a PC to other network users by means of software alone.

Figure 10.2 diagrams the basic relationships between the major DOS emulation components on a UNIX workstation. The DOS emulation product is shaded. Notice that the PC emulation aspect is divided into hardware and software components. (Some products do not require physical hardware.) The PC Emulation Hardware

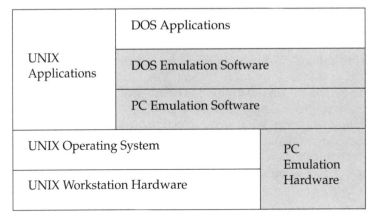

FIGURE 10.2 Running DOS emulation on a UNIX workstation

includes a real Intel CPU and video graphics accelerator. The PC Emulation Software converts the DOS hardware calls to UNIX hardware calls, for the sake of the mouse, memory, drives, and ports. It may also duplicate the CPU and video, if physical hardware is not used. The DOS Emulation Software layer provides the DOS command structure and BIOS link between DOS application and the hardware.

Workstation Requirements

Before you get started on the installation process for an emulator, check to see that you can run DOS sessions acceptably on your UNIX workstation. We look at the hardware from the standpoints of functional requirements and performance.

Functional Requirements

DOS emulators often support both the Motif and OpenWindows graphical user environments. Before purchase, you need to find out if an emulation product would force you to switch GUIs.

Keyboard support may be restricted to only certain models of any workstation manufacturer. However, the 101 key-style keyboard is a safe bet.

Some products suggest that the workstation can run DOS emulation with as little as 12 megabytes of RAM, but that is probably wishful thinking. Windows requires at least 4M of RAM to run acceptably. Perhaps 2M might be used by the emulation program. UNIX consumes 6M+ just to load itself, which doesn't leave any room for applications. Most new workstations are shipped with 20-24M of RAM, which is a better target for DOS emulation. 16M may be acceptable, as long as you don't open multiple Windows sessions. If you do not have enough memory, creating a larger disk swap space is an option on some machines. However, this solves only so much of the problem, and disk access is also much slower than memory access.

A significant amount of disk space is also needed to run DOS emulation. DOS itself takes up 2-3M of disk space, Windows another 8-12M, and extra swap space can consume 12-50M, depending on how large an area you need. (The emulators for Sun OpenWindows recommend 2-3 times the amount of system memory.) All this before installing any DOS applications, which may require as little as a few kilobytes to as much as 20M each. If you don't have at least 100 megabytes free, it won't be worth your time to install DOS emulation.

You can run DOS from X-terminals attached to the UNIX workstation, because a DOS emulator is just another X application. However, they can bog down the workstation, just as any CAD or analysis package might.

Performance

On most workstations, DOS emulation runs at least as fast as a 286 PC. For anyone who has ever used a 486, that can bring you to tears. Modern DOS/Windows software usually requires more processing power than a 286-level machine provides. Here are ways to speed it up.

Workstation CPU and memory

The primary requirement of a workstation is a fast CPU. If your workstation is an entry-level or old machine (up to 30 SPECmarks) you must either live with 286-level performance or add an accelerator. Mid-range to high-end machines (50-100 SPECmarks) provide 386SX- to 486SX-level performance, often without an accelerator.

The amount of workstation memory also affects performance. The more memory, the more applications can be loaded at once, and the less swapping to disk must take place. Swapping to disk is a slow, mechanical function.

Accelerator cards and emulation servers

Accelerator cards boost performance by replacing some of the emulation software with 486 hardware. Obviously, if hardware is present, the software does not have as much overhead to deal with, and it can run programs faster. The software can't totally pass along the speed of the 486, but it certainly upgrades the DOS emulation to the 386 level. Accelerators provide numeric co-processors for faster calculations, and video controllers for faster VGA-mode operation under DOS. Accelerators can also provide support for Windows 386 enhanced mode, and Windows applications that run in protected mode. Figure 10.3 shows a 386-level accelerator.

On the downside, an accelerator requires a bigger outlay of cash than software, and it is more difficult to install. An accelerator also consumes a slot you may need for another accessory. (Does your workstation have a free slot?) But the performance advantage pays for itself quickly. At least one vendor has tackled the performance problem with a multiuser solution. Logicraft, Inc.'s Omni-Ware converts a PC into

FIGURE 10.3 Puzzle Systems' Synergy II puts a PC inside the Sun

an emulation server for up to four users. Omni-Ware's PC accessory boards redirect PC hardware functionality across the network to your workstations. The server emulates PC video controllers, hard disk controllers, keyboard, and parallel printer port. Only the PC's Intel CPU remains, to be emulated in software. Since the workstations do not require hardware, and the server is multiuser, workstations can run DOS programs on a first-come, first-served basis.

Preparing for Installation

DOS emulators require you to make a few special preparations before you install. While the things you must do aren't difficult, don't be surprised if the preparations themselves cause you to re-plan your deployment of DOS emulation.

Shared Memory and Other Kernel Options

If you are running on a Sun with SunOS 4.x (a BSD machine), you may have to activate some System V drivers. Sun provides these drivers for the standard GENERIC kernel, but not in the small kernel. You can find and activate them if they are not already active.

One item to check is shared memory. Has it been turned on in the kernel? To find out, locate your kernel configuration file, usually called **/usr/sys/sun(x)/conf/ GENERIC**. You can load that file into an editor and search for **IPCSHMEM** (Inter-process Communication Shared Memory Facility), a System V enhancement, added for the sake of third party software. If you no longer use **GENERIC**, find the configuration file you do use. This will be indicated in the file **/usr/etc/config**.

SunSelect's SunPC documentation lists its kernel requirements. In case you have altered your kernel and may be missing one or two, here is the list to give you some advance warning. Options: VDDRV (the SunPC driver), IPCSHMEM, NFSSERVER. Pseudo-devices: clone, time64, tirw64, sp, snit, pf, nbuf, tcptli32. Device-drivers: zs, fd, sbus (the SunPC accelerator), bwtwo or cgsix or cgthree (video acceleration), audioamd.

Swap Space

Swap space is especially important to DOS emulators, which require a ton of memory. A swap area is disk space that has been reserved for temporary storage purposes by the operating system. The kernel moves data and/or hunks of idle programs out of memory and into the swap space when it needs the memory to load an activating process. CPUs are designed to perform only the program instructions in RAM, so if a portion of a program must be re-activated, it must first be brought back into RAM from disk, or 'swapped' for what is in memory. The more RAM you have, the less swapping must be done. However, you must also have a large swap space, because according to Murphy's Law, if users can, they will always run more programs to fill up all available RAM. Having adequate swap space prevents the ultimate performance problem—system lockup, where the window manager goes on a vacation without you. Your vendors may ask you to check swap space before you install, to insure themselves that they won't be embarrassed. For example, a minimum configuration of SunSelect SunPC requires approximately 11M to **a**) run the SunPC window and **b**) provide 2M for program space. Ordinarily, Windows runs much better with 8M for programs, requiring 6M of additional swap space.

 **Popping the Kernel**

Don't take kernel modifications lightly, because modifications incorrectly done can make your machine unbootable. Especially watch any changes you make to Sun's **/sys/sun/conf.c** file. If you can't boot on a Sun, try executing **vmunix.old** in your home directory from the boot prompt.

To find out what swap space you have currently on a Sun, type **/usr/etc/pstat -s**. One rule of thumb is to have swap space equal to two times the memory in the machine. To make programs run like cheetahs, you can increase the swap area to six or seven times the machine's memory, though allocating that much swap space consumes a lot of disk space. You should not do any swapping over the network to another machine—that is a no-no. While it can be done, you won't like the performance, or the potential interruption to your work if the network link goes to pot.

If your swap space is too small, you may have two options for increasing it. The painful option is to re-partition (reformat) the disk with a larger swap partition. If you have an SCO machine, this is your only choice. (The swap partition identifier displays at boot time as a part of the kernel boot messages. The kernel also warns you, through the SWAPWARN option, when you reach a low level of available swap space.) For the easy way to add swap space, create a supplementary swap area in a spacious filesystem using the **mkfile** command. The following commands create a 32M swap area in **/home** on a Sun SPARCstation with SunOS.

```
SUN_HOST% su
SUN_HOST# mkfile -nv 32m /home/extraswap
```

Next, **edit /etc/fstab** to include:

```
/home/extraswap swapdir swap rw 0 0
```

Finally, execute these commands to make **extraswap** available and exit superuser:

```
SUN_HOST# swapon -a
SUN_HOST# exit
```

You should get an acknowledgment from **swapon** that it is "Adding /home/extraswap as swap device". If there is no way to find enough space on your local drive, you can prepare a swap file on a remote host, then use NFS to mount that swap file on your local system. (But again, this is not recommended.) Another call to **pstat** should show the increase in swap space. If it does not, or if you do not get the acknowledgment from **swapon**, check to see if the **extraswap** file exists and is the right size. Then check for errors in **/etc/fstab**. There may even be an error on a previous **fstab** line that prevented the swap line from being reached. Reboot if you need to—the **rc** startup script also runs **swapon**, and you may find a mount error for line x of **/etc/fstab**, giving you a handle on where to find the error.

Installing DOS Emulation Hardware

There is not much about installing the hardware that the vendors don't address in their instruction books. However, here are some general principles to guide you.

You can install accessory boards in Sun SPARCstations, IBM RS/6000s, and other UNIX workstations yourself. The first step is to shut down your UNIX machine properly. This requires using the appropriate command—usually **shutdown**. See Appendix A for further details. Then turn off the power to the peripherals, then the system unit, then the monitor. Detach the cables from the system unit, move it to a clear area, and plug the power cord back into the unit and the wall outlet to help protect against static electricity. Remove the cover.

At this point, take time out to worry about frying your $15,000 workstation or the accelerator board with a static discharge. SunSelect provides a static protection wrist strap for use in installing SunPC—wear it. Make sure you are discharged on something other than your electronics. Handling the card by its edges, insert the card into its designated slot according to vendor instructions. Then replace the cover, return the system unit to its peripherals and reconnect the cables. Turn the power on to the monitor first, followed by the peripherals, then the system unit.

When you start a DOS session, there should be a confirmation of the accelerator's presence. If you do not get a confirmation, try the diagnostics supplied with the card. The card should automatically connect with the emulation software.

Logicraft's Omni-Ware does not place any board in the UNIX workstation. Rather, it turns a dedicated PC into a DOS server by adding extra hardware and networking the PC with UNIX. Products such as this have extensive, specific instructions for their installation.

Installing DOS Emulation Software

Vendors distribute DOS emulation products on either QIC tape (quarter-inch cartridge) or CD-ROM, with possible additional floppy diskettes. Make sure you have the right hardware before you place an order.

Configuring the UNIX Environment

Just as with any UNIX software, installing the software is usually a three-step process: loading the files, running a configuration script, and fixing up the rest of the details by hand. Here is a quick overview of the process.

A general procedure

Emulation products for UNIX generally require you to login as root before installing. Some, such as Insignia Solutions' SoftPC, also require you to exit your windows system (OpenWindows). This is a good idea. You can copy the files onto your disk with no problem, but restarting the windows system makes sure any changes to startup scripts take effect. You may have to reboot the computer after the product is loaded.

Your installation manual may instruct you to set environment variables or path names in your **.cshrc** or **.login** script, either before or after you install the files. See Chapter 1 for a discussion of shell scripts. You can make the changes from the convenience of your favorite editor. Here are some sample lines from **.cshrc** for Insignia Solutions SoftPC 3.0:

```
setenv SPCHOME /home/softpc
setenv XAPPLRESDIR $SPCHOME
setenv FONTPATH $SPCHOME/fonts/x
set PATH=($PATH $SPCHOME/bin)
```

On a Sun, you may have to set the **LD_LIBRARY_PATH** variable with the location of the OpenWindows libraries.

Load the files, then run the configuration program. This step installs the driver(s) in the UNIX kernel, edits startup scripts such as **rc.local**, and hopefully fixes up everything else.

Running DOS emulation for network clients

If the DOS emulation product permits itself to be supplied over the network to other UNIX users, there are a couple of hurdles to clear. First, export the directory that contains the emulation. NFS and the mount daemons must be running to export, and the file that defines exported directories is **/usr/etc/exports**. Type **exportfs -a** to see if the emulation is being exported. If it is not, use an editor to place the directory in the file.

The second task is to mount the exported directory on the remote machine(s). If you find **automount** in the remote machine's process list (via the **ps** command), you're in luck—go home early. If not, you must create both a new directory to use as a mount point and a new entry in the **/etc/fstab** file. You can then reboot the machine to mount the server's DOS emulation directory automatically, or use the **mount** command without rebooting.

Finally, you must configure each client machine to run DOS. This involves executing the previously mentioned configuration program from each client workstation, to rebuild its kernel. On an X-terminal, however, you may be able to start the emulator with a display flag, or set the DISPLAY environment variable.

Configuring the DOS Environment

In order to run DOS you will have to set and maintain DOS environment variables such as **PATH**. Most variables are set in the DOS startup scripts, along with commands to automatically run programs. (See Appendix A for details on DOS startup scripts and file editing.) Nearly all of your DOS configuration can be done in the file **AUTOEXEC.BAT**, unless you have a PC LAN, in which case you may need to edit **LASTDRIVE** in **CONFIG.SYS**. If, on the DOS boot, you get a message that you are "**Out of environment space**", increase it by placing **SHELL=COMMAND.COM / E:512 /P** in your **CONFIG.SYS** file. The default environment space is only 160 bytes; this raises it to 512 bytes.

The other major aspect of configuring the DOS environment is setting up the DOS drives. Utilities can make this a simple matter, as shown in Figure 10.4.

Selecting Fonts

Emulators provide special DOS fonts to imitate the DOS command lines, etc. In order to use them in a DOS window under the Motif window system, you need to have Motif-compatible DOS fonts. Products usually provide DOS fonts for the Motif

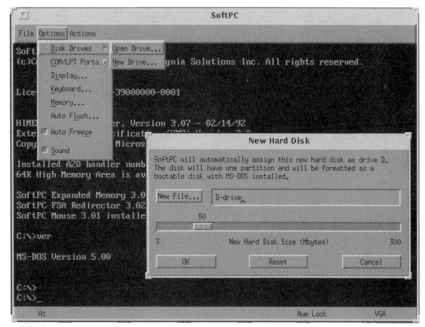

FIGURE 10.4 Emulating a hard drive in software with Insignia Solutions' SoftPC

and OpenWindows environments. You may select which set of fonts to access in **FONTPATH**, a variable in your UNIX startup script. The normal fonts for a Sun OpenWindows machine are kept in **/usr/lib/X11/fonts**.

If the product does not find the DOS fonts after you have specified their location, run **xset**, the user preference utility for X. That should clear up the problem. Here are the commands:

```
xset +fp (dos_font_directory)
xset fp rehash
```

Installing Microsoft Windows

Most DOS emulators allow complete compatibility with Microsoft Windows 3.0 and 3.1. They accomplish this with special drivers, which you may have to install as a separate action. Once the drivers are installed, all you must do is load the Windows software, as supplied by Microsoft. (Some vendors now bundle Windows with their emulators.) Figure 10.5 shows Microsoft Windows running on a Sun inside of a SoftPC DOS emulation box.

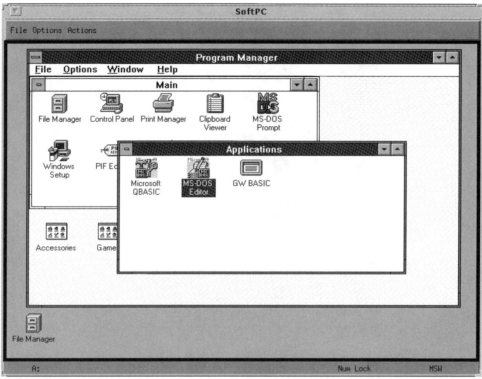

FIGURE 10.5 Windows with an OPEN LOOK border, as viewed from the Sun

Running DOS Emulation

Now it's time to get behind the wheel. What does the scenery look like under DOS? Here is a short travelogue.

The Basics

The primary capability you want is, of course, to run DOS applications. As for UNIX, typing the name of an executable application file starts the program. From then on, you follow the vendor's user interface until you leave the program and return to DOS.

C: is the designation (DOS prompt) for the local DOS hard drive, which happens to be a reserved area on your UNIX drive, if not a real PC drive across the network. With some products, the entire C drive is actually one large UNIX file. DOS uses the UNIX design of hierarchical directories and path designations prefixed to files, but you're in for a shock—slashes have been replaced by backslashes! Commands and keystrokes are cross-referenced in Appendix A to help you get up and running quickly.

If you have Windows compatibility with your DOS emulator, you have an advantage in learning DOS programs. Windows-compatible applications have a standardized user interface, so you won't have to wholly retrain when you fire up a new one. DOS-only programs often make use of a Menu bar at the top of the window, but there may be little else the same between applications.

HOT TIP	"Bad command or file name"
	This is the standard 'Sorry' message from DOS. It means that a) you incorrectly spelled a command at the DOS prompt, or b) the command is not in the **PATH**, set in **AUTOEXEC.BAT**. DOS checks for the file in the current directory first, followed by the root (**C:**), followed by the **PATH** list. Also, make sure the file exists. Parameters you affix to a command do NOT generate this error.

You can connect your printer to DOS so that you can copy or print text files from the command line, print screens (using the PrintScreen key), and send formatted print jobs from applications. You may have access to both UNIX printers and PC network printers, depending upon the product.

When you enter the DOS window, all of your UNIX programs continue running as before. Leaving the DOS window may either suspend DOS temporarily, or you can have the window remain active and running. When a DOS program running on a PC hangs, you have to CTRL-ALT-DEL or power down to reset—now you must kill the emulation window.

You can cut and paste text between the UNIX and DOS environments, but not graphics, even under Windows. You also won't find drag and drop support across environments.

Accessing Workstation Hardware

DOS emulation provides an entirely new way of accessing workstation hardware. You will have to make some adjustments. Here are the major enhancements.

Floppy drives

One nice feature of using DOS emulation on a Sun workstation is that the floppy drive is easier to use. Usually you can just click on a diskette drive button to attach it or eject the floppy. This is much faster than mounting the **pcfs** file system. Under DOS, the drives are still referred to as A: or B:. You can perform any regular DOS command, including **FORMAT**.

Printer and communication ports

The parallel and serial ports on a workstation take on new names under DOS. DOS uses the standard names LPT1, LPT2, etc. for parallel ports and COM1, COM2, etc. for serial ports. DOS emulators provide a means of assigning the new names to the devices you have defined on your workstation. For example, you can assign COM1 to Sun's **/dev/ttya** device and LPT1 to the **lp** printer defined in **/etc/printcap**. You might also assign LPT ports to files. There is a small caveat, however: if you have multiple DOS sessions open, only one can have control of a particular communications (COM) port at a time.

Mouse

The DOS window requires its own mouse, so the emulator creates a Microsoft-compatible mouse out of, say, a Sun mouse. When you enter the DOS window, you have to attach this mouse, but doing so disables it for use outside the window until you detach it. Mouse control can be a problem if you need to cut and paste between the DOS window and other UNIX windows. Using SoftPC or SunPC, you must re-attach the mouse every time you return to the DOS window, unless Windows is running in that DOS window.

Connecting to Novell NetWare and Other PC LANs

Some DOS emulation products for UNIX do support connections to PC LANs, especially Novell NetWare. Such connections allow you to access DOS file servers so that you can share data and programs with other PCs on the network. If there is a file server with the application you need, you don't need to reinstall it on the workstation.

Setting up a NetWare connection

There are usually scant requirements for setting up a NetWare connection, as long as you have a network set up between the UNIX workstation and the NetWare file server. If your workstation is not connected to the NetWare cabling, Chapters 4 and 5 will help you. (Also, Chapter 7 can give you instructional background in being a NetWare client.) Outside of the network, the DOS emulator must include an IPX protocol driver to allow connection over the workstation's Ethernet adapter.

NetWare and other PC LANs are non-graphical in nature, so there are no special requirements in that regard. Also, normal PCs run the LAN client software from within DOS script files **CONFIG.SYS** and **AUTOEXEC.BAT**) which you also use under DOS emulation, so you should not have to go through any contortions that an ordinary PC user wouldn't have. The only real task you must perform is to edit the DOS startup files. Unless instructed otherwise, the commands you place in **AUTOEXEC.BAT** will probably look similar to these:

```
IPX
NETX
(drive_letter:)\LOGIN SERVER_NAME/USER_NAME
```

There may be additional commands ahead of **IPX** to locate to a Novell program directory. 'Drive_letter' is the letter of the network drive used for logins. This is typically F:, but may be different either because 1) the NetWare server system login scripts map a different letter to the login drive, or 2) the DOS emulation software requires another letter. You may have to set a variable in **CONFIG.SYS** called **LAST-DRIVE**, and the NetWare system administrator may have to modify your user startup scripts to map the drives properly. In addition, you may have to change a network attribute called *frame type*, but that is usually easily remedied with econfig. See Chapters 5 and 7 for specific instructions on any of these changes.

The DOS emulation allows you to have more than one DOS session open at a time from a single workstation. However, only one of these sessions can be connected to NetWare.

WABI and Friends

Sun Microsystems hopes to replace DOS emulators with WABI technology (Windows Application Binary Interface). Sun promises full Microsoft Windows compatibility. That is, Windows applications can run out of the box on a UNIX workstation without Windows or paying for a Windows license. Just click on the Word for Windows icon in the corner of your UNIX desktop, and you get Word for Windows. The original Windows look and feel remains, without the application vendor having to recompile any source code.

The technology works by translating Windows system calls into equivalent UNIX system calls, skipping some of the emulation steps. WABI should operate much faster than existing DOS emulators because it spares most of the overhead of duplicating the PC and DOS in software. However, there are limitations to WABI. First, only certified applications are guaranteed to work. These are top-selling Windows applications that also conform to the Windows API. Second, those parts of a Windows program that do not use the API, such as most help systems, will not work at all without the presence of a Windows license and emulator. Third, DOS applications are still out in the cold. They will not work under WABI.

Meanwhile, Insignia Solutions and Bristol Technology have teamed up to run shrink-wrapped Windows products with a significant advantage: Microsoft's blessing. Similar to WABI, their product, called SoftWindows, translates Windows system calls to UNIX calls on the fly and avoids PC/DOS emulation steps, with 486 performance. However, since Insignia Solutions is licensing source code from Microsoft, they can keep abreast of Windows technology better than Sun, who is reverse-engineering the Windows API. SoftWindows requires a modified Windows 3.1 software license, and compatibility with all Windows applications is virtually guaranteed.

The cost of SoftWindows is expected to be higher because Insignia Solutions has to pay for a Windows license for each copy of SoftWindows. In addition, it is highly likely that WABI will be bundled by the workstation vendors with their workstation operating systems.

IBM, HP, USL, SCO, and other UNIX vendors have agreed to license WABI from Sun. Insignia Solutions is emphasizing the compatibility advantages to their technology. Both sides plan to have initial products available by the end of 1993. Windows software vendors will have to adapt their licensing strategy, but they won't have to port their products to UNIX unless they really need the capabilities and performance a native port provides. (You may see fewer native UNIX ports.) Microsoft has threatened to sue Sun for 'intellectual property infringements,' but Sun seems confident.

11

Connecting Printers

Introduction

For the purposes of this book, connecting printers represents more than just stringing a serial or parallel cable between your computer and printer. In this chapter we emphasize networking printers—making a UNIX printer available to DOS users or making DOS printers available to UNIX users. If you are a novice UNIX user, you will find setting up UNIX printers to be a formidable task—perhaps the most difficult and aggravating of all. If you are a novice DOS user, printer setup is easier, but you still have new things to learn. Conceptually, networking printers is not difficult to master. Just remember to mind your Ps and Qs (print servers and queues, of course).

For this chapter we depart from our standard format. The previous how-to chapters mentioned many products, but did not discuss their specific installation in detail; we reserved that for the product evaluation chapters in the last part of the book. With regard to printer connections, however, we choose to walk through several product installations with you in order to better illustrate the procedures involved.

Starting with the Basics

Many system administrators find printing to be a driving force in establishing a network. Printers and plotters are perfect devices for networking because they spend less time sitting idle when available to many users. As you network DOS and UNIX computers, the list of pooled equipment invariably includes one or more laser or dot-matrix printers.

Concepts and terminology for network printing

As discussed previously, a TCP/IP network represents the common medium for networking UNIX and DOS computers over Ethernet. Printers can be attached directly to this network cabling, or indirectly through one of the networked computers. Please review Chapter 5, Setting Up a TCP/IP Network, if you do not currently have a network in place. As an alternative to TCP/IP, some products provide forms of

UNIX-DOS connectivity over other protocols such as Novell's IPX/SPX. However, the setup procedures remain the same.

You have three choices when connecting a printer to the network: 1) attach the printer to a UNIX workstation, 2) attach the printer to a PC, or 3) attach the printer directly to the Ethernet cabling. The printer requires an interface to whichever cable you use, of course. Dot-matrix printers have either a serial or parallel interface—sometimes both. Laser printers have both. Direct Ethernet connections require special adapters (similar to computer LAN adapters) that may be either internal cards or external boxes. These adapters most commonly provide BNC connectors for attachment to thin Ethernet, but you can get other varieties.

Knowledge of certain terms comes in handy. If the printer attaches to a computer via serial or parallel cable, the printer is *local* to that computer. Each print job goes directly from the computer to the printer. Thus, the computer may have to wait on the printer receiving the data if there is no spooler active. (A spooler simply grabs all of the print job and delivers it in the background to the printer—allowing the computer user to go on with computing.) If the printer connects to the network cabling, it is called a *remote* printer. Even if the printer attaches to a network station via serial or parallel cabling—if it becomes available to network users, it also is termed a remote printer.

On the network, a *spooler* places each print job into a spool directory or *print queue*—a special holding area on the file server. Another program, the *print server*, waits continually for jobs to appear in the queue—plucking from the queue each stored job in its turn and transferring it to a designated printer. This print server/print queue arrangement does several things for you. It keeps print jobs separated (with banner pages to identify the source, if desired). It allows flexibility; multiple printers can serve a single queue on a first-come, first-served basis, or several print queues can feed one printer. In addition, print server software allows each network user to manage their print job(s). Such management can include deleting jobs, reordering them, shifting them to other printers, as well as additional functions.

PCL versus PostScript

For a majority of managers, a relevant question is: Do I want auto-switched PCL and PostScript capability? If all you have is a dot-matrix printer, this is not an issue—these printers do not provide either PCL or PostScript capabilities. However, they can serve the network by printing ASCII text files from either DOS or UNIX. Laser printers are more versatile. PostScript is a graphics-oriented page description language used by desktop publishing software. Since UNIX workstations provide good platforms for desktop publishing, PostScript laser printers have come to dominate the UNIX laser market.

DOS software, on the other hand, typically generates files for laser printers in the PCL (Printer Control Language) format developed by Hewlett-Packard, giant of the laser printer market. PCL-compatible applications create graphic images using

LaserJet-specific commands. Such applications are commonly found in general business settings—accounting, sales, etc.

HOT TIP **What'cha Readin'?**

Did you know that you are reading PostScript files? The PostScript page description language is excellent for desktop publishing—allowing you to integrate text, diagrams, photographs, clip art, and many other types of graphics. If we had printed the PostScript output for this book on a non-PostScript printer, it would have made tough reading, the book would have been three feet thick, and we would have had to charge $849.95 for it! PostScript files are necessarily huge, so PostScript printers require 3-4 more megabytes of memory than their non-PostScript cousins.

You no longer have to choose one or the other format. You can retrofit existing printers to automatically sense the format of an incoming file. A stock HP laser printer can print PostScript files if you purchase one of several add-on products. Newer printers can master either type of job without an accessory.

Product Types

You can get a variety of printing functionality with different products. This section gives a bird's-eye view of the field of products.

If you need only to share a printer between 2-16 non-networked computers, your simplest and cheapest solution is to buy a manual switchbox or *print buffer*. For example, you can connect both a Sun SPARCstation via serial cable and a DOS PC via serial cable to a serial A-B switchbox. This in turn feeds the printer's serial interface. When your Sun user needs the printer, the switch must be set on A before pressing **Print**. When the PC user needs the printer, the switch is turned to B. A print buffer handles the switching automatically. The print buffer also has the memory to store (buffer) the entire print job—preventing you from having to wait around for the printer to receive and print your job, one page at a time.

On the other hand, if you place the printer on a network you can service many more users. One way of connecting to Ethernet LANs is through an Ethernet adapter board, similar to what you find in PCs. These boards slide into the expansion slot on the printer and provide communications with network operating system protocols—principally TCP/IP and Novell NetWare IPX/SPX. The boards have an on-board processor to handle all network communication tasks, leaving the printer's own processor free to do its primary job. Some printers include an Ethernet adapter as standard equipment—such as the HP LaserJet IIIsi and 4si MX.

External print servers climb a little higher on the ladder of functionality. They connect as many as three printers/plotters at once to the network cabling. They also act as servers for network print queues.

For PostScript printing on a non-PostScript printer, you need to convert the Post-Script file to a bit-mapped image the printer can deal with. You can obtain software to do interpret the file at the workstation, or use a PostScript cartridge to interpret at the printer. The cartridge slides into one of the font cartridge slots and translates incoming PostScript files to the printer's native language. However, without some auto-switching mechanism, EVERY file will be treated as PostScript. While you are at the store, remember to pick up a couple megabytes of extra memory for the printer—PostScript needs it. Incidently, there are no PCL cartridges for converting PostScript printers.

Accelerator cards offer increased speed and more. These cards mount in the I/O slots of printers and speed up printing—in addition to providing auto-switched PCL and PostScript emulation capabilities. At this time such products do not provide an Ethernet adapter, but they should be compatible with any adapter supported by the printer.

The easiest, though most expensive, way to solve all of your problems at once is to purchase a new printer. Some models can detect the format of the print job automatically and immediately switch to either the PostScript or PCL interpreter. These printers come network-ready, so all you provide is an Ethernet cable to the onboard adapter.

We used an HP LaserJet III in our lab, which does NOT network or emulate PostScript out of the box. Most of the installation examples in the chapter apply to that printer. Many of the procedures will be identical for other LaserJet family models and similar for other printers on the market.

Selecting a Hardware Interface

Before you swan dive into purchasing a printer accessory from a salesman, such as a manual switchbox, print buffer, Ethernet adapter, or print server, you need do a little planning. Some options make more sense for connecting a printer to your company's network. You should select a cabling plan and hardware interface in conjunction with any purchase of accessory devices, because some products could force a dead-end solution on your company.

Comparing Interfaces

There are three types of interfaces—serial, parallel, and Ethernet (coax or UTP). There are advantages and disadvantages to each one. Under a 9600 baud *serial* connection, the speed of transmission is roughly 1200 characters per second. All seven bits that compose each ASCII character—with their accompanying stop bit—(a typical scenario; this can vary) must travel single-file across the wire to their destination. *Parallel* interfaces are several times faster because the bits are sent in parallel over different wires. Practically speaking, you cannot detect any difference in speed between serial and parallel interfaces for short text files. Where the parallel interface does make a substantial difference is in downloading soft fonts to the printer, and in printing graphics.

An *Ethernet* connection requires more hardware than either serial and parallel interfaces but provides greater performance, theoretically approaching 1,250,000 characters per second—the speed of Ethernet. However, Ethernet connections always require spooler and server programs, which cause varying delays. Keep in mind that many users will notice little difference between interfaces, speed-wise; they must usually walk to the printer, anyway.

Serial interface allows a long maximum distance between computer and printer—50 to 250 feet, depending on which expert you listen to. (See Chapter 9.) In fact, serial can span distances of over a mile with boosters/drivers, but you might find the hike a little long merely to pick up a printout. Parallel interfaces can only tolerate 10 feet (some stretch to 15). Ethernet interfaces allow the most flexibility, because you can move the printer around the network without running new cable or having to place the printer close to a computer. For example, a parts counter clerk in an automotive dealership using an Ethernet interface could have the bill printed out and waiting for you at the cashier's desk simply by pressing a key at his or her own station.

The serial interface provides one special asset that the others do not—the ability to receive print jobs via modem. A computer application, if specially programmed, can send a print job to a remote modem connected only to a printer for remote delivery of printed material—similar to a fax. However, applications making use of this capability are rare. More commonly, you can find fax modems that connect directly to a printer to print out faxed documents.

Setting Up a Hardware Interface

Hooking up the cable to the printer is simple. Let us draw your attention to just a few points. Serial cables for printers differ from serial cables for modems. Printers using the serial interface require null modem cables, which have lines 2 and 3 crossed between ends. (Note: terminal cables are also null modem cables, but they usually don't work as printer cables because they have different ends and too few conductors.) If you intend to use a serial cable between, say, a Sun workstation and an HP LaserJet, it should also have male DB25 connectors on both ends (or you can use a gender changer). Sun provides an adapter that converts its DIN-style serial port jack to a female DB25. Parallel printer cables are all the same, but a parallel interface may not be provided on some workstations. If you have network cabling, you will need a network-ready printer, or, a network adapter and a bit of time for installation. See How to Install an Internal Network Adapter, and How to Install a

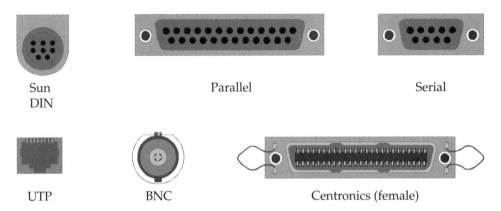

Sun
DIN

Parallel

Serial

UTP

BNC

Centronics (female)

FIGURE 11.1 Common cable/port connectors used in printing

Print Server, later in this chapter. Figure 11.1 can help you identify the ports and/or cables you have currently.

You must set the printer to use one of its hardware interfaces. On an HP LaserJet, do this by taking it off-line, then holding down the Menu button until the display changes to the configuration options. Advance through the options by pressing the Menu key until it displays **I/O=**. Scroll through the options using the Plus (+) key—**PARALLEL, SERIAL**, or perhaps **OPTIONAL** (for Ethernet). When the interface you want is showing, press Enter. If you chose **I/O= SERIAL**, touch Menu again to show **SERIAL=RS-232, BAUD RATE=9600, ROBUST XON=ON**, and **DTR POLARITY=HI**—the default values. You might later boost the baud rate to 19,200, but 9600 is safe to start with. The line speed should be set to the highest baud rate possible; however, for most files and installations the line speed makes practically no difference.

Networking a Printer Under UNIX

In this section, we intend to help you solve the mystery of networking printers with UNIX—be they PostScript or PCL printers, local or remote. We have reached the tricky part. If you master setting up the UNIX details, you get an 'A'.

Overview of UNIX Printing

UNIX printing remains a difficult process to describe. No one program has control from start to finish, which, while it makes for good modular programming, also makes the process hard to follow. We will break up the problem into two parts: preparation and process. In general, before you print you must make the following preparations:

●Select a device interface file to match your cabling to the printer. Often printing is handled through a serial port, but it can be a parallel port if your workstation has one. Device drivers for managing all ports are pre-installed into the system kernel, but to use a port you must still reference the appropriate interface file.

●Define the printer. The printer must be told which device driver to use, what filter programs to apply, where to find the spooled files, etc. The same printer can be defined in more than one way for different end results.

●Ensure that the print server daemon is operational.

When the preparations have been made, we can define the UNIX printing process in four basic steps:

●The user issues a *print command* to start a print job. The print job is stored in a *spool directory*, and a message is sent to the print server that a job is waiting.

●The print server daemon always waits for notification of a new job. When one appears, it creates a clone of itself (a *child*) to print the job, while the original keeps waiting for another. If the printer is located on a remote machine with its own print server, the local server forwards the job.

●The new print server daemon runs the print job through a filter to convert the file into an acceptable format for the printer.

●The formatted job is transmitted along to the printer device driver, and the child daemon dies.

We now explore the basics of how you can prepare for printing. Eventually we will return to the subject of print and queue management commands.

Selecting a Device File

On the UNIX filesystems, the **/dev** directory contains *device* or *special* files. You must select one of these for use in talking to the printer. (We talk to cars, computers, and plants; why not to printers?) Software applications and print commands use the device file as an interface to the kernel's built-in device drivers. Actually, a device file is not really a disk file at all, but rather a path to an I/O channel. There are two types of device files, *character* (or *raw*) and *block*. Character devices move data one character at a time, while block devices move data in chunks. (If you type **ls -l** in a directory of devices, lines starting with **c** are character devices, files starting with **b** are block devices.) A hard disk is a block device, but often has a character interface as well for the sake of some applications. Printer ports normally use character devices. For our purpose in this chapter, you only need to select the file that matches your port. Your system documentation will help you identify the file you need.

To print a file, you write it to a device file, which funnels the data to the device driver, which in turn passes it to the physical port on the back of the computer. A serial port device file on a Sun may be called **/dev/ttya**. A parallel port file may be identified as **/dev/lp0** or **/dev/bpp0**. If the printer is connected to the Ethernet cable, you do not use a device file since in such a case the network handles communication.

Configuring a Serial Port

Our Sun SPARCstation IPC provides two serial ports, but it isn't always enough to just attach a cable to one of them. Serial ports must be reconfigured on occasion.

Serial ports are by default used for terminal communications. You have to modify a data file in order to inform the system that you have a printer, rather than a terminal, connected to one. On a BSD system, **/etc/ttytab** contains a table filled with *tty* devices. A **tty** is simply another name for a terminal. (In the olden days, Teletype Corporation was a major manufacturer of interactive, printer-like terminals—hence, TTY.) System V uses the file **/etc/inittab**. System V Release 4 adds **/etc/ttydefs** and the configuration programs **sacadm** and **ttyadm**. You'll need to be on your toes to properly wade through any of these terminal configuration procedures. The format of definition files can also vary between systems. (Again, see Chapter 9.) Several UNIX processes use the **tty** configuration file to initialize and control terminals.

The serial port we used for the printer was **ttya**, the first serial port listed in **/etc/ttytab**. Be certain to check whether or not a login has been enabled on the serial port you have chosen. On a BSD Sun, **ttya** should indicate 'off', disabling **login** and **local**. For more extensive information about serial ports, see Chapter 9, Making Serial Connections.

Defining a Printer

The following discussions show how to edit the low-level files needed for printing. No matter how you connect a printer to a TCP/IP network—whether through parallel, serial, or Ethernet cabling, you have to modify a printer definition file. On BSD systems, this is done by editing the **/etc/printcap** file. System V UNIX uses *interface* files for the same purpose.

Newer UNIX systems include setup utilities, so that you don't have to dig around in files. With SCO, you use **sysadmsh** to do the configuring. IBM's AIX provides the **smit** utility; UnixWare has **Setup** utilities; HP-UX has **sam**, and Sun Solaris 2.x has the **admintool**. They help you select the device file and set up the port, as well as defining the printer. All of these utilities are much simpler to deal with than editing files by hand.

Modifying /etc/printcap for BSD UNIX printing

Printcap is short for "printer capability database," and describes how to access each printer. Be cautious when modifying this file—it is extremely touchy, like some people before they've had their morning coffee. In addition, if there is trouble, your

printcap may not be set up to send you error messages, so you won't know what is wrong.

Find the manual page for **printcap** and study it. (See Appendix A, under Getting Help. For the Sun SPARCstation, see the System and Network Administration manual.) The listing below shows a sample **/etc/printcap** file with definitions for a few common printer connections.

```
1|serial_for_Sun|lp|HP LaserJet III (Sun):\
            :lp=/dev/ttya:br#19200:\
            :ms=pass8,ixon:\
            :sd=/home/pc/pcnfsd/spool/sun:\
            :lf=/home/pc/pcnfsd/spool/lpd-errs:
2|serial_for_PCs|HP LaserJet III (PC):\
            :mx=0:lp=/dev/ttya:br#19200:\
            :ms=pass8,ixon,raw:sf:sh:\
            :sd=/home/pc/pcnfsd/spool:\
            :lf=/home/pc/pcnfsd/spool/lpd-errs:
3|remote_printer|HP LaserJet III (remote):\
            :mx=0:lp=:sf:sh:\
            :rm=scopc:rp=laser:\
            :sd=/home/pc/pcnfsd/spool:\
            :lf=/home/pc/pcnfsd/spool/lpd-errs:
4|ps|HP LaserJet III (Pacific Data):\
            :mx=0:lp=/dev/ttya:br#19200:\
            :ms=cs8,-parenb,-cstopb,-clocal,-cread,-ixon,-ixoff,crtscts:\
            :sd=/home/pc/pcnfsd/spool/sun:\
            :lf=/home/pc/pcnfsd/spool/lpd-errs:\
            :if=/usr/lib/hpf:sh:
5|microplex|HP LaserJet III (Pacific Data):\
            :lp=:rp=qprn:rm=microplex:\
            :ms=cs8,-parenb,-cstopb,-clocal,-cread,-ixon,-ixoff,crtscts:\
            :sd=/home/pc/pcnfsd/spool/sun:\
            :lf=/home/pc/pcnfsd/spool/lpd-errs:\
            :if=/usr/lib/hpf:sh:
6|laserjetIII:\
            :mx=0:lp=/var/spool/printers/laserjetIII/.null:sh:\
            :sd=/var/spool/printers/laserjetIII:\
            :lf=/var/spool/printers/laserjetIII/log:\
            :of=/usr/lib/hpnp/hplj.of.sh:\
            :if=/usr/lib/hpnp/hplj.if.sh:
7|parallel_ALM:\
            :mx=0:lp=/dev/mcpp0:sh:\
            :sd=/home/pc/pcnfsd/spool:\
            :lf=/home/pc/pcnfsd/spool/lpd-errs:
```

The first definition is the default printer, as evidenced by the name **lp** for line printer. The Sun prints to the printer identified as **lp** if no other printer is specified. This printer connects to the UNIX host directly via serial cable (**lp=/dev/ttya**), and also prints a burst page. Definition 2 is designed for use by PCs. It differs from definition 1 in that the automatic form feed and automatic header page are surpressed (**sf** and **sh**). Printer 3 is connected directly to a remote SCO UNIX PC named **scopc**, which can be accessed over the network (**lp**=nothing). Note that **rm=scopc** sets the remote host name, and **rp=laser** sets the remote printer name. Definition 4 was added for the Pacific Data PE/XL product—again, accessed through Sun's serial port. The name **ps** is a common name for PostScript printers under UNIX. Definition 5 is a variation of 4, using **PE/XL** with the Microplex M200 Print Server over the network. Definition 6 uses the HP JetDirect Ethernet network adapter. This printer is accessed remotely through a device called **.null**. Finally, definition 7 is used for a parallel printer connected to a Sun via an ALM-2 board. Note that parallel and ethernet device drivers do not require a baud rate (**br**) or terminal mode (**ms**) parameters.

The first line of each definition shows the name(s) of the printer. First comes an optional printer number (a matter of convention only, but some TCP/IP products, such as SunSelect PC-NFS, need it). Then follows a very important short printer name, followed by a long descriptive name and other aliases. Subsequent lines contain two-character parameter names and their values. Here are the most common parameters.

```
br: baud rate for tty devices
if: input filter
lf: log file name for errors (can be /dev/console or a file)
lp: device driver name - ttya is first serial port, ttyb is second, (blank) is Ethernet
ms: terminal modes for tty devices
mx: maximum file size (0=unlimited)
of: output filter
rm: remote machine-host that has a printer (rp)
rp: remote printer name
sd: spool directory
sf: suppress form feed
sh: suppress header (burst) page
```

Note that printers can be given restricted access with the **rg** and **rs** commands. These are not commonly used, but check for their existence if you are having trouble printing to a device.

Observe these important rules of thumb when editing **/etc/printcap** for a Sun SPARCstation or other BSD machine:

•Do not multiply definitions needlessly. A long file length can reportedly cause problems as well as provide more bug habitat.

•Do not use spaces, apostrophes, or punctuation in the short printer name field, or the definition will be ignored.

- Separate the names on the first line with the " | " character.

- One (and ONLY one) definition must have"**lp** as an alias. This will be the default printer, used by the spooler commands.

- Each line in a definition except for the last line must be terminated with a "\\",(no blank space) and a carriage return.

- Each line in a definition after the first must be preceded by a tab or blank space.

- Use a colon to separate each parameter—one at the beginning and end of each line (except the first).

- Make sure that any paths are entered correctly and that they exist.

- Start simply and make changes slowly. Double-check your syntax.

- Set permissions for directories and files when you are through. (See below.)

- Kill and restart the print daemon. (See below.)

- Kill and restart the **rpc.pcnfsd** daemon to let DOS machines know of a new printer or spool directory.

Some software products prepare a new **/etc/printcap** entry for you during the install/configure process. Others, such as FrameMaker, provide a sample entry that you can type in.

Selecting a model file for System V UNIX printing

You must have a *model file*, or interface script, for each printer on the network. These files are typically stored in the **/usr/spool/lp/model** directory. As they do for the BSD **/etc/printcap** file, vendors usually supply sample System V interface model files for you. The files contain commands for placing the printer in landscape/portrait mode, generating banners, setting the number of copies, etc. The model file supplied by SCO OPEN DESKTOP for the LaserJet is thousands of bytes long and supports the PCL level 5 features of the printer. If there is no model file for your printer, look for a **standard** model file to provide minimal printer access.

Vendors may require changes to your interface file. Interface file programming is shell script programming—not hard, if you know what you are doing and understand printing on a detailed level, but mind-boggling to the average businessperson. If you do not have the bent to modify one of these large programs, look to the vendor for assistance. Usually, you can just use one of the vendor's scripts whole hog.

To complete spooler setup, bring down the print server and reconfigure it. Run **/usr/lib/lpshut** to stop the server daemon. Then run **/usr/lib/lpadmin** to configure the printer database. You must add parameters to this command in order to make it do something worthwhile. Here are some commonly used parameters:

-A (alert)	send an alert via mail, console message, etc.
-d (printername)	make printername the default printer
-F (fault_action)	recover from a printer fault
-I (contenttype)	restrict types of files to this list
-p (printername)	assigned name of printer
-m (modelname)	selected model file
-T (printertype)	type, from /usr/lib/terminfo
-u allow:(userlist)	allow any user on the list, or 'all'
-u deny:(userlist)	deny any user on the list
-v (device)	selected device file name

Finally, run **/usr/lib/lpsched** to restart the server. You can also use **enable** and **disable** with a printer name to activate and deactivate specific printers without bringing down the server. Another pair of commands, **accept** and **reject**, permit (or prevent) print jobs to be queued for a printer.

Filters

Filters are useful in printing. A filter program may be run to transform a text file in some manner. For instance, a filter might convert a text file to PostScript format for printing on a PostScript-only printer. Some filters require you to include parameters; e.g., name of the host accounting file, login, width and length of page, and more. Common UNIX filters include the **pr** filter for breaking up text into columns. Often, a vendor includes a filter with a print server.

Permissions

If you have specified a device such as **ttya** in your **printcap** file, make sure that the network users have permission to access that device. Spool directories, log files, and filters defined in **printcap** must also be accessible. To check permissions on the **ttya** device, for example, type **ls -l /dev/ttya**. This command displays a line that shows the permissions field, the number of links, the owner, the size in bytes or the major and minor device numbers, and the time of last modification. The permissions field reveals the following.

Character 1: type of entity (d=directory, l=symbolic link, c=character file, "-" =plain file, etc.)
Characters 2-4: owner permissions
Characters 5-7: group member permissions (owner's group)
Characters 8-10: non-group member permissions

The last three sets are all similarly constructed. Usually you will have four options available: **r**=readable, **w**=writable, **x**=executable and **-**=no permission granted. For the **ttya** example above, permissions of **crw-rw-rw-** are typical, indicating that this special character file allows all users to read and write to the device. Use **chmod** to change the mode to new permissions, **chgrp** to change the group ownership of a file/directory, and **chown** to change the owner of a file/directory. See Chapter 6 for instruction in using these commands.

Print Daemons

Similar to a DOS TSR (terminate and stay resident) program, a daemon waits in the background for work to do. There are two primary daemons that affect printing. One is the UNIX print server (in two flavors, BSD and System V), and the pcnfs server for PCs.

BSD LPR server

When you boot a BSD UNIX system **/usr/lib/lpd** is invoked, usually from the **/etc/rc** file. **Lpd** stands for *line printer daemon*, but a more accurate description is the spool area manager. It doesn't place jobs in the spool directory, but it does schedule print jobs and causes them to be printed. Another name for **lpd** is 'lpr server', because the **lpr** command initiates and spools the print requests.

When the **lpd** daemon first wakes up, it reads the **/etc/printcap** file to determine which printers are out there; then it restarts any print jobs that might have been left-over from before a crash. Next, it waits for requests. Note: if you ever change a definition in **/etc/printcap**, you should type **lpc restart (printername)**. Or, the long way is to determine the **lpd** process number (**ps -ax** will list them all on a Sun system), kill it (e.g., **kill 115**), and restart (**/usr/lib/lpd**) so that the daemon identifies your current configuration.

The various commands supported by **lpd** cause it to print or remove files that are in a queue, display queue status, and control printers. An actual print job begins with the user executing **lpr**, the print requester. **Lpr** stores the file to be printed in a spool directory under a unique job number beginning with the letters **df** for *data file*. A **cf** file is also created as a *control file*, showing who sent the job, the job name, and other fascinating items. **Lpr** sends a message to the LPR server (**lpd**).

Lpd then forks, or begets, a child **lpd** to perform the task. It also creates a lock file to prevent another daemon from being started in the spool directory holding the print job. Afterward, the parent **lpd** returns to listening. The child **lpd**, being more ambitious than its parent, checks **/etc/printcap** for itself, to learn about the printer to which it must send the file. If that printer requires a filter, the child **lpd** sends the file through the filter on its way to the printer. At the conclusion of the task, the lock is removed and the child process dies.

For remote users, **lpd** uses **/etc/hosts.equiv** (see Chapter 5) and **/etc/hosts.lpd** for authentication. If the remote host is not found in **hosts.equiv**, its name is then checked for a match in **hosts.lpd**. Here is a sample of the **/etc/hosts.lpd** file, which has a similar format to **/etc/hosts.equiv**—[+ | -]hostname [username]. However, unlike **hosts.equiv** it restricts remote hosts only to print functions:

```
+Bonnie
gomer Gini
barney+
-Roger
-goober
```

User Bonnie can access the printer from any host, but Roger has no remote access. Gini can use the printer from host gomer, and anyone can print from host barney, but no one can print from host goober. To let everyone in, just have the single entry '+'.

System V server

The primary daemon server for System V UNIX is **/usr/lib/lpsched**. This daemon starts the print service. Just as for BSD UNIX, the print service starts at every multiuser boot. Another command, **lpshut**, stops it.

In order for **lpsched** to print a file, the printer must be enabled (using **enable**, previously described). However, even if a printer is disabled, **lpsched** can still schedule print jobs as long as the **accept** command has been issued. Users on some System V systems can be restricted using **lpadmin**, as described previously.

Some System V UNIX machines can use the LPR protocol as well as **lpsched**. SCO provides an **lpd** server for printing on remote UNIX hosts, requiring you to build a **/etc/printcap** file. Others that do not support **lpr** require you to transfer the print job to a host that does and print it using **rsh**.

PCNFS server

If you are running an NFS client product for PCs, you can redirect your print jobs to a UNIX printer. NFS spools the files for you, and the normal print server takes over. Kill and restart **/usr/etc/rpc.pcnfsd** (the name of the PC authentication daemon on a Sun—**bwnfsd** is the name of the Beame & Whiteside version) following a change to /etc/printcap. **Pcnfsd** reads **printcap** to know where the spooling directory is located.

Pcnfsd comes in two versions, which have differing impact upon the printing process. Version 1 provides two fundamental services—mounting remote printers and invoking a print job. The user-friendly frills are added by Version 2—obtaining the status of a queue or printer, obtaining a list of available printers, cancelling a job, and browsing for network printers under Windows. See Chapter 6 for more details about NFS and **pcnfsd**.

Printing and Queue Management Commands

You can send a print job to the printer in more than one way. Applications and desktop software provide utilities and drag-and-drop methods for printing, which make life simple. Many UNIX users print and manage spooler functions from the command line. In that case, users of BSD and System V UNIX must use different commands. Here are your options.

Printing from the BSD UNIX command line

BSD's LPR protocol supports several commands. Print a text file on Sun, DEC, or other BSD systems with lpr (filename). The lpr command creates a print job in a spooler directory. Add -h to suppress a burst page, or -P (printer) to select a printer. You can also redirect the console output of other commands to the printer using a vertical bar |, called a *pipe*. For example, ps -x | lpr -h prints hard copy of your current process list (this might be helpful in documenting what was running at the time an intermittent problem occurred).

CAUTION

WATCH
YOUR
STEP

Killing Daemons

Do not kill a process if someone on the network needs it up. If you kill **rpc.pcnfsd** in order to correct a problem with printer access, users will temporarily lose access to the server's drives as well. Should this occur, have users sit tight and wait for the server daemons to come back up. They will probably be able to continue where they left off, experiencing nothing more serious than an increased heart rate. But, it's better to warn them.

There are several commands you can exercise to manage your queues. Look at the print queue contents with **lpq**. It outputs information similar to the following:

```
lp is ready and printing
Rank          Owner       Job          Files          Total Size
active        ken         964                         /home/ken/schedule
3248 bytes
1st           mike        965          /bigfile       154775 bytes
2nd           gini        966          release.doc    40156 bytes
ps:
no entries
```

The command **lprm** removes all of the jobs belonging to you from the print queue. Or, add a job number as a parameter to kill just one print job. Most of the time you will use **lpc** to control the queue. Add parameters to **lpc** to select a control function. With most of the parameters you can add **all** or a specific printer name to limit the scope of your action. Here are a few examples:

```
lpc ?                       show help
lpc down pr_name            disable the pr_name queue
lpc status                  show state of daemons & queues
lpc restart pr_name         restart pr_name daemon for abandoned jobs
lpc up all                  enable all print queues
lpc                         run lpc in interactive mode
```

All of the above commands can be issued by any user. The superuser can use additional parameters such as **abort**, **clean**, **disable/enable**, **start/stop**, and **topq**. See the manual for additional information about these commands. (Reference Appendix A under Getting Help.)

There is another way to print files from a BSD UNIX command line. You can use the remote command **rsh** to access a remote printer. **rsh** (remote shell) connects to a remote host running **rshd** (the **rsh** server daemon) and executes a user command; then terminates the connection. For example, you might type the command **rsh (remote_host) lpr -h (filename)**. You do need permission to access the remote host without an interactive login. This you get from the **/etc/hosts.equiv** file (for trusted hosts) or **.rhosts** in an individual user's home directory on the remote machine. If the **hosts.equiv** file contains your hostname, and your username is recognized, you're in. The **.rhosts** file is similar—for only one host. If neither have been configured, all you get is **Permission Denied.** To create an **.rhosts** file for yourself on a remote host, login via **telnet**. Then, in your home directory, use a text editor to create the file. The format should be **hostname username**, and all you need is one line.

Printing from the System V UNIX command line

You can print files from System V UNIX machines such as SCO UNIX or Novell UnixWare by typing **lp (filename)**. Adding other parameters such as these after **lp** can make life easier: **-d (printer)** selects a printer; **-o nobanner** disables the banner page; **-o onlcr** adds carriage returns before linefeeds; and **-o ff** adds a formfeed at the end of the job. However, these options are not universally supported by model scripts.

Two commands let you manage the print queues. The primary command is **lpstat**, which displays information such as the following:

```
lp-1280        34119 ken        on lp
lp-1281        645 mike
```

To remove a print job from the queue, use **lpstat** to find the identifying number of the job; then use the **cancel** command, e.g., **cancel lp-1281**.

On a System V system you can also use the remote command **rcmd** for printing. This command is exactly the same as BSD's **rsh**, described above.

Printing from graphical desktops and applications

Under the newer graphical desktops there are easier ways to print text files. SCO OPEN DESKTOP and Novell UnixWare let you drag and drop text file icons to the printer icon. Or, use a tool such as Sun's OpenWindows Print Tool, shown in Figure 11.2.

If your machine has been previously set up to print text files, printing from within applications usually becomes a simple matter under UNIX. The two procedures—printing applications and printing text files—require the same printer configuration. If you are familiar with DOS, you will notice a similar setup function

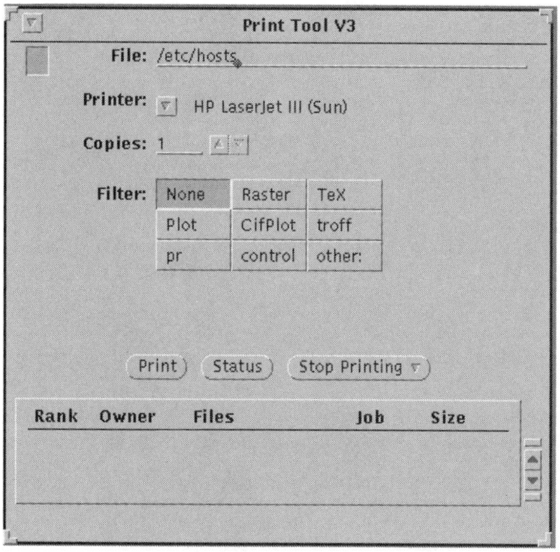

FIGURE 11.2 OpenWindows Print Tool

within the UNIX application to let you select the printer and print parameters. When that function has been completed, find the Print button, and click on it to print the document.

Printing from IBM AIX

IBM took their own route through the printing maze, rather than conform to System V or BSD (although they can support **lpr/lp**). During a brainstorm, IBM hit upon the idea of calling everything in their system 'q____' to identify queue components. For example, AIX users type **qprt (filename)** to print a file. The printer configuration file is called **/etc/qconfig**, and the spooler daemon is called **qdaemon**. Check your system user manual for details.

Although we would prefer not to have this added complexity for multivendor environments, IBM did do us a favor by creating the System Management Interface Tool (SMIT) for the purpose of managing system resources—including print queues. The Spooler section of SMIT provides a push-button approach to queue management. Note that AIX has no **/etc/printcap** file, but it does support **lpr**. See Figure 11.3.

Troubleshooting basic connections

Firing up even a simple dot-matrix printer can often be more of a headache than you expected. If the commands provided above do not work and you do not immediately understand why, take a step back and try using the **cat** command to print. You can bypass the **lp** system and redirect output from the **cat** command directly to the device file. The following example prints the **hosts** file to a SPARCstation LX's parallel port:

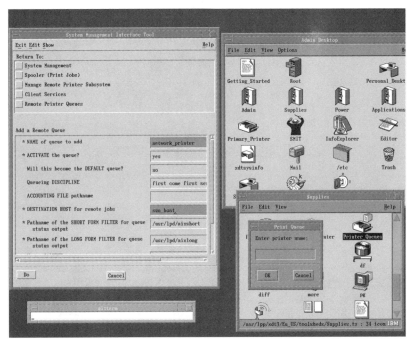

FIGURE 11.3 Setting up a print spooler from IBM's SMIT

cat /etc/hosts > /dev/bpp0

If the printer does not respond, check the following:

• The cable may not be properly connected, it may be defective, or it may not be a printer cable. A serial cable must be a null modem cable (pins 2 and 3 and switched between ends), not a modem cable (which is wired straight through).

• The printer may be broken. If you are uncertain about this, swap in another printer.

• The printer may be configured through internal switches or front panel selections to use another cable interface, if it has more than one.

• The device file you referenced does not match the port to which the printer is connected.

If you can tell that the printer receives characters but does not print them correctly, or at all, check these points:

• The printer's internal configuration switches or front panel selections may be incorrect.

• The printer may be expecting PostScript output. If you do not have a Post-Script file handy, you can generate one with these commands:

```
$cat > testprinter.ps
%!
/Times-Roman findfont 12 scalefont setfont
300 400 moveto
(I am a PostScript printer) show
showpage
CTRL-D
$cat testprinter.ps > /dev/ttya
```

Supplying IP Addresses to Devices

Depending upon the product you implement, you may be able to skip this section. Network-aware devices including print servers, printer LAN adapters, and network-ready printers need an IP address in order to exist on the network. You must give them a host IP address, just as you would any computer or X-terminal. However, they usually do not have a console with which you can enter that address, so the device must obtain it from another machine. There are several ways to do this.

All of the methods below require you to first enter a host name and IP address into your **/etc/hosts** table (or master host table under NIS). After you have entered this information, use one of the methods below to configure the device. Then, ping the node with **ping hostname** to test the connection.

RARP and BOOTP

We discussed **RARP** servers in Chapter 5. Your system must have a **RARP** daemon running before you can use this method. Use an editor to create a new entry in the **/etc/ethers** for the device. Then power up the device, and it should locate its IP address without further help. Thereafter, the device always uses **RARP** to boot.

See Chapter 5 for help in setting up a BOOTP server. Your print server vendor may also provide instructions.

ARP and TELNET

You can use **telnet** to configure a device with an IP address. Here is a general procedure you can use if your product supports **telnet**. First update the ARP table with the host name and address of the device. The syntax for this command is:

```
arp -s hostname ethernet_address
```

For example, this line could read **arp -s pserver 0:40:x8:0:d:f3**. When you have completed this task, start a **telnet** session to the device:

```
telnet hostname {portnum}
```

A port number value such as 2002 may be supplied by the vendor for use rather than the default **telnet** port number. At this point, the vendor may or may not have you login as root, usually ignoring the password. You should then see a command-mode prompt. Follow the vendor's instructions to configure the device. Use Control-D to leave **telnet**. The device stores the address in non-volatile memory, so it will keep it through power-down.

Connecting a terminal to the device

Some devices, such as the Microplex and MiLAN print servers, allow you to connect a terminal to their serial port. The vendor gives you all of the communication settings for this link. When you power-up the device, it will send you a configuration screen of some sort, on which you can enter an IP address, netmask, and user passwords. Again, the device will store the address in non-volatile memory.

How to Access UNIX Printers from DOS

DOS machines networked via TCP/IP can use UNIX printers. Here are the three methods of network printer access which are usually supported by TCP/IP networking software.

All three of these methods usually utilize a software program called a *redirector*. A redirector is a TSR or DLL program which watches a DOS interrupt for incoming data and re-routes it. In the case of these programs, the redirector steals data intended for the local printer port and ships it to a remote spooling directory. Redirectors can serve different print protocols. Where the data goes, and what happens along the way, depends on the method of printing used. Some vendors supply more than one redirector.

Printing via DOS-based LPR client

A DOS version of the UNIX **lpr** command can be used to communicate with a remote **lpr** server. To set up a redirector and **lpr** client, you would typically enter commands such as these, used by Wollongong's PathWay, in your **AUTOEXEC.BAT** file:

```
lprint
lprq lpt1: servername:printername
```

Then, from a DOS prompt you can use the typical print commands without modification. The DOS **PRINT** command can be used as long as it is loaded before the redirector. The **COPY** command and the DOS application **Print** menu choice can also be used with the **lpr** client.

Another **lpr** client option may not require a redirector, but may be a self-contained command for sending a file. Wollongong also supplies one:

```
lpr -S servername -P printername filename
```

Lpr clients are considered almost a manual method of printing. They are useful for DOS-based printing, but not typically for Windows because NFS provides superior benefits. Nearly all TCP/IP products provide **lpr** print capability.

Printing via remote commands

A large percentage of the products we examined provided remote command capability. Remote shell commands can be used to run **lpr/lp** clients on a remote host. These commands would ordinarily be entered from a DOS command line. For example, you might print a text file through an LPR server on an RS/6000, using the **rsh** command:

```
rsh rs6000 lpr -h autoexec.bat
```

Printing via NFS

The easiest way to access and manage UNIX printers from a DOS PC is through NFS. Before you get the wrong idea, on the UNIX host side the LPR protocol still handles the print jobs. The difference is that the PCs interface to the UNIX print system is through the more functional **pcnfs** server rather than through the **lpr** server. **Pcnfs** has particular advantages to Windows users.

Just as for **lpr** client programs, output to local printer ports can be redirected to a network printer. In order to do this under NFS, the printer must be mounted (connected). The **pcnfsd** daemon must be running on the host, because it must supply the location of the spool directory to the connecting PC. (And that directory must be in a mounted drive under NFS.) Later, when a print request is made from either DOS or Windows, the redirector routes all of the print file to the remote spooling directory. It also informs **pcnfsd** of the new print job—including some control data as well as information on which filters should run. At the other end, **pcnfsd** passes the responsibility to the local print spooler.

Once the printer has been mounted the first time, most NFS products allow you to automatically mount it thereafter. The printer mount is usually handled by the PC boot scripts—either through an explicit command in the **AUTOEXEC.BAT** startup file or by an NFS executable program which runs at boot time. After mounting, you define the printer for Windows.

Let's consider an example. In the case of SunSelect's PC-NFS, mount the printer initially through the **NFSCONF** utility. Select **Define Printer**; then enter 1) the name of the server which has access to the printer, 2) the name of the printer (the abbreviated name from **/etc/printcap**), 3) your selection for when output is to be queued for printing (usually after a 30-second time-out—user adjustable), and 4) the output filter. Output filters force print files to match the type of printer, whether PostScript or non-PostScript. In our case, where we used both PostScript and non-PostScript files, our best option was to leave the files unfiltered (**raw**).

Another popular product, Beame & Whiteside's BW-NFS, requires you to specify your mount commands explicitly in **AUTOEXEC.BAT**. The syntax resembles the drive mounting syntax, namely:

mount lpt1:\\sun_host\\serial_for_PCs

Both PC-NFS and BW-NFS allow you to register your user name and password automatically with **pcnfsd** to avoid having to stop and validate them each time you mount the printer.

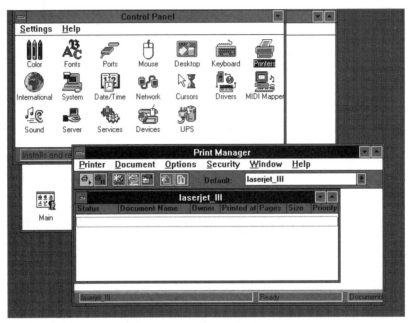

FIGURE 11.4   The Microsoft Windows NT Print Manager

Phase 1 mounted the printer; phase 2 informs Windows of the printer's availability. Enter the Control Panel and select the Printers icon. If you are using Windows NT, the Print Manager has been upgraded from plain Windows (see Figure 11.4).   You must access the printer as a shared resource through an SMB-compliant server, unless you install a third-party LPR client. Chapter 14 has more details about Windows NT.

If you use plain Windows 3.1, here is the procedure to connect a network printer. Click on the **Add Printer** button on the **Printers** window to get the ball rolling. Select **Connect/ Network/Browse** (see Figure 11.5). At this point you should see the name of the server—double click on it (or select it and **Show Printers**), and a list of the **/etc/printcap** printers appears in the bottom window. Select the one you want and double click (or select it and click on Printer Info)—the printer status should show **Enabled**. Click on **Select**, then **Connect**—now the connection will be displayed in the Current Printer Connections window. If there is an option similar to **Restore All Connections at Startup** under the Control Panel's Network icon, make sure it is selected.

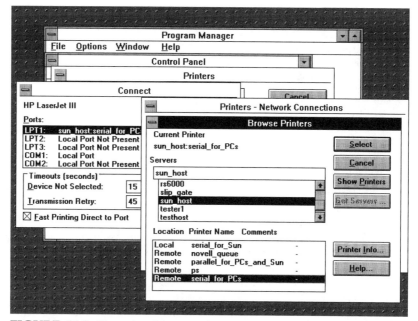

FIGURE 11.5 Browsing for network printers with Windows 3.1 Print Manager

Now print to the printer from any Windows application, just as you would to a locally-connected printer. The Print Manager can display information about the status of this remote printer, and you can either kill jobs or reassign them.

Networking a Printer Under DOS

Attaching printers to DOS stand-alone computers or to a PC network is, in our opinion, much easier than UNIX. Mainly, there are no complicated configuration files to edit. However, you must still do some setup—most of which is handled through utilities.

Configuring PC Ports

If you connect your printer directly to the network cabling, you do not need to be concerned about PC parallel or serial ports. However, if the printer has no LAN adapter or print server to attach it to the network, you must attach the printer directly to a PC via serial or parallel cable.

Parallel ports and cables are the easiest to work with. PCs usually have at least one, called LPT1. At the PC, the parallel port is a 25-pin female D-style jack. LPT1 is the default printer port—requiring no setup.

Serial ports, also called communication (COM) ports, are a little more complicated, but not much. Most PCs have two: COM1 is a 9-pin male D-style jack; COM2 is usually a 25-pin male. If you connect a printer to a COM port rather than the LPT port, you should place a **MODE** command in the PC's **AUTOEXEC.BAT** file to redirect all default printer output to the COM port. Use this line if the printer is on COM1:

```
mode lpt1:=com1:
```

Some users never have to print files from the DOS command level; they always print from applications. If you do print from DOS, you also need a line to configure the serial port attributes, similar to:

```
mode com1:9600,n,8,1,p
```

The parameters stand, of course, for 9600 baud, no parity, 8 data bits, 1 stop bit, continuous retry. This parameter set is supported by nearly all PCs and printers. See Chapter 9 for more serial connection information.

DOS Print Commands

You can print from the DOS command line in several ways. One way is to issue the **PRINT** command; e.g., **print c:readme.txt** spools a text file located on the **C:** drive to the default printer (PRN, or LPT1). If you wish to use other than the default printer, use the **/d** switch with another device name such as LPT2 or COM1. To remove a file from the DOS print queue, place a **/c** switch before the file(s) to be removed. To add files, use **/p** similarly. **PRINT** is a TSR which remains in memory after you call it, and it consumes a little less than 6K or memory.

HOT TIP 	**Getting Hard Copy of a DOS Session** If you wish to record on paper the DOS commands you enter and the console output they generate, you can press **Ctrl-P** before you begin—and again when you have finished the series of commands. Everything between the **Ctrl-P**s will go to the printer in addition to the console. Be sure to turn it off, or a basket of paper may show up at your door! The handy **PrintScreen** key (sometimes **Shift-PrintScr**) sends an image of the current console display to the printer. These commands are not suitable for network environments, since they can interrupt or be interrupted by other user's jobs.

Another way to print a file is to **COPY** it to the printer. Do this by entering **copy c:readme.txt com1**, for example. This method does not leave a TSR resident in memory. A third method you can use is to redirect output. For example, you can print out a directory listing by typing **dir c:\develop >lpt1**. The CTRL-P and PrintScreen keys can also be used to redirect output. However, of all print commands, only **PRINT** will automatically eject the last page.

Printing from Windows

Once a printer is set up under Windows, it can be used without fuss from every Windows application. To configure a printer under Windows 3.1, go to the **Control Panel/Printers**. Click on **Add** to see a list of supported printers. Have your original Windows diskettes handy if you select a printer model not previously installed, because Windows will need the information to find the right printer driver. As Figure 11.6 shows, when the driver is installed, you can click on **Connect** to change the port, followed by **Settings** to configure the port attributes.

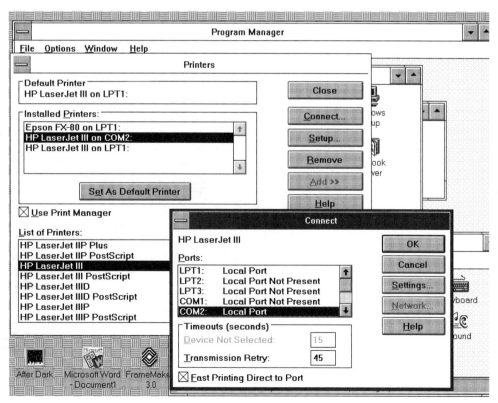

FIGURE 11.6 Windows lets you define and switch between several printers

When in a Windows application, merely click on the printer icon or select **File/ Print** from the action bar in order to print to the default printer. Or, choose **File/Print Setup** to select a different output printer.

Some TCP/IP products can obtain better performance on network printing if the print manager is turned off. This eliminates wasted time sending the print job to the local spooler in addition to the remote spooler. To turn off the Print Manager; go to **Control Panel/Printers**, and toggle off the **Use Print Manager** box.

Novell NetWare Print Servers and Queues

NetWare represents the most ubiquitous PC network operating system out there. NetWare utilities are easy to understand and operate, and in all NetWare utilities you use the arrow keys to select the next menu and **Escape** to go back to the previous menu.

The **PCONSOLE** utility configures your network printers, servers, and print queues. You should log into the network either as the supervisor or a print queue operator to change the configuration.

First, define a print queue for each printer. A NetWare print queue is comparable to a UNIX spool program. It creates a directory on the server (under **SYS:\SYSTEM**) to hold print jobs. Use the Insert key to add a new print queue name. Descriptive names might include **ENG_QUEUE_1** or **QMS_QUEUE**. A print queue functions independently of the print server—its only responsibility being to accumulate print job files for the print server.

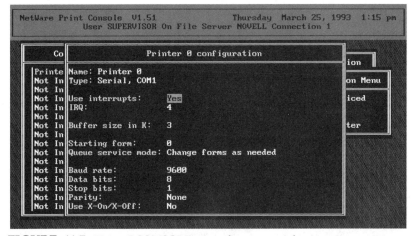

FIGURE 11.7 Using PCONSOLE to configure a serial printer

PSERVER, the NetWare print server, pulls jobs from the queue and sends them to the printer. Define a printer from the Print Server Configuration Menu (see Figure

11.7). Depending upon the product you are installing, you may state the printer type as "Defined elsewhere" or as a Remote printer. Select the queue or queues to which this server must respond.

On a PC, run **PSERVER**. On a UNIX computer that has been outfitted with Novell server software, the print server program may have a different name.

Print servers can be remote; that is, the print server software may be located on another computer, while the queue is defined at the file server. The print server on a remote UNIX host works regardless of whether the local PC attaches to one of the UNIX host's drives. This is due to the fact that the print server logs into the file server—the file server does not seek the print server. If the file server goes down, the print server will re-establish connection when that file server comes back up. A print server is a NetWare user that always tries to find and serve its queue, and **USER-LIST** will display it if upon the completion of login.

The **CAPTURE** command redirects normal LPT1 (parallel port) output to the print queue specified. It allows you to print files from the command line and use the Shift-PrntScr key to print screens. **NPRINT** is similar—printing files from the command line. **CAPTURE** can be placed in the system login script—similar to the following line which redirects LPT1 output to print server **NOVELL** and print queue **PQ0**—with a request for **No Banner page**:

```
F:\PUBLIC\CAPTURE S=NOVELL Q=PQ0 NB
```

Windows applications do not require the use of **CAPTURE**. Instead, the Print Manager can connect the network printer and manage the formfeeds as long as the queue has been set up. Figure 11.8 shows an example of how this is done.

Accessing DOS Printers from UNIX

UNIX users can print to DOS printers if the DOS printer is controlled by an LPR server. An LPR server is provided by some TCP/IP products (see Chapter 13) and runs as a DOS TSR in the background. All spooling for that printer goes on at the PC. Any UNIX or DOS computer which runs an LPR client can print to the DOS printer. However, at least one vendor admits that its LPR server should only be run on a machine dedicated to that purpose. This is partly due to a performance sag for the user at the server machine—that person who is trying to work on a spreadsheet at the same time that a file from a remote client is printing. We find even more compelling this vendor's acknowledgment that if a remote job comes in at the same time as a local job from Windows, the printouts may have errors. It would be best to check with your vendor about this if a background LPR server is important to you.

You can find only a small variety of other products which access DOS printers from UNIX computers. One product provides an LPR server for a Novell NetWare network printer. Another enables a UNIX workstation to function as a NetWare client with full rights to NetWare printers.

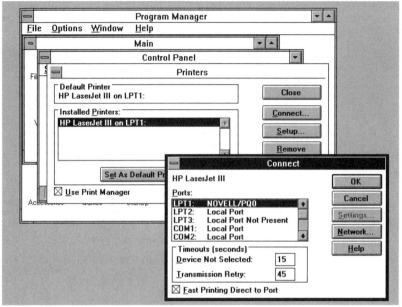

FIGURE 11.8 Connecting a Windows printer to a Novell print queue is easy

How to Print PostScript Files on Non-PostScript Printers

When you link UNIX and DOS computers, you may find that your UNIX users cannot print to the same printers as the PCs. The PostScript file format is often the reason (most PC applications get along fine without it). You may have to find an interpreter.

Color Age Freedom of Press

Freedom of Press is a software-only solution for the problem of printing PostScript files on non-PostScript printer. The software loads on a SunOS 4.x, Macintosh, or Windows 3.1 PC computer, and it intercepts every PostScript print job and converts it to a bit-mapped graphics image. Freedom of Press works with system print spoolers and is compatible with over 100 output devices, making it nearly hardware-independent. However, a numeric coprocessor is strongly advised for a PC or Macintosh running Freedom of Press. Without one, a 286 or 386 machine will likely function more slowly than the printer cartridge solution.

Hewlett-Packard PostScript Cartridge Plus

Turning an HP LaserJet into a PostScript printer is more complicated than just plugging in a cartridge. There are three major requirements: memory, auto-switching, and fonts.

We tested HP's PostScript Cartridge Plus, which includes Adobe Type Manager fonts for Windows. We also installed an HP 2-megabyte RAM expansion board. You need at least 2 megabytes of RAM to print PostScript files, but only a small percentage of the world's installed LaserJets have more than 1 megabyte. In reality, having at least 3 megabytes is preferred for speed, more downloadable fonts, and fewer problems with legal-size paper.

Installation

First, tackle the memory. Unplug all cables and the power cord from your LaserJet III. Position the printer so that the left side (as you face it) overhangs the edge of the table. Remove the plastic cover over the RAM Expansion slots by pulling out in the middle. Loosen, but do not remove, the three screws holding down the metal cover plate, and then slide off the plate. Take the memory board from its static pouch. (Guard against static electricity, or you could fry any board before it is ever installed!) Push the board firmly into place in the forward slot. Since you cannot see the slot, and it is very resistant, you might wince as you do this. Replace the metal and plastic covers.

Next, push the PostScript cartridge into one of the cartridge slots on the front of the printer. If you ever owned 8-track tapes, you may be tempted to do this while the power is on, BUT DON'T! *Never* insert or remove a cartridge while the printer is on. This is an electronic device, in no way similar to a tape cartridge. Now reconnect the cables and turn on the printer.

The first thing you notice is that the *00 READY* in the display window has been replaced by *POSTSCRIPT READY*. Next, the startup page should print. Both events are managed by the cartridge. Print out a test page by taking the printer off-line; then hold down the Test key until the display shows the page is being printed (or *05 SELF TEST* in PCL mode). Print a font page by taking the printer off-line and touching **Test** once. Note that the test page displays a list of new parameters you have not seen before.

Configuration

Go into the printer's configuration menu. (Take the printer off-line; then hold down the Menu button until you see the *AUTO CONT* parameter.) The menu for PostScript mode differs from normal PCL mode. It stores a second set of parameters, meaning that you may have to reconfigure your printer's hardware interface. Touch the Menu button repeatedly until you see *START PAGE=ON*. Turn off the start page by touching the Plus (+) key; then Enter. Continue through the Menu to the *SW MODE=PS* switching mode parameter. This controls the printer's initialization in PostScript mode. You can change this default to PCL if you usually have more non-PostScript files printing. When you have completed the Menu, press On-line.

To switch between PostScript and PCL manually during the course of the day, take the printer off-line, then hold down the Plus (+) button and touch Reset. Turning off the computer and removing the cartridge also works to force the printer into PCL mode, but is not recommended as a habit due to wear-and-tear on the cartridge and printer slot.

Setting up language-switching

If you have defined the printer to the UNIX network, you can immediately print PostScript files from UNIX nodes. The printer displays *PROCESSING DATA* while accepting a print job. However, if you send a PostScript file to the printer while the printer is in PCL mode, you will get out an unformatted document—along with many pages of PostScript programming. If you send DOS PCL files or ordinary text files from UNIX or DOS, the printer will get stuck on *PROCESSING DATA*, because PostScript printers cannot handle any non-PostScript files. Auto-switching between jobs is important, and HP gives you a few ways to handle it.

In the first method, you set up device drivers (TSRs) on your DOS machines and leave the printer in PostScript mode. An install program sets everything up for you—even the interface with Windows, if you have Windows. You can choose to route PostScript/PCL print jobs through different ports on the PC or through the same port. HP supplies another method for PCs—namely, the batch file approach. This lets you switch modes from the DOS command line.

On a network such as Novell NetWare, auto-switching becomes even more complicated. However, HP provides a booklet of instructions for setting up the NetWare **CAPTURE** and **NPRINT** commands. A TSR device driver is again involved.

Only one question remains; how do you print ASCII text files from UNIX? HP does not discuss this in its documentation, but there are two remedies. One is to go to the printer and physically switch it to PCL mode. The second involves switching to PCL mode remotely—copy the **TOPCL.ASC** file from one of the DOS diskettes up to the UNIX drive (via FTP or NFS from a TCP/IP networked PC). This file was supplied for downloading by DOS batch files, but it works from UNIX as well. Use **lpr -h topcl.asc** to download the file.

Installing fonts

Desktop publishing software, whether for UNIX or Microsoft Windows, requires a variety of fonts. You may already own all the fonts you need, since font files are included with desktop publishing software as a matter of course. However, most users benefit from having more fonts for Windows applications. The HP PostScript cartridge provides many fonts at the printer which are unusable without similar display fonts on the PC. In order to make use of the PostScript fonts, you need to have PostScript fonts with Windows. These can be provided with packages like Adobe's

Adobe Type Manager (ATM). Without PostScript fonts, you cannot use a PostScript printer or cartridge.

Software which comes with PostScript Cartridge Plus includes ATM, fonts, and PostScript drivers for Windows. You can install these programs and fonts easily from Windows using another HP-supplied install program. The fonts require lots of disk space, but they are necessary.

How to Install a PostScript/PCL Print Accelerator

PostScript cartridges and extra memory represent a good solution, but an accelerator provides a better. Accelerators offer ten times faster print speeds than cartridge-based solutions alone. Plus, these products tend to roll all of the things you need into one package. In addition, they target multiprotocol platforms and provide for easier installation. We installed Pacific Data PE/XL on our LaserJet, but see Appendix B for other products including BetterYet IV, from Output Technology Corporation.

Pacific Data PE/XL

With this product we were able to print a FrameMaker PostScript document from a UNIX workstation, followed immediately by a Microsoft Word for Windows document from a PC, and text files from either direction. The best part was that we didn't have to do any setup on the DOS machines. We used this product extensively through the course of our writing and found it invaluable.

The PacificPage PE/XL includes a PostScript cartridge, an accelerator expansion card with 4 megabytes of additional RAM, matching Windows fonts, and drivers. You do not have to jump through any hoops to do language-switching, because the PE/XL automatically senses the format of the incoming print job at the printer.

Installation

Using the instructions found earlier under How to Install PostScript, install Pacific Data's cartridge and accelerator card. Slide the PE/XL board into the hindmost RAM expansion slot—any RAM board already there should be moved to the front slot. Put the printer back together and turn it on.

After the printer has initialized, it will kick out a startup advertisement, and the front panel will display *PacPage PE/XL* instead of the usual *00 READY*. This indicates that the printer is in PostScript mode. If you send a PCL or text document to the printer while it is in PostScript mode, you will see and hear the printer give a little hiccup and reboot itself as a PCL printer, thus displaying *00 READY* before it starts printing the document. Conversely, if the printer is in PCL mode when it receives a PostScript document, it will again reboot itself as a PostScript printer. Pacific Data's product gives your printer a split personality. You can manually change to the other mode by taking the printer off-line; then holding down the **Continue** key, and briefly touching **Menu**. Print a test page for reference.

Configuration

Make sure the printer is in PostScript mode; then take the printer off-line. Press **Menu** briefly until *STARTPG=ON* appears. The welcome page prints every time the printer is powered on, but you can turn it off by pressing "+", then **Enter**. Press **Menu** until *PacPage PE/XL* again displays. Now hold down **Menu** until the second menu of parameters starts. Proceed through the list by pressing **Menu**. Note certain values in particular: *I/O=ALL* allows incoming files via parallel, serial, or Ethernet cable—all can be connected at once. *AUTO SENSE=ON* recognizes the type of incoming file, whether PCL or PostScript, and print both properly. (If this feature causes problems in your environment, Pacific Data recommends you disable it and switch the printer manually.) You may wish to change *DEF EMUL*, the default emulation mode on power up. Use "+" to select either PostScript (PS) or PCL mode, and **Enter**. Press **On-line** when you are through.

If the printer has been used on the network before, try printing a PCL file from the PC and a text file from the workstation. You should not have to do anything extra accomplish this, but you will notice a delay in printing if the printer must change modes. If the printer is new to the TCP/IP network, you must first enter a printer definition in the BSD UNIX server's **/etc/printcap** file, or prepare an interface model file for use by System V UNIX. Unfortunately, Pacific Data supplied only a quick example for the BSD **printcap** file, and nothing at all for System V.

You can prepare a UNIX system such as a Sun workstation to print PostScript documents, but it requires extra steps. Hopefully, later versions will streamline this process. Appendix A of the User's Guide describes how to do this for a serial connection between host and printer. You will be required to type a small C-language program (given) into an editor and save the file as **hpf.c**. To complete the job, compile this file into an executable file and copy it into the **/usr/lib directory**. The compile command (which Pacific Data did not provide) is **/bin/cc -o hpf hpf.c**. Remember that in a C program you cannot use '#' for remarks as you can in UNIX scripts. The **hpf** file is called an *input filter* and serves to regulate the speed at which the characters go to the printer.

You can now select a PostScript file in, let's say, FrameMaker and print it to the printer defined in the new **printcap** entry. If your printer does not reset after a PostScript job, and the form feed light continues to flash, either the printer is alerting you that the computer is telling it dirty words, or it received some unrecognizable characters. Check the Appendix A process again.

Pacific Data claims that their product currently senses PostScript files better than many PostScript printers. Most products accomplish this by looking at the first two characters of the file (usually "%!" for a PostScript file), but Pacific Data claims to look at the first 4K of characters. Regardless of the validity of this claim, the product certainly works well.

How to Install an Internal Network Adapter

Serial/parallel connections are great for local connection to a particular computer, but they are inflexible from the network point of view. You can place a printer anywhere on the network if you add a network adapter. These cards usually come with server/spooler software for configuring a spooling host.

Hewlett-Packard JetDirect for UNIX

We mounted the previous products, accelerators, and RAM cards in the RAM expansion area on the side of the LaserJet. A network adapter goes in the "I/O" slot on the back of the printer. We selected an HP JetDirect for UNIX card with thin Ethernet BNC connector (shown in Figure 11.9) for attachment to our TCP/IP network.

To install the card, position the LaserJet so that the back side hangs over the edge of a table, facing you (the printer should have all cables/power cord removed whenever you install options). Remove the screws from the "Optional I/O" cover. Take the card from its anti-static bag and carefully fit it into the mounting slots inside the printer. When the card is nearly in (within 1/2 inch or so) there will be resistance— push the card firmly until it seats. Then replace the screws to hold in the card. Note, if you have thick fingers it is practically impossible to connect the Ethernet cable to the printer—the space is extremely tight; find a friend with strong, thin, perhaps double-jointed fingers. When you complete the connection, turn on the printer.

FIGURE 11.9   The Hewlett-Packard JetDirect for Unix printer adapter

Configuration

As described earlier under Selecting a Hardware Interface, change the LaserJet hardware interface from *PARALLEL* or *SERIAL* to *OPTIONAL*. Now, press the tiny Status button on the adapter. The printer will print out a status report—in five languages! The adapter's Ethernet hardware address is provided on the report, along with many pieces of information which tell you the state of the connection. The report references the packets received and packets transmitted up to that point in time—also showing a *CLOSED* TCP connection status. The JetDirect card automatically tries to configure itself via **bootp** from the network, but the UNIX software must first be installed to insure its success.

Installing the workstation software

We obtained the software SunOS, but you can get HP-UX and SCO versions also. Place the tape containing the JetDirect software into the Sun's tape drive and follow the instructions to install it on the Sun. This software is organized in two parts: startup and spooler software. The startup software makes changes to the files **/etc/inetd.conf** and **/etc/services** to enable a bootp server. Start the configuration utility **/usr/lib/hpnp/hpnpcfg**.

     Hpnpcfg displays an interactive menu, which you should follow sequentially. Step 2 performs the BOOTP/TFTP configuration which requires answers to several questions—most importantly questions regarding the hardware address, printer name, and IP address. Steps 3-5 verify that **BOOTP** is operational, that the connection is viable, and that test pages can be printed. At this point you can print another status page at the LaserJet—it should show a **Listen** connection status and display the information you just entered. Step 6 sets up the spooler directory. You can choose between PCL and PostScript language support. If you have a product such as Pacific Data PE/XL installed which will do auto-switching at the printer, create one spooler for each type, and name them as different printers. Considering all that **hpnpcfg** does for you, this utility certainly represents the easy way to set up the card.

Expanded features

The newest generation of JetDirect cards, which we did not test, add two welcome capabilities. The first is SNMP support, for remote management of the printer. The second is enhanced protocol support for NetWare and NETBIOS-based LANs.

How to Install a Print Server

External adapters are much simpler to connect to printers than their internal counterparts, but there is still much to do on the software end. We tested two popular models: the Microplex M200 TCP/IP Printer Adapter and the Milan FastPort 3000 Network Print Server. You can find others from companies such as Xircom, Inc.; Castelle, Inc.; Extended Systems, Inc.; Rose Electronics; AXIS Communications, Inc.; and Corollary, Inc. Most of these companies can supply a multiprotocol model to support both TCP/IP and Novell IPX.

     Here are the general steps for installing most external print servers:

1. Lay out a plan of which job-spooling computers (queues) are to be served.
2. Create a host name for the device in the host tables of print spooler machines.
3. Attach the printer and network cabling to the print server.
4. Configure the device, particularly with its IP address.
5. Interface the UNIX host's print spooler with the print server.

With regard to step 5, which involves interfacing the print spooler with the print server, we recommend two primary methods. The simplest way is through the LPR protocol, which nearly every product supports and which requires no extra software for the host. The other method requires installing host software which uses UNIX sockets. Installing and configuring host software is more of a hassle than using LPR, but this method provides an opportunity to build more features into the product.

Microplex Systems Ltd. M200/M201 TCP/IP Printer Adapter

We installed the M200 easily on our thin coax Ethernet. (The M201 is identical, except that it is used with unshielded twisted pair.) This device has enough memory to support up to about 30 directly-connected TCP/IP hosts. You can simultaneously print on three printers connected to the one parallel and two serial ports.

Installation

To install the M200, first modify the **hosts** table on a UNIX server to include a new IP address for the device. Then connect the cables between the M200, the network, and the printer. (Remember to configure the printer for the interface you use, whether serial or parallel.)

A diskette is included for installation on the UNIX server. However, this software remains optional (the M200 supports both LPD and sockets). We did not install it, but for those who wish to, the process is not rigorous. The software provides a) a setup program for the IP address, b) socket-based software to interface with the UNIX spooler program, and c) sample interface files for System V UNIX machines. We found the documentation to be thorough—right down to pin-out specifications for all of the cables. However, we did not need to read much of it—which was the best part.

Your only remaining task is to inform the device of its IP address. There are four methods to choose from. The first requires the previously mentioned host software installation utility. The other three methods use RARP, ARP/TELNET, or the attachment of a terminal to the COM1 port. We elected to use the RARP method. See our earlier section, Supplying IP Addresses to Devices.

Configuration

Printing through the M200 can be handled directly, through **rsh/rcmd** or a proprietary pseudo-tty host daemon. The host daemon allows bi-directional communications from a PostScript printer. Most users print indirectly, however, through the usual LPR protocol and print spoolers. Microplex provides excellent instructions on the use of M200 with both BSD and System V UNIX spoolers. On our Sun, this involved entering a new printer description in **/etc/printcap** and creating spooler directories. Then we were able to print from either DOS (via NFS) or UNIX. The M200 does not autosense the PostScript/PCL protocols, but you can add Pacific Data's PE/XL for that.

You can configure the M200 with a routing table, allowing it to service requests from other networks. You can also control which hosts can access the printer(s), setup login users, and configure other options.

Expanded features

Version 4 of the ROM software (targeted for 3Q 1993) adds Novell IPX print server capability but remains at the price of Version 3—$795. You gain the ability to send print jobs from TCP/IP hosts and NetWare print queues indiscriminately. Additionally, it manages up to 32 NetWare print queues on 8 file servers. Updates can be installed over the network via FLASH memory. The new version also supports SNMP (Simple Network Management Protocol) to make the M200/M201 recognizable to most LAN management software.

MiLAN Technology FastPort 3000/3100 Network Print Server

The FastPort 3000 we tested was a multiprotocol version 3.0—serving both TCP/IP clients and Novell print queues. This unit, shown in Figure 11.10, autosenses whether the Ethernet frame type is Ethernet_II or Novell's Ethernet_802.3. More importantly, FastPort runs IPX as a NetWare print server.

The device comes with both a BNC and a UTP jack, a big advantage for companies with a mixed environment. The FastPort has one parallel and one serial printer port, which can be used simultaneously. Unfortunately, the FastPort does not autosense PostScript and PCL files. The FastPort is indeed fast, faster than perhaps any other print server—it will never cause a bottleneck. The model 3000 (and the faster 3100) can easily outpace all printers and nearly all plotters on the market. Additional features allow you to restrict printing to certain hosts, and send error messages to the manager via e-mail.

Installation

You can use RARP, ARP/TELNET, or a terminal to set the IP address. We tried each of the first two methods to no avail, until we realized we had not set the cable type switches on the back of the FastPort for BNC (a bad case of 'user error'). For more help, see our previous section, Supplying IP Addresses to Devices.

FastPort Version 3.0 requires that you install host software because it does not support the LPR protocol. Host software allows FastPort to do niftier tricks than LPD—such as creating a bank of related printers. (The first printer free gets the job.) We found the software easy to install—requiring, however, a small amount of con-

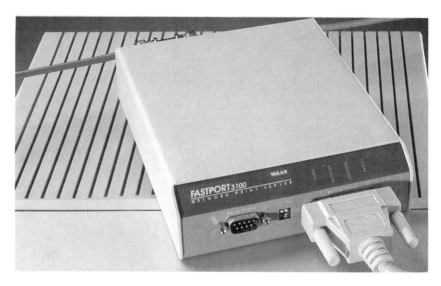

FIGURE 11.10 Photo of MiLAN Fastport 3100

figuration time. After installation, a cold reboot of the FastPort is all it takes to start printing from UNIX. Getting Novell PCs to work is as easy as defining a server/ queue in **PCONSOLE** and executing one setup command.

Expanded features

MiLAN's instructions come well-tuned to a variety of individual environments— including BSD, System V, VMS, Wollongong's PathWay Access, SunSelect's PC-NFS, FTP's PC-TCP, NeWSPrint, Adobe TranScript, and more. Version 4.0, due out shortly and priced at $695, will include support for both LPR protocol and Ethertalk, which should make any printer look like an Apple LaserWriter. By the time this book is published, FastPort will also have NETBIOS support for use with Microsoft LAN Manager and Windows for Workgroups.

How to Install a Network-Ready, Multiprotocol Printer

We choose not to spend major time here, since you can obtain succinct instructions from your printer vendor. Installation is somewhat simpler than for most other products, because you can connect your network cable directly to the printer. Nevertheless, you must still configure the UNIX side with host software, printer IP address, and description—an installation process similar to that for print servers. Several vendors offer network-ready printers—many of which can autoswitch between PCL and PostScript jobs. Some provide huge input buffers to spool hundreds of pages. Printers in this category include the QMS 860 and QMS-PS 1700, the COMPAQ PAGEMARQ, the HP LaserJet 4M and 4Si MX, and the IBM LaserPrinter 4039. If you have the bucks, such a printer makes a tidy solution for a multiprotocol network.

12

E-Mail, Terminals, and More

Introduction

This chapter was a brilliant stratagem, allowing us to organize all of the remaining types of products we think you should know about. We also made this chapter easy to read (or not read) by conveniently grouping products under the categories, Software and Hardware.

As in the last chapter, we discuss individual products within the text, rather than using a separate chapter at the end of the book for Product Evaluations (with the exception of e-mail products which we cover in Chapter 18). We walk through the installation procedures for several products in order to more effectively illustrate the techniques involved.

Software Products

E-Mail Options

Not every DOS to UNIX connectivity situation necessitates direct application and peripheral sharing. Having one large internetwork might involve more cable than you care to swallow. Often your goal is simple communication or file transfer. You want the network of DECstations in Engineering to be able to communicate with the rest of the company running a Novell network. Your answer may be an e-mail connection between the two networks. In particular, e-mail is suited to bridging long-distance relationships. Consider the needs of a corporation with its headquarters in Chicago and branch offices scattered throughout the Mid-West. Application interoperability may not be necessary—just the ability to exchange files and to communicate without playing telephone tag. Dedicated Wide Area Networks can provide the same options, but at much higher expense and with significantly more effort.

"Ah, e-mail," you say. "Why that is obviously an easy and elegant solution to my problem." If it were only so! Even though e-mail itself is a simple, commonly accepted application, there is a dearth of e-mail applications supporting both DOS and UNIX. In fact, if you already have an e-mail application in place, you may be forced into gateways and commercial e-mail systems in order for your current PC e-mail system to speak to a UNIX e-mail setup.

There are some available options. We examine the basics of each and tell you how they might best work in your situation. We touch on as many innovative solutions as possible given the few commercial packages straddling these two operating systems. Chapter 18 evaluates some of the more popular options on the market.

The E-Mail Acronym Shuffle

We can't begin to give you a detailed tutorial in the world of e-mail standards and protocols. It is confusing, constantly changing, and difficult to pin down. Here we give you a handle on the differences separating the two e-mail worlds of DOS and UNIX—the differences that make e-mail difficult to integrate across platforms.

In general, all e-mail systems have in common certain components. They have a way to send messages from one machine to another. This is the protocol or *mail transport agent* (MTA). The MTA takes responsibility for determining how to get the message to the right place. In addition, e-mail systems have some method for storing and maintaining addresses. This is often referred to as directory services or Post Office. Each user has a unique address stored in the Post Office list, so each piece of mail can be sent to the correct station. Finally, an e-mail system needs a user interface—a way for you to create, read, forward, store, and delete mail. This is termed the *mail user agent* (MUA).

With these basic terms filed in our heads, we can examine some of the particulars of the DOS and UNIX e-mail markets—as well as look at various options for bridging these worlds.

DOS and PCs

Within the DOS realm, each e-mail vendor took it upon itself to work with a proprietary protocol. This means that cc:Mail users cannot send mail to Microsoft Mail users, even if they are on the same LAN. Novell attempted to improve the situation by creating a standard protocol called *Message Handling Service* (MHS). However, most vendors ignored MHS (a few like Beyond Mail didn't). MHS requires a separate server on the Novell network in order to handle the mail. Many vendors have placed software gateways on top of MHS (appropriately named *MHS Gateways*) to allow their e-mail packages to talk to MHS-based e-mail systems.

Three primary vendor coalitions have launched attempts to standardize DOS e-mail. An MHS standards group is attempting to make MHS and its Novell connections the standard. A second alliance, the VIM (Vendor Independent Messaging) Interface Group, hopes to develop a standard API for vendors to use when going from one mail system to another. Members include IBM, Lotus, Apple, and Word-Perfect. A third group, MAPI (Messaging Application Programming Interface), is being led by Microsoft. Unfortunately, the API and methods endorsed by MAPI are not compatible with the APIs endorsed by VIM. In fact, none of these so-called standards has received full marketplace acceptance.

UNIX and larger machines

Three primary standards, or acronyms, are associated with UNIX e-mail products—SMTP (Simple Mail Transport Protocol), X.400, and MIME (Multipurpose Internet Mail Extensions).

SMTP is a part of the Internet Protocol suite mentioned in Chapter 5. The standard protocol used between UNIX workstations, SMTP is directly supported by products like Z-Mail and UNIX's own **sendmail** program. SMTP represents a tight, small protocol that scales well across machines. Also used by the Internet for e-mail transfer, SMTP has become a well-established standard. Many products support it either directly or through a gateway.

X.400 is an international standard for connecting different e-mail systems and has as its basic purpose to determine how messages are handled. It represents a whole set of standards and specifications considered a part of the OSI model. X.400 excels in its ability to connect all manner of e-mail systems—hence, its acceptance as an international standard. However, X.400 has its problems. First, the specification is sufficiently huge that it presents implementation difficulty for smaller machines. X.400, therefore, migrates towards connecting larger machines and enterprise-wide networks. Second, because of its size, many vendors do not implement the entire X.400 specification. The result has become the proliferation of incompatible or incomplete X.400 e-mail solutions. These factors have slowed the acceptance of X.400 in the U.S.

MIME extends beyond both X.400 and SMTP. It sets a specification for how to send non-text data such as graphics, video, and other aspects of multimedia. Since the MIME standard can be built on top of existing networks, it becomes fairly easy to send attachments and enclosures that contain non-text. MIME is being adopted by the Internet Engineering Task Force and will eventually become an accepted Internet protocol. Only a handful of products are MIME-compliant as of the summer of 1993, but many vendors in the UNIX arena are in the process of adopting it.

Dual Platform Products

In terms of simplicity, the preferred e-mail solution is a product that works on your DOS network and on your UNIX machines. Chapter 3 clearly lays out some of the pros and cons of this approach. Training is simplified. Administration centers around one product rather than many. Functionality is high. However, the cost of giving up your present e-mail system could be prohibitive.

There are a limited number of dual-platform products available in the DOS—UNIX environment. Significant players include cc:Mail from cc:Mail, a division of Lotus Development Corp.; Z-Mail from Z-code Software Corp.; WordPerfect Office from WordPerfect Corp.; Select Mail from SunSelect; and The Wollongong Group

Inc.'s Messenger. Only WordPerfect Office and cc:Mail have any substantial following in the DOS marketplace. The remaining three products are relatively new.

You should find minimal setup and configuration problems with this set of products. They all require a TCP/IP connection, but when that is in place, the configuration becomes straight-forward as shown in Figure 12.1. This provides a major reason to consider a dual-platform product rather than use a gateway or a commercial provider. Dual platform products require careful consideration, however, if you are required to rip out an e-mail system already in place.

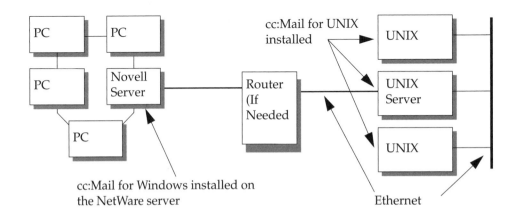

FIGURE 12.1 E-mail across networks using cross-platform e-mail products

E-Mail Gateways

When you have two incompatible e-mail systems, often an e-mail *gateway* is the only available option. An e-mail gateway converts the transport protocol of one system into the protocol of another system. Unless you use a commercial network, a gateway is the only way to move between two disparate e-mail systems. There are two basic types, X.400 and non-X.400 gateways. Your choice depends largely on your present e-mail system and the degree of flexibility you require.

X.400

X.400 products by design often serve as backbones or gateways for various e-mail systems. Available also from non-e-mail vendors, these products often supply more than a single interface gateway. An X.400-based gateway can give you flexibility to access other e-mail systems depending on how it is implemented. The X.400 gateway can also facilitate the transition to a X.400 e-mail system if such is your plan.

Other gateways

Many popular DOS-based and Novell-based e-mail products sell assorted gateway packages. Each of these gateways support access to a specific e-mail system. Some are implemented strictly in software while others require a separate gateway machine, such as a node on the LAN. There are gateways to IBM's PROF, DEC's ALL-IN-ONE, various mini-computer mail systems, and to UNIX systems. For example, cc:Mail has a gateway to SMTP which can be beneficial if you are not using their cc:Mail for UNIX product. Microsoft Mail has gateways for IBM PROFS and AppleTalk Mail. Though limited in scope, these gateways serve an important niche.

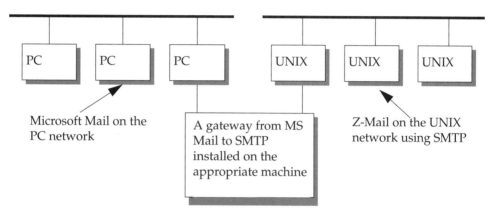

FIGURE 12.2 E-mail network using an e-mail gateway product to route the mail

Commercial E-Mail Networks

One option for e-mail over long distances is to use a commercial e-mail provider. There are several services available that do not require a specific type of computer or type of operating system. These include MCI Mail, CompuServe GENIE, AT&T Mail, America Online, and Prodigy. Some of these systems lean more toward providing information to the consumer; and, therefore, e-mail becomes a secondary priority. For most businesses, these become too expensive and cluttered to be considered for regular e-mail transactions. In Chapter 18, we discuss CompuServe and MCI Mail as two services particularly suited to businesses.

Most of the advantages and disadvantages of commercial e-mail are laid out in Chapter 3. After making the serial connection and installing the terminal emulation software, you should have no difficulties connecting to a commercial e-mail provider. We think more businesses should take advantage of this solution for contact with branch offices, suppliers, and customers.

UNIX Commercial Networks

UNIX machines have been connected to networks long before many DOS users had even heard of networks. Many online networks are geared more to UNIX users. However, the proliferation of computers and the need to internetwork has opened these networks up to all users who can get into the system. There are a number of these systems including UUNET, PSInet, usenet, and the most famous of them all, The Internet. The Internet and UUNET are discussed in Chapter 18.

UNIX commercial networks have similar advantages and disadvantages to the regular commercial e-mail providers. There are some differences, however. Some of the networks require you to use **uucp** to access them. **uucp** is the UNIX to UNIX copy program that was one of the first methods for UNIX systems to send mail back and forth. Systems like UUNET require a **uucp** type connection. You cannot use a standard DOS or Windows terminal emulator, but you can purchase DOS-based **uucp** products to make the connection.

The Internet is also a bird of a different feather. It is really a host of internetworks spread across the country. The main components of the Internet are file transfer, e-mail, and remote login. You can access the Internet by logging directly into a network that is connected via TCP/IP, dialing into an Internet via PPP or SLIP, or dialing into a host with standard terminal emulation software. Individuals, small businesses, or departments must use some type of dial-in service to access the Internet. The Internet is discussed in more detail in Chapter 18. There are many commercial providers supplying access to the Internet.

Sneakernet

There seems to be no end to the acronyms and jargon of the computer world, but at least here's one that sounds interesting. "Sneakernet" is the term applied to a special kind of file transfer—manually copying files to a disk and carrying them to another computer. Actually, the sneakernet factor was the major reason for the invention of network cables. As shoe costs went up, employees (who were not allowed to wear Nikes to the office at that time) developed sore feet as their soles wore through from transferring files between computers. In more modern times, however, employees have taken to longer-lasting, rubber treads, and sneakernet has revived due to the rampant desire for information-sharing with dissimilar and/or offsite computers.

One major obstacle to sharing files between DOS and UNIX is that text file structure differs between the two (see Appendix A). The second major problem is that diskettes are formatted differently between DOS and UNIX. For example, you cannot put a DOS-formatted 3.5 inch diskette into a Sun floppy drive and read it without doing a **mount /pcfs**. We are aware of no standard utility to read a UNIX diskette at a DOS machine.

ftp (File Transfer Protocol) is the primary network solution, but requires cabling, adapters, and TCP/IP network software. TCP/IP network products for PCs invariably include **ftp**, and often, integrated file conversion utilities. **ftp** is explained in Chapter 5.

If you are interested in inexpensive networks using sneakernet rather than cables, check out Common-Link, from Pacific Microelectronics, Inc. at (415) 948-6200. Install Common-Link software on an SCO UNIX or Sun computer and the computer will instantly be able to read and write in DOS or Macintosh formats. Under DOS, Common-Link supports both 720K and 1.44M capacity diskettes. Under Macintosh, Common-Link supports only the 1.44M format, not 400K or 800K. The product also formats diskettes and allows you to manipulate diskette directories. And, even if your UNIX machine does not need any files from the DOS or Mac machines, it can still function as a translation station between the two. Macintosh can easily read DOS files through the Apple SuperDrive, but DOS machines have no inherent ability to read Macintosh.

Internetwork Management Tools

Once your company amasses multiple networks with tens to thousands of nodes, it becomes obvious that you need help to manage them. A system administrator cannot afford to physically go to each computer to make little changes in the system setup for accommodating a new server feature. Growing networks run into traffic problems periodically, problems which are difficult to trace and correct without an analyzer/monitor. Malfunctioning equipment, software metering, inventory, virus detection, user support ... all of these challenges and more can be solved with network management software.

Of course, multiprotocol networks (using TCP/IP, IPX/SPX, AppleTalk, and other types of packets) make any problems harder to deal with. Internetwork management software makes life simpler for the system administrator, providing a remote control for managed PCs and workstations.

How Network Management Software Works

Network management software is organized in a client-server fashion. *Agent* software runs in the background on each managed computer on the network. As an alternative, a *proxy agent* runs on a second machine which watches the first from a distance. The agent learns specifics about the computer system and its interfaces, and monitors particular communication events that go on. The *manager* software retrieves agent information, collates it, and reports the information in tabular or graphical format. With some products, the manager can exert control over the remote agent to gain access to files and directories, allowing remote configuration and user support. Additionally, *trap packets* can be generated by many agents to alert the manager to a variety of events as they occur. On a PC, the agent is a TSR; on a UNIX workstation it is a daemon. As with other TSRs, PC agents have a downside—

they consume DOS memory (usually no more than 20-30K), making it harder to load applications.

The concept of the Management Information Base, or *MIB*, is key to the manager/agent scheme. The MIB is simply a database for certain types of information, stored at each site. The agents continually gather data about network configuration and node status, traffic statistics, resource accounting, and security, and store the data in the MIB. The manager software can query this distributed database via the agent and put together trends and analysis for the network as a whole. The MIB-II standard, containing many groups of monitored variables, is described in RFC 1213. Note: Vendors are allowed to claim compliance with the MIB-II standard even if they do not support all parts of it. Vendors also have wide latitude to invent their own additional MIBs for DOS, Windows, or other information.

Standards for Network Management

Most network management software supports the *Simple Network Management Protocol*. SNMP has also been implemented by all major bridge and router manufacturers. Designed in cooperation with the Internet Activities Board (through numerous RFCs, including RFC 1157), SNMP is the most prevalent network management protocol in use today. It has recently been updated as SNMP Version 2.

Just because a product is "SNMP-compatible", however, doesn't mean that you can interoperate with another management product in the way that you want. SNMP-based agents can supply information to third-party managers, but the managers may not be able to use much of the information the agent gathers.

The *Common Management Information Protocol* (CMIP) is coming on strong as the eventual replacement for SNMP. CMIP is brought to you by the International Standards Organization, makers of the OSI model. CMIP is richer than SNMP in capability, but is also more complicated to implement. Many vendors have developed interfaces to CMIP, as well as to SNMP.

The Open Software Foundation (OSF) plays a large role in standardizing network management. OSF's *Distributed Management Environment* (DME) charts much of the course for network management tools from the general standpoints of software management (distribution, installation, etc.), software license management, and printing services. OSF has endorsed both SNMP and CMIP as the protocols of choice for network management.

One old friend that has made a big impact in network management is IBM. NetView, an IBM mainframe-based product, has been managing SNA networks for years. Several SNMP products interface with NetView, although those interfaces are technically limited in scope. But, if you are joining an SNA network and a PC LAN, your investment in IBM probably dictates consolidation under NetView. You should look for NetView-linking products—products which act as intermediaries between IBM and other major network management systems. See the Appendix for a list of a few such products.

Network Management Utilities

As a system administrator, you face a difficult job in selecting network management software, partly because there has been an explosion of new products to choose from within the last two years, and partly because no one product does it all. Even more than X server or TCP/IP network products, each network management product bundles its own set of widely-varying utilities. Often, you must select more than one product to obtain your chosen mix of functionality. Here are some general categories of functions. Bear in mind that we are only scratching the surface of capabilities.

Performance monitoring

Performance monitoring is the primary function of most network management tools. The monitoring function can help you determine the causes of certain problems and consequently, develop ideas of how to fix them.

Network slowdown is directly related to the amount of traffic over the network. You can identify users who generate continuous traffic using the monitor. Or, if a network is having collisions (errors) because there are simply too many users, you can get ideas on how to best correct the situation via bridges, scheduling, or other means. Malfunctioning Ethernet adapters and intermittent cable connections can also cause extra traffic. You can pinpoint these faults with a monitor.

Protocol analysis

One of the most-needed functions, usually lumped together with performance monitoring, is filled by the *protocol analyzer*. (Other names include *packet analyzer, packet decoder* or *network analyzer*.) In addition to the traffic statistics discussed above, this product gives you detailed information about the *types* of packets being generated, and lets you view the contents of each. Having this information can usually lead you to the source of a network problem, including perhaps a buggy application. Some analyzers are expensive, hardware-based units for use on larger networks of at least 250 nodes. Other less-expensive analyzers make use of special network interface cards or are based completely in software. If you are on a shoestring budget, the cheaper analyzers can adequately spot most of the trouble you'll face.

Many types of packets, corresponding to multiple software and hardware protocols, can be filtered and reported. Common packet types include ARP, IP, UDP, ICMP, TCP, and NFS (UNIX); IPX (Novell); AppleTalk; NETBIOS (LANtastic and others); DECnet (Digital); SNA (IBM); XNS; OSI; Banyan Vines; data link protocols such as Ethernet 802.2, 802.3, SNAP—a hodge-podge of protocols. Some packets encapsulate other packet types. You can also re-group packets under different categories, such as packets containing errors, broadcast packets, packets to/from the current station, etc. Many protocol analyzers allow you to program your own filters.

The user interface is very important, especially if you do not have a strong background on the technical side of a LAN. Debugging a network is not easy, so look for products which can explain the problem in language you can understand.

Once you obtain an analyzer, be sure to collect and store baseline network data from a typical day. This information will be invaluable to review when an abnormal situation comes up.

Traffic pattern analysis

To save some users from inequitable delays on the network, find a product that can help you analyze the flow. Such products can determine the most active servers and client stations and graph the traffic levels. Many products can generate bogus traffic to stress-test the system. This can help determine where the bottlenecks are.

Graphical network representation

Select a product which can show a diagram of your network. Not only does this allow you to get the visual lay of the LAN (you might forget about the laptop in Finance), it also gives you a means of managing nodes via mouse clicks. Click on the laptop to get the inside view.

With the aid of mapping software, some products can even provide diagrams of the enterprise superimposed over a map of the world, states, or city streets. See an HP OpenView demonstration if you want a treat.

Resource inventory

You can take inventory of your networked equipment automatically, without ever having to pry a lid off of a computer. Products such as Microcom Inc.'s LANlord 2.0 provide so much PC information you probably couldn't find half of it in the PC vendor's printed documentation. This function can show the brand and configuration of many kinds of boards installed on a machine, microchannel or otherwise: video controller, disk controller, serial/parallel board, and network interface adapter. Unfortunately, AT bus (non-microchannel) PCs don't keep track of which boards are in which slots, as microchannel PCs do.

But that's not all. Inventory software can also tell you intimate information about the filesystems, how the drives are mapped, what the startup files contain, the versions of network drivers used, what device drivers are loaded into memory and where, quantity and type of memory, and much more. You can be alerted by the software if a user is running short of hard disk space. Having this information at your fingertips makes software installation and user support a snap.

Remote node configuration

Any network management tool that can inventory the network hardware/software should also be able to let you configure the entire station remotely. On PCs, this includes editing startup files, modifying the environment, rebooting, copying new files, executing programs, and much else.

User support

The best way to help a user out of a jam (and prevent having to help them again) is to show them how to fix it themselves. You can do this with the remote control functionality of some software, taking control of the user's keyboard and mouse to lead them through the solution. Combined with the messaging (below), the user can be trained on the spot to deal with future emergencies.

Real-time messaging

Messaging is known under a few names, including CHAT and SEND. This function allows one user (for instance, the network manager) to send messages back and forth with a network user. This is similar in concept to e-mail, except that the mail daemons are not used. Communication occurs in real-time, enabling users to hold conversations over the network with reasonable (immediate) response times.

Virus detection

PCs, more so than UNIX computers, are vulnerable to viruses. A *virus* is a program that, unknown to the user, can do anything from playing time-activated jokes to destroying filesystems. The virus can gain entrance to your network through a contaminated disk loaded on a single machine, or perhaps through contact with computers outside of your firm. Then, it can replicate itself whenever the program it is attached to is executed. You do not want to let a viral infection run rampant through your network. To combat this menace, some network management products integrate virus protection software, which can identify and remove a thousand viruses.

Perhaps more importantly, virus detection functionality on a network manager can often identify the point of entry of any virus and track the potential spread of the virus from machine to machine. This gives you a chance to catch and exterminate all replications of a virus before there is too much damage to user files.

Software application metering

Software license violations are illegal, and they can be expensive if a company is found guilty of them. Most UNIX products utilize license servers to police the licenses. However, much of the DOS/Windows software on the market performs no elaborate license-checking. Hit squads of computer-literate enforcers have been known to 'move in' on a company to search for license violations and pirated software. Metering functions can spare you the effort of maintaining adequate licenses for your users (or the agony of court sessions). Agents can inform the manager of each application as it is run, and threshold levels can alert the company to potential liability. The information can also aid in making software purchasing decisions.

Security

"Be careful, little hands, what you do" might be the motto on some modern networks. Permissions control the security of networks, but sometimes companies wish to know more about what their employees do, such as playing computer games, modifying configuration files without authority, and—you name it. For those occasions in which a company deems it appropriate, monitoring can certainly be done. Records of program activity can be kept with no trouble, and trap alerts can be set for many types of activity.

Selecting an Internetwork Management Tool

Network management tools come in a variety of shapes and sizes. Most of them support networks of a specific variety, such as Novell NetWare LANs, or TCP/IP networks. Therefore, they are not internetwork tools at all. The protocol monitoring functions can indeed identify many types of packets, UNIX- or DOS-based, flowing over the cable, but most products support only their own agents on a single platform. This means that there is no remote control, inventorying, or other monitoring of the non-supported platform. Some tools provide different agents for other platforms, such as DEC or Apple; these will be more expensive than single-platform products. Limited internetwork support is provided by virtue of SNMP compatibility, which can make data available to managers on other systems.

Heavy-hitting products in the Novell realm include Intel Corporation's LANDesk Manager, which can also monitor UNIX packets, and Microcom Systems, Inc.'s LANlord, which manages LAN Manager networks in addition to Novell. You can get tools such as NetScope, from Qualix Group, Inc., for monitoring and analyzing UNIX packets on Sun systems. When it comes to enterprise-wide network management (true internetworking packages), the most popular products include HP's OpenView, SunConnect's Sun Net Manager, and IBM's NetView. These three have become standards of their own due to their widespread presence in the marketplace. Most vendors try to include interfaces to those systems with their products.

Which GUI you want to work from sometimes narrows your search for management software. Some products are designed for the Motif graphical interface, others for OpenWindows, the X Windows system, Microsoft Windows, or OS/2 Presentation Manager. Others use whatever GUI HP OpenView or SunNet Manager use.

The price of network management software varies widely with the functionality, from as little as $400 for single-networks to tens of thousands for enterprise-wide packages. Also, some vendors charge by server license, others by number of nodes.

Macintosh Connectivity

We wrote this section for the System Administrator who is wondering how to incorporate his Apple Macintosh computers. You can choose from several types of Macintosh connectivity, including DOS or terminal emulation, TCP/IP and NFS, X Window System, and more. One of these solutions is to connect the Mac to an Ethernet LAN and run SoftPC software from Insignia Solutions Inc. SoftPC installs on the Mac and helps it emulate a DOS PC, running DOS programs and talking with other

PCs. SoftNode completes the interface by providing ODI drivers and NetWare shells to let the Mac be at home in a Novell LAN environment.

Another option combines hardware and software. Cards from Cubix Corporation run DOS sessions inside the NetWare server box for remote clients, including Macintosh computers, if you install pcMACTERM software from Symantec Corporation. The solution allows the Mac to remotely control a Cubix card, which in turn executes DOS applications.

Artisoft LANtastic for Macintosh networks Mass on a peer-to-peer PC network with TCP/IP access. Try also Locus Computing's PC Interface for Mac for UNIX client capability. FutureSoft Engineering has a Mac version of DynaComm, their communications and terminal emulation software package. For dial-up access to UNIX computers for news and file transfer, try InterCon Systems Corporation's UUCP/ Connect. InterCon supplies the more general purpose TCP/Connect II and NFS/ Share as well. Try Webster Computer Corporation for a variety of Mac-integrating products ranging from DEC PATHWORKS print managers to multiprotocol routers. Connectix manufactures Hand Off II, Maxima and Virtual 030. SunTOPS from Sun-Select makes a Sun workstation act as a non-dedicated file server and NFS gateway for Macintosh.

If X is your thing, contact White Pine Software, Inc. for eXodus. Cayman Systems Inc.'s XGator lets you control the Mac from an X station. Check with other manufacturers mentioned in this book for Mac versions. See your Apple dealer for additional ideas. Apple Computer has Apple Access II, Macintosh PC Exchange, MacTerminal & MacX. For other connectivity options, see the Sneakernet discussion above, and the UnixWare product evaluation in Chapter 14.

Hardware Products

Character-Based Terminals

Character-based terminals, sometimes called *alphanumeric, serial, or dumb terminals*, are the "cheap seats" on a UNIX system. Connected via ordinary twisted pair, multiconductor, or telephone cable, these display/keyboard stations let users run character-based applications on the UNIX host. Character-based applications comprise approximately 75% of UNIX applications at this time; newer applications seek the GUI look. The display requirements for character-based programs are small, in terms of memory, size and capability, holding the cost down on terminals. Only one program (or "session") can be run at a time unless you have multisession software for the host which we mention later.

Wyse Technology is probably the best-known manufacturer of general purpose terminals. Their popular WY-60 offers a choice of green, amber or white display, 44-

line/132 column capability, ASCII, ANSI or IBM AT-style keyboards, a small amount of built-in software (clock, calender, calculator, setup) and a list price of $599.

Installing a Serial Terminal

We connected a WY-60 (see Figure 12.3) to our SCO UNIX host via that computer's COM2 serial port and a DB25 M/F cable. Most organizations will install a multiport board in the computer to service many terminals. Large organizations can have as many as 64, 256, or more terminals connected through concentrators or hubs. See our comments on terminal servers and multiport boards later in the chapter.

There really is not much to setting up a terminal. Normally, you plug into the modem port on the back of the terminal. The other port is for a local printer. The cable must be a null modem cable (with lines 2 and 3 crossed), and you don't need more than 3 conductors. Most terminals such as the WYSE are set from the factory to boot properly on power-up, without installing any new software on the UNIX host. Your biggest problem is making sure the UNIX port is sending out a **getty**. Chapter 9 outlines the method for setting up the UNIX host. If you wish to change any boot parameters, such as colors, cursor style, rows/columns, or terminal emulation mode, you can access the setup information from a setup screen. You can reach the WY-60 setup information using the Shift-Setup keys. There are a slew of parameters. You should write down your settings—sometimes an electrical surge, a host crash or a quick trigger finger will set one or more parameters to the wrong settings.

FIGURE 12.3 WYSE-60 character-based terminal

Multisession Software

There are a few UNIX products that let character terminals have multiple sessions. Terminals with multiple pages of screen memory best support this technique. When you switch from screen 1 to screen 2, the contents of the second screen are immediately visible because they have been saved in memory. In most cases, these sessions are full screen windows that are switched by the use of a set of control keys (such as CTRL-F1). This capability is not exactly like having an X-terminal or even an Alpha terminal, but it is certainly beneficial to many users.

SCO has always supported multiscreen on the console unit and now supports a similar utility on terminals. This utility is called **mscreen**. It allows up to 20 separate screens, each with its own login. Another product is Facet Term from Structured Software Solutions. It also supports 10 multiple sessions on a terminal plus gives you the ability to split the screen in two and cut and paste between sessions. JSB Corporation sells MultiView Mascot, a windowing software product that runs on character-based terminals and provides a Motif-like interface. It also supports cut and paste and a set of accessories. This capability, while not the same as having a GUI interface, certainly goes a long way.

Character Terminal versus PC

As with all terminals, there is a time and place for them. A PC is not always the best solution. The character terminal is low-cost (under $500 on the street), simple to set up and foolproof. However, serial connections and terminal emulation from a PC to a UNIX host provide many attractions. We make the following recommendation. If you do not have PCs and are installing a new application where the users are only doing one task, use character-based terminals where possible. If you have PCs or need access to a PC network, use a PC with a terminal emulation program.

Multiport Boards

When you need to attach several terminals to a UNIX host, you can install a *multiport board* in your UNIX PC. A single multiport board often provides 4, 8, or 16 serial ports. These intelligent boards effectively off-load communications from the central CPU to the multiport board itself, freeing the central CPU from the menial details of talking to the terminal. They also provide RAM to buffer communications and processing. Besides performance, your main benefit is an expanded system for a good price per user. Multiport boards can be found with DB-9, RJ-11, or RJ-45 connections. A typical board for 8 terminals can be found for $100 to $170 per user.

There are not a lot of negatives to multiport boards. They do not allow Ethernet communications (for that task you should consider a terminal server). They also consume a slot or two inside your computer, but you get a lot in return. Nearly all the models selling today run a cable from the actual adaptor to some type of exterior box

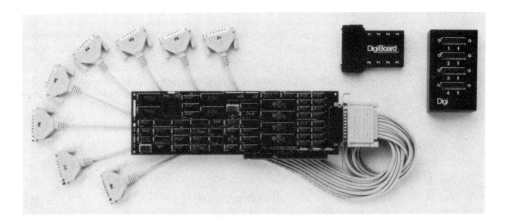

FIGURE 12.4 Digiboard PC/16e multiport board

where the cable connection is made to the terminal. The Digiboard PC/16e multi-port board (shown in Figure 12.4) is one example of the newest multiport boards with on-board processors. Other vendors are listed in Appendix B. Given the low additional cost of intelligent boards and their increased processing power, you should give them a close look.

Terminal Servers

Rather than use a standard multiport board, a newer connectivity option is the *terminal server* (also known as a *communications server*). Found in many forms, the key to a terminal server is the ability to tap into the UNIX host via an Ethernet connection and run serial terminals from it. There are a number of reasons to consider purchasing a terminal server. First, it moves much of the processing off of the host and onto the server. Second, the Ethernet connection from the host to the terminal server increases throughput. Third, many servers allow terminals to access multiple hosts thereby eliminating the restriction of a single-host based network. The major disadvantages are the cost and complexity. If you are not using Ethernet on your system, the terminal server forces you to use it while the multiport board does not.

An example of a terminal server with multiple protocols is Corollary Inc.'s CNS-1600. The CNS-1600 supports TCP/IP, IPX/SPX and LAT all on the same network. You can connect 16 serial devices, 2 parallel printers and use it with either 10Base-T or AUI Ethernet connections. The CNS-1600 supports RS-422 serial connections. RS-422 supports RS-232 devices but allows them to use higher speeds, up to 115.2K bps. Terminal servers are generally slightly higher in price than a multiport board.

X-Terminals

X-terminals are graphics-based terminals—much more functional (and expensive) than character-based terminals. X-terminals can run GUI-based programs (graphical user interface) designed for OpenWindows, Motif, and other UNIX windowing environments—something that character-oriented terminals cannot do. They also have built-in network connectivity other than through a serial port, i.e., thin-net (BNC), thick-net (AUI), and twisted-pair (10Base-T) connectivity. The X comes from the X Window System, a technology first developed by MIT and now the standard across all UNIX workstation platforms. X server software can be installed on a PC, allowing a PC to run X applications and be a competitor of an X-terminal. Chapters 8 and 15 discuss X concepts and PC-based X servers in great detail. In this section we focus on the hardware-based X solutions, X-terminals.

X-terminals have no local disk drive with which to boot. Therefore, they are designed to interrogate the network to find their boot configuration, a configuration which must be set up ahead of time. If that fails, you can boot them manually via the internal boot ROM program. If you boot manually, you will not have to load software on the UNIX server workstation. However, the centralized boot file system makes administration easier for multiple installations.

In our lab, we used two X-terminals. One was a high-end engineering-style terminal from Tektronix: the TekXpress XP337 (shown in Figure 12.5). The other was an NCD 17c, a mid-range X-terminal. The TekXpress XP337 has a 19-inch color display with 1152 by 900 pixel resolution, 5M of RAM, a MIPS R3000 CPU, and has a list price of $4995. The NCD 17c has a 17-inch color display with 1024 by 768 resolution,

FIGURE 12.5 Tektronix XP337 color X-terminal

8M of RAM, and a 68020 CPU. The NCD 17c has been replaced with the NCD mcx17 which uses a Motorola 88100 RISC processor and sells for $4,295.

Installing an X-Terminal

Connecting the cables on the Tektronix XP337 hardware proved to be intuitive—you don't need instructions. We hooked up the system to a Sun SPARCstation IPC via TCP/IP thin coaxial Ethernet.

Configuring the software was more challenging (usually true for all brands of X-terminals). The time-consuming part was to edit a configuration file—xp330.cnf—the file this terminal looks at to boot. When the XP337 boots, it attempts to get its startup information from a server. It uses BOOTP and/or RARP to find the *boot server* (see Chapter 5), which then downloads the appropriate configuration file to the terminal. If there is no boot server, you can boot the terminal manually. We inserted the host IP number and name into the configuration file, along with many other options. On the XP337 you can pre-configure the network IP tables, file hosts, the X environment, boot procedure, TCP/IP, DEC options, serial port options, keyboard, SNMP (for network management software), and other items. Setup screens make maintenance of the terminal information simple.The installation manual describes in detail the process for setting up the various options needed on the Sun, e.g., TFTP, SNMP, etc. Since the Sun had been a stand-alone machine, we had to make the Sun ready to do TFTP (Trivial File Transfer Protocol), or in other words, become a boot server. In our case, this meant unremarking a line in the **/etc/inetd.-conf** file that said:

```
TFTP DGRAM UDP WAIT ROOT /USR/ETC/IN.TFTPD IN.TFTPD -S /TFTPBOOT
```

The **-s /tftpboot** portion is called a secure path, required for **tftp** file transfers. This secure path is, intentionally, the path to the boot files. Then, we restarted the **inetd** process. We also had to spend time setting up the X Display Manager (**xdm**) on the Sun—see Chapter 8.

X-Terminal versus PC

In comparison with PC's running X-servers, X-terminals have certain differences. Since an X-terminal has no disk drives, it boots off of the host computer or in some occasions uses an onboard EEPROM to initiate the startup. PCs invariably boot from the local hard drive. Centrally-managed boot software can be either an advantage or a disadvantage to your organization, depending upon your current bias toward centralization/decentralization.

The typical display for an X-terminal is much beefier, both in size and resolution. The size alone is limiting to a PC, since on smaller displays windows are crowded together. X-terminals can have much more memory than a PC, allowing them to open dozens of windows. (The Tektronix XP330 models can have up to 52M.)

X-terminals are *multitasking*. That is, if you open up several programs under X and set each monitoring, or recalculating (as a spreadsheet), or doing whatever it does—each will continue running to completion even though its window is not in the foreground. A PC must run X-server software to multitask.

If you are trying to decide between purchasing a PC and an X-terminal, factor the costs of the following PC items into your analysis:

1. high-performance CPU—at least a 386, preferably greater
2. large, high-resolution display
3. graphics accelerator
4. extra memory
5. network adapter
6. TCP/IP software
7. Windows and DOS software
8. X-server software

Last, but not least, don't forget the "fiddle factor" cost of getting the software up and running on the PC. An X-terminal provides nearly an "out-of-the-box" solution, excepting the boot software setup.

AlphaWindows Terminals

The Display Industry Association (DIA), composed of terminal, multiport board and software manufacturers, has proposed a new standard as a cheaper alternative to X. While X-terminal sales are not nearly rivaling the sales figures for serial terminals, they nevertheless represent the future and dazzle the eyes of buyers. DIA members stand to lose significant market share to X-terminals and PCs with X servers unless they can in some fashion imitate the benefits of the X-terminal.

AlphaWindows is their response to this challenge. This new intermediate class of terminals provides windowing, multiple program execution, mouse support and cut and paste of data between applications. They run existing character-based UNIX applications (which amount to 3/4 of all UNIX applications) without modification on the same serial cabling that has always been used, and share the same host processor as before—a typical scenario for small business. In contrast, while X-terminals function under the same shared-processor environment and can also run character-based applications, X can additionally thrive in a LAN environment where there may be distributed processing (several servers). X also is the doorway to the newer GUI-based applications.

Is AlphaWindows a viable long-term standard or just a stopgap measure? Just how different is this technology? Windowing on an AlphaWindow terminal is accomplished in part by software which runs on the UNIX host. This requirement is not shared by an X-terminal, which has several megabytes of memory, PROMs and a processor to manage windows. Except for getting around in the window manager, the AlphaWindow terminal's mouse will not be that handy for the user since character-based applications do not typically use a mouse. Data entry (the usual purpose of terminals) doesn't normally require the user to cut and paste between applications.

The ability to run multiple sessions concurrently is the main benefit, and may be well worth the price to some. Alpha terminals are manufactured by ADDS, Cumulus, Link Technologies, and others, and cost only slightly more than their older counterparts ($50-100 more for monochrome versions). Note, however, that multisession capability has been provided for years through software alone. Structured Software Solutions FacetTerm and JSB Multiview Mascot are two software solutions that accomplish the goal of multiple sessions on ordinary terminals. Indeed, both companies are members of DIA and now provide window management software for many of the Alpha terminals.

Whether the AlphaWindows standard catches on or not depends mostly upon the price differential between ordinary serial terminals and X-terminals. Prices are narrowing rapidly. For the business that considers X to be overkill at this time, the incremental advantage of AlphaWindows is worth considering. However, we think the price of X-based products will fall enough that AlphaWindows has a short life.

Uninterruptible Power Systems

A *UPS* is one of the least glamourous and most important purchases you can make for a network. Power protection is a wise investment because of the three Ds: damage, data loss, and downtime. You placed all of the PC's in the office on surge-protected power strips many months ago—excellent! However, that is only a partial solution when it comes to networked computers. Each user station on the network, whether PC, terminal or workstation, is dependent upon constant communication with its server-host. Users need advance warning of a network shutdown to give them time to save their work. The best protection possible is needed to guard expensive machines' circuitry and prevent unnecessary work stoppage from downtime. Power protection and smooth shutdown are essential to a well-managed network. A modern UPS provides these benefits, plus the ability to monitor UPS status from a network station.

What a UPS Does

Power problems come in a variety of flavors; only a couple are guarded against in the typical power strip. Surges are periods of increased (abnormal) voltage and are often caused when a large electricity user in the building stops. The duration and/or frequency of the surges are hard on sensitive electronics. Spikes are overvoltages as well, but these are short-duration, very high voltage hits. Often caused by lightning, but also by large electrical loads, spikes can do anything between corrupting data and blowing chips. Sags are the opposite of surges—under voltage situations. These can cause disk errors, disk crashes, and computer lock-ups. Brownouts are longer-duration sags, lasting minutes or hours. Noise and harmonic distortions are impulses on the power line that can cause erratic problems, introducing errors into data streams and damaging circuitry. For blackouts, get out the flashlights.

All of the above, including blackouts, can be effectively dealt with by a UPS. Our UPSs have effectively 'cleaned' the power to our equipment through countless power fluctuations. If the power fluctuates too severely or quits altogether, a UPS contains a battery that can run the server long enough for it to go through its shut-down procedure. The UPS may warn network users as part of that process, although their terminals/PCs may be dead at this point anyway. With UNIX operating systems an orderly shutdown is a must; otherwise the filesystems will not be synchronized and files can be corrupted, requiring a long process of rebuilding at the next start-up. Novell file servers also need time to get their affairs in order. See Appendix A, Shutdown Procedures for further information about shutdown processes.

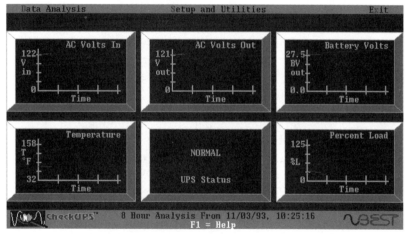

FIGURE 12.6 Best CheckUPS lets you monitor a UPS remotely

On a lesser scale, power strips such as the American Power Conversion Surge-Arrest Plus provide protection against lower levels of spikes and surges and do noise filtering. APC offers a $25,000 guaranty against equipment damage when using this product. However, if you are running a PC off of the strip (not through a UPS) and the power goes down, you could lose a significant amount of the PC user's recent work. Laser printers, copiers, fax machines and terminals are ideal users of power strips since data does not depend upon the state of these devices.

You should also consider protection for your communication lines. *Surge protectors* can be connected in-line on the RS-232 serial port of a laser printer or on the AUI cable to your workstation. Power strips such as SurgeArrest Plus can optionally pro-

tect telephones and modems from phone line spikes. Best Power Technology manufactures spike protectors for long-haul Ethernet cable. The more exposure you have
in equipment and distance between equipment, the more you should invest in these
devices.

One of the nicer features of power protection systems is remote monitoring. A
system administrator can instantly view the status of a remote UPS over the network. Some can even graph the power data over time for you. Figure 12.6 shows the
status of the UPS attached to a server on another floor.

Planning for a UPS

Uninterruptible power systems come in various "capacities", depending upon how
much power is needed to drive equipment. Capacity is measured in volt-amperes.
To determine the capacity you need for a UPS in say, the server closet, a simple, con-
servative method is to add up the volt-amperes of that equipment. The vendors can
provide assistance with this, but here is how to get the information for them.

- Look at the information plate on each piece of equipment that has a power
cord. If you cannot find one (or you need a front-end loader to move the piece),
go to the specifications page in its user manual. Note the amp rating and associated voltage. For example, 14" color monitors typically draw 1.0 amperes of
current at 110 volts (household voltage). Occasionally you will see something
like "5/2.5a 115/230v", which means 5.0 amperes at 115 volts or 2.5 amperes at
230 volts. Nearly all circuits in North America (Canada, USA, Mexico) are 110-
120 volts and use the standard household outlets. In the rest of the world 220-
240 volt circuits are the norm. On PC's you may need to find a sticker inside the
box on the power supply to get these ratings. (Look at the "input" ratings—the
"output" ratings are generally for powering the monitor outlet.) If you find a
watt rating instead of amperes, copy that down in a separate column and go on
to the next piece.

- Multiply each voltage rating by its associated amp rating to get volt-amperes,
e.g., 115V x 5A = 575VA. If the watt rating system was used, use the equation
#Watts x 1.4 =?VA.

- Total the volt-amperes for all of the equipment. This is the maximum capacity
you would need, ignoring future growth.

The volt/amp ratings are expressed as if the unit were fully configured, with
every card slot, chip socket and drive bay filled. The plate ratings may be based on
the internal fuse rating, a level of current draw that would never be attained under
ordinary circumstances. In practice, then, a PC and monitor rated at 700 volt-
amperes may only use 1/3 to 1/2 of that. Laser printers really do draw high volt-
amperes, mostly during the initial 20 seconds of warm up, and they also cycle the
heating element periodically for a split-second. Network interface cards are fairly

insignificant power loads, but extra memory and hard disk drives (@ 100VA each) are not. Workstations may consume half of their rating. A desktop "pizza-box" PC with 14″ color monitor might use 150VA, but a 19″ monitor for CAD may use 300VA. Also, equipment usually draws its maximum current on start-up, so unless you turn on all of your equipment simultaneously, you probably have a little room to fudge there. In short, calculating your UPS requirements based upon plate ratings will probably give you twice as much UPS as you actually need, providing a good comfort margin.

Installing a UPS

We used several Best products in our lab, one of which was the $1049 Fortress LI950 with $99 CheckUPS II remote monitoring software. The UPS hardware consists of one heavy, compact box and a power cord. All you need to do is turn it on and let the batteries charge before you plug in the equipment. One terrific feature is that the front panel shows you the exact power consumption as the equipment is running. You can also see, among other things, how long the attached computers would survive on battery power if the power were to go down. This model supplies 950 VA— enough to power a Sun SPARCstation IPC with external hard drive, tape, CD-ROM and 17-inch color monitor, a 486 tower PC with 14-inch color monitor, and an IBM RS6000 with tape drive and 19-inch monitor. This configuration uses 100% of the UPS's capacity, and gives 18 minutes' warning before shutdown.

Installing the CheckUPS II software on the workstations was not difficult but does require compiling source code on the target system. Compiling instructions are provided, but you can get help along the way from Best's technical support as well. Connect the supplied RS-232 cable and adapters between the computer and UPS serial ports. When all is ready, run a live test—kill the power to the UPS!

13

TCP/IP Networking Products

Introduction

You can find many products that enable TCP/IP networking. Some are feature-rich, others are "lean and mean." Here we summarize 22 of the most popular products. You can usually find these demonstrated at the major trade shows, including Interop and Comdex. We purposefully selected products for review that represent the best each vendor has to offer. All of these products install on the PC. Most of the products have NFS. Windows compatibility is important to a large percentage of users, so we selected a Windows-compatible product from each vendor to evaluate over a DOS-only version. Some vendors take the modular approach to products, requiring you to purchase the modules you need. In that case we obtained a combination of modules to attain the basic feature set for purposes of comparison.

Evaluation Criteria

As a standard test, we attempted to connect a product to each workstation through NFS and to the Novell server—all concurrently. We did not attempt connection to Microsoft LAN Manager, Banyan Vines, or other network operating systems, although most of the products do that as well. We tried to follow the following principle during installation: *Do it the easy way, but get the job done.* Hard-core academic types may protest, but businessmen want ease of mastery and a quick installation. Thus, we did not pursue every elegant but complicated enhancement.

We installed the products on an ALR PowerPro 486-50 PC, or an Insight 486-50 PC, which ran MS-DOS 5.0 and Microsoft Windows 3.1. The primary UNIX hosts were 1) a Sun SPARCstation IPC for user authentication and NFS drives, and 2) an IBM RS/6000 for NFS drives only. When we needed an SCO server, we used a 486 Insight Distribution Network Inc. PC running the SCO Open Server Enterprise System. We did not use the NIS (Network Information Service) on the UNIX machines, choosing rather to rely solely on the local files (**hosts**, **passwd**, **group**, etc). This helped us tailor the discussions to smaller installations that do not run NIS. The Novell server was an IBM Model 90 486 PC. All computers were connected via Ethernet thin coaxial cable. When the product supported Novell NetWare, we used the ODI LAN adapter driver. With others (such as SunSelect PC-NFS) we used the NDIS driver. NetWare compatibility is largely a matter of installing the right drivers.

The Ease of Installation section helps you save time—"our pain, your gain." You can consider ahead of time the potential trouble areas of certain products by reading that section. How smoothly the installation utility works does not necessarily indicate the quality of the user product, but it does reflect the company's follow-through and commitment to the product. (For troubleshooting help on particular subjects, see Chapters 4, 5, and 6.) The Ease of Use section is a catchall for the "warm fuzzy" issues: flexibility, degree of intuitive operation, functionality, appearance, and documentation. The Summary section provides our independent and esteemed opinion of the product, if you care. As a bonus, we have included a tabular list of features at the end of the chapter for your comparison of products at a glance.

HOT TIP

Coffee, Soft Drinks, TCP/IP?

If you will be using one of these products with another network operating system such as NetWare, Vines, or LAN Manager, you should set up the other product(s) first. That way you will be able to answer all questions during configuration of a multiprotocol TCP/IP product. Some products positively require the other networks to be operational before they will load.

3Com TCP with DPA 2.1, and NFS with DPA 1.0

This maker of network interface adapters, transceivers, hubs, and other network hardware goodies has naturally gravitated to network software. They have had their hands into network standards for years, along with the likes of Microsoft, Intel, and others. Demand Protocol Architecture (DPA) is 3Com's title for multiprotocol connectivity mechanisms. The product interfaces with NetWare and most NetBIOS-based LANs.

We were not able to get a copy of 2.1 to try, but we did install an earlier version of the product, version 2.0. We had a bad experience with that installation, for several reasons. First, it forced us to install a 3Com adapter driver. (We had to replace it later by hand with the SMC driver.) During configuration, the program asked us to confirm our confirmations, change entries it could just as well have changed itself, lost information, and used certain keys in odd ways. Finally, the program caught itself in a loop, asking for a disk we couldn't supply. We found it difficult to get assistance. We received a "fix" diskette which was unreadable. A product shouldn't be judged entirely on the basis of its install program, but this series of misfortunes consumed so much time that we were prevented from being able to grind through to a conclusion. See the table at the end of this chapter for a list of features.

Beame & Whiteside BW-NFS 3.00

BW-NFS is one of the most solid products we tested. It provides an abundance of features—including an NFS daemon for the UNIX host and an NFS server TSR for the PC.

Ease of Installation

A DOS program copies all software onto the PC and leads you through basic configuration. Use **BWCUSTOM** to make subsequent changes. All of the Windows groups and programs were configured automatically. A **hosts** file must be created by hand; there is no utility.

BW-NFS was one of the few products we tested that provides an NFS server daemon for the UNIX host. BW's daemon, **bwnfsd**, is similar to **pcnfsd** Version 2—providing file locking/sharing and Windows support. As a result, **pcnfsd** can be used instead of **bwnfsd**. In such a case, skip the **bwnfsd** compilation section and go directly to the NFS testing pages. Unfortunately, BW does not provide an NFS setup utility for the client PC, and the directions for making the hookup are cryptic. Here is some help:

1. If the PC always uses the same account on the UNIX host, type **net password (filename) (username) (password)** from the DOS prompt. This saves your login information in a file in the root directory called ***(filename)**, e.g. *johnson, and prevents your having to enter it at boot time.

2. Add a line to **AUTOEXEC.BAT** (just before the **win** line or the end of the file) for authentication purposes. If you performed step 1 above, type **net register *johnson**. If multiple persons with different accounts use this same PC, type **net register** with no filename parameter so that users must enter their username and password at boot time. (You should have a user reboot when done with the PC.) This step helps to automate mounting but does not actually login to the UNIX host, so you should verify that you can login at the host with your username and password.

3. Insert more lines in **AUTOEXEC.BAT** for each resource you wish to mount. For example, **net link G: \\sun_host\/home/pc *nfsuser** mounts the UNIX hosts /**home/pc** directory as virtual drive G. Mounting printers requires a different syntax: **net link lpt1: \\sun_host\laserjetIII**. The printer *laserjetIII* must be defined in /**etc/printcap** on the UNIX host.

4. Reboot. If the product hangs before **net link** line, there is likely a problem authenticating the user for that resource. Check the login information.

We're not done yet! If you run Novell NetWare from this PC, load the BW Network Driver from the Windows Setup program to let Windows control the access to both networks. (If you have not set up Windows for NetWare yet, do that first; then rerun **Setup** for BW over the top of it.) We found the instructions for NetWare connections to be on the skimpy side overall.

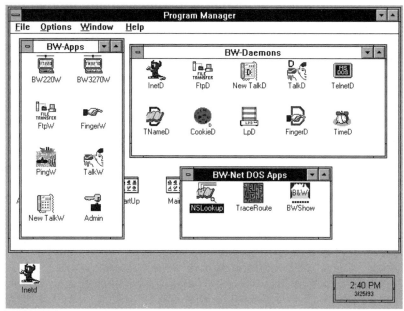

FIGURE 13.1 BW-NFS has one of the best assortments of utilities and services

Ease of Use

We like the **ftp** utility—it is very easy to use. The other Windows utilities have a plain (non-graphical) appearance—BW could have made them a little more exciting. However, they are simple to use, which is most important. BW-NFS includes talk communications programs for interactive messaging between network nodes.

The real difference from competitors comes in the network utilities and server daemons BW-NFS provides. Figure 13.1 shows the three major groupings of BW programs. DOS-based utilities include **NSLookup**, which queries domain name servers interactively. **TraceRoute** is a great diagnostic tool which helps track your packets through gateways and networks. **BWShow** dredges up handy information about your PC system hardware and DOS/Windows startup scripts. (This utility is very useful for helping debug many setup problems.)

BW-NFS provides a liberal number of server daemons, for maximum advantage in a PC network. The **inetd** PC daemon (TSR) provides a unique server to other PC's, patterned after that for UNIX. As remote PCs make requests for services, **inetd** spawns new programs for them. The services include **telnet**, **ftp**, **finger**, **lpd**, and some UDP programs.

Summary

What is it missing? Windows look-and-feel seems to lag behind the best competing products, but is ahead of most. BW should have put more care into the installation process—the only real sub-standard performance in our opinion. But, you only have to deal with that once, right?

Beame & Whiteside's BW-NFS is very full-featured. It is not surprising that Novell and 3Com have adopted parts of it as their own. Considering the functionality, BW-NFS is priced reasonably at $349, and we think you will be happy with this solid product.

Cogent Data Technologies WinNET plus 1.2

Cogent's product is actually different from every other product in this chapter. WinNET plus adds no new TCP/IP networking capability to your existing setup, but it does provide multiprotocol support to Windows. Its sole purpose is to provide *simultaneous* access to multiple networks through Windows. You can see UNIX and NetWare drives together on the File Manager if they were set up in advance under DOS. However, you cannot connect a new resource without getting out of Windows and adding another mount command at the DOS command line, then rebooting.

Windows 3.1 Setup utility only allows one network protocol driver to be loaded at a time. This means that, while you may see several mounted drives under the File Manager, the full capabilities of one or more networks may not be realized. Without help, the Network window on the Control Panel can only display one network's configuration options. For example, if you set up Novell NetWare in Windows first, then a TCP/IP network, you have no ability to enable and disable console messages through NetWare. To regain the NetWare configuration parameters, you must *switch* networks, re-loading the NetWare driver from Setup (but then you lose TCP/IP). Windows for Workgroups helps this situation a little by supplying a button to make switching between two networks easier.

An even bigger problem is that applications which use network-specific API calls can only run when the right network is loaded. If you have one application that needs NetWare, and another that requires Vines, you must switch the network setup before you can run each.

WinNET plus not only lets you define up to 5 different networks, it lets you use each of them concurrently, without switching. The resources from each network can be connected at will, without leaving Windows, and API-specific applications just run. WinNET plus supports: Apple File Protocol (using Farallon/Timbuktu for Windows 1.0), Banyan Vines 4.11-5.5(1), DEC PATHWORKS for DOS 4.1, FTP Software PC/TCP 2.2, IBM LAN Server 1.3+, Microsoft LAN Manager 2.0-2.2, Microsoft Windows for Workgroups 3.1, Novell LAN WorkPlace for DOS & NFS Client 2.3, Novell NetWare 2.15-4.0, SunSelect PC-NFS 4.0 and 5.0, and 3COM 3+Open 1.1+. It requires Microsoft Windows 3.1 and MS-DOS 3.0 or higher. WinNET plus does not consume any conventional (DOS) memory.

Ease of Installation

WinNET plus installs quickly using a Windows-based setup program. You must have your other networks working first. The installation program tracks down all other network drivers on your disk (even multiple copies of the same driver) so that you do not have to give it directions. What WinNET plus does is to replace your existing Windows network drivers with itself. Acting as a middleman, WinNET calls the other drivers as needed.

If your PC does not currently have multiprotocol capability, but you want it to access multiple networks, Cogent supplies a program with WinNET plus called MpNET to help you. MpNET sets up the low-level, multiprotocol support for your LAN adapter. It enables you to link with several network OSs at the DOS level, before proceeding to Windows networking. This can be very handy if you mix LAN WorkPlace for DOS (which only uses ODI drivers) with NDIS-based LANs.

Ease of Use

WinNET plus affects three areas of the Windows environment, the File Manager, Print Manager and Control Panel. If you click on **NetWork Connections** from the File Manager or Print Manager, you see a new screen. It lists your current connections, along with icons indicating the source networks. You can **Browse** for additional resources and connect them. As you might expect, the Network utility on the Control Panel leads you to the individual dialog boxes for each network driver.

If you want to change any of the above types of information quickly, without entering the Windows utilities mentioned, you can use a Hot-Key. The hot key window displays a menu that lets you change drives, printers, and network settings.

Summary

Cogent's WinNET plus is a huge advantage to companies which have need for simultaneous connection to more than network, for the sake of their API-specific applications. WinNET plus also makes it possible to modify network connections from within Windows rather than having to jump out to DOS. Given these capabilities, we think the $149 per node price is reasonable.

Distinct TCP/IP 3.0

Distinct TCP/IP is a visually-oriented product, making use of Windows exclusively (no DOS programs). Distinct provides no NFS functionality, but it does allow concurrent connections with NetWare, LAN Manager, and other network operating systems. "Simple to use" is the motto of this product.

Ease of Installation

Judging from the small size of the manual, you would guess the installation would take 10 or 15 minutes. You're right. We found it a fast, two-disk install process. The Windows-oriented installation and configuration programs were easy to understand. Since Distinct TCP/IP provides no NFS capability, you need do very little editing in the startup files—unless it becomes necessary to shuffle some lines for concurrent connections with NetWare, Vines, or LAN Manager. Distinct's approach is to set up the TCP/IP protocol and hardware drivers to work under a general scenario, then tell the user how to change them for particular driver preferences. You do not need to worry about the Windows interface at all—that is done for you. Distinct TCP/IP does not use a standard **hosts** file, but it provides an editor for you to build a list of reachable hosts. Direct or dialup SLIP connections can be configured from the utility as well. And it only uses 4K of DOS memory.

Move any **win** line after the network lines in **AUTOEXEC.BAT**. We configured Distinct TCP/IP three separate ways for NetWare compatibility. Our first method was to use Distinct's NDIS driver with an NDIS-compliant **IPXLND.COM** to replace our current **IPX.COM**, as outlined in the **\ETC\IPX.TXT** file. Distinct's IPX modules (**IPX.COM** and **IPXLND.COM**) default to the normal Novell-style Ethernet_802.3 frame type. Since we were using Ethernet_II, we had to change the frame type on **IPXLND.COM** using **ECONFIG**. Place the **DISTINCT** driver (the TCP/IP kernel) after the **IPXLND** and ahead of NetWare's **NETX** driver.

The second method was to load Distinct's packet driver instead of the **NDIS** driver, change the interrupt number on the packet driver line in **AUTOEXEC.BAT**, and swap in Distinct's **IPX.COM** for packet drivers. If your Novell network uses the Ethernet_II frame type, remove the **-n** parameter from the packet driver line.

Finally, we experimented with the ODI driver method. Obtain **LSL.COM** and **IPXODI.COM** from Novell or your LAN adapter vendor and install them first. Then, when you install Distinct, go ahead and install the packet driver, ignoring the configuration options presented. You have to go back by hand and set **AUTOEXEC.-BAT** and **NET.CFG**. Be sure to add the **ODIPKT.COM** and **DISTINCT.EXE** programs after **IPXODI**.

Ease of Use

FTP is pretty slick. You can select multiple files on one host with the mouse, then drag/drop them on the other host to start file transfer. (Or, press the Get or Put button—see Figure 13.2.) Click on buttons to rename files, delete, or print them. If you fire up your FTP Server program and identify other Distinct TCP/IP PC users to it, those users can log in to your PC for file transfers as well.

Telnet is an ugly baby—hard to dress up—but Distinct does the best job of making it presentable. There are buttons to Connect/Disconnect. Telnet supports **Copy/Paste** to and from the Windows Clipboard, so you can grab info from your RS/6000 and paste it into a Microsoft Word for Windows document. Or, you can capture

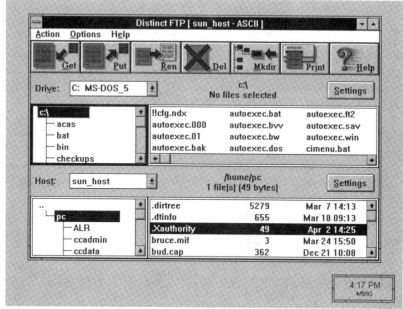

FIGURE 13.2 Push-button file transfer using Distinct TCP/IP

entire sessions to a disk file. There is an automated script capability for telnet, but it is not well-integrated with the rest of the product.

Printing is not any easier under Distinct TCP/IP. Since Distinct provides no LPD/LPR capabilities, you have no access to UNIX printers except by transferring the file to the UNIX host and executing a print command through **telnet**.

Summary

We think Distinct has done a fine job of providing an easy-to-use TCP/IP product for Windows users. The lack of NFS capability is a severe drawback, however—many users would like NFS' "invisible" use of network drives and printers. Distinct TCP/IP attempts to alleviate this in part by providing a good FTP client and server capability for passing files between machines. The price is $395 per single user, or $1995 per 10 users.

Esker TUN*PLUS 7.1

You can find the emulation portion of the TUN*PLUS product discussed at length in Chapter 16. Here are some significant points we wish to make about the TCP/IP stack, utilities, and NFS client. The installation and configuration makes use of a combination of DOS and Windows configuration utilities. The DOS utility is well-organized, and lets you enter network information, edit the **hosts** file, and test connections with **ping**. There is also a facility for sharing remote printers and tape drives (using **tar**). You can even do your NFS mounting from this utility—an improvement over most of its competitors, which require you to edit startup scripts. Our main complaint is that there may be too much information displayed—less knowledgeable users may get lost in the details.

TUN*PLUS includes a small set of TCP/IP utilities for DOS and Windows. The list includes **ftp**, **telnet**, **rsh**, and **rexec**. There is no support for SNMP, but there is an e-mail utility and support for the SMTP, POP2, and POP3 e-mail protocols. There are no servers for the PC. TUN*PLUS supports ODI, NDIS, and packet drivers. The documentation provides setup instructions for the drivers, plus helpful but minimal information about setting up the UNIX side of NFS.

The strongest point about TUN*PLUS is that it includes several terminal emulation types. TUN*PLUS retails for $295.

Frontier Technologies Super TCP/NFS for Windows 3.00

SuperTCP is one of only a few products which are true Windows products—fully DLL. They are also the first to offer a Windows VxD product, due out in January 1994. However, Frontier also lets you go the DOS-only route if you choose, with another set of applications supplied. SuperTCP/NFS provides a broad feature set. Figure 13.3 shows a list of them.

Ease of Installation

After you run through the Windows installation utility once, the program asks what additional options you wish to install (quite a number of them). Run through installation again for those options, if you want them (and have room on disk). The options are discussed in the first third of the user manual; plan on killing a little time there. Select *LAN OS Coexistence* if you run NetWare, LAN Manager, Banyan Vines, or another network and want to use NDIS drivers. DO NOT select it if you use ODI drivers with NetWare.

If you selected the *Express* option you get an easier configuration screen than for *Custom*. If you installed extra modules, you get the *Advanced* screens. You don't have to touch most of the information on the Advanced screens, except for **SubNetwork Address Mapping**. That window is where you enter your IP Address and choose a driver type. A flurry of other windows come at you before the configuration phase is over, depending upon the options you installed earlier. Don't spend hours on them at first; you can go back later, if need be.

Our installation of NFS did not work for some reason—it did not set up **AUTOEXEC.BAT** with **NFSINIT**, among other things. We uninstalled, then re-

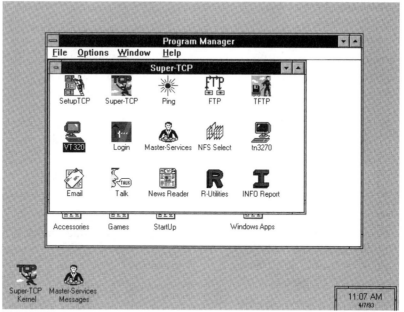

FIGURE 13.3 The wild Frontier—SuperTCP's handy services for TCP/IP

installed it by running the INSTALL program again. That fixed our problems. NFS consumed 72K of DOS memory; the rest of the product consumed virtually none.

Ease of Use

Frontier provides VT320 terminal emulation for **telnet** and environment-changing buttons in the **telnet** window. We found that by pressing some of them we could make the host session unreadable—be careful how you use the fonts and autosizing buttons. Window size is limited by your selected font. You can record keystrokes into a macro for automated host access, or you have the option of programming a script from scratch.

Although you can swap in a standard **hosts** file for the one created during installation, the **ftp** utility keeps its own list of up to five frequent **hosts**. We created a bogus host called *root* accidentally when we entered a username for a host name, and we could not remove it.

We could exchange e-mail with the RS/6000 using the E-mail utility. Since our Sun was not set up quite right, we could only receive mail from that end. We found an unfortunate shortage of troubleshooting information from any source for those needing help on the UNIX side. Fortunately for us, the UNIX printer was already working and gave us no trouble.

Summary

Super TCP/NFS for Windows is more difficult to configure than it needs to be. It also doesn't hang together as solidly as some others. We found ourselves annoyed by glitches here and there. This $495 product packs a ton of capability into a Windows interface, but Frontier has to work out the bugs and simplify configuration before we can give an unqualified 'Yes'. SuperTCP/NFS has some features that make it stand out, though. If you need MIME support to tack graphics onto E-mail, this is your only choice. It has servers galore, X.25 support, E-mail, Network News, SNMP, NFS, 100% DLL programs, and a WinSock-compatible TCP/IP stack.

FTP Software PC/TCP 2.11 with InterDrive

FTP provides the richest feature set of all products in this guide. PC/TCP features a **pcnfs** daemon for the UNIX server, along with adequate information on how to set up the UNIX side of TCP/IP. However, although PC/TCP is a venerable product, it does lag behind the times in its user interface.

Ease of Installation

FTP wins first prize for the most daunting set of documentation and diskettes. It also took top honors for the lengthiest installation time. The best way to approach FTP is to place the first diskette into the drive and type **a:\install** at the DOS prompt. Then, let the program lead you along. If you get stuck, start flipping pages. You can always **ESCAPE** out of the install if you have to, or reconfigure parts of the software later. The configuration program will also allow you to change most of your responses.

On the Operating Environment screen you should pay particular attention to the technical matrix of driver options—this is very important to making the software work with the LAN adapter. If you connect to Novell NetWare, select one of the *ODI* options. If you do not know what type of driver you need, choose an option in the middle *NDIS* column. The *DIX Ethernet* row is for normal BNC-connector Ethernets; use of the *IEEE 802.3 Ethernet* is rare.

The EMACS-style configuration program automatically prompts you to insert information for the main data file, **PCTCP.INI**. Use DownArrow to go through the file, accepting the defaults or making additions/changes. The **tn** section is for Telnet attributes, **idrive** is for NFS functionality.

Assuming you installed **idrive**, be sure to fill out the **host** name of the remote file server, the exported path on that machine, your chosen drive letter, the security key and username, and turn on file sharing/locking.The drive letter must be less than the **LASTDRIVE** statement in **CONFIG.SYS**, if that statement exists. If you are using NetWare, mount UNIX drives as **D:** or **E:** if those letters are available.

PC/TCP always looks for **pcnfsd** (the authentication daemon) running on the server where a drive is to be mounted. If you are mounting drives on two servers but only one runs **pcnfsd**, enter the **pcnfsd** server's IP address for **NIS-server**. FTP does not support NIS yet, but this will let all drives be mounted.

When you have saved the configuration file (F5) and exited the configuration utility (Esc), immediately start an editor to work on **AUTOEXEC.BAT** and **CON-FIG.SYS**. Our **CONFIG.SYS** was a shambles after FTP got through with it—our SCSI controller driver was **REM**arked out, another driver was removed, and it didn't even place the right paths on its own files.

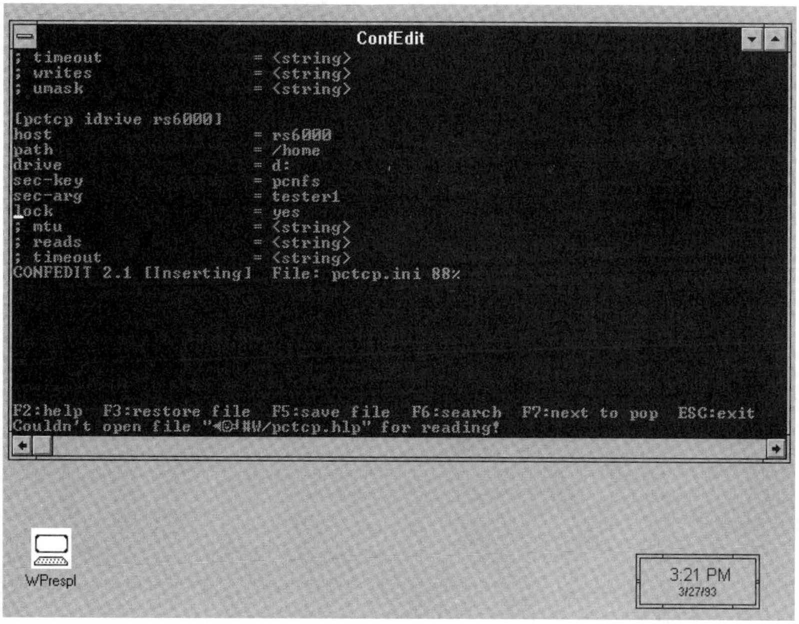

FIGURE 13.4 Not pretty, but it works—the DOS-based ConfEdit program

If you have an NDIS driver, you may need to find the protocol manager files on the supplementary FTP diskettes and copy them on. Edit **PROTOCOL.INI** with your LAN driver information. ODI installation also requires you to roundup files.

There is no configuration utility icon for maintaining NFS drives, printing, mail, and other features under Windows. Use the **confedit** program for this purpose—see Figure 13.4. (Create a DOS icon for Windows using **File/New/Program Item**— you will use **confedit** a lot.) Enter the names of NFS machines under **[pctcp idrive]/ default**. Then prepare a **[pctcp idrive (NFS machine)]** section for each NFS drive. Enter the line **idmnt -a** into **AUTOEXEC.BAT** after **IDRIVE**, and make sure **CON-FIG.SYS** has a **LASTDRIVE=** command with a value at least as big as your new drive letters.

Printing works with the aid of a print redirector. You configure printing with **confedit** and the program **WPrespl**, not through the network connections feature of

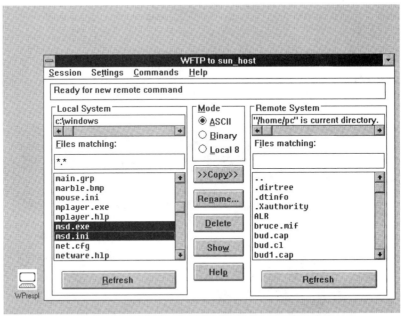

FIGURE 13.5 Ftp is easy with PC-TCP—just select files and click on Copy

the Windows Print Manager. Make sure the **[pctcp print]** and **[pctcp lpr]** setup fields are completed through **confedit**, and that **PREDIR** is executed before you start Windows.

Ease of Use

Most of the utilities run under Windows in DOS-compatibility boxes. PC/TCP includes four true-Windows utilities: **ftp**, **telnet**, **ping**, and **netstat**. The **ftp** utility (shown in Figure 13.5) was not the easiest of all we tried, but it was one of the best, providing simultaneous display of local and remote drives. **Ping** and **netstat** (**Winet**) were well-planned—probably the best of those we evaluated. **Winet** even had a screen oriented toward debugging a network, showing not only the basic activity level but the quantities and types of receive and transmit errors.

Memory is a concern if you load PC/TCP into conventional memory. When we had the product loaded there, at times we could not load the Windows File Manager, even if all of the PC/TCP group and utility windows were closed. This caused us some concern, but we had no perilous incidents, only inconveniences. We were able to load all but **PREDIR** (the print redirector) into high memory and fix the problem. Here are sample lines from AUTOEXEC.BAT which load the main protocol drivers into high memory (for a NetWare/ODI configuration).

```
ETHDRV -M
LOADHIGH IDRIVE
IDMNT -A
PREDIR
```

Setting up printing was difficult. FTP Software supplies so many options and details that it is easy to get lost—we needed help troubleshooting more than one problem. When pursuing printing problems, don't enter **CONFEDIT** if **Wprespl** is also running—you will only get a Sharing violation error message. Version 2.2 reportedly does away with both **Wprespl** and **PREDIR**, and provides better support for printing.

Summary

If you really like knowing the guts of what you are doing, this product is for you. But, if you care at all about the person that may have to pick this up if you get run over by a bus, think twice. Although the Windows utilities are among the best graphically, product maintenance (configuration) remains a hardship. FTP has packed more capabilities into the product than the average business person wants or needs. However, the product is like a Swiss Army knife—if you need a particular feature in your TCP/IP software, look here first. PC/TCP lists for $400, and Interdrive is $100 more.

IBM TCP/IP for DOS 2.1 with NFS Kit

Even though TCP/IP works against the SNA doctrine, IBM can provide you with the connectivity. We found the Windows interface in this version to be startlingly good, and the feature set was substantial. However, we had quite a few problems getting our version of the product to work.

Ease of Installation

IBM's installation program is DOS-based. IBM wants you to complete forms with your setup information, then hand them to an installer. However, we think that if you can fill out the forms, running the install program with illustrated documentation at hand will pose no additional challenge for you.

The **CUSTOM** configuration program only supports NDIS and SLIP connections—your NDIS driver is likely to be in the list. You also can set up routing information, NetBIOS, a Windows icon group, printer services, **PROTOCOL.INI**, and which daemons start at boot, from **CUSTOM**. We suggest you take it slow and don't activate all your services at once. You do have to insert some host names and addresses by hand into the **HOSTS** file, and NFS values into TCPDOS.INI. Memory requirements are average, but not as good as for the Windows DLL products—66K of DOS RAM for the stack and NFS, 30K for each additional utility server.

Ease of Use

IBM has developed a distinctive and appealing look for their Windows applications, making them among the best graphically. They are remarkably ease to understand and use. TCP/IP for DOS has five true Windows applications: **telnet**, **ftp**, **lpr**, **ping**, and **mail**. All of these except **mail** are duplicated as pure DOS applications. IBM also supplies **ftpd**, **lpd**, **routed**, and **snmpd** servers.

Windows-based FTP allows you to define buttons for each of your file server hosts (see Figure 13.6). Establishing connection is as simple as clicking a button. The **Ascii/Binary** button is a toggle that places you in either mode for file transfer. You can easily manipulate directories, rename or delete files, or look at file attributes (**Detail**) using the tool bar.

Telnet is also a pleasure to use. For any host session you can define an order in which emulations are offered to the host. The available modes include VT100,

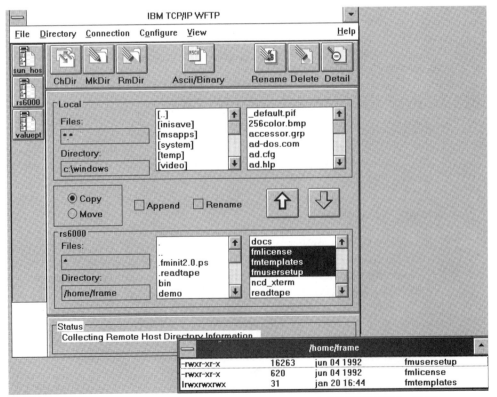

FIGURE 13.6 Push-button connection to the RS/6000 with IBM TCP/IP for DOS

VT220, IBM 3278, ANSI, and TTY. You can also define options for each, such as using extended attributes and setting a 43 x 80 screen size for 3278 emulation. (The 3270 emulation is one of the few to be fully compatible.) The same options can be defined for DOS-based **telnet** sessions using the **SETTERM** utility.

The **mail** and **lpr** applications held to the same high standard. **Mail** is SMTP-compatible. DOS-based remote commands are also provided, though not iconized for the group window.

NFS mounts of remote filesystems is handled through DOS commands, as usual. We were able to mount drives on the RS/6000 and Sun simultaneously, and with no problem.

Summary

A lot of imagination and good sense have gone into this product. IBM's TCP/IP for DOS is one of the less expensive products you can buy, at $230 (the NFS Kit is $135 more). If you need NetBIOS networking/application support, IBM supplies a kit for that as well for $125. There is a developer's kit for taking advantage of the four API libraries TCP/IP for DOS supports. The product's biggest failure is that the documentation does not help you with concurrent NetWare connections or provide a driver for NetWare (although you can indeed make the connection through Novell's ODINSUP driver). We think the product needs a Windows-based configuration utility, but we consider this IBM product to be a leader in ease of use, nevertheless.

InterCon Systems TCP/Connect II for Windows 1.0

InterCon has always concentrated on the UNIX-Macintosh connection, so TCP/Connect II represents InterCon's first entry into the DOS/Windows market. For shops mingling Macintoshes, PCs and UNIX, InterCon is one of the few companies that can serve all three.

TCP/Connect II for Windows (mostly OEM'ed from Frontier) was introduced too late for us to evaluate (October, 1993). It provides full support for TCP/IP and NFS, including **ftp** for file transfers between the dissimilar equipment, and NFS client and server software. Terminal emulation includes VT320, tn3270, and support for any INT 14 emulator. For e-mail, TCP/Connect II includes a MIME mail handler, an NNTP news reader, and the ability to add multimedia attachments. It supports remote commands, has a TALK utility, and provides an SNMP agent and Finger server for LAN management purposes. On the technical side, the product uses Dynamic Link Library technology, making it go easy on your PC memory. TCP/Connect supports the WinSock API, Ethernet and Token Ring, and most network adapter drivers (including ASDI, PDS, NDIS and ODI). It retails for $495.

Ipswitch Piper/IP 1.0

This new product was introduced too late for us to test, but it has an impressive feature list. Although Piper/IP provides only DOS-based applications, it also has a Winsock-compatible DLL-based stack, and it consumes under 6K of DOS (conventional) memory. The product supports all types of popular adapter drivers and networks. NetBIOS applications can use Piper/IP to run on large routed networks, and there is SQL support as well.

Piper/IP includes a long list of TCP/IP utilities including the usuals: **telnet**, **ftp**, **tftp**, **lpr**, **cookie**, **finger**, **whois**, **arp**, **route**, **netstat**, and **ping**. Remote commands include **rexec**, **rsh**, and **rcp**. There are server daemons for **telnet**, **tftp**, **ftp**, **finger**, remote commands, an SNMP agent, and others. Both an NFS client and server are included. Piper/IP also supports remote tape access, mail, and a news reader. The price of Piper/IP 1.0 is $375. Also, check out Vantage/IP if you have an OS/2 machine.

James River ICE.TCP 2.1

This product was one of the first TCP/IP products to market for SCO UNIX/Xenix environments. James River concentrates most of their documentation on the SCO market, although the product can be used to reach any UNIX host. They provide no NFS option. IceTCP is not a Windows application, but some niceties are provided to make it run under Windows. ICE.TCP enables concurrent connection to Novell NetWare and Microsoft LAN Manager servers.

Ease of Installation

The DOS install program takes only a minute or two to copy the software onto your hard drive and place a couple lines in your startup files. Then you must do several things by hand: set up your adapter driver, create a hosts file, and run a utility to configure the TCP/IP driver and create a data file. James River strongly advocates packet drivers and discourages the use of other types, but they do offer ODI- and NDIS-to packet shims. We tried their ODI shim so that we could coexist with NetWare, but the shim, which uses software interrupts, did not work with the After Dark screensaver. If you are running with Windows, be sure to execute WINSHIM and perform the other Windows-compatibility instructions in the Release Notes.

The DOS-based configuration utility (**SETTCP**) would not run without a call to tech support. We chose a non-standard directory path for the files, but the install program set a wrong path for them in **AUTOEXEC.BAT**. We had to swap that line. **SETTCP** could use some help for user-friendliness. Accessing the menu bar options was confusing. We even found it difficult to Exit. Fortunately, there is little you really have to change.

James River uses special file transfer and print server daemons on the UNIX host. (The print server only comes with the multiuser version.) Simple instructions are provided for installation. The DOS **HOSTP** print redirector call should be placed in **WINSTART.BAT**, and you must also create a **HOSTP.DAT** printer definition file.

Ease of Use

James River supplies one **telnet** window icon for Windows users. When you click on it you are immediately required to select a host for a **telnet** session. (James River calls their **telnet** DejaVu.) You can set up many parameters for the session at that point, including resetting screen size and colors. You can **Copy** and **Paste** text between the ICE.TCP window and other Windows applications. We would have liked to see **Help**, but there is none. You can open up as many as 5 host sessions.

Other features of ICE.TCP can be reached from a DOS prompt. There are DOS versions of DejaVu, PING and TFTP. To transfer a single file you can use TFTP, but the FTCOPY file transfer command from James River is easier. (It requires the UNIX daemon previously mentioned.) Use FTCOPY as you would a DOS COPY command, complete with wildcard capability. ICE.TCP also includes a copy of a public domain network monitor, NETWATCH.

We had a problem with ICE.TCP hanging the computer when leaving Windows, forcing a hard reset. Removing the call to SHARE fixed that problem. The aspect of ICE.TCP that we liked best was that it consumed less than 2K of RAM, all for Windows support.

Summary

We think James River should do more of the setup for you—ICE.TCP requires more steps to be taken by hand than perhaps any other program we tried. They do rightly recommend packet drivers for the sake of performance, but those minute gains often don't matter to users who already have NDIS and ODI drivers set up. We believe James River could do more to accommodate those users. Overall, the bugs we encountered worked against our confidence in the product.

ICE.TCP is a low-end product for those sites that need **telnet** sessions and file transfer, with few Windows frills. At $245 for a single PC ($995 for 10 users), it is moderately priced; but, in our opinion, you can find better values.

Lanera TCPOpen/Plus 2.1

All of Lanera's utilities are DOS-based and very similar to their UNIX counterparts. TCPOpen/Plus includes an NFS client.

Ease of Installation

Lanera's installation utility was straightforward and fast. The product tells you to insert two lines of information in **PROGMAN.INI** if you are a Windows user—something most programs do for you. Run **TCPSETUP** to configure the software for the network, LAN adapter, printer, FTP client and server, and other information. We selected the ODI driver option for coexistence with NetWare, requiring us to ignore a warning on exit that an interface was not specified.

The user interface in **TCPSETUP** was a little odd; Backspace deleted the character to the right, and having to hit Enter before modifying each field was hard to get used to. If you make a change under any category, remember to press F10 to save it! The **hosts** file setup screen, for example, is extremely aggravating unless you press F10 after each new entry—it is much easier to use an editor to create the file if you know the format. Setup documentation for the hosts and networks database was one useless paragraph; the rest was marginal, although there was a section for networking concepts that could be somewhat helpful. Overall, the configuration utility was more taxing to use than those of competing products.

Finishing the configuration required placing lines into **NET.CFG**. These lines bind two new protocols to the LAN adapter. (If NetWare uses Ethernet_II Frame type, be sure you have a Protocol line for it as well.) Also, edit **AUTOEXEC.BAT** to insert lines for LSL, the ODI driver, **IPXODI**, **NETX**, and **LOADTCP**. All but the latter you must get from Novell or another source—a drawback. Move the **SET TCPOPEN=** line ahead of **LOADTCP**, or **TCPIP_xD** if you do not use **LOADTCP.-BAT**.

As with many of these products, NFS requires a separate installation procedure. The NFS configuration program, NFSADMIN, allows you to create filesystem mount and user/group tables without editing startup files by hand. You can also test network connections (ping) and view network statistics from this utility.

Ease of Use

Windows users can execute the DOS commands from the Windows DOS-compatibility box, or they can set up PIF files and icons for them. That is the most you can do to give this product a GUI, unfortunately.

The DOS utilities (commands) in TCPOpen/Plus satisfy user demands for **ftp**, **tftp**, **rcp**, **rsh**, **rexec**, **lpr**, **ping**, **ifconfig**, **netstat**, and others. **Telnet** emulations are limited to VT100 and support for third-party interrupt 14 emulators. Lanera patterned all commands after the UNIX versions of the same, so if you are a UNIX professional you should come up to speed quickly. Lanera throws in some extra programs to sweeten the pot, such as **ftp** and **tftp** servers, a local-and-remote **tar** archiver, **arp**, **finger**, and more still.

Summary

At \$295 with an NFS client, TCPOpen/Plus is one of the least expensive products you can buy for TCP/IP and NFS networking. The lack of a Windows interface accounts for the price advantage. You can get just the TCP/IP kernel and a development kit if you have a programming project in mind. (They are WinSock and BSD-compatible.) On the whole, this product makes sense for anyone who is comfortable in DOS and has no need for Windows.

NEI UniHost and PCWorks

This two-product set offers an inexpensive solution for sites that need only file transfer, e-mail, terminal emulation, and remote commands. UniHost is a command server for the UNIX and VAX platforms. Its job is to manage PC requests received from the PC terminal emulation product, PCWorks. (Incidently, PCWorks has a twin sister for Macintosh called MacLine.) PCWorks sports VT220 and ANSI emulation, and it can be configured for direct or dial-up serial host connections in addition to Ethernet TCP/IP. It uses either XMODEM or a proprietary protocol for file transfer, and it provides a pre-made script for multiple file transfers. UniHost and PCWorks do not afford NFS capability.

To install UniHost, first get the PCWorks product running. UniHost must be uploaded to the UNIX host using PCWorks. The rest of the installation is routine. The terminal emulation is easy to use, and of the full-screen variety. UniHost is a \$395-795 platform-specific product, and PCWorks adds another \$195 per user (quantity discounts available).

NetManage Chameleon NFS, Newt 3.1

Chameleon is 100% DLL; it is totally a Windows application and it does not function under DOS. This decreases its RAM consumption to less than 10K in low memory—a welcome sight to anyone who has suffered cRAMps. This product provides some valuable additions to the basic function set: 3270 emulation, IP routing, and SNMP agents. To function concurrently with NetWare you need the extra-cost option, IPX/link. A developer's kit is also available.

Ease of Installation

Execute the installation program from within Windows. It immediately starts the Custom configuration program when the files have been installed. Select the adapter card you are using, and Custom will set default values which you can edit. Enter the IP address and other standard information; then a summary screen is displayed. Custom provides an easy way to build the configuration files without editing files at

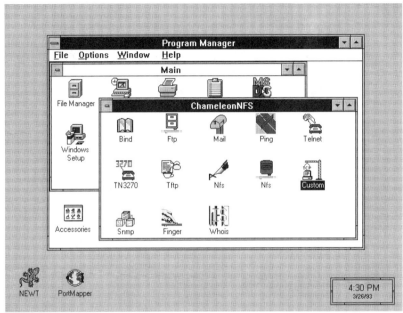

FIGURE 13.7 A sturdy array of programs greets the ChameleonNFS user

the DOS level. It even helps you build the **PROTOCOL.INI** and **host**s files from scratch. (If you have a **hosts** file, go ahead and place it with the Chameleon files.) Chameleon keeps its **.INI** and configuration files tidy in the **\NETMANAG** directory, out of the occasional confusion of **\WINDOWS**. Before you reboot, make sure the **win** line is moved AFTER the Chameleon-generated lines in **AUTOEXEC.BAT**—this may be the only thing you have to do from a text editor.

The only problem we had in installing the product was in setting up the device driver for the SMC adapter. NetManage supplies device drivers, but the driver it installed was old. We had to use the *Other* category to enter the new SMC drivers, but noticed that the driver file name was lost after power-down, apparently preventing Chameleon from making any connection with the host. (However, the **tcpip.cfg** file does contain this information.) We found that doing a warm reboot (Ctrl-Alt-Del) magically fixed the problem without even entering the data again—the program booted properly the second time. This two-boot fix is somewhat annoying. NetManage has pledged to fix this in a future version. Check this and every networking product by powering down to see if the connections are restored on power-up.

Ping, **ftp**, and other utilities have the nice bonus of individual configuration. If you frequently access a particular host, you can save time by letting Chameleon store your startup parameters. To mount UNIX drives and printers you use the Windows File Manager, Print Manager, and Control Panel. The Chameleon windows knit seamlessly with those applications.

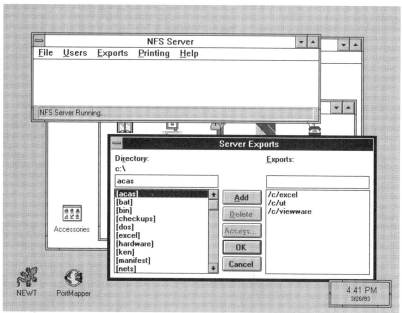

FIGURE 13.8 Serve your files to other PCs via Chameleon's NFS Server

Ease of Use

If MS-Windows represents your environment of choice, Chameleon is a good selection for a TCP/IP product. Not only is it 100% DLL, it also does a good job of being a Windows GUI application—from the appearance of the windows to the maximum use of standard Windows tools.

But, since people also choose a product by its feature list, NetManage insured success by building in one of the most comprehensive set of functions and utilities of any product. Figure 13.7 shows the program icons. Extras include 3270 emulation for connection to IBM mainframes, SNMP agents for remote network management, electronic mail, routing, peer-to-peer resource sharing, and an NFS server (see Figure 13.8). We found these functions to be easy to use and intuitive. A developers kit is also available for developing client-server applications.

Summary

Chameleon NFS is perfect for Windows users and one of the simplest products to install. The DLL design represents a salvation for the user plagued with memory shortage. Windows users on a Novell LAN will be happy with the IPX/link option. The feature set is great, but you would expect that from a $495 product (a little pricey). Our only disappointment was that the product does not provide much help on the UNIX server side; neither did tech support. If you have a gap in your UNIX knowledge, get a Chameleon demo first. You will find it worthwhile to work that end out and watch the Chameleon run.

Novell LAN WorkPlace for DOS 4.1 and NFS Client 2.3

Just as for all of their products, Novell supplies a sturdy tool in LAN WorkPlace. The name is a little misleading, because the major utilities are fully interfaced with Windows. Take note that the NFS Client is actually a Beame & Whiteside Software product, so it does not feel as 'Novell', even though it is packaged in red.

LAN WorkPlace for DOS supports DDE (dynamic data exchange), allowing DDE-compliant products such as DEC's ACA Services to be used to program distributed client-server applications.

Ease of Installation

The first thing you will notice is that Novell provides LOTS of documentation. They provide so much, in fact, that some points (Installation, for example) are discussed in four places across different manuals. This can be confusing, unless you are a card player and can hold several papers/books at a time in one hand. However, it is well-written and helpful—you won't be as lucky with some other products. Before you begin installation, **REM**-out the **SHARE** and **WIN** lines in the **AUTOEXEC.BAT** file. You can replace them when the install program has finished.

Novell provides uniform, easy-to-use installation and configuration utilities for nearly everything you want to do in Novell-world, and the WorkPlace install is no exception. The install program checked all drives including Novell network drives and offered to be installed there. We agreed, since most purchasers of this product have a Novell network and require multiple licenses. The install program does change **AUTOEXEC.BAT**, **CONFIG.SYS**, **NET.CFG**, Windows **.INI** files, and creates **LANWP.BAT** on the local (**C:**) drive. It also places a few new files in the root directory.

Edit **SHARE** and **WIN** back into **AUTOEXEC.BAT** (place **WIN** after the new line(s). **REM** any lines that formerly executed **IPX**, **NETX** and logged in to the Novell server. These programs will now be handled from within **LANWP.BAT**. Look in **LANWP.BAT**—if you will always want to establish connection, **REM** the first two lines which ask that question and test the response. Here is our **LANWP.BAT**:

```
rem C:\yesno "Do you want to load the networking software? (y/n)"
rem if errorlevel 1 goto noload
PATH J:\WKPLACE\BIN;%path%
C:\lsl.com
C:\SMC8000
C:\ipxodi.com
C:\netx.com
```

```
F:login NOVELL/ken
tcpip.exe
set name=tester1
break on
:noload
```

If you chose **Other** when asked to select your LAN adapter from the adapter list, you must enter the name of its ODI driver file after the LSL line. Novell requires you to use an ODI driver with the LAN adapter; NDIS or packet drivers are not even mentioned in the literature. You may have to obtain an ODI driver from the board manufacturer (check ahead). Novell displays a clear bias toward Eagle adapters. Also, edit **NET.CFG** with a Link Driver section for that driver, being sure to specify the proper adapter settings and frame type.

All Windows setup was performed automatically for us, but we had to select Window/Arrange Icons in the Program Manager to find the new program group. Your first task can be to obtain a **hosts** file from the UNIX server, using Rapid Filer, or, create a **hosts** file from scratch.

When you have LAN WorkPlace for DOS working, install NFS Client for LAN WorkPlace, a separate product. You can install the files in the same location as LAN WorkPlace, but you will find a hitch if you installed LAN WorkPlace on a NetWare network drive. NFS Clients needs a special driver to be loaded (from **CONFIG.SYS**) before any network drives are attached, so you must place a copy of **ETHDRV.LWP** on your local hard drive. Also, the installation program asked for the name of our first NetWare Drive, then used it as **LASTDRIVE**, ruining our ability to login to the Novell server. To fix this, edit **CONFIG.SYS** by bumping **LASTDRIVE** down one letter, e.g., from **F** to **E**. Documentation is pretty poor about what you must do next. Here are some sample lines from our **AUTOEXEC.BAT** file that show 1) how to load NFS, and 2) how to mount a UNIX drive and printer:

```
CALL C:\LANWP.BAT
loadhigh J:\WKPLACE\NFSCLNT\lwprpc
loadhigh J:\WKPLACE\NFSCLNT\lwpnfs pcname /r:4096 /w:4096
net register *PASSFILE
rem Now mount the drive and printer
net link D: \\192.9.200.1\/home/pc
net link LPT1: \\192.9.200.1\laserjetIII
```

Although the documentation said otherwise, we could not succeed with a **NET LINK** if we used the host name instead of IP address. If you use **NET REGISTER** to help speed up the boot process, be sure to create **PASSFILE** with the **NET PASS-WORD** command.

Ease of Use

Not being a company to slack off when it comes to visual output for the user, Novell gives you 24 different icons to look at under Windows (see Figure 13.9), nearly all of them orange-red, of course. The first eight are true Windows applications—the rest are DOS-based programs, most of which you may never use . . . but you can never have too many programs around. There are nine DOS utilities for remote commands plus **telnet**, **ftp**, **ping**, TSU, and a services and statistics utility called **LWPCON**. The Windows utilities include, again, **telnet** (Host Presenter), **ftp** (Rapid Filer), and **rsh**, plus an **ftp** server, IP resolver, **finger** and finger server, and talk. NFS Client adds UNIX-to-DOS and DOS-to-UNIX file converters.

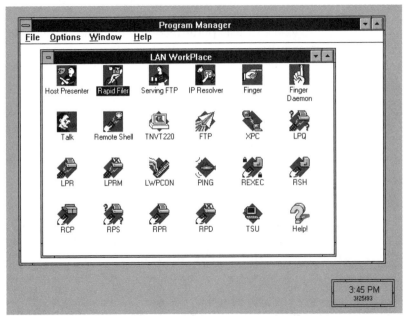

FIGURE 13.9 A host of program icons greet the LAN WorkPlace user

We liked the Rapid Filer **ftp** program. It was simple to understand and use. (See Figure 5.3 in Chapter 5.) Its hard to make a **telnet** session presentable—the Host Presenter does about as well as all the other products. The Talk utility is handy for holding conversations with other users over the network. **Rsh** finds a home under Windows with a full-fledged utility. You can redirect the response from the host to a file or the clipboard.

LWPCON was the most unusual of the utilities, as it was the only one to bring a Novell-style interface into the Windows environment. We easily viewed tables, statistics, and port mappings across the network. It figures that Novell would do a good job with this one.

Summary

LAN WorkPlace is typical high Novell quality, but the NFS Client is a bit shaky from the standpoint of documentation. However, you will not have any disappointments with these products, once they are installed—they are among the best. A 10-user license of LAN WorkPlace for DOS costs $1995—not bad. However, 10 licenses of NFS Client for LAN WorkPlace adds another $1395, placing it more in line with its competitors.

Pacific Softworks Fusion 3.4

Fusion is a DOS-based NFS product that provides a rudimentary Windows interface. Fusion allows concurrent connection with Novell NetWare.

Ease of Installation

Fusion supplies a DOS install program. The questions and screens were among the easiest to understand of all we tested, but they didn't go the distance in setup. The install program supplies NDIS drivers and some for the Western Digital family of adapters. Loading the NDIS driver is a good idea—mandatory if you purchased the IPX Concurrency option (it uses an NDIS-to-ODI shim). However, the SMC NDIS driver we loaded was too old and would not let the adapter ping. If in doubt, get a newer driver from the adapter manufacturer.

After installation, Exit to DOS and edit your **AUTOEXEC.BAT** file immediately. If you wish to use NFS, Fusion requires you to edit in lines to start and configure that capability. For example, **nfs** starts the NFS client. Then, **mount Sun_server:/home/pc G:** mounts the UNIX server's exported directory **/home/pc**, calling it drive G. Fusion 3.4 is incompatible with the SHARE program under Windows **(NFS, NSTAT, NET-SETUP,** and other utilities won't work), so remove that line from **AUTOEXEC.BAT** if you have it. Also make sure that your **CONFIG.SYS** file contains a **LASTDRIV-E=(letter)** command. There will be additional steps to perform later for Windows setup, but reboot for now to make sure the basic connection under DOS is working.

As the computer boots, if you installed the IPX Concurrency option you will notice that a Fusion-compatible version of IPX and Spry Concurrent are loaded. Fusion displays that it is "now up." Then the Novell NETX program attaches the Novell server and you are ready to go as a DOS machine. Note that the Fusion **IPX.-COM** defaults to Novell's Ethernet_802.3 Frame type. If your server runs some other frame type, you will have to change IPX using Novell's **econfig** command. If you are a Windows user, you must follow additional instructions in the Appendix to bring the Fusion icon group to life.

Fusion does not read a standard hosts file, so you have to enter host names and IP addresses by hand from the **Netsetup** program. We suggest that you avoid using **Netsetup** to modify the DOS Environment after the first time. It tries to be a smart utility but really makes dumb changes to your **AUTOEXEC.BAT** and **CONFIG.SYS** files, duplicating lines, setting its own path incorrectly, and putting new lines after **win**. If you use **Netsetup** and things suddenly fall apart, check over these files. When possible, make the changes through a file editor instead.

The printer requires special attention. Fusion uses the DOS **PRINT** program, so enter **print /D:PRN** into **AUTOEXEC.BAT** after **NETBIND**. Also enter any **SET** variables that are missing, according to the Fusion documentation. You may need to risk **Netsetup** for this.

Ease of Use

Windows users will be disappointed with this product. All applications are for DOS and run in DOS windows—only the startup icons are Windows-like. The Windows programming is not very bullet-proof, and there are several ways to generate sharing violations and screen glitches. Some of the utilities such as **ping**, **finger**, and the remote commands require you to edit their PIF files ahead of time with static information about one host. There is no way to dynamically select hosts from these programs—you would have to set up several PIFs and icons to do that. Fusion does not make use of the Control Panel or Print Manager as other NFS products do.

Outside of the problems with Windows, Fusion does supply a good list of TCP/IP utilities, including VT220 **telnet**, an **ftp** client and server, a list of remote commands (**rcp**, **rlogin**, **rsh**, **ruptime**, and **rwho**), and several network utilities for network statistics, packet monitoring, **ping**, and **finger**. We mentioned the NFS client, which lets you access UNIX drives from either DOS or the Windows File Manager.

Printing files becomes a severe weakness, because you must go to the DOS prompt and type **lpr (filename)**. There is no ability to use the UNIX printer via the Windows Print Manager. Consequently, you cannot print from Windows applications.

Summary

Fusion 3.4 is a good attempt at multiprotocol connectivity with Novell concurrency, NFS and an FTP server, but we would not recommend it for several reasons. The product is too difficult to set up and maintain, and the product had no true Windows compatibility. The price is reasonable, at $295, but the product features are more restrictive than they need to be. Overall, there are just too many glitches and drawbacks compared with other products.

Solid Computer PCShare 1.3.1

PCShare is a product designed from a different, but usable, perspective. Considering that it comes from Germany, whereas most of the others are from the United States, one wonders if perhaps Americans all got thinking on the same track from looking at each other. PCShare places part of the burden on the UNIX workstation; it includes software for both the UNIX machine and the PC. Therefore, PCShare has been tailor-made for the major UNIX computer systems, including DECStation 3100, IBM RS/6000, NeXT, Sony News RISC, Sun, and MIPS Magnum.

The UNIX platform requires a PCShare server. This server makes printers, disk drives, tape drives, etc. available to the PCShare client, installed on the PC. PCShare requires only 25K of RAM on the PC, and that can be moved into high memory, so you won't have any RAM problem with this product. All communication makes use of the TCP/IP and UCP/IP protocols over Ethernet. NFS is supported.

Installation and basic configuration can be performed through menu-driven utilities. These utilities, whether for UNIX or DOS, edit the system startup files for you. Except for the Glossary, which was non-alphabetical, we thought the documentation was laid out logically and thoroughly. The central configuration file is **pcshare.conf**, stored at the server. This file contains many parameters to govern file locking, terminal attributes, and more. It must be created and edited by hand, if you do not wish to use the PCShare default values.

The resource-mounting process is different than anything we saw for other products. Instead of having to place mount commands in AUTOEXEC.BAT, the PCShare client automatically seeks the PCShare server defined in its local **hosts** file. If it finds the server, it reads that host's **/etc/exports** file and mounts any exported filesystem that begins with the word "Public" as a drive. (At least one filesystem, called Public Disk and containing PCShare files, will always be mounted.) Printers whose names begin with "Public" are handled similarly, being assigned to LPT ports. Each UNIX user can use a **.exports** in their home directory for mounting additional resources, also.

PCShare uses ANSI terminal emulation. You can either execute single commands remotely, such as **unix pwd**, or start a shell with **unix sh**. PCShare supports remote tape backup and restore through **tar**. The product also makes use of the **lpr** protocol for print services. There are brief instructions for coexisting with Novell NetWare and Microsoft Windows, but this product is obviously not designed with those environments in mind. The price of PCShare is $2915 for a 3-user license— pretty steep in our book. Solid Computer currently has no U.S. office.

Spry AIR for Windows 1.2

Spry has several networking products on the market, including an X server and a Sun/NetWare peer-to-peer product. All of their products are targeted toward the low-performance, low-price market.

Ease of Installation

We had trouble with the Windows-based install—it did not make the changes to **AUTOEXEC.BAT** and **CONFIG.SYS** that it said it would, and we ended up calling tech support for help in inserting lines. We also installed the AIR MAIL product and NFS client (which is Beame & Whiteside's), again, with help from tech support. Both of these options had to be installed from the DOS level, although they were supposed to install from Windows.

The nicest thing about the installation process was that the utility asks for pertinent network information during the install. When done, you should not have to do any more configuring to make it work.

Ease of Use

All of AIR's functionality is tied to a single "Console" window. The sub windows for **telnet** and **ftp** were essentially DOS windows without much to dress them up except a menu bar of options. The **telnet** session supposedly allowed connection via script file, but there were no instructions or facility to set up a script. **Ftp** was actually easier to use if you knew the commands and entered them on-screen, rather than trying to use Spry's menu bar of commands. If you don't know **ftp** commands, the menu bar is painfully slow to use.

We tried the **ftp** server, and we were able to pass files to and from the PC with no trouble. There is also an RCP server. The **mail** utility (AIRMAIL) had the best GUI-feel. It was adequate, as mail tools go, with a mail composition window. However, long status messages were cut off on either end. Also, if you change the font for messages, this also changes the button fonts for some obscure reason, perhaps forcing some buttons out of view. AIRMAIL requires a POP3 server for the UNIX host—you can get one from Spry.

Spry's documentation was always a weak point, but the latest set is quite good. However, it mentioned a **tar** program included with the NFS client, but that program was not supplied on our diskettes. Neither was the **bwnfsd** daemon for the UNIX host. Spry utilities violated Windows system integrity more than once. After the problems with installation, we wonder about Spry's quality control.

Summary

At $375 with an NFS client, Spry's mediocre capabilities and user interface seem over-priced. Look for the 2.0 release (with a better Windows GUI) by the time this book is done. Also check out Concurrent, which provides an IPX stack over NDIS. This product helps you access NetWare, LAN Manager, Vines and other networks without rebooting.

SunSelect PC-NFS 5.0

PC-NFS is a mature product, having been around since the mid 80's and boasting over 1 million users. It is one of the few products to provide UNIX help and NFS server daemons (primarily **pcnfsd**)—a necessity for some sites that don't already have them. PC-NFS is compatible with many other networks, including Novell NetWare and Microsoft Windows for Workgroups. A toolkit is also available to help you create client-server applications.

Ease of Installation

PC-NFS was one of the trickier products we installed. The actual software installation was not so unusual, but configuration turned out to be lengthy and confusing. Unfortunately, SunSelect's installation information spans different manuals, so it does not always flow in a step-by-step manner. We ended up making a lot of separate changes and rebooting several times before it was all put together.

Installing the PC software

If the **INSTALL** program drops out of sight with a message that it could not create a file on the target drive, the problem may be with lines in your **CONFIG.SYS**. On some machines you need to use the DOS version of EMM386 rather than the Windows version; so be sure to change the path. We had to add a **C:** path on the front of **COMMAND.COM** in the **SHELL** command. It doesn't hurt to increase environment space (**/E**) temporarily, either.

Configuring a 3Com Etherlink II (3c503) network adapter for PC-NFS requires extra attention. You may NOT use the card's shared memory feature with PC-NFS, so be sure that you disable that option on the board by setting a jumper (this should be the default setting, however.) Take out any MEM line in **NET.CFG**.

The installation program runs **NFSCONF** for you to allow you to configure the product. You should complete the Network section immediately so that the network will be active when you reboot. Then exit to DOS and install the Windows portion.

PC-NFS did a fairly good job of editing our startup files for us, inserting lines between our existing ODI modules, but we still had to add lines. RTM was needed for Windows and the print server. **RNMFILE** was needed for running a local **hosts** file instead of NIS. You should add **LISTENER** if you want the console messaging feature (and install the **msgserv** daemon). There are other TSRs for SNMP and for receiving e-mail.

The **LASTDRIVE** command in **CONFIG.SYS** plays havoc with most NetWare sites, since you must choose a last drive greater than the default NetWare login drive, drive **F:**. NetWare uses drives after **LASTDRIVE**, and PC-NFS needs a minimum of four drive letters for one filesystem and printer, so your **SYS** volume must be mapped to drive **H:** or higher. You will probably have to change the NetWare login script drive mappings, as well as your **AUTOEXEC.BAT** login line, to accommodate PC-NFS. This also means that user configuration files for network applications such as WordPerfect may have to be edited to find the new storage drives.

Another problem we had was in finding enough DOS memory. With NetWare and adapter drivers pre-loaded, we could not complete installation until we moved the TCP/IP stack into high memory. With its full complement of programs, but less outside drivers, PC-NFS needs about 149K of memory. Nearly all modules can be loaded high, however.

Installing the UNIX software and mounting NFS resources

Since Sun does not normally supply the PC authentication and printing daemon for NFS with their workstations, SunSelect provides it with the NFS client. If your host already runs **rpc.pcnfsd**, it may be the older Version 1 program that does not support the Windows **Browse** function. Unfortunately, most TCP/IP products provide only some general suggestions if they say anything at all. But if you want documentation on UNIX (SunOS) systems, you can get plenty of it from SunSelect in the Administration Guide and the Reference Manual.

Even with step-by-step instructions, though, if you are a UNIX neophyte you had better strap yourself in and bring a lunch. UNIX-side configuration involves preparing daemons for printer sharing, user authentication, file locking, and local mail. Beside the daemons, you will probably need to edit UNIX data files such as /**etc/printcap**, /**etc/exports** and /**etc/passwd**. You may need to create directories and user-groups, as well as set permissions for groups. The process can be performed from the PC through PC-NFS' **telnet**. This low-level set up is required for any TCP/IP network product, but most manufacturers leave what goes on in the UNIX box to your system administrator (which may be you). See Chapter 6 for details.

When the daemons are running on the UNIX server, run **NFSCONF** from a DOS prompt (not a Windows DOS-shell). This time through you will perform the first mount of each drive and set them into a batch file for mounting at startup. **NFSCONF** can be confusing because data can seem to disappear—pay attention to using Show, List, and Delete from Startup to manage the data files. Do not mount the printer at this time—reboot instead.

Once you have entered the authentication server information you will be asked for login information each time you boot the PC. You can eliminate the user name and password entry by placing them in **NETWORK.BAT**, the repository for startup authentication information (see the Reference Manual Commands). Once you are authenticated by the **pcnfsd** server, you can mount drives and printers from Windows, but it is best to do it from the startup file, **DRIVES.BAT**. **NFSCONF** maintains **DRIVES.BAT** through the Mount and Delete from Startup selections under Connections; but, if you choose, you can edit this file yourself. The last startup file is **PCNF-SRES.INI**, which is the master list of user-defined resources. If you change your system around frequently, as we do, chances are good that **DRIVES.BAT**, **PCNFS-RES.INI**, and Windows will get out of sync with each other and not do the proper mounts. If your installation has a problem such as losing the printer at startup,

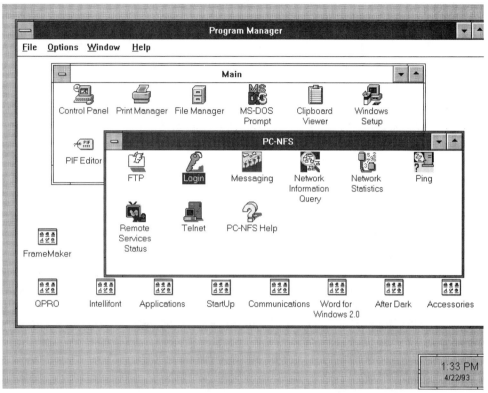

FIGURE 13.10 PC-NFS supplies a well-rounded group of utilities for the Windows user

delete any improper entries from Startup; then unmount and remount the correct printer, adding it to Startup.

Ease of Use

In spite of the excellent amount of general information in print, PC-NFS documentation supplies no printed information about operating the Windows versions of **ftp**, **telnet**, etc.—use Windows Help. See Figure 13.10 for a display of PC-NFS utilities.

FTP was not one of the easier Windows **ftp**'s to use, in our opinion, but we could do everything we wanted to do. **Telnet** had a plain look, but packed in a ton of setup options—including VT320 emulation, Kermit file transfer, and script command files. One unique **telnet** feature caught our eye—a WordPerfect mode for running with VAX/VMS WordPerfect. This mode lets you use your PC templates and keystrokes with the VAX program. You can see network statistics, updated in real time, or scan the port services on remote hosts. Network Information Query is provided, but only works if you have NIS.

We had the most trouble with printers. SunSelect gives you good instructions for setting up an HP LaserJet printer on a Sun workstation. However, **NFSCONF** didn't sync with Windows, and the resulting confusion required us to do repeated testing in order to make things work. The boot process said it mounted the printer as LPT1, but 1) **NFSCONF** did not really mount it, and 2) Windows did not use it, although Windows would not let us reallocate LPT1. The only way we could get Windows to configure LPT1 for the printer was to mount the printer from **NFSCONF** and go immediately (without reboot) to Windows for setup. If you have already rebooted, delete the printer from Startup in **NFSCONF** first; then reboot and try the method outlined.

We loaded several PC products onto the Sun and used it as our NFS file server with perfect success. File locking capability, however, should be installed on the server so that you and your neighbor do not access and overwrite the same file.

Summary

If a product's installed base means a lot to you, go with PC-NFS. It has the basic features you need, plus NFS, NFS server daemons for the UNIX side, and a few frills. However, given the arduous installation process, we are tempted to look elsewhere. Nevertheless, we do credit them for having the best documentation on UNIX issues. Developers support PC-NFS as a league-leader for the TCP/IP protocol stack. The price of the product is $415 with documentation, $345 without.

Ungermann-Bass TCP/Next 1.0

Ungermann-Bass has long had NetOne-TCP. That product is now being replaced by TCP/Next, and existing clients are being converted. We were not able to obtain a copy of TCP/Next for evaluation. According to a UB representative, TCP/Next integrates TCP/IP applications from FTP Software.

Walker, Richer & Quinn Reflection/TCP Connection 2.0

We installed two WRQ products to attain basic configuration. TCP Connection (the TCP/IP stack) supports concurrent connection to Novell NetWare, DEC LAT, HP NS/VT, and NDIS-compliant networks. The terminal emulation package Reflection 2 for Windows 4.0 completed the system.

Walker, Richer & Quinn provides a proprietary file transfer protocol along with standard FTP. The new protocol (called WRQ) is designed primarily for modem users, and takes advantage of data compression and error correction technology. Though a little slower than FTP on a network, WRQ is faster than Kermit over the phone lines.

Reflection supports DDE (dynamic data interchange), which means that Microsoft Excel and other DDE-compliant applications can trade information with the UNIX host across the TCP/IP network—all without user interaction. With the proper software you can capture real-time host data, send commands, and create compound documents.

Ease of Installation

Install Reflection 2 for Windows first—TCP Connection will need to know its location in order to complete the entire installation. The Windows-based install program is user-friendly.

TCP Connection also installs easily via a DOS program. The manuals are well-structured and helpful. If you have a **hosts** file you can provide a path for Reflection to find it, or else build one from scratch. Of all the products we tested, this was the only one to place its lines in **AUTOEXEC.BAT** before the **win** line, providing a strong chance that you will not have to edit any startup files by hand (unless it doesn't have the driver for your LAN adapter). The product seems a little outdated on LAN adapter drivers—we had to select **Other** for our SMC 8013, then install the driver and edit **PROTOCOL.INI** with the missing information.

PROTOCOL.INI is the WRQ's storage place for all TCP/IP parameters on the PC. Its options are described in the manual along with some of the UNIX-side configuration files that you may have to alter.

After basic configuration there is more to do. The WRQ file transfer configuration is a bit scary, relative to other TCP/IP networking products for PCs, because it takes liberal actions on the UNIX host. Choose **File/Transfer Setup** and press **Predefined Settings**, then select *WRQ to UNIX*. This action will complete the boxes for you, but you must also load software on the UNIX host. Choose **File/Open**, run a **Command** file as explained in the reference manual, and watch it copy files to the host and compile them there in the user's home directory. Then choose **File/Transfer** and press **Show Host Files**. If you get a message that the "Transfer link failed", go back to the Transfer Setup and select the 7-bit Transfer Link.

A standard **ftp** is included with TCP Connection, if you want it. Create a program item to call **ftp** from the Reflection group window. **Ping** can also be programmed in this fashion for a certain host, but **stat** cannot.

A **File/Print** Setup box is also available, but it does not handle network printers since there is no NFS. When you leave Reflection 2, choose **File/Save** to save your basic connection and file transfer information for next time.

WRQ does not support ODI drivers, only NDIS. However, you can make simultaneous connection with NetWare via a dedicated IPX shell that talks to WRQ's NDIS converter.

Ease of Use

Reflection made little use of the Windows environment; it supplied only one **telnet** window as the center of the product. Menus for file transfer and other features all hung off of that one window. The WRQ file transfer utility shows tree-structured directories, but an entire branch of files cannot be transferred en masse except using wildcards—directory by directory. See Chapter 16 for a discussion of Reflection's terminal emulation capabilities and host sessions via **telnet**.

Summary

Using intelligent programs, WRQ does a lot of the installation for you—making the Reflection product one of the easier ones to install. Modem users will appreciate the WRQ file transfer, but network administrators may resent it. Reflection certainly focuses on being a TELNET-oriented solution. We were surprised that NFS was not offered since Reflection provides excellent connections to other LANs. If you need a DDE-compatible product with a TCP/IP stack, only this product and Novell's LAN WorkPlace for DOS can help you. WRQ's main strength lies in its ability to communicate concurrently with DEC and HP hosts. Reflection has options for the hard cases; if it had NFS support and better use of Windows, it would be a clearly superior product. Reflection 2 for Windows costs $269 and the TCP Connection $179, if purchased separately, or $424 if purchased together.

Wollongong Group PathWay Access 2.1

Wollongong has been a powerful and stable force in the networking industry for several years, and this experience shows through in their product. PathWay Access is not as flashy as some, but it proves to be easy to use and has plenty of unique features.

Ease of Installation

Installation proved to be a multistep process—a bit more complicated that for other products we tried. We selected the ODI driver for compatibility with NetWare. We found that we had to install ODI first (by hand) before the runtime modules would install. Start the LSL and ODI adapter driver going at a minimum, but you can get it all going: **IPXODI**, **NETX**, and **LOGIN**. The Link Driver & Link Support sections are sufficient in **NET.CFG**. Reboot and start the DOS-based install program, **PWSETUP**.

Wollongong provides an editor for **NET.CFG**, as well as a startup file viewer. You may have to adjust **NET.CFG** to remove duplicate lines and add others—possibly a Protocol line for IPX if you didn't have it before. The editor is not terribly handy since it does not allow you to also edit the other startup files. You will probably have to edit them using a DOS editor.

Install Access for DOS applications next. Enter the printer server host. The program doesn't tell you, but it wants the "Access for DOS" diskette. Install it even if you use Windows—the Access for WINDOWS diskettes will be installed later. Then run through the configuration and supply information for TCP/IP. Check your startup files before you reboot.

Next, run Windows and install Access for Windows applications using the **File/Run** option. This will move some group icons and programs onto the PC. Exit Windows; then install the Client NFS for DOS option. Unfortunately, Client NFS has only a spartan install program that merely copies its files to a **\PATHWAY** directory. If you placed the Runtime and Access files elsewhere, you will have to move the files by hand: **copy \pathway*.* (newpath)**.

Next, load the Pathway NFS Network Driver through Windows Setup. Edit **CONFIG.SYS** with a **LASTDRIVE=** entry. Access restricts the drive letters you can use for NFS drives to those up to and including **LASTDRIVE**. (Novell uses the letters after **LASTDRIVE**.) If you want a Novell drive as **F:** and the NFS drive as **G:**, you are out of luck. Place **nfs** in the **AUTOEXEC.BAT** file after **PWTCP** and reboot.

You can mount NFS drives and printers from within Windows, but you can only browse the drives there. You should mount them from **AUTOEXEC.BAT** anyway, because then they will still be available if you exit Windows. It also means fewer mount messages to acknowledge on Windows boot.

Wollongong provides an authentication and locking daemon for the UNIX host, called NFSAD. However, we were frustrated to find no printed instructions for installing it. Pathway's documentation is excellent except on this point—call them.

Ease of Use

Most of Pathway's capability hangs on a single window's action bar. **File** leads you to terminal, file transfer, and printer sessions. You can save the startup parameters for any session under a name you choose, recalling it later to speed connection. (The terminal emulation includes VT340, IBM 3270, and others.) Under **Edit** you can find options for modifying the aforementioned session configuration files. There are Copy/Cut/Paste options for pasting text between a local application and a terminal session—you can even copy graphics from (but not to) the terminal session. You can also trigger a Capture mode to record the terminal session. The **Commands** and **Size** menu bar selections let you set fonts, colors, and other terminal attributes after logging in to a remote host, or run a script. The **Windows** menu selection lets you activate previously opened session windows.

Providing a script language that remains second to none, Wollongong is the only vendor to supply a script compiler with its product. We built a simple script in just a few minutes, shown in Figure 13.11. (It logs in to the UNIX host and opens our e-mail while we load the coffee-maker.) If you have a programmer's bent, this will be fun, but anyone can do it.

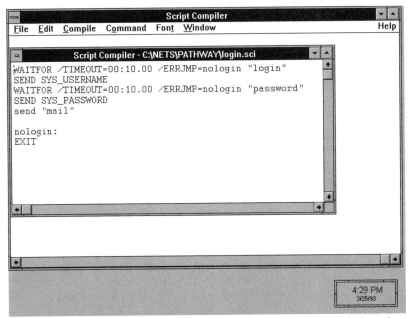

FIGURE 13.11 Wollongong's Script Compiler automates your daily tasks

Access provides plenty of options for keyboard configuration. The Keyboard Remapping utility shows at a glance what functions are assigned to each key, and makes it easy to assign special functions, such as end of transmission (Ctrl-D) to a single key.

Summary

Wollongong provides some unique and beneficial enhancements in the $350 Access, but occasionally we were surprised by some minor throw-back implementations. Access could use some internal standardization, but otherwise represents a solid, easy-to-use product.

Our Recommendations

Network environments are almost as unique as snowflakes. No one solution fits all needs. Even so, we believe some of these products have particular strengths and are best suited for specific environments. Given the large number of products, we feel compelled to make some judgment calls between them and to choose our personal favorites. However, take these with a grain of salt and double-check your own selections with the vendors. In most cases, they are happy to provide a demo.

If you want the answer to every DOS—UNIX networking question, and you want lots of peculiar options, go with FTP Software's PC/TCP. FTP provides the reputation and market presence to insure things will work.

SunSelect's PC-NFS has top-notch documentation for the UNIX side. However, we thought Wollongong's PathWay documentation, while not as helpful for UNIX, was the most generally thorough, well-organized, and clearly written.

If you need a lot of help for UNIX, including the pcnfs daemon, you have four choices: Beame & Whiteside's BW-NFS, SunSelect PC-NFS, FTP TCP/IP, and Wollongong's PathWay Access.

If terminal emulations and keyboard remapping is your thing, select Wollongong's Pathway Access. It even lets keyboards speak many more foreign languages than we can recognize on sight. Wollongong also provides a very powerful script language which increases efficiency by automatically performing routine tasks. Buy this in place of a robot, if you can do simple programming.

Windows users will love Distinct's TCP/IP for **telnet** and **ftp**. If you need NFS drives and UNIX printing, however (which Distinct does not supply), choose IBM TCP/IP for DOS or NetManage ChameleonNFS. There are other similarities between Distinct and NetManage: both were the easiest to install of all we tried, and each also goes easy on DOS RAM. If you frequently have problems with loading programs due to insufficient DOS memory, try one of those two.

If you are price conscious, choose ... IBM??? Yes, basic TCP/IP services and a good Windows interface cost just $230 for a single user! However, if you need multiple licenses check each of your favorite products—quantity discounts always apply.

We could give a Novell Peace Prize to several of these products for concurrent TCP/IP-NetWare connectivity. Of course, Novell's own LAN WorkPlace for DOS provides the most assurance on the Novell side, and it did a good job with the UNIX tasks as well.

Accessing multiple networks represents a problem for some readers. If you need simultaneous access to as many as five networks at once, get Cogent's $149 network accessory, WinNET plus.

Which product did we like the best, all things considered? We'll hand that one to Beame & Whiteside's BW-NFS. It seemed to balance the most features and flexibility with ease of use.

Product Comparison Table

Most features in Tables 13.1, 13.2 and 13.3 are *client* applications for your PC; that is, they rely on support daemons running on a UNIX host. PC products with *server* capability provide the stated service to other client PCs; e.g., an FTP Server allows other computers to make an FTP link to your PC without UNIX host involvement.

Several network operating systems are grouped in the table under the title 'NetBIOS'—for NetBIOS/NDIS-compatible LANs. The category includes the following

LANs: Microsoft LAN Manager, Banyan Vines, IBM LAN Server, DEC PATH-WORKS, 3Com 3+Open, DCA 10Net, HP LAN Manager, AT&T LM/X LAN Manager or StarLAN, SCO LAN MAN/X, Hayes LANStep, Tiara10Net, and perhaps others. We did not test the products against those LANs, but the vendors claim to support some or all of them. Contact the vendor to verify support for your particular NetBIOS LAN.

DOS memory (low memory) consumption is a complicating factor in many sites. To illustrate the problem, by the time you start a couple telnet sessions, ftp, e-mail, and an SNMP agent, you may not be able to load your spreadsheet—even under Windows. Only 640K of DOS memory is available, and into that must fit the DOS system, hardware drivers, Windows paraphernalia, Novell and TCP/IP network protocol stacks, terminal emulation, and utility TSRs. Much of the cramp can be relieved by loading those various portions into upper memory beyond the 640K boundary. Commands to memory managers such as EMM386, QEMM, and 386MAX are required to load DOS-based programs high. On the other hand, Windows DLL-based programs are loaded into the appropriate memory space without special effort on your part. Be aware that very few programs are 100% DLL-based. That is, a vendor may supply the WinSock DLL or Telnet as a DLL and claim DLL compliance, but the underlying stack and NFS client may still be memory-gobbling TSRs. Products with DLL stacks and NFS clients use little or no DOS memory.

We noted the amount of DOS memory consumed by each tested product under typical installation—with EMM386 (NOEMS parameter) providing the memory management. We made no special effort to load anything into high memory unless necessary to make it run. The memory figure given represents the amount of low memory consumed by the TCP/IP protocol stack and NFS support programs. It does NOT include adapter and NetWare drivers. Fair enough?

Lack of UNIX Info remains the chief failure with all products. Some companies say up front that they do not provide UNIX-end customer support for their product. You shouldn't need such assistance if the UNIX host is already networked, but if you are creating the network from scratch, this will be your most difficult task. Certain products provide both information and the UNIX server daemons for NFS.

Note that Beame & Whiteside supplies their NFS client product in an identical form, or nearly so, to Novell (NFS Client for LAN WorkPlace), Spry (AIR for NFS) and 3Com (NFS w/DPA). Those table columns are marked with an asterisk "*". For the reasons of space, time, appropriateness, and/or lack of information, the Cogent Data Technologies WinNET plus, Ipswitch Piper/IP, Solid Computer PCShare, and Ungermann-Bass TCP/Next do not appear in this table.

Table 13.1: **TCP/IP Networking Products for PCs**

Product	3Com TCP with DPA 2.1*	Beame & Whiteside BW-NFS 3.0	Distinct TCP/IP 3.0	Esker TUN*PLUS 7.1	Frontier Technolog- ies Super TCP/NFS for Windows 3.0	FTP Software PC/TCP 2.11
Single-User Price	$350	$349	$395	$295	$495	$400
Utilities/Functions						
Telnet Emulations	VT100	VT220, 3rdParty	VT100	VT220,ANSI, IBM3151, WYSE, other	VT320, 3rdParty	VT220, 3rd Party
Concurrent Sessions	32	20	60	32	Multiple	10
FTP/FTP Server	Yes/No	Yes/Yes	Yes/Yes	Yes/No	Yes/Yes	Yes/Yes
TFTP/TFTP Server	Yes/No	Yes/No	Yes/Yes	No/No	Yes/Yes	Yes/No
Print Client/Server	NFS/No	lpr,NFS/lpd	No/No	rsh,NFS/No	lpr,NFS/No	lpr,NFS/No
Remote Commands	rsh,rcp	rsh,rcp	None	rsh,rexec	rsh,rexec,rcp	rsh,rexec, rlogin,rcp
TN3270 Emulation	Yes	Yes	No	No	Yes	Yes
Mail, Messaging & News	No	SMTP,POP2, POP3,TALK	No	SMTP,POP2, POP3	SMTP,POP2, POP3,TALK, NNTP,MIME	SMTP,POP2, POP3,PCMA IL,NNTP
Ping	Yes	Yes	Yes	Yes	Yes	Yes
Finger	No	Yes	No	No	Yes	Yes
Statistics/Table Display	Yes/No	Yes/No	Yes/ARP Only	No/No	Yes/Yes	Yes/Yes
SNMP Agent	No	MIB-II	No	No	MIB-I,MIB- II,Ext-MIB	PC/SNMP Tools @$300
Other Utilities Included		Telnet server				
NFS Support	NFS w/DPA 1.0 @ $175	Standard	None	Standard	Standard	InterDrive @ $100
Client/Server	Yes/No	Yes/No	No/No	Yes/No	Yes/Yes	Yes/No
File Conversion	Yes	Yes	N/A	Print only	Yes	Yes
File Name Mapping	Yes	Yes	N/A	Yes	Yes	Yes
File Attribute Setting	Yes	Yes	N/A	Yes	Yes	Yes

Table 13.1: TCP/IP Networking Products for PCs

Product	3Com TCP with DPA 2.1*	Beame & Whiteside BW-NFS 3.0	Distinct TCP/IP 3.0	Esker TUN*PLUS 7.1	Frontier Technologies Super TCP/NFS for Windows 3.0	FTP Software PC/TCP 2.11
Configuration/Support						
Operating System Support	Win,DR,NW, NetBIOS	Win,NW, NetBIOS	Win,NW, NetBIOS	Win,DR,NW, NetBIOS	Win,NW, NetBIOS	Win,DESQ, NW,NetBIOS
Cabling Support	Ethernet, Token-Ring	Ethernet, Token-Ring, SLIP	Ethernet, Token-Ring, ARCnet, SLIP,PPP	Ethernet, Token-Ring, ARCnet,SLIP	Ethernet, Token-Ring, SLIP,PPP option	Ethernet, Token-Ring, SLIP,PPP, StarLAN
Driver Support	NDIS,ODI	NDIS,ODI, ASI,Packet, Board	NDIS,Packet	NDIS,ODI, Packet	NDIS,ODI, Packet,ASI	NDIS,ODI, ASI,Board, Packet,DLL
API Programming Support	BSD,BAPI, RCP, WinSock	WinSock (Ver. 3.0c)	WinSock	WinSock	WinSock	WinSock (Ver. 2.2)
Unix Info/Pcnfs Daemon	Scant/Yes	Adequate/ Yes	Scant/No	Scant/No	Scant/No	Adequate/ Yes
Install/Config Utility Type	DOS	DOS	Windows	DOS and Windows	Windows	DOS
Applications Type	DOS	DOS, Windows non-DLL	Windows DLL	DOS, Windows	DOS, Windows DLL, VxD shortly	DOS, Windows non-DLL
DOS Memory Consumed	27K	28K	4K	104K	72K (all NFS)	60K
Utilities Pre-config	Scripts	Telnet,Ftp	Telnet	Telnet,Ftp	Telnet	Telnet, Ftp
Context-Sensitive Help	No	Yes	Windows	No	Yes	Windows Apps Only
UNIX Backup Support	No	Tar	No	Tar	No	Tar,Rmt, Ddates
Related Products	OS/2 version @ $350	See Appendix B	Dev kit @ $495, Stack @ $200	Stack @ $190	Dev Kits @ $695, X.25 @ $1995, LPD Server @ $395, PPP @ $95, NetBIOS @ $295, Stack @ $195	LPD @ $400, DNS @ $500, OS/2 ver. @ $400,Dev kits @ $500,Stack @ $200

Table 13.2: **TCP/IP Networking Products for PCs**

Product	IBM TCP/IP for DOS/ Windows 2.1	Intercon TCP/ Connect II for Windows 3.0	James River Group ICE.TCP 2.1	Lanera TCP Open/Plus 2.1	NEI PCworks/ UniHost	NetManage Chameleon NFS 3.11
Single-User Price	$230	$495	$245	$295	$395-795	$495
Utilities/Functions					PCworks @ $195 (add.)	
Telnet Emulations	VT220,ANSI, TTY	VT320, 3rd Party	VT220,Wyse 60,AT&T605, IBM3151, ANSI	VT100, 3rd Party	VT220,ANSI, TTY	VT220,ANSI
Concurrent Sessions	Multiple	Multiple	3	10	1	32
FTP/FTP Server	Yes/Yes	Yes/Yes	Yes/No	Yes/Yes	Yes/No	Yes/Yes
TFTP/TFTP Server	Yes/No	Yes/Yes	Yes/Yes	Yes/Yes	No/No	Yes/Yes
Print Client/Server	lpr/lpd	lpr,NFS/No	Proprietary/ No	lpr,(NFS in 2.2)/No	ftp only/No	NFS/NFS
Remote Commands	rsh,rexec,rcp	rsh,rexec,rcp	None	rsh,rexec,rcp	Yes	rcp Server
TN3270 Emulation	Yes-includes ext attributes	Yes	No	No	No	Yes
Mail, Messaging & News	SMTP,POP2	SMTP,POP2, POP3,TALK, NNTP,MIME	No	No	Yes	SMTP,POP2, POP3
Ping	Yes	Yes	Yes	Yes	No	Yes
Finger	Yes	Yes	No	Yes	No	Yes
Statistics/Table Display	Yes/No	Yes/Yes	Yes/No	Yes/No	No	Yes/Yes
SNMP Agent	MIB-II	MIB-I, MIB-II, Ext-MIB	No	No	No	MIB-II, DOS, Windows
Other Utilities Included	Router	Modem server, POP server				Router, Domain Name server
NFS Support	NFS Kit @ $135	Standard	None	Standard	None	Standard
Client/Server	Yes/No	Yes/Yes	No/No	Yes/No	No/No	Yes/Yes
File Conversion	Yes	Commands	N/A	Commands	N/A	Yes
File Name Mapping	Yes	Yes	N/A	Yes	N/A	Yes
File Attribute Setting	Yes	Yes	N/A	Yes	N/A	Yes

Table 13.2: TCP/IP Networking Products for PCs

Product	IBM TCP/IP for DOS/ Windows 2.1	Intercon TCP/ Connect II for Windows 3.0	James River Group ICE.TCP 2.1	Lanera TCP Open/Plus 2.1	NEI PCworks/ UniHost	NetManage Chameleon NFS 3.11
Configuration/Support						
Operating System Support	Win,NW, NetBIOS	Win, NW, NetBIOS	Limited for NW,NetBIOS	Limited for NW,NetBIOS	DR	Win,NW, NetBIOS
Cabling Support	Ethernet, Token-Ring, SLIP	Ethernet, Token-Ring, SLIP	Ethernet, Token-Ring, ARCnet	Ethernet, Token-Ring, SLIP	Ethernet, SLIP	Ethernet, Token-Ring, FDDI,SLIP
Driver Support	NDIS	NDIS, ODI, Packet, ASI	Packet, NDIS,ODI	NDIS,ODI, Packet	None provided	NDIS,Board
API Programming Support	WinSock, BSD, ONCR-PC,FTPAPI	WinSock	None	WinSock, BSD	None	WinSock
Unix Info/Daemons	Scant/No	Scant/No	Scant/No	Scant/No	Scant/No	Scant/No
Install/Config Utility Type	DOS	Windows	DOS	DOS	No Utility	Windows
Applications Type	Windows DLL, DOS	Windows DLL, DOS	DOS, Windows	DOS	DOS	Windows DLL
DOS Memory Consumed	66K (Stack & NFS)	72K (all NFS)	1.4K	120K	0 on PC	6-10K
Utilities Pre-config	Yes - buttons	Telnet, FTP	Telnet	Telnet	Ftp scripts	Save/Learn
Context-Sensitive Help	Yes	Yes	No	Ftp only	No	Yes
UNIX Backup Support	No	No	No	Tar	No	No
Related Products	NetBIOS kit @$125, Dev kit @$550	Mac version @$495 + NFS client @ $295 & LPR client @ $195		Dev kit @ $295, Stack @ $150, Router @ $295, SNMP @$100	Mac version @ $145, specialty network products	Dev kit @ $500, DOS version @ $400

Table 13.3: TCP/IP Networking Products for PCs

Product	Novell LAN WorkPlace for DOS 4.1	Pacific Softworks Fusion for DOS 3.4	Spry Air for Windows 1.5*	SunSelect PC-NFS 5.0	WRQ Reflection for Windows 4.0 & TCP Connection 2.0	Wollongong PathWay Access 2.1
Single-User Price	$399	$295	$275	$415	$424	$350
Utilities/Functionst						
Telnet Emulations	VT220, 3rdParty	VT220	VT220	VT320	VT320	VT340,Tek41 05/4010
Concurrent Sessions	10	4	15	Multiple	18	12
FTP/FTP Server	Yes/Yes	Yes/Yes	Yes/Yes	Yes/DOS svr	Yes/No	Yes/Yes
TFTP/TFTP Server	Yes/Yes	Yes/Yes	No/No	No/No	No/No	Yes/No
Print Client/Server	lpr,rpr,NFS/No	lpr/No	lpr,NFS/No	lpr,NFS/No	No/No	lpr,NFS/lpd
Remote Commands	rsh,rexec,rcp	rsh,rcp, rlogin,rwho	rcp server	rsh,rcp,rdate	None	rsh,rlogin,rcp
TN3270 Emulation	No	Option	$199 option	$ option	$199 option	Yes, plus TN3179G
Mail, Messaging & News	No	No	POP3	send	No	send only
Ping	Yes	Yes	Yes	Yes	Yes	Yes
Finger	Yes	Yes	No	Command	No	Yes
Statistics/Table Display	Yes/Yes	Yes/No	Yes/No	Yes/Commands	Yes/Yes	Yes/No
SNMP Agent	MIB-I	No	No	MIB-II	No	Yes
Other Utilities Included	Finger server, XPC				WRQ transfer, DDE server	
NFS Support	NFS Client 2.3 @ $295	Standard	AIR for NFS @ $100	Standard	None	PathWay Client NFS @ $95
Client/Server	Yes/No	Yes/No	Yes/No	Yes/No	No/No	Yes/No
File Conversion	Commands	No	Yes	Commands	N/A	Yes
File Name Mapping	Yes	Yes	Yes	Yes	N/A	Yes
File Attribute Setting	Yes	Yes	Yes	Commands	N/A	Yes

Table 13.3: TCP/IP Networking Products for PCs

Product	Novell LAN WorkPlace for DOS 4.1	Pacific Softworks Fusion for DOS 3.4	Spry Air for Windows 1.5*	SunSelect PC-NFS 5.0	WRQ Reflection for Windows 4.0 & TCP Connection 2.0	Wollongong PathWay Access 2.1
Configuration/Support						
Operating System Support	Win, NW, NetBIOS, DESQview	Win,NW	Win,NW, PCSupport, NetBIOS, DECnet	Win,DR, NW, NetBIOS	Win,NW, NetBIOS	Win,NW, NetBIOS
Cabling Support	Ethernet, Token-Ring, ARCnet, SLIP,PPP	Ethernet	Ethernet, Token-Ring, ARCnet, FDDI (SLIP, PPP w/NDIS version)	Ethernet, Token-Ring, SLIP	Ethernet, Token-Ring, SLIP,PPP	Ethernet, Token-Ring, SLIP,PPP
Driver Support	ODI Only	NDIS	Packet,NDIS ODI (versions)	NDIS,Board	NDIS (ODI in TCP Conn. 2.1)	NDIS,ODI, ASI,Packet
API Programming Support	None	None	WinSock, NetBEUI	WinSock	NetBEUI, (WinSock in 4.1)	NetBEUI, BSD, Win-Sock (Ver. 2.1.1)
Unix Info/Daemons	Scant/Yes	Scant/No	Scant/Yes	Good/Yes	Scant/No	Good/Can supply
Install/Config Utility Type	DOS	DOS	Windows	Partial Win	DOS, Win	DOS, Win
Applications Type	DOS, Windows non-DLL	DOS	Windows non-DLL	DOS, Win-dows non-DLL	DOS, Win-dows non-DLL, DLL (ftp)	DOS, Win-dows DLL
DOS Memory Consumed	24K	78K (all NFS)	53K	149K	39K	83K
Utilities Pre-config	Scripts	Telnet script	Scripts	Telnet	Yes	Scripts
Context-Sensitive Help	Yes	No	No	Yes	Yes	Yes
UNIX Backup Support	No	No	Tar	No	No	No
Related Products	OS/2 & Mac versions @ $399	Dev kit @ $100	AIR for DOS @ $275 Concurrent @ $249	See Appendix B	Reflection X adds X server @$599	Mac ver. @ $295, OS/2 ver. @$245, enterprise e-mail

14

PC LAN—UNIX Products

Introduction

Our focus here is on products that integrate UNIX and DOS computers on a whole-sale basis—PC LAN to UNIX networks. Chapter 7, Linking UNIX with PC LANs, provides the background for this chapter. All of the following solutions cover hardware platforms with frosting, making them palatable to new users who are unfamiliar with more than one type of hardware and operating system. Bigger drives, more printers, remote logins and remote program execution, X Windows support—the menu offers a little of everything. Some of the products bear remarkable similarities to TCP/IP networking products for stand-alone PCs, but their target market is networks, not stand-alones; you load them on a server for use by all PC LAN clients. Others disguise a computer to look and act like a client or server of the opposing network. There is something here for every PC LAN.

Evaluation Criteria

In the following evaluation of products, we have chosen to focus on ease of installation and general product usability, but we ignore most of the details of setup. We note setup challenges in a more cursory manner than we did for other chapters, giving you the general idea of what to do, e.g., "Create a user account under UNIX." For nitty-gritty information about hardware drivers, TCP/IP functionality, startup files, printer setup, commands, etc., investigate other related chapters. This chapter complements Chapter 7, Installing PC-LAN to UNIX Hybrids. Note also that we have not tested any of the products under significant network traffic.

It makes sense to categorize these products by function. Some products allow PC LAN clients (of several varieties) to access a UNIX server. Others work the other way, providing PC LAN resources to UNIX clients. Still others try to work bi-directionally in a peer-to-peer design.

UNIX Resources for NetWare Clients

Beame & Whiteside MultiConnect Server for Solaris 1.0

If this product measures up to the level of Beame & Whiteside BW-NFS (a TCP/IP networking software package), MultiConnect should be a hit soon after release. We were not able to get a look at MultiConnect, since it won't be out until the first quarter of 1994, but here are a few of its anticipated features.

MultiConnect Server for Solaris places a streams driver into the Sun's kernel which makes the Sun look like a NetWare 3.11 file server. The Sun then supports all of the usual NetWare utilities, including **LOGIN**, **MAP**, and **ATTACH**. MultiConnect also provides NetWare clients with access to UNIX printers, and can reroute print jobs queued on other NetWare servers to its own printers. The MultiConnect Server can capably function as the only NetWare server on the network.

Beame & Whiteside will also roll-out two other products with the MultiConnect Server for Solaris—the MultiConnect Server for Windows NT, and the MultiConnect Client for Solaris (see a description later in this chapter). The servers each cost $849 for a 5-user setup, $5395 for 100 users. A Canadian firm originally, Beame & Whiteside moved its corporate headquarters to North Carolina in October, 1993.

Firefox Communications NOVIX for NetWare 1.0

Firefox provides a middle-of-the-pack product. The purpose of NOVIX is to enhance existing NetWare clients with UNIX host session capability. Installed on the NetWare server, NOVIX provides a pool of UNIX host sessions on a first-come, first-served basis to PC users. Only the standard **telnet**, **ftp**, and **rlogin** commands are included—enough to run UNIX character-based applications and go out to the Internet for e-mail—but NOVIX integrates with LAN WorkPlace for DOS to provide a stronger TCP/IP utility set. UNIX users can print to Novell printers, but not vice-versa. The product does not use a separate communications gateway PC, as some products such as Ipswitch Catipult do, so it is some burden on the file server. On the other hand, Novix does not require special software or configuration for the NetWare client PCs—a boon to the system administrator.

Ease of Installation

You can install NOVIX on NetWare 2.2 servers or router PCs (which use Value Added Processes) or 3.11 servers (which use Network Loadable Modules). Firefox recommends that the server be dedicated, not for partial use as a DOS workstation (which only makes sense—the DOS capability won't be that fast anyway). Software installation is unique—first you attach a Configuration Pack (a sentinel device) to the parallel port of a workstation on the network. (Firefox says this Configuration Pack will be scrapped in the next version.) Next, you login at that machine as SUPERVISOR and run the DOS-based install program.

As you run the installation program, you need to have configuration information about the server's LAN adapter handy (IRQ, I/Q Base, etc.). The product keeps an installation log which you can view on-screen or print from the installation menu. As you feed diskettes into the installation program, it updates the Configuration Pack with the number of concurrent host sessions you have purchased; it also creates licenses for the number of concurrent users (overkill, in our opinion). Remember that each **ftp** session requires two host sessions. When you are finished with the installation procedure, remove the Configuration Pack and attach it to the parallel port of the NetWare fileserver. If you have a printer connected there, don't worry—the Pack works in-line with the printer.

Next, run **NVCONFIG** to set up the host services and features you require for the Netware clients. The screens work similarly to NetWare screens. Firefox has you specify port numbers for use in connecting workstations to a UNIX host. This approach allows flexibility to support cases where non-standard ports are used, but that is rare. The port numbers are important, so either enter the sample numbers from the manual or check your **/etc/services** file on the UNIX host. If you need both **telnet** and **ftp** services from a particular host, you must create two different host sessions using different access types and port numbers. You should lower the *Number of Connect Retries* and *Interval Between Retries* values.

To set up a Novell printer for use by UNIX users, do the Novell side first from **NVCONFIG**. Each queue needs a unique IP address. On the UNIX side, set up **/etc/ hosts** and **/etc/printcap** with the new information. NOVIX does not support printing by IBM AIX workstations.

Plug the Configuration Pack onto the parallel port of the server. Without it, the NOVIX software will not load. If you have NetWare 2.2, create a **SERVER.CFG** file to allow NOVIX to load automatically. For routers, create **XBRIDGE.CFG**. If you have NetWare 3.11, you must edit **AUTOEXEC.NCF**. We found the installation manual to be quite redundant between the three types of NetWare versions supported, making it easy to get lost in the wrong section.

Finally, run NetWare's **SYSCON** to give your group(s) trustee access to the **SYS:\TCPGWAY** directory (Read and Filescan rights only), and a search drive mapping. NOVIX can run from Windows if you also run some TSRs for task switching (supplied).

You can use the **NVHCM** utility to perform **ping** and other diagnostics. **NVHCM** needs more instructions. Don't type **TCPC** on the front of your commands. That only works under NetWare 2.x. Use F10 to exit. Note that if you make changes or additions to any of the existing setup through **NVCONFIG**, be sure to run **NVHCM** afterwards—once inside, type **READ** to absorb your changes. Unfortunately, there is no troubleshooting section in the documentation.

Ease of Use

We had a difficult time using the product, mainly because the documentation had poor instructions (it seemed to beat around the bush, but never flush the fox). It took us some time to figure out how to start and use the various features. The documentation could use some screenshots or illustrations—there were none in the user manual.

All utility screens were, again, similar to Novell NetWare screens. To use **telnet**, type **VT220-1** (for single session, **VT220-4** for 4-session) from the command line. A menu comes up showing your list of connectable hosts. If there is only one host, it automatically brings up a login for that host, bypassing the menu. You can also supply parameters to load pre-built configuration files.

The **ftp** screen was more complicated, as Figure 14.1 shows. Enter a minimum of the user name and password. Press F6 to see files on the remote system. You cannot see directories on the local system.

Rlogin also requires a separate service definition and TCP port number. Use *VT220* as the **Access Type**.

ETHVIEW is an add-on utility from a previous product. It is a simple LAN analyzer, but it only works with selected LAN adapters via VLLI drivers.

We had an unexplained problem with editing the configuration, then trying to start a session. The bug forced us to reload the NOVIX NLM at the server to clear it; this problem has received attention for the coming Version 2.0.

Summary

We hit this product hard on documentation. The manuals looked promising, but they did not convey clearly how to use the product. Firefox agreed, and has already

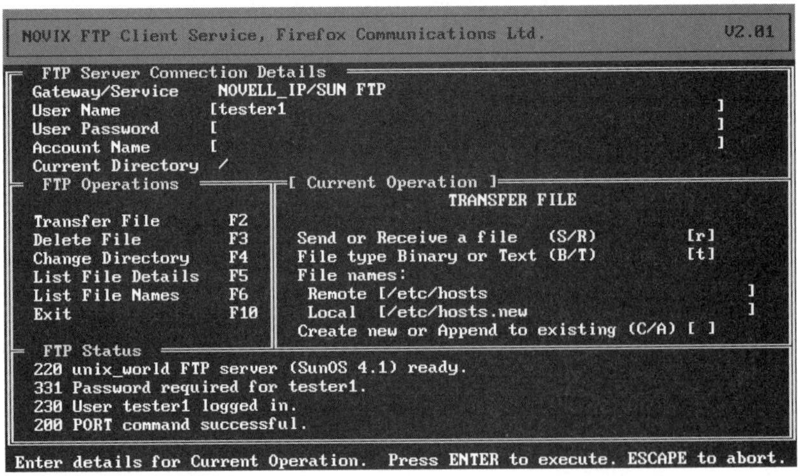

FIGURE 14.1 File transfers using NOVIX take some getting used to

rewritten the manuals for Version 2.0, due out shortly. That version will also provide fully controlled access to services by User/Group name. Hopefully, Version 2.0 will be a more solid product with fewer deficiencies.

The server software costs $995 for 5 concurrent sessions, and workstation software is an additional $500 for 5 concurrent users. For the price, NOVIX 1.0 is no bargain. You can get more utilities plus NFS for less money on other products. However, NOVIX is one of those products that requires no changes to the workstations—no additional memory drain on limited-RAM machines and none of the repetitive configurations.

Locus Computing PC-Interface 4.1

Of all the products in this chapter, PC-Interface is one with higher-than-average name recognition, since it has been bundled with some releases of UNIX. PC-Interface uses UDP, a sister protocol to TCP that does NOT provide the TCP utilities **telnet** and **ftp**. However, PCI does provide its own proprietary terminal emulation, NFS capability, and allows you to use familiar DOS commands to access UNIX resources. Note that PCI does NOT integrate PC-LANs with UNIX, but rather, standalone PCI clients with the PCI server. However, you can have concurrent connections with NetWare. This product does not fit any category well, but we decided this was the best place for it.

Ease of Installation

PCI is a client/server product, requiring a server component on the UNIX side. SCO Open Server Enterprise System comes with the PCI server, but you can order the server from Locus if your UNIX package does not have it. The installation is easy. Our only problem was that our 4.1 version did not support DOS 6.0, so the program hung on boot until we used the **SETVER** command to trick PCI. PCI also provides a Windows network driver, and it adjusts the Windows **.INI** files for you.

HOT TIP   **Out of Sync**

Sometimes a PC networking product or other application suddenly fails after you install a newer version of DOS. For example, you may get a disquieting message that Drive C: is an invalid drive. You can often use **SETVER** as a work-around. First, make sure **CONFIG.SYS** contains a line such as **DEVICE=C:\DOS\SETVER.EXE**. Then, type **setver (executable name) (version)** from a command line to set the executable program's needed version number into a table; e.g., **setver pciinit.exe 5.00**.

Ease of Use

After booting the PC with PC-Interface loaded, we were immediately able to do a login to the SCO Open Server machine. PCI supports both Ethernet and serial connections, selectable from the login line. The UNIX drive was mounted as drive D: in our case, and we could use all of the usual DOS commands to access it. However, expect to see foreign-looking file and directory names—they must be truncated for display and access under DOS. We stored and executed DOS programs on the UNIX drive with no trouble. There is also a utility to let you use UNIX, instead of DOS, commands.

PCI provides a basic terminal emulator with most of the characteristics of a VT220. This emulator can be run from within Windows, but only in the DOS mode. You are limited to a single host session. PCI does not use the typical telnet protocol to establish the session, but you end up with a login to the UNIX host just the same.

Printing a DOS file on a UNIX network printer requires setup through a redirection command. Then, you can print using the usual DOS commands (except PRINT), or print through the Windows Print Manager.

Summary

PC-Interface is a stripped-down product for businesses that need only dumb terminal emulation and the ability to share UNIX drives and printers with DOS PCs. It has few of the amenities of the TCP/IP products listed in Chapter 13. At $235, it strikes us as being a little expensive, pound for pound, especially when concurrent connection with NetWare (via the NetWare Companion option) costs $100 more. You also need to buy a PCI server, if it did not come with your UNIX operating system.

For a full TCP/IP protocol stack (still without telnet, ftp, and other utilities, however), ask for PC-Interface Plus ($369). It also allows 8 terminal sessions from Windows via Century's Tiny Term, includes the NetWare Companion, and provides UNIX/DOS peer-to-peer printing.

Novell LAN WorkGroup 4.1

If you read the evaluation of LAN WorkPlace for DOS in Chapter 13, you have a basic conception of what LAN WorkGroup is all about. This product, which installs on the NetWare file server, provides NetWare clients as a group with remote UNIX resources via TCP/IP utilities. LAN WorkGroup offers a long list of DOS-based utilities such as ftp, telnet, remote commands, lpr/lpq/lprm, and others. In addition, several are also included as full Windows applications. A few, including ftp, talk, and finger, provide both client and server functionality.

LAN WorkGroup dynamically assigns IP addresses to the client machines. It also includes an SNMP agent which allows a network manager to remotely monitor the TCP/IP activity of a WorkGroup node. (The nodes can also monitor TCP/IP activity on remote machines via SNMP.) If you desire serial or modem connections to the NetWare server, you can install the SLIP and PPP drivers on the remote nodes.

LAN WorkGroup 4.1 and its single-user sister product, LAN WorkPlace for DOS, are easy-to-use products. They give NetWare clients access to UNIX resources through a familiar set of GUIs (DOS, Windows, NetWare) with a minimum of training. A 50-user license lists for $4995. However, you should plan on also buying the optional NFS Client for LAN WorkPlace for the ability to mount UNIX drives as extra storage. IBM shops can also purchase a 3270 terminal emulation utility for connectivity with their mainframe.

Novell NetWare NFS Gateway 1.1

NFS Gateway product takes care of NetWare clients who need more disk space. It provides an easy and transparent link to UNIX drives for extra file storage. To the NetWare user, files stored on the remote UNIX NFS-mounted drives can be accessed in the usual fashion as DOS files in a NetWare volume.

This product is a "gateway", meaning that NetWare clients access the UNIX drives through a single machine. (NFS Gateway installs on a NetWare file server.) However, there is no communication or functionality in the opposite direction, from UNIX clients to NetWare, with the exception of remote NetWare administration from an X Window System console. NFS Gateway can run alongside Novell's NetWare NFS product, which does enable UNIX clients to access NetWare drives. NFS Gateway is able to access remote Network Information Service and Domain Name Service databases, which help NFS Gateway locate remote NFS servers and provides user and group information.

The installation process is the same as for other NetWare server products. However, you must have TCP/IP communications configured before installing the NFS Gateway—see your TCP/IP Transport Supervisor's Guide. Novell supplies a new administration utility for the NFS Gateway called **NFSCON**. From **NFSCON** you can do such things as login to multiple NFS Gateway servers, mount/dismount volumes (remote filesystems), and view activity levels for NFS drives. There is an error reporting feature. **NFSCON** also lets you copy (using **ftp**), edit, and create configuration files to pass between servers. You can create NIS or DNS databases from local files or vice-versa.

On the UNIX computers you must also make some changes. You must export filesystems to the NFS Gateway, and make sure the NFS server is active. You must also define the NetWare users and groups for the UNIX system, and define the NFS Gateway as a new host on the TCP/IP network. Novell provides welcome information on these procedures for AIX, NeXT, SCO, Solaris, SunOS, System V, ULTRIX, and UnixWare.

NetWare NFS Gateway is a good way to make use of unused disk space on big UNIX drives. At $4995 for 50 users, NFS Gateway isn't the cheapest of this type of solution, and it does require modifications on both the Novell file server and the UNIX server. However, dyed-in-the-wool NetWare fans will like the thorough Novell manual and administration utility.

Puzzle Systems SoftNet Utilities 1.07

Puzzle's SoftNet Utilities make a UNIX Workstation look and act like a NetWare file server. This is the opposite scenario to NetWare NFS, which makes a NetWare server look like a UNIX server. Also, UNIX users can login to NetWare as NetWare clients, and NetWare clients can login to the UNIX workstation as UNIX clients. TCP/IP software is not required by the NetWare clients to communicate with the new server—Puzzle uses Novell's native IPX. SoftNet Utilities presently work with the following hardware platforms: Sun SPARC, HP PA-RISC, and Silicon Graphics.

Ease of Installation

We installed SoftNet Utilities on a Sun SPARCstation IPC. The product allows you to locate the files in any filesystem, which is a good thing if your **/usr** filesystem is full. Tar the files off of the diskette, then make simple edits to your login script.

The configuration program is easy to use. Figure 14.2 shows some of its windows. Enter the network number for the Novell network (go to a NetWare client and run **SLIST** to find it). The **Process Priority** field is particularly important, because it affects the speed at which NetWare operations perform in relation to UNIX operations. You can optimize the Sun for one or the other operating system. You can set the frame type to *Ethernet_802.3* or *Ethernet_II*. SoftNet works under the older NetWare 2.2 as well as 3.11.

Next, select the users who need access to the Sun server. The list of current UNIX users is displayed to select from. Each Novell user who does not also have an account on the Sun must be given one, either now or later. (Create new accounts in **/etc/passwd**.) SoftNet's configuration utility automatically sets up the *supervisor* account and *softnet* user group.

Create a mount point for each NetWare volume—SYS is set up automatically. Then run the diagnostics. If you have an improper network number, SoftNet will suggest a more appropriate one. Start the Puzzle fileserver on the Sun. From a NetWare node **SLIST** should show the Sun as an available Novell file server. Login to the Novell network as *supervisor*, attach the Sun, and map a drive to it. Then, create user home directories on the Sun with **syscon**. For the sake of NetWare clients you should insert **attach** and **map** commands into their login scripts, so that they can use the new server automatically.

Any trustee rights you set from NetWare apply only to the NetWare directories on the Sun and do not modify rights under UNIX login. Some additional differences

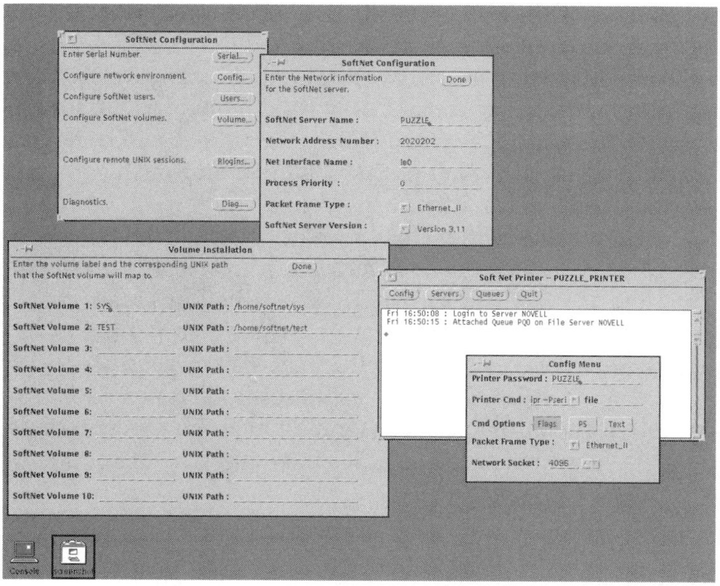

FIGURE 14.2   Puzzle SoftNet Utilities configuration screens

also exist in the permission structure as viewed from NetWare. Filenames are converted automatically.

UNIX and NetWare users can have their choice of UNIX or NetWare printers. To allow UNIX users to use a printer on the Novell LAN, install the spooler program on the Sun. This program redirects **lpr** print jobs to the NetWare print queue after automatically logging in as a NetWare user. Conversely, we connected our Novell users to the UNIX printer by creating a new print server and print queue using **pconsole** on the Sun, then running the printer configuration utility.

Place the SoftNet server daemons into the **rc.local** file so that they run automatically on boot. You need **snfs** (the SoftNet server) in the list, and either **snsp** (for the spooler) or **snpr** (for the NetWare print server.) Here is an example:

```
        if [ -f /home/softnet/snfs]; then
                cd /home/softnet
                /home/softnet/snfs &
                /home/softnet/snpr puzzle_printer NOVELL PQ0 &
                cd /
        fi
```

Ease of Use

When Novell clients login, the Sun drive (if attached in the login script) appears in their drive mappings, allowing them to use the drive as any other. Simple as that. Under Windows, the File Manager shows the new drive. Then you can load new applications on the Sun, or off-load the applications for particular work groups from the most burdened server to the Sun.

Puzzle does not set up the extra capability to do a NetWare login directly to the Sun, although you can make this work by copying **LOGIN.EXE** from your NetWare server to the Sun's **SYS:\LOGIN** directory. Puzzle does not provide any of the utilities you might normally find in **\PUBLIC** and other NetWare directories, but you can copy them from another NetWare server.

You can print to the UNIX printer by using the usual **CAPTURE** command in **AUTOEXEC.BAT** or the system login script, or by using **NPRINT** from the command line. If you also run Windows, use the Print Manager to connect the new network printer.

To login to the Sun as a UNIX client, run **unxlogin**, either from the DOS prompt or from the **AUTOEXEC.BAT** startup script. This program starts a remote session on the Sun, using VT100 terminal emulation. Login, then execute UNIX commands in the UNIX filesystems. You can do a **unxlogin** whether or not the workstation drive is attached for NetWare.

Summary

We found this product to be a good one for system administrators, because it is simple and because it does not alter normal procedures. The price, at $1295 for 16 users, is cheap compared to a new file server. SoftNet Utilities makes use of the Sun's big drives without a lot of fuss. It is easy to understand and set up, and it makes few claims on your UNIX files. The documentation is a little shy on printer configuration, but it is good otherwise.

One of the best features is that SoftNet uses the NetWare IPX protocol for communication, eliminated the need to place TCP/IP or NFS on the Novell side. This avoids a lot of clutter, extra install time, and expense.

SunSelect NetWare Sunlink 1.0

This product is one implementation of Novell's NetWare for UNIX (an OEM product), turning a Sun box into a full-featured Novell server. As with Puzzle SoftNet Utilities, the product targets existing NetWare users who wish to add a Sun fileserver into the resource list. However, you can set up a NetWare network using this product even if you don't have any other Novell machines. You will have lots of setup to do and documentation to read, just as you would with NetWare. This product includes the workstation drivers LSL, IPXODI, NETX, and a small assortment of ODI drivers to get your PCs connected. It also includes Novell NetWare Workstation for Windows software, to help you set up the Windows PC drivers.

Ease of Installation

NetWare SunLink installs on a Sun running SunOS. SunSelect supplies SunLink only on CD-ROM media, so you need a CD-ROM drive attached to the Sun. Since Sun knows its own system and is content to modify it, the SunLink installation program makes changes in quite a few UNIX files, as well as building a new kernel.

This program requires boot files on the PC, so the installation program offers to place the files on a bootable diskette for you. However, if you don't have a 3Com, Eagle, or IBM Token Ring LAN adapter in the PC, it will only do half of the job—SunSelect only supplies drivers for 11 cards from these three manufacturers. You can build the diskette anyway for reference, then modify it with a board driver to match your particular hardware.

HOT TIP

In Search of the Bootable Diskette

To make a bootable disk, insert a diskette into the 3 1/2" drive (probably the **B:** drive) and type **format b:**, then **sys b:** to transfer the PC operating system. You may need to add extra parameters for the **format** command, depending upon your version of DOS and your brand of hardware.

The installation program lets you install the software into whatever filesystem you choose. Ignore SunSelect's default network number—find out your Novell physical network number, and enter it instead. Complete the installation of SunLink by installing the SunNet License software and licenses. This requires you to call Sun-Select to tell them all about yourself and ask for some keys.

You have to make additional changes by hand. Use **sconsole** (Figure 14.3) to adjust the frame type or change any parameters. (You can't edit frame type, just delete the existing Network Assignment entry, then add it back with corrected parameters.) We found **sconsole** to be more difficult to use than most other configuration utilities, partly because the menus were somewhat unclear, partly because editing and menu movement were antiquated. It was simpler to load the configuration data files into an editor for our one-shot test, but for the long haul you will have to learn **sconsole**.

When you are comfortable with the configuration, type **/nwreboot**. The new **vmunix** NetWare-like kernel will be copied into your root directory over the top of the existing **vmunix** kernel. Then you can reboot the Sun. As you do, notice that several NetWare drivers are now loaded automatically during the early boot process. If all is well, your NetWare client PCs will now be able to recognize the new server and attach to it or login. Use **SYSCON** (Novell's **SYSCON** and many other utilities come with SunLink) to create user accounts and login scripts.

```
+------------------------------------------------------------------------+
|                                                                        |
|                         Add A NetWare Network                          |
|                                                                        |
|                                                                        |
|                                                                        |
|       New Network Number:          03030303                            |
|       Adapter Device Name:         /dev/dsd                            |
|       Adapter Type :               ETHERNET_DLPI                       |
|       Interface Name:              le0                                 |
|       Frame Type:                  ETHERNET_II                         |
|       Module Name:                 NULL                                |
|                                                                        |
|                                                                        |
|                                                                        |
|                                                                        |
|                                                                        |
|                                                                        |
|       Added IPX Network 03030303                                       |
|             Press RETURN to continue...█                               |
|                                                                        |
+------------------------------------------------------------------------+
```

FIGURE 14.3 Configuring a NetWare network with SunLink's sconsole

Finally, configure for network printers. UNIX users cannot print to Novell print-ers, but Novell users CAN access UNIX printers. Use **PCONSOLE** to set up the print queues and servers. Use **sconsole** to configure UNIX-based printers.

Ease of Use

We noticed one thing right away—the SunNet license server used by SunLink may conflict with other license servers. FrameMaker's license server would not start as long as SunLink was up. We had to use the **stopnw** command to bring down the Sun NetWare server, then load the FrameMaker license server, then type **startnw** to bring SunLink back up.

SunSelect includes most of the standard NetWare utilities with NetWare Sun-Link. They are a welcome sight to Novell system administrators, and help shield them from day-to-day involvement with UNIX. However, the UNIX system admin-istrator still has to monitor processes and configure files infrequently. This is a little bigger job than for some other products, since SunLink modifies the kernel and sev-eral other files. It is not as self-contained as we would like. Printer maintenance does require both **PCONSOLE** and **sconsole** setup, if the printer is UNIX-based.

We had problems using **stopnw** when OpenWindows was loaded—the Sun locked up. We recommend exiting OpenWindows before downing the SunLink server using **stopnw**. **Stopnw** and **startnw** also caused problems on occasion by not unloading or loading everything they were responsible for.

SunSelect supplies a utility, **NVT** (Novell Virtual Terminal), to support NetWare clients logging into the Sun as UNIX users. This utility allows a third-party terminal emulation package to find a UNIX server using the IPX protocol. Configure this fea-ture from **sconsole**, then set up a user account on the Sun. Run **NVT** (a DOS TSR program), then press Alt-T to select the server, then start your terminal emulator in *Interrupt 14* mode.

Summary

As with PC-NFS, Sun has gone after providing a full-featured software product in SunLink. Novell takes some of the credit, because they licensed the engine to Sun. But creating a SunLink server is twice as complicated as setting up a Novell server on a PC, and also harder to maintain on the UNIX side. There are more ways for the system to fail. There is still a large burden on the UNIX system administrator. Most businesspeople would be happier with a less obtrusive and more friendly solution. After all, in this scenario the Sun is an add-on to the NetWare LAN, not the default server, right? The base 2-user kit costs $995, and 10 additional licenses are $1000.

UNIX Resources for Non-NetWare Clients

Artisoft LANtastic and LANtastic for TCP/IP 5.0

Artisoft has established itself as the low-cost networking leader for DOS users with its LANtastic peer-to-peer LAN. LANtastic for TCP/IP extends PC connectivity inexpensively to the UNIX realm. With a feature list similar to that of the TCP/IP single-user products described in Chapter 13, LANtastic for TCP/IP gives multiple DOS users access to UNIX through TCP/IP and NFS.

Artisoft's latest version of LANtastic, version 5.0, has several advantages over 4.1—primarily support for NDIS drivers. This gives you more hardware options than just NetBIOS. Installation is very close to that for the 4.1 product. However, take note that you cannot mix 5.0 nodes with 4.1 nodes on the same LAN. Artisoft charges only $50 to upgrade an entire 4.1 LAN, so do it.

Ease of Installation

Artisoft sells network adapters and cables (at least, for the time being), but Eagle, SMC, Xircom and some other NetBIOS- or NDIS-compatible adapters work if you buy LANtastic/AI software (adapter independent). In keeping with the spirit of interoperability, the following discussion assumes you are using AI.

LANtastic 5.0 peer software should be installed on each networked PC first. LANtastic 4.1 and previous versions defaulted to the Ethernet_802.3 frame type and also had trouble talking to certain NetBIOS adapter drivers (such as Xircom). The new 5.0 uses TCP/IP's Ethernet_II frame type out of the box, and you can purchase

NDIS support software which allows you to use whatever NDIS driver the adapter vendor supplies

Use the **NET** program to mount a remote server's shared resources, or **NET_-MGR** to share resources as a server. When you are satisfied that the PCs are interrelating, install LANtastic for TCP/IP on a node designated as the TCP/IP server. You do the TCP/IP configuration from a DOS program called **LTCP-MGR**. Set up the default account information first, then specify a block of IP addresses to use. Finally, for each PC, select an IP address from the range, and finish defining an associated user account. The user name you enter for an account must be a valid user name on the UNIX host.

The Central Station, a $595 accessory, performs several functions, including laptop connection, dial-in support, and print server. It is simple to set up, but don't buy it if you only need a laptop docking station—a Xircom adapter is much cheaper.

To configure NFS, you must manually enter **nfs** into the **TCPSTART.BAT**, followed by commands for NFS mounts of UNIX drives and printers. Create a **hosts** file as well. To complete the installation phase, configure each PC workstation to find the TCP/IP server, run the **nfs** command again, and mount the drives/printers.

Ease of Use

The Windows interface is easy to use—we recommend you get it if your machine has Windows. For instructions you need to go to the online Help rather than the 5.0 manual. The TCP/IP utility window (which is the take-off point for telnet and ftp) is quite bland, for a Windows utility. On the other hand, the management of LANtastic itself was very GUI, as you can determine from Figure 14.4.

LANtastic 5.0 helps you share DOS resources (drives and printers) among many PCs. It also provides other helpful utilities, including "chat" capability, an e-mail tool, voice mail messaging (using LAN Radio and an Artisoft Sounding Board), and the Network Scrapbook for saving Windows clipboard items permanently. You can also modify communication parameters for extra performance.

Using LANtastic for TCP/IP, we were able to mount UNIX drives directly from each node. Remote UNIX printers can also be mounted and used via the LPR protocol, and print queues can be managed from long distance. The LANtastic nodes easily logged into the Sun and RS/6000 for host sessions or file transfer. The telnet-and-ftp utility was adequate under Windows (which means that it was easier than using UNIX commands). Telnet supports VT340 and TN3270 terminal emulations.

LANtastic for TCP/IP also includes other goodies for the DOS command line: an **ftp** server, **tftp**, **ping**, **stat**, **finger**, an LPR server, an SMTP mail interface, and the remote commands **rlogin**, **rsh**, and **rcp**. There is an SNMP agent, supporting MIB-I and II, for remote monitoring by LAN management software.

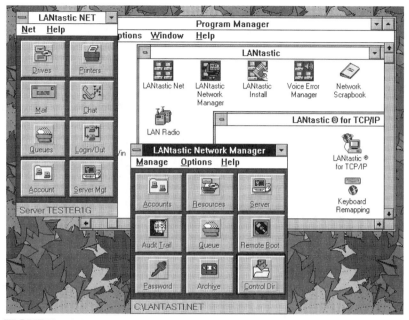

FIGURE 14.4 Artisoft's push-button network configuration

Summary

We liked the capability built into the product. The configuration process was confusing at times, however. We did not find configuration to be completely clear and got lost in the early stages between similar-sounding buttons and options. Still, once configured, it was an easy system to use. This product includes a broad set of functions and has good value. The only thing that would make it better would be a Windows interface for all of the TCP/IP utilities, not just **telnet** and **ftp**.

Artisoft's LANtastic for TCP/IP has done a good job of carrying PC users to the door of UNIX. LANtastic makes sense for operations that primarily need resource-sharing—the product fits the peer-to-peer philosophy of TCP/IP well. Artisoft's technical support crew is knowledgeable if you have trouble. If you need NetWare connectivity as well, try LANtastic for NetWare 5.0, an add-on product that supports ODI drivers and the NetWare shell. LANtastic/AI for Windows 5.0 is $779 per 6-pack, and the TCP/IP module is $1199 per 5 floating licenses. The NetWare option is $499, for up to 500 users. NDIS Support is $199.

Banyan VINES for SCO UNIX 1.0

VINES, as you might imagine from the name, entwines computers (PCs) in a network. Banyan preaches the 'enterprise network' philosophy, which takes a more global view of networking than Local Area Networks. VINES networks offer advantages to large networks, including single login to the entire host of hosts, upward expansion or network scalability, and a distributed directory service (Street-Talk).

Banyan's initial path to UNIX trails through the doors of SCO. VINES for SCO UNIX installs on a UNIX server outfitted with either SCO UNIX V/386 Release 3.2 Version 4.x or SCO Open Desktop Release 2.x. The product's primary purpose is to let PCs wrap tendrils around UNIX resources, but it provides no similar advantage to snare PC resources for UNIX users. Once an SCO computer is ensnared as a VINES for UNIX server, other UNIX resources can be passed through it to the VINES enterprise network, including printers and NFS-mounted drives.

Ease of Installation

We did not install this product, but the documentation provides an excellent layout of the product. To install VINES for SCO UNIX with all options, you should have at least 30M of disk space. Of course, SCO UNIX requires another 40M, or ODT up to 90M. You also need at least 12M of memory, and a LAN adapter card that is supported by SCO. Install SCO software first, then use SCO's **custom** program to install VINES for UNIX base and optional software. Once you get it installed, initialize VINES with the **vinesadmsh** program first, then specific services through the Manage Services menu. Relink the kernel to support communications drivers. After full initialization of the server, create user PC boot diskettes in the usual VINES manner. Manage the network with **vinesadmsh**, and control network access (set up users, groups, and rights) with MUSER, MGROUP and SETARL.

Certain modules are not part of the base product and must be purchased separately. Unfortunately, these are the real goodies. The main 'option' is File Services, which lets users share files on the UNIX server. Other modules include Asynchronous Terminal Emulation, to allow VINES users to login to SCO as UNIX users. Another is the Print Service, which PC users may desperately want if the only PostScript printer is on the UNIX network. Other modules include the Network Mail Service, Remote Network Management, and Server-to-Server IP which encapsulates VINES packets in IP format for transmission over the Internet. The base product includes the StreetTalk global directory, NetBIOS support, security, and fundamental services.

Ease of Use

VINES services run as VINES-only applications on the UNIX machine. For file sharing, VINES clients have access both to the usual Banyan File Service protected areas defined on the UNIX machine and to new UNIX Connectivity File Service areas that are accessible to UNIX users as well. However, UNIX users cannot login as VINES clients and cannot run DOS programs in the UCFS.

VINES clients can print to any printers on the network, including those attached to non-VINES UNIX workstations. Unless intentionally restricted, UNIX users can conversely print to any of the VINES network printers, except that workstations cannot access printers attached to PC VINES 5.0 servers. VINES for UNIX makes use of the UNIX lp daemon.

DOS users (VINES clients) can run character-based programs on the SCO side through the terminal emulation module. However, only direct connection is supported; dial-up connections require third-party products. If you have installed the Remote Network Management option, your VINES on UNIX machine can provide limited information about itself to non-UNIX VINES servers.

Using the electronic mail option, you can send mail across the network between VINES clients. But you can only send mail to a non-Vines mail system (such as SMTP) if you program a gateway between the two. Banyan provides API tools to software developers for this purpose, but look for an existing gateway product first.

As with discount airline tickets, "some restrictions apply." WAN connectivity is missing, and remote dial-in is not available. Although diskless workstations can boot from regular VINES servers through Remote Program Load, they cannot boot from VINES for UNIX servers. DOS PCs must run DOS 3.1 or greater. IBM shops cannot run OS/2 Version 2.0 or use the Extended Attributes. Macintosh users are hurt the worst—they cannot access a VINES for UNIX server at all.

Summary

The SCO platform makes a good choice for initiating UNIX connectivity. NFS links SCO to any other UNIX computer. Banyan's network database access performance on SCO PCs (versus similar applications on NetWare PCs) is attractive to many DOS shops. The price of VINES for UNIX per SCO server varies between $3995, which includes the base utilities and StreetTalk, to $13,960 for all options.

Invisible Software InvisibleLAN 3.4

InvisibleLAN is a NetBIOS-compatible, peer-to-peer LAN. The product includes support for TCP/IP and Windows 3.x. TCP/IP connections require the addition of a third-party TCP/IP protocol stack product, such as FTP's PC-TCP or Lanera's TCPOpen. Special features include electronic mail, remote control of network nodes, and UPS monitoring. InvisibleLAN is priced at $449 for a two-user network, with hardware.

InvisibleLAN has also developed the ULTRA Server 3.3, a $399 software package which turns a PC into a dedicated file server for the peer-to-peer network. Invisible claims benchmarks that show ULTRA Server is faster than a NetWare 3.11 server for a small number of users. ULTRA targets smaller operations that need the performance of a dedicated file server without the added functionality of NetWare.

Microsoft LAN Manager for SCO Systems 2.2

While LAN Manager does not have a large market of the PC LAN business, it does have its adherents. One reason is the availability of LAN Manager on UNIX servers. SCO markets and supports LAN Manager for UNIX 2.2. This product is a full fledged version of LAN Manager and does not require any additional purchases. It does requires SCO Open Server Network System or Enterprise System as the base operating system. It includes complete DOS clients and OS/2 clients.

Installing LAN Manager for UNIX proved to be much easier than setting up an OS/2 server, but part of the reason was that we already had the SCO system running. LAN Manager uses the SCO **custom** utility and loads all the files from disks. The only major installation or configuration requirement is to determine whether to use TCP/IP or NetBEUI. Either choice requires you to use **netconfig** and set up a chain. There are excellent instructions.

LAN Manager for UNIX operates exactly like the OS/2 version in regard to client support. You would purchase this product if you are already using LAN Manager and SCO in your shop.

LAN Manager for UNIX 2.2 does a number of things for internetworking. First, it is similar to Puzzle Systems's SoftNet Utilities in that it allows a UNIX host to act as a DOS LAN server, in this case LAN Manager, rather than NetWare. Second, it can act as a connection to other LAN Manager servers. A DOS client registered on the UNIX server could access other servers with the appropriate **NET USE** commands. Third, LAN Manager for UNIX allows DOS clients and UNIX clients to share DOS executables and data files. A program such as Lotus 1-2-3 could reside on the SCO machine and would be accessible to both the LAN Manager clients and to UNIX clients running DOS Merge. See the discussion of SCO Open Server later in this chapter, and see Chapter 17 for more information on Locus Computing's DOS Merge.

At present, there is no LAN Manager client support within LAN Manager server. This means that UNIX clients cannot access other OS/2-based LAN Manager servers. The lack of driver support in the older LAN Manager client is the problem. In fact, if you plan to load LAN Manager for UNIX, you must remove any LAN Manager client software before installation.

LAN Manager for UNIX might be a better deal than purchasing LAN Manager directly from Microsoft. The UNIX operating system is a better platform than OS/2 in our opinion, particularly since Microsoft is not supporting OS/2 in the long run. The advent of Windows NT Advanced Server, which is Windows NT with LAN Manager, is another reason to consider LAN Manager for UNIX as a product to bridge the gap. It makes the most sense if you already are using either SCO or LAN Manager in your business, but also can be considered in a new installation.

Microsoft Windows for Workgroups 3.1

Windows for Workgroups (WFW) is an expansion of Windows 3.1, adding peer-to-peer networking. An add-on TCP/IP stack is available to support third-party applications. The TCP/IP stack is WinSock-compatible, so it can be used by WinSock-aware applications.

Ease of Installation

If you install Microsoft Windows for Workgroups for use in a NetWare environment, you use NDIS, not ODI, drivers. The SETUP program will install NDIS drivers for you and remark-out or remove the ODI driver lines. The MS$IPX section of PROTO-COL.INI contains a *MediaType* field that initially indicates *Novell/Ethernet*, the Novell frame type. If you use the Ethernet_II frame type, you must change this field so that you can find your Novell server. Enter the Windows **Control Panel/Network** program. Select **Network Settings/Adapters/Setup/Protocols**. Select *Novell IPX* and click on **Settings**. Change the **Media Type** to *Ethernet_II (DIX)*.

Make sure your **LASTDRIVE** command in **CONFIG.SYS** is set to a high enough letter to support mounting workgroup drives. You may have to change your NetWare login script and/or **AUTOEXEC.BAT** to accommodate **LASTDRIVE**.

Windows for Workgroups has no native NFS capability or TCP/IP utilities. For that you must go to third-party software, as before. If you load Windows for Workgroups on a machine that currently uses an NDIS adapter driver for a TCP/IP (and NFS) network product, you may have trouble getting TCP/IP to work again. Our SunSelect PC-NFS 5.0 Protocol Manager setup was commandeered by the aggressive WFW install program and changed so that it no longer loaded the drivers properly in **CONFIG.SYS**. SunSelect provides special instructions to get it working again. If you have PC-NFS 4.0, your only option is to upgrade to 5.0, which supports WFW. Other products such as NetManage ChameleonNFS and FTP Software PC-TCP have also been upgraded to new versions which support WFW.

Ease of Use

The **Control Panel/Network** utility has changed dramatically from Windows 3.1. The main difference? It allows two networks to be defined at once. Currently supported networks include Microsoft LAN Manager, Novell NetWare, and SunSelect PC-NFS 5.0. You must still switch between networks, however, by clicking on a button—only one can be loaded at a time. As shown in Figure 14.5, you can also modify your adapter settings and login information from this utility.

Sharing drives using WFW is easy, as long as all machines are in the workgroup. Just click on the drives, directories, or printers you want to share with other users, and they will see them automatically when they connect remote resources. On the other hand, UNIX drives and printers can only be mounted using the NET USE com-

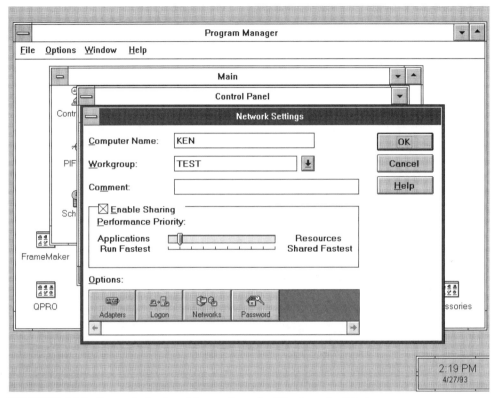

FIGURE 14.5 Expanded networking options for Windows for Workgroups

mand at a DOS prompt. (This is similar to the way LAN Manager does it.) For further details, see the Microsoft Windows NT evaluation below.

Summary

We found Windows for Workgroups easy to install and use. The product focuses on making network connections easy, and it largely accomplishes that task, although it requires involvement with the NetBIOS/NetBEUI protocol. If you are networking Novell PCs with UNIX already, adding a third protocol may be out of the range of sanity, although you can do it. This is a logical first step to Windows NT, since WFW creates Windows clients in a peer-to-peer arrangement. A Windows NT machine can function on the network as either a client or server. You can get a WFW upgrade for Windows 3.1 for $99.95, or add Windows 3.1 for $150 more.

Not having an integrated NFS client is a serious deficiency of the new Windows products, Windows for Workgroups and Windows NT. Another is the absence of TCP/IP utilities in WFW.

WFW is clearly a DOS peer-to-peer networking solution. If you don't need Net-BIOS networking for the sake of an application, but need UNIX connections, you would be better served to get a TCP/IP for Windows product from another vendor. You can network your PCs as peers using NFS instead of NetBIOS, if the product provides NFS server daemons for PCs.

Microsoft Windows NT 3.1

Microsoft has high hopes for its new operating system—intending that it become the platform of choice for the world's PC computing. At the very least, it is a much more powerful replacement for LAN Manager. Like UNIX, NT is a 32-bit operating system, has fault tolerance capabilities, and can run on multiprocessor Intel and RISC platforms. NT applications can access up to 2 gigabytes of RAM. The NT product contains both client and server capabilities, so it can function as a Windows for Workgroups peer, as a dedicated file server, or as a client of a RISC workstation. A related product, the NT Advanced Server, adds support for domains. NT runs Windows 32-bit applications, OS/2 applications, and POSIX-compliant applications, as well as older 16-bit DOS programs (via Insignia Solutions DOS emulation).

Microsoft doesn't want to burn any bridges that potential users might need in migrating to NT. Since Microsoft doesn't want to alienate UNIX users, a few standard TCP/IP utilities have been included, as well as a WinSock-compliant TCP/IP stack. Microsoft is hoping to establish NT as the ideal platform for application development, so there is a heavy emphasis on software development tools to help large and small organizations develop custom applications. NT supports distributed applications through Remote Procedure Calls compliant with the Distributed Computing Environment standard. DCE-compliant servers running on UNIX machines can be integrated.

Ease of Installation

Windows NT is one of the few DOS software products to be distributed on CD-ROM. If you don't have a CD-ROM on your machine, you can install it over a network, from a CD-ROM on another machine. We installed Windows NT using Windows for Workgroups 3.1, creating a peer-to-peer network on the CD-ROM machine and the target machine.

The installation procedure is very familiar to Windows 3.1 users. NT uses a Setup program similar to that for Windows 3.1—the major difference being that it takes 7-8 times as long to perform due to the volume of this operating system. There was nothing difficult about the installation. Windows for Workgroups functionality (drive sharing) was maintained in NT, so we could re-access our CD-ROM.

Driver setup under NT is different from Windows for Workgroups in a couple respects. NT sets up your LAN adapter early in the Setup process and replaces

WFW's NDIS 2.0 drivers with 3.0 drivers, which do not use **PROTMAN**. Also, instead of configuring.INI and startup scripts in the Network tool, as WFW does, NT uses a registry—a database which supervises all network protocol connections.

The TCP/IP and SNMP utilities have to be installed in a separate procedure after the main body. Login as administrator, then go to the **Control Panel/Network** utility to **Add Software**. Select the *TCP/IP Protocol* software. If you have a hosts file, you can copy it or merge its contents with NT's **HOSTS** file in the **SYSTEM32\DRIVERS\ETC** directory. (If you have a LAN Manager hosts file, import it.) Regardless, screens will be presented for capturing new IP addresses.

One option to note is the *Scope ID for Windows Networking*. Windows uses the NetBIOS protocol for networking, and affixes the scope ID to the NetBIOS name to delineate target machines for any communication. However, when a TCP/IP stack is available the NetBIOS packets can be converted to TCP (or UDP) and IP packets. A module called NBT (NetBIOS over TCP/IP) provides NetBIOS translation to IP addresses. This NetBIOS to TCP/IP interface is defined in RFC 1001 and 1002.

Ease of Use

Windows 3.1 and Windows for Workgroups 3.1 users will immediately notice that NT's organization is nearly the same, with some additional tools but no major rearrangement. The **Network** tool on the Control Panel has been redesigned from the single-network scenario of Windows 3.1 to a mix-and-match utility. You can have several network protocols defined at one time through the **Networks** button. (However, only one can be used at a time.) An additional button controls **Bindings**.

The File Manager user interface has changed a little, mostly due to the addition of buttons on a toolbar. These buttons handle drive connection, directory sharing, file sorting, and general functions for copy, delete, etc. The **Disk/Connect Network Drive** window could not find our NetWare or UNIX drives—we had hoped for something new and easy, but this is the way it's always been. Every remote drive must be a workgroup resource, *shared* by the remote machine and *connected* at the NT machine. The SMB (Server Message Block) protocol, developed in 1987 by Microsoft and Intel, dictates how the resource may be shared. Some UNIX add-on software products provide SMB servers, allowing them to participate fully in Windows networks. Without an SMB server, the NT machine must have an NFS client to share the UNIX machine's exported resources. NT does not currently provide an NFS client, but it supports third-party NFS products such as SunSelect PC-NFS. Novell supplies a protocol driver for accessing NetWare drives from NT.

The Print Manager has changed similarly to the File Manager. There is new toolbar. UNIX printers must be known to the Microsoft Windows workgroup via an SMB server or through a third-party LPR client.

The list of TCP/IP utilities includes **ftp** and an **ftpd** server, **tftp**, **telnet**, **arp**, **route**, **netstat**, **ping**, **finger**, and the remote commands **rsh**, **rexec**, and **rcp**—but no **lpr**. Amazingly, all TCP/IP utilities are DOS-based programs (an afterthought?),

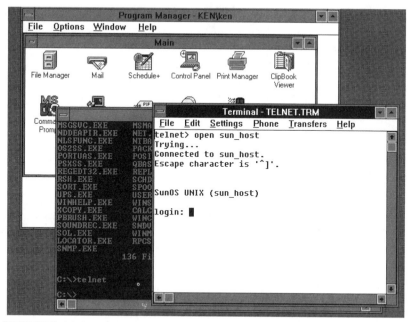

FIGURE 14.6 Logging in to the Sun from a Windows NT machine

designed to run from the MS-DOS Prompt compatibility window. This creates an additional hardship. Telnet does automatically start the Windows Terminal Emulation utility in Telnet mode—the closest thing to a Windows utility (see Figure 14.6).

Summary

Given the fact that there is little-to-no Windows orientation to the TCP/IP utilities, no UNIX printing, and no NFS client, NT is obviously weak in the area of UNIX connectivity. We wouldn't recommend NT's TCP/IP utilities for frequent use.

Microsoft has provided a TCP/IP protocol stack for use with TCP/IP- and Win-Sock-aware applications, so NT may still be just what you want. However, no one should consider the $495 Windows NT simply for its present UNIX connectivity—there are much better (and cheaper) products available for that purpose. (The $2995 NT Advanced Server additionally offers domain support.) As we said for Windows for Workgroups, if you need peer-to-peer networking with UNIX, network using NFS products instead. Will NT offer Windows-based TCP/IP utilities and an NFS client later on? Only if you (and a few hundred others) demand it.

Performance Tech. POWERfusion for Workgroups 1.3

POWERfusion is a peer-to-peer PC networking product which uses the NetBIOS protocol for communications and the Server Message Block protocol for distributed file system capability. The product uses these protocols not only to network PCs but also to access remote UNIX disks for PC client file storage, without using the slower TCP/IP and NFS. (However, UNIX users cannot access DOS disks.) POWERfusion provides VT220 and ANSI terminal emulation for connection with UNIX hosts, a file transfer utility, and remote program execution—none of which are standard UNIX utilities. UNIX and DOS users can share each other's printers. Performance Technology provides concurrent connection with Novell and Banyan networks through special NetBIOS/IPX or NetBIOS/Vines modules.

The product requires SMB server and NetBIOS programs to be installed on the DOS and UNIX machines. POWERfusion for Workgroups supports primarily the SCO and RS/6000 markets, with additional support for aging Motorola systems. It does not work with Sun SPARCstations, DECstations, or other UNIX varieties, although a SVR4 version will be available before this book is out. The DOS components are designed to be easy on RAM, consuming only 43K of DOS memory.

POWERfusion can directly connect with all PC LANs that are SMB/NetBIOS-compliant. That list includes Microsoft's Windows for Workgroups and LAN Manager, and IBM's LAN Server. However, most of their clients purchase POWERfusion to link standalone PCs with UNIX. POWERfusion can function as a boot server for diskless PCs, and can also network UNIX boxes without TCP/IP. POWERfusion's main assets are fast LAN communications, coupled with peer-to-peer disk and printer sharing, but its feature set beyond that is limited. The price of the 5-user SCO version is $750, or choose an unlimited user SCO version for $3000.

UniPress Software LAN Manager 2.2 for Sun

Right before we went to final copy, UniPress Software announced a port of LAN Manager to the Sun SPARCstation. This package is similar in concept to LAN Manager for SCO systems (see the earlier discussion). Its major use is to integrate Sun users with Microsoft Windows and, particularly, Windows NT. Windows users have full access to the disk and print services located on the Sun UNIX host. Administration of LAN Manager for Sun can be done from any workstation on the network. Due to the lateness of the release, we were unable to evaluate the product. A 48-user license is $2,995 and an unlimited user license is available for $7,995. Individual LAN Manager clients are priced at $50. In addition, UniPress Software offers LAN Manager for UNIX for AT&T UNIX, Consensys, and UnixWare.

PC LAN Resources for UNIX Clients

Beame & Whiteside BW-Server 1.0

For those sites with PC resources to spare, BW-Server provides UNIX users with the means to use them. BW-Server converts a PC into a full-fledged NFS host. UNIX users can access inexpensive and ubiquitous PC drives and peripherals such as printers, CD-ROM, etc. The BW-Server PC can operate either in a dedicated mode, or provide NFS services in the background while allowing use of DOS and Windows in the foreground. Also, the BW-Server can provide Unix users with easy access to Net-Ware drives without reconfiguring the NetWare server. Remote users can browse the BW-Server for available resources. Released in September, 1993, the BW-Server (including TCP/IP kernel) lists for $245.

Beame & Whiteside MultiConnect Client for Solaris 1.0

Beame & Whiteside plans to release the MultiConnect Client in the first quarter of 1994, simultaneously with MultiConnect Server for Solaris. MultiConnect Client for Solaris installs on a Sun, allowing a Sun user to mount NetWare volumes as UNIX file systems. The product supports UNIX file permission and user id/group id mapping. As a bonus, a Sun user can also print to NetWare printers using either the UNIX **lp** system or NetWare's **NPRINT**.

Novell NetWare NFS 1.2

NetWare NFS makes a NetWare 3.11 server look familiar to UNIX clients, letting them use NetWare drives the same as any NFS-mounted UNIX filesystem. Both UNIX and NetWare clients gain the use of each other's print servers. X terminals can be used as NetWare management consoles.

Ease of Installation

Before you install NetWare NFS, you need to make sure your 3.11 file server understands the Ethernet_II frame type used by TCP/IP networks. If your server presently uses Ethernet_802.3 (the default for pre-4.0 NetWare), you have a choice of how to alter this: either reconfigure the server and each NetWare client machine to use the new frame type, or bind the IP and IPX protocols to two different adapter definitions. The second method is the easiest, since it requires only modifications to the server's **AUTOEXEC.NCF** file. If you choose the first method, you must both reset the frame type in **AUTOEXEC.NCF** and run a configuration utility (**ECONFIG**) at each node. There are perils to configuring the nodes: if any node uses a third-party IPX shell that is not programmable, you have to obtain a new shell from the vendor.

Installing the software is trivial; configuring it takes time—you must enter data on the UNIX users and user IDs, network hosts, and printers that will inter-relate with this new server. Printing out your primary UNIX host's **/etc/passwd**, **/etc/hosts**, and **/etc/printcap** files (or NIS maps) ahead of time is good advice. You must issue commands to install the NFS name space on this server. You can perform all other configuration through a NetWare-style utility.

Export the NetWare filesystems of your choice, except for the main system directories sys/login, sys/public, etc. You can place ownership and permissions on the filesystems just as you would UNIX filesystems. Then, select a NetWare print queue and the LPD server to service the UNIX users, add print filters, trusted hosts, etc., and create an **/etc/printcap** entry for the NetWare queue. For the sake of your NetWare clients you can also define a print queue and server to use a UNIX printer through the LPR Gateway feature. The necessary commands to start the new services are automatically inserted into the server's startup scripts, so all you need to do is reboot.

Once the server is back up, you should be able to **ping** it from another UNIX host. If it does not respond, run **CONFIG** at the server console to see if the IP protocol is listed as available, and check its IP address and subnet mask. If it is not listed at all, check the **AUTOEXEC.NCF** file line which binds IP to the network adapter—it should follow a line which loads TCP/IP. In our case, the binding defaulted to an NE2000 adapter, which was not the adapter we had.

Ease of Use

Once installed, the NetWare file server's exported drives can be mounted and used by remote hosts just as any NFS drive. There is no separate login to the NetWare server. Remember to use the correct mounting syntax; e.g., **mount -o soft novell_server:/volname/directory /mountpoint**. There is a difference from UNIX drives, however—NetWare servers have automatic caching for disk I/O, an optimization which accelerates throughput and response time beyond that for a typical NFS-mounted drive. UNIX workstations can be set up to do the same caching and attain similar performance, but this takes some extra effort under UNIX.

You can give both NetWare and UNIX clients access to the same files for the sake of sharing complex documents, spreadsheets, databases and CAD/CAM files. For example, we composed a TCP/IP products spreadsheet using Microsoft Excel for Windows, saved it in text format, and imported it into Chapter 13 (a FrameMaker document) on the Sun, just by plucking it from the common directory.

Printing from UNIX to NetWare or from NetWare to UNIX alike are configured totally on the NetWare side, except for an entry in **/etc/printcap**, outlined in the documentation. This makes printing easy to maintain, if you understand the NetWare print maze. If your UNIX machine does not support the LPR protocol, you must pass the print job via **rsh** to a machine that does.

An **ftp** server runs on the file server, primarily for allowing remote administration from an X terminal. A special version of **RCONSOLE**, called **XCONSOLE**, is supplied with NetWare NFS.

Summary

At $4995, NetWare NFS is much more expensive than buying another disk drive, if all you want is more disk storage. There are side benefits, however, which may boost its value in your particular scenario—notably, increased performance, the ability of NetWare and UNIX clients to share the same data files, and other things such as the means to perform UNIX user accounting. Bringing all network printers into play for all users is also worth good money. Remember that NetWare NFS still runs on a dedicated PC, so don't expect to gain a workstation out of the deal. NetWare NFS is a unique product, designed to appeal to NetWare-centric system administrators, but its particular strengths should be compared to those of alternative products. If all you need is file transfer, but not NFS networking (such as for point of sale), try the $995 NetWare Flex/IP 1.2, a product with a subset of the NetWare NFS features.

Puzzle Systems SoftNet Client 1.0

SoftNet Client enables a UNIX box to mount Novell filesystems and store UNIX files there with permissions and attributes retained. It also supports UNIX printing on NetWare printers.

Ease of Installation

Installing the SoftNet Client is as simple as can be—just **tar** the files off of the disk and set a serial number. Use **slist** to display a list of NetWare servers. Then, mount a server's NetWare drive on your chosen mount point. You must specify a NetWare user name and password with the mount command for login, or you can use a utility to preset this information into a data file. There is no kernel reconfiguration or disk partitioning required, and no export process for the NetWare filesystems.

To set up the print facility, run another utility to funnel all print jobs through a specific NetWare user account. On the NetWare side, you may need to run **SYSCON** to prepare any more user accounts.

Ease of Use

Storing new files or accessing existing files is as easy to do as it is from any NetWare PC, with no difference. If you use the same user account to login from a PC or a Soft-Net Client, you have all the same permissions.

UNIX SoftNet Clients can print jobs on NetWare printers using the usual **lpr** command. Specify the NetWare print queue name as the *-P* printer.

Puzzle supplies an unmount command which you can use to disengage from NetWare. The command logs off of NetWare, unmounts the filesystem, and terminates the client daemon. However, it will not execute if the filesystem is in use by a UNIX user.

Our copy of version 1.0 had a few flaws that Puzzle Systems is aware of. By the time you get this book we would hope SoftNet Client has everything ironed out.

Summary

This may be a brand new product, with a few bugs, but it shows the expertise and good sense of the Puzzle programmers. As with other Puzzle products, SoftNet Client attains a level of simplicity, while providing functionality, that is unrivaled. There just isn't that much do to make it work with your NetWare network. SoftNet Client lists for $395 per single user, or $1495 for a 5-user license.

Bi-Directional Networking

DEC PATHWORKS

Just as with all software, PATHWORKS is in transition. However, Digital would not let us evaluate the product, because they believe there are too many major changes being made. Here is our limited view of what PATHWORKS is and where it is going.

PATHWORKS is a cornerstone of NAS (Network Application Support), Digital's variety of an open systems standard. PATHWORKS is sought by DEC shops, because it only supports the high-end number-crunchers and UNIX workstations manufactured by DEC.

Built as a peer-to-peer, client/server network operating system, PATHWORKS can integrate UNIX, VMS, Novell NetWare, Microsoft LAN Manager, and other operating system platforms by trading DECnet, TCP/IP, and IPX packets. A PC running PATHWORKS has full rights and responsibilities as a DECnet node.

On PCs, PATHWORKS is based upon Microsoft's LAN Manager, which means that it uses Microsoft's protocols to store sharable files across the network (not NFS). The product supports NetBIOS and NetBEUI, and ties in both OS/2 and DOS/Windows PCs. The current product requires a TCP/IP option for **telnet** (VT320) and **ftp** capability. If you have NetWare, you need the NetWare Coexistence option.

You may connect to DECstations running Ultrix and PATHWORKS for Ultrix. Or, connect to your VAX server with PATHWORKS for OpenVMS. Macintosh is not left out, either. DEC's most recent offering, PATHWORKS for SCO UNIX server software, allows other PATHWORKS clients to share applications and peripherals on an SCO UNIX PC.

DEC provides two notable features with every PATHWORKS for DOS/Windows client. The first is PC DECwindows Motif, an X Window System server. With an X server you can run UNIX graphics-based programs from your PC. Components are required for the VAX or DECstation. The second feature is a license for DEC MAILworks, a full-featured electronic mail system.

The next generation, which we could not see just yet, concentrates on OSF/1 support. DEC Alpha machines running OpenVMS or OSF/1 will be the new preferred platform. All current PATHWORKS clients will be migrated to OSF/1.

Here is the price structure for existing products, showing prices for full product and license only:

> PATHWORKS for DOS client 4.1 $695/$205
> PATHWORKS for DOS TCP/IP Option $170/$100
> PATHWORKS for SCO UNIX server 1.0 $295

Ipswitch Catipult 1.2

Catipult will loft your OS/2—NetWare network into UNIX connectivity by functioning as a communications gateway between NetWare and TCP/IP. NetWare clients can access UNIX hosts via **telnet**, **ftp**, e-mail, and remote commands. On the other hand, UNIX users can also **telnet** or **ftp** to Catipult client PCs running the **telnet** or **ftp** server daemons. The price is $2975 for 30 concurrent users.

Catipult installs on a PC running OS/2 Versions 1.21 or 1.3. This structure offloads the UNIX connectivity functions from the NetWare server while providing UNIX access to NetWare clients. Catipult requires LAN adapters that support the NetWare Requester for OS/2; Ipswitch recommends NE2000, 3Com 3C503 and 3C523. It supports ODI, NDIS, and Token-Ring Communication Manager drivers for OS/2. The NetWare server requires NetBIOS support to be loaded, and also needs up to 6 megabytes of disk space for storage of the Catipult TCP/IP applications, depending upon how much you store at the gateway machine.

The installation process includes definition of a single IP address to cover all Catipult clients. However, UNIX users who wish to **telnet** or **ftp** to a particular Catipult PC running the associated server daemon can do so, because each server PC has a unique port number at the central Catipult server.

Except for **telnet** and **ftp** servers, all TCP/IP utilities are character-based DOS utilities. However, the applications can run from Windows' DOS-compatibility window. **Telnet** provides VT102 terminal emulation, or you can use third-party terminal products that support Interrupt 14. In an IBM shop you may want 3270 terminal emulation, which Catipult has. Other utilities include several for network information and diagnostics (**FINGER, COOKIE, NETSTAT**, etc.), mail (POP3 or Catipult's own), printing via LPR (to BSD UNIX computers), and a multiuser maze game.

The major drawback to Catipult is that there is no NFS—NFS is too slow over their gateway. There is no ability to mount the big UNIX drives for direct use by NetWare clients.

Version 1.3, which came out too late for our testing, has substantial improvements, including DOS printer redirection for printing from applications to network printers. It will support the new WinSock standard. Catipult will have a full-screen, graphical installation program with online help. While the TCP/IP applications remain DOS-based, a Windows front-end will iconize the applications, simplifying them for users.

Mini-Byte Software NetCon 5.1

If there is a "sleeper" in our book, it is probably NetCon. The name Mini-Byte Software is known to few people, but we talked to a couple of NetCon users, both of which really liked the product. After trying it ourselves, we think NetCon is well worth your attention.

This product functions as a NetWare client for UNIX users, a NetWare file server and UNIX terminal emulation server for NetWare users, and a UNIX peer-to-peer network—all bundled into one! NetCon is based upon a proprietary protocol called TFS, which according to Mini-Byte also increases performance by 2-8 times over the speed of TCP/IP and NFS. What more could anyone ask for?

NetCon connects DOS, OS/2, and NetWare PCs with SCO UNIX/ODT and SunOS 4.1.x servers. The SunOS version of NetCon is also marketed by Sprysoft, Inc. as Sprysoft NetWare Client for UNIX. NetCon works with NetWare 3.11, but not easily with the older 2.2. At this time it does not yet support NetWare 4.0.

Ease of Installation

All installation occurs at the UNIX servers—nothing is required for the DOS PCs. The installation instructions are very brief and simple. The process rebuilds the UNIX kernel with the ability to converse with NetWare servers using NetWare's native tongue, IPX. (IPX is a faster protocol medium, because it does not do as much packet checking.) We were not too happy with NetCon's manual, which is small, and, in some places, confusing. If you are installing NetCon on a Sun, you must power-down twice during the installation process, although the manual mistakenly says only to "reboot". Installation on SCO has several more steps than for installation on a Sun.

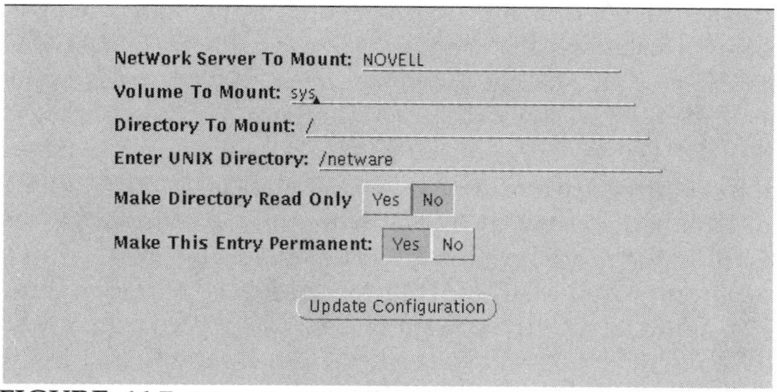

FIGURE 14.7   Mounting NetWare drives is a breeze with NetCon

The installation and configuration process is quite easy to perform, although you must wait on Mini-Byte midway through for an Activation Key. Netcon supplies a configuration utility (called **netcon**) to make life easy on the administrator. It enables you to manage file servers, mount network server drives, map users and groups between UNIX and NetWare, set up print servers and queues, and much more. We liked **netcon**'s ease of use. One of its windows is shown in Figure 14.7.

You don't have to set up all NetWare users under UNIX. Instead, you can create a generic user on the UNIX host and map it to a group of NetWare users. NetCon cannot grab a userlist from NetWare.

Ease of Use

The main rule of operation is to always bring up the NetWare file server BEFORE the NetCon server. If you don't, NetCon cannot find a NetWare server, and it marks even itself as "down". Once running, you can change servers without logging in.

From a NetWare client PC you can see the Sun and/or SCO machine as a new NetWare server (using **SLIST**). The NetWare LAN Supervisor should edit the login scripts for PC users to map the UNIX filesystems to drive letters. Then, as PC users login to NetWare they gain automatic access to these new NetWare volumes.

From the reverse side, mount a NetWare file server volume for use in storing UNIX files through the **netcon** utility (refer again to Figure 14.7). If you have a DOS emulator, you can also run DOS programs stored on the NetWare file server.

We did have some difficulty with user passwords. NetCon couldn't handle mixed-case passwords on the UNIX side, forcing us to change some of them. This will be fixed in the next release.

As if it didn't have enough great features, NetCon provides a special bonus, an SPX terminal server coupled with its ANSI terminal emulation, allowing multiple host sessions and command shells from the same console. You can have a single login session and up to three command shell windows from DOS, with HOT-KEY switching between the windows. If you use MS-Windows, you can expand the number of sessions to 6 (18 total windows), depending upon available memory. The emulation is also compliant with the ANSI extensions for the SCO Console.

Summary

We think Mini-Byte has a good product in NetCon. It gives everyone—both UNIX and DOS users—what they want without a lot of fuss. We especially liked the fact that it installs and is maintained on a single platform. We wondered about introducing a proprietary protocol (TFS) instead of TCP/IP and NFS, but you can only make the standard UNIX protocols go so fast. Overall, NetCon was one of the easier products to install and use, as well as being full-featured.

A three-user version of NetCon costs $995; an unlimited user version—$3995. You can also get a stand-alone version which networks DOS PCs with UNIX *without* a NetWare server for a slightly higher price.

Network and Communications Mgmt TCP Gateway 386

Here is a product which integrates two separately-cabled networks running Novell NetWare and TCP/IP. TCP Gateway 386 installs on a dedicated NetWare client PC running OS/2, and allows complete bi-directional communication. It requires both hardware and software components to function.

The hardware is an intelligent Ethernet controller, the NP600/XL. This board links the PC to the thin- or thick Ethernet TCP/IP network via BNC or AUI ports. To interact with the NetWare network, the PC also needs a regular Ethernet adapter. NCM recommends that this *TCP Server* be at least a 386-25 PC with 6M of RAM and a 40M hard drive. It requires OS/2 1.2 or 1.3 and the OS/2 Requester.

The software component also installs on the TCP Server and supplies the cross-communications across the two adapters. The software includes **ftp** and SMTP (mail) server daemons which route requests from UNIX users to the NetWare file server. It also routes requests from NetWare PCs to the UNIX servers—you must install NCM's TCP/IP client utilities on each NetWare workstation. The client utilities include **ftp**, **telnet**, SMTP **mail**, **rsh**, **rcp**, **netstat**, and **ping**. All of these are DOS utilities (not Windows) and can be accessed from a Novell-like menu. The **telnet** utility emulates VT220 terminals, and it supports interrupt 14 emulators as well.

NCM claims greater throughput for the TCP Gateway 386 at higher network traffic levels than for their competitors. This is due to the off-loading of TCP/IP communications to the separate microprocessor on the NP600/XL board, as well as to the ability to adjust packet size for optimum performance. The price of TCP Gateway 386 is $5995 for 64 concurrent users (the maximum), or $2495 for 8 users.

Quarterdeck DESQview/X 1.0

DESQview/X is unlike any other program we review. It is a combination X server, DOS emulator, and TCP/IP connection utility. We put our main evaluation in this chapter since you can access another PC using DESQview/X, run X, Windows and DOS programs all at the same time. However, there are discussions of DESQview/X in Chapters 15 and 17 as well.

DESQview/X is an exciting program. If you are having difficulty finding a solution to an internetworking problem, DESQview/X may be the answer. While Quarterdeck first thought DESQview/X would appeal to DOS users, it has become a major attraction to X users who want to run X programs from a PC without using MS Windows.

Ease of Installation

For DESQview/X to work across a TCP/IP network, you need to have the DESQview/X to Other X Systems Network Drivers package. This costs $200 and does not come with the standard DESQview/X. You also need a TCP/IP networking product such as Sun's PC/NFS or FTP's PC/TCP. The installation process for DESQview/X is not trivial and requires significant patience.

The biggest problem with DESQview/X is DOS memory. In order to use DESQview/X as a connection between DOS and UNIX, you have to have enough memory to run the network drivers, the TCP/IP protocol and DESQview/X. Certain TCP/IP products including Sun PC-NFS use a great deal of low memory for their drivers. When we ran DESQview/X with these drivers in low memory, there was not enough memory left for DESQview/X to make a remote connection. When we tried to load the drivers high, we ran into many problems. One of these problem is the busmastering SCSI controllers used on EISA machines. A second problem is with LAN adapter drivers. In particular, **PROTMAN.SYS** (part of an NDIS driver setup) requires a large amount of RAM and often does not load into high memory.

Quarterdeck attempts to solve installation problems by shipping a new version of QEMM with DESQview/X. It allows the QEMM Stealth program to recover various high memory segments and install **PROTMAN.SYS** high. We were successful in using Stealth on our IBM Value Point 486 machine. We did have to change the address of the SMC network card and rearrange the loading location of some drivers. Here are a few pointers to make your life easier.

- Only use the version of QEMM provided with DESQview/X. It has been optimized for networks.

- Save copies of your **CONFIG.SYS** and **AUTOEXEC.BAT** files—multiple installs make it difficult to keep track of the various copies.

- Use the Stealth and Optimize programs to optimize memory placement.

•Move your network RAM address to be contiguous with other video RAM. This is frequently D000-D3FF, but use Quarterdeck's Manifest to determine the location.

•Use the ASPI drivers with a SCSI hard disk.

•Do not load DOS high, because it only needs about 48K of the 64K space in HMA (High Memory Access) under DOS 5.0. Instead, let DESQview/X load high, as it takes the entire 64K space, saving 16K of low memory.

•Do not use Windows **SMARTDRV.EXE** in **CONFIG.SYS**. QEMM can do the buffering work with the DB=10 parameter. You still can use **SMARTDRV.EXE** in the **AUTOEXEC.BAT** file.

•Set stacks at 0,0.

•Call Quarterdeck. The possible options number in the thousands, and Quarterdeck has done its homework. Even the most skilled PC power user may find it difficult to correctly install DESQview/X.

Ease of Use

Once successfully installed, you have many options to make use of a UNIX system. The simplest is to open a DOS window within DESQview/X on your PC. Then use Quarterdeck's version of **telnet** to make a connection. After you log in to the remote host, you can run character applications from the **telnet** window.

You can run X applications from your **telnet** window in the same fashion as you do from UNIX or from an X server. For example, when you type the following command, the xclock displays on your screen.

```
xclock -display <your machine>:0
```

DESQview/X uses its own window manager unless you configure DESQview/X to use Motif or OPEN LOOK.

DESQview/X also supports the **rsh** and **rexec** commands. These allow you to run a remote program from a command line.

We ran a variety of X applications with DESQview/X and found it to be as stable as any MS Windows X server. You can use DESQview/X's own File Manager program to copy files from your PC to various UNIX hosts. You can also configure the system with users and give them specific access rights. DESQview/X provides customizable menus. You have the option of giving the menu item a name, a command to execute, a host name, and a user name. It is simple to create the menu item—another thing altogether—to make sure it works. We found it difficult to diagnose what happened when our command did not come up.

Summary

Once past the involved installation procedure, DESQview/X, at $475 has no equal. If you have enough RAM and processing power (12 MB and 486 33MHz as a minimum in our opinion), a whole new world opens up. If you use DOS applications and need X application access, DESQview/X is possibly the best solution on the market. If your main need is Windows and X applications, a Windows-based X server makes more sense because Windows 3.1 runs more slowly under DESQview/X. As a DOS server for UNIX machines, DESQview/X makes an excellent option. However, we think the DOS server should be a dedicated machine for such purposes. DESQview/X gives you access to other PCs, NFS drives on UNIX servers, Windows applications and X applications.

SCO Open Server Enterprise System

The Santa Cruz Operation Inc. has revamped their product line to compete head-to-head with UnixWare. The long history of SCO and its penetration in the small business world give SCO a leg up on the market. When it comes to DOS—UNIX networking and internetworking, SCO provides many possibilities. We examine the SCO Open Server Enterprise System because it is the option most likely to be used in a mixed networking environment.

The Enterprise system is SCO UNIX System V Release 3.2 Version 4.2 at its core. The networking options cover about every possible base, including TCP/IP, NFS, IPX/SPX, NetBIOS, LAN Manager Client and Locus PC Interface. The basic user interface is the same as SCO Open Desktop and includes X11, X.desktop from IXI, the Motif Window Manager, and Locus DOS Merge. This level of cross-network support compares well with UnixWare.

Ease of Installation

Getting Open Server Enterprise System up and running can be done either by upgrading from any previous version of SCO Open Desktop, or by doing a completely new installation from scratch. An original installation requires 3 floppies and a CD or a tape. There is no version of SCO Open Server supplied on floppy diskettes. If you are upgrading, you can easily preserve any DOS partitions and programs or data left over from the previous version of ODT. The upgrade saves the network and mouse configuration.

The entire installation takes about 1.5 hours. It goes flawlessly, if you have done your homework. SCO provides a detailed worksheet on the various information you need to fill out in advance. This installation is nothing you jump into without preparation. You have to collect a significant amount of information about your machine. One major advantage of SCO is the large degree of support for various peripherals such as video cards, hard disks, and tape drives—more than anyone in the industry.

TCP/IP and NFS

The TCP/IP and NFS module from SCO is relatively easy to configure. You get the complete TCP/IP protocol stack, utilities, and the NFS daemons. The only real job to do for TCP/IP is to set up the proper chains through **netconfig**. You have to link the board driver to the TCP/IP protocol. NFS is less user-friendly. You must do all NFS drive mounting and exporting from the command line. Both the mount and the export commands are well documented, and you can mount a filesystem permanently. Normally, only the superuser can mount file systems but SCO does provide a method for users to mount filesystems if desired. However, UnixWare's icon-driven NFS mounting and exporting is many times easier than the command line method used by SCO.

NetBEUI

Besides TCP/IP, you get NetBIOS and NetBEUI support with SCO Open Server. The NetBIOS module supports both the newer Transport Provider Interface (TPI) and the older DO_NCB. This makes Open Server compatible with all versions of LAN Manager. NetBIOS runs over TCP/IP. You normally only need NetBIOS if you are using either the LAN Manager client or running LAN Manager 2.2.

PC-Interface

The Open Server Enterprise System supplies a Locus Computing PC-Interface server that installs automatically. While you can purchase the SCO server from Locus directly, getting it pre-installed is a great way to save time and money. PC-Interface is discussed earlier in the chapter. In general, a UNIX machine equipped with PC-Interface can run DOS applications stored on the UNIX host, use UNIX host resources such as printers, and run UNIX character-based applications through a terminal emulator. PC-Interface supports serial, TCP/IP and IPX/SPX connections.

IPX/SPX

SCO IPX/SPX provides Novell NetWare users access to the SCO UNIX host and its files, enabling them to run SCO UNIX applications in character mode. Unless you purchase the one X server that supports X applications over IPX/SPX (Hummingbird's eXceed/W), you are limited to character applications. No TCP/IP or serial connections are necessary. Including the IPX/SPX product in SCO Open Server provides better Novell connectivity, but nothing that challenges UnixWare. The major advantage is speed. It does not allow SCO clients to access any NetWare servers, nor does it allow the SCO UNIX machine to act as a NetWare server.

If you happen to purchase SCO IPX/SPX as an upgrade to SCO Open Desktop, some installation will be required. With Open Server, IPX/SPX comes ready to go.

The IPX/SPX module installs through **custom**. The entire process requires about 1 hour. You need to know what type of Ethernet frame type you are using on the Novell network—Ethernet 802.3 or Ethernet II. You must also reinstall some of your original links in **netconfig** if you had TCP/IP, NFS or Lan Manager installed.

There is a DOS component, Novell Virtual Terminal (NVT), to SCO IPX/SPX. While not a true dual stack, NVT resides as a TSR and must be loaded after **IPX** or **IPXODI** is loaded in your **AUTOEXEC.BAT** file. It consumes 38K of memory. However, you still need a terminal emulator program that supports INT 14 or INT 6 such as Futuresoft's DynaComm. You can also create applications that use SCO IPX/SPX and interact directly with the NetWare client, but it requires programming.

LAN Manager Client

You also get a LAN Manager client with Open Server. Ostensibly, this gives you the option of logging into a LAN Manager server and accessing the applications residing on the server. However, there are two fundamental problems with this approach. First, it is unusual to go from the UNIX host to a LAN Manager server for file support. Second, the LAN Manager client provided with SCO Open Server is version 1.1. It does not work well with newer 2.2 servers because 1.1 did not support validation. So when you try to log into the LAN Manager server with a 1.1 client, you have to alter the procedure. SCO is still considering plans for a 2.2 client.

Nonetheless, you can use the older client to access a LAN Manager server. You have to either login as *guest* or setup a special account on the LAN Manager server to allow you to get in without any validation. The best reason for accessing the LAN Manager server is to let UNIX clients share data with other LAN Manager clients. For example, Lotus spreadsheets and Microsoft Word documents can be shared across the platforms in this environment.

DOS/Windows Compatibility

SCO uses Locus Computing's Merge product as UnixWare does. SCO supports the latest release and it gives you Windows 3.1 access. A DOS icon is automatically inserted on the desktop at boot time. You can find more details in Chapter 17 on DOS Emulators. The **C:** is the root subdirectory while **E:** is the DOS partition (if one exists). The DOS emulation appears to be slower than when running under UnixWare, but in this case we were running without a lot of extra RAM. There is no separate Windows 3.1 icon like that supplied by UnixWare.

Summary

SCO has a strong following among small businesses. SCO intends its Open Server product line to extend beyond the traditional core users. The Open Server Enterprise System is an excellent platform for UNIX applications and has a variety of connectivity options. SCO platforms can serve as hosts to Banyan VINES or Microsoft LAN Manager. TCP/IP and NFS are well-supported. We like SCO in a mixed PC environment that involves anything but Novell. Even then, products such as Mini-Byte's NetCon give SCO excellent Novell connections. SCO is a well-tested and stable environment with thousands of available applications. Open Server Enterprise System sells for $2,195 for 16 users and only $3,195 for up to 512 users.

Spry NetWare Client for UNIX 5.0

Spry selected a poor name for this product, in our opinion. This product is not only a NetWare Client for UNIX users, but also a NetWare Server, a UNIX terminal emulation server for NetWare users, and a UNIX peer-to-peer network. The product installs on Sun systems only. NetWare Client for UNIX is the same product as Net-Con (SunOS version), developed by Mini-Byte Software, Inc. (see earlier evaluation). NetWare Client for UNIX lists for $995.

Novell UnixWare 1.0

UnixWare blends the best of DOS, Novell NetWare, and UNIX. The core product is UNIX Systems Laboratories (USL) UNIX System V Release 4.2. UnixWare was initially developed and released by Univel, a joint partnership of USL and Novell. However, in mid-1993 Novell bought USL and the Univel name was dropped.

From our point of view, UnixWare does two things. First, it enables you to run either DOS, Windows or UNIX applications without modification and without terminal emulation. Secondly, it seamlessly integrates Novell NetWare, giving you full access to NetWare services over IPX/SPX, in addition to support for TCP/IP. We concentrate our review on the aspect of cross-platform interoperability.

Ease of Installation

UnixWare comes in two configurations. The Personal Edition is designed as a UNIX workstation for users who need both UNIX applications and access to the Novell server. The Application Server brings full TCP/IP support, multiuser licenses, and a complete UNIX utility package into the picture. The Application Server handles application installation, application and printer sharing, and network administration. Typically, the Application Server is a development platform and file server for other clients. The Personal Edition (P.E.) can be either stand-alone or networked to a Novell Server. You have to purchase the TCP/IP option if you want to connect the P.E. to another UNIX box (although this will become standard in the next version). UnixWare comes either on CD-ROM or tape. Installation is simple, as long as you have compatible hardware. As a new operating system, UnixWare does not have as much driver support available for the vast array of PC hardware options as SCO.

Installation requires you to make some decisions about your network card and mouse but otherwise is uneventful. After installation, we explored the UnixWare GUI desktop and found that our NetWare servers were available for login—RIGHT OUT OF THE BOX! No other operating system provides this degree of internetworking so easily.

TCP/IP and NFS

TCP/IP and NFS software must be loaded as a separate module. This process is easily done from the Application Setup desktop icon. Until you load TCP/IP & NFS, you do not have access to remote UNIX hosts, drives, and printers. (You always have access to NetWare LAN peripherals.) This installation adds two new setup icons for Internet Setup and File Sharing. Internet Setup establishes your local machine address and creates a list of remote hosts. Once you create an entry for your primary remote UNIX host, UnixWare grabs the remote host's **/etc/hosts** file and provides your system with a list of all available hosts.

NFS setup is trickier. You use the File Sharing icon to do this configuration. Enter the name of the remote host, then let UnixWare browse that host for exported filesystems. Next, select the filesystem and enter a folder name to serve as its mount point. You should not drag shared-file folders into other folders once they have been placed.

DOS and NetWare

We tested DOS and NetWare compatibility in a number of different ways. We reviewed a Beta version of the new Locus Computing's Advanced Merge for Windows module. This module is the standard distribution of both UnixWare offerings. See more about how Locus's Merge product works in Chapter 17 on DOS Emulators. UnixWare provides a partial copy DR DOS 6.0 (another Novell product), but lets you decide if you want a full version of DR DOS or MS-DOS. You must have a user account on the Novell server to login, but otherwise startup configuration is minimal. You can make NetWare servers available for login through the NetWare setup icon.

UnixWare places a default **COMMAND.COM**, **AUTOEXEC.BAT** and **CON-FIG.SYS** in the root directory (**C:**), right next to **.login**, **.profile** and **UNIX**. When you fire up the DOS application window, these files load **EMM386**, a mouse driver, **IPXTLI** and **NETX** to attach to NetWare disks. The default **AUTOEXEC.BAT** does not do a NetWare login, nor does it set up your paths and environment variables. However, each user can place new startup files in the **C:\HOME\(username)**, also known as **D:**, directory to override the default startup files. You complete the installation by loading the UnixWare NLM on the Novell fileserver.

Ease of Use

UnixWare supports the X Windows System, and the Moolit toolkit provides you with either the Motif or OPEN LOOK GUI. The desktop itself is the standard SVR4 desktop, and we found the icons, drag and drop operations, and menus to be quite usable. Users can run a character- or X-based UNIX application either by selecting an icon and running the product from the GUI or running it from an xterm.

Using NetWare servers from UnixWare is probably the simplest networking action we experienced of any product we tested for this book. If you choose to use the GUI, you click on the NetWare icon and UnixWare asks you to authenticate your username and password for access to the NetWare server (this is your username on the NetWare server, not on UnixWare). It then presents you with a folder showing all available NetWare servers. As you select icons, you can move to a particular application and select it. A DOS emulation window is opened by UnixWare and an **AUTOEXEC.BAT** file runs, attaching you to the server. Then you must login. If you only want to copy or link a file, these actions can be done directly from the desktop through drag and drop operations. The Advanced Merge for Windows module also provides Windows 3.1 support in standard mode. Figure 14.9 shows UnixWare's window to the NetWare server.

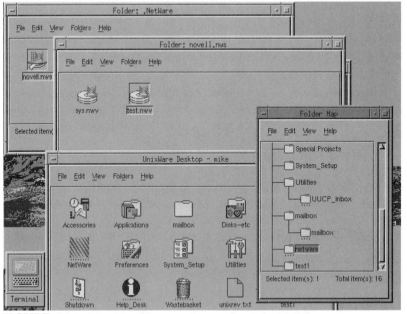

FIGURE 14.8   UnixWare shows volumes about the NetWare server

Both PE and AS have access to NetWare services from the NetWare fileserver. These services include file sharing, printer services, and MHS mail. In fact, nearly every NetWare service or NLM (NetWare Loadable Module) is accessible from Unix-Ware. Printers can be set up from an icon-based setup menu, and you can send print jobs to any printer connected to the Novell network. To print a file, simply drop it onto the printer icon.

UnixWare uses icons for connections to other UNIX systems. For example, if you create an icon called RS6000 through the Internet Setup menu, when you select the icon, UnixWare uses **rlogin** to open up an xterm window on that remote host. You must have a **.rhosts** file on the remote host with your system name and user name.

UnixWare includes a copy of NVT. Using NVT, NetWare PCs can login to the Application Server and run character-based UNIX programs. However, those PCs still need a third-party terminal emulator with support for interrupt 6b or 14. See Chapter 16 for products that support these interrupts. You cannot store DOS applications on the UnixWare platform for access by PC clients.

Troubleshooting documentation for the desktop environment is weak. There is no troubleshooting in the User Handbook. The rest of the manuals (more than 10 of them for the Application Server) give background for the administrator, but not for the desktop. They are poorly cross-referenced.

Novell/Univel was anxious to get the first release out, and some bugs were missed in the early release. Remote printing was particularly difficult to get going. Logging into the NetWare file server can take a long time because of a problem Unix-Ware has with arbitrating the NetWare requests across the network. A workaround is to move the **LOGIN.EXE** program to your UnixWare **D:** directory. Then when you access DOS programs, make sure you are in the program's directory rather than relying on the **PATH** environment variable.

Summary

Notwithstanding the above weaknesses, we found UnixWare to be a well-organized product, and heading in the right direction. You get DOS and Windows support through Locus Merge, and you have access to all of the NetWare services on the network. Having Novell's marketing muscle behind the product certainly gives Unix-Ware a strong chance for success. Overall, UnixWare is much more than just an enhancement to a NetWare LAN. No other product provides the degree of integration between NetWare LANs and UNIX systems. It is also a relatively inexpensive solution—list price for the Personal Edition is $249, the Application Server is $1299 for unlimited users, and the TCP/IP and NFS option is $295.

Recommendations

The wide range of products in this chapter obviously serves several niches. What looks beautiful to the beholder depends upon the specific requirements at the site.

However, we thought some of the products exhibited a better price/performance ratio overall.

UnixWare is hard to beat for close integration between UNIX and NetWare. Windows NT doesn't pack much punch for UNIX connectivity, but then, they would like to replace UNIX. We think Puzzle's SoftNet Utilities are a simple but potent solution for anyone who needs an extra Novell server. Their NetWare client is just as easy. Artisoft is a capable company and should be considered for new installations. They seem to be effectively pushing the peer-to-peer solution in numbers of nodes, ease of use, and now, connectivity with NetWare and UNIX. Mini-Byte's NetCon has the best bi-directional connectivity between UNIX and DOS/Novell of any non-operating system product. DESQview/X makes a great solution for any site that needs internetworking flexibility, providing a wide range of connectivity options.

Table 14.1: **PC LAN to UNIX Internetworking Products**

Product	Host Platform	NFS Support	TCP/IP Utilities	NetWare Support	NetBIOS Support	Windows Utilities
Artisoft LANtastic for TCP/IP 5.0	DOS PC	Client	Yes	Client Option	Yes	Yes
Banyan VINES for SCO UNIX 1.0	SCO UNIX PC	Server/Client	N/A	No	Yes	No
Beame & White-side BW-Server 1.0	DOS PC	Yes	No	Yes	No	No
Beame & White-side MultiConnect Server for Solaris 1.0	Sun w/Solaris	No	No	Server	No	No
Beame & White-side MultiConnect Client for Solaris 1.0	Sun w/Solaris	No	No	Client	No	No
DEC PATHWORKS	UNIX & DOS	Yes	Yes	Client	Yes	Yes
Firefox NOVIX 1.0	NetWare Server PC	No	Yes	Yes	No	No
Invisible Software InvisibleLAN 3.4	DOS PC	Third-party	Third-party	No	Yes	Yes
Ipswitch Catipult 1.2	OS/2 Server	No	Yes	IPX/SPX only	Yes	No
Microsoft LAN Manager for SCO Systems 2.2	OS/2 Server	Client	No	No	Yes	No
Microsoft Windows for Workgroups 3.1	DOS PC	No	Available	Support	Yes	Yes
Microsoft Windows NT 3.1	PC	No	Yes	Support	Yes	Yes
Mini-Byte NetCon 5.1	SCO PC or Sun	No - TFS	No	Server/Client	Yes	No
NCM TCP Gateway 386	OS/2 Net-Ware PC	No	Yes	Client	Yes	No
Novell LAN Work-Group 4.1	NetWare Server PC	Client	Yes	Yes	No	No

Table 14.1: PC LAN to UNIX Internetworking Products

Product	Host Platform	NFS Support	TCP/IP Utilities	NetWare Support	NetBIOS Support	Windows Utilities
Novell NetWare NFS 1.2	NetWare Server PC	Server	Yes	Yes	No	No
Novell NetWare NFS Gateway 1.1	NetWare Server PC	Client	No	Yes	No	No
Novell UnixWare 1.0	PC	Server/Client	Yes	Client	No	No
Performance Technology POWERfusion 1.3	DOS PC	No - SMB	No	Yes	Yes	No
Puzzle SoftNet Utilities 1.07	Sun	No	No	Server	No	No
Puzzle SoftNet Client 1.0	Sun	No	No	Client	No	No
Quarterdeck DESQview/X 1.0	DOS PC	No	Some	IPX/SPX	Yes	No
SCO Open Server Enterprise System	SCO UNIX PC	Yes	Server/Client	IPX/SPX only	Yes	No
Spry NetWare Client for UNIX 5.0	Sun	TFS	No	Server/Client	Yes	No
SunSelect NetWare SunLink 1.0	Sun	No	No	Server	No	Yes
UniPress LAN Manager for Sun 1.0	Sun	Client	Yes	No	Yes	No

15

X Servers

Introduction

In Chapter 8, we looked at how to install, configure, and use an X server in a variety of scenarios. In this chapter we review the leading X servers—using market research information from the X Business Group (Fremont, Calif.) to make that determination. We also restricted our testing to the Microsoft Windows-based X servers discussed in Chapter 8. Many additional servers, however, are given brief coverage at the end of this chapter.

X servers differ from the average application. For the most part, you do not interact with the X server itself, but with an application on the UNIX host. The role of the X server is to provide a convenient conduit to the X applications. For that reason, we evaluate an X server with a different set of criteria than we used with other productivity applications.

Evaluation Criteria

We tested X servers in three categories: ease of installation, configuration options, and ease of use. System administrators will most likely scrutinize the configuration options, while ease of use is on the top of the list for end users. Ease of installation, on the other hand, should interest everyone.

Ease of Installation

In our installation evaluation, we consider how well the product installs, how well it handles the different available networks, what installation options are available, the quality of installation instructions and documents, and how well it handles errors. We look for X server flexibility in the areas of installing multiple fonts and handling more than one protocol. Although all of us prefer thinking of installation as a one-time event, the fact remains that networks shift, and PCs must be altered or reinstalled. Installation also includes the process of getting the X server to be initially recognized by the network—including any drivers or other run-time utilities. Since getting an X server up and running is such a big job, it must be easy to install.

Configuration Options

Each X server uses a control panel or dialog box to provide configuration options. These options represent your points of interaction with X server operations. Typical options include window configuration, font management, and communication options. We evaluate how easy it is to use the configuration options, how many options the product has, and how well they integrate with the product.

Ease of Use and Compatibility

With regard to the ease-of-use category, we feature X servers that create icons for easy login, support **xdm**, are compatible with various X applications, and provide adequate documentation. In a day-to-day work environment, this category represents regular interaction between the user and the X server. We are particularly concerned with how well the X server lets you place icons on the screen and with how well it mimics Windows applications during X client operation and start-up.

With regard to compatibility, we comment on how well the X server works with a variety of X applications. In some cases, we found applications that X servers did not handle correctly. We looked for consistency and reasonable response time. By nature, UNIX workstations are more powerful than the average PC. Trying to run high octane applications on a PC X server can provide some real performance disappointments. Keeping that in mind, we looked for telltale signs of sluggish response time.

AGE Logic XoftWare/32 for Windows 2.0

XoftWare/32 for Windows is produced by AGE Logic Inc. Relatively new compared with Hummingbird's and VisionWare's products, XoftWare/32 represents an upgrade from XoftWare for Windows and is the first 32-bit Windows X server. AGE supplies the X server component for both JSB Limited's JSB MultiView/X and Walker, Richer, & Quinn's Reflection X. We mention both of these later in the chapter. XoftWare is available for a number of platforms—Windows NT, SCO UNIX, and DOS. We discuss the other members of the family at the end of the chapter. At the end of 1993 AGE will ship a new version of Xoftware/32 for Windows.

Ease of Installation

AGE uses a Windows-driven, configurable installation. You need over 10.5 megabytes of disk space to install the server, all the many fonts, and the tutorial. It took us over 30 minutes to install. Xoftware/32 automatically changes your **AUTOEXEC.-BAT**, **SYSTEM.INI** and **VSI.INI** file, but it also creates a backup and lets you change these files manually if you prefer. Like other X servers, it follows the same pattern of using TSRs for some networks and Windows DLLs for others. The latest upgrade supports the WinSock API for all networks as they become available from the network vendors. You can use the **WINSTART.BAT** option in some networks to reduce the amount of low DOS memory consumed by the X server TSR.

At installation time, you select the network communication protocol from a list and choose whether to load the 75dpi fonts, the 100 dpi fonts, or both sets. You can also select your own program group in Windows. This avoids adding an unneeded program group that you later have to delete. Xoftware lets you only select a single network type during the installation.

Xoftware/32 supports 11 different networks including all the popular ones. Xoftware/32 can be purchased with a copy of Novell LAN WorkPlace for DOS, the TCP/IP connection product from Novell (see Chapter 13). While this adds additional cost ($100) to the product, it makes it easier to get up and running on your TCP/IP network. The user's guide provides installation instructions, and the install program has a complete set of dialog boxes for installing LAN WorkPlace. Other X servers are beginning to offer TCP/IP network software bundles with their software.

Configuration Options

All XoftWare/32 configuration options are located on the options menu that pops up when the server icon is single-clicked with the mouse. There is no separate control panel, nor can any options be set before you run the server. The menu contains seven options: display, server, performance, mouse, keyboard, fonts, and clipboard. Color options are found under the display option. XoftWare/32 provides four-color maps, and Version 2.1 should have TrueColor which supports more than 256 colors. There is virtual screen support in single window mode but no true panning like that found in XVision.

Keyboard country settings are provided by AGE. You can use the X11 xmodmap utility, but you cannot map the keyboard keystroke by keystroke as you can in XVision. You get three sets of fonts—75 or 100 dpi and fixed-width fonts. A font compiler comes with Xoftware, but it is accessed from outside the program. You can convert X fonts to Windows fonts with the utility. Xoftware/32 uses a font substitution routine that finds a matching Windows font if the requested X font is not available.

Ease of Use and Compatibility

AGE provides both XDMCP support and a program starter for you to launch programs. The program starter as shown in Figure 15.1 supports **telnet**, **rsh**, **rexec**, **rlogin**, or **xdm** methods of connection. You can specify the host, user name, password, and command in the prgogram starter and then save the results. In addition, you can attach an icon to a specific program and save it. Xoftware/32 also lets you click on a number of icons simultaneously. If you have multiple hosts, this option brings up whatever application responds first, irrespective of the order in which you clicked on the icons.

AGE does not supply any other utility programs or X clients with its server. There is no full-featured **telnet** like those provided by XVision or Exceed; rather, AGE expects you to depend on the **telnet** provided by your network (which sometimes are not very robust). You do not get a separate configuration program; instead, you do all configuration within the X server once it is started. The XoftWare/32 version provides no network monitoring like that of XVision or PCXware, nor does it offer a separate launch program like eXceed's Launch Pad.

The documentation provides a few pages of error messages but little troubleshooting information. We found only one troubleshooting example in the program section. Unless you are a highly technical and UNIX-knowledgeable user, Xoftware will disappoint you with its weak documentation—which equals only about a quarter of the pages found in eXceed/W from Hummingbird. The online tutorial is good but provides no information not already found in the manual.

We encountered some minor incompatibilities with X clients—such as DECWrite for Sun SPARCstations and Metacard. Most applications worked fine. There is a performance feature that allows you to adjust the number of resources dedicated to the

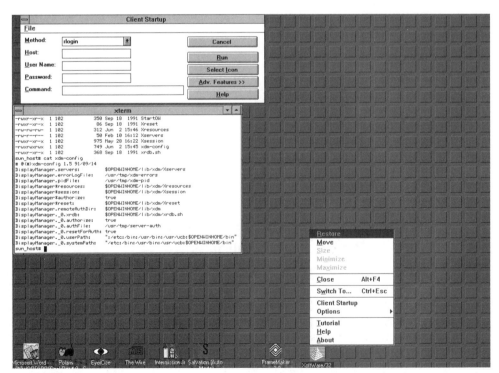

FIGURE 15.1   XoftWare Client Startup box and configuration menu

X server. This adjusts the speed of the X server in general and drawing speed in particular.

Summary

XoftWare/32 has some excellent power user features—such as the 32-bit engine, font substitution, and automatic client startup. Installation is flexible. However, it lacks other key features. It provides fewer configuration options than some products, and its automatic routines to set up and run programs seem less robust than equivalent options from other vendors. It does, however, provide a wide variety of platform versions which allow you to use XoftWare on DOS, Windows, and Windows NT machines. The availability of a bundled TCP/IP communication protocol stack is a big plus. Xoftware/32 is $495, and $595 with the TCP/IP stack.

Hummingbird Communications eXceed/W 3.3

Hummingbird Communications Limited's eXceed/W (eXceed) has a large share of the PC X server market. Notably, Hummingbird is one of only two companies that provide X servers for both DOS and Windows. This flexibility allows companies with a mix of previously installed machines to provide X servers to all their users without buying new hardware. Our review covers eXceed's 3.3 release for Windows. In addition, we also discuss other products in the family at the end of this chapter.

Ease of Installation

eXceed/W uses a Windows-based install program. Laid out clearly, it gives you the option of automatically making changes to your system configuration files. eXceed/W excels in flexible installation options for networks. You install eXceed/W according to how it will be used. The options are personal, user, shared, or copy. Personal installation covers a single user on a single PC. The remaining options allow eXceed to run on a network. A user install puts the configuration files on the local disk or in a user directory and assumes the remaining files to be located on the server. A shared install copies all files to the server. Hats off to eXceed for this user-thoughtful flexibility.

Unlike most X servers, eXceed lets you select multiple TCP/IP protocols from a list of 20-plus supported protocols for installation on your system. Each protocol installs its specific files in a separate sub-directory. You can also install all the font sets, including 75 dpi, 100 dpi, Andrew, and standard IBM PC fonts.

eXceed/W uses a configuration program—Xconfig/W—to specifically set up your machine. We mention some of the options in the Configuration section that follows. Xconfig/W provides detailed information in the form of a help screen on what you need to do for each network protocol and how it should be setup. With release

3.3, eXceed/W supports the WinSock API, revision 1.1. HCL works nicely with those networks that provide a WinSock standard API. For older networks, you must use one of HCL's APIs (usually in the form of a TSR). For example, the PCNFS API requires 64K of low DOS memory. This memory consumption becomes of primary concern when switching from Windows to DOS. If you use an older version of Sun's PC-NFS, Hummingbird's installation guide says to use their own RTM files. However, you should ignore their words of wisdom and instead use Sun's own files. This goes for other X server products that give the same advice. We regularly crashed our PC with a 3COM 503 Ethernet II card by using the vendor's **RTM.EXE** files. The newest version of eXceed/W eliminates the need for a special driver (**XPORT.EXE**) required for earlier versions.

Configuration Options

HCL supports more TCP/IP products than most other X servers. All major vendors plus a number of minor vendors are supported by HCL. Of great interest to the vast hordes of NetWare users is HCL's decision to support the IPX/SPX protocol—a protocol used both by Novell's NetWare and UnixWare. Any Netware client machine can access a UnixWare host without having to load dual protocol stacks.

The configuration program, Xconfig/W, is Windows-based and dialog box driven. Most of the settings in Xconfig/W have no effect on the current server session—forcing you to restart the server. Xconfig/W options include changing the mouse timing, setting color models, assigning font aliases and usage, and controlling certain X Protocol settings. eXceed/W now supports broadcast mode of **xdm** and uses its own Access database to restrict host access to your X server if you desire. This reduces the number of broadcast packets on the network.

If your X font requirements go beyond standard specifications, eXceed provides excellent support. As seen in Figure 15.2, eXceed represents a full implementation of X11.5. This takes advantage of X11R5's better XDMCP security, scalable fonts, and support for font servers. Font databases or a font server are where all clients look for requested fonts. The font database compiles fonts as well as imports and exports aliases. The eXceed/W font management facilities are the most advanced of all the X servers. Within a dialog box format you can view fonts, change properties, create aliases, and scale fonts.

Color support extends to **pseudo_color**, **static_color**, and **true_color**. HCL lets you edit the RGB database as well as compile it. Some of the options in the Xconfig/W are more informational in nature. This applies to the **README** file and the transport section. HCL's **X/CONFIG** program provides all the expected X server options. You can set up backing store(how X keeps track of windows that are covered by other windows), determine how eXceed/W connects to the host, name a default host, set up keyboard options, and configure mouse emulations.

Ease of Use and Compatibility

As with most X servers, eXceed/W grants login access through **rexec**, **rsh**, and XDMCP. eXceed/W provides an icon driven method of starting up programs called Xstart. With Xstart you can specify an X program to run automatically when you click on the icon and open the connection. You supply user id, host name, password, and the command sequence when first setting up. Similar to XVision's Program Starter, you can name, save, and attach icons to these Xstart scripts. The documentation provides some examples on how to start certain UNIX commands depending on which shell is being used.

Hummingbird provides a substitute shell that can be used with, or in place of, Window's Program Manager. Called the Launch Pad, it is menu driven and can be reconfigured by the user to open any Windows, DOS, or eXceed/W program. You can also start any X client with the Xstart program through Launch Pad. However, we did not like it as much as other shell replacements—either those geared as UNIX connectivity products such as JSB MultiView Desktop or straight Windows programs such as Symantec's Norton Desktop.

With HCL, you get a load of extras. These include a full-featured **telnet** utility and an **ftp** file transfer utility. You can run multiple sessions of **ftp** to different hosts, but each session can be connected only to a single host. HCL's implementation represents the client side of **ftp**; the host must be running a server version of **ftp**. You

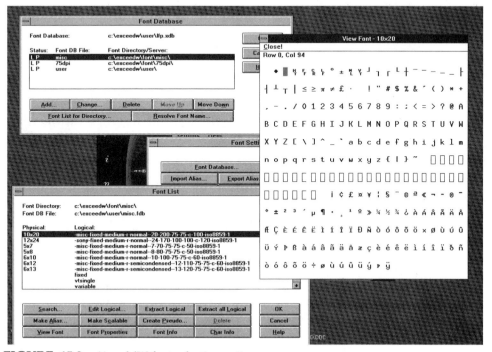

FIGURE 15.2 eXceed/W font selection options

can copy and paste text or graphics between X and Windows with eXceed using a full range of options. You can, for example, copy a rectangle using a camera icon, copy the entire visible screen, or copy whatever exists in the X selection. The resultant text goes into the Windows clipboard or into the X selection depending on the direction of the cut and paste.

HCL provides an option to let you run local X clients. A few such as **ico**, **maze**, and **xlogo** are provided for a test basis, and you can purchase a separate xdk toolkit. No other X server provides this level of convenience. However, unless you are the programmer type, you may find its usefulness limited.

A new Performance option on the server menu gives you some of the flexibility found in other products. This includes the ability to control such items as Windows System Resource Usage, the amount of time before network data is flushed out, and buffer caching. We found eXceed/W to excel in compatibility, and we give it an overall good performance rating as well.

Summary

eXceed/W shines in a number of areas when your X server needs go beyond the norm. Font support and font management are outstanding, and even non-programmers can use them correctly. The Xstart facility and Launch Pad make it easy to integrate eXceed/W into a Windows environment. The family of HCL products includes a DOS product (mentioned later in the chapter) and IPX/SPX support. eXceed/W permits a heterogenous computing environment to use an X server. eXceed/W is expensive at $545, but site licenses are available.

Integrated Inference Machines X11/AT 3.2

X11/AT from IIM was one of the first Windows-based X servers on the market. Although initially the market leader, X11/AT has lost ground in recent times. It is not based on X11R5, and it is available in versions for other operating systems.

Ease of Installation

X11/AT uses an entirely Windows-based installation routine. It alters your **AUTOEXEC.BAT** or **CONFIG.SYS** file. You can choose to install any number of fonts and see what impact it will have on disk space before installing. X11/AT allows you to load only one network protocol at a time. In order to load multiple protocols, you have to circumvent the setup utility. You can purchase X11/AT in a bundle with FTP's PC/TCP TCP/IP protocol.

Version 3.2 relies on a combination of DLL files and TSRs when loading the network protocol. X11/AT automatically selects the proper protocol if it is running.

X11/AT provides an unload from memory option if you are using a TSR. This is useful if you have run DOS programs outside of Windows.

We did run into problems with the **PATH** statement found in **AUTOEXEC.BAT**. X11/AT installation corrupted the path. The next time we went into Windows, we got error messages concerning missing drivers. Changing the **PATH** back to its original directories corrected the problem. X11/AT uses a **NETWORK.DLL** file normally located in the **C:\IIM\NETWORK** directory. If X11/AT cannot find this file, it will not load.

Configuration Options

X11/AT uses a dialog box method to configure the server. You click on the selection you want to change. Standard options include keyboard compatibility, backing store, and font paths. One feature available in X11/AT, but found in only one other product is three methods of window management. All products let the X clients be managed independently by Microsoft Windows or operate collectively using a UNIX window manager (Motif, Open Look, etc.) inside one large Microsoft Windows window. X11/AT introduces a third scheme. You can choose a UNIX-based window manager to directly control each client. You invoked it by calling the window manager directly from within an xterm.

The command, **mwm &**, executed in an xterm window opens the Motif Window Manager and prompts X11 to ask if you want to switch from the Microsoft Windows window manager to the X-based window manager. This allows you to use Motif and Microsoft Windows for each appropriate application. However, it did not always work correctly. If you enable Raise Assist, the Motif windows can move to the top over the MS Windows applications.

X11/AT supports text copy in both directions but supports graphical copying only from X to MS Windows. Clicking on the server icon brings up a short menu. You select copy from the menu and the cursor changes into a different shape. Text transfers rely on selecting text and using either the standard X or Windows clipboard commands.

There is only marginal color palette support in X11. There are four RGB databases, but we missed the common ones such as **pseudo_color** and **direct_color**. The standard color set, however, is acceptable.

Ease of Use and Compatibility

X11/AT does not have as many login capabilities as other X servers. It provides no **rexec** or **rsh** connections, but you can use **xdm**. We also could not use a hostname when using the **WTELNET** connection and were forced to use the Internet address.

X11/AT supports a launch command for automatically starting an X client. Unlike XVision and eXceed/W, the launch command does not allow for separate parameter files. If you want to create separate icons to load specific programs, you have to create the entire command line and then save it as a file. For example, building a permanent xterm icon requires you to go to the Windows Program Manager and select New Program Item. In the command box, you might type the following in the Command Line.

LAUNCH RS6000 MIKE "NOHUP XTERM -DISPLAY INSIGHT:0 &"

Because the Program manager is limited to 60 characters, you may need to create a batch file called by the command line. You need to create a new command line for each program you would start on the X server. Once invoked, a dialog box asks for the password. Launch uses **WTELNET** to make connections. While it worked with our sample scripts, we prefer the methods used by products such as eXceed/W and XVision where you use a dialog box to make selections and save the result as the parameters for the launch command.

The single manual found with X11/AT is reasonably thorough. There is excellent information on how fonts work with X11/AT and in the X server. Information on setting up the server is detailed. The troubleshooting section is large, but we still came across two errors during the setup that were not in the guide. Some of the best detail on **xdm** and **XDMCP** are provided in the X11/AT manual. A sample **xsession** file is provided.

We could get multiple xterms from multiple hosts up and running with X11. MetaCard worked correctly and used the correct fonts. (This application is particularly difficult.) The speed of the MetaCard tutorial compared similarly with other X servers. We tested Z-Mail on both the Sun SPARCstation and the IBM RS/6000. It worked, but the cursor occasionally became confused. FrameMaker for Motif ran but locked up more than once.

Summary

X11/AT costs $295 and has adequate configuration and functions. Font support is good and it is one of two products to support a third windowing option. It does, however, show its age. It does not yet support X11R5. A bigger problem is the weak login support, no **rexec** or **rsh**, and the difficulty in making icons that the user can click on to start an X application. Until the next release, we would think twice before purchasing X11/AT.

NCD PC-Xware 1.0

NCD purchased the GSS Division of Spectragraphics Inc., in order to break into the PC X server market to compliment their X terminal line. NCD's newest product, PC-Xware, completely replaces their previous Windows X server, PC-Xview. However, the DOS version of PC-Xview is still available. PC-Xware is unique among X servers because it replicates the server software provided with NCD's line of X terminals. We looked at a late Beta copy of PC-Xware.

Ease of Installation

PC-Xware uses a Windows script, with an option for a selective install or standard install. A selective install lets you load whatever fonts you choose. You can use the integrated stack sold with PC-XWare or your own. NetManage's Newt is the stack supplied with PC-Xware, and you can read more about it in Chapter 13. It is a Windows-only stack. The install asks you detailed questions about your network setup and is entirely Windows-based. There is even a utility to test the network connection. However, when we used the wrong I/O RAM address for the network card, Newt still passed the test, but PC-XWare would not load as would be expected.

Overall, the installation is extremely user-friendly. Its biggest shortcoming is the inability to load multiple protocols or different network attachments. You can load only network stack and that includes NCD's XRemote, a compressed X data serial protocol. However, you can run through the selective install for each network and then they are all available. The manual is clear for installation of both the basic product and the integrated stack.

Configuration Options

There are 15 different TCP/IP network stacks supported by PC-Xware. You can also use NCD's Xremote for serial connections, which is a compressed X data transmission protocol between a PC and a host. PC-Xware supports telnet, rexec, and xdm connections to any host. You can configure the startup dialog box to access any host by any of these methods.

PC-Xware really excels in the configuration of the X server. Instead of the typical control panel for configuring the X server, NCD includes PC-Xservices, a utility which closely replicates the software NCD provides with its X terminals (Figure 15.3). NCD supports three window manager variations: a local Microsoft Windows window manager, a Motif window manager supplied by NCD (called ncdwm) or the window manager on the host. PC-Xware is the only X server that allows you to run a Motif-like window manager locally (X11/AT uses Motif over the network). You can change window managers on the fly and this is unique to PC-Xware.

The PC-Xservices allow you to set user preferences and setup parameters. Both of these menus are extensive, and both support features not found in other products. Under the PC-Xservices, the User Preference menu is a large set of parameters. They affect keyboard mapping, the mouse, the screen background and compatibility. Within setup parameters, there are options pertaining to SNMP (Simple Network Management Protocol), network interfaces, licenses, diagnostics, fonts, and file services.

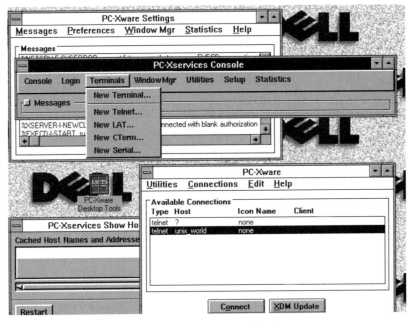

FIGURE 15.3 PC-Xware console services and settings menu

Whenever you want, you get a complete console of messages where you can see the status of the connections as it occurs. Great for troubleshooting. If you login in via telnet, a VT320 window is provided complete with a menu of configuration options. You can set the standard features found in your Xterm including blink cursor, jump scroll and reverse video. PC-Xware lacks some of the font and keyboard control found in products such as eXceed/W. There is a font compiler, but no font tools. There is also no way to remap keys on the keyboard.

Ease of Use and Compatibility

Creating applications and setting them up as icons is not as easy in PC-Xware as in some products. Initially, you have a limited set of icons provided by NCD, but there are more in the library. In the Settings box, you can set a type of connection, the host name, a client to run and an icon. PC-Xware automatically places the icons in the Windows Program Manager. You have to move them manually to place them in another Windows group. The end result is basically the same.

The user can easily make changes by clicking on the root or background window. When using the local ncdwm, a menu pops up on the root window. You can make changes from this menu (which is like a true root Motif menu) plus get different status updates. There is a memory status and an X connections choice where you are informed about the status of each X connection to any host. The same information is also available from the PC-Xservices

Some of the more common features, such as cut and paste, are available from a separate icon called PC-Xware Desktop Tools. This resides on your desktop and is invoked by clicking on it. PC-Xware supports all the copy and paste options.

Running Metacard, a demanding X application, worked fine with PC-Xware. **xdm** is supported and not difficult to setup. If you have multiple hosts available, a dialog box appears with a list of the possible hosts. When you login via **xdm**, you get a console dialog box giving you the status of any available hosts and what is happening on them. Xterm worked well.

Summary

PC-Xware is an X server of a different breed. The inclusion of the PC-Xservices provides significantly more configuration options than any other product. Some of these would not be used by users, but having them for administration is great. The on the fly Window Managers and separate Desktop Tools are benefits as well. The basic X server works well and contains all the bells and whistles. With the integrated network stack and support for NCD's Xremote for $545, PC-Xware deserves a close look.

VisionWare XVision 5

XVision from VisionWare is a market leader in the Microsoft Windows X server market according to The X Business Group. First introduced in 1989, XVision never saw life as a DOS product. Its introduction straight into the Windows market can be seen in its clean install, strong configuration options, and well written documentation. We initially reviewed XVision 4.1, but XVision 5 became available right before our manuscript went to press so we have incorporated the changes here.

Ease of Installation

Installation uses two separate programs, but they are integrated in the install process so there are few difficulties. XVision takes a layered approach to the communication links. The VisionWare Communications package is the base level for all of Vision-Ware's products. This saves some redundancy when working with multiple Vision-Ware products. VisionWare Communications combines Windows DLL files and a set of Network Communication Interfaces (NCI). The communication guide for Vision-Ware communications is clear and detailed, but there are some things you should know up front. The NCI is usually a TSR program and must be loaded before Windows. It also must be loaded after all the network drivers and devices required by your particular network. Not every network version requires an NCI for XVision to work, but the majority do. Some of the NCIs can be loaded in the **WINSTART.BAT** file, but you have to check with XVision since it is not documented. Basically, you load a small TSR (12K) before loading Windows and let the NCI load high. This saves considerable memory.

XVision requires a serial number be entered during install. A separate setup manual guides you through the installation process. The default list did not show some of the most recent upgrades to popular TCP/IP protocols. This becomes a problem if your network is new. Significant changes may not be reflected in the drivers sent by Visionware. You can only load one TCP/IP protocol at a time, but you can load a TCP/IP stack and another protocol (such as a serial protocol or DECNet). You can get around the single stack limitations by copying the protocol files off the disk. XVision 5 automatically detects what network you are running and configures your software for that network.

XVision 5 allows you to load multiple sets of fonts at installation. There are 75 dpi, 100 dpi, Andrew, and miscellaneous fonts. One useful feature in XVision 5 is the ability to automatically sense fonts that are not available and makes appropriate substitutions.

Configuration Options

XVision uses a control panel, shown in Figure 15.4, similar to the one in Microsoft Windows from which you make changes to the underlying X-server settings. In all the X-servers we reviewed, we found this one of the easiest ways to change settings. Most settings require the server to restart before they take effect. If you let the server go down, all your X applications go with it. The server has to be running to access the dialog box.

The XVision 5 desktop, a new feature, allows you to configure the applications and the connection. The desktop is very similar in concept to the program manager. It lets you do what Program Manager does as well as let you launch network applications, all from a single place.

XVision supports the NCD XRemote protocol for sending data over a serial line. The only other X servers with serial line support is eXceed/W Express and PC-Xware. The XRemote protocol has its limits—you can have only one XRemote connection open at a time. Also, while faster than straight serial, it is relatively slow. XRemote is, however, a good compromise if you need X connectivity over a serial line. The XRemote protocol is bundled with XVision.

XVision supports at least 16 networks including the best selling networks FTP PC/TCP, SunSelect PC-NFS, and Novell's LAN WorkPlace for DOS. It does not support many of the newer and smaller vendors' products such as Frontier Technologies Super TCP and Spry Air for Windows. However, Version 5.0 supports the WinSock API which allows it to connect to many newer TCP/IP stacks.

Multiple windows are supported by XVision, in a similar fashion to most X servers. XVision supports six levels of visual color classes—more than any other product.

You can let Windows use its default colors for all applications—Windows and X, or you can use the specific colormaps supplied with the X client. In addition, you can set the visual default to have the Windows color palette included in the X color palette.

Ease of Use

XVision 5 attempts to make the X server work and act just like any other Windows application. In that respect, XVision comes from the opposite direction of PC-Xware which attempts to make the X server appear more like an X terminal. Once loaded, you click an icon to invoke XVision. The new desktop allows you to manage all your local and remote applications. You can choose to use the X windows background, rather than the MS Windows background. There is a new desktop metaphor in XVision that provides drag and drop support across Windows and X applications. Online help is available when using the configuration menu. The help is fully hypertext-based and detailed. Even a novice can learn how to correctly configure the X server using this help.

The primary method of connecting to remote applications is through the desktop in a manner similar to PC Connect (discussed in Chapter 16). The desktop is

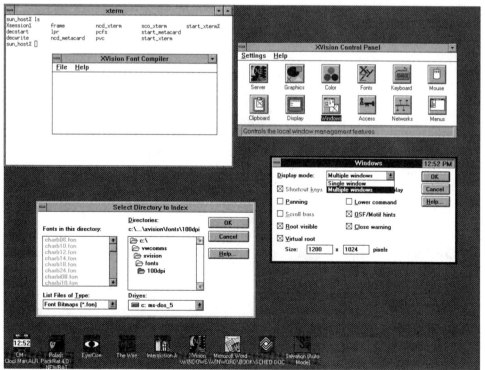

FIGURE 15.4 XVision Control Panel and Font Compiler windows

object oriented in design. You set up each host with all the information about the host. Next you tell an application which host to use or even drop an application icon on to a host icon to invoke the application. This prevents having to repeat information for each application.

XVision 5 also supports an automatic program launcher called Program Starter, which is the primary method of launching. Similar to the technology provided by other X servers, each program can have a title, associated commands, host name, user name, and password. You can save and name each program starter set. If you want to place an icon in the Program Manager group that runs your application, you select **XPS.EXE** and put the program name with an **xps** extension afterward. The primary reason to support it in XVision 5 is for compatibility.

XVision supports XDMCP mode with all its different options. You can specify a local authorization file that matches the file on the UNIX host. The XVision control panel makes it easy to make changes to the system. You can also access the Windows Task Manager from the Motif Menu Button if you keep the root window visible.

We were impressed with both the cut and paste options, which included graphics, and clearly illustrated documentation. Performance tuning is readily available with XVision. In setting the color visual classes, you can tell XVision not to let Microsoft Windows update the color maps of all its applications. With XVision you can also control the accuracy and speed of the graphic redraws. Three precision modes are provided, the greater the precision, the slower the speed.

Summary

XVision 5 is a solid product with many configuration options. The new desktop metaphor provides a single place to work with all your applications and gives quick access to X applications. The color options represent some of the best. Those wanting serial access to their X applications will appreciate the option of using XRemote. Performance-tweaking choices exceed those found in competing products, and the install is well done. XVision sells for $495 and is also bundled with LAN WorkPlace for DOS for $100 more. The newest version gives XVision the look and feel of being an integral part of your Windows desktop.

Additional X Servers

There are additional X servers on the market—perhaps more by the time you read this book. The products mentioned in this part of the chapter are either family members of products we reviewed earlier, relicensed versions of the X servers we reviewed, or ones with incomplete Windows support. Depending on your situation, you may prefer to purchase from a vendor with a family of products.

AGE Logic XoftWare Family

The XoftWare family of products is one of the largest available. It covers some unique niches in the X server market. AGE also provides their engine on an OEM basis for other vendors' products including Reflection by Walker, Richer and Quinn and JSB Multiview/X. All XoftWare products cost $100 more with the bundled network stack.

XoftWare/32 for Windows NT

The NT version of XoftWare/32 contains all the features found in XoftWare/32. It is a complete NT product that makes use of Microsoft's embedded TCP/IP support in addition to the normal network options. NT's TCP/IP support, though not stellar, does the trick, if you choose not to purchase additional networking software. The NT version adds TrueColor support and the XScope utility for network management. It sells for $495.

XoftWare for DOS

The DOS version of XoftWare is an older product. It is designed to run on 286, 386 and 486 machines, although we would be reluctant to use an X server on a 286. It supports most of the standard X server features like virtual screens, XDMCP, Motif Window Manager, and full font availability. You can purchase the DOS version with a bundled network protocol stack. XoftWare for DOS runs in a native DOS environment or in a DOS compatibility box within Microsoft Windows. You can hotkey to DOS or back to Windows. The main advantage of the product is to allow you to stay with a single X server vendor across all your platforms. The DOS version sells for $295.

XoftWare for Windows, Desktop Edition

AGE has responded to the changing X server market by creating a low-end product for MS Windows. The XoftWare for Windows/Desktop product provides the key elements of an X server without the power-user bells and whistles. It is priced at $195, lower than any other product on the market. For the user who simply wants access to one or two X applications, this product has real potential. The server engine is a full-fledged, 32-bit product with no crippling limitations. It does not include the font compiler, the multiple application start-up, and the extra fonts found in the full version of Xoftware. You can get it bundled with the TCP/IP stack as well.

Hummingbird Communications eXceed Family

Hummingbird, with its family of X server products, is well positioned to provide complete support to an entire company. Besides the Windows version we reviewed, Hummingbird has versions for DOS, Windows NT, and serial connections. We tested the serial product, and most of our comments will be in that direction. The Windows NT product was not available at publication.

eXceed/Xpress

Hummingbird has chosen to tie in with Tektronix's serial communication protocol called Serial Xpress. This protocol resembles NCD's Xremote, and it allows you to use serial lines (direct or over a modem) to access a UNIX host and its X applications. We loaded and tested eXceed/Xpress between an Insight 486 50MHz PC and a Sun SPARCstation IPC. See Chapter 9 for issues related to making the serial connection. Xpress comes either as an add-on to eXceed/W or as a separate product. As an add-on to eXceed/W, you get a host module($125) and the PC module. If you purchase it as a separate product ($249), you do not get network support for TCP/IP, Xstart, FTP support, or the **Xstartd** program. Xpress is based on eXceed/W release 3.3.

eXceed/NT

Hummingbird has recently released a version of its X server for Windows NT. This product is substantially the same as the 3.3 release of the eXceed/W product. It sells for $645. The NT product has its own development kit (a separate product for $695) for local X clients, is fully X11R5 compliant, supports Windows Sockets, and supports two windowing modes.

eXceed for DOS

Hummingbird also sells a DOS version ($545) of their X server. This gives a complete PC family to the Hummingbird X servers. The DOS product is much more difficult to setup than the Windows version. It supports the standard X server features.

JSB Multiview/X

JSB Corp., in Scotts Valley, Calif., sells an X server named Multiview/X. This product is a relicensed version of Age Logic's Xoftware for Windows which we reviewed earlier. The major difference lies with the integration of MultiView Desktop into the X server. Essentially, when you purchase Multiview/X, you get both an X server and the MultiView Desktop suited for character applications. This provides an excellent desktop for those interested in providing users with an easier connection to UNIX and other systems. For a discussion of JSB Multiview Desktop, see Chapter 16.

The X server is the basic Xoftware Windows engine. The addition of the Multiview Desktop overcomes the weak client configuration options found in Xoftware, making the X server more attractive. Multiview/X also supports its own fonts in addition to the standard set of X fonts. However, Multiview/X still has the same limited X server engine configuration options found in Xoftware like no keyboard mapping. Products like PC-Xware and XVision 5 have many more options for setting up the X server and customizing how it operates. In a pure X environment, other products are more appropriate. However, if you have users with a mixed need for character and UNIX applications, Multiview/X is well worth considering because of its many connection options and the flexibility of the desktop.

NCD Family

NCD's DOS X server, PC-XView for DOS, has a full range of features including support for X11R5, a local Motif Window Manager (but not the NCDwm found in PC-Xware), VGA support, backing store and font support. The current version 4.0, is not nearly as integrated as the new PC-Xware. In a mixed DOS/Windows environment, NCD is a good solution to remain with a single vendor.

NCD XRemote is a special serial protocol just for use by X servers. It was once a part of a separate product package, but now is bundled with NCD's PC-Xware and VisionWare's XVision.

Quarterdeck DESQview/X

At first glance, you might think that DESQview/X is not at all an X server. In some respects, that is correct—DESQviewX is more than an X server for PCs. It is also not Microsoft Windows-based, but it can run X applications in the same manner as any Windows-based X server. We evaluate its strength and weaknesses in Chapter 14, PC-LAN Products, because of its many different features.

If you are considering an X server, you would be wise to consider DESQview/X. DESQview/X provides a graphical user environment with access to the cut and paste ability associated with X servers. You can alter the DESQview/X menu system to place your X clients directly on the menu. When you double click on these items, the X server portion of DESQview/X opens a window with your application. We liked the flexibility of DESQview/X and the ease of accessing X applications. You can use either the DESQview/X window manager, Motif, or OPEN LOOK. If you want a graphical environment but do not want to use Microsoft Windows, DESQview/X is the best choice on the market.

White Pine Software eXodus 5.0

White Pine Software relicenses and distributes XVision produced by Visionware in the U.K. and renames it eXodus for MS Windows. We noted no major differences between the versions. White Pines produces a Macintosh-based X server and a Next X server as well. White Pines is the only vendor to provide this multiplatform support. However, the Macintosh server is not from Visionware and therefore does not follow the same design forms. This reduces the incentive to purchase from the same vendor, although it is only a small factor. When you purchase eXodus for MS Windows, you get all of your support from White Pine Software.

WRQ Reflection X

Walker, Richer & Quinn just recently entered the X server market. Their product, Reflection X, is an OEM'd version of AGE Logic's Xoftware/32 for Windows product. We installed Reflection X and examined some of the differences. Overall, the basic X server is nearly identical to Xoftware. The method of connecting to X clients, the settings options, and basic engine similar.

There are two main differences—set up and configuration menus. Reflection X uses a slightly different setup routine. It is well laid out and allows you to make selections on which network and fonts to load. Reflection X also supports WRQ's own TCP/IP stack. In addition, all the TCP/IP protocols supported by Xoftware are also supported. The configuration menu used by Reflection is different from all other X servers and resembles the configuration used by Microsoft Word. A set of icons is displayed on the left-hand side of the screen. When you select an icon, the main dialog box changes the available options. The actual configuration options are almost exactly the same as Xoftware and are limited. For example, there is no desktop or a way to alter the performance. The window manager options are standard. You also get a Windows **ftp** interface and module. The **ftp** module makes it easier to transfer files without having to use the UNIX command line. For the available options, the configuration method used by Reflection X is the best of all the products we reviewed. We just wish there were more options. There is virtual screen support, limited keyboard mapping and enhanced client start-up routines.

Unlike the major addition Multiview/X makes to the basic Xoftware engine (see later in the chapter), Reflection X does not alter Xoftware. The major reason to purchase Reflection X is to have a complete WRQ environment. You can purchase a terminal emulator, a TCP/IP stack and an X server from WRQ, all as one product called the Reflection X Connectivity Suite. This integrated approach is the market niche being pursued by WRQ—it makes an administrator's job easier if all the network support is coming from a single vendor.

Recommendations

The X server market does not easily sort itself out. There are a number of excellent products. See Tables 15.1 and 15.2 for comparisons. Both eXceed/W and XVision have strong features and excellent configurations. We lean towards eXceed/W because of its stronger font support and various versions. If you need to use both character and X-based applications, JSB's MultiView/X is worth considering, although we think the X server is weaker than the best products. Finally, the new PC-Xware from NCD is a whole new approach to configuration and maintainence. Similar to the NCD X terminal software, PC-Xware may well change the way vendors look at X servers. We liked the multitude of options and the flexibility of the configuration menus.

Table 15.1: Reviewed X Server Features

	eXceed/W	XVision5	XoftWare/ 32	X11/AT	DESQview /X	PC-XWare
X11R4 or X11R5	X11R5	X11R5	X11R5	X11R4	N/A	X11R5
File Transfer	Yes	Yes	No	Yes	Yes	Yes
Telnet Full/Partial	Full	Full	Partial	Full	Partial	Full
rsh/rexec Support	Yes/Yes	Yes/Yes	Yes/Yes	No/No	Yes/Yes	No/Yes
XDMCP (Broadcast, Indi-rect, Query)	All	All	All	Partial	No	All
Can Use winstart.bat?	Yes	Yes	Yes	No	N/A	Yes
Auto Client Starter	Yes	Yes	Yes	Yes	Yes	Yes
Windows Fonts	Yes	Yes	Yes	Yes	N/A	Yes
Font compiler/server	Both	Both	Both	No	Complier	Compiler
BDF/PCF fonts	Both	Yes	Both	No	Yes/No	Yes
Install multiple fonts	Yes	Yes	Yes	Yes	No	Yes
Virtual Screen & Panning	Yes	Yes	Yes	No	Yes	No
Graphics Copy and Paste	Yes	Yes	Yes	Yes	Yes	Yes
Backing Store	Yes	Yes	Yes	Yes	Yes	Yes
# of Networks Supported	20	16	13	13	7	15
Install more than one TCP/ IP protocol	Yes	No	Yes	No	Yes	No
Winsock Support	Yes	Yes	Yes	No	N/A	Yes
Color Options (true, static, pseudo	Allt	All	All	One	None	All
Local X clients	Yes	No	No	No	Yes	Yes
Keyboard Mapping	Yes	Yes	No	Yes	Yes	No
Bundled Network Stack	No	Yes	Yes	Yes	Yes	Yes
Price	$545	$495 $100 more with TCP	$395 $100 more with TCP	$295 $345 w/ TCP/IP	$475 - includes Networking	$545 - includes TCP/IP

Table 15.2: **Unreviewed X Servers and Their Features**

	eXceed/NT	White Pines eXodus	WRQ Reflection X	JSB Multiview/ X	XoftWare/ 32 for NT	Xoftware Desktop
X11R4 or X11R5	X11R5	X11R5	X11R5	X11R5	X11R5	X11R4
File Transfer	Yes	Yes	Yes	Yes	No	No
Telnet Full/Partial	Full	Full	Partial	Full	Partial	Partial
rsh/rexec Support	Yes/Yes	Yes/Yes	Yes/Yes	Yes/Yes	Yes/Yes	Yes/Yes
XDMCP (Broadcast, Indirect, Query)	All	All	All	All	All	All
Can Use winstart.bat?	NA	Yes	Yes	Yes	NA	Yes
Auto Client Starter	Yes	Yes	Yes	Yes	Yes	Partial
Windows Fonts	Yes	Yes	Yes	Yes	Yes	Yes
Font compiler/server	Yes	Both	Both	Both	Both	No
BDF/PCF fonts	Yes	Yes	Both	Both	Both	Yes/No
Install multiple fonts	Yes	Yes	Yes	Yes	Yes	No
Virtual Screen & Panning	Yes	Yes	Yes	Yes	Yes	Yes
Graphics Copy and Paste	Yes	Yes	Yes	Yes	Yes	Yes
Backing Store	Yes	Yes	Yes	Yes	Yes	Yes
# of Networks Supported	1	16	14	15	1	13
Install more than one TCP/IP protocol	No	No	No	Yes	NA	No
Winsock Support	Yes	Yes	Yes	Yes	Yes	Yes
Color Options (true, static, pseudo	All	All	All	All	All	No True Color
Local X clients	Yes	No	No	No	No	No
Keyboard Mapping	Yes	Yes	No	Yes	No	No
Bundled Network Stack	No	No	Yes	Yes	Yes	Yes
Price	$595	$495	$469 $199 with TCP/IP	$495 includes TCP/IP	$495	$195 $100 with TCP/IP

16

Terminal Emulators

Introduction

Chapter 10 provides details on making a serial connection between your PC and UNIX machine—in many cases, the cheapest and easiest type of connection to put into place. If you have read Chapter 10 and chose to make a serial connection, you are now interested in the second half of the equation—terminal emulation and related products.

Though generally less expensive than buying a full fledged TCP/IP software solution, terminal emulators are also more limited. For example, you cannot use X applications with a terminal emulator. Still, many UNIX programs do not require anything beyond character-based emulation. Accounting programs, job scheduling, and inventory are typical text-based UNIX applications.

Given its inability to run X applications, the extensive support for different networks among terminal emulation products surprised us. Since most of these products began in the serial communications market, their expansion into TCP/IP, IPX/SPX, LAT, and other network protocols is notable. Of course, if you already have a network card in your PC and you need access to character-based UNIX applications, buy a product that supports your present protocol rather than running another serial cable.

In the following pages, we evaluate some of the best-selling Windows terminal emulation programs, some popular serial products with UNIX components, and products that provide unique features. Since space and time limit us from a thorough evaluation of every product on the market, we provide brief coverage of additional products at the end of the chapter.

Evaluation Criteria

As with each of our product chapters, we use a set of categories to measure the effectiveness of each product. With terminal emulators, ease of use and power features come to the forefront. Since these programs usually end up on the desks of secretaries and clerks, if they are overly difficult to use, they will not be.

Installation and Configurability

With regard to product installation, we consider whether each product automatically sets up your system, what options are available during setup, and what are the system requirements. Configuration issues include terminal emulation modes and keyboard mapping.

Connectability

Connectability features include what types of network support are provided (such as TCP/IP and LAT), how dial up options work, what type of file transfer support is provided, and whether there are other network services—printing, for example.

Ease of Use

When we think of ease of use, our minds center on how well the menus are laid out, how easy it is to use shortcut keys, and whether there are icon bars and autologin scripts that can be used by non-programmers. We also consider the quality and clarity of help systems and manuals.

Power Features

This section looks at special options such as a scripting language, platform support, the presence of an editor, remote control options, and UNIX-specific features—such as support for the SCO UNIX **mscreen** utility.

Windows Terminal Emulators

We divide terminal emulators into two groups. The first group consists of popular PC-based programs that run under Microsoft Windows. While not particularly geared to UNIX systems (most are directed at modem communications to on-line services), these programs are popular on PCs and make access to UNIX easier by their familiar interface. The second group are products with UNIX components for file transfer.

Datastorm PROCOMM PLUS for Windows 1.0

PROCOMM Plus for Windows is a new Windows communications program following in the footsteps of Datastorm's PROCOMM PLUS for DOS. The Windows version is an entirely new program with compatiblilty to the DOS version.

Installation and Configurability

The basic installation is trouble-free. The communications configuration created during the initial install can be changed when running the program. PROCOMM PLUS offers 34 terminal emulation modes including Televideo and DEC emulations. The ANSI version did not work well with SCO UNIX applications. Setting up PROCOMM PLUS to access your modem is done by clicking on the setup icon. A dialog box with buttons defines the various options. We found the keyboard mapping in PROCOMM PLUS to be better than any product of any type except for maybe Hummingbird's eXceed/W X server. You can pull up the keyboard map for a VT320 and remap the delete key (or any key) through a graphical keyboard.

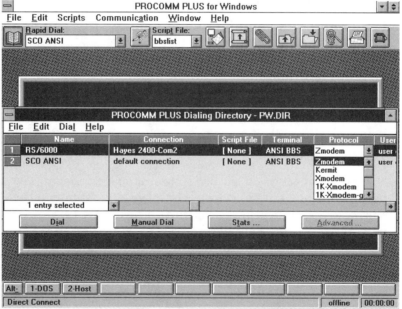

FIGURE 16.1   Datastorm's Procomm Plus for Windows with dialing directory

Connectability

There are 11 different download options—including being able to view GIF files while they are downloaded. There is INT 14 support for communication servers but no other network support and no network-particular printer support. Like FutureSoft's DynaComm, PROCOMM PLUS uses a Dialing Directory—the new trend in Windows communications programs. Rather than storing settings for online services in separate files, the Dialing Directory allows you to pick a number off the screen, and PROCOMM PLUS begins dialing as shown in Figure 16.1. The new settings are automatically loaded, making it a snap to go between a direct UNIX connection and, say, CompuServe.

Ease of Use

PROCOMM PLUS calls its icon bar an action bar. Instead of placing common actions such as **File/Open** on the action bar, PROCOMM PLUS has created innovative actions such as the scroll icon (giving you direct access to the 31 pages of buffer). The clipboard icon can pick file names off a listing and save them for later placement in a download command. While these different icons take a little getting used to, they prove their value by condensing multiple keystrokes into a single mouse click. PRO-COMM PLUS has done an excellent job of making the options accessible. In some ways, however, this is the typical first port to Windows. Although the user interface is polished, there are times when the Windows menu choices do not fit the standard Windows interface. For example, the File menu does not contain the standard **Open**, **Print**, and **Save** options. Generally, this is only inconvenient, but it might require some adjustment for Windows users.

Power Features

PROCOMM PLUS loads itself with features, but none of them are UNIX-specific. You can program the Meta keys that display at the bottom of the screen to send a command, run another program, or run an ASPECT script. ASPECT is the scripting language provided with PROCOMM PLUS. Truly Windows-based, it challenges DynaComm by providing a complete script option. PROCOMM PLUS supports a host script that allows others to log into your machine, giving you extra communication options. You can call your machine late at night from home or let another site download files from your system. There is no editor provided so PROCOMM PLUS uses Windows Notepad to edit scripts.

Summary

The $179 workstation price of PROCOMM PLUS adds another big plus to an already strong program. We found PROCOMM PLUS solid in the use of innovative icons, terminal emulation, and scripting. In addition, the keyboard mapping is simply the best. What PROCOMM PLUS doesn't do well is make any overtures to UNIX, nor does it have a wide variety of Novell communication server support. It is a general PC communication program designed to handle the gamut of needs in that area. Even so, we think if you work in a Windows environment, PROCOMM Plus for Windows is possibly the strongest program on the market.

DCA Crosstalk for Windows 2.0

Crosstalk for Windows is the Windows version of DCA's popular Crosstalk Mark 4. Historically, Crosstalk has been a market leader in the DOS communications market.

The Windows version is well-designed and easy to learn because it makes excellent use of the Windows interface.

Installation and Configurability

The standard Windows install script goes without a hitch. When you first start up Crosstalk it offers you the opportunity to select a login profile. If you need to create a new profile, a simple script walks you through the settings. Crosstalk supplies 22 terminal emulation options including WYSE, Televideo, and DEC as well as PC-terminal and ANSI. These are important emulations for UNIX systems. Once you are running the program, configuration lets you make changes to any parameter.

Connectability

We had no trouble logging into our SCO system on a direct connection and to our IBM RS/6000 over U.S. Robotics 2400 baud modems. When running in full screen, the default fonts gave us 24 lines in about 3/4 of the screen space, leaving 10 lines of leftover space. Crosstalk does not automatically use the entire screen.

Over a dozen file transfer options put Crosstalk at the head of the pack. It includes Kermit, DART, and CompuServe. You do not get **ftp** support, since Crosstalk lacks TCP/IP support. Crosstalk lets you take a snapshot of any particular screen and save it to file or printer. While there are network connections for NASI and Int 14h, Crosstalk is less suitable for network communication operations than DynaComm or SmartTerm. If you are using a network API or have multiple COM ports, Crosstalk allows more than one session at a time.

Ease of Use

Nearly everything in Crosstalk exudes the look and feel of Windows. The interface is full of shortcut keys, dialog boxes, buttons, and icons. An icon bar across the top of the screen, as well as the icons within setup dialog boxes, make Crosstalk commands easily accessible. In terms of pure Windows aesthetics and simplicity, Crosstalk is one of the best.

Crosstalk supplies a set of auto login scripts for services such as MCI Mail, CompuServe, and Delphi. These scripts provide the correct settings and lets you put user name and password information into the login script. The ANSI emulation supplied with Crosstalk did not work well on our SCO machine, but VT100 did fine. We were able to use function keys and get full screen support without any noticeable bugs. Setting up a connectivity session, setting the terminal emulation options, and establishing the file transfer rules are all done from well-designed and usable dialog boxes. Documentation clearly lays out the features found in Crosstalk.

Power Features

The supplied editor contains only simple editing options, but does have a compile option for scripts. The scripting language, CASL, allows for full Windows functions such as dialog boxes. One feature we really liked, the QuickPad, lets you design simple commands and scripts for use with different sessions as shown in Figure 16.2. Similar to DynaComm's function key buttons, the QuickPad can be buttons, icons, text, or graphics. A number of preconfigured QuickPads are provided. This feature allows a DOS user to invoke simple UNIX commands without learning how to write UNIX script files.

There are no UNIX-specific options with Crosstalk. You cannot use SCO's **mscreen** or **ftp** file transfer. The page buffer is easily increased up to the 64K limit. While there are no true remote control options, Crosstalk still enables other users to log onto the PC and download files.

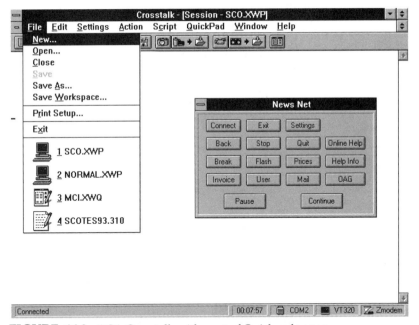

FIGURE 16.2 DCA Crosstalk with a set of Quickpads open

Summary

We were impressed with the QuickPads, icon tool bar, and the configurability of Crosstalk for Windows. At $195, it is moderately-priced, but it ranked as one of the easiest-to-use packages with the greatest flexibility. It lacks UNIX-specific features that might be needed by individuals doing a large number of file transfers. It also does not support a wide variety of network connection options. However, for general communications in the Windows environment, Crosstalk is a cut above.

FutureSoft DynaComm 3.1

DynaComm was one of the first Windows communications packages on the market. In fact, the terminal program found in Microsoft Windows is a scaled-back version of DynaComm. As such, DynaComm has had a leg up on the competition when it came to getting the interface right and is just now coming under stiff competition from other Windows-based communications programs.

Installation and Configurability

DynaComm 3.1 uses a Windows-based installation program that is both flexible and uneventful. It gives you the option to not load tutorials and optional scripts. Installation goes smoothly, with all networks loaded and available from DynaComm's menus and no unusual system requirements. There are 16 terminal emulation options including DEC, Televideo, and AT&T 605, as well as full keyboard mapping.

Connectability

DynaComm provides support for 12 different network options beyond standard serial communications, including NASI, NetBIOS, DEC LAT, and TCP/IP. There is support for Novell's NVT over a Novell network to a UNIX host. DynaComm has perhaps the most options for connecting to Novell. It also provides support for all major TCP/IP networks. DynaComm boasts six different binary file transfer options but no **ftp** support. Interestingly, one of its serial options accesses all four COM ports. DynaComm uses a Dialer mode to dial out to pre-built autologin services.

Ease of Use

The Dialer in DynaComm replaces the Director script found in previous versions of DynaComm. For some users this is a negative, but most will find the Dialer (Figure 16.3) a useful tool that makes automatic logins easier. Dynacomm depends on setting files and scripts to make a login; sometimes this can be confusing. In the Dialer, you set the various options and then save the information as a settings file. The Dialer can be used to track the costs of your login sessions. All appropriate settings such as user name, password, phone number, and terminal emulation are set in the Dialer.

Check boxes, radio buttons, and dialog boxes are logically laid out and easy to find. DynaComm supports a new toolbar which improves upon the programmable function keys of earlier versions. Excellent use of icons and the Function key status bars gives DynaComm users multiple methods of invoking commands—icons, menus, or shortcut keys. We found the User's guide, while better than previous editions, a tad on the dry side. On-line help is just a regurgitation of the manual.

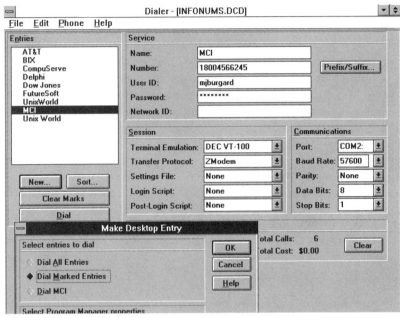

FIGURE 16.3 DynaComm dialer window

Power Features

One of the strengths of DynaComm is the completeness of the scripting language. FutureSoft did not just take a DOS scripting language and port it to Windows. Full support for popup menus, dialog box, radio buttons, and other Windows features are provided. This means your script looks and feels like a Windows application. Scripts are full-featured and can be created in the document editor provided. There is also a script recorder that does a good job of capturing commands. DynaComm uses separate setting files for individual login scripts.

Summary

At $249, DynaComm falls into the middle of the pack in pricing. It is PC-centric as are products such as PROCOMM PLUS and Crosstalk. It does not have any overly specific UNIX features such as Blast or TERM. The advantage to DynaComm is its ease of use, the strong scripting language (one of the best) and its Dialer. If you need a Windows product for modem communications to various hosts including UNIX, DynaComm is an excellent choice.

Hayes Smartcom for Windows 1.0 and Smartcom III

Smartcom for Windows 1.0 from Hayes Microcomputer is the child of Smartcom III, the DOS version. Smartcom is one of the last entries into the Windows communications market. Smartcom for Windows is a full-featured, PC directed communications program. We reviewed both the DOS and Window versions of Smartcom.

Installation and Configurability

Installation is a no-brainer with Smartcom for Windows or DOS. There are only five terminal emulation modes in DOS and only eight in Windows including four VT modes, but no Wyse, Televideo, or SCO Console—definitely a weakness for UNIX connectivity. The ANSI mode did not work well in our tests. There is no special keyboard mapping, and you will have difficulty using this emulation program with programs that need function key assignments in UNIX.

Connectability

Configuration is done through a settings file. Smartcom for Windows gives you only a couple of preconfigured setup files. No connections to CompuServe, MCI or any other popular on-line system are preset. Using the setup file, you choose standard configuration items such as modem settings, terminal emulation, file transfer and speed. One beneficial feature is the ability to set the speed to maximum. Smartcom supports some network connections including NASI/NCSI, interrupt 14 and two TCP/IP connections (but none in the DOS version). There are eight file transfer protocols in the Windows version and six in DOS. There is no ftp support and no UNIX specific file transfer options. Overall, the network and configuration options of Smartcom for Windows are fewer than other products.

The limited terminal emulation options reduce the flexibility of the program for UNIX. There is a separate keyboard preference where keystrokes are assigned program actions or edit functions. All the keys are assignable and can be done without any programming.

Ease of Use

The use of the phone book metaphor is easy to understand for most users. It also reflects Smartcom's propensity towards modem based communications. The use of a status bar with commands options clearly labeled shows Smartcom's DOS leanings. The phone book metaphor is detailed in Smartcom. There are a large number of choices for the expert but most of the defaults work. You can access network printers through Smartcom, TCP/IP support, various serial connections, dial up options, ftp support, printing setup, and other network services.

Unlike some DOS to Windows switch-overs, SmartCom maintains the Windows standards well. It does it better than PROCOMM or Crosstalk making Smartcom for Windows easier for Windows users. When you are actually placing a call, Smartcom for Windows gives you clear icons updating the progress of the call. A large text buffer called the peruse buffer lets you cut and paste text.

Like all good windows communications applications, Smartcom for Windows uses buttons called Smart Buttons to provide different functions, seen in Figure 16.4. Beside invoking Smartcom for Windows scripts and menu selections, these buttons can invoke other Windows applications. There can be multiple rows of buttons, you can create your own buttons and attach macros to them, and there are given 36 default conditions that can be attached to a button.

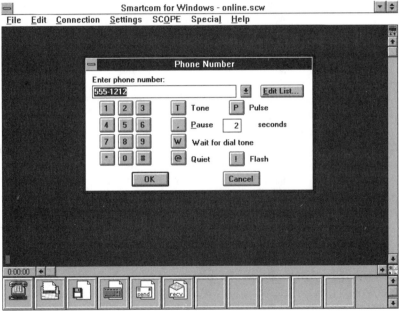

FIGURE 16.4   Hayes Smartcom For Windows toolbar and phone dialer

Power Features

There is a complete editor in the Windows version that is a separate program. The editor can be used for creating scripts. It has complete ANSI control, a special character selection option and standard word processor options such as word wrap, search and replace. The editor is much better than the default Windows editor and can be used outside of Smartcom. The DOS editor is much weaker.

If you want to play hard ball, Smartcom for Windows is the only communications product we reviewed that supports ISDN. If you use a Hayes ISDN system adapter, Smartcom for Windows works with it. It supports circuit-switched and packet-switched networks.

Scope is the Smartcom for Windows scripting language. It is 100% percent compatible with previous versions of SmartCom making it attractive for Execucom and SmartCom III users. Scripts can be called up via key combinations, debugged with the Watch Window and has a learn mode.

Summary

Smartcom for Windows shows its 1.0 genesis. While it has standard Windows features such as buttons and toolbars, it does not have some of the extras found in second and third generation programs. Smartcom for Windows, at $149 is a bargain and is suited to anyone with extensive SCOPE scripts from previous Smartcom products, and its editor is better than most. UNIX connectivity is only marginal. There are too few terminal emulation options and only two TCP/IP connection options.

Persoft SMARTERM 420 for Windows Version 3.0

Persoft SmarTerm 420 for Windows is a communication program designed for connections in the DEC world. SmarTerm has the typical array of Windows features plus it includes a TCP/IP module, DEC LAT support, and **ftp** server utility. The new version of SmarTerm makes better use of Windows than did version 2.0. Its biggest weakness, SmarTerm has limited terminal emulation options for UNIX connections.

Installation and Configurability

The Windows-based install allows you to select directories, keyboard maps, and network connection options. You can create default setups at the time of installation. There is a file server version and a stand-alone version. You cannot load the stand-alone version on a network drive even if you are the only user. The program fails to load in this scenario.

The install and configuration routines are easy to use. You can choose a number of network options and set most of the parameters from within the Windows install program. You decide on your primary connection option at installation.

SmarTerm 420 is still primarily geared towards the DEC market and the only emulation available is from the VT series of terminals. Not all of the VT emulations worked with our tested UNIX applications; some function keys worked erratically in certain programs. Only the VT100 emulation seemed to have a complete set of function keys that was understood by most UNIX programs. Shortcut keys are everywhere in SmarTerm. There are also four basic keyboard maps provided with SmarTerm. Keyboard mapping is well-laid out and done from a graphical interface.

For example, you can define the backspace key to match the UNIX system you are using.

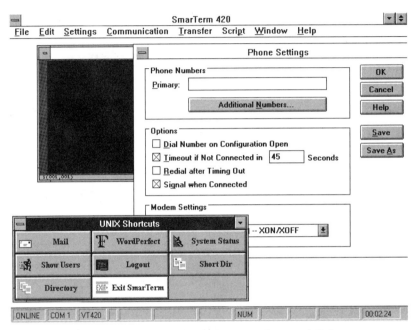

FIGURE 16.5 Persoft SmartTerm 420 button palette and dialer.

Connectability

SmarTerm provides a broad base of connection options, including LAT, INT 14, NASI/NCSI, and Digital Pathworks. Version 3.0 comes with complete TCP/IP support and SmarTerm has many DEC options. If you run a strong DEC shop, Smar-Term has excellent connection options to DEC hardware. There is **ftp** support over TCP/IP connections but not over serial lines. The **ftp** option supports drag-and-drop file transfers. There is also Winsock TCP/IP support provided. The TCP/IP module supports NDIS and ODI drivers, **ftp**, **RARP**, **ping**, and domain name server. For many users, it is all that is needed for a basic TCP/IP connection. The Windows-based TCP/IP module is new to version 3.0 and we do not review it in Chapter 13.

Persoft has improved its communication options in Version 3.0. A new dialing directory has been added that is much better than the previous method of making a connection. Version 2.0 did not let you specify the initialization commands and startup configuration of your modem. However, SmarTerm still is not the most convienent program for modem communications.

Ease of Use

Persoft follows most Windows ease of use guidelines in the design and setup of menus and dialog boxes. Version 3.0 is full of useful shortcuts and options. The button palette, mentioned later, is an excellent idea and the start-up scripts and configuration options are many. We did find the various configuration scripts to be somewhat confusing, if only for their thoroughness. Documentation is well-written and well-illustrated, but there is no tutorial to walk you through the process of logging on to other systems.

Power Features

The scripting language allows you to build special scripts for logging on and transferring files. Version 3.0 adds a script recorder. SmarTerm calls up Windows Notepad if you choose to edit a script. Persoft provides a set of sample scripts including logging on to MCI Mail and Dow Jones. It also uses a button palette, a user-configured set of buttons to invoke scripts or short commands. The button palette, seen in Figure 16.5, can be created for specific applications or tasks. Besides choosing the graphic and label, each button can execute a command, pass a string, or run a script. LAT (DEC's protocol) is strongly supported in SmarTerm as are multiple sessions.

Summary

SmarTerm 420 3.0 for Windows is a good Windows-based program. It has excellent connections to DEC equipment but is less suited for UNIX connections. Its Windows interface is vastly improved in version 3.0. The Button palettes make better use of colors and icons. In a DEC environment or one where VT emulation is high on the list, SmarTerm has much to offer. In a generic setting, it is less suitable. SmarTerm sells for $295.

Walker, Richer & Quinn Reflection 2 for Windows 4.1

The Reflection Network Series of DOS and Windows emulators is geared to the DEC market as opposed to being a generic terminal emulator, although WRQ is trying to increase the appeal of their product line. It also has appropriateness to the UNIX market because of its proprietary file transfer protocol and because WRQ has an entire series of products including TCP/IP and X servers.

Installation and Configurability

The setup program is Windows-based and configures Reflection based on your answers to questions. It does make changes to a number of .**INI** files without an option to view the changes first.

Reflection supports only VT emulations. While a drawback in certain UNIX markets, VT emulations are still some of the most popular in the world and work with nearly any UNIX application. Still, this limits who might be interested in Reflection. To use the first four function keys in the standard keyboard mapping, we had to enable the embedded numeric keypad. There is full graphical keyboard mapping in Reflection.

Connectability

Reflection has some of the widest connection options of any product. Besides serial, INT 14, and NASI, you can choose from CTERM, LAT, HP-NSVT, BAPI and a total of 13 altogether. WRQ's own WRQ protocol is one available file transfer option. There is also **ftp** support. The WRQ protocol requires a program called **uxlink2** to be installed on the host. If you have not used a previous version of Reflection, there is a script that uploads and compiles the necessary program. This mini-boot strap method is supposed to work on any UNIX system. It failed on our SCO system because SCO does not supply **cc** (a UNIX compiler) with its personal edition of SCO Open Desktop.

Ease of Use

Reflection is a standard Windows interface with the addition of a button palette. The button palette is like PROCOMM'S Meta keys and SMARTERM button palette. It is a programmable group of commands with icons attached. You go into the Define Button option to assign a command or script to the button. WRQ includes a wide variety of .bmp files to be symbols in the buttons. However, even with the button palettes, Reflection is not as easy to use as PROCOMM PLUS or DynaComm.

We had difficulties getting Reflection to not use our embedded numeric keypad in our laptop. It would not let us use the numlock key and it assumed the numeric keypad was on. The presence of a mouse clickable Numlock option in the Reflection status bar saved the day. The dialer appears to have room for only four options in it. We found certain items difficult to follow like having the file transfer options under the File Command. The help system online is detailed and easy to use.

Power Features

A scripting language with record options and Window-aware commands is a central part of Reflection. No document editor or special multiple screen support exists. The ability to use a special protocol makes Reflection UNIX-aware. However, where Reflection shows its prowess is in the DEC environment. The manuals deal with many DEC issues such as answerback mode and printer control characters. The ability to trace all communication events and send the file to WRQ is available. You also get some basic statistics under the troubleshooting option.

Summary

In general, we thought Reflection at $299 was more difficult to use than it should have been. The organization of the menus and the way you set up different dial options did not come easily. We had difficulty making the UNIX transport option work. Where Reflection really shines is in an all-DEC environment or where you need access to ULTRIX- based DECstations and VAXes. In a more generic UNIX environment with Windows users, products such as PROCOMM PLUS and Dyna-Comm will serve you better.

UNIX-Aware Terminal Emulators

In this category, we include a number of DOS or Windows-based terminal emulator products which have UNIX components. In most cases, the UNIX component is designed to provide a file transfer mechanism between PCs and UNIX. There are other options that make these products ideal in a mixed environment.

Century Software Term—Windows, DOS, and UNIX

Century Software has a reputation for making its products available on a wide variety of UNIX platforms. We examined the DOS, Windows and SCO UNIX versions of Term. The Windows version is the newest and we concentrate our comments on it. The features and the interface between the products are similar, but the Windows product is the most advanced.

Installation and Configurability

TERM installs without difficulty in all environments. The UNIX version brings you to the setup menu immediately, letting you configure the system. The DOS version requires you to start up TERM first. All versions support a variety of network connections including TCP/IP. TERM supplies 15 terminal emulation options in DOS and 17 in Windows. All the choices are excellent for UNIX Connectivity.

All versions of TERM use a serialization scheme and if you attempt to install it on a network drive, TERM senses it and only allows one user. You have to purchase the server version to install on a network drive. There are moderate keyboard mapping facilities. You can remap any set of keys, but it has to be done in a script file, which is not convenient. The Windows product does not automatically setup your communications environment (like which port to use) upon installation.

Connectability

TERM on the PC side (DOS or Windows) can connect not only to UNIX via serial lines but also over TCP/IP using Sun PC/NFS, FTP PC/TCP, and others. There is also support for NetBIOS, Novell IPX/SPX and Locus PC-Interface protocols. IPX is through Novell's NVT to a UNIX host that has an IPX/SPX protocol installed such as SCO's IPX/SPX product. Network support is definitely geared towards TCP/IP rather than Novell-based communication servers.

TERM has a file transfer sliding window protocol called WTERMCRC which is similar to Blast's. If your UNIX host has a copy of TERM, you can run it in server mode from the PC and then do file transfers. We did not have any problem with file transfers. At least 10 other protocols are provided with TERM.

Ease of Use

The UNIX and DOS versions of TERM do not win any awards for ease of use, both using the outdated Lotus-style menu. The DOS version uses the ALT-F1 key to invoke the menus. On the plus side, many configuration options are set in popup windows.

The Windows version is a different story. As shown in Figure 16.6, there is an icon bar across the top and many dialog boxes have further pull-down menus when there are selections. TERM did not supply any sample common login scripts such as for MCI or CompuServe, but, like many programs, it lets you save configurations in a file. There are no shortcut keys in the Windows version and you cannot easily program function keys. There is a session window that lets you start multiple sessions, but there is nothing such as Dynacomm's dialing directory. Overall, the Windows version is a snap to use.

There is no index in the DOS manuals, but the Windows help is great. TERM supplies excellent information on how to get your serial connections correct and how to set up your UNIX host. Some of the shortcomings include no autologin scripts for the DOS version, a weak help system, and non-standard actions (help is ALT-F2).

Power Features

TERM supports multiple sessions or multiple screens within a single session. You can have nine multiple sessions, but only two of them can be serial connections, and these have to use separate serial ports from your PC. Other sessions have to be over a network. If you have need for terminal emulation access to a TCP/IP network and over a serial line simultaneously, TERM is one of a few programs capable of providing that option in a single package. Both the DOS and Windows version provide this option. TERM supports the SCO mscreen utility making it a good choice for SCO terminal emulation. Scripting, automatic recording of scripts, and the option to use one of the system editors are included with TERM. The Windows version uses the Windows Notepad and does not provide an editor.

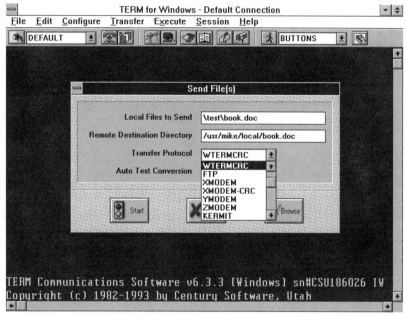

FIGURE 16.6   Term For Windows makes good use of dialog boxes and pop-ups

Summary

We liked TERM's multiple session ability and its support for a variety of networks. Its own file transfer protocol is also an advantage. The Windows product is done well, just missing a few extras. We did not like the odd use of function keys and wished Century supplied some start-up scripts. At $195, TERM for windows is an excellent choice for a Windows environment connecting to UNIX machines. The UNIX version is $495.

Digiboard DoubleVIEW Version 1.3

DoubleView comes from Digiboard, well-know for its multiport serial boards. DoubleView is meant to piggyback on this success in the UNIX serial connectivity market. DoubleView is a solid program without extras and without a graphical interface. It is also inexpensive for multiple users.

Installation and Configurability

On the PC, DoubleView installs easily. Once installed, you load DoubleView and run through a setup script. All the setup options are done through multiple full-screen setup menus. As a TSR, DoubleView is similar to ICE.TEN.PLUS. You can work in DOS applications and pop-up the terminal emulation over other applications. There are only five emulations available but they include SCO, AT&T and Wyse 60 which make DoubleView ideal for SCO environments. There is color and keyboard configuration support. There is no keyboard mapping but you can see how the emulation mode maps certain keys by pressing Alt-H. DoubleView requires about 67K of RAM and it can be unloaded from memory.

Connectability

DoubleView is strictly a serial connection tool. There is no support for any other networks or protocols. Any printing from the host to a DOS printer connected to a PC is done only if the host UNIX box is using a Digiboard intelligent serial board. In that case, you can print data to a printer attached to your PCs serial or parallel port at the same time communications are occurring.

Using DoubleView for modem communications is not the best idea in our mind. You can insert only one modem setup string in the setup. You could code a set of softkeys to handle different modem commands but given that most communication programs provide you with pre-configured setups for hundreds of modems, it hardly seems worth the effort.

Ease of Use

Starting up DoubleView is easy as is bringing up the setup screen. There are not many options in DoubleView. You make a direct connection with the Alt-V key. We found the emulation modes solid. The UNIX applications used the function keys without any difficulty while the DoubleView hot-keys also worked well. There is no MS Windows option to DoubleView. You can use it within a DOS compatibility box under MS-Windows but that seems like a waste.

Power Features

Power is not DoubleView's claim to frame. The only file transfer option is the Dcopy command. You can copy either text files or binary files. In an ASCII transfer, the DOS-to-UNIX translation is handled automatically.

There is a small scripting language in DoubleView. It is adequate for logging into a system but it is nothing such as the powerful and complete languages found in DynaComm or PROCOMM PLUS. There is no record mode or editor in which to write the scripts. DoubleView does provide the screen switching ability necessary to support SCO's mscreen utility giving you multiple UNIX screens one at a time.

Summary

DoubleView, at $239 for 8 users, is a simple terminal emulator that runs as a TSR in DOS machines. It is particularly well suited to SCO machines using DigiBoard multiport boards because of the extra printing options. We only recommend Double-View for direct connections because of its weak support for modem communications. We also would not use DoubleView in a Windows environment or where you needed to access many different machines.

Esker TUN*EMUL 7.0

Esker provides a line of UNIX to DOS internetworking products including TUN*-EMUL, a terminal emulator; TUN*TCP, a TCP/IP kernel, TUN*X11, a DOS-based X server and TUN*PLUS, a combination of TCP/IP and EMUL. We looked at TUN*-EMUL as a comparison to other terminal emulation products.

Installation and Configurability

If you purchase TUN*PLUS, you get TUN*EMUL and a TCP/IP kernel. The installation is complicated because there are different modules and assorted instructions. There are 14 terminal emulation types to choose from. The ANSI version was one of the few applications to work with applications running SCO console emulation. There is complete keyboard mapping in TUN*EMUL, including the ability to map the escape keys. This means you can make TUN*EMUL into any emulation if you know the proper configurations. Other options are configured in the menu, but there are not as many as in, say TERM from Century Software.

Connectability

TUN*EMUL supplies a file transfer module called RCOPY that you load on the UNIX host for file transfer. There are versions for SCO UNIX, and C source versions for other systems. TUN*EMUL converts the DOS CR and LF to the UNIX LF and vice versa. You can also use **ftp** when a TCP/IP connection is used.

TUN*EMUL supports Interrupt 14H and TCP/IP connections. TUN*PLUS provides its own TCP/IP kernel making the product suite more complete than emulators that rely on third party TCP/IP kernels. If you want to use TUN*EMUL with a Novell Network in conjunction with TCP/IP, the manual supplies a reasonable discussion of implementing the dual stacks. There is also complete keyboard remapping options in TUN.

When purchased with TUN*TCP, you get an NFS module. This is a big improvement over Esker's previous non-NFS resource sharing product. File transfer without the NFS is limited to Esker's proprietary method.

Ease of Use

TUN*EMUL does not win any awards for making it easy for users to work with terminal emulation. The Windows part of the program has numerous shortcomings and is far from a true Windows implementation. The menus do not follow the Windows standard, and the first program you open does not do much but allow you to open the emulator. You can not make many real changes once in the emulator mode. The new Version 7.0 includes scalable fonts and icons to make the interface more lovable. The File Transfer menu is confusing and does not make it clear that you are invoking a line-by-line send or receive. There is limited support for modem communications. The manuals have been completely rewritten in the latest version.

Power Features

With TUN*EMUL, you get the remote copy option allowing you to move files from DOS or Windows. A scripting language is including in version 7.0. However, there are more things missing. There are no fancy smart buttons or icons that are programmable. There is no document editor. Multiple sessions are supported only if you are using TCP/IP or INT 14H or using Mscreen.

Summary

In general, our impressions of TUN*EMUL, at $245, is not favorable. If you need an easy-to-use program, this is not it. You might consider it if you have SCO systems and want direct file transfer options but we prefer other products such as ICE.TEN and Blast in those situations. If you need a full TCP/IP kernel, NFS and emulation, TUN*PLUS provides a solution to consider.

James River Group ICE.TEN.PLUS 3.4

ICE.TEN.PLUS is a DOS-based and MS Windows terminal emulator designed for over 20 different UNIX machines. We tested the SCO/Intel UNIX version under both DOS and Windows. It offers some unique file transfer and command options that make it attractive in an SCO setting.

Installation and Configurability

There is some work involved in getting all the components of ICE.TEN up and running. You have to install the DOS and Windows software and then run an install program to set parameters. Because the terminal emulation component of ICE.TEN, Dejavu, is a TSR program, you need to configure it before starting the program. The older DOS configuration routine has been replaced and now allows all configuration changes to be made on the fly similar to the Windows version.

ICE.TEN.PLUS has a set of components to install on the UNIX machine. These files copy directly into the **/usr/bin** directory. You run a **chmod** command to make the files executable. ICE.TEN does support keyboard mapping and color but the options for these choices are not menu driven.

Connectability

What ICE.TEN lacks in beauty it makes up in power. It was one of only a few programs that properly implements the SCO console ANSI emulation. If you want to access SCO, this is one of the best ways. ICE.TEN.PLUS supports 11 different emulation modes. It includes Wyse, ANSI (SCO and non-SCO), and VT100 which are the three most common for an SCO UNIX box. The ANSI console emulation worked flawlessly in 25 line mode.

There is no support for network APIs or TCP/IP connections. Serial support is the extent of ICE.TEN. As a TSR, Dejavu requires about 58K of memory. This makes it difficult to load into high memory, but if you have space Dejavu will load into high memory. James River has its own TCP/IP product, but it does not work with Dejavu.

Ease of Use

ICE gets both a thumbs up and a thumbs down in the ease of use department. On the positive side, the simplicity of the Dejavu pop-up emulator makes it easy for any one not familiar with UNIX. The quality of the ANSI emulation eliminates some of the hassles found with other products. James River supplies a UNIX utility called the **dshell** which makes life much easier for the DOS user. Running **dshell** from the UNIX prompt lets you use all DOS commands instead of UNIX commands. To get a directory listing, you need type only dir instead of ls -x. Hiding the UNIX prompt behind the DOS prompt is an ingenious idea, at least for DOS users.

The Windows product has fewer rough edges than does the DOS version of Dejavu, but it is not a complete Windows implementation. There are a few icons (in the newest version), but no special configuration keys or other graphical options. You can capture the screen in Windows and the configuration file uses 3-D buttons rather than a text mode.

On the thumbs down side, the lack of significant configuration options while in the terminal emulation mode makes it hard to correct a potential problem. Through a pop-up menu, you can make changes to baud rate and parity and access the print options. The manual is OK but there is no on-line help in either the DOS or Windows version.

Power Features

There are two other features in ICE.TEN that make it well worth looking at for the SCO (or any UNIX) environment. First is the ucopy command. When installed on the UNIX host, you can copy a file from UNIX to DOS and vice versa. Ucopy requires the connection to be open via Dejavu, but all the work is done from the DOS prompt. Ucopy uses either Xmodem or Ymodem for transfers.

The second feature is the Host Print which allows a DOS user to print to a UNIX printer. Host Print lets you attach either LPT1, 2 or 3 to Dejavu. When you print from within Lotus 1-2-3 or Wordperfect, the output goes to the UNIX printer. Host Print also works within Windows 3.1 but requires loading a TSR before starting Windows.

We found Dejawin (the WIndows version of Dejavu) to be slower than other Windows-based communication programs in screen redraws. The ucopy option is somewhat unstable in the Windows environment. ICE.TEN.PLUS does not have any scripting or editing facilities.

Summary

ICE.TEN.PLUS is appropriate in an SCO or other UNIX environment where you need to easily work between the PC and the UNIX host. It has some attractive features. If users unfamiliar with UNIX need access to UNIX printers and files, ICE.T-EN.PLUS is one of the only products with printer, file transfer and DOS command support on an SCO platform. It is not designed for modem communications. Starting at $395 for an unlimited user license, this product is a bargain.

U.S. Robotics Blast 10.7

Blast continues to be a character-based program. We include it in our review for two reasons. It is available on a wide variety of platforms and can be used for PC to UNIX and UNIX to PC communications. Secondly, the Blast protocol is well known and highly regarded for file transfer.

Installation and Configurability

Blast installs quickly on either PCs or UNIX machines. You do not make many selections during setup, but leave them until you start up the program. Blast does not require much memory or disk space on a PC. There are 17 terminal emulation modes. You can map the keyboard but you have to create a special ASCII text file.

Blast uses a full screen setup file that includes nearly every parameter needed for dialing into a system. You can specify a separate script to start up with actual dialing instructions, logon names, and so on. The setup routine seems long and difficult given the dialog box method common in Windows products.

Connectability

Blast started life as a serial communication product and that remains its strength. It now has TCP/IP support on the UNIX host, but that is secondary to its modem and direct connections. There is support for many different modems including the entire U.S. Robotics line. Blast does not allow peripheral sharing nor can you use ftp to transfer files.

In the file transfer area, Blast can start up another copy of Blast on the remote UNIX host and then use the Blast protocol to make transfers. The Blast protocol is a sliding frame full-duplex protocol. This means it both transmits and sends blocks of data at the same time. It also supports sophisticated error correcting and noisy-line recognition and correction. You can also use Xmodem, Ymodem, Zmodem and Kermit. Without Blast on the UNIX machine, you can only capture files.

Ease of Use

Blast uses a Lotus-style menu with status lines at both the top and the bottom of the screen. Blast uses an odd combination of control key shortcuts that may be confusing at first. For example, to leave the terminal mode, the default is CTRL-K CTRL-K. Menus respond by selecting the capitalized character in the word.

You have access to both a reference manual and a user's guide. Being a character-based program, there are no icons, fancy graphics or other neat tricks to make the program easier to use. While there are many options in the configuration, Blast does not provide a single auto-login script for any public e-mail service or other scenario. Help is context-sensitive.

Power Features

We included Blast in our evaluations due to its excellent platform support and its proprietary protocol. Blast is available on over 40 different platforms including nearly every form of UNIX. We loaded Blast on both PCs and SCO UNIX and used the Blast protocol to transfer files. In a controlled environment, it is one of the best serial-based file transfer options available, fast and reliable. A simple text editor is provided with a CTRL-key interface. Scripting is supported.

Blast offers a remote control module different from nearly any other product. With Blast, you can control PCs from your SCO UNIX host. The remote module loads as a TSR on the PC and allows you to use the Access command from the UNIX host to control the PC. This is an excellent remote diagnostics program. Unfortunately, it is difficult to set up and consumes 85K of RAM on the DOS machine.

Summary

We can't say much good about the Blast interface—it is plain and unassuming. However, the file transfer protocol is excellent and the variety of platform support makes Blast an ideal terminal emulation product in some situations. Its remote control DOS option is also a one-of-a-kind option that gives added flexibility. The DOS product is $169 while the UNIX product, one of the best on the market, is priced at $495.

Windows-Based Serial Desktops

Serial desktops are a combination Windows shell program and terminal emulator. They tend to be easier to use than communication programs, have more network options, and are highly configurable for the system administrator.

JSB MultiView Desktop 3.1

JSB MultiView Desktop is one of a series of connectivity products from JSB Computer Systems Limited. MultiView Desktop provides an alternative Windows desktop from which you can launch applications residing on a variety of different hosts. MultiView Desktop supports not only serial connections, but also many network connections. It can replace the Window Program Manager and it comes close to providing users with seamless connections.

Installation and Configurability

Installation is a matter of running the Windows script on the PC and using Custom on the UNIX host, in our case SCO Open Server. The Windows setup lets you decide if you want to alter the AUTOEXEC.BAT file and makes you select a network connection. Most of the configuration is done from the desktop once you start the product. Everything went smoothly during the install on the UNIX host. We had some minor problems with installing JSB over a network. A couple of .ini files install locally and need to be copied to other machines.

Configuration is done in two steps—nodes and applications. Each node is given a network type and a terminal emulation type. If you choose RS-232 or modem, you have to set the normal serial parameters. Everything is done from dialog boxes. There are not many terminal emulation modes. The SCO Console worked well in our tests, but there are no Wyse or Televideo modes. There is fairly extensive keyboard mapping and programming available in JSB.

Connectability

You get a wide variety of network support with MultiView Desktop. It includes FTP PC/TCP, SUN PC-NFS, and LAN Manager support. Overall, there are over 20 different network options, but no Novell IPX/SPX. JSB was the originator of the WinSock specification that Microsoft adopted so you will find WinSock support whenever the network vendor uses it. Network options are as good as any product.

Making a connection is done from a series of menus and dialog boxes. The hosts themselves are not displayed on the desktop like they are in PC-Connect. Instead, you create nodes by identifying network connections, names, and specific login actions. Then each application icon is attached to a particular node, whether it is local or remote.

MultiView Desktop supports multiple connections over a serial connection because of the host support module. This is a big plus over nearly all other products. Host support extends to over a dozen different UNIX machines. File transfer is simple and done from a series of dialog boxes, and automatically converts UNIX text files to DOS. The UNIX print services require your Windows applications to print to file, but the file is moved to the UNIX host and spooled automatically.

Ease of Use

Once configured, JSB MultiView Desktop is remarkably simple. Click on an icon and an application starts up. It doesn't matter to the user whether the application is a Windows spreadsheet on the local hard disk, a accounting program on the UNIX host, or even an X application running across TCP/IP (with the help of an X server).

In some respects improvements in the generic Windows 3.1 interface and the proliferation of third-party desktops reduces the need and benefits of a serial-based desktop. However, JSB serves as both a Windows shell, a terminal emulator, and as a configuration utility. In this respect, it is still a good combination given its simplicity.

You get a complete set of icons to use when configuring a desktop, but you don't get much in terms of default setups. JSB provides a file transfer, remote shell and remote login icon all configured for direct RS-232 connections. Help is the standard Windows hypertext-based system. It is mostly a rehash of the manual.

Power Features

JSB MultiView Desktop does not have some of the high-end options found in the best Windows terminal emulators. There is a learn mode that builds scripts, but is not complete and so there is no way to create buttons for specific options. The ability to customize icons to run specific applications goes along way, but MultiView Desktop is not a leading edge product at the interface end. Products such as Norton's Desktop for Windows are more intuitive. The ability to have multiple serial sessions is one of the more important aspects of JSB MultiView Desktop. The file transfer module uses DDE and you can create programs between DOS and UNIX that make use of DDE technology.

Summary

Overall, JSB MultiView Desktop is a solid program. The ability to configure various icons without the user knowing where the application resides makes sense. Even more helpful is the ability to have multiple sessions over a serial line. At $955 for a 5-user pack, you might find the price at little steep, but functionality is great. Even if you use TCP/IP or NFS, JSB MultiView Desktop is a strong integration product for bridging DOS and UNIX.

VisionWare PC-Connect 6.1

PC-Connect is a one of a group of connectivity products from VisionWare. We review VisionWare's X server in Chapter 15. PC-Connect, like JSB Multiview, is a MS-Windows product that provides an alternate desktop and has a host component. It is more than a terminal emulation program and is targeted at large corporate environments where a common desktop is needed.

Installation and Configurability

VisionWare products can be difficult to set up. You must first install the communications drivers from the VisionWare Communications package. This comes with PC-Connect, but it requires a separate installation. The host module installs via a script and populates four different directories. You do not rebuild the kernel with the SunOS version.

There are only five terminal emulation modes supported in PC-Connect. While on the sparse side, VisionWare claims they are well done. We did not like the fact there was no SCO ANSI emulation and that you had to run the setup from the floppy disks to change the default terminal type. That isn't hassle-free computing in our minds. However, you can now select the terminal type when you load new applications and that takes away most of the sting. Within a terminal emulation mode, there are many options that allow you to configure your particular emulation requirements.

Connectability

PC-Connect supplies full TCP/IP and serial connection options. VisionWare supports at least 11 different TCP/IP packages. PC-Connect supports WinSock. At present, many of the network connections use TSRs. When connecting to hosts that reside on the PC-Connect desktop, other network options include LAT, CTERM, Netware via NVT, AT&T Starlan and others.

When you connect with any host via a direct serial connection or a modem connection, you have the ability to run a single login session. This assumes there is no PC-Connect host module installed. You can run one application at a time. If you purchase the host module (available for over 30 UNIX machines), you can create a multiple channel login. For example, you can run multiple applications over the connection even if it is RS-232. None of the regular terminal emulators provide this option.

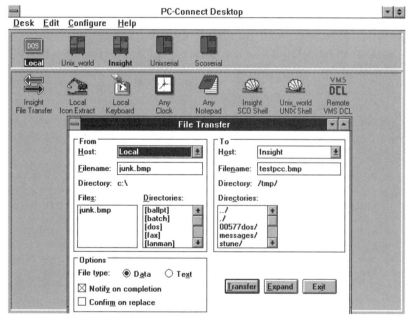

FIGURE 16.7 PC-Connect has its own desktop with a menu-based file transfer
dialog box

The host module provides other options as well. There is file transfer, as seen in Figure 16.7, and remote printing options in PC-Connect. The UNIX component of the file transfer uses Microsoft's DDE. The remote printing is a two step process and not smooth. You have to print to a file and then start a process on the UNIX host that picks up the file and prints it.

You can run X applications from PC-Connect by using a TCP/IP network and buying XVision from VisionWare. If you go to all that trouble, we are not sure having PC-Connect is much of an advantage. Another option is to use third-party emulators within PC-Connect. Crosstalk or PROCOMM PLUS can be used over DOS interrupt 14H within PC-Connect.

Ease of Use

The overall desktop is all graphical and simple to use. It can be used to replace the program manager or run with it. The idea with the desktop is to create icons that represent applications located on various machines in the network. You create either new hosts or new programs. The hosts can have any name you desire. Once you have identified the hosts, you create programs. You can identify an application with a host or allow it to access any host. You can also drag an application onto the host.

Once all the network connections are established, PC-Connect is transparent to the user. They click on an icon and an application runs. Many icons are provided by VisionWare. Each application runs in its own window whether it is a Windows application, a character-based UNIX application or an X applications.

The desktop itself is not particularly innovative. It does not support fancy drag-and-drop operations, and it serves as a glorified program manager for networks. The icons are created in a similar fashion as in program manger and you can not assign properties to icons so they automatically call up an application. You can start multiple applications on multiple hosts with one click of the mouse by setting up the correct configuration.

The documentation found with PC-Connect is thorough and easy to follow. There is a lot of it and unfortunately, a novice will not get far with PC-Connect until the documentation is read. The paradigm is just different enough.

Power Features

Most of the high-powered features of PC-Connect have to do with its connectivity options. With the ability to act as a multiplexor on serial lines as well as Ethernet, PC-Connect is one of the most flexible connection options for PC to UNIX. The multichannel option is essentially the equivalent of using SCO mscreen in that you can run multiple sessions over a single line.

PC-Connect provides more than the standard serial connection. You can configure the host module so portions of the desktop are stored on the host. This allows the system administrator to give every user the same desktop and access to the same applications. There is also a security option where the system administrator can restrict access to programs on a user-by-user basis. The system administrator can also configure the desktops and lock out users from changing their desktops. You get 100% control over the applications they can put on the desktop. You can purchase an optional development kit called the PC-Connect Development System which is an API that allows you to create applications on the host that can interact with PC-based applications via DDE. This is a step toward interoperability that goes beyond the call of duty. A UNIX notepad is also provided for editing on the UNIX side. Shell scripts on the UNIX host can be written to work with file transfer and the notepad.

Summary

PC-Connect and MultiView Desktop are surprisingly similar. The differences are more in how you setup the desktop than the final result. PC-Connect gives users an integrated network desktop where all applications run from a single screen. Multiple serial connections and ease of use are two big features. PC-Connect sells for $2045 for 10 users.

Other Terminal Emulators

A short description of additional UNIX-aware terminal emulators is provided here. These products all specialize in UNIX to DOS connectivity. They all support UNIX to DOS file transfer and many support remote or local printing. Company information is listed in Appendix B.

Alpha Software produces PCVision, which is an OEM'd version of WRQs Reflections for DOS. The major differences is the additional non-DEC terminal emulation modes added. PCVision is full-screen, DOS-based and supports remote printing.

Arnet Corp.'s ArneTerm is very similar to DoubleView from Digiboard. It is a TSR emulator that works best when used with Arnet's own multiport serial boards. It supports local printing through the multiport boards, but has only a few configuration options. It is an OEM'd version of Hansco Information Technologies Inc's, HIT/Ansi, which is also available directly from Hansco.

Cactus Software produces Multi-Scream for the SCO market only. It has excellent SCO ANSI support and a simple, but easy to use interface. File transfer is supported via Kermit and it supports multiple sessions through shell layers.

NEI's PCWorks is a DOS-based terminal emulator with strong modem support as well as additional features. The full screen configuration menu is one of the more complete among UNIX-aware emulators. Besides easy to use modem options, PCworks has an interface to UNIX mail, and supports other network services such as printing through its UNIX module.

Specialix's Aterm is a basic terminal emulator with file transfer support. There is only one emulation mode with Aterm, and it did not work well with SCO in our experience. Both remote and local printing are supported, but we found the documentation to be severely limited.

Tundra Software's Rapport is designed to be a UNIX-only terminal emulator. It is the only product to provide a special emulation mode and not use any standard emulations. It supports an easy to use file transfer method, but does not support modem connections. We found the documentation to be lacking and the single terminal emulation mode to be limiting in many situations.

Recommendations

When it comes to terminal emulation, there are many products to choose from. Use Tables 16.1, 16.2, and 16.3 to get a better handle on the features of each product. Here's our advice. If you are connecting to a UNIX host occasionally and also need to access other hosts or on-line services, go with PROCOMM Plus or DynaComm. Both are easy to use and flexible. When connecting to a UNIX host is your only purpose and you need to have dial-up capability, we think Century Software's TERM for Windows is an excellent program. It is the best mix of features, ease of use, and flexibility. However, it is also expensive if you have to purchase the UNIX module. Each of the other UNIX-aware programs has a niche. Finally, Blast is a good choice for a multiple operating system environment.

The serial desktop products are in a category all by themselves. For direct connections to a UNIX host, be it serial or over a network, both products have advantages. The consistent desktop and the ability to configure multiple hosts make them more friendly to the average user. Of course, it often makes good sense to upgrade from your current product rather than buy an entirely new one. Many emulators come from a line of connectivity products, and you can get benefits by using more than one product from the same vendor. For example, when you need a TCP/IP kernel and a terminal emulator, you can consider PCworks or TUN*Emul and their TCP kernels.

Recommendations

Table 16.1: UNIX-Aware Terminal Emulators

	Blast	TERM for Windows	ICE-TEN PLUS	TUN*EMUL	Double View
# of Terminal Emulation Modes	12	17	11	14	5
Keyboard Mapping (Advanced, Moderate)	Moderate	Moderate	Moderate	Yes	Moderate
FTP	No	Yes	No	Yes	No
UNIX print services	Yes	No	Yes	Yes	Yes
Scripting	Yes	Yes	No	Yes	Yes
TCP/IP Support	No	Yes	No	Yes	No
WinSock Support	No	No	No	Yes	No
LAT Support	No	No	No	No	No
Total Network Connection Options	Serial	16	Serial TCP/IP	7	Serial
132 Columns Screen Support	Yes	Yes	Yes	Yes	Yes
File Transfer (Xmodem,Ymodem, Zmodem,Kermit, CompuServe)	Xmodem, Ymodem, Zmodem, Kermit, blast	All plus wtermcrc & termcrc	Xmodem, Ymodem	Proprietary Only	Kermit
Dial-up Options	Yes	Yes	Yes	Yes	Yes
Multiple Sessions	Yes	8	Yes	4	Yes
Remote Control	Yes	No	No	No	No
Platform Support (Windows, DOS or UNIX)	DOS, UNIX	Windows, DOS, UNIX	Windows, DOS	Windows	DOS
Document Editor	Yes	No	No	No	No
Auto Logins Provided	Yes	Some	No	Yes	No
Graphics File Viewers	No	No	No	No	No
Toolbars	No	Yes	No	Yes	No
Price	$169 DOS $495 UNIX	$195 $495 UNIX	$395/unlimited license	$245	$239 -8 user

Table 16.2: Windows-based Terminal Emulators

	DynaComm	Crosstalk	SmartTerm	Smartcom	ProComm PLUS	Reflection
# of Terminal Emulation Modes	13	22	8	8	34	4
Keyboard Mapping	Yes	Yes	Yes	Yes	Yes	Yes
FTP	No	No	Yes	No	No	Yes
UNIX print services	No	No	No	No	No	Yes
Scripting	Yes	Yes	Yes	Yes	Yes	Yes
TCP/IP Support	Yes	No	Yes	Yes	No	Yes
WinSock Support	No	No	Yes	No	Yes	
LAT Support	Yes	No	Yes	No	No	Yes
Total Network Connection Options	13	4	5	6 plus ISDN	2	10
132 Columns	Yes	Yes	Yes	Yes	Yes	Yes
File Transfer (Xmodem,Ymodem, Zmodem,Kermit, CompuServe)	ALL	ALL	ALL	ALL	ALL	Zmodem, Kermit, Xmodem
Dial-up Options	Yes	Yes	Yes	Yes	Yes	Yes
Multiple Sessions	No	Yes	4 (telnet)	No	No	Yes
Remote Control	No	No	No	No	No	No
Platform Support (Windows, DOS or UNIX)	Windows	Windows	Windows	Windows	Windows, DOS	Windows, DOS
Document Editor	Yes	Yes	No	Yes	No	No
Auto Logins	Yes	Yes	Yes	Yes	Yes	Yes
File Viewers	Yes	No	No	Yes	Yes	No
Toolbars	Yes	Yes	Yes	Yes	Yes	Yes
Price	$249	$195	$295	$179	$179	$299

Table 16.3: Windows Desktops for UNIX

	JSB Multi-view Desktop	PC-Connect
# of Terminal Emulation Modes	7	5
Keyboard Mapping	Yes	Yes
FTP	Ver 3.7	No
UNIX print services	Yes	Yes
Scripting	Yes	Yes
TCP/IP Support	Yes	Yes
LAT Support	No	Yes
WinSock Support	Yes	Yes
Total Network Connection Options	32	16
132 Columns	Yes	Yes
File Transfer (Xmodem,Ymodem, Zmodem,Kermit, CompuServe)	Proprietary Only	Proprietary Only
Dial-up Options	Yes	Yes
Multiple Sessions	Yes	Yes
Remote Control	No	No
Platform Support (Windows, DOS or UNIX)	Windows	Windows
Document Editor	No	No
Auto Logins	Yes	Yes
File Viewers	No	Yes
Toolbars	No	No
Price	$995 5-pack	$2045 - 10 user $295 UNIX Module

17

DOS Emulators

Introduction

We looked at a few DOS/Windows emulators and servers, to see how difficult they are to install and use. Surprisingly, there are very few products available. For general background and installation hints, see Chapter 10.

Evaluation Criteria

The most important aspect of a DOS emulator is. . . (drum roll) . . . its DOS emulation! If it won't run the programs, it's no good. Compatibility is key. Secondary (but still vital) concerns include performance and system resource consumption. In short, DOS emulators hog memory, disk space, and CPU cycles. Not only do they gobble up resources, without fast hardware underneath, they are as slow as flies in winter.

A couple products which come bundled with PC UNIX obviously have use of the same PC hardware. In this case, they need only create a *virtual machine* to forge interaction between DOS and the hardware, circumventing the UNIX access paths. DOS compatibility and performance are never problems for these products.

DOS servers can provide an alternative to DOS emulators, but they usually require the private use of networked PC—which you may not have. We have mixed the emulators, virtual machine products, and servers together in this chapter. The table at the end of the chapter indicates at a glance the character of each product.

IBM AIX Personal Computer Simulator/6000 1.2

If your shop is Big Blue through and through, you can find an IBM DOS emulator for your RS/6000. The AIX Personal Computer Simulator/6000 (also known as pcsim) supports only the ancient versions of IBM DOS—3.3 and 4.01—as well as old Windows 286 or 3.0. Pcsim can only use Windows 3.0 in real—not protected—mode. If you have a particular software package to implement, you had better clear the version number with IBM. Other than Windows itself, we saw no true Windows business applications on the list of supported programs.

However, it does emulate extended memory, the LIM 4.0 standard for expanded memory, 80287 numeric coprocessors, and VGA graphics. You can access IBM internal CD-ROM drives. You can also share DOS data files with AIX applications and between DOS sessions.

Pcsim remains one of the few products that does not install DOS for you. You need to create a file for the emulated C drive and then use FDISK to create a DOS partition on it. Bothersome as this may be, it is a small matter when weighed against pcsim's limited DOS software compatibility. If we were you, we would shop around for a better DOS emulator than pcsim 1.2. Price varies by RS/6000 configuration.

Insignia Solutions SoftPC 3.0/3.1

Insignia Solutions' SoftPC supports practically all UNIX workstation platforms: Sun SPARCstation, Silicon Graphics, NeXt, Apple Macintosh, DEC, HP, and IBM RS/6000. It does not, however, support Intel-based UNIX (dominated by Locus Merge). Insignia Solutions OEMs the SoftPC for SPARC engine to SunSelect, which adds an accelerator card forming the SunPC product (which we discuss later in the chapter). Insignia Solutions also OEMs SoftPC to Microsoft, of all companies, which integrates it with Windows NT as the 16-bit DOS compatibility mode.

SoftPC does not use an accelerator card but instead duplicates all CPU and other chip traces in software. This makes the memory requirement somewhat higher than for SunPC, which does use physical chips on the accelerator card. Not having an accelerator also hurts SoftPC performance on the slower machines, which is sensitive to the speed of the UNIX processor. On a SPARCstation II with 32M RAM, SoftPC runs DOS programs at a speed roughly equivalent to a 386-20 megahertz PC. On a SPARCstation IPC with 24M RAM, which runs at only about 20 SPECmarks, all you get is 286 performance. 100-SPECmark machines boost performance to the 486 level.

Ease of Installation

We installed SoftPC on our Sun SPARCstation IPC with 24 megabytes of RAM. The optimum swap area size on a Sun with OpenWindows is three times the amount of RAM—e.g., in our case, 24M X 3 = 72M. SoftPC supplies fonts for both Motif and OpenWindows. Motif machines (Sun or otherwise) require much less swap space— typically equal to the RAM. The install program created drive **C:** with DOS 5.0 (included), though it was small. You can easily create additional drives in separate container files, including drives networked with NFS.

SoftPC uses FSA, a proprietary "file sharing architecture" similar to NFS, which allows users to store DOS files in UNIX filesystems. The installation program automatically builds an **AUTOEXEC.BAT** file for you that links the UNIX root filesystem as Drive **E:**, subject to normal UNIX permissions. You can create new directories and store files outside of the reserved DOS drives.

Ease of Use

The mouse is active as a UNIX mouse by default. Inside DOS mouse-aware programs, such as Quattro Pro for DOS, you must use the Attach Mouse function to make the mouse act like a Microsoft mouse. This can be a problem, if you don't remember how to Detach the mouse when you want it to serve UNIX again. For example, we lost all mouse control when we exited MS Diagnostics (which, by the way, thought it was running on a loaded 286 of unknown origin). Without a mouse, you are stuck in the DOS window until you power down, unless you detach the mouse from DOS. Insignia gives you a key sequence to regain control under UNIX.

There isn't much to the SoftPC menu bar—only functions you seldom need—making the product extremely simple to use. The Options menu contains configuration options including new drive setup, communication port configuration, and a few other less important things. The Actions selection (Figure 17.1) exposes a menu for those odd discrepancies between the operating systems—the mouse activator, floppy disk ejector, etc. You will have to click on these items occasionally, especially if you load a large application from floppies. When you push the mouse out of the DOS window, Auto-Freeze takes over, halting the window operation to prevent the waste of CPU cycles. You can turn this off.

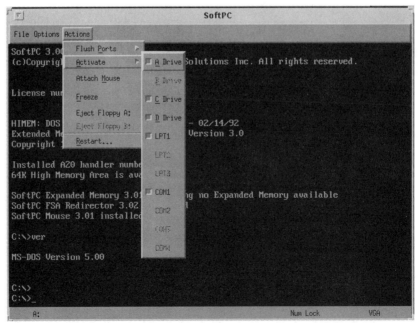

FIGURE 17.1 SoftPC lets you select and define your "PC" hardware

We loaded Microsoft Windows from floppies onto our freshly-made **D:** drive. When you try this, don't immediately panic if the process seems unbearably slow. Instead, check the following items. Make sure you follow the instructions to set up Windows with the SoftPC display and mouse drivers—this will fix the speed. Additionally, MS Windows likes to use the 256 color mode which causes display problems outside of the DOS window. In other words, if you are in the DOS window running a Windows application, the rest of the display becomes a hideous color combination—worse than that Baggie in the back of your refrigerator. To solve this problem, make sure the SoftPC Display option is set to 16 colors, and load the SoftPC display driver instead of the driver chosen by Windows for the Setup options.

The SoftPC mouse driver lets you go back and forth between MS Windows and UNIX windows without fiddling with the mouse attachment/detachment. We actually had to go into the Control Panel to make the mouse less responsive. It's not foolproof, though. Sometimes, the SoftPC window rejects any movement of the mouse within its borders, throwing the mouse back into the UNIX part of the display. This happens if you do the following: 1) request Windows to put up a new window, 2) move the cursor out of the window to start a UNIX program—without waiting for the new window to display, and 3) set Auto-Freeze to ON. On another occasion, we lost the mouse until we performed the detach sequence (above). Windows automatically places a line to execute **SMARTDRV** in your **AUTOEXEC.BAT**. Take it out. SoftPC does its own disk-caching, so **SMARTDRV** only slows down the window.

You can set your DOS program to use any of four different COM (serial) ports or three LPT (parallel) ports (all emulated in SoftPC software). You can also tie LPT1 to the UNIX system's **ttya** port for talking to the serial printer.

We tested some DOS applications for proper operation within the DOS compatibility box and had no problems with compatibility (which is Insignia Solutions' primary emphasis over performance). Windows and DOS programs worked as usual. Even the Windows screensaver worked. (At least we saved part of the display from burn-in!) Programs also ran from the Windows MS-DOS Prompt window—which is a little like looking at a reflection of a reflection. One minor problem—after exiting the DOS prompt window, we had to wiggle the mouse to fully engage Windows again. With SoftPC, just as with a real PC, an application can hang the computer so badly that Ctrl-Alt-Del will not reboot. With a real PC you reach for the Reset button or the Big Red Switch—with SoftPC you press the Restart button.

On a PC, DOS compiles each command before execution. SoftPC improves performance at the command line by saving the compiled forms to avoid recompiling. This makes it faster for repetitive tasks.

Summary

Version 3.1 for SPARC, while not yet available for our test, will be compatible with Solaris 2.0/2.1. Insignia Solutions will also be bundling Microsoft Windows 3.1 with it—all for $549. Note that Insignia Solutions manufactures SoftPC for many platforms, including Macintosh—a good way to get everybody singing from the same songbook. We were happy with the faithful imitation of the PC and the total DOS/Windows application compatibility. Although there are ways to get caught in limbo between Windows and UNIX, if you let the Windows application finish its current task before jumping out, you should have no trouble. The main downside is lack of speed. Without a fast machine or the ability to add an accelerator, this product runs like a 286.

Locus Computing Merge 3.1

Merge is a product that runs DOS or Windows programs on Intel-based UNIX systems. It is not true emulation because the DOS applications actually execute on the Intel processor. Merge creates a virtual machine where the application executes its instructions. As such, Merge maintains a high degree of compatibility and high performance when running DOS and Windows applications on UNIX-based hosts.

Locus does not market Merge directly, but instead supplies it to several OEMs who integrate it with their Intel-based UNIX products. These companies include SCO, IBM, Unisys, Siemens, Dell, Microport, Novell, and others. We tested Merge on a UnixWare Application Server and on a SCO Open Server Enterprise System.

Merge supports either a separate DOS partition or using the UNIX partition to store DOS programs. Merge comes on its selected platforms with a copy of DOS, but if you want to run Windows applications, you need to purchase a licensed copy of Windows and install it. The biggest advantage of maintaining a separate DOS partition is the ability to change the boot partition and use only DOS. In SCO's case, you can type in **DOS** at the boot prompt and never use **FDISK**.

Normally, Merge gives the DOS partition a drive name of **E:** when running. **C:** is reserved for the UNIX partition while **D:** is given to the user's home directory. You should keep separate files—one for native DOS and one for Merge under UNIX. Once over this hurdle, there are no installation issues.

Merge supports using a mouse if you turn it on with the popup menu. VGA and EGA graphics are supported in a full screen mode. Locus has a *zoom* feature that you use when graphics are necessary. On SCO and UnixWare machines, the zoom feature puts the application on an alternate screen, allowing you to switch back and forth between DOS and your UNIX desktop.

The newest version of Merge overcomes nearly all of the limitations of DOS emulation and previous versions of Merge. Merge supports MS-DOS 5.0 and DR DOS 6.0, but not MS-DOS 6.0 (until next version). You can run both Windows 3.0 and 3.1 applications. Our experience was surprisingly pleasant. Windows programs ran crisply—no problems. Merge also has enhanced its memory support. It now works with DOS programs using LIM/EMS memory above 640K and it also supports 16M of extended memory. You can print to either DOS or UNIX printers, and any device driver written for one works with the other.

Merge can still have problems with applications that write directly to the hardware and do not use any device drivers. Thankfully, these are few and far between. While we still prefer to run Windows applications natively, running DOS applications under Merge produces no noticable degradation on a 486 machine.

Logicraft Omni-Ware for UNIX 2.0

Omni-Ware is a DOS server product. By placing extra DOS hardware in a PC on the network, that PC can supply DOS services such as video graphics, parallel printer port, keyboard, and hard disk control to UNIX workstations. The workstation runs the DOS application, but Omni-Ware redirects all DOS system calls to the PC server.

The first step in installation is to convert a PC into a dedicated Omni-Ware server. Install the Omni-Ware Gate Array coprocessor board, and the optional VGA board. The server comes in both Ethernet and SCSI versions, each of which also connects to thin or thick Ethernet notework cabling. This hardware installation requires you to not only set DIP switches, but also remove redundant controller boards for VGA video and the parallel port. You usually either remove the hard disk controller, or reconfigure it as the secondary controller. You must install a Status Display panel in an unused half-height drive bay slot on the front of your PC case. The Omni-Ware hardware installation is rigorous, compared to that for a typical PC accessory. However, Logicraft supplies well-illustrated documentation. Logicraft also supplies pre-installed PC servers, including a four-user variety.

On the other hand, the Omni-Ware software must be installed on the UNIX host. Omni-Ware supports many platforms, including Sun, IBM, DEC, Intel, HP, and Pyramid. You also have your choice of running MS-DOS 5.0 or OS/2 1.3 as your PC-mode operating system. The UNIX software includes Windows drivers, configuration utilities, and programs to help the PC server do a remote boot.

Just as for other products, Omni-Ware lets you switch between PC and UNIX environments without logins, and run PC applications designed for DOS, Windows, or OS/2. Hard disk emulation routes disk requests from a local disk to logical network disks, which can be physically located on remote VMS or UNIX hosts.

Omni-Ware is expensive, starting at $3495 ($19,995 for multiuser). However, this approach provides advantages that others don't, such as centralized file storage and support for ISA-bus PC accessories.

Puzzle Systems Synergy II

Going for the money, Puzzle Systems has concentrated their efforts on products for the market leader, Sun. Synergy II includes both software and one SBus master slot board with an Intel 486 CPU. It supports SVGA and lower video standards, with 1M of video RAM. Synergy II provides 540K of RAM cache. The Synergy II board is socketed for an optional math co-processor, and it can be upgraded to newer CPUs as well. Performance is equivalent to the Intel CPU installed; i.e., a 486 chip gives 486 performance. Disk operations are faster than typical PC disk operations due to the faster SCSI drives. Synergy II can recognize up to 26 NFS-mounted drives. It operates with both OpenWindows 2.0/3.0 and SunView user environments. Software comes on floppy diskettes, including DR DOS 5.0.

Synergy II can direct LPT2 output to either of the Sun's serial ports, but COM1 communications and LPT1 printer output go through the on-board RS-232 serial and Centronics parallel ports, respectively. (Modem communications do not affect SunOS processes.) Providing a parallel port means that if you attach a Xircom adapter you can network the computer with Novell NetWare, Microsoft LAN Manager, Banyan Vines, and other PC LANs.

Puzzle avoids swapping memory to disk (except under Windows), instead appropriating memory as any other UNIX program would. You can specify how much workstation memory to use for DOS, but Puzzle recommends at least 24M for a 4M DOS configuration. If there is not enough memory available to satisfy the DOS configuration, Synergy II will not boot, but 24M should satisfy DOS extended and expanded memory requirements. Synergy II is compatible with Windows 3.0/3.1.

The mouse pointer controls the DOS compatibility of the floppy diskette drive, the keyboard mapping, and the mouse type (Microsoft compatibility under DOS). If you move the pointer out of the DOS window, these devices instantly revert to UNIX compatibility; move it back—DOS again.

Just as with the SoftNet Utilities, Puzzle has minimized the impact of DOS on the UNIX system while providing high functionality. Its networkability also commends Puzzle to your attention. Synergy II with a 486-DX33 CPU is priced at about $2100, varying by distributor.

Quarterdeck DESQview/X 1.0

We provide a significant amount of information on DESQview/X in Chapter 14 on PC LAN-based internetworking solutions. However, DESQview/X also acts as a DOS server. If you have numerous UNIX workstation users who need only occasional access to DOS programs, you can put DESQview/X on a single PC at a relatively low cost.

Ease of Installation

Installing DESQview/X is a complex procedure already discussed in Chapter 14. You need a TCP/IP network installed before you can use DESQview/X as a DOS server for a UNIX host. Once you have installed the product, two issues remain—fonts and security. For the UNIX host to use a DOS window, a set of fonts for DOS applications needs to be set up on the UNIX host. This involves copying the three PC font sets from DESQview/X to the UNIX host. Once on the host, the fonts must be moved to the appropriate font directory. You can use the **xset q** command to find where the fonts are located on your machine. Next you have to convert the fonts from **bdf** format to **snf** format. Most, if not all UNIX machines, have a **bdftosnf** executable in /**usr/bin** (Sun's is **convertfont** found in /**openwin/bin**). Once the fonts are converted, you have to reboot the machine or run **xset fp rehash** to make the fonts available. If you attempt to run the DOS window without the fonts, it may not work.

Security issues remain the biggest problem with DESQview/X. You must have access to the UNIX workstation from the PC and vice versa. Normally, the UNIX machine must have at least an **xhosts** file that lists your PC. You can just place a '+' in the **xhosts** file which provides access to all hosts, but we think it is better to list your host PC individually. Before attempting to start a DOS window, you can also run **xhost +**. This opens access to every host.

Ease of Use

In order to get a DOS window up on your UNIX workstation, you need to use the **rsh** or **rexec** command. A typical command looks like this:

```
rsh valuept -L mike DOSR
```

The first parameter after **rsh** is the machine you are logging into. The **-L** gives you the option of listing a user name. The **DOSR** is the program that runs on the DESQview/X PC. This should open a DOS session in an xterm window on your workstation. The window can also be opened by executing the **RUN DOS** command on the PC and sending the output to the UNIX workstation.

The resultant window is not a DOS compatibility box because you are actually using the DOS PC—*its* processor and memory. Ill-behaved DOS programs should be just fine as long as they run smoothly under DESQview/X directly.

The actual emulation is a joy. Unlike some other products, DESQview/X provides immediate mouse focus—if you move your mouse into the DOS window, it works! As with all DOS emulators, however, speed remains a problem. In this case, the problem is not so much the speed of the UNIX workstation, but the speed of your PC. Since DOS programs run on the PC and not on the workstation, you need at least a 486 machine for an adequate DESQview/X server. While the PC can be operated by a user at the same time a DOS session is running from the UNIX workstation, we discourage this unless the UNIX users log on only occasionally. For constant access, you need to dedicate the PC as a DOS server.

In theory, you can run Windows from the DESQview/X machine or even bring up Windows from your X station, but we had little luck with that option. We also found that on an IBM ValuePoint 486 25MHz PC, MS Windows crawled when running under DESQview/X.

Summary

When you have a number of UNIX workstation users who need infrequent access to certain DOS character programs, DESQview/X at $475 is a an excellent choice. We are satisfied with both its compatibility and its reasonable response time. Our major concern focuses around getting memory and network requirements set up on the PC side and establishing the correct security permissions. For full-time DOS or Windows emulation, however, we recommend going with another product; and if you do not currently have a networked PC, DESQview/X makes even less sense.

SunSelect SunPC 3.1 and Accelerator

SunSelect OEM's the SoftPC software engine from Insignia Solutions. However, in order to increase performance from a miserable 286 to a tolerable 386 on slower Suns, SunSelect packages an accelerator card with the software. To gain an impression of its installation process, characteristics, and capabilities, see our evaluation of Insignia Solutions SoftPC, earlier in this chapter.

Since hardware is supplied with this product, it demands less system memory and disk space than does SoftPC. SunSelect recommends installing SunPC on a system with at least 12M of memory—a minimal requirement in our opinion.

The accelerator card in effect creates a 486 PC inside the Sun. Card installation is a simple matter, and the documentation measures up to SunSelect's usual high standard. SunSelect also supplies a wrist strap to help you discharge static electricity—protecting the accelerator against an untimely death. Before you purchase, make sure you have a free slot on your 2- or 3-slot SPARCstation.

The accelerator automatically attaches to the SunPC window—but only one. You can run extra SunPC windows, but they do not have access to the accelerator hardware. If you do not need added speed for some applications, run them in the non-accelerated window and save the accelerated window for the performance hogs.

SunPC also includes an IPX driver for accessing NetWare servers. The product costs $1795 with a 486DX accelerator, $1195 with a 486SX, or $395 for a single software license without an accelerator.

SunSoft VP/ix

VP/ix is similar in type to Locus Merge, but integrates DOS with SunSoft's INTER-ACTIVE UNIX System V/386 Release 3.2—a variety of UNIX for the PC. It will also be ported to the Solaris 2.0 operating system for PCs. The product currently includes MS-DOS 3.3, but supports other versions of DOS and Windows 3.1. SunSoft bundles VP/ix with the operating systems, and does not sell the product separately.

TERA Technologies Network PC Access 2.0

NPA was originally developed for remote control of PCs and scientific instrumentation by UNIX workstations. It requires a dedicated PC server as well as client software that runs on the UNIX machine. It is not multiuser, because the PC is not multiuser. However, from the UNIX side you can access DOS from either the workstation or an X-terminal. You can also control multiple PCs running NPA servers. Any network to which the PC server is attached—be it Novell NetWare or Microsoft Windows for Workgroups—remains available from the UNIX client station. The NPA server also supports other DOS machines running the NPA client.

We tested a beta version of NPA 1.0, but there has been a lot of revision since then. At that time NPA had serious compatibility problems—we could run very few DOS software packages without some problem. The vendor states that the compatibility has improved through version 2.0, and that there are "no known problems with Windows applications." We suggest verifying the compatibility of your applications with NPA in advance of purchase.

Network PC Access allowed us to use the PC printer and modem for UNIX purposes. PC peripherals are often cheaper and more ubiquitous than their UNIX counterparts, which means that you can save money buying NPA instead of duplicate peripherals. However, if you don't have a PC to dedicate, you will have to buy one of those. Get a higher-end model—a 386 or 486.

NPA Server software costs $495, and the Client software $195 each. You also need TCP/IP networking software for the PC. NPA supports FTP's PC/TCP, Novell's LAN WorkPlace for DOS, and SunSelect's PC-NFS.

Recommendations

With so few products on the market, it is difficult not to name them all. Among the emulators, we think Insignia Solutions' SoftPC is a good bet for compatibility; we also like its availability for multiplatform UNIX environments. However, if performance improvements head up your wish list, the accelerator boards of other products might make more of your dreams come true. If you have an older or slower Sun, for example, you really need SunSelect's SunPC or Puzzle's Synergy II. If you have a UNIX PC, you have little choice—Locus Merge 3.0, or SunSoft VP/ix.

We are not inclined toward hardware-based servers, such as Logicraft's, since for the price of the single-user product you could buy and network a couple PCs. DESQview/X makes more sense as a server solution, and it is a multifaceted product to boot. However, we found setup to be on the difficult side. TERA's NPA can provide the best PC LAN connectivity of all emulators and servers in the list, but stay heads up on the compatibility issue. For further details, see Table 17.1.

Table 17.1: DOS Emulators and Servers

	Type	Max Sessions	Platforms Supported	GUIs Supported	Networks Supported	DOS Software
IBM AIX PC Simulator/ 6000 1.2	Emulation Software	5	IBM	Motif	TCP/IP, NFS	Supports IBM DOS 3.3, 4.1, Windows 3.0
Insignia Solutions SoftPC 3.1	Emulation Software	Memory-dependent	All UNIX except PC-based, MAC	Motif, Open-Windows	TCP/IP, NFS	Includes DOS 5.0, Windows 3.1
Locus Computing DOS Merge 3.1	Virtual Machine	Memory-dependent	System V, SCO, MAC	Motif	N/A	Includes DOS 5.0, supports Windows 3.1
Logicraft Multiuser Omni-Ware 2.0	Server PC w/multiple 486 boards	4	Sun, IBM, DEC, HP, System V, SCO	Motif, DEC, Open Windows, Sun-View, HP	TCP/IP, XNS	Includes DOS 3.3, w/OS/2 1.3 option, supports Windows 3.1
Puzzle Systems Synergy II	Emulation Software w/ Accelerator	1	Sun	OpenWindows, Sun-View	TCP/IP, NFS	Includes DR DOS 5.0, supports Windows 3.1
Quarterdeck DESQview/X 1.0	Server Software	Memory-dependent	All X work-stations	Motif, Open-Windows	TCP/IP	Supports all
SunSelect SunPC 3.1	Emulation Software w/ Accelerator	4	Sun	Motif, Open-Windows	TCP/IP, NFS, NetWare	Includes DOS 5.0, Windows 3.1
SunSoft VP/ix	Virtual Machine	Memory-dependent	INTERACT-IVE, Solaris	Motif	N/A	Includes DOS 3.3, supports Windows 3.1
TERA Technologies NPA 2.0	Server Software	1	Sun, SCO, INTERACT-IVE	Motif, Open-Windows	TCP/IP, NFS, NetWare, NetBIOS	Supports all

18

E-Mail Options

Introduction

Chapter 12 discusses some of the issues you need to consider when looking at e-mail solutions in a mixed DOS—UNIX environment. In this chapter we review actual products. However, in the process of selecting these e-mail solutions for evaluation, we ran into two problems. First, there are few products that are interoperable across UNIX and DOS. Nearly all the favorite DOS and Windows-based e-mail packages such as Beyond Inc.'s Beyond Mail, Microsoft Corp.'s Microsoft Mail, and DaVinci Systems' eMail have avoided the UNIX marketplace. Second, there are various methods of interconnecting e-mail systems, and the options available are not all products you just purchase off the shelf. There are specific products such as Lotus Development's cc:Mail, commercial e-mail networks such as MCI Mail, and internetworks such as the Internet. So our task was by no means an easy one.

We have chosen as our goal to make you aware of the options and give you some guidance as to which solution might best fit your needs. In this chapter, we review a sampling of products and commercial networks, listing them alphabetically. Based on this information, you can do some test driving and acquire an e-mail solution to fit your needs. For additional information, Appendix B lists many good books that provide in-depth discussions on topics like modem communications, the Internet, and UUNET.

Evaluation Criteria

Because of the tremendous variety of different products and services, we could not review every option. For those specific products we did review, we utilized four criteria: ease of installation and configuration, user interface issues, interoperability across platforms, and smart features that make e-mail more useful in the corporate environment.

Installation/Configuration

We look at the software installation, system requirements, administration issues (such as setting up users and address directories), and security issues.

User Interface

Interface issues include the use or non-use of a GUI and icons, whether or not you can substitute long mail addresses with aliases, and the simplicity of the address directories. We consider how you edit messages, what mechanisms are available for replying and forwarding mail, what types of attachments (graphics, binary files, etc.) can be used, and what message organization options are available.

Interoperability

In the interoperability area we emphasize the number of platforms the product supports, its ability to work with other applications, how easy it is to send mail across to other platforms, and what support exists for standards such as X.400, SMTP, and MAPI.

Smart Features

This category includes certain unique features such as the ability to create macros, the option to customize the interface, the range of automatic message routing options and automatic filtering options, and time management options like calendars and appointments.

CompuServe

CompuServe represents the most popular on-line service in the U.S. It offers a wealth of options to users including shopping, news, technical support, and electronic mail. Of course, we are only interested in discussing CompuServe's ability to transmit mail to and from the Internet, giving you access to many UNIX networks.

Sending mail from CompuServe to the Internet is not difficult. Avoid using the Receipt Requested option since the receiving end might not be able to respond. Also, the address must have the word **INTERNET** stuck in front of the destination address, which has to be in domain address form. A message to **mikeb@uworld.com** would look like this:

    INTERNET: mikeb@uworld.com

Sending mail to a CompuServe user from the Internet requires you to know the recipient's CompuServe ID number. Note that you must use the ID number with a period instead of the comma normally separating the two numbers.

INTERNET: 72345.412@compuserve.com

The domain name used is **compuserve.com**. The person sending the mail does not insert the word **INTERNET** because it shows up automatically on the receiving end. If the CompuServe recipient has a private CompuServe mail area, then the address would list his or her name followed by title of the organization.

mikeb@ABC.compuserve.com

CompuServe charges a minimum $2.50 monthly subscription fee. In addition, there are on-line fees ranging from $6 to $23 dollars per hour depending on the service in use and your baud rate. When using CompuServe for Internet mail, there are other additional pricing issues. Unlike regular CompuServe mail, which includes only sending charges, you are charged for both sending and receiving mail when the the Internet is involved. On the standard Compuserve plan, you get about 60 messages per month for a $9.00 charge with the mail charges based on file length. An alternative plan lets you pay connect charges only when sending or receiving mail. This is better if you are sending large files through the Internet.

Many larger cities have local number connections to CompuServe. In addition, you can use TYMNET or other public packet-switching networks. Don't forget, however, that there are no 800 number connections like those provided by MCI Mail.

Lotus Development cc:Mail 1.0

While E-mail on DOS machines has taken off in the last few years, no popular DOS vendor has ventured to tie-in the UNIX side of the house except through the use of expensive and sometimes hard-to-use gateways. In late 1992, Lotus Development Corp. released cc:Mail for UNIX. Now, with the proper versions, cc:Mail allows e-mail interoperability across DOS, Windows, OS/2, Macintosh, and UNIX platforms.

Installation/Configuration

cc:Mail for UNIX installation is a multiple step process. Currently, the administration module is a DOS program and can be run only on a PC. You also need your PCs connected to a Sun SPARCstation with NFS, the only supported platform in the initial release. cc:Mail for UNIX will not work without an NFS connection. You install the post office on the NFS drive and administer the mailboxes from a DOS PC. This can be inconvenient in a UNIX environment with no networked PCs, but should present no problem in a mixed environment. Lotus intends to create a UNIX-based administration module in early 1994. There is also a Macintosh version of the administration module.

The administrator creates user accounts and mailboxes and identifies the post offices for those accounts—a straightforward process. You can configure cc:Mail to store your messages either locally or on the NFS drive. The product also provides for encryption of messages. Each user can maintain his or her own address directory or access directories already existing on the UNIX network.

User Interface

The strength of cc:Mail is in its GUI-based interface. When used in a combination Microsoft Windows/Sun SPARCstation environment, cc:Mail provides an easy-to-use product for even the most computer-phobic person. Icons control nearly all common mail functions such as Prepare, Send, and Read. In addition, it fully supports the Open Look specification on the UNIX side.

We like the way you can send messages by clicking on the Send icon, then clicking on a directory and selecting a destination. cc:Mail for UNIX also supports incremental searching (the process of typing in only a few letters to find the correct address) when you are addressing a piece of mail. You can also assign priorities to mail messages before they are sent. Nearly any file type can be sent as an attachment in UNIX—fax, audio, graphics, or images—as many as 20 per message.

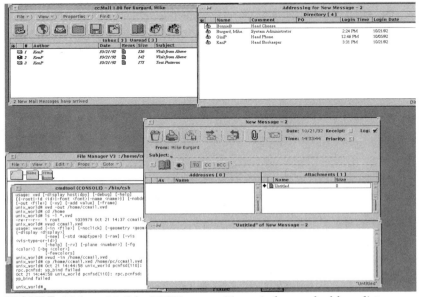

FIGURE 18.1 cc:Mail for UNIX composition window and address list

An inbox stores all your incoming messages clearly, with labels describing the subject and sender. Available actions include automatically forwarding a message, storing it locally, or sending a reply. Storing a message locally can be done in an archive mode. The process of reading mail, as well as forwarding and managing it, can be done entirely with icons. These icons are extremely clear, as shown in Figure 18.1.

We regret the lack of one ease-of-use feature—aliasing. Unlike other common UNIX utilities, cc:Mail does not let you take a long address such as **mike.info@bozeman.MT.com** and use **mikeb** as the alias. The point and select nature of the interface reduces the need for aliases, however. We like the clear documentation; the variety of illustrations and clear step-by-step instructions.

Interoperability

With respect to working on mixed platforms, cc:Mail rates both a good score and a poor one. Serving as perhaps the most interoperable of independent e-mail packages, cc:Mail runs on DOS, Windows, OS/2, Macintosh, and UNIX. This gives it tremendous market potential. While cc:Mail does not support Novell's MHS or SMTP on non-UNIX platforms, its own transport protocol has become something of a standard.

On the UNIX side of the cross platform house, cc:Mail is less supportive of multiple platforms. Its initial release is available only for Sun SPARCstations. Further releases in 1994 are planned for IBM RS/6000, SCO OpenDesktop, and other workstations. Even so, this leaves cc:Mail covering only a portion of the UNIX market. Products such as Z-Mail cut a much wider path through the UNIX jungle.

From the UNIX machine, cc:Mail allows you access to regular UNIX mail users and lets you send messages over the Internet via whatever mechanism your machine uses. This means anyone on the UNIX network can communicate with you, even if they are not using cc:Mail. cc:Mail offers its own gateways as options to the base product. We expect few users will need more than one per system.

Smart Features

cc:Mail trails the high-end DOS-only packages such as BeyondMail with regard to smart email features. Nevertheless, cc:Mail messages can easily be sorted into different folders. For long term storage, you can archive messages to your local drive. The sort options are easy to use, and the Find command will locate a particular message for you. However, there are no automatic routing options with cc:Mail, nor is there any automatic filtering. Other DOS and some UNIX products allow you to bring messages from a specific user (such as the boss) to the top of the pile. Other options such as appointments, calenders, and time management are not available in cc:Mail. Lotus has put them into the Windows version and plans to incorporate these features in early 1994 in the UNIX version. Without them, cc:Mail lags slightly behind the single platform products such as BeyondMail with regard to richness of features.

Summary

If you already use cc:Mail, the UNIX version is an excellent match. If your operation does not use any kind of e-mail, cc:Mail is also an attractive product. It works on the most popular platforms with user friendliness. cc:Mail starts at about $125 per user but drops to under $50 when over 100 users are on the network. We like the icons, the consistent interface, and the support for attachments. In short, cc:Mail stands as the most complete product DOS—UNIX email package of all the ones we reviewed.

Lotus Notes 3.0

Lotus Notes defined the workflow and groupware market when it was first released. It is far more than an e-mail package and is not designed just for e-mail situation. At $495 per user license, Notes is expensive. It is designed to automate your workflow, of which e-mail is just one portion. You use Notes to electronic manage and manipulate your work far differently from any other product. Notes is a client/server technology and requires a server machine in the loop.

Notes supports the VIM API specification. The e-mail aspects of Notes are formidable. It e-mail enables other Lotus applications like 1-2-3 and Ami Pro. There are full delivery notification options, personal address books, aliases, and customizable forms. The e-mail portion of Notes is merely a template within Notes as are all applications. Notes templates support filters and special functions that allow you to customize your e-mail. The real strength of Notes is that sending graphics, spreadsheets, and whatever is not an attachment process. These activities are a key element of Notes, thereby allieviating many of the problems and difficulties with attachments. For example, you can import a spreadsheet directly into a routing form and send it off to another user who can view the sheet immediately.

Lotus Notes 3.0 is a totally interoperable application. It has clients for Windows, Macintosh, UNIX, OS/2 and Windows NT. The Sun Solaris 1.1 client was released in late 1993 while clients for SCO UNIX, HP/UX, Solaris 2.x, and IBM AIX will appear in 1994. All clients will be available in a Motif GUI. Lotus Notes for UNIX will use TCP/IP. In order to interoperate with PCs, either a TCP/IP stack needs to be running on the PCs or IPX/SPX has to be available for the UNIX machine. Lotus states the UNIX version will be fully compatible and interoperable with all other Notes clients. We were unable to test Notes due to its late release date on UNIX.

The Internet

The Internet is a large internetwork of networks all around the world. We have covered some of the basics of the Internet in other chapters. Here we want to give you an overview of what can be done on the Internet when it comes to e-mail and DOS—UNIX internetworking. The Internet is not a product you can buy. Nor is it even a commercial network you can sign up for in the traditional sense. In order to use the Internet you may need to purchase an e-mail product or use one of the terminal emulators mentioned in Chapter 16. Nonetheless, the Internet has some tremendous advantages in the e-mail world. A sampling of books describing the Internet can be found in Appendix B.

What is Available?

There are three main features available from the Internet: e-mail, file transfer, and remote login. File transfer is the ability to get programs and other files downloaded from somewhere on the Internet. Remote login allows you to login to another computer and access its facilities. But, of course, our main focus here is e-mail.

If you have a direct connection via TCP/IP to the Internet, you need a basic e-mail front-end, which all UNIX systems include. If you are signing on from a DOS machine, you must have an e-mail program that is compatible with the Internet protocols. This usually means something SMTP-based. You also need to know the addresses of the recipients. Unlike LAN-based e-mail or online services, the Internet provides no catalog or directory of addresses. The Internet uses the Domain Name System of naming. If you send e-mail to **mikeb@gooblatz.com**, the Internet will accept the mail and attempt to deliver it. You may get a message back later saying that there is no such address.

When it comes to e-mail in the DOS—UNIX internetworking department, the main advantage of the Internet is that many UNIX networks are already connected. Thus, you can reach the largest audience with the Internet. Because much of the Internet is made up of backbone networks run by the government, there are certain limitations to commercial traffic. Exactly what those limitations are and how they are enforced is vague. The "acceptable use" policy of the the government portion of the Internet simply states that commercial traffic is not allowed. What "commercial" means is not clearly defined. There are large grey areas. In addition, many network portions of the Internet do not have a commercial limitation. Depending on what you want to do and what connection method you are using, it makes sense to check out any possible limitations.

Where Do You Hook Up?

Once you decide you need an Internet connection, you need to decide where to make the physical connection. There are a variety of options. The traditional connection is through a local university or government facility. These were the only connection points for the Internet during its genesis, and many universities still offer connections. A second option is to sign up for one of the commercial services designed primarily for Internet connection. These include CERFNet, UUNET, and PSI. For a monthly fee, these organizations give your business a direct connection to the Internet. Thirdly, you can use a broad-based commercial service—such as MCI Mail, CompuServe, and America Online—as your gateway to the Internet. If your mail needs are small, these services can be economical, although they offer neither file transfer nor remote login to the Internet.

How Do You Connect?

Having found a place to connect, you now need to decide how to connect to the Internet. Not all methods of connection work for all the various providers and services. The simplest connection method is a direct TCP/IP connection from your own organization. Many universities and large corporations have a continuous TCP/IP connection to the Internet. A second, related option is to use a dedicated leased phone line to dial into an Internet site. With leased lines, you also have full Internet access to file transfer and remote login. These may or may not be 24 hours a day.

You can dial into the Internet over regular public phone lines with at least three variations. First, you can use SLIP (Serial Line Internet Protocol) or PPP (Point-to-Point Protocol) to connect directly to the Internet. This option gives you full services. Second, you can use terminal emulation software and dial into a computer which has Internet access. In this case, you might get full Internet access, but any file transfers will go to the computer you are logged into and not to your computer. Third, you can use off-line software. The software dials your connection, sends and receives your mail, and logs off. When you read your mail, you are no longer logged on to the Internet. This represents the fastest, cheapest solution if all you need from the Internet is an e-mail connection. Your choice of options largely depends on your budget, your expected rate of use, and your need for full Internet services. Most smaller businesses use a dial-up service to a commercial network. Larger businesses often find leased lines to be more advantageous and economical.

If you are going to connect directly to the Internet, you need a to register your network. This involves being assigned a unique Internet IP network number and a unique domain name (such as mikeboz.com). Once you have this information, you can assign specific addresses to each machine on your network.

You request the IP number and the domain name from the Defense Data Network (DDN) Network Information Center (NIC) operated by Government Systems Inc. You have to provide detailed information about your network and you have to complete two separate forms. The phone number and address of DDN NIC is listed in Appendix B. It requires 8-10 working days for the application to be completed.

One other issue should be mentioned. Each network on the Internet is assigned a class of A, B or C. The class number is directly related to the size of the network. In almost all circumstances, your business or home use will only require a Class C network. A class network can support 254 hosts. This should be sufficient for all but the largest organizations. The DDN NIC carefully guards Class A and B networks and only provides them when warranted.

MCI Mail

MCI Mail is a popular public e-mail network service. While MCI Mail is beginning to branch out as a gateway to other services, it was never intended to be a collection of services such as CompuServe. Rather, MCI Mail is primarily an e-mail system and a gateway to other mail systems.

Access MCI Mail with a terminal emulation program. MCI Mail's role as a gateway makes it attractive for DOS-UNIX e-mail connectivity. If you, as a DOS user, want to send a message to a UNIX user on the Internet, you can do so directly. The key element is specifying an External Mail System (EMS) and choosing Internet—as per our example below. MCI Mail actually uses UUNET (discussed later) to make the connection, thereby allowing you to connect to UUNET addresses as well. The reverse works as well. A UNIX user connected to the Internet or UUNET can send e-mail directly to an MCI subscriber. This type of arrangement is ideal for DOS and UNIX sites that might send only occasional e-mail connections.

Once you know your recipient's Internet e-mail address, all you have to do is use MCI Mail's EMS option. Here's how:

1. At the "**To:**" prompt, type the recipient's name followed by the letters EMS in parentheses.
2. At the "EMS:" prompt, type "**INTERNET**."
3. At the "**MBX:**" prompt, type the recipient's Internet address.

Example:
TO: Mike Burgard (EMS)
EMS: INTERNET
MBX: mikeb@uworld.com

MCI Mail charges $.50 per each 500 character message sent. Longer messages cost $.10 for each 1000 characters. There is no charge for receiving messages. You have no connect charges since MCI Mail can be reached via 800 numbers anywhere in the continental U.S. Expect a $35 annual fee. However, there is a Preferred Subscription rate for frequent users. For a flat $10 per month, you pay no subscription fee and can send up to 40 5,000 character messages per month. MCI Mail also provides gateways to CompuServe, Dialog Information Services, Dow Jones, and a wide assortment of other network services.

MCI Mail is command driven and not particularly user friendly. You get a DOS program called COMMAccess to use as a terminal emulator. It was less than adequate all the way around. A better choice is to look at a Windows-based menu interface to MCI Mail called The Wire, from SWFTE International Ltd.

SWFTE International The Wire 2.1

If you choose MCI Mail as a gateway to various UNIX systems, you can use an MS Windows application called The Wire from SWFTE International. The Wire allows you to create, read, delete, and manage your mail off-line and is much easier to use the normal MCI interface.

The advanced Windows interface provides a handful of different icons representing mail in various states of writing and reading. Folders and messages can be placed on the screen, and drag and drop technology works with The Wire. There is a complete button bar across the top of the screen for actions such as send, save, and delete.

The Wire allows you to store your incoming and outgoing messages in desktop folders for better organization. You can have many different folders. Drag a message and drop it into a folder, or create an address book for each user to whom you regularly want to send mail. If you want to send mail to Internet users, check the EMS box, and put the Internet address in the options box. Although it is much simpler than using MCI Mail direct, if you want to send a one-time message, you still have to enter the person's address in your address book—a bother.

To create a message, click on the address in the address book. A composition window opens, and you can enter the message. You can add **cc:** addresses or additional **To:** users. You can also build user groups in the address book. Messages received can be forwarded or replied to. You can schedule The Wire to call multiple times a day or only at night. There is no interactive on-line method of using The Wire. The Wire sells for $99.95 and actually makes MCI Mail user-friendly.

Notework Corp. Notework/UUCP 2.0

Notework is a TSR-based e-mail system that runs on Novell networks. It ties into a UNIX network by using its sister product, Notework/UUCP. Notework/UUCP works in conjunction with a Novell MHS communication server to connect and transfer mail to a UNIX-based UUCP mail system. We look at both Notework products here, but concentrate on Notework/UUCP.

Installation/Configuration

Installation is all done on the Novell and DOS side of the equation. Notework/UUCPcontains no UNIX components. On the Novell side, you need MHS software and a PC to act as the MHS gateway/communication server. MHS, which runs continually on a dedicated machine and is bundled with Notework, installs quickly. The Notework/UUCP gateway product installs on the MHS machine. Your knowledge of UNIX is limited to learning the login information of your UNIX host and basics about UNIX UUCP addressing schemes.

Notework/UUCP uses standard UUCP addressing such as **uunet!uworld.com!-mike,** or you can use Internet domain style addresses such as **mikeb@uworld.com**. In either case, you must build a dictionary of UNIX addresses and store these on the MHS gateway. However, users need not know these addresses since the system administrator can create a set of aliases. A user can just address a message to mikeb, and the address directory takes care of converting it to the proper format.

User Interface

There is no user interface to the Notework/UUCP. We give you an idea of what the Notework e-mail interface is like, since that represents the most likely candidate for the front-end. If you use another e-mail front-end, Notework/UUCP still uses the MHS directory. On the UNIX side, you use your normal **uucp** mail program. The interface to Notework is simple and effective. As a TSR, you can pop up Notework over any DOS application using a hot-key. In addition, there is a Windows version that we did not test. Notework uses a variety of graphics to handle the different mail features. For example, when mail arrives, a small airplane flies across the screen. You can also highlight addresses from the directory to select mail recipients. Overall, we thought the basic product had a good interface.

Interoperability

Because Notework/UUCP does not provide UNIX components, it might be considered less than an integrated e-mail solution. Notework/UUCP is not appropriate if you have all your systems on the same TCP/IP network, and you want the same e-mail front-end. There is no support for SMTP, MAPI, X.400, nor any mail standards other than MHS and UUCP. You can, however, use Notework/UUCP as the gateway between UNIX and other MHS-based mailing systems such as BeyondMail. The serial connection can be through either a dial-up modem or a direct RS-232 serial connection. Direct connections can check for e-mail as frequently as every minute. If you use a modem to make the connection, Notework/UUCP autodials from the PC at user-defined intervals.

Smart Features

There are no smart features in Notework. The product handles standard e-mail tasks but has no automatic routing of messages or automatic filtering options; nor does it provide scripting or macro language.

Summary

As an e-mail solution, Notework does the job. It is not a leading edge product, but its connection to UNIX via UUCP makes Notework worth considering in those situations where the UNIX LAN and Novell LAN are already in place. A complete Notework solution is not expensive since it has no UNIX components. If you start from scratch with no e-mail on the Novell network, you need to purchase Notework, Notework/UUCP, and the MHS Gateway. Purchased together, you can get a 10-user pack for $1497. If you already have an MHS e-mail front-end, the remaining components cost $999.

SunSelect SelectMAIL for Windows 1.0

Sun Microsystems Inc. hopes to piggyback on the success of its workstations with a slew of PC-to-UNIX connectivity products. We have reviewed a number of these products in earlier chapters. SelectMail is the newest entry. SelectMail connects DOS and Windows users to a TCP/IP e-mail network of UNIX workstations. Though there is a DOS client, we only reviewed the Windows version.

Installation/Configuration

Like all dual platform products, SelectMAIL requires a TCP/IP connection to the UNIX network. This can come via PC-NFS or any other TCP/IP product such as those reviewed in Chapter 13. You can use SelectMAIL from a Novell network if you run a dual protocol stack on your PC or if your network uses a network-wide TCP/IP stack such as LAN Workgroup for DOS. Installation is a basic Windows install, and we experienced no problems. If the mail server, which is a UNIX workstation, is not running a POP (Post Office Protocol) server, you will have to provide one. In the case of SPARCstations, SunSelect supplies a POP2 and POP3 server as well as providing source code for other UNIX workstations. Copy the files from the install disks to the UNIX host via NFS—a simple process.

You need to provide a few basics about the POP server when you first start-up SelectMAIL. Unfortunately, the seven page configuration form does not adequately explain the entries, and you cannot access the documentation until you are in Select-MAIL since the documents are entirely on-line. The main items needed are the Internet address of your Internet mail domain, the type of POP server, and the Post Office host name. You cannot use IP addresses for the POP server; you must use the host name. Sendmail or some type of SMTP mail transport agent must be running on the UNIX host.

User Interface

Given Sun's lead in the GUI on the UNIX side, we expected a sharp Windows interface. We weren't disappointed. There is an icon bar across the top with multiple menus and dialog boxes everywhere. You can have your inbox, outbox, and compose box all open at the same time. The icons allow you to do such things as open a message, compose a new message, and open your personal address book. You can create your own address book, but the global address book should be created and maintained by the system administrator. The address book also supports aliases.

When you want to address a letter, open your address book and drag and drop an address into the **To** spot or the **CC**. When you open a folder, double click on messages to open them. We did find a few idiosynchroncies. There were times we thought a double-click should open a message, but it didn't. We also experienced situations when a window stayed under another window even when selected. Nevertheless, we liked the interface overall.

You can perform all the standard functions such as forward mail, reply, store mail locally, and add attachments. With the availability of subject and address headers, composing mail is straight-forward. You can use any of the available screen fonts and apply them separately to different folders. There is a spell checker and you can compose and reply to mail off-line.

Interoperability

As you might guess, SelectMAIL is well-suited for a Sun SPARCstation environment. However, your PC can connect to any UNIX workstation or TCP/IP machine on the network that is running a POP server. There are no UNIX clients with SelectMAIL since Sun assumes you already have a UNIX client running on the network. SMTP is supported as the sending protocol, but you will find no X.400 or MAPI support. Since the directory service is all proprietary, you cannot use X.500 directories or any current directory or address book you might have residing on the UNIX hosts. The POP server is provided for the convenience of the PC users. Sendmail delivers the mail to the mailbox, and the POP server gathers the mail and delivers it when the PC is up and running. This eliminates the need for the PC to be running 24 hours a day. It supports any TCP/IP stack that uses TCP/IP

Smart Features

With SelectMAIL you get a basic e-mail package. It has no bells and whistles, nor is it customizable like Z-Mail. You will find no macro language, nor is there any method to change the icons or buttons. The mail routing features are standard. You cannot mark a priority on a message, though you can indicate delivery notification. There are no smart routing features either, such as automatic filtering or automatic message routing. There are also no calendars, schedulers, or other time-management tools. SelectMAIL is designed to meet basic e-mail requirements, and it fulfills those with ease, but it is not intended to be an e-mail groupware product.

Summary

SelectMAIL fits well into certain niches. For an UNIX—DOS network, where Windows users need access to the Internet mail system and you are already using TCP/IP, SelectMAIL is a good choice. The Windows client costs $130.

UUNET

UUNET is a on-line commercial service dedicated to providing connections between systems using UUCP (UNIX to UNIX Copy). UUNET grew from a series of regional and national networks that AT&T (among other companies) provided gratis to universities and research labs during the 70s. The vast majority of present subscribers represent the same type of organizations who were taking advantage of earlier networks provided by AT&T. Today there are no restrictions on who can sign up for UUNET, and it is open to commercial network traffic.

In general, the main reason to consider UUNET as a DOS—UNIX e-mail connection is if the two parties are separated by distance, and UNIX is the dominant operating system in one side of the company. In this type of situation, UUNET works well. Obviously, it also works well for UNIX users desiring to reach other users across the globe.

UUNET works by collecting your messages through your UNIX mailer (**mail** on a BSD machine, **mailx** on a System V UNIX box, or whatever e-mail front-end you are using) and forwarding them to your company headquarters or to a vendor. Normally, e-mail messages are collected and sent out at night when rates are lower. Your system uses **uucp** to contact UUNET. Messages are forwarded to the central UUNET system in Falls Church, VA. UUNET then reads the addressing information and forwards the messages on to another system. Often the other system is the final destination. In some cases, the message is forwarded further, particularly when addressed to foreign destinations.

UUNET provides a number of service options. The primary option is a mail store and forwarding system that allows you to send and receive mail from other UUCP e-mail sites. UUNET also provides the USENET news service. USENET is somewhat similar to CompuServe's forums in which users exchange information about specific subjects. The USENET also contains many articles and general news information about particular topics. There are over 1,000 news feeds (sources of information) available.

Costs and subscription options vary depending on your needs. The lowest cost option is to sign up as a low volume, dial-up customer for $300 a year. This gives you 3 hours of connect time per month. If your company has few sites and only occasionally needs to exchange e-mail, this option is the cheapest. For $180 more, you get the 800 number for connection. More substantial e-mail requirements require the monthly account cost of $36 plus the cost of hourly connect charges. These fees range from $2.60 to $16.00 per hour depending on the type of connection and time of day. You can also save money if you are making long distance direct connect calls to various UUCP hosts throughout the country.

UUNET is also a gateway to the Internet and can act as an Internet mail forwarder. One advantage of UUNET for intercompany e-mail across the country is that the network is up 24 hours a day. Your e-mail does not depend on some intermediary. All UNIX systems come equipped with UUCP as part of the operating system. User guides generally explain its operation. On the DOS side, you must purchase a UUCP program. Besides Notework/UUCP which we mention earlier, others are listed in Appendix B. The market is not large; many of these products are shareware.

Wollongong PathWay Messenger 1.0

Perhaps the most far reaching e-mail integration attempt of any vendor to date is PathWay Messenger from The Wollongong Group. Messenger has client components on MS Windows, Macintosh, SCO UNIX, SunOS, and Interactive UNIX. The server portion loads on either Interactive UNIX or SunOS. Messenger is entirely GUI-based and supports many e-mail standards including SMTP, X.400, X.500, and POP. Its biggest limitation is the requirement for the Windows clients to be running Wollongong's PathWay as the TCP/IP stack and the $10,000 server price tag.

Installation/Configuration

While you can use just the client portions of Messenger, the product works best when the server component, called Messaging Services, is installed on your UNIX workstation. The installation requires about 1 hour on a Sun SPARCstation. Be forewarned, you need to create all your PC mail user accounts first. One advantage of the server is its ability restrict the access of PC users to Messenger mail services and not give them a full UNIX login.

Since Messenger requires PathWay from Wollongong as the TCP/IP transport, users who already have another transport or stack are at a significant disadvantage. (The next version will support WinSock allowing you to use any stack.) However, if you don't have a stack, PathWay is a good one to consider. Look for further comments on Wollongong's PathWay transport in Chapter 13. Messenger supplies a runtime PathWay TCP/IP module for Windows. It uses a typical Windows install and takes only minutes. Installing the Windows client is not difficult. You don't need to have the Messaging server facilities running on the UNIX host in order to use Messenger e-mail, but it makes more sense to do so.

Each user can have a personal address book. In addition, the system administrator maintains a global or system-wide distribution list. There can be some confusion about what you should put down for the name of the mail server and POP server. These are usually both the same names and the same host. You will have to run a POP3 server or an IMAP server. If you load the Messenging server on the UNIX workstation, **sendmail** is replaced by these services.

User Interface

The interface on the Windows side of Messenger is clean and well-laid out. The UNIX client is also GUI-based and uses Motif. There are many menus across the top and a toolbar of buttons below. Thus, composing, sending, and reading mail can be done quickly. You can create folders in which to store your messages based on any mechanism you deem appropriate such—as subject or date. Nearly all folders and selection items work with a double-click. For example, you can store messages locally in a folder, and then open a message by double-clicking on it when the folder is open. Messenger does not support drag and drop, however.

A mailbox or address can store an X.400 address, fax and voice phone numbers, and domain-style Internet addresses. When you want to address a message, you open either your personal address book or a public mailing list. Double-click on potential addressees, and they appear in your the message. Attachments supported include spreadsheets, data, pictures, and fax. There is no limit to the number of attachments. By virtue of a set of passwords, there can be a number of e-mail users from a single PC. The mail window acts such as a mini-desktop, letting you leave folder icons open on the screen along with mail in various stages of creation and handling. The mail composition editor is easy to use, though not as complete as a word processor.

Interoperability

PathWay Messenger is a strong supporter of accepted standards. It uses SMTP as the mail transport agent (MTA), and it provides support to X.400 and X.500 directory services. Messenger is the only cross-platform product we found with support for X.500 services. The server utilities allow the administrator to maintain a single global directory of users.

Pathway runs on Windows and Macintosh in addition to UNIX. In order to deliver the mail from the server to a PC, it uses either POP or IMAP. These servers act to keep the mail ready, eliminating the need for the PC to be up 24 hours a day. You can, however, send mail from the PC without these servers. If you have a separate fax server, you also get the benefits of being able to store fax numbers and send mail via fax. Support for USENET connections is supplied with Messenger.

Smart Features

Messenger does not attempt to enter into the domain of groupware. There are no scheduling routines or smart mail functions such as automatic filtering or automatic routing . There is, however, an automatic message forwarding based on patterns, as well as message notification and prioritizing of outgoing messages. There are no macros or any ability to customize the interface. However, the Messenging server module contains many administrative utilities, making it easy to configure and administrate a large mail network.

Summary

PathWay Messenger is an ambitious e-mail product. It represents an excellent choice for a large company with PCs, Macs, and UNIX workstations—a company which needs access to X.500 directory services and frequently sends mail outside of the organization. Messenger is more cumbersome for internal mail than Z-Mail or cc:Mail, however. The Windows client sells for $195, while the UNIX mail server is $9,995. At that price, Messenger is an Enterprise wide solution for large companies.

WordPerfect Corp. WordPerfect Office 4.0

WordPerfect Office gives you more than just an e-mail package. WordPerfect Office is a groupware product designed to manage your appointments, schedules, e-mail, and tasks. We include WordPerfect Office for two primary reasons—first, because it is one of only a few products with a planned release across a variety of platforms and, second, because WordPerfect has a large share of the DOS and UNIX word processing market. In fact, WordPerfect has the distinction of being the only word processing package with a sizable following on both platforms. This makes it an ideal package to consider for internetworking.

Unfortunately, WordPerfect Office was caught in our inevitable publishing deadline. Version 4.0 was released in the summer of 1993 for Windows and Macintosh clients, and the UNIX client is not available till late 1993, so it came too late for us to fully install it. 4.0 is a significant change from 3.0, however, and here is an overview of its features. (Some of these features may not be present in the UNIX client.)

The administration module for WPO 4.0 is DOS-based, but the clients are GUI through and through. The Windows interface uses plenty of icons, dialog boxes, and automatic selection routines when you double-click on an item. Addressing can be done by point and click or by incremental searching as you type a user name. Drag and drop is supported in the Windows and Macintosh versions.

The scheduling and groupware portions of WPO 4.0 are significant and closely tie with e-mail functionality. You can schedule a meeting by opening the Meeting option on the Schedule icon. Not only can you send e-mail to all the meeting participants, but WPO searches their calendars and determines what times are available. You can send messages and attachments as part of a scheduling item.

WPO 4.0 is a leading, if not the leading, e-mail package for cross-platform interoperability when we consider smart mail features. First, you can filter and manage both incoming and outgoing messages. You can control what messages appear in your inbox and which messages are displayed. Outgoing messages have tremendous amounts of information with them, including priority settings, receipt acknowledgements, and other delivery notification features (such as the ability to withdraw a message that was delivered, but not yet read).

In addition, there are complete rules-based mail filters and work-flow options. These are state-of-the-art. You can create a rule—for example, you can delegate mail and meetings to a different individual by checking a series of buttons. Many rules can be written without complicated if-then statements. WPO 4.0 works with Word-Perfect's new forms software to allow you to manage paperwork such as invoices and purchase orders without actually passing the paper from desk to desk.

Overall, our first impressions of WordPerfect Office 4.0 are laudatory. Not only does it compete with the best groupware on any platform, it is one of only two (Lotus Notes being the other) to cross DOS—UNIX platforms and provide the type of interoperabilty necessary in today's environment.

Z-Code Software Z-Mail 2.1

A relative newcomer to the e-mail market, Z-Mail is a UNIX-based program that got its start as a public domain UNIX mail front-end. The present Z-Mail product is a full-fledged product that runs under Motif, supports SMTP, and has character-based modules for terminals and DOS. The GUI is easy to use, and it is a great improvement over standard UNIX front-ends.

Installation/Configuration

Z-Mail works on a wide variety of UNIX platforms. It runs under Open Look, Motif, and character-based UNIX operating systems. Its new DOS version, Z-Mail Lite provides Z-Mail with a wide range of interoperability across UNIX and DOS machines.

Installation on the UNIX side varies by machine but is generally handled by an installation script. The script uses the **tar** command to download the files and then runs the **install** program. The script asks you to supply directory names, an activation key, and other pertinent information. It takes 15 minutes to run and gives you the option of changing default directories. We experienced no problems and found the script to be typical UNIX—a little cryptic, but otherwise smooth sailing. The Z-Mail Lite DOS version requires copying off the files and setting some parameters in text files.

User Interface

A full GUI interface, as seen in Figure 18.2, puts Z-Mail at the head of the pack when it comes to UNIX- based e-mail systems. One drawback, though, the PC package is character-based. It runs in Windows only in a DOS compatibility box. This sole factor makes Z-Mail less attractive to companies running mixed UNIX and MS Windows environments. However, the flexibility of Z-Mail's interface and the dearth of competing products make it worth considering.

The Z-Mail interface consists of seven sections, including a menu bar and message summary. Each section can be enlarged or reduced in size. The Menu Bar uses Motif-style, pull-down menus. A Button Panel comes with six default actions and the option to create more. Z-Mail also has an icon toolbox that allows you to skip the menu. We didn't like the toolbox much, since we found it difficult to fit on the screen. The icons are not closely fitted to the menu like they are in cc:Mail. Reading, composing, and sending e-mail is a simple process in Z-Mail. Selecting a button designated Compose brings up a window for you to enter the message text and routing information.

Z-Mail Lite has nearly all the functionality of the parent product, but not nearly as much style. The character interface is weak by comparison and does not support the types of graphics found in many DOS character products. However, it uses pull-down menus and follows the same layout as Z-Mail. If you are familiar with Z-Mail, you should require no additional training to use Z-Mail Lite.

Z-Mail fully supports aliasing and attachments. If you regularly send messages to a person with an address of **CutiePie@Workshop.bigplace.com**, you can create the alias, **cute**. There is access to global address directories either created by the administrator or through centralized services. Message encoding is handled automatically, and sending attachments from the UNIX side can be done by dragging an icon from your desktop and dropping it on Z-Mail if you are using IXI's X.desktop or Motif 1.2.

Interoperability

Part of the reason there are so few cross-platform packages comes from the lack of standards in the market. Z-Mail attempts to support many of the prevailing standards on the UNIX side of the market while virtually ignoring the PC side of the market. It runs on a wide variety of UNIX workstations including Data General, DEC, HP 9000, IBM RS/6000, SCO Open Desktop, Silicon Graphics, and Sun. Z-Mail also offers a character-based product that lets any terminal use Z-Mail.

Z-Mail uses SMTP as the transport protocol across all versions. It does not require a POP server on the UNIX host for its DOS client. Z-Mail also supports MIME (Multipurpose Internet Mail Extensions) and X.400. Support for these two standards provides a degree of interoperability with Z-Mail not found in other products.

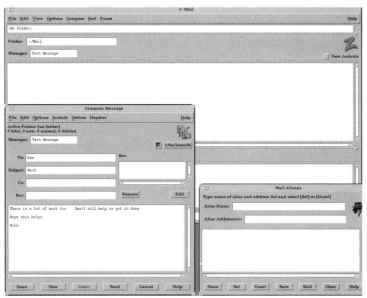

FIGURE 18.2 Z-Mail GUI interface

Smart Features

In addition to its interoperability, Z-mail is a strong competitor in the DOS-UNIX internetworking mail group due to its customization features. Z-Mail supports over 100 variables that you can use to configure your system. These variables are set through the Variables menu or as initialization files. They include the ability to change how Z-mail operates, how the screen looks, and what menu defaults are invoked.

Z-mail also supports Z-Script, a language which lets you set up macros to handle your mail in specific manners. In its simplest form, scripting is used to program the buttons found in different parts of Z-Mail. You can write a Z-Mail script to automatically put messages from your boss into a specific folder and inform you when such mail arrives. This degree of smart mail routing is terrific! There may be some pure UNIX products and some pure DOS products that do more, but they don't have Z-Mail's interoperablity.

Summary

Z-Mail breaks some of the pricing molds for UNIX-oriented software. Platforms do not enter into the pricing scheme—only the number of users. Starting at $295 per user, Z-Mail is priced all the way down to $125 per user for 500 or more. There is an additional, one-time charge of 10% of the purchase price for a network license server. Since few people need documentation, Z-Mail prices it separately.

As we went to press, Z-Code is releasing version 3.0 of Z-Mail. New features include an improved scripting language, directory services across all platforms, full MIME compliance, and POP support. These additions enhance Z-Mails attractiveness.

Recommendations

This is not a race with a clear winner. Each product has a niche. For cross-platform groupware, Lotus Notes 3.0 and WordPerfect Office 4.0 are both high quality products. If you already use WordPerfect, WPO 4.0 is an excellent product. Lotus Notes, meanwhile, is much more than e-mail or groupware and can be used in an enterprise-wide scenario, but it is too costly for e-mail only. In the pure e-mail category, cc:Mail is the most advanced product, and it is the easiest to work with. It also does the best job of covering all the major platforms—although Wollongong Messenger is a close second among pure e-mail packages. Messenger, with its server module, should certainly be considered for the large organization. Z-Mail has an excellent set of UNIX front-ends, but the DOS client is not attractive for a Windows user. Table 18.1 lays out other pertinent differences between several products.

If you need only occasional e-mail access to UNIX systems not under your control and not in your building, the Internet and commercial services such as UUNET are a good choice. Use a gateway such as MCI Mail if you need to communicate with a more diverse group of users.

Table 18.1: **E-Mail Features**

	Lotus cc:Mail	Notework/ UUCP	Sun Select MAIL	Wollongong Messenger	WordPerfect Office 4.0	Z-Code Z-Mail
Supported Platforms	DOS, UNIX, MAC, OS/2, Windows	DOS, Windows	DOS, UNIX, Windows	Windows, MAC, UNIX	DOS,UNIX, MAC, WIndows	DOS, UNIX, MAC
Supported Standards	SMTP	uucp, MHS	SMTP,POP	SMTP, POP, IMAP, X400	MHS	SMTP, POP MIME, X.400
Automatic Filtering	No	No	No	No	Yes	Yes
Automatic Routing	No	No	No	Partial	Yes	Partial
Message Prioritizing	Yes	No	No	Yes	Yes	Yes
Auto Replies	Yes	No	Yes	Yes	Yes	Yes
Store & Forward	Yes	Yes	Yes	Yes	Yes	Yes
User Archiving	Yes	No	Yes	Yes	Yes	Yes
GUI Interface	Yes	Yes	Yes	Yes	Yes	UNIX-only
Macros	No	Yes	No	No	Yes	Yes
X.400 Support	No	No	No	Yes	Yes	Yes
Reports	No	No	No	Yes	Yes	No
Drag and Drop	Yes	No	Yes	No	Yes	Yes
Attachments (Voice, Fax, Spreadsheet, Graphics, Video)	All	All	Text and Binary	All	All	All
Customizable Interface	No	No	No	No	No	Full
Gateways Available	Yes	No	No	No	Yes	No
Encryption	Yes	No	No	No	Yes	Yes
Aliases	Partial	Yes	Yes	Yes	Yes	Yes
Multiple Directories	Yes	No	Yes	Yes	Yes	Yes
Price	$895 - platform pack $345 - 10 user pack.	uucp: $999 $40 per user	$130 per user	$9,995 - server $195 - client	Admin -$295 5-users-$495	$295 -single user -lower for multiple users

Appendix A

Survival Kit

Common DOS/UNIX Commands and Keys

Have you ever tried to find your way around in a foreign country? A foreign-language dictionary becomes your best and most indispensable friend. The same holds true when you cross the borders into DOS or UNIX country. And so we offer you our foreign language dictionary in Table A.1—a list of the most frequently-used commands and keys under DOS and how they translate into UNIX. There are many similarities between the two, due to DOS's ancient origins in XENIX. The keys indicate general usage, but they may vary by machine configuration and application. Parentheses indicate required parameters; braces designate optional parameters, and operating systems appear within square brackets. Some DOS commands may only be available under later DOS versions. Some of the UNIX keys appear only on Sun keyboards. Remember that the case of commands does not matter under DOS—only under UNIX.

Table A.1: **Command and Key Translator**

DOS Command	UNIX Command	Purpose
Key: \	Key: /	Separates directory and file names.
Key: * or ?	Key: * or ?	Replaces unknown characters.in filenames. (Wildcards)
Key: |	Key: |	Filters output of one command through another command. (Pipe)
Key: < or >	Key: < or >	Redirects input/output of a command to another source/destination.
Key: Backspace	Key: Delete or Backspace	Erases the character to the left of cursor.
Key: Delete	Key: Shift-Delete	Erases the character at the cursor.
Key: Home/End		Moves the cursor to the beginning or end of the current line.
	Key: Home/End	Moves the cursor to the beginning or end of the current file.

Table A.1: **Command and Key Translator**

DOS Command	UNIX Command	Purpose
Key: F1	Key: HELP	Requests context-sensitive help.
Key: F3	Key: !!	Repeats the last command.
Key: Ctrl-C or Ctrl-Break	Key: Ctrl-C	Breaks out of the current task or script.
Key: Pause or Ctrl-S	Key: Ctrl-S	Halts current operation until a key (Ctrl-Q under UNIX) is pressed to continue.
attrib (-r filepath /s)	chmod (-R 777 filepath) or chmod (-R a+rwx filepath)	Changes the attributes/permissions of files and subdirectories in filepath to read-write-execute for all users.
attrib (+r filename)	chmod (444 filename) or chmod (a-wx filename)	Reduces the attributes/permissions of filename to read-only for all users.
cd	pwd	Displays the current working directory.
chdir (dir) or cd (dir)	cd (dir)	Changes to the directory 'dir'.
chkdsk	df	Measures filesystem free space.
chkdsk /f	fsck	Checks and repairs filesystems.
cls	clear	Clears the screen
copy {sourcefiles targetdir}	cp {sourcefiles targetdir}	Copies sourcefiles to targetdir directory.
date, time	date	Displays date and time. Can also use to set them.
del (file) or erase (file)	rm (file)	Deletes the file.
del *.*, then use rd	rm -R (directory)	Deletes all files, removes subdirectories.
dir	ls -l, ls -al	Lists all files in current working directory.
dir /w	ls	Lists all files in abbreviated format.
edit (file) or edlin (file)	vi (file) or ed (file)	Edits the text file.
exit	exit	Exits from an interactive shell.
find {/n /i string filename}	grep {-in -e string filename}	Searches for occurrences of string in filename, ignoring case and displaying line numbers.
help (command) or (command) /?	man (command)	Displays help text for command.
mkdir (dir) or md (dir)	mkdir (dir)	Creates a directory called 'dir'.
more < (file) or type (file)|more	more (file) or cat (file)|more	Pages through a long text file.
print (filename)	lpr -h (filename) [BSD & AIX], lp (filename) [System V]	Prints filename with no banner page.

Table A.1: **Command and Key Translator**

DOS Command	UNIX Command	Purpose
rename (filename) (newname)	mv (filename) (newname/newdirectoy)	Renames filename as newname. Mv can also move filename to newdirectory.
rmdir (dir) or rd (dir)	rmdir (dir)	Removes the directory called 'dir'.
set	set and setenv	Lists environment variables.
set (variable=value}	setenv (variable value)	Sets an environment variable to value.
shell (or dosshell)	sh	Begins an interactive shell.
type (filename)	cat (filename)	Lists the filename to the console.
ver	uname -a	Displays operating system version

Other Important Commands and Keys

The following two Tables A.2 and A.3 describe DOS and UNIX commands. They also list the keys with no close counterparts in the opposing operating system—keys which come in handy, nevertheless. The UNIX commands are specifically for the Sun SunOS, but they approximate other UNIX system commands as well.

Table A.2: **DOS-Specific Commands and Keys**

Command	Purpose
Key: Escape	Cancels the current operation.
Key: PrintScreen	Sends screen image to parallel port.
Key: Ctrl-P	Starts/stops directing screen output additionally to the printer.
Key: Alt-(?)	Typically used to access DOS application menu bars, e.g., Alt-F for File.
diskcopy (A:) (B:)	Copies the entire A: drive disk to B: drive, formatting B: as it goes.
format (A:) {/X}	Formats the diskette in A: for use by DOS. See DOS manual for /X options.
mode {com1: 9600,n,8,1,p}	Initializes the first serial port for use by DOS programs. 9600 baud, no parity, 8 data bits, 1 stop bit, continuous retry. Not needed for Windows programs.
mode {lpt1:=com1:}	Redirects output for the parallel port (including print screens) to the first serial port. This would be done if com1 is attached to the printer.
undelete	Restores a file deleted in error. DOS 5.0 or higher, only.

Table A.3: **UNIX-Specific Commands and Keys**

Command	Purpose
Key: Escape-(?)	Usage depends upon the character attached.
Key: Ctrl-D	Logs user off of the system or out of the current shell.
Key: Cut, Copy, or Paste [SunOS]	Allows command-line text to be captured, removed, and/or pasted to a new location.
cc (-o outfile source-file)	Compiles sourcefile (written in C), leaving the executable version as outfile.
chgrp (-R newgroup) filepath	Changes the group ownership of all files in filepath to newgroup.
chown (-R newowner filepath)	Changes the owner of all files in filepath to newowner.
du [-a] (directory)	Displays the sizes of directories (and files) in blocks.
file (filename)	Examines filename to determine its type, e.g., ascii text, c program text, etc.
find (file) -ls	Finds file(s) and displays general file information, e.g., date, permissions, owner, etc.
kill -9 (process#)	Stops the currently running process. Determine process# using ps.
ln (-s) (old) (new)	Links old file/directory name to new equivalent name. -s creates a symbolic link.
ps -ax [SunOS], ps -ef [Solaris], ps -A [AIX], ps -a [SCO]	Lists the currently running processes (daemons). A status of 'D' indicates that the process is stuck in a non-interruptible state (swapper and pagedaemon are always D.) 'I' and 'S' processes are waiting, 'R' processes are running, 'T' means stopped.
ps -aux [SunOS], ps -Af [AIX], ps -af [SCO]	Lists the processes with more information in wide format. Widen the window first.
ps -x|grep process-name [SunOS]	Checks to see if a particular process is running. This command always returns a line for "grep".
su {username}	Set user (switch to a new user id - root assumed). Starts a new shell, requires login, and changes user and group ID's to match new user name.
touch (filename)	Creates an empty file, or updates the last modified time to an existing file.
which (filename)	Finds the location of filename in the PATH.
who, whoami	Shows who is logged on to the system.

Search Paths for Executable Programs

Both DOS and UNIX make use of a search path variable placed in the environment by the startup scripts. The order of search varies between DOS and UNIX, however. When a DOS executable program is typed at the command line, the current directory is automatically searched first, followed by the paths listed in the **PATH** variable.

Under UNIX, the **PATH** variable is searched, but not the current directory (unless '.' is one of the entries in the **PATH** variable).

If you must execute a UNIX program which is not in the search path, you have two options. Either type the complete path in front of the program name, (e.g., **/home/test/newprog**); or, if you are already in the /**home/test** directory, place **./** ahead of the program name (e.g., **./newprog**.)

Editing Text Files Under DOS and UNIX

DOS and UNIX each provide basic text editors which you can execute from the command line. Graphical interfaces supply more editors, which are usually easier to use than the basic models. However, just in case you have to edit a file in a hurry and your editor of choice is not available, here are instructions for the common editors.

DOS Editors

DOS provides two editors with its 4.x and higher versions, **EDIT** and the older **EDLIN**. Use **EDIT** for full-screen editing—you will catch on quickly; plus, it provides on-line help. You can either load your text file at the command line with **edit textfile** or load it after starting **EDIT**. Both **EDIT** and **EDLIN** are commonly stored in the **\DOS** directory, so if you find yourself with no search path, start **EDIT** with **\dos\edit**.

Start **EDLIN** by typing **edlin textfile**. When it has loaded your text file, you will see End of input file, followed by a * prompt. First, type l to list the first 23 lines of the file. If you need to see later lines, precede l with a starting line number.

Next, to change a line, type its line number. This will display that one line and provide a blank area for the new copy underneath. Use the Right-Arrow/Left-Arrow keys to locate on the starting position, or retype the line from the beginning. You can use the Insert, Delete, and F3 keys to help. When finished, press Return to go back to command mode. If you do not wish to make changes to the selected line after all, leave the new copy blank and press Return.

To insert lines ahead of, say, line 6, type **6i**. **EDLIN** will keep issuing new lines as long as you keep using them. When you are through, press Ctrl-Z and Return.

Deleting lines is a little more tricky. Type **6d** to delete line 6, but remember that all of the subsequent lines will be bumped up (line 7 becomes line 6, etc.). If you must delete lines 6-8, type **6,8d** (or **6d** three times in succession.) If you are in doubt about your line numbers, list them out with l.

When you are through editing, enter **e** to end and save the file or **q** to quit without saving. You can get to know **EDLIN** better if you look over your DOS manual; but, frankly, most people want something more.

UNIX Editors

You can find several UNIX text editors, including **vi**, **ed**, **emacs**, **INed**, and others. To get up and editing quickly, use the editor that comes with the graphical desktop. If you don't have one, here are basic instructions for two of the most popular UNIX editors.

vi

If our experience is any indication, you will find the UNIX **vi** editor difficult to use. It overwhelms you with more options than anyone could remember and annoys you with beeps whenever you change command mode. (It sounds like you are hitting wrong keys.) Curiously, it has a cult following of loyal users. It is a full-screen editor. Start it with **vi textfile**. If **vi** complains that it has no terminal type when you try to start it, issue the command **TERM=vt100; export TERM** first. Below we discuss a few of the most useful commands—enough to get you through.

Use the arrow keys to locate the cursor at the edit point. Then press ESCAPE to enter command mode. Specify **a** to begin inserting text AFTER the current cursor position. Remember that if you must retrace—going back to correct a typing error, for example—you must type ESCAPE-a again.

You can delete characters at the cursor by typing ESCAPE-x. Keep pressing the x key until all of the characters you wish to delete are gone. To do a line delete, press ESCAPE-dd.

To conclude the edit session, enter **ZZ** to save and quit, or enter ESCAPE-COLON (:). Finally, choose from the basic options **q** (quit) or **q!** (quit without saving). Do NOT use **e** (or **e!**) unless you wish to abandon your changes and start over on the file.

ed

Ed is the basic line editor, similar to **EDLIN** in DOS. Start it with **ed (filename)**, quit with **q**. You must do a write **w** before you quit in order to save your work.

When **ed** starts up it displays the byte count of your file and then . . . nothing. List a range of lines, for example 1-20, using the format **1,20n**. If the file has no a line 20, **ed** lamely returns only a **?**. If you type **h** you will get the reason. Type just a line number to display a single line.

You can enter change mode at line 14 by typing **14c**. Every line you type after that replaces its corresponding line in the file, until you type a period ".". Use **6i** to insert lines before line 6. Just type line after line until you are done adding lines, then use a period to end the insert mode. To delete lines 4-6, use the command **4,6d**. **Ed** renumbers the remaining lines after a deletion.

Boot Processes

Computers can fail to boot properly for many reasons, including bad path or file names, hanging programs, poorly-written scripts, etc. Here are some facts about the various boot processes that may help you put the finger on difficulties.

DOS Boot

The DOS kernel is contained in hidden files of the boot disk root directory. You cannot see them without special software tools. **COMMAND.COM**, a visible file, rounds out the set by interpreting DOS commands entered at the system prompt.

When the computer powers up, the DOS system files automatically execute the instructions contained in **\CONFIG.SYS** and **\AUTOEXEC.BAT**—in that order. **CONFIG.SYS** contains information about environment variables and device drivers. Each driver loads in order of appearance in the file. After that list executes, the system calls the **AUTOEXEC.BAT** batch (script) file—its final act before yielding control to the user. **AUTOEXEC.BAT** can load other drivers, as well as set additional environment variables. Network login commands are usually placed in this file. **AUTOEXEC.BAT** can also call other **.BAT** files. As a final line in the script, the user may start Windows or another favorite program automatically.

Windows reads several **.INI** files when it starts. The most important one **\WINDOWS\SYSTEM.INI**, tells Windows which drivers to load. After reading the **.INI** files, the Startup window controls which applications are loaded automatically, displaying icons at the bottom of the screen for each. One additional script file may be executed during this process—**WINSTART.BAT**. This file loads user-specified, memory-resident programs (TSRs) using the Windows memory-handling drivers. (The use of windows drivers saves conventional memory for DOS applications.)

OS/2 Boot

OS/2 machines integrate nicely with many networking products for PCs. The startup procedure resembles that of DOS, and the kernel is again contained in several hidden files.

CONFIG.SYS is much expanded over its DOS counterpart and is the primary source of startup information. It contains many more drivers than under DOS, and in it you can set environment variables and search paths. With help from the **OS2.INI** and **OS2SYS.INI** files, **CONFIG.SYS** also starts the Presentation Manager.

After the list of instructions in **CONFIG.SYS** has been executed, instead of running **AUTOEXEC.BAT**, the system executes **STARTUP.CMD** if one has been created. On a LAN Manager server machine **STARTUP.CMD** is used to issue the command **NET START SERVER**.

CMD files are the OS/2 counterparts of DOS **BAT** files. If you open the DOS-compatibility window under OS/2, **AUTOEXEC.BAT** does control that DOS shell, allowing you to customize your DOS environment. This is the only case, though, in which **BAT** files play any importance under OS/2. **BAT** files are ignored altogether by OS/2 1.3—you cannot execute them. Under OS/2 V2.0 and higher, **BAT** files are honored as executable alternatives to **CMD** files, but **CMD** files still take precedence.

UNIX Boot

UNIX boot processes are extremely complicated in comparison with the DOS or OS/2 boot processes. Here we provide an overview of the boot process for a Sun SPARC-station running SunOS (a BSD UNIX) with brief notes about differences for System V UNIX.

The system firmware first performs a self test which reports either that the Self Test completed successfully or leaves the screen dark. The firmware then loads the bootblock code program from the beginning of the default local drive. That program in turn reads a program typically called **boot**. (If boot is ever changed, it must be reinstalled.) Boot mounts the root filesystem and loads the *kernel*, called **vmunix** (System V: **unix**.) The kernel initializes the hardware interfaces and process framework. Finally, the kernel starts a daemon called **init**, which gets the processes going.

Init is responsible for initializing the single- and/or multiuser mode of the computer. In multiuser mode, **init** creates a getty process for each active communication line. **Getty** is the program that controls user login, password verification, and starts a shell to accept user commands.

Init also invokes a series of run command (**rc**) script files which account for most of the startup messages you see on the screen. The content of the **rc** files varies between UNIX versions, and users/administrators often add more variety by making their own changes as well. The first script, **/etc/rc.boot**, performs the primary tasks of setting the machine name, configuring the network interface, and running **fsck** to check and repair the filesystems. If **fsck** finds no problems, **init** starts **/etc/rc**. Rc calls **/etc/rc.local** as a sub-script.

Rc.local is a lengthy file that starts daemons and also accesses the Network Information Service. The NFS daemons are started here and remote filesystems are mounted. Most specific system configuration changes go into **rc.local**. When the instructions in this file have all been executed, **rc** regains control in order to start the standard daemons, as well as networking and accounting functions. Two daemons of particular interest in networking are **inetd** and **lpd**. Inetd, together with **inetd.-conf** and the **portmap** daemon, prepares the Remote Procedure Call system for **ftp**, **telnet**, remote boot, and other services. **Lpd** is the printer daemon. The final act of **rc** is to leave you with a login prompt to a multiuser system.

System V UNIX provides a twist to the previous discussion—**init** calls a file called **/etc/inittab** to tell it what to do. **Inittab** provides a list of gettys and script files to run under different run levels (level 3 is for multiuser NFS networks). The script files include **/etc/rc, /etc/bcheckrc**, and others.

When you login, more scripts run, depending upon your chosen shell. These include **.cshrc**, **.login**, **.kshrc**, and **.profile**. Their purpose is to configure the environment. See Chapter 1 for information about these files.

If your workstation hangs on boot after you have made a change to one of the system startup scripts (such as **/etc/rc.local**), you may be able to reboot in single-user mode to fix the problem. In single-user mode, gettys and many other processes do not run—allowing you to find and fix problems. Power down the computer; then, after you turn it back on and have the introduction screen, press Stop-A (on a Sun) to generate the monitor prompt >. Type **b -s** to boot in single-user mode. When you see the # prompt, edit the file you suspect. To boot in single-user mode without **rc.local** execution, type **b -sb**. In System V, you are often given the opportunity to go into single-user mode at the time of booting.

Shutdown Processes

No matter how pretty a box it comes in, your new product may still hang your system in some fashion, forcing a shutdown and reboot. Or, software may suggest a reboot to start new daemons. DOS and UNIX computers have different shutdown/reboot procedures.

DOS Shutdown

There is no universal rule, as such, for rebooting or turning off a DOS machine except closing any open application. If you have Windows 3.1, you can close all applications by double-clicking on the upper left-hand box on the Program Manager window. Windows makes sure any applications you have open will be closed and the work saved. Other PC operating systems such as OS/2 and desktop manager software often have a Shutdown button or menu option.

Do a warm reboot (leaving the hardware on) by pressing Ctrl-Alt-Del. If that does not work because the machine is hung, try the more drastic Reset button on the computer chassis, or reach for the Big Red Switch. There are no filesystems that can be corrupted unless the PC is a network file server (see Chapter 7). Make sure the PC is not running a multiuser DOS before you end up crashing other users.

UNIX Shutdown

UNIX systems, which are multitasking, are designed to remain running. However, a process may run amok occasionally, creating severe slowdowns, making the display go bonkers, etc. You can usually kill the offending process (if you can identify it with **ps**), though occasionally a process won't die. To clear it, you should always run a shutdown routine rather than simply turning off the computer. Such a routine typically warns all other users on the system, writes a message to the error log, and makes sure the filesystems are in sync before going into its self-inflicted coma. If you just flip the switch you can suffer data loss or a corrupted file system.

Check your User or System Administrator manual for specifics about the proper commands and vendor-specific options for shutting down your system. You must have root authority to do a shutdown, but you don't need to exit from the graphical desktop manager first; sometimes these even provide a shutdown icon.

On many UNIX machines, including the Sun and IBM RS/6000, you have several command-line shutdown options that overlap each other. Under normal multiuser circumstances you should use **shutdown + (minutes)** because it warns any users. If the system is a stand-alone, or if you must shutdown in a hurry, use **halt** to skip the warning delays. You can both shut down and reboot by issuing a **reboot** command, although like **halt**, **reboot** does not warn users.

SCO OPEN DESKTOP provides a System Terminate option in the **sysadmsh**. You can also issue **shutdown -g (minutes)** or **haltsys** commands from a command line. Novell UnixWare provides a shutdown switch icon to do a total shutdown, or go to the root directory to type **shutdown**.

Getting Help

Most UNIX systems supply on-line manual pages. To get information on, say, the /etc/fstab file, type **man fstab** from a command line. If there is help available, it will be listed for you. Use the spacebar for screen-by-screen display. Or, you may find the same manual page in the printed Reference Manual. The number in parenthesis after the command or file name signifies the category to which it belongs, e.g., **1** for Commands, **5** for File Formats, etc. Practically any command or file can be unobfuscated in this manner, although the details may not be entirely current.

Under DOS 5.0 and higher you can obtain help at the command line by typing **HELP (command)** or **(command) /?**. Under older versions there is no command line help other than the DOS manual. Within DOS applications, however, you can generally receive context-sensitive help by pressing the F1 key. In Windows applications, the menu bar has a HELP option.

What to Do with Core Files

As you work with software products on UNIX systems, especially during installation, you may generate a **core** file if the system bombs (crashes). A **core** file is a memory dump which can be debugged by an experienced technician using **sdb** (the symbolic debugger). Assuming that you do not have such skills, at the least you can type **file core** to see what application caused the crash. Then call the vendor and delete the dump. **Core** files consume vast amounts of disk space in your filesystems.

Core files can be recognized under graphical file managers (including the Sun Solaris file manager) as a bright red icon with a bomb inside. Dragging the bomb to the wastebasket may only set the file in a holding status. To really get rid of it, **cd** to the directory that contains the **core**, then type **rm core**.

Copying Files Between DOS and UNIX Computers

UNIX files are stored on disk in ISO format, and the ISO format is not compatible with DOS. Binary files can be moved between systems simply by reading and writing a new disk format. However, moving text files requires translation, as well.

All text files have a Linefeed character (0x0A) at the end of each line. DOS text files throw in an extra character—a Carriage Return (0x0D or CTRL-M). In order to transfer a UNIX text file to a DOS machine, first translate the file using the unix command **unix2dos**, e.g., **unix2dos (/path/)unix_name_can_be_long (/newpath/)dos8-char.txt**. There is a similar command for converting DOS files to ISO format, **dos2unix**. You can use either command to place the converted file in a new location.

System V UNIX (such as SCO) file names can be up to 14 characters long. BSD UNIX (such as SunOS) names can be up to 255 characters long (hard to remember at that length, though). Remember that UNIX filenames can have multiple periods within. DOS filenames, on the other hand, can be a maximum of 8 characters followed by a period and a 3-character extension.

If NFS is installed between the computers, place the file(s) in the shared filesystem for direct access. If copying the file(s) onto a floppy disk for transfer to the DOS machine, you need to do two things: 1) obtain a DOS-formatted diskette, and 2) mount the UNIX floppy drive as a DOS floppy drive. You can mount the drive as a DOS drive on the Sun workstation by typing **mount /pcfs**, as long as the **/etc/fstab** file indicates that **/dev/fd0** is of type *pcfs* (PC filesystem). For example, our **/etc/fstab** file contains the line:

```
/dev/fd0 /pcfs pcfs rw,noauto 0 0
```

The line also signifies that the **/dev/fd0** filesystem directory is read/write and should not be automatically mounted on boot. The remaining two zeros are for UNIX options irrelevant to the floppy—leave them zero. If **/etc/fstab** does not have a line similar to this, edit one in; then create the directory by going to the root directory and typing **mkdir pcfs**.

Next, insert the floppy and copy the text files either to or from it with the **cp** command (if the file is already translated), or use the redirecting capability of the **unix2dos** or **dos2unix** commands. Wild cards (*) can be used in the file names. Use the **ls** command to see a list of the files now on the floppy, e.g., **ls /pcfs**. Note: ls with the **-l** option does NOT provide the expanded listing when used on a DOS diskette if **/pcfs** is a symbolic link to another directory, e.g. **/home/pcfs**. In this case, type **ls -l / home/pcfs** to get the expanded listing. Eject the floppy with **eject**. Ejecting the disk also restores the drive to its original UNIX configuration.

Appendix B
Books and Vendors

Books

UNIX

Arthur, Lowell Jay. *UNIX Shell Programming*. New York: John Wiley & Sons Inc., 1990

Coffin, Stephen. *UNIX System V Release 4: The Complete Reference*. Berkeley, CA: Osborne McGraw-Hill, 1991

Mansfield, Niall. *The Joy of X*. Great Britian: Addison-Wesley Publishers Ltd., 1992

Moore, Mike and Michael Burgard. *X.desktop Cookbook*. Great Britain: Prentice Hall International, 1992

Peek, Jerry, Tim O'Reilly, Mike Loukides, and other authors of the Nutshell Handbooks. *UNIX Power Tools*. New York: Bantam Books, 1993

Southerton, Alan X. *Modern Unix*. New York: John Wiley & Sons Inc., 1993

Levine, John and Margaret Levine Young. *UNIX for Dummies*. San Mateo, CA: IDG Books Worldwide Inc., 1993

Winsor, Janice. *Solaris System Administrator's Guide*. Emeryville, CA: Ziff-Davis Press, 1993

X Windows References. Sebastopol, CA: O'Reilly & Associates Inc. Eight volumes.

DOS & Windows

Gookin, Dan. *DOS for Dummies: 2nd Edition*. San Mateo, CA: IDG Books Worldwide Inc., 1993

Livingston, Brian. *Windows 3.1 Secrets*. San Mateo, CA: IDG Books Worldwide, Inc., 1992

Stinson, Craig and Nancy Andrews. *Running Windows*. Redmond, WA: Microsoft Press, 1990

Wolverton, Van. *Running MS-DOS*. Bellevue, WA: Microsoft Press, 1993

Networking

Comer, Douglas E. *Internetworking with TCP/IP*. Englewood Cliffs, NJ: Prentice Hall, 1991

Kochan, Stephen. *UNIX Networking*. Carmel, IN: SAM, 1989

Miller, Mark. *Troubleshooting TCP/IP*. San Mateo, CA: M&T Books, 1992

Derfler, Frank. *PC Magazine's Guide to Connectivity: Second Edition*. Emeryville, CA: Ziff-Davis Press, 1992

Derfler, Frank. *PC Magazine's Guide to Linking LANs*. Emeryville, CA: Ziff-Davis Press, 1992

Dvorak's Guide to PC TeleCommunications, Berekely, CA: Osborne-McGraw Hill, 1992

Fitzgerald, Jerry. *Business Data Communications, 4th Ed.* New York: John Wiley & Sons, 1993

Florence, Donne. *LAN, Developing Your System For Business.* New York: John Wiley & Sons, 1989

Handbook of LAN Cable Testing, San Diego. Wavetek/Beckman Industrial Corp., 1992

LaQuey, Tracy and Jeanne C. Ryer. *The Internet Companion.* Reading, MA: Addison-Wesley Publishing Co., 1993

Madron, Thomas. *Local Area Networks.* New York: John Wiley & Sons, 1990

Madron, Thomas W. *Enterprise-wide Computing.* New York: John Wiley & Sons, 1991

Malmud, Carl. *Exploring The Internet.* Englewood Cliffs, NJ: PTR Prentice Hall, 1992

Spinney, Byron. *Ethernet Pocket Guide.* Horsham, PA: Professional Press Books, 1992

Vendors

Alpha Terminals

Applied Digital Data Systems Inc.
100 Marcus Blvd.
Hauppauge, NY 11788
800-231-5445, 516-231-5400

Cumulus Technology Corp.
1007 Elwell Ct.
Palo Alto, CA 94303
415-960-1200

Link Technologies Inc.
46959 Landing Pkwy.
Fremont, CA 94538
800-448-5465, 510-651-8000

Bridges, Concentrators, Hubs, and Routers

Allied Telesis
575 East Middlefield Road
Mount View, CA 94043
800-424-4284, 415-964-2771

Cabletron Systems Inc.
35 Industrial Way
Rochester, NH 03867
603-332-9400

Cisco Systems Inc.
1525 O'Brien Drive
Menlo Park, CA 94025
415-326-1941

Gandalf Premier
1051 Perimeter Drive-6
Schaumburg, IL 60173
800-354-4224

LANTRONIX
26072 Merit Circle, Suite 113
Laguna Hills, CA 92653
800-422-7022, 714-367-0050

Standard Microsystems Corp.
80 Arkay Dr.
Hauppauge, NY 11788
800-762-4968, 516-273-3100

3Com Corp.
P.O. Box 58145, 5400 Bayfront Plaza
Santa Clara, CA 95052
800-638-3266, 408-764-5000

SynOptics Communications Inc.
4401 Great America Pkwy.
Santa Clara, CA 95054
800-776-8023, 408-988-2400

Well Fleet Communications Inc.
15 Crosby Drive
Bedford, MA 01730
617-275-2400

Character Terminals

Applied Digital Data Systems Inc.
100 Marcus Blvd.
Hauppauge, NY 11788
800-231-5445, 516-231-5400

Digital Equipment Corp.
146 Main St.
Maynard, MA 01754
603-881-3914

Link Technologies Inc.
46959 Landing Pkwy.
Fremont, CA 94538
800-448-5465, 510-651-8000

Televideo Systems Inc.
550 E. Brokaw Road
San Jose, CA 95161
408-954-8333

WYSE Technology
3471 N. First St.
San Jose, CA 95134
408-473-1200

DOS Emulators/Servers

IBM
1133 Westchester Ave.
White Plains, NY 10604
914-642-5458

Insignia Solutions Inc.
6 Campanelli Drive
Andover, MA 01810
800-848-7677, 508-682-7600

Locus Computing Corp.
9800 La Cienega Blvd.
Inglewood, CA 90301
310-337-5286

Logicraft Inc.
22 Cotton Road
Nashua, NH 03063
603-880-0300

Books and Vendors

Puzzle Systems Corp.
16360 Monterey Road, Suite 250
Morgan Hill, CA 95037
408-779-9909

Quarterdeck Office Systems
150 Pico Blvd.
Santa Monica, CA 90405
310-392-9851

SunSelect
Two Federal St.
Billerica, MA 01821
508-442-2300

SunSoft
2550 Garcia Avenue
Mountain View, CA 94043-1100
800-346-7111

Tera Technologies Inc.
7755 SW Cirrus Dr.
Beaverton, OR 97005
503-643-4835

E-Mail—Public Providers

America Online Inc.
8619 Westwood Center Drive
Vienna, VA 22182
800-227-6364

Cerfnet
BOx 85608
San Diego, CA 92186
800-876-2373

CompuServe Inc.
5000 Arlington Centre Blvd.
P.O. Box 20212
Columbus, OH 43220
800-848-8199

Defense Data Network (DDN)
Network Information Center (NIC)
Government Systems Inc.
14200 Park Meadow Drive, Suite 200
Chantilly, VA 22021
800-365-3642, 703-802-4535

MCI International
201 Centennial Ave.
Piscataway, NJ 08854
800-444-6245

PSInet
11800 Sunris Valley Dr,Suite1100
Reston, VA 22091
703-620-6651

UUNET (Alternet)
3100 Fairview Park Dr., Ste 570
Falls Church, VA 22042
800-488-6383

E-Mail—Software

cc:Mail Inc.
2141 Landings Drive
Mountain View, CA 94043
800-448-2500, 415-961-8800

Notework Corp.
320 Washington St.
Brookline, MA 02146
617-734-4317

SunSelect
Two Federal St.
Billerica, MA 01821
508-442-2300

SWFTE International Ltd.
Stone Mill Office Park, P.O. Box 219
Rockland, DE 19732
800-237-9383, 302-234-1740

Wollongong Group Inc.
1129 San Antonie Rd.
Palo Alto, CA 94303
800-962-8649, 415-962-7100

Word Perfect
1555 N. Technology Way
Orem, UT 84057
801-225-5000

Z-Code Software Corp.
4340 Redwood Highway, Suite B-50
San Raphael, CA 94903
415-499-8649

Mail Order Suppliers

PC Connection
6 Mill St.
Marlow, NH 03456
800-800-5555

Qualix Group Inc.
1900 S. Norfolk St., Suite 224
San Mateo, CA 94403
415-572-0200

UNIX Central
474 Potrero Ave.
Sunnyvale, CA 94086
800-532-1771

UNIDesk
Technology Park, 2 Wall Street
Billerica, MA 01821
800-477-1793

UniPress Software Inc.
2025 Lincoln Hwy.
Edison, NJ 08817
800-222-0550, 908-287-2100

Modems

Boca Research Inc.
6413 Congress Avenue
Boca Raton, FL 33487-2841
407-997-6227

Hayes Microcomputer Products Inc.
P.O. Box 105203
Atlanta, GA 30348
404-840-9200

Intel PC Enhancements Division
5200 NE Elam Young Parkway
Hillsboro, OR 97124
800-538-3373

Practical Peripherals Inc.
375 Conejo Ridge Ave.
Thousand Oaks, CA 91361
805-497-4774

Supra Corp.
7101 Supra Drive SW
Albany, OR 97321
503-967-2400

Telebit Corp.
1315 Chesapeake Terrace
Sunnyvale, CA 94089
408-745-3068

U.S.Robotics Inc.
8100 North McCormick Blvd.
Skokie, IL 6007
708-982-5010

ZoomTelephonics Inc.
207 South St. #61
Boston, MA 02111
617-423-1072

Multiport Boards

Arnet Corp.
618 Grassmere Park Drive, Suite 6
Nashville, TN 37211
800-366-8844, 615-834-8000

Chase Research
545 Marriott Dr., #100
Nashville, TN 37210
615-872-0770

Comtrol
2675 Patton Rd
St. Paul, MN 55113
800-926-6876, 612-631-7654

Computone
1100 Northmeadow Pkwy
Roswell, GA 30076
800-241-3946, 404-475-2725

Corollary
12802 Kelven
Irvine, CA 92714
800-338-4020, 714-250-4040

Digiboard
6400 Flying Cloud Drive
Eden Prairie, MN 55344
800-344-4273, 612-943-9020

Equinox Systems
6851 W. Sunrise Blvd.
Plantation, FL 33313
800-275-3500, 305-255-3500

Maxpeed
1120 Chess Dr.
Foster City, CA 94404
415-345-5447

Specialix
745 Camden Ave.
Campbell, CA 95008
800-423-5364, 408-378-7919

Stallion Technologies
4708 Abbay Dr.
Nashville, TN 37211
800-729-2342, 615-333-6096

Stargate Technologies
29300 Aurora Rd.
Solon, OH 44139
800-782-7428, 612-349-1860

Network Interface Adapters

Allied Telesis
575 East Middlefield Road
Mount View, CA 94043
800-424-4284, 415-964-2771

Boca Research Inc.
6413 Congress Avenue
Boca Raton, FL 33487-2841
407-997-6227

D-Link Systems Inc.
5 Musick
Irvine, CA 92718
714-455-1688

Eagle Technology
1160 Ridder Park Dr.
San Jose, CA 95131
800-733-2453, 408-441-4003

Standard Microsystems Corp.
80 Arkay Dr.
Hauppauge, NY 11788
800-762-4968, 516-273-3100

Thomas-Conrad Corp.
1908-R Kramer Lane
Austin, TX 78758
800-332-8683, 512-836-1935

3Com Corp.
P.O. Box 58145, 5400 Bayfront Plaza
Santa Clara, CA 95052
800-638-3266, 408-764-5000

Ungermann-Bass Inc.
3900 Freedom Circle, P.O. Box 58030
Santa Clara, CA 95052
408-496-0111

Xircom
26025 Mureau Rd.
Calabasas, CA 91302
818-878-7600

Network Management Software

FTP Software Inc.
2 High St., No.
Andover, MA 01845
508-685-4000

Hewlett Packard Co.
11311 Chinden Blvd.
Boise, ID 83714
208-323-3560

IBM
1133 Westchester Ave.
White Plains, NY 10604
914-642-5458

Intel PC Enhancements Division
5200 NE Elam Young Parkway
Hillsboro, OR 97124
800-538-3373

Novell Inc.
122 East 1700 South
Provo, UT 84606
800-453-1267, 801-429-7000

Peregrine Systems, Inc.
1959 Palomar Oaks Way
Carlsbad, CA 92009
619-431-2400

SunConnect
2550 Garcia Avenue
Mountain View, CA 94043
800-241-CONX

Systems Center Inc.
1800 Alexander Bell Drive
Reston, VA 22091
703-264-8000

3Com Corporation
5400 Bayfront Plaza, P.O. Box 58145
Santa Clara, CA 95052
800-638-3266, 408-764-5000

PC LAN /UNIX Software

Artisoft Inc.
Artisoft Plaza, 575 E. River Road
Tucson, AZ 85704
602-293-4000

Banyan Systems Inc.
120 Flanders Road
Westboro MA 01581
508-898-1000

Beame & Whiteside
706 Hillsborough St.
Raleigh, NC 27603-1655
919-831-8989

Digital Equipment Corp.
30 Porter Road (LJO2/C10)
Littleton, MA 01460
508-486-2291

Firefox Communications
P.O. Box 8165
Kirkland WA 98034
206-827-9066

Invisible Software Inc.
1215 N. Highway 427, Suite 135
Longwood, FL 32750
407-260-5200

Ipswitch Inc.
580 Main Street
Reading, MA 01867
617-942-0621

Locus Computing Corp.
9800 La Cienega Blvd.
Inglewood, CA 90301
310-337-5286

Microsoft Corp.
One Microsoft Way
Redmond, WA 98052
206-936-3227

Mini-Byte Software Inc.
1154 St. Georges Ave.
Avenel, NJ 07001
908-855-9660

Network & Communications Mngnt. Inc.
6803 Whittier Ave.
McLean, VA 22101
703-847-0040

Novell Inc.
122 East 1700 South
Provo, UT 84606
800-453-1267, 801-429-7000

Performance Technology
800 Lincoln Center, 7800 IH 10 West
San Antonio, Texas 78230
512-349-2000

Puzzle Systems Corp.
16360 Monterey Road, Suite 250
Morgan Hill, CA 95037
408-779-9909

Quarterdeck Office Systems
1901 Main Street
Santa Monica, CA 90405
213-392-9851

The Santa Cruz Operation
400 Encinal St., P.O. Box 1900
Santa Cruz, CA 95061
408-425-7222

Spry Inc.
1319 Dexter Ave. N., Suite 150
Seattle, WA 98109
206-286-1412

SunSelect
Two Federal St.
Billerica, MA 01821
508-442-2300

UniPress Software
2025 Lincoln Highway
Edison, NJ 08817
908-287-2100

Power Protection

American Power Conversion
132 Fairgrounds Road, P.O. Box 278
West Kingston, RI 02892-9906
800-800-4APC

Best Power Technology Inc.
P.O. Box 280
Necedah, WI 54646
800-356-5794, 608-565-7200

Printer Products

Castelle Inc.
3255-3 Scott Blvd.
Santa Clara, CA 95054
408-496-0474

Color Age Inc.
900 Technology Park Drive
Billerica, MA 01921
508-667-8585

Hewlett Packard
11311 Chinden Blvd.
Boise, ID 83714
800-752-0900

LANTRONIX
26072 Merit Circle, Suite 113
Laguna Hills, CA 92653
800-422-7022, 714-367-0050

MiLAN Technology Corp.
894 Ross Dr., Suite 105
Sunnyvale, CA 94089
408-752-2770

Microplex Systems Ltd.
265 East 1st Ave.
Vancouver, BC
Canada
604-875-1461

Pacific Data Products
9125 Rehco Road
San Diego, CA 92121
619-552-0880

QMS Inc.
One Magnum Pass
Mobile, Alabama 36618
205-639-4400

Rose Electronics
10850 Wilcrest, #900
Houston, TX 77099
713-933-7673

Xircom
26025 Mureau Rd.
Calabasas, CA 91302
818-878-7600

TCP/IP Software

Beame & Whiteside
706 Hillsborough St.
Raleigh, NC 27603-1655
919-831-8989

Cogent Data Technologies Inc.
175 West St., P.O. Box 926
Friday Harbor, WA 98250
206-378-2929

Distinct Corp.
14082 Loma Rio Dr.
Saratoga, CA 95070
408-741-0781

Esker Inc.
1181 Chess Drive #C
Foster City, CA 94404
415-341-9065

Frontier Technologies Corp.
10201 N. Port Washington Rd.
Mequon, Wisconsin 53092
414-241-4555

FTP Software Inc.
2 High St., No.
Andover, MA 01845
508-685-4000

IBM
1133 Westchester Ave.
White Plains, NY 10604
914-642-5458

InterCon Systems Corp.
950 Herndon Parkway
Herndon, VA 22070
703-709-9890

Ipswitch Inc.
580 Main Street
Reading, MA 01867
617-942-0621

James River Group Inc.
125 North First Street
Minneapolis, MN 55401
612-339-2521

Lanera Corp.
1762 Technology Dr., Suite 108
San Jose, Ca 95110
408-453-6150

NEI
16 Technology Drive, Suite 210
Irvine, CA 92718
714-753-8588

NetManage Inc.
20823 Stevens Creek Blvd., Suite 100
Cupertino, CA 95014
408-973-7171

Network Research
2380 N. Rose Ave.
Oxnard, CA 93030
800-541-9508, 805-485-2700

Solid Computer
D-8042 OberschleiBheim, Germany
Bruckmannring 32
0 89 / 31 57 19 - 0

Spry Inc.
1319 Dexter Ave. N., Suite 150
Seattle, WA 98109
206-286-1412

SunSelect
Two Federal St.
Billerica, MA 01821
508-442-2300

3Com Corp.
P.O. Box 58145, 5400 Bayfront Plaza
Santa Clara, CA 95052
800-638-3266, 408-764-5000

Walker, Richer & Quinn Inc.
2815 Eastlake Ave. East
Seattle, WA 98102
206-726-7368

Wollongong Group Inc.
1129 San Antonio Road, P.O. Box 51860
Palo Alto, CA 94303
800-872-8649, 800-962-8649 (in CA)

Terminal/Communication Servers

Corollary Inc.
2802 Kelvin
Irvine, CA 92714
800-338-4020, 714-250-4040

LANTRONIX
26072 Merit Circle, Suite 113
Laguna Hills, CA 92653
800-422-7022, 714-367-0050

Network Products Corp.
1440 W. Colorado Blvd
Pasadena, Calif. 91105
818-441-6504

Terminal Emulation

Cactus International Inc.
13987 West Annapolis Court
Mt. Airy, MD 21771
301-829-1622

Century Software
5284 S. 320 West, Suite C134
Salt Lake City, Utah 84107
801-268-3088

Corporate Microsystems Inc.
P.O. Box 2059
Lebanon, NH 03766
603-448-5193

Esker Inc.
1181 Chess Drive #C
Foster City, CA 94404
415-341-9065

FutureSoft Engineering
12012 Wickchester Lane, Suite 600
Houston, TX 77079
713-496-9400

Hayes Microcomputer Products Inc.
P.O. Box 105203
Atlanta, GA 30348
404-840-9200

James River Group Inc.
125 N. First St.
Minneapolis, MN 55401
612-339-2521

JSB Corp.
108 Whispering Pines Drive, Suite 115
Scotts Valley, CA 95066
800-359-3408, 408-438-8300

NEI
16 Technology Drive, Suite 210
Irvine, CA 92718
714-753-8588

Persoft Inc.
465 Science Dr., Box 44953
Madison, WI 53744
608-273-6000

Software Moguls Inc.
12301 Whitewater Dr., Suite 160
Minnetonka, MN 55343
612-933-8790

Specialix Inc.
745 Camden Ave.
Campbell, CA 95008
800-423-5364, 408-378-7919

Structured Software Solutions Inc.
4031 W. Plano Parkway, Suite 205
Plano, TX 75093
214-985-9901

Tundra Software
3455 Harvester Road #19
Burlington, Ontario
Canada L7N 3P2
416-681-3322

U.S.Robotics Inc.
8100 North McCormick Blvd.
Skokie, IL 6007
800-342-5877, 709-933-5329

Walker, Richer & Quinn Inc.
2815 Eastlake Ave. East
Seattle, WA 98102
206-726-7368

Wollongong Group Inc.
1129 San Antonio Road, P.O. Box 51860
Palo Alto, CA 94303
800-872-8649, 800-962-8649 (in CA)

Transceivers

Allied Telesis
575 East Middlefield Road
Mount View, CA 94043
800-424-4284, 415-964-2771

LANTRONIX
26072 Merit Circle, Suite 113
Laguna Hills, CA 92653
800-422-7022, 714-367-0050

MiLAN Technology Corp.
894 Ross Dr., Suite 105
Sunnyvale, CA 94089
408-752-2770

Standard Microsystems Corp.
80 Arkay Dr.
Hauppauge, NY 11788
800-762-4968, 516-273-3100

3Com Corp.
P.O. Box 58145, 5400 Bayfront Plaza
Santa Clara, CA 95052
800-638-3266, 408-764-5000

UNIX Workstations

Digital Equipment Corp.
30 Porter Road (LJO2/C10)
Littleton, MA 01460
508-486-2291

Hewlett Packard Company
300 Apollo Drive
Chelmsford, MA 01824
800-752-0900

IBM
1133 Westchester Ave.
White Plains, NY 10604
914-642-5458

Silicon Graphics
2011 N. Shoreline Blvd.
Mountain View, CA
415-961-0595

Sun Microsystems Inc.
MS M6-86, 2550 Garcia Ave.
Mountain View, CA 94043
415-960-1300

UUCP Software

R.M. Greenberg Software Concepts Design
594 Third Ave.
New York, NY; 10016
212-889-6431

Tim Pozar
Late Night Software
671 28th St.
San Francisco, CA 94131
415-788-2022

Vortex Technology
P.O. Box 1323
Topanga, CA 90290
213-390-3920

X Servers

Age Logic Inc.
9985 Pacific Heights Blvd.
San Diego, CA 92121
619-455-8600

Digital Equipment Corp.
30 Porter Road (LJO2/C10)
Littleton, MA 01460
508-486-2291

Hummingbird Communications Ltd.
2900 John St., Unit 4
Markham, Ontario
Canada L3R 5G3
416-470-1203

Integrated Inference Machines
1468 E. Katella Ave.
Anaheim, CA 92805
714-776-8958

JSB Corp.
108 Whispering Pines Drive, Suite 115
Scotts Valley, CA 95066
800-359-3408, 408-438-8300

Network Computing Devices Inc.
350 N. Bernardo Ave.
Mountain View, CA 94043
415-691-2558

Visionware
1020 Marsh Road #220
Menlo Park, CA 94025
415-325-2113

Walker, Richer & Quinn Inc.
2815 Eastlake Ave. East
Seattle, WA 98102
206-726-7368

White Pine Software
40 Simon St., Suite 201
Nashua, NH 03060
603-886-9050

X Terminals

Hewlett Packard Company
300 Apollo Drive
Chelmsford, MA 01824
800-752-0900

Human Designed Systems Inc.
421 Feheley Drive
King of Prussia, PA 19406
800-HDS-1551, 215-277-8300

Network Computing Devices Inc.
PC-Xdivision
9590 SW Gemini Drive
Beaverton, Oregon 97005
415-694-0650

Tektronix Inc.
26600 S.W. Parkway, P.O. Box 1000
Wilsonville, Oregon 97070
503-682-3411

Visual Technology Inc.
120 Flanders Road
Westboro, MA 01581
800-847-8252, 508-836-4400

Index